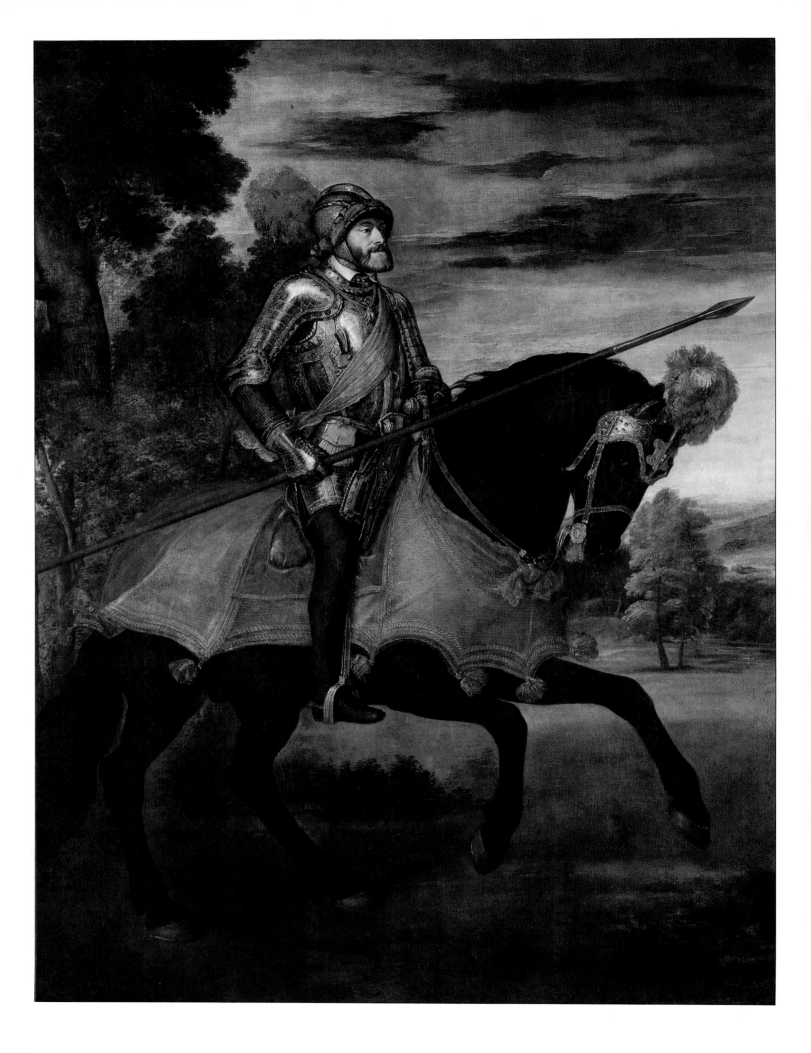

The History of Painting and Sculpture

GREAT
TRADITIONS

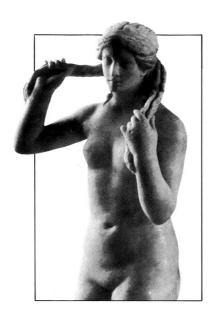

MITCHELL BEAZLEY

The Mitchell Beazley Library of Art

Editor-in-Chief and Editor of Volume 1
Jack Tresidder
Senior Executive Art Editor
Michael McGuinness
Senior Editor and Editor of Volumes 2 and 3
Paul Holberton
Editor of Volume 4
Jane Crawley
Editors
Ian Chilvers
Jane Cochrane
Katharine Kemp
Jean McNamee
Roslin Mair
Judy Martin
Susan Meehan
Senior Designer
Marnie Searchwell
Designers
Paul Bickerstaff
Alan Brown
Peter Courtley
Gerry Douglas
Jane Owen
Chief Picture Researcher
Flavia Howard
Picture Researchers
Celestine Dars
Tessa Politzer
Sandy Shepherd
Researchers
Julian George
Andrew Heritage
Tony Livesey
Julian Mannering
Kate Miller
Robert Stewart
Editorial Assistants
Barbara Gish
Amber Newell
Proof Reader
Gillian Beaumont
Indexers
Hilary and Richard Bird
Production Controller
Suzanne Semmes

THE MITCHELL BEAZLEY LIBRARY OF ART
was edited and designed by
Mitchell Beazley Publishers, Mill House,
87–89 Shaftesbury Avenue, London W1V 7AD

ISBN 0 85533 177 1 Slipcased set

ISBN 0 85533 356 1 Volume 2

Composed by Filmtype Services Limited, Scarborough, England
and Tradespools Ltd, Frome, England

Origination by Gilchrist Bros, Leeds, England
and Scala Istituto Fotografico Editorale, Florence

Printed in the Netherlands
by Koninklijke Smeets Offset b.v., Weert

The Mitchell Beazley Library of Art

Volume 1

UNDERSTANDING
ART

The principles of art
appreciation – themes,
methods and techniques

Volume 2

GREAT
TRADITIONS

Ancient and Medieval,
Renaissance and Baroque
– Western art to 1789

Volume 3

NEW
HORIZONS

Art of the modern world
from 1789 to the present,
and art of the East

Volume 4

ART AND
ARTISTS

Biographical entries on
more than 3,000 artists,
with a glossary of terms

STRUCTURE AND ORGANIZATION

This book is one of four independent but inter-related volumes designed to provide a wide range of knowledge about painting and sculpture within a compact but comprehensive library of art. The exceptionally high proportion of illustrations reflects the importance given to visual information. Words about art lose much of their impact when they cannot be related directly to the works they describe. In general, if a work of art is mentioned in the text it is also illustrated – and described in further detail – on the same page.

The organization of the history is, with few exceptions, chronological and geographic, but a particular school or movement is usually followed through to its final development, not treated piecemeal. Though enough context is given to orientate the reader, the aim is not to provide a socio-cultural history but to keep the focus of interest fixed firmly on the paintings and the sculptures themselves.

Particular subjects, or aspects of them, are usually encapsulated within a single two-page "spread". This allows the reader either to begin at the beginning in the conventional way or to enter the book at any point, finding each spread more or less self-contained, though it connects with the others to build up a coherent whole. The spread system allows a double approach; the broad development of art is unfolded in "narrative" spreads, which begin usually with background information and then cover a particular period, movement or region. In the course of the story, some artists arrive of such stature that they have one of these spreads to themselves. An alternative kind of spread, a "focus", is recognizable by a large-scale illustration. Here, the opportunity is taken to pause and contemplate a single work of art. The aim is to convey its essential flavour, sometimes to show why it was specially significant or influential, sometimes to trace out the process of its creation, always to make the reader look at it again, with deeper understanding.

EDITORIAL AND INDEXING METHOD

The locations of works of art shown in this book are not given in the captions but can be found, together with the dimensions and medium, in the list of illustrations that precedes the index. Entries in this list are headed, as are the captions themselves, by the name of the artist or, if this is unknown, by the place of origin or original location of the work. This may be different from the present location; thus "*The Virgin of Vladimir*" appears under the heading CONSTANTINOPLE, where it was made, though it is kept in the Tretyakov Gallery in Moscow.

Titles of works of art are given in italics, but if translation is inappropriate, or the title is a popular one which may not properly describe the image, it is also placed in inverted commas and capitalized – thus "*The Embarkation for Cythera*", "*La Toilette*". The names of monuments or buildings, notably churches, are usually the local names – thus Ste Madeleine, the Residenz. "S." is used for all the Italian variations, San, Santa, Sant', Santo. For Chinese words the pinyin rather than the older Wade-Giles system is used (though the Wade-Giles spelling is cross-referenced to the pinyin in the index). The Latin form of an ancient Greek name has been used except in the historical section on ancient Greek art; thus Hercules in Renaissance art, Herakles in Greek art.

COMPANION VOLUMES IN THE LIBRARY

Though this book is self-contained, with its own index, there are some cross-references to companion volumes in the Library. The introductory *Understanding Art* volume (vol. 1) covers both the formal and the technical sides of painting and sculpture, providing a basic course of art appreciation. *Great Traditions* (vol. 2) begins the history of painting and sculpture with Palaeolithic images and traces the development of the Western tradition from Egypt, Greece and Rome through medieval art to the Renaissance and the era of Baroque before the French Revolution ushered in the modern world. In *New Horizons* (vol. 3) the arts of Islam, Asia and Japan are introduced before the story is told of Western art in the nineteenth and twentieth centuries. Finally *Art and Artists* (vol. 4) provides succinct accounts of the lives and works of more than 3,000 artists, a gallery of portraits and self-portraits, and a comprehensive glossary of art terms and techniques.

Contents: GREAT TRADITIONS

Art from Prehistory to the French Revolution by DAVID PIPER

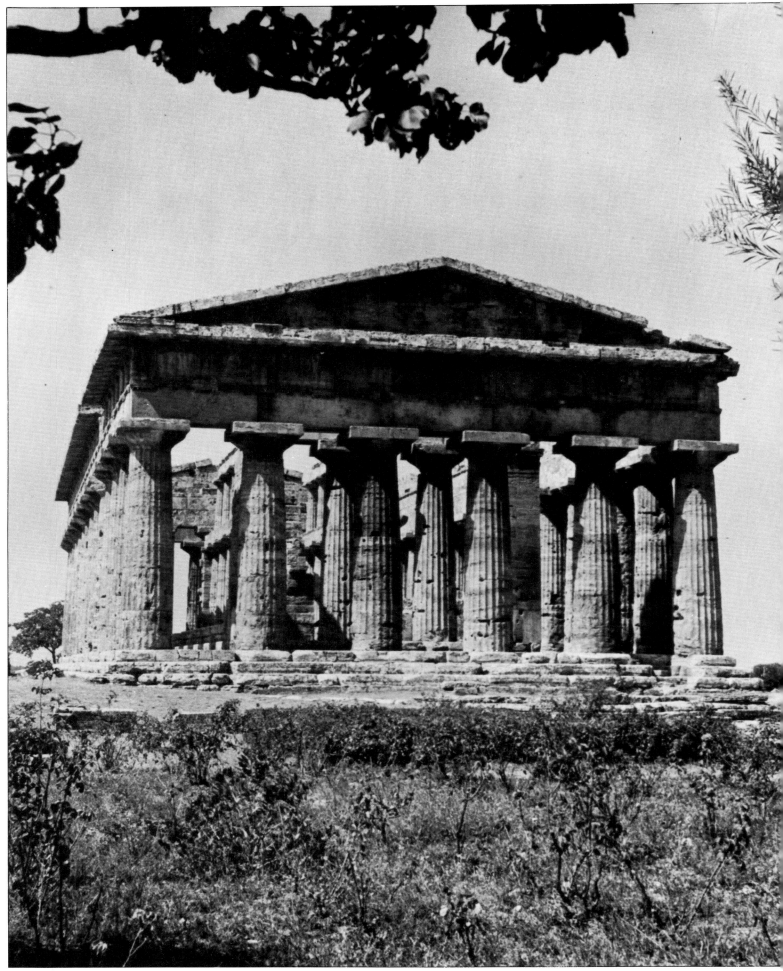

ANCIENT WORLDS

In this volume and in its following companion the history of art has been organized in the usual way region by region and in chronological sequence, which may wrongly imply a distancing not only in time and space but in sympathy. In a way it is true of course that the several and disparate worlds considered in this opening section are fundamentally remote. They are mostly "dead" cultures, their languages sometimes entirely unrecorded, sometimes impossible for us to read. Most people in the twentieth-century West can look at a statue by Michelangelo and think they know what it means – and will not be too far wrong; among ancient cultures, the context, function and meaning of a work of art are often less clear, even to scholars.

Yet ancient artefacts have an interest not only as the objects they were but as the objects they are. If the history of art shows anything it is that art does not always move forward in linear progression. It frequently turns back for inspiration, as the Renaissance turned back to the classical world, and as modern art has again turned back to the force of "primitive" sculpture. We may well feel closer in spirit to a Palaeolithic image than to one produced in a sophisticated court of the eighteenth century.

There are two major departures from chronology in the course of this history. One is that the art of Asia is placed at the beginning of the next volume, though the civilizations of China and India emerged hardly later than those of Mesopotamia and Egypt. Apart from acknowledging the fact that the arts of East and West have not much cross-fertilized except in the modern era, this shift allows ancient and modern Eastern art to be treated coherently.

Secondly, the tribal arts of Africa, Oceania and North America are considered immediately after Palaeolithic art. In the naturalism and powerful immediacy of cave-paintings millennia old there are parallels with Aboriginal and some African art of quite recent origin; and parallels again between Oceanic, North American Indian and some African tribal art and the cultures that preceded the rise of states and civilizations. As Pre-Columbian art (for convenience treated here also) shows, images produced in the context of the earliest organized states tended to become more formal and stylized, not because naturalism was unattainable but because it was almost irrelevant. The art of many early civilizations was intended to convey, in forms that were approved and perpetual, images of gods and rulers or of the duties of the community towards them.

It was against a background of almost imperceptible change in the art of the Middle East that Greek art of the sixth and fifth centuries BC developed with the swiftness of a revolution. The human body became the focus for sculpture and soon for painting, too, a basic subject of Western art ever since. Though its primacy might be challenged – in the medieval era, or again in our own century – the human figure, together with the making visible of light and space that is its stage, has proved an inexhaustible Western theme.

PAESTUM, ITALY (left)
The Temple of Neptune,
c.470-460 BC

PALENQUE, MEXICO (right)
The Pyramid of the
Inscriptions, c. AD 700

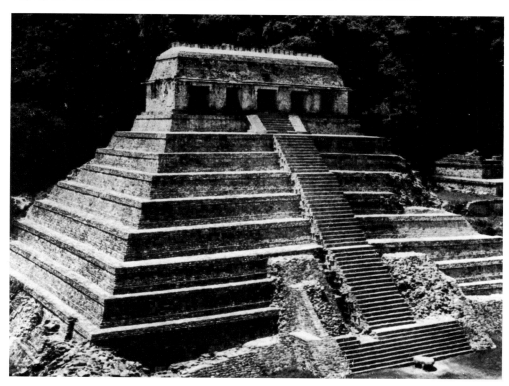

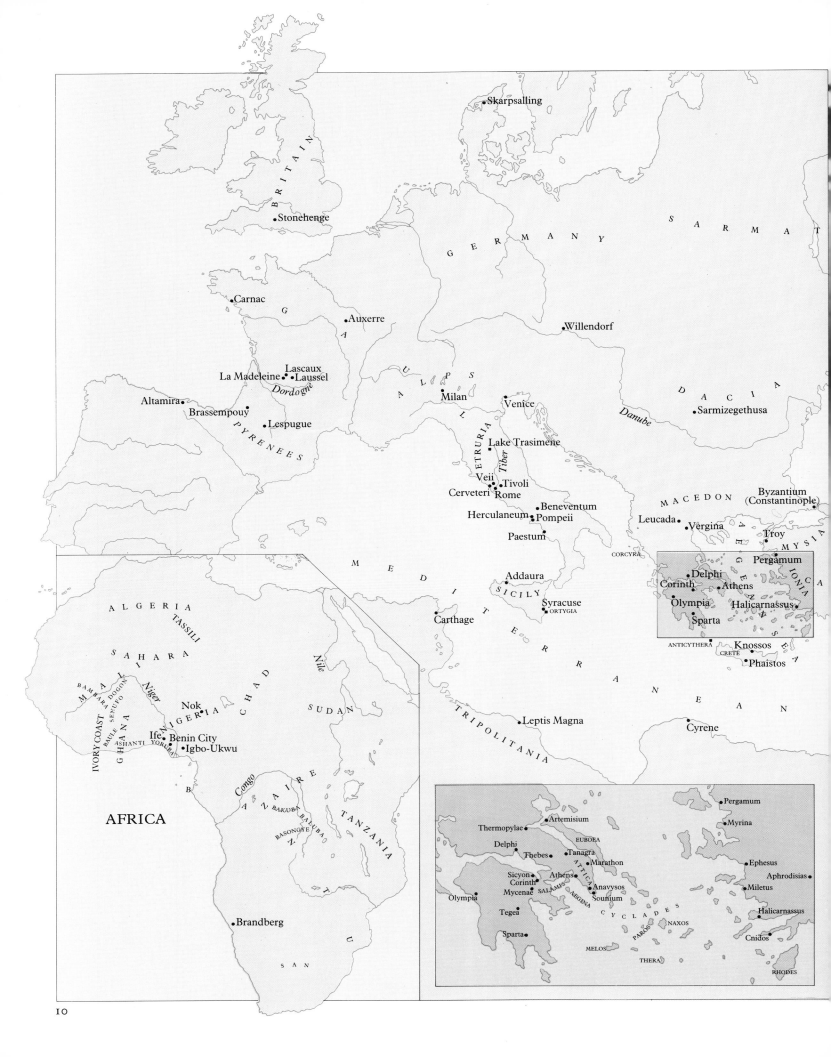

• Skarpsalling

B R I T A I N

• Stonehenge

S A R M A T

G E R M A N Y

• Carnac

G
A
U
L

• Auxerre

• Willendorf

D A C I A

• Lascaux
La Madeleine • • Laussel
Dordogne

Altamira •
Brassempouy •
• Lespugue

P Y R E N E E S

A
L
P
S

• Milan

• Venice

Danube

• Sarmizegethusa

ETRURIA
Tiber

• Lake Trasimene

Veii • • Tivoli
Cerveteri • Rome

• Beneventum
Herculaneum • • Pompeii
• Paestum

M A C E D O N

Byzantium
(Constantinople)

Leucada • • Vergina
• Troy

M Y S I A

CORCYRA

• Pergamum

M E D
I T E R R
A
N
E
A
N

• Delphi
Corinth • • Athens
• Olympia
• Sparta

I O N I A

A E G E A N

• Addaura
S I C I L Y
• Syracuse
ORTYGIA

• Carthage

ANTICYTHERA

• Knossos
CRETE
• Phaistos

A L G E R I A
T A S S I L I

S A H A R A

M
A
L
I

Niger

BAMBARA DOGON
SENUFO
GHANA
IVORY COAST
BAULE
ASHANTI
YORUBA

• Nok

N I G E R I A

C H A D

Nile

S U D A N

T R I P O L I T A N I A

• Leptis Magna

• Cyrene

• Ife • Benin City
• Igbo-Ukwu

Congo

Z
A
I
R
E

BAKUBA
BALUBA
BASONGYE

B

AFRICA

T A N Z A N I A

U
T
U

S A N

• Brandberg

• Artemisium
Thermopylae •
• Pergamum
• Myrina

Delphi •
• Thebes • Tanagra
EUBOEA
• Marathon

ATTICA
Sicyon • Athens •
Corinth •
Mycenae • SALAMIS
Olympia • AEGINA • Anavysos
• Sounium

• Ephesus

• Aphrodisias

• Miletus

Tegea •

C Y C L A D E S

PAROS
NAXOS

• Halicarnassus

Sparta •

MELOS

• Cnidos

THERA

RHODES

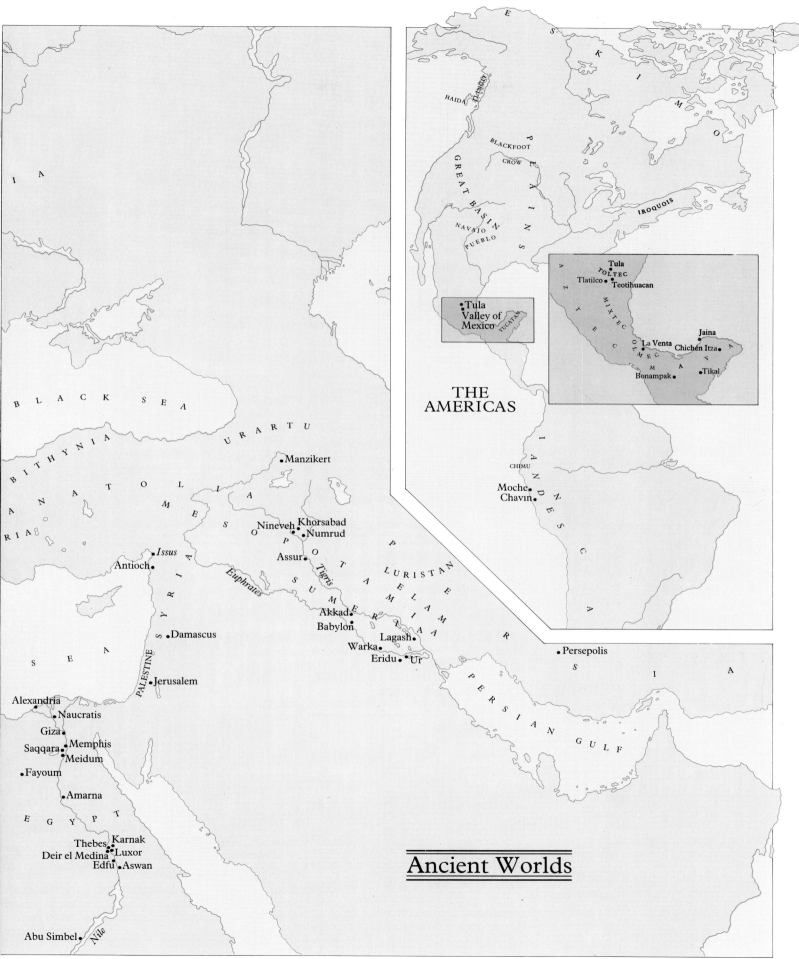

THE
AMERICAS

Tula
Tula
Valley of
Mexico
YUCATAN

TO·L·TEC
Tlatilco•
Tula•
•Teotihuacan
A
Z
T
E
C
MIXTEC
La Venta
O·L·M·E·C
•Jaina
Chichén Itza•
•Tikal
Bonampak•
M·A·Y·A

S·K·I·M·O

HAIDA·TLINGIT
BLACKFOOT
P
L
A
I
N
S
CROW
GREAT BASIN
NAVAJO
PUEBLO
IROQUOIS

CHIMU
Moche•
Chavin•
A·N·D·E·S

B L A C K   S E A

BITHYNIA
ANATOLIA
URARTU
•Manzikert

M·E·S·O·P·O·T·A·M·I·A
Nineveh• •Khorsabad
•Numrud
Assur•
Issus
Antioch•
SYRIA
Euphrates
S·U·M·E·R
Tigris
LURISTAN
E·L·A·M
P·E·R·S·I·A

•Damascus

S E A
PALESTINE
•Jerusalem

Akkad•
Babylon•
Warka•
Eridu• •Ur
Lagash•

•Persepolis

P·E·R·S·I·A·N   G·U·L·F

Alexandria•
•Naucratis
Giza•
Saqqara• •Memphis
•Meidum
•Fayoum

•Amarna

E   G   Y   P   T

Thebes• Karnak
Deir el Medina• •Luxor
Edfu• •Aswan

Abu Simbel• *Nile*

Ancient Worlds

Palaeolithic Art

The creative impulse to make images – objects without any apparent mechanical use – emerged very early indeed: it was almost simultaneous perhaps with the arrival of man as we know him now, *homo sapiens sapiens*, superseding Neanderthal man.

The earliest surviving man-made works that qualify as art come mainly from Europe, and date from within the huge range of time known as the Upper Palaeolithic period, from about 30000 to about 10000 BC. The Upper Palaeolithic comprises in sequence the Aurignacian, Gravettian and Magdalenian periods, measuring approximately from 30000 to 20000 BC, from 20000 to 14000 BC, from 14000 to 10000 BC. Then, as the climate thawed, mankind entered the Mesolithic era, and a food-producing neolithic culture appeared in Europe about 8000 BC.

The context in which Palaeolithic art was produced was one of developed hunting and food-gathering cultures, which possessed tools and weapons made of stone, wood or bone. Small-scale sculptures, engravings or reliefs have been found on former dwelling-sites – this kind of art antedates the cave-paintings by several thousands of years. Early work tends to concentrate on the human figure; later, more attention is given to animals. The most famous of the early sculptures are the so-called "*Venus*" figures, and the best-known amongst them, the limestone "*Venus of Willendorf*", may also be the earliest, from between 30000 and 25000 BC. Small though she is, she is charged with significance: in the swell of her breasts, belly and buttocks she is a personification of fecundity. The carving is accomplished with a satisfying control, and the interrelationship of the spherical volumes has provoked admiration and emulation in the twentieth century, for instance from the sculptor Brancusi. Comparable figures have been found in France, in Italy, in the Danube basin and as far east as Asiatic Russia. They are often more stylized, ranging from the outstanding ivory "*Venus*" of Lespugue (in the Dordogne) to mere symbols; all are generalized, faceless. Quite as early, however, the first faces in art appear, at the same sites: from Brassempouy in the Dordogne comes a clearly defined head in ivory, conveying the impression of a real woman lurking through the abrasions of millennia – with a sophisticated, almost Egyptian-looking hairstyle.

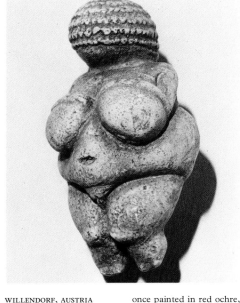

WILLENDORF, AUSTRIA
"*The Venus of Willendorf*", c.30000-25000 BC
Carved from a pebble and once painted in red ochre, the "*Venus*" is of a size to be clutched in the palm of the hand – like an amulet.

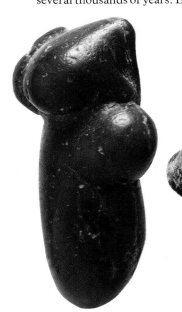

LAKE TRASIMENE, ITALY (above) "*Venus*" figure, Aurignacian period? Sometimes the feminine form was reduced to its essentials, to an evocative symbol. But there is not enough evidence to assume a consistent development, whether towards greater abstraction or away from it.

LESPUGUE, FRANCE (left)
"*The Venus of Lespugue*", c.20000-18000 BC
The figure is damaged, but it is still apparent that the stylization is complex, that this is a relatively sophisticated work of art. On her back, not shown, is incised a hanging cloth. On many of these figurines details may once have been indicated by colour (eaten away by acids in the soil).

LA MADELEINE, FRANCE (below) *Bison*, c.12000 BC
The form of the animal is ingeniously adapted to the shape of the weapon, a club that could be thrown, of reindeer antler. Decorated objects begin to survive in abundance from the late Magdalenian period (named after the cave where this object was found); animal designs predominate, plant forms, geometric and spiral patterns appear very rarely.

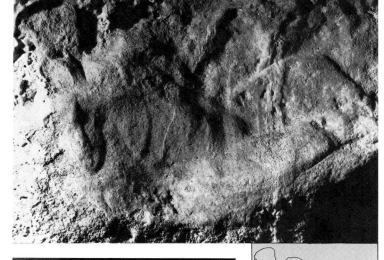

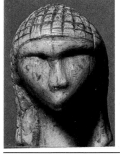

BRASSEMPOUY, FRANCE (left) *Female head*, c.22000-20000 BC
The ivory fragment is one of a group of statuettes of the late Aurignacian; but its clearly delineated features are almost unique amid the hundreds of finds made in prehistoric sites in the Dordogne caves.

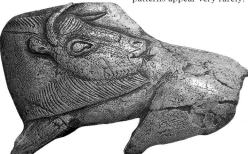

LAUSSEL, FRANCE (right)
"*The Venus of Laussel*", c.20000-18000 BC
Prominent in the woman's hand, the horn suggests later, Bronze-Age, bull-cults. From a rock shelter in the Dordogne, the slab is 45cm (almost 18in) high, and similar in conception to "*Venuses*" in the round.

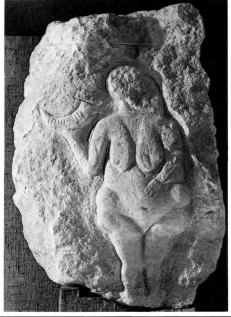

THE DORDOGNE, FRANCE (above) *Reclining woman*, c.12000 BC
The relative naturalism, unexaggerated proportions and relaxed disposition are highly unusual in the later Magdalenian period. The contour is expressive, the body is understood to have volume, in an era when figures were usually caricatured; naturalism was reserved for animals, which were represented more frequently. A flint was probably used to cut away the rock, and bumps and hollows in the natural surface were incorporated in the sculptor's design.

Techniques of engraving – scratchings or incisions on surfaces of bone, stone or horn – are probably as old as those of carving or modelling, but the best works of this kind are mostly later, of Magdalenian times. True sculpture in relief is much rarer, but was carved sometimes in the openings of caves, where there was enough light to see by, sometimes into rock in the open air. One Gravettian relief, from the Dordogne again, shows, for the first time in Palaeolithic art, a human figure in relationship to an object: with one hand on her belly, she holds with the other a bison-horn up to her face, seen in profile. Later, a more accomplished mastery could produce images of sensuous ease, such as the reclining nude from a cave in the Dordogne.

The earliest paintings were perhaps simply outlines of hands traced in red or black, but pictures of animals came very soon, and the two are found together at the earliest sites so far known, in the Dordogne. Caves with paintings are all in limestone areas, and virtually confined to south-western France and northern Spain; the most famous, the caves at Lascaux and Altamira, were not dwelling-sites but sanctuaries, in use perhaps for hundreds or

thousands of years from early Magdalenian times or just before. Lascaux, discovered in 1940, caused a sensation when it was published after World War II: in the "Hall of the Bulls" the bison and horses seemed to come thundering out of the darkness of prehistory in the vitality of their line and colour – and their size. The "Hall" is some 21 metres (70ft) long, and the beasts are mostly well over life-size. The paintings deep within the cliffs at Altamira, which has a gallery almost as long but much less high, were the first to be discovered, in 1879: they were then hardly to be believed, and the genuine and huge antiquity of these and other sites has been demonstrated only recently by the radiocarbon method and by stratigraphical analysis.

Both caves were devoid of light, and the painting must have been done by crude lamplight, with the broad black or brown contours of the drawing applied with rough felt-tips (as it were) made of moss or hair; at Lascaux the colour was blown on through a tube – red, yellow, brown, violet, but not green or blue – while at Altamira something like a brush was used. The animals are shown in a limited repertoire of positions, and always in profile: at

Altamira the animals do not relate to a ground or base but seem to float across the surface of the rock all ways up – this in spite of a much stronger feeling for mass and volume than at Lascaux. Only at Lascaux do human figures appear – schematic "matchstick" figures that anticipate the greater stylization emerging at the close of the Magdalenian period.

The magical purposes behind the depiction of these animals can only be guessed, but connections with some form of propitiatory hunting cult seem logical, since we find comparable images produced in tribal cultures that have survived almost to the present day – such as those of the Bushmen in South Africa (see over) or the Aborigines in Australia (see p. 23).

Neolithic culture, characterized by the development of ceramics, weaving and agriculture, emerged with the changed climate in Europe from about 8000 BC. Its most prominent relics fall into the category of architecture – stupendous megalithic complexes such as Stonehenge or Carnac – but there also survive painted clay figurines, and many pots incised, modelled or painted with an abstract, often geometric decoration, to be developed further in the metalwork of the Bronze Age.

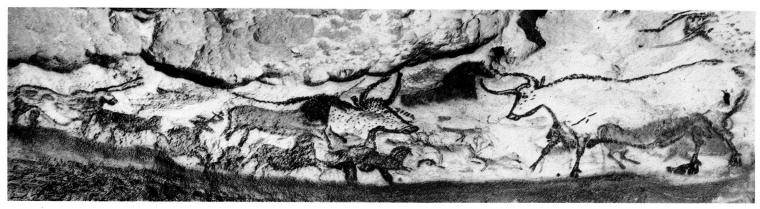

LASCAUX, FRANCE
"The Hall of Bulls",
in use c. 15000 BC?
Superimposed bison, horses and deer seem to stampede across walls and ceiling.
The pictures were renewed, or new images painted over old ones, countless times,

possibly for centuries; the site fell into disuse perhaps only in Mesolithic times. Lascaux was a miracle of survival, and a few years after its discovery had to be closed to the public, since the paintings were deteriorating alarmingly.

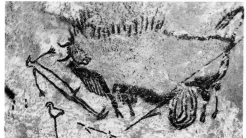

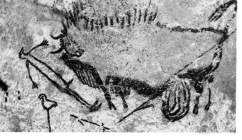

LASCAUX, FRANCE (above)
Detail: *Man and bison*
The man seems drawn less naturalistically than the animal he attacks (?) with a weapon. One theory is that painting the beasts was thought to bring them under the hunter's control.

ALTAMIRA, SPAIN (left)
Detail: *Two bison*,
c. 13000 BC?
The beasts represented at Altamira include horses and deer, but are mostly bison. Several of these may have been copied from a dead model, trussed when it had been killed – for instance the lower of the two here.

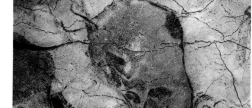

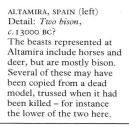

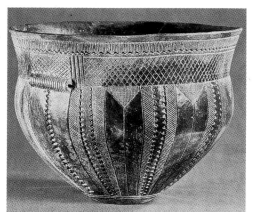

ADDAURA, SICILY (above)
Human figures, c. 10000 BC?
Some figures are clearly male, but none is definitely female. They are engaged in a ritual that perhaps involved dancing or acrobatics, and possibly some performers wear masks.

SKARPSALLING, DENMARK
(left) Decorated bowl,
3rd millennium BC
A long series of neolithic cultures in northern Europe and Russia contributed to a tradition of ornamental decoration that culminated in Celtic art (see p. 66). Such ornament was applied also to tombs and megaliths.

African Art 1: Prehistoric and Historic

The traditional art of the continent of Africa can be divided roughly into two kinds – first, the "prehistoric", which has much in common with that of European neolithic culture, but in parts of Africa persisted even into the twentieth century; secondly, much better known, the art that was once called "primitive" or "negro" but is better described as "tribal".

The dating of the prehistoric art is still speculative, but its origins probably go back to at least 7000 BC. The earliest art has been found in the region that is now the Sahara, and consists of images at first scratched or engraved rather than painted on rock surfaces. The most ancient imagery, up to about 4000 BC, is of the chase, of wild animals – elephant, rhinoceros, hippopotamus, giraffe, antelope, ostrich – depicted fairly naturalistically, sometimes on a very large scale: a rhinoceros at Tassili is more than eight metres (26ft) high, and the human hunters can be more than three metres (11ft) tall. There follows (perhaps 4000-1200 BC) the "Cattle" or "Pastoralist" period, and the subject matter expands to include domestic cattle as well as wild animals. The style is at once less vital, smaller in scale, and less naturalistic, yet it shows an awareness of the needs of perspective. Then horses, dogs and a kind of wheeled chariot are included, but increasingly stylized. Horse-driving later gives way to horse-riding; and the drawing of humans can become almost geometrically schematic (a double triangle indicating the body). The scale shrinks, so that images are 30 centimetres (12in) or less high. Finally, the "Camel" period, which lingered on in remote areas until quite recently, shows domestic animals, and even fire-arms and cars, but, taking its name from the Saharan beast of burden, signals the desiccation into desert of a region once populated and life-supporting.

The images of the San (Bushmen) of South Africa were at first engraved on rock surfaces, but later quite vivid colour was employed. The beginnings of their tradition have been put as early as 4000 BC or as late as the fourteenth or fifteenth century AD (the more usually accepted estimate), but their art is an expression of a hunting and food-gathering existence that has been continuous from the remote past. In the earlier work animals seem to be represented in symbolic roles – the elephant is thought to represent rain clouds; also flora appear as well as fauna. In later work a somewhat cruder, more emphatic manner develops, often showing tribal battles, tribes or races (latterly white Europeans are included) being identified by colours. The style is traceable in some variety in the south and far up into the eastern areas of Africa, but is found very rarely in the different terrain of Central or West Africa. In most areas, however, two-dimensional representation is common in other media – notably on cotton, clay or wood – though the motifs and styles do not seem to be related to those of the prehistoric rock-paintings.

It is particularly in these areas, in Central or West Africa, in forest and grassland regions, that the best sculpture, especially in wood, has been created (see over). Surviving examples are mostly not earlier than the nineteenth and twentieth century, but they bear witness to far more ancient traditions. The disappearance of earlier evidence is largely due to the perishable nature of most of the media used; nevertheless, while archaeological exploration in much of Africa is still in its infancy, some startling discoveries have been made. The Nok culture of central Nigeria seems to go back nearly 2,500 years: terracotta figures and heads have been found in the ancient tin fields there which

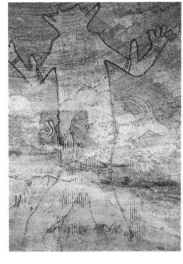

TASSILI, ALGERIA (right)
Rock-painting
In the Sahara desert and its surrounding area there has recently come to light the best and most varied collection of prehistoric rock art in the world; in 1956-57 the shallow caves of Tassili revealed what are probably the earliest known African paintings.

TANZANIA (below)
Rock-painting
Tanzania in East Africa is comparatively rich in rock-paintings, but they are usually less interesting and more recent than those of the Sahara or of South Africa. In technique and pigments they are no more than generically similar: no link need be presumed.

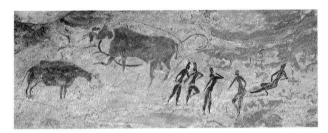
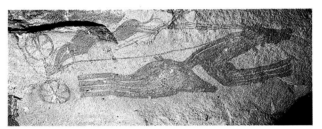

TASSILI, ALGERIA (left)
Rock-painting, of the "Pastoralist" type
Many of the paintings of Tassili show cattle being herded or tended; though bulls and cows are usually distinguishable the same is not true of men and women. The relaxed, hand-on-hip pose of some figures was first used in this phase.

TASSILI, ALGERIA (left)
Rock-painting, of the "Wheeled Chariot" type
Knowledge of the wheel is one sign of progress; and, though the stylization of the figures has increased, the artist has shown them consciously in profile. It is thought that the images depict myths rather than the traffic of everyday life.

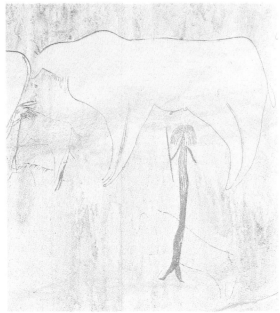
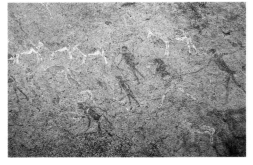
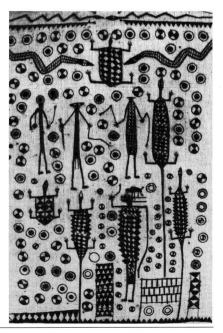

BRANDBERG, SOUTH AFRICA (above) "The White Lady"
Despite its nickname, the striding figure of this famous southern painting is believed to represent neither a lady nor white skin, but a male native in white paint. In this way it can be related to present Bantu practice – that of painting the body white in initiation ceremonies.

IVORY COAST (right)
Embroidered cotton
An agricultural fertility dance is illustrated on the hand-woven cotton, worked by the Senufo tribe. Near the middle of the lower row of figures, surrounded by hunters and reptiles, is a magician, wearing a "fire-spitter" mask. Its marked patterning distinguishes this from rock-painting.

probably date from the fourth or fifth century BC. Excavations in the 1930s at the religious centre of Ife, somewhat to the west of the Nok region, revealed some remarkable heads and figures, stylistically perhaps the distant descendants of the Nok culture, but more than 1,000 years later. Some of the terracotta heads found were extremely stylized, others, particularly those in bronze, were vividly naturalistic, and cast with a sophisticated control of the *cire-perdue* technique. More recently bronzes of perhaps the eighth century AD have been unearthed at Igbo-Ukwu in eastern Nigeria. Surely developed from these traditions are the better-known and far more numerous artefacts of the court of Benin, which was the royal and administrative centre of a great empire.

Early Benin bronzes, of perhaps about AD 1500, show a greater technical sophistication of casting and finish than those of anywhere else, though from the beginning more stylized, more hieratic than the more naturalistic ones of Ife. Later, the stylization became still more pronounced, and the handling progressively less sensitive, though the technique continued into the early twentieth century. The Benin repertoire included the famous *Queen Mother*

heads, with their formal coherence and elegance which to Western eyes evoke immediate recognition of a "classical" quality; these bronze heads, both female and male (the male ones, often with enormous finials of ivory, are in fact more frequent), were essentially commemorative but had also some religious role. Vivid bronzes of birds and animals were also produced, and animated bronze plaques in high relief in which representations of European (Portuguese) figures appeared from very early on. While some discern Western stylistic influences in Benin art, there seems little doubt that both techniques and style were originally indigenous. Bronze was not its only medium; ivory, too, was a favoured material, and was carved at Benin and elsewhere, often for export to Portugal, with great sensitivity.

Further west, the Ashanti cast in bronze and brass small weights that have become justly famous. Recent archaeology has also unearthed evidence (mostly in the form of terracotta sculpture) of long-established, hitherto unknown traditions in nearby Ghana, Chad and Mali – providing some prehistoric context for the greatest achievement of African art, which is surely its woodcarving.

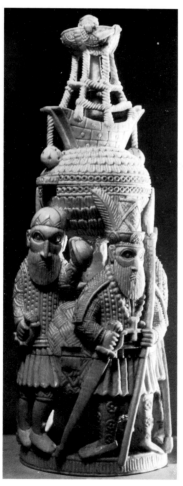

NIGERIA
A Benin king and his retinue
A Dutch visitor to the Benin court in 1667 noted the great splendour of the king's palace and also "the bronze plates decorating the rectangular pillars". The reliefs showed scenes from Benin life; here the king, distinguished by his high beaded collar (and his size and central position) is flanked by soldiers and music-making boys. The narrative quality suggests European influence; and Portuguese engravings were possible inspiration.

NIGERIA (right)
Human head
The subtractive – cut into rather than modelled up – style of Nok terracottas is the basis of suggestions that they reflect a lost tradition of woodcarving. This head is life-size.

NIGERIA (below)
Human head
The fine parallel lines of many Ife bronze *Heads* represent the effects of ritual scarification. Hair was possibly once set in the holes. Again the style calls to mind woodcarving.

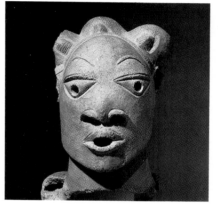

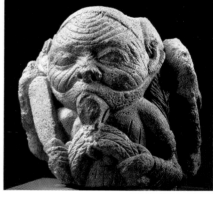

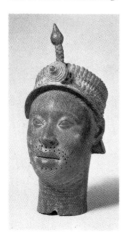

NIGERIA (right)
Queen Mother head
According to tradition, the men of Ife were asked to send a master bronze-worker to the Benin court, to initiate its artists. In later *Heads* – similar, but male – the emphasis on the regalia – the head-dress, the neck-rings – increases, moving distinctly away from natural proportions.

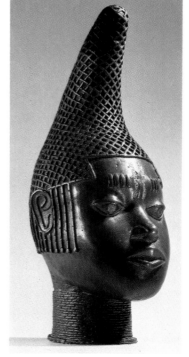

GHANA (below)
A weight
This type of brass weight, used by the Ashanti for weighing gold-dust, their currency, is unique to the region. The weights are inventively varied; they often illustrate proverbs.

NIGERIA (above)
Human head
The Ife culture shared with its Nok predecessor a curiosity about disease and deformity, reflected perhaps in this terracotta, an old man's head backed by the image of an owl.

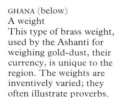

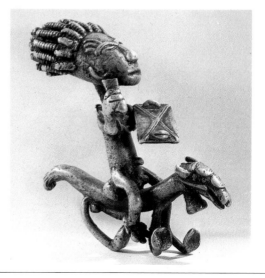

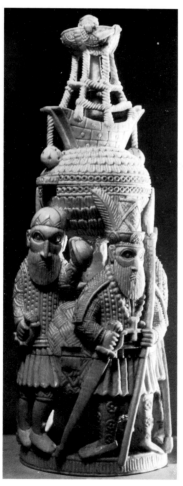

NIGERIA (above)
Salt-cellar
The Portuguese, who first set foot in Africa in 1494, soon appreciated the skill of the local ivory workers and established a trade in objects (such as this, made for export) and craftsmen.

African Art 2: Tribal

European artists and collectors began to take an interest in what was called "primitive" art – mainly the art of black Africa – from about the beginning of this century. They were primarily concerned, however (see vol. 3 p. 126), with the handling of certain formal problems, and very little with the function for which the images were made. To Western artists, from the Cubists onwards, African art suggested ways of escape from the dominant, but seemingly exhausted, academic tradition of naturalism. For Africans, however, art had a quite different function in a quite different way of life, and was essentially an integral part of an all-pervading religion. Individual images were agents, even embodiments at times (though not "idols" to be worshipped, as many Europeans used crudely to think) of the vital forces divined in all living matter. Often they spoke for the spirits of the dead, so perpetuating the vital essence of the ancestry of the tribe, and becoming identified with the ancestral spirits.

Though there are secular aspects to most of the forms used, and some objects are clearly purely decorative and ornamental, generally African tribal artefacts were created for a particular ritual or ceremonial use. This is true not only of masks and figurines but also of carved pieces ranging from musical instruments, sceptres and ceremonial axes to stools, doorposts and doors. Although the individual artist or craftsman might be recognized and highly regarded – sometimes as an exceptional member of the community – the conception of the thing made as a "work of art" in museum terms was very rare. In no instance is this more clear than in that of one of the most widespread of African forms, the mask.

In Europe, African masks are generally shown emotionally and physically stilled in a glass case, taken out of time, but their true context was in motion, in dance. Masks have been made in many different forms – some to be worn not on the head but on the arm or at the hip; many designed as the apex of a whole attendant regalia, of a cloaking garment of straw, twine, bark-cloth, furs – enriched perhaps by a medley of shells or ivory or metal objects. Transfigured, virtually transubstantiated in all this, the masked wearer lost his own personality, and became the vehicle of superhuman spiritual power. When this spirit spoke through the masked, cloaked dancer, he became its sounding-board and mouthpiece.

MALI
Walu mask: *An antelope*
Based on a rocky plateau near the Niger river, the Dogon tribe, creators of this mask form, are both farmers and hunters, many of their masks and figures representing the animals they keep and hunt. The antelope mask is worn at funeral festivals; its high stylization may reflect the penetration of Islam, but its rectangular recessed shape recurs in Dogon building.

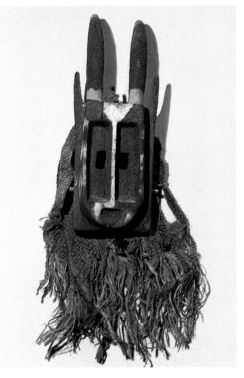

MALI (right)
Dogon dancers
The *kanaga* and the *sirigé*, two masks associated with funerary rites, are being "danced". The story told to the uninitiated is that the *kanaga*, surmounted by a cross, symbolizes a bird; to the initiated, mankind's relationship to the earth and the sky. The *sirigé* dancer bends to touch the earth with the "blade" of his mask and with whirling movements represents the genesis of the universe.

IVORY COAST (below)
Weaving pulley
The function of the pulley was to raise and lower the heddles holding the warp threads. It is Baule work: it is by exception among African artefacts simply decorative, without ritual purpose. This is perhaps reflected in the coolness of the image; the shape of the face beneath a topknot is a formal variation on the shape the pulley needed to be. Its assurance is easy for Westerners to admire.

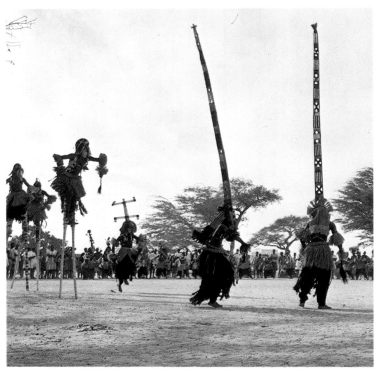

ZAIRE (below)
Kifwebe mask
Heavily hooded eyes, a box-like mouth, incised linear decoration and white and red colouring typify this striking Basongye form. This tribe, who live near the Bakuba in the wet Congo forests, used masks like this in ceremonies intended to ward off sickness.

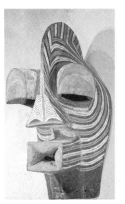

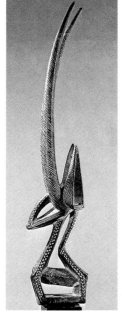

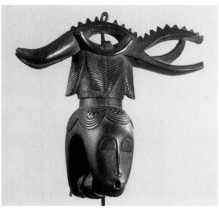

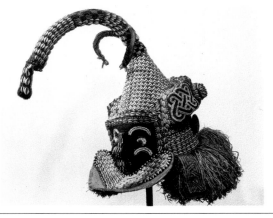

ZAIRE (left)
A mask: *Woot*
The mask is elaborately embellished with beads and cowrie shells; it was made by the Bakuba tribe for use in the initiation rites of a young man's society, and it represents *Woot*, the Bakuba equivalent of Adam. It may be worn only by persons of royal blood.

MALI (above)
Chi wara head-dress: *An antelope*
The Bambara, neighbours of the Dogon, also produce antelope masks, and yet the *walu* is very different from the graceful *chi wara*. There is a Bambara legend that the antelope spirit taught men agriculture; so the mask is worn at fertility rites.

The total image obviously often had to be awe-inspiring, both to satisfy the spirit as a worthy medium for its temporary habitation and to convince those who beheld it of its authority. Yet the forms which masks have taken throughout West and Central Africa, though they can be categorized, as forms, into various stylistic divisions and subdivisions, are not at all consistently related to their meaning or function. Very similar spiritual or emotional concepts could find very different physical expression in different tribal cultures, even if the use of white pigment on a mask, for example, usually indicated a direct connection with the dead (colour other than black, white and the hue of the wood is not usual, many Yoruba masks providing a notable exception). A lofty forehead seems generally (as in the West) to be associated with wisdom, but relatively naturalistic, though superbly simplified masks, which to Western eyes suggest a serene classicism, are found amongst a large range of different tribes with very different associations and functions, including aggressive ones. Once the connection of a carving with its original function is lost, it is difficult to establish with any certainty the purpose for which it was made. Most masks are no doubt anthropomorphic, though portraiture in any sense is very rare; the faces of the masks may show scarifications, recalling the fact that one important medium of art for many tribes is the ritual painting or scarring of the living body to traditional patterns. Bird masks and animal masks also occur (often antelopes or bush-cows); in some areas permeated by Islam, masks nevertheless persist but often in forms stylized almost beyond recognition.

Much tribal ritual is centred on initiation into age-groups – into the young men's or old men's "societies" – each of which has its separate emblems and cult; many carved figures, as well as masks, are associated with such "societies", and often represent patron deities – the god of thunder, the god of fire. Carved figures are as widespread and numerous as masks, and likewise relate to ritual, though some tribes – the relatively prosperous and settled Baule on the Ivory Coast, for example – made carvings almost as luxury goods. The Yoruba in Nigeria were adept carvers of figures in the round, and often crowned their sometimes massive masks with groups of several manikins, highly animated, as if a party were in progress. Among the Yoruba, too, and in some other tribes sculptors could achieve a status and prestige somewhat similar to that of a successful artist in the West.

Study of African tribal art is still at an exploratory stage, and the geographical area involved is enormous – the whole of West and Central Africa, with significant traditions, too, in East Africa. Wood, the dominant medium, is vulnerable to use, to the climate and to the ubiquitous termites or white ants, and the other materials used are also mostly perishable – raffia, for instance, or cotton. After the incursion of Europeans new materials and new motifs – such as the Portuguese musket-bearer, recurrent in West Africa – inevitably followed: both the subject matter and the context of the traditional African arts have been altered by the impact of other cultures not only recently but over a long period of time – Islam and Christianity have been present in Africa for hundreds of years. As the new states of black Africa gradually stabilize into a modern identity, the reconciliation of native traditions with the penetration of Western artefacts and culture should stimulate fresh and original forms of art.

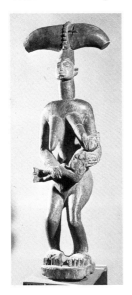

CONGO (right)
A chief's stool
Within their established tradition, workshops or individuals could develop a "manner": this Baluba piece is carved in the "long-faced style of Buli", which is a local region.

NIGERIA (left)
Shango cult figure
Shango is the Yoruba god of lightning and bringer of fertility to women; this is one of his followers.

NIGERIA (below)
Egungun cult mask
This type of mask, which varies in its features, has the dual purpose, in dance, of amusing the crowd and of commemorating an ancestor – jovial acrobats cavort on this Yoruba piece, polychrome, busy with figures.

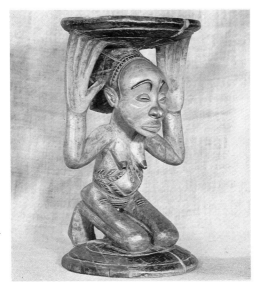

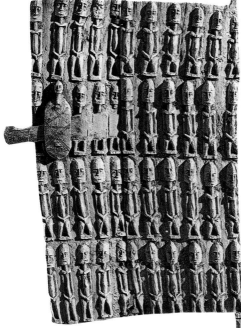

MALI (below)
A granary door
Millet is the staple diet of the Dogon, and the need to grow, harvest and store it safely is imperative. Granaries, built on stone bases to keep it free from damp, adjoin the dwelling-places and are sealed with wooden doors carved with ranks of ancestor figures. It is believed that these will protect the precious harvest from harm; they are sometimes carved with upstretched arms, a plea for rain. The geometrical verticality of Dogon masks recurs in these carvings.

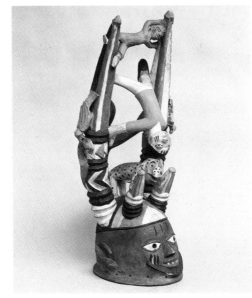

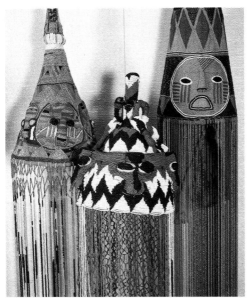

NIGERIA (left)
Bead-embroidered crowns
The identity of a Yoruba king is secret and on his rare public appearances he always wears a beaded crown with hanging fringe to hide his face. These crowns are usually conical, and patterned with faces, often painted faces. Some beads are native, of coral or glass, but most were manufactured in Europe; there are some crowns, too, which mimic Arab turbans or European regalia. The Yoruba were always happy to incorporate extraneous motifs in their versatile art.

Pre-Columbian Art

Civilization in America before the coming of Columbus flourished chiefly in Central America or "Mesoamerica", especially southern Mexico, and on the coastal borders of the Andes mountains of northern South America. In time it spanned approximately between 1800 BC and AD 1500, when it was destroyed by European invasion, and it developed in complete isolation certainly from Europe and probably from the East – an isolation that had lasted from late in the Upper Palaeolithic period, when the original Americans-to-be crossed from their native Asia by the link, now vanished, between Siberia and Alaska. In those 3,000 years civilizations of great complexity came and went and came, some of them practising a highly original and technically accomplished architecture, as well as ceramic, stone and wood sculpture, and painting. Pre-Columbian art developed in considerable diversity over a wide time scale and a vast area, inhabited by many shifting and inadequately recorded peoples; nevertheless certain characteristics, recurrent throughout the region, are forcibly striking – above all a strong and vivid sense for a rather angular linear pattern, but also a feeling for ceramic in three dimensions.

The Mesoamerican cultures are divided into three approximate periods – Pre-Classic, up to AD 200; Classic, 200-900; and Post-Classic, 900 up to the Spanish conquest. From the Pre-Classic period comes mainly simple pottery, including figurines, but also the sophisticated products of the highly developed Olmec culture, which flourished between about 1200 and 600 BC. Most famous are their jade figurines (not shown) and their colossal heads in stone, formidable in the mystery of their purpose, sometimes two metres (8ft) or more in height. The heads are startlingly naturalistic, with a disquieting intensity in their heavy-lipped mouths and frowning expressions. The Olmecs seem to have initiated the Mesoamerican tradition of large ceremonial centres built in stone, and of date-keeping.

The Classic period saw the consolidation of agricultural communities ruled by theocracies centred on cities or religious complexes. They varied in different areas but had common factors – hieroglyphic writing, an advanced astronomy and massive pyramid temples, with the accompanying ritual of a mysterious ballgame and comparable iconographies of sometimes inhuman deities. One distinctive culture was centred on Teotihuacan, a city of about 85,000 people in central Mexico. Better known is the widespread Mayan civilization. The imagery of Mayan art is much concerned with rain and agricultural fertility; formally, the sculpture tends rather to relief, to surface decoration, than to fully three-dimensional expression. Nevertheless, both in stone and in wood, Mayan sculptors show remarkable control of free, cursive, but also densely intricate design: often glyphs (many of which have now been deciphered) proliferate across the surface, filling out the space round the highly stylized but vivid figures. Such carving occurs notably in the temples, on door jambs and lintels, but also on free-standing stelae (not shown) sometimes up to ten metres (30ft) high. One most striking and abundant kind of Mayan art is in fired clay, whether in the form of pots – often painted – or figurines. A few copies of Mayan manuscripts have survived, and rare survivals of mural painting, from the late Classic period, show a developed style and imagery, with profile figures outlined in thick black, filled in with flat colour.

The Post-Classic period was dominated by the emergence of new warrior aristocracies –

TLATILCO, MEXICO (right)
Female figure,
Pre-Classic period
Several early agricultural communities in the Valley of Mexico produced round figurines of this type. The woman is hollow, made of unglazed terracotta, with white slip used to define the eyes, mouth and ears.

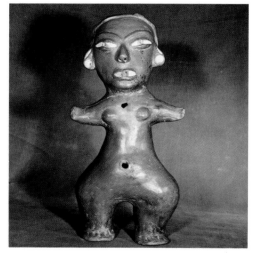

TIKAL, GUATEMALA (below)
Door lintel, *c.* AD 747?
The Maya decorated their ball-courts and temples with stucco, murals and stone- and woodcarving, showing refinement both in handling architectural masses and in decorating surfaces. The lintel came from the interior doorway of a Mayan pyramid temple.

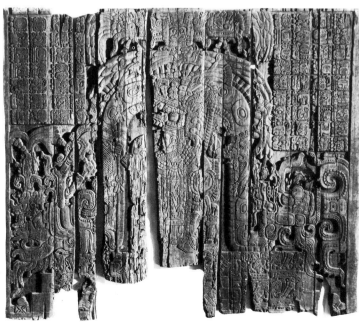

MEXICO (right)
Head, 1200/600 BC
These massive basalt heads were possibly linked to a cult of the jaguar; they are uniquely Olmec. In some jade carvings on a smaller scale feline features are imposed on human faces.

MEXICO (below)
The cosmos, AD 1250/1500
The opening page of this Mixtec manuscript shows the world's five regions – centre and four directions. Various symbols represent the complex constituents of the Mixtec (and also the Aztec) calendar cycles; the fire god holds the centre.

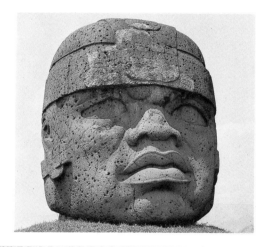

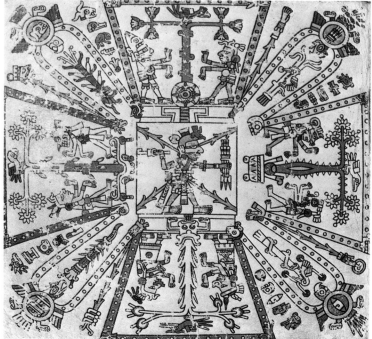

the Mixtecs, the Toltecs and, best known, the Aztecs. They seem to have shared an ever-increasing dependence on gods that required nourishment by human sacrifice. Their sculpture was correspondingly brutal, and often brilliantly and disturbingly expressive. The Toltecs produced colossal free-standing stone sculpture – for example the celebrated male column-figures at Tula – which has a harsh, angular, abstract and massive quality that has much impressed modern sculptors. The Mixtecs produced murals, and especially manuscripts, with flatly coloured figures in complex geometric designs, and were superb craftsmen, in precious stones, in featherwork, in pottery and in cast gold. Aztec art found its most characteristic expression in sculpture – horrifically dramatic, massive (on whatever scale), and handled, often in the hardest of stones, with extraordinary finesse. One of its most famous images is a female deity in childbirth, ruthlessly expressing agony.

In South America, a considerable civilization had flourished from at least 1000 BC, known as the Chavin culture after a temple complex some 3,000 metres (10,000ft) above sea-level in northern central Peru. A chiefly

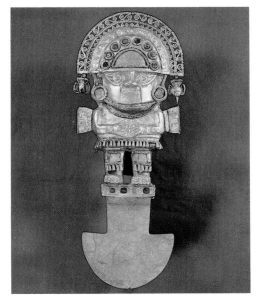

of northern South America is of outstanding quality. The Chimu personage is of gold inlaid with turquoise.

small-scale sculpture – birds and complex zoomorphic figures – is associated with it; also pottery and goldwork. Some of the finest goldworkers were the Chimu on the north coast of Peru (c. AD 1200-1470), but also in Colombia and Ecuador metalwork of great sophistication was made – jewellery, vessels and figures in many techniques, including gold cast by the *cire-perdue* method. There still exist superbly worked textiles from Peru, and a rich harvest of vessels has come to light there, either painted or, most notably, modelled into astonishingly naturalistic heads, sometimes so vivid that it seems they must be portraits.

The best-known culture in South America is that of the Inca, though their dominion was in fact brief (AD 1476-1580). They were superb masons, and their most impressive remains are architectural; of their statuary only miniature stone and metal figures have survived in any quantity. These show a marked tendency towards stereotype, an abstract handling of geometric volumes. The Mesoamerican culture fell first to the Spanish, with the conquest of the Aztec Empire by Cortés; the power of the Inca was finally broken by about 1580, and the vital root of the indigenous culture cut.

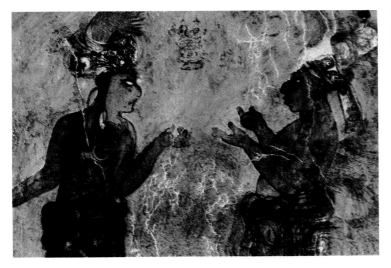

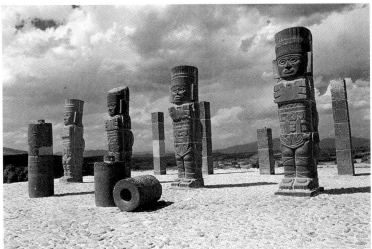

BONAMPAK, MEXICO (above)
Two warriors, c. AD 750
When the Mayan city of Bonampak was discovered in 1946 unique murals came to light, depicting battles and raiding parties which had been launched perhaps in order to obtain enemy prisoners for sacrifice; a religious procession is also shown. These gesticulating, possibly arguing, Indians are lively and expressive; as often in Mayan reliefs, the figures are in profile, in animated silhouette.

JAINA, MEXICO (right)
Priest or *official?*
AD 600/900
The heavy chain, bracelets and tall head-dress suggest a ceremonial functionary; even the markings beside his mouth are scrupulously noted, and this little Mayan, too, seems barrel-chested like a sergeant-major.

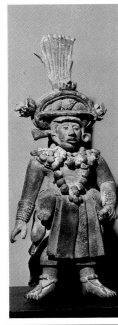

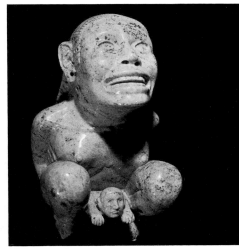

MEXICO (above)
Tlazolteotl, AD 1300/1500
An iron necessity seems to drive forth the child and excruciate his mother, the Aztec birth-goddess.

PERU (right)
Ex voto, c. AD 1500
Spanish interest in Inca gold and silver did not extend to its workmanship. Only small items survive.

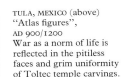

TULA, MEXICO (above)
"Atlas figures",
AD 900/1200
War as a norm of life is reflected in the pitiless faces and grim uniformity of Toltec temple carvings.

PERU (right)
Head, c. AD 500
The small ceramics, often in the shape of heads, of the early, Moche culture are among the finest in Peru.

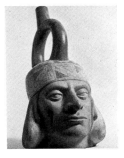

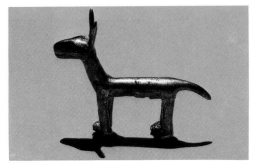

A Tlingit House-Post

The Indians of North America developed no such states and civilization as the natives of South and Central America, but consisted up to the time of the European conquest and after of mostly small tribal groups, culturally distinct and speaking different languages. They developed a variety of life-styles in different parts of the continent, and their art was correspondily diverse. Artistry was everywhere applied to the embellishment of everyday objects – tools and weapons, household utensils or clothing – and in some regions rich traditions of painting and sculpture developed, in association with an elaborate religious ceremonial. Some of these traditions have continued to the present, though the societies in which they developed were destroyed or drastically altered with the progressive westward expansion of European settlement. Surviving works of North American Indian art in museums around the world date mostly from the nineteenth or early twentieth centuries, when European control was already firm.

While the northern and western parts of the continent were inhabited by peoples living by various modes of hunting, fishing and gathering, the Indians of the eastern and southern areas were predominantly farmers leading more settled lives. Sixteenth-century European narrators described large-scale architectural sculpture and murals in the prosperous villages of the south-east, and archaeology has revealed numerous smaller artefacts – including pottery, stone sculpture and engraved shell. Sculpture was less developed in the north-west woodlands, though the tradition among the Iroquois of carving "false-face" masks is noteworthy; both painting and embroidery, however, were common techniques, applied to clothing and equipment often in complex geometric designs. The painting was on hide; for embroidery dyed porcupine quills and moose-hair were used until trade with Europeans introduced coloured cloth, glass beads and extraneous floral designs.

In a similar way European trade enriched and transformed the arts of the Plains tribes. These peoples depended for their livelihood on the hunting mainly of buffalo: hide was their basic material, and their art was applied mainly to costumes and essentially portable possessions. A strong tradition of painting developed, executed in two contrasting styles. Traditionally the women painted such objects as rawhide travelling bags and hide robes in a bold geometric style; men created naturalistic paintings of warlike exploits on robes and tepees, and also symbolic designs for objects associated with rituals. Among the farming Pueblo Indians, dwelling in adobe villages in the south-west, the women plaited baskets and painted pottery in sophisticated, usually abstract designs, also applied in weaving; the men were responsible for the symbolic forms, representational but often highly stylized, applied in murals painted in underground sanctuaries and in elaborate masked costumes representing spirits in public festivals staged by the clans of the village. Some rituals, notably among the Navajo, involved the famous "sand-paintings" (one is reproduced on page 210 in volume 3) in which powder was sprinkled on sand in symbolic, stylized motifs

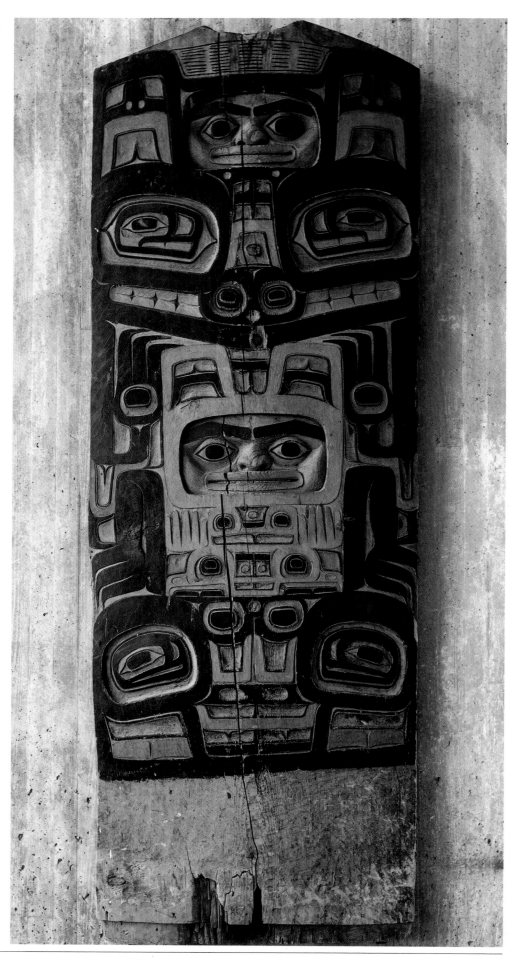

from a rich mythological repertoire. Here, in the south-west, archaeology has revealed that the artistic tradition extends back several hundred years before the arrival of Europeans.

Further west, in the Great Basin and California, where the Indians lived in smaller, scattered groups and supported themselves by gathering and hunting, some extraordinarily fine basketry was produced but painting and sculpture were less developed. These arts had their greatest flowering on the north Pacific coast, which was exceptionally rich in natural resources – especially timber – and supported a relatively large and settled population, who lived mainly by fishing. During the winter months much time and energy were devoted to elaborate festivals; for both ceremonial and utilitarian objects the Indians employed a sophisticated woodcarving in a distinctive style. Perhaps most spectacular were the massive house-posts and the free-standing poles carved with figures proclaiming the ancestry and status of wealthy leaders. This sculpture was usually conceived in relief, and often painted, and a similar vocabulary of stylized motifs was applied to two dimensions – painted on wood, hide or cloth, or woven.

In contrast, the living of the scattered, nomadic Eskimos in the Arctic region was hard-won, but the mastery of bone and ivory carving which these people displayed is hardly less remarkable. On tools or weapons, in toggles or amulets on clothing, in decorative studs for things of wood, the Eskimos depicted with fine feeling the birds and mammals of land and sea on which they depended for their livelihood. They were both carved in the round and engraved, in lively hunting scenes. Eskimo woodcarving was less sophisticated, though expressive masks were made.

Contact with Europeans at first stimulated many local traditions, notably on the Plains and on the north Pacific coast, but the subsequent conquest generally had disastrous effects. Nonetheless Indian culture has proved resilient in some areas. Indian artists have worked to supply collectors since the nineteenth century, and sometimes traditional arts have been revived, though not usually for their old purposes. The Haida Indians, for instance, of the north Pacific coast, perfected the art of carving a local stone, argillite, using traditional themes (not shown) as well as novel ones based on European models.

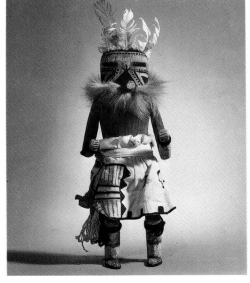

THE SOUTH-WEST (above)
Kachina doll
These small wooden figures represent *Kachina* spirits as they appear impersonated in the sacred dances of the Pueblo – in masks and patterned cloths. Those made for collectors tend to show European influence in pose.

THE SOUTH-WEST (below)
Weaving a blanket
The arts of the hunting and herding Navajo were greatly influenced by the Pueblo, their neighbours. With the simplest of finger-weaving techniques, the woman runs a geometric pattern; men had a different repertoire.

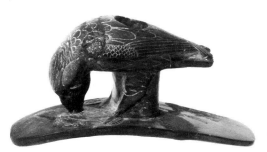

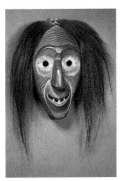

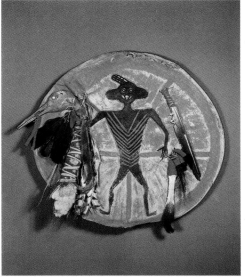

THE MID-WEST (above)
Stone pipe-bowl
Pipe-bowls shaped into quite naturalistic birds or animals are frequent among the numerous small stone carvings, dating to the early centuries AD, of the south-east. This one is from prehistoric Ohio: the bowl is in the bird's back, the legs are a tube.

EASTERN WOODLANDS (above)
"False-face" mask
The deliberately grotesque "false-face" masks played a part in Iroquois rituals intended to cure disease.

NORTH PACIFIC COAST (left)
Carved house-post
A work of the Tlingit tribe, the post is a characteristic example of the architectural carving of the north Pacific coast. Its principal motif is a bear in a squatting pose. Though local variations occur, north Pacific coast art was governed by strict conventions, by a language of abstracted curvilinear motifs almost impossible at first sight to relate to the objects they represent.

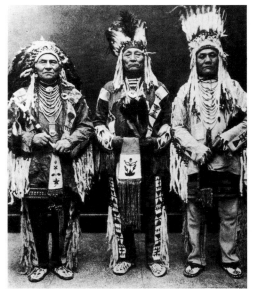

THE PLAINS (above)
Hide shield
Made of buffalo hide, the shield protected not only physically but magically; the stylized figure is the moon-god. It is Crow work.

THE PLAINS (left)
Blackfoot dignitaries
The costumes were adorned with ornamental tassels, with embroidery in floral and geometric patterns and with other accessories, all, like the eagle-feather headdresses, indicative of ritual powers and of social status.

ARCTIC REGIONS (right)
Arrowshaft straighteners
The Eskimo tools are both carved – with polar bear or seal heads – and engraved – with caribou and energetic "matchstick" human figures. (The tool was used on a shaft held over a fire.)

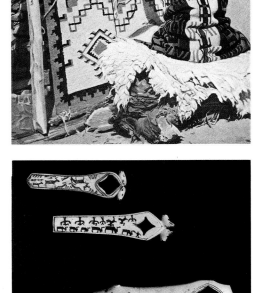

Oceanic Art

The term "Oceanic" is used to describe an enormous geographical zone – nearly 10,000 kilometres (6,000 miles) from north to south and some 14,500 kilometres (9,000 miles) from east to west. The area embraces a continent (Australia), the second largest island in the world (New Guinea), various other large islands such as those of New Zealand – and a multitude of smaller islands spangling the huge swell of the Pacific between New Guinea and South America. Inevitably, the art produced in so vast an area is very diverse in form, and for ethnic as well as geographical reasons. Its makers are the descendants of successive settlings by migrants from the west of mixed origins, some Mongoloid, some Melanotic or dark-skinned. There are often affinities with the art and culture of the tribal peoples of South-East Asia (see vol. 3 p. 28), though these less isolated peoples have mostly come into contact with Buddhism, Hinduism or Islam.

Like the indigenous art of Africa, Oceanic artefacts were not made with any idea of their being "art" as the word is used in the West. Oceanic paintings and sculptures were conceived as an integral part of the religious and social ceremony of everyday island life, and

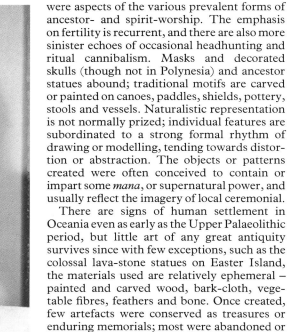

were aspects of the various prevalent forms of ancestor- and spirit-worship. The emphasis on fertility is recurrent, and there are also more sinister echoes of occasional headhunting and ritual cannibalism. Masks and decorated skulls (though not in Polynesia) and ancestor statues abound; traditional motifs are carved or painted on canoes, paddles, shields, pottery, stools and vessels. Naturalistic representation is not normally prized; individual features are subordinated to a strong formal rhythm of drawing or modelling, tending towards distortion or abstraction. The objects or patterns created were often conceived to contain or impart some *mana*, or supernatural power, and usually reflect the imagery of local ceremonial.

There are signs of human settlement in Oceania even as early as the Upper Palaeolithic period, but little art of any great antiquity survives since with few exceptions, such as the colossal lava-stone statues on Easter Island, the materials used are relatively ephemeral – painted and carved wood, bark-cloth, vegetable fibres, feathers and bone. Once created, few artefacts were conserved as treasures or enduring memorials; most were abandoned or sometimes destroyed once their immediate

SEPIK, NEW GUINEA (above)
Ancestor figure
Squatting ancestor figures recur not only in Oceania but in tribal South-East Asia (see vol. 3 p. 28). Such figures could be channels for ghostly power; their pose perhaps had connotations of fertility and rebirth.

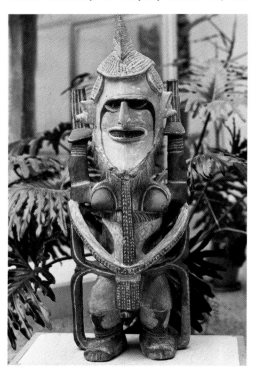

NEW IRELAND (left)
Uli (Ancestor figure)
These bisexual images were created for the climax of a series of ceremonies in a three-year cycle. Then huge painted figures were erected, in front of which ritual dances were enacted; this is one of the smaller statues that surrounded the central structure.

NEW IRELAND (below)
"Soul-boat"
Local custom ordained that the body of a dead chief should be laid in a canoe and sent out to sea. His companions are thought to be relatives or supporters, and enemies he had slain. The figures resemble *uli*; every surface is enriched.

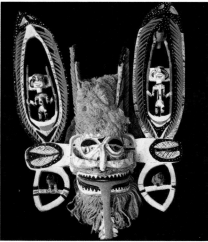

SEPIK, NEW GUINEA (above)
Crocodile head
The crocodile was one of the most favoured animal motifs of the Sepik area, and often, as here, adorned the prows of Sepik canoes. Since it can glide swiftly through the water, it was both appropriate and helpful magically as a figurehead.

NEW IRELAND (left)
Malanggan
New Ireland *malanggans* ("carvings") show a wider variation of design than is common in Oceanic art. Brightly painted, they were used in funeral rites or in initiation ceremonies; the wearer of a mask like this would represent a spirit.

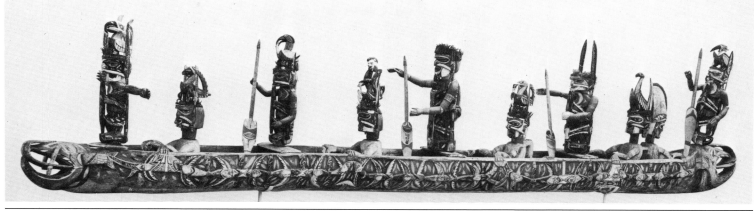

purpose had been fulfilled. However, since foreign intrusion into many parts of the region is fairly recent, the traditions in which they were conceived have often remained unadulterated and stable well into this century.

Ethnologists usually distinguish three main areas in Oceania – Melanesia, Polynesia and Micronesia. The most aesthetically rewarding art comes from Melanesia, which includes New Guinea and the fringes of smaller islands to the north and east: here there is great variety, even within small, but fairly populous, areas such as the Sepik River in New Guinea. Melanesia is also the region closest to Indonesia, where there is a strong feeling for decorative brilliance and fanciful ornament. Carving in wood, often coloured, predominates, and the ancestor figure and the human head are recurrent themes, both in woven or carved and brightly painted masks and in pattern form as decoration on all kinds of surfaces. To a Western observer, unfamiliar with their symbolism, the visual intensity of these images – sometimes horrific, but by no means always so – can be haunting. In parts of New Guinea, craftsmen's work was prized, even collected, and specialist artists emerged.

Besides New Guinea, the sculpture of New Ireland, one of the major islands in the Bismarck Archipelago, has attracted particular attention in the twentieth-century West – especially the ancestor figures known as *uli*, and the closely related decorative sculpture, *malanggan*, displayed at festivals. One product of New Ireland, preserved in a Western museum, the so-called "soul-boat", is famous, not least for its impressive size. The figures in the canoe are human in scale but awesomely demonic and inhuman in appearance; as in the *uli*, significant parts of the body are ferociously emphasized – eyes, teeth and genitalia.

The artefacts of Polynesia, the wide scattering of islands over the Pacific from New Zealand to Easter Island, may seem in comparison less vital, more decorative. Ancestor figures and masks are rare; unfortunately early missionaries were responsible for a thorough and widespread destruction or mutilation of sculpted ancestral deities. But the Polynesian delight in complex rhythms of surface patterning finds many variations in many media, from the spectacular featherwork of Hawaii to the intricately carved wood and greenstone of the New Zealand Maoris – and including the

"living art" of tattoo. The Maori fascination with curvilinear surface ornament was almost obsessive; highly complex linear patterning is found in the carved decoration of canoes and of the doorposts and lintels of meeting-houses, and still persists, even if the original vitality appears only rarely in modern work. Remote in the east, Easter Island produced colossal human figures in stone, sometimes 18 metres (60ft) high, presiding enigmatically over a windswept, treeless landscape.

Australian art was somewhat different in kind: after a first migratory wave Australia remained isolated. The Aborigines' images are mostly drawn or painted rather than carved in the round; scratched on rock surfaces and painted in caves or on the ground, they range from simple figurative images, human or animal, to formal and abstract patterns. Among the most famous are the Wandjina paintings in the north-west – tall white-faced and red-haloed figures (not shown) – and the so-called "X-ray" paintings of Arnhem Land.

Micronesia, the group of islands to the north-west of the Pacific, shows in contrast a handling of form often spare, smooth and austere, at times almost streamlined.

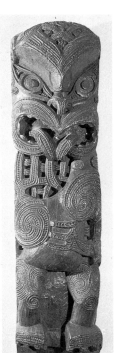

HAWAII (right)
Kukailimoku
The ferocious Hawaiian god of war is made out of vivid feathers on netting over a wicker framework. Natives presented Captain Cook, when he landed, with a similar object: this god demanded human sacrifice.

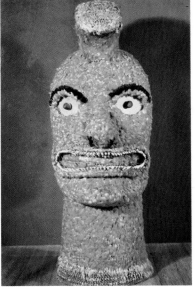

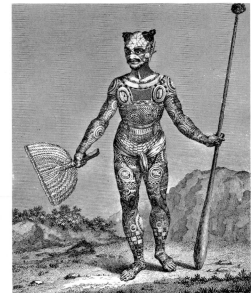

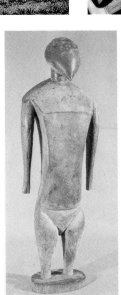

NEW ZEALAND (above)
Carved house-post
A high degree of finish is characteristic of most Maori art. Craftsmen – and the tools they used – were accorded honour, since they did their work under the authority and guidance of a divinity.

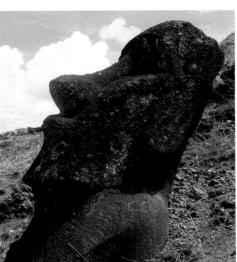

(above) *Tattooed warrior*
This early 19th-century engraving may represent a native of the Marquesas Islands: there the entire skin surface was covered in elaborate designs. In New Zealand the Maoris used to confine tattoos to certain parts of the body; and the more elaborate the tattoo, the greater its wearer's social status or wealth.

EASTER ISLAND (left)
Ancestor figure?
Insufficient wood grew on the island for the making of boats, and the settlers became isolated. Yet many not dissimilar megaliths are found on Sumatra or Nias (see vol. 3 p. 28). Sheer size and their bleak setting make them the most awe-inspiring creations of Oceanic art.

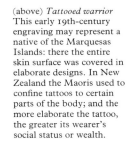

AUSTRALIA (above)
A kangaroo
The portrayal of an animal in the "X-ray" style is a feature limited to the art of Australian Aborigines: it is the depiction, inside the outer shape, of inner organs and the skeleton of their quarry. The image is painted on a strip of bark; its purpose was symbolic, co-ordinating man and Nature.

NUKURO (left)
Tino
Tinos, in Nukuro, one of the Caroline Islands, were the creators of the world. Such Micronesian images in smoothly carved wood were sometimes yet further refined, with hands and feet altogether eliminated, and the smooth, beaked head made still more prominent.

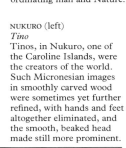

Egyptian Art 1: The Old Kingdom

Prehistoric and tribal art is essentially instinctual, and lacks an architectural context. It is spatially disorganized, without frame or distinction between the figure and the ground on which it stands. The emergence of a highly organized, schematic and structured art about 3000 BC is almost abrupt, and coincides with the rise of civilization itself, suddenly articulate with a written language. The focus of this flowering was those central lands on which Asia, Africa and Europe pivot, and in them especially the basins of the great rivers of Egypt and Mesopotamia; it came perhaps a little earlier in the latter than in Egypt, but Mesopotamia (see p. 28) was to prove much more vulnerable to disruption.

The traditional structure of Egypt's history rests on the account given by one Manetho in the early third century BC. Its chronology is divided into Kingdoms, Old, Middle and New (with two intermediate periods), and these into dynasties calibrating some three millennia. About 3000 BC, a monarch named Menes is said to have united the regions of the northern and southern Nile below Aswan, and to have founded the first of the Old Kingdom dynasties. Menes is often thought to be identical

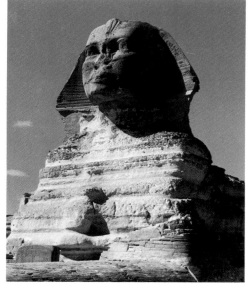

GIZA (above)
The Sphinx, c. 2530 BC
The Egyptian Sphinx was a regal symbol rather than a monster; the Giza Sphinx's head is the head of the 4th-Dynasty ruler Chephren. It was cut from the living rock which provided the stone for nearby pyramids.

with Pharaoh Narmer, and a large cosmetic palette featuring Narmer – one of the earliest specimens of Egyptian art – exemplifies, almost unheralded, its basic and enduring conventions. The low relief is set in a frame of regular shape; within its perimeter, the ground is divided precisely into bands, or registers, on which the images are placed. These are seen in profile, clear cut, and generally directed from left to right. There is no real sense of perspective, but instead an ordering in terms of scale, more important figures being bigger than minor ones. Extreme stylization is already established, and some conventions of drawing: the profile in which the human figure is almost always shown is not strictly true, having usually two left (or two right) hands and feet, with part of the torso and the eye rendered frontally.

Specialists now view with scorn the platitude that Egyptian art continued unchanged for 3,000 years, but for the ordinary spectator the extraordinary consistency of style is striking. Egyptian art had a religious, or magical, purpose, and the stamina of its conventions was due to the stability of religious dogma and the fact that the state was an expression of

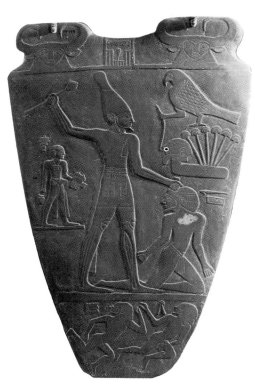

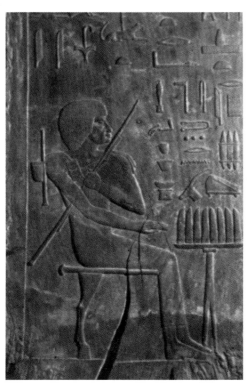

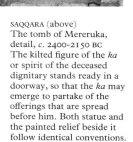

SAQQARA (left)
Hesy-ra before an offering table, c. 2650 BC
In one of the five carved wooden reliefs in Hesy-ra's 3rd-Dynasty tomb, he sits beneath hieroglyphs which list not only his titles but also the libations and the offerings that he hopes to obtain in the after-life. He carries writing materials.

SAQQARA (above)
The tomb of Mereruka, detail, c. 2400-2150 BC
The kilted figure of the *ka* or spirit of the deceased dignitary stands ready in a doorway, so that the *ka* may emerge to partake of the offerings that are spread before him. Both statue and the painted relief beside it follow identical conventions.

MEMPHIS (above)
The palette of Pharaoh Narmer, c. 3100 BC
The slate relief, a rare 1st-Dynasty survival, shows Narmer victorious, overcoming those who opposed his unification of Egypt. The god Horus assists.

SAQQARA? (right)
Servant straining beer, c. 2400 BC
The style of this brightly painted wooden statuette (she guarantees ale for her master's after-life) contrasts with the stiff gravity of royal statuary.

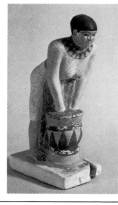

SAQQARA (right)
The tomb of Mereruka: *Cutting a hyena's throat, c. 2400-2150 BC*
The 32-room *mastaba* (a low flat-topped type of tomb; only Pharaohs built pyramids) of Mereruka is extensively decorated with painted reliefs of daily life. Hieroglyphic signs above the farm servants are like cartoon captions: the one using the knife is saying to the other: "Grip it tightly!"

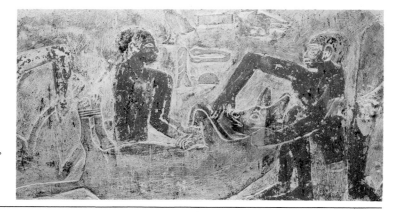

that dogma, indeed was largely a religious institution. The king, or Pharaoh, was a god, and the hierarchy of society beneath him was exactly and divinely fixed and ordered.

In the Third Dynasty, in the late twenty-seventh century BC, the Old Kingdom entered its prime. The capital was established at Memphis above the delta of the Nile; the royal pyramids were located nearby at Giza and Saqqara. Most Egyptian art now extant, even the temple art and colossal outdoor sculpture, was designed not for the use of living patrons but to accompany or adorn the dead. Unlike later European arts, which commemorate the past or the present, this art was prospective, looking to the future, though indissolubly linked with death; and it had an essentially practical purpose. Prayers were meant to be recited by the living which would bring to life the objects surrounding the dead, and all the trappings – clothes, ornaments, weapons, jewellery and so on, and the painted or relief decorations on the walls of tombs showing hunting, feasting and the pleasures of earthly life – were intended for the future delectation and maintenance of the dead man's or woman's *ka*, or spirit, in the after-life.

Painting and relief in Egypt were closely related, reliefs being usually coloured, and conceived in one plane rather than in the round. The walls of tombs and temples were often completely covered with decorations, but always in a disciplined format, within a precisely controlled framework, as in the early palette of Pharaoh Narmer. The subject matter ranged widely, from formal hieratic imagery, closely related to the accompanying hieroglyphics, to representations of earthly life, sometimes enchanting in their naturalism, especially towards the end of the Old Kingdom, notably in the tombs of nobles of the Fifth and Sixth Dynasties. The tomb of Vizier Mereruka has particularly fine reliefs, proving the vivacity possible within set formulae. The famous "*Geese of Meidum*" are as brilliant now as when they were painted, about 2550 BC.

The quality of the monumental sculpture of the Old Kingdom was never to be surpassed. The earliest royal portrait known anywhere, the seated life-size statue of Pharaoh Djoser, of about 2680-2660 BC, is unfortunately much damaged (not shown); it was originally painted, with eyes of inlaid quartz. The statue of Pharaoh Chephren 100 years later demon-

strates the same set form. Both seem still to dwell in concentrated gravity within the cubic block from which they were cut, and on which they were first drawn, in profile on the side, frontal on the front. But though still bound by these limitations of pose, viewpoint and handling such statues are sometimes strikingly naturalistic, like *Prince Rahotep and his wife Nofret*, seated forever as if they had just been groomed by the make-up artist. Especially when the person represented was of comparatively low rank, remarkably realistic images could appear, though in the best of them inessentials continued to be discarded to retain the essential form of the whole. The *Seated scribe* now in the Louvre is indeed the eternal essential bureaucrat. He is less than life-size, but Egyptian sculptors could manage any scale, from small wooden models to the desolate giant rock Sphinx rising 20 metres (65ft) above the desert at Giza.

Middle Kingdom statuary became increasingly static, but could also be softer and more human in feeling, and was also set up not only in tombs but also in public places. But it was in truth an interim period, awaiting the richer and more ambitious art of the New Kingdom.

GIZA (left)
Pharaoh Chephren,
c. 2585-2560 BC
Chephren is carved in a hard stone taking a high polish, and shaped to an established regal formula.

MEIDUM (below)
Prince Rahotep and his wife Nofret, c. 2550 BC
The statues are so vivid that the diggers who first discovered them in 1871 fled in terror. Although the postures follow rigid formulae, the paint on the faces is as bright and real as life, and the eyes gleam with rock-crystal irises; the details are rendered with minute truthfulness.

SAQQARA (below)
Seated scribe, c. 2450 BC
This small painted statue of the early 5th Dynasty is one of the finest of a large group of very similar *Scribes*. Other dignitaries were also represented about their characteristic tasks, in typical postures. In this cross-legged pose the kilt was stretched taut, and so could be used virtually as a desk on which to write.

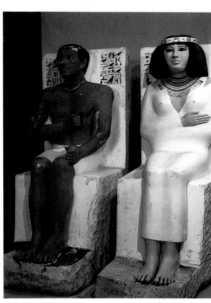

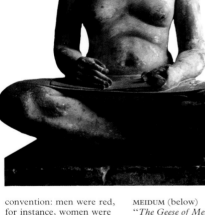

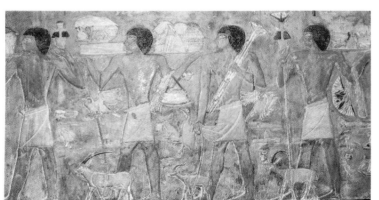

SAQQARA (left)
The tomb of Ptah-hotep, detail: *Funerary procession, c.* 2400 BC
Figures in Egyptian art were not only drawn but also coloured according to convention: men were red, for instance, women were yellow. The artist first drafted an outline, then chiselled the relief, before applying flat colours to set forth figures and objects.

MEIDUM (below)
"*The Geese of Meidum*",
c. 2550 BC
The procession of various species of geese belongs to a rural scene, stylized but full of vivid incident.

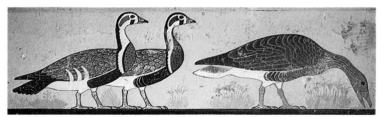

Egyptian Art 2: The New Kingdom

Between the close of the Old Kingdom in 2155 BC and the beginning of the New Kingdom in about 1554 BC the political stability of Egypt was somewhat disrupted; in 1785 BC the Middle Kingdom had collapsed, and Egypt was ruled by alien invaders. But the monarchs of the Eighteenth Dynasty (1554-1305 BC) not only expelled the intruders and re-established internal order, but transformed Egypt into a major world power, with an empire embracing at its peak Palestine and Syria. The Eighteenth Dynasty is usually considered the Golden Age of Egyptian art.

Thebes was now the capital, the centre of enormous architectural projects – the temples of Karnak and Luxor and, above all, across the Nile, the tombs of the Theban rulers tunnelled into the cliffs, the famous "Valley of the Kings". The colossal pyramids and *mastabas* of the earlier periods had proved indefensible against generations of tomb-robbers, but even the hidden rock-cut tombs were not inviolable. Most of the mortuary sculpture has been lost, but surviving examples from the early Eighteenth Dynasty show a development towards a softer, more graceful style, though the poses are much the same. In many tombs the murals remain, often in gouache on a mud-and-plaster ground rather than in coloured low relief (which the poor quality of the stone precluded); perhaps partly as a result, these paintings, though still carried out within the old conventions, depict the pleasures of earthly life, from fowling to dancing girls, often with greater brilliance and freedom. There is even often more than a hint of movement.

In the midst of the New Kingdom's prosperity there occurred an interlude of a mere couple of decades, about 1379-1361 BC, which has fascinated posterity. Under Amenhotep IV a new art was stimulated by a new religion, a form of sun-worship. This was the cult of Aten, the sun-disk, and Amenhotep, his representative on earth, changed his name to Akhenaten and established a new capital at Amarna.

The individual personality of Akhenaten stands out in surviving statuary uniquely among the severely formal representations of centuries of Pharaohs. Amidst some changes in subject matter arising out of the new cult, the dominant image in Amarna art is that of Akhenaten himself, whose idiosyncratic features, long-faced, large- and loose-lipped, almost dreamily visionary, contrast with the classic clarity of the busts of his wife Nefertiti. The earliest portraits of the new art are often unflattering to the point of caricature, which has sometimes been attributed to the Pharaoh's insistence on truth and sincerity, but later ones are softened. Generally, Amarna art is more vivid than before, more sensual, and seeks response on a personal rather than on an ideal level; it is much more sympathetic to modern sensibility than the orthodox stream of Egyptian art. Fortunately a significant quantity of Amarna art has survived the ruthless destruction of the subsequent reaction.

The reversion to orthodoxy is, however, far more richly represented, largely owing to the chance of history that preserved the tomb of one of Akhenaten's successors, Tutankhamun, intact from the ravages of tomb-robbers. Assembled about 1361-1352 BC, its store of literally thousands of objects deposited to accompany the dead man into his after-life remained unsuspected until 1922. The overriding impression of this hoard is of sheer ostentation in wealth, with its silver, precious stones, intricate inlay and carving – and gold. The innermost of the layers of Tutankhamun's coffin is made of 110 kilograms (243lb Troy)

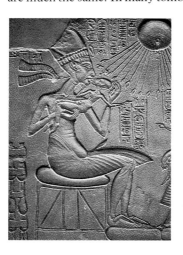

AMARNA (left)
Akhenaten with his baby daughter, c. 1379-1361 BC
Incised in limestone, the heretic Pharaoh sits under the sun-disk he worshipped. The sweeping, quite harsh freedom of line is in quite startling contrast beside the rigidity of earlier art.

THEBES (right)
A banquet, c. 1413-1367 BC
Wine, women and song are a recurring theme in the tombs near Thebes. What is remarkable here is the shimmering movement in the hair and robes of the musicians, the feeling for the twining gestures of the dance in the girls beside.

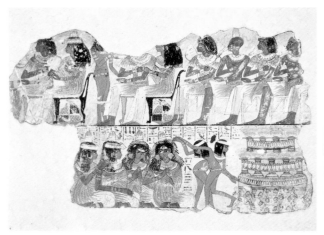

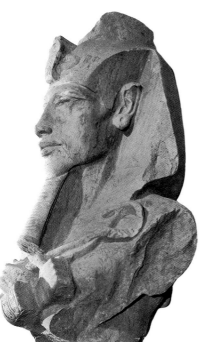

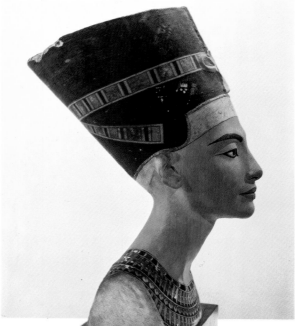

KARNAK (right)
Akhenaten, c. 1379-1361 BC
An inscription says that Akhenaten took a personal interest in the art he had commissioned, and himself briefed the master mason. His crown, his beard set in a cylinder, his flail and crook, are the intimidating symbols of authority; his face is equally stern, but not impersonal. This head is a fragment of a column figure, one of 30 found in a courtyard at Karnak.

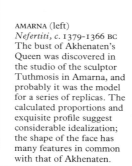

AMARNA (left)
Nefertiti, c. 1379-1366 BC
The bust of Akhenaten's Queen was discovered in the studio of the sculptor Tuthmosis in Amarna, and probably it was the model for a series of replicas. The calculated proportions and exquisite profile suggest considerable idealization; the shape of the face has many features in common with that of Akhenaten.

THEBES (above)
One of four cases for Tutankhamun's viscera, *c.* 1361-1352 BC
The four miniature coffins, of beaten gold inlaid with cornelian and coloured glass, covered inside with magical texts, are craftsmen's work of extraordinary quality. The design repeats that of the mummy-case proper.

THEBES (below)
Tutankhamun hunting ostriches, c. 1361-1352 BC
The ostrich feathers which completed Tutankhamun's long-handled golden fan

(a treasure of his tomb) are lost, but the embossed hunting scene is perfectly preserved. A walking *ankh* hieroglyph behind the car holds out an identical fan.

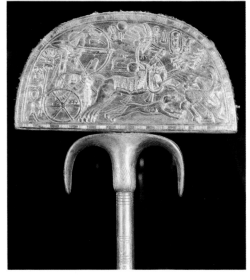

of gold. The proliferation of riches and the virtuosity of the workmanship tend to dazzle our eyes to some unevenness in quality: the return to the old formulae results in rather blatant, though splendid, forms, empty in emotion beside the subtlety of Akhenaten's art – even though here and there the more naturalistic approach stemming from Amarna is maintained, indeed many of the objects in Tutankhamun's tomb must have been made during Akhenaten's reign. Where this freedom persists, notably in reliefs, for instance on the back of Tutankhamun's throne, the art has a touching quality; the sheer profusion staggers the imagination, and its documentary importance for the social, political and religious history of the period is immense.

During the next thousand years Egypt slowly declined in power, becoming subject eventually to a series of invasions. The later New Kingdom Pharaohs were at first intent on the consolidation of the imperial image: the proliferation of colossal statues of Ramesses II suggests an attack of megalomania. These are conceived entirely in traditional terms, being severely simple and hieratic, though often extremely impressive, if mainly in their scale

and in the enigma of their impersonality. Wall-painting and relief carving continue but are conventional in quality – time-worn motifs repeated without variation – and the same is true of most of the manuscript illumination. This, however, was a remarkable Egyptian invention: from these beaten strips of papyrus reed the line leads to vellum, paper and to mass-production printing.

In the last millennium BC patrons and artists continued to imitate and sometimes to refine earlier styles, and the brief Saite Dynasty (664-525 BC) made the past almost into a cult. In the seventh century, Greek traders had been permitted to establish a city at Naucratis on the Nile delta, but though Egyptian influence on Archaic Greek art is quite distinct (see p. 34), Greek culture had no apparent effect on the Egyptians. The conservatism of Egyptian art survived even the final extinction of the indigenous dynasties, and the establishment of the Ptolemaic Kingdom in the wake of the conquest of Alexander the Great. Some of the Egyptian images most popular today date from this time – the animal sculpture, with its distinctive smooth clarity, and the hauntingly cold, implacably sinister animal-headed gods.

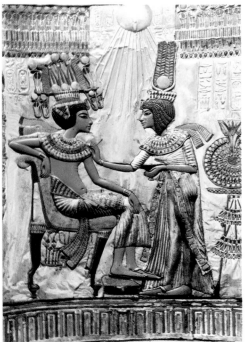

THEBES (left)
A panel of Tutankhamun's throne, before 1361 BC
His Queen offers scented oil to her husband in an ornate pavilion; the style and relative intimacy recall Akhenaten's reliefs, and the throne must have been made during the Amarna period.

ABU SIMBEL (right)
The Temple of Ramesses II, c. 1304-1237 BC
Four statues of Ramesses, more than 20m (65ft) high, form the imposing façade, cut from the living rock. The features are bland, the forms squared and weighty. (The entire monument was moved up the cliff in 1967.)

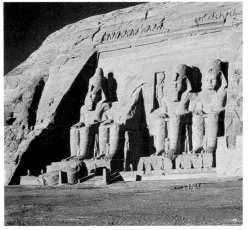

EDFU (below)
The Falcon of Horus, 3rd century BC
A long procession of carved gods and priests lines the steps of Horus' temple, and the capitals of the columns are richly sculpted in low relief. This seems more an idol than a representation: naturalism is subservient to the sacred symbolism.

DEIR EL MEDINA (below)
Cha' and Mere pay homage to Osiris, c. 1405-1367 BC
The brightly illustrated papyrus manuscript is *The Book of the Dead*, a series of prayers to the gods to assure resurrection.

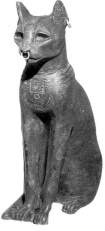

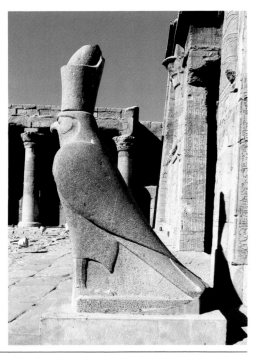

SAQQARA? (above)
Cat, after 30 BC
The hollow-cast figurine inscribed with protective symbols served as a votive offering probably to the goddess Bastet. Many elegant, highly detailed images of animals survive from the later periods.

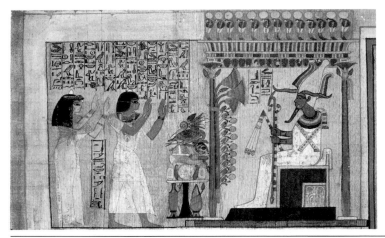

Western Asian Art

A second major artistic culture of early antiquity was more or less contemporaneous with that of Egypt, developing in the regions stretching from the Persian Gulf to the Black Sea and from the eastern littoral of the Mediterranean as far as the frontiers of modern Afghanistan, but tending always to centre on the basins of the two great rivers Tigris and Euphrates (Mesopotamia). The art of the whole area is embraced by the term "Western Asiatic", but is often labelled according to whichever temporarily dominant strain is under discussion – as Mesopotamian but also as Sumerian, Akkadian, Babylonian, Assyrian, Persian. Geographically less firmly defined than was Egypt on the strong life-line of the Nile, the political development of Western Asia proved as unstable as its frontiers, its continuity ever broken by invasion and alien occupations. Art nevertheless developed fundamentally along consistent lines, reflecting persistently the concepts of divinity and kingship, closely interlocked.

By the fourth millennium BC – somewhat earlier than in Egypt – what had been a scattered agrarian society in the fertile region of the lower Euphrates was tending to coalesce in urban settlements under a deified ruler. The characteristic focus of this culture, the Sumerian, was the man-made staged hill, the *ziggurat*, topped by a temple. From about 3500 BC religious observances were enhanced by remarkable developments in the arts, followed by the invention of a cuneiform writing. Closely allied to the early pictographic symbols was the imagery used in one of the most persistent of all Western Asian media – the cylinder seal, carved with stylized figures or glyphs. Though miniature in scale, these seals tend to survive far better than larger work, which was often in ephemeral materials: stone was very scarce in lower Mesopotamia. In them abstract geometric designs are enlivened by formal images of elemental gods, of animals, of religious ceremonial. The feeling for frieze-like design in low relief, characteristic and persistent in all Western Asian art, is clear, but sculpture in the round was also obviously highly developed, though well-preserved survivors are very rare. The best examples show a sophisticated ability to reconcile the human body with abstract form, but there are also some that look by comparison crude or grotesque. The Sumerians, like the ancient Egyptians, prepared

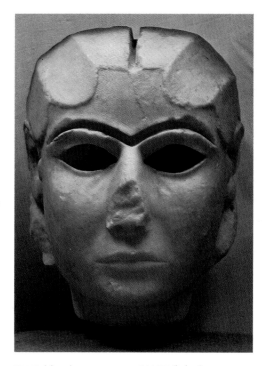

MESOPOTAMIA (right)
Cylinder seal and its impression: *Gilgamesh grapples with a bull and with a lion, c.* 2300 BC
Such seals of stone or fired earth were rolled on damp clay to produce a relief impression, which served as a signature. Myths such as the deeds of Gilgamesh, a great Mesopotamian hero, were often represented.

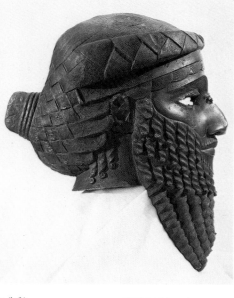

WARKA (above)
"*The Lady of Warka*", *c.* 3500 BC
The marble head, once part of a body perhaps of wood, is witness to the "Proto-literate" period. Eyes and eyebrows were inlaid with coloured stone: the hair, which is summarily cut compared to the superbly modelled face, was covered by beaten gold or copper.

LAGASH (below)
The ruler Gudea, c. 2100 BC
More than 30 statues or parts of statues of Gudea have been identified. Most are carved from the hard stone called diorite, which can be worked to a smooth, subtle finish, with the body largely undifferentiated. But the hands, clasped in worship in a gesture found very early, are well formed.

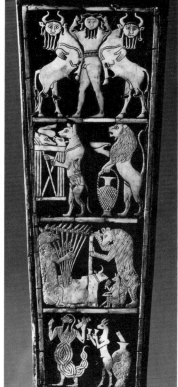

ERIDU (above)
Male figure, c. 4500 BC
This clay idol is one of the earliest sculptures in the round yet unearthed in Mesopotamia. Similar female terracottas survive, their shoulders also being dotted with lumps, which are presumed by some to represent tattooing. They are a mysterious prelude to the rise of civilization.

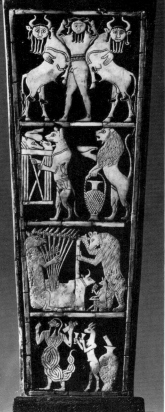

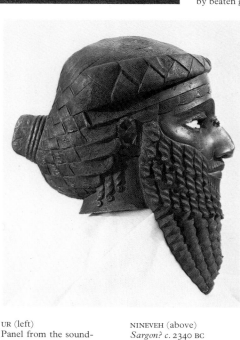

UR (left)
Panel from the sound-box of a harp; *A hero* and *Fabulous animals, c.* 2600 BC
The harp is treasure from one of the chambers of the royal tombs at Ur. On the panel, inlaid with gold, is a scene of an ass playing a harp of the same type. There is a new naturalism in this most famous piece.

NINEVEH (above)
Sargon? c. 2340 BC
This powerful image of an Akkadian ruler shows an accomplished handling of bronze – with distinct textures for the face, hair and beard. The Akkadians adopted Sumerian culture but gave it their own form. The head is hieratic and magnificent, fully assured in its stern simplification.

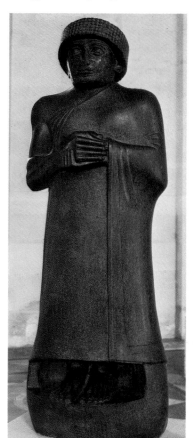

for an after-life with well-furnished tombs, and excavations, for instance at the famous royal graves of about 2600 BC at Ur, have revealed fragments of a luxurious civilization, rich in gold and silver and precious stones; copper was used extensively for horse-trappings and on furniture.

The Sumerian dynasties were supplanted about 2340 BC by Sargon of Akkad, who for a time unified the Mesopotamian city states on a centre further to the north (near modern Baghdad). The Akkadians, taking over most of the Sumerian artistic conventions, produced some almost fiercely vigorous and more natur-alistic images. The Akkadian era was de-stroyed in its turn by the insurgent Guti from the north, and from about 2125 BC to 1594 BC there ensued a long period of flux all over Western Asia. The shifting, often violent pat-terns of restless movement affected the forms of art, as new ideas and styles flooded in from all quarters, from Egypt and Syria or from the Aegean; Mesopotamian styles likewise were widely exported. During the domination of the Guti there was, however, briefly a stable regime, apparently inspired by one remarkable ruler, Gudea, about 2100 BC. During his rule a very impressive, monumental, life-size statu-ary was developed, highly formalized but with great feeling for the balance of naturalistic representation with abstract sculptural mass. These qualities seem to recur in the sophisti-cated, hieratic style, remarkably consistent in various media, developing in an empire cen-tred on Babylon by the time of the great law-maker Hammurabi (about 1792 BC).

A major turning-point in the art of Western Asia came with the consolidation and then spectacular territorial expansion of the As-syrian dynasties from their centres in the northern Tigris valley. The most remarkable and highly distinctive achievement of Assyrian art came in the form of the continuous low relief frieze (see over).

Briefly, even before the collapse of Assyria to the Medes in 612 BC, Babylon had re-emerged as a political and cultural centre, but it, too, succumbed to these new northern invaders. Persian, or Iranian, art, while tend-ing to be influenced predominantly by Meso-potamian example, had already produced its individual styles – very early in the area of Elam and most notably perhaps in the numerous surviving bronze fittings of between about 1200 and 800 BC from Luristan. The art of the Persian Empire, however, was pre-dominantly architectural in character, with decoration drawing on traditional Meso-potamian themes; the Persians, too, deployed long ceremonial relief friezes, but also deve-loped skilled metalworking techniques. Per-sian rule was extended from the magnificent capital at Persepolis both east and west.

Other peoples on the periphery produced over the centuries their own variations on Mesopotamian and Egyptian styles – the Hit-tites in Asia Minor, for example, and the peoples of Syria – and the regions bordering on the Mediterranean looked both ways. Early Greek art shows strong traces of Meso-potamian influence, but in the fourth century BC the Asian thrust westward was finally reversed by Alexander the Great. A Greek influence persisted long after the fragmen-tation of Alexander's Empire by the Parthian dynasties, although Persian tradition gradu-ally reasserted itself and, under the Sassanian dynasty (AD 224-642), the Hellenistic tradi-tions were reorientalized. In the seventh century AD art in the whole area was funda-mentally altered by Islam (see vol. 3 pp. 22ff).

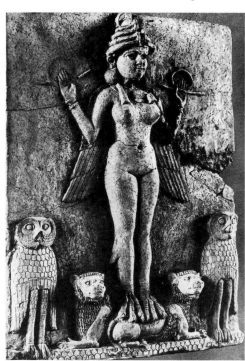

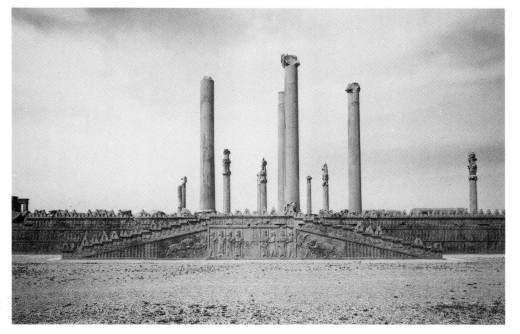

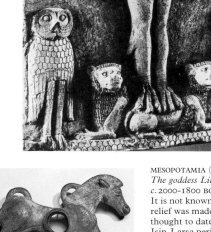

LURISTAN (above)
Horse bit, 9th century BC
Small bronzes showing a wide diversity of elegantly stylized motifs (sometimes Mesopotamian in origin) accompanied prehistoric Iranians to their graves.

MESOPOTAMIA (above)
The goddess Lilith,
c. 2000-1800 BC
It is not known where the relief was made but it is thought to date from the Isin-Larsa period – after the collapse of the last dynasty of Ur, before the ascendancy of Hammurabi. The goddess Lilith was a goddess of death: in each hand she holds a length of rope, which signifies the span of man's life; at her feet are her attributes, the lion and the owl, in whose guise she sometimes appeared. The awesomely magnetic terracotta was coloured red and black.

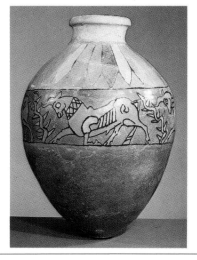

PERSEPOLIS (above)
Processional stair,
c. 500 BC
The magnificent ruins of Darius I's Palace attest his power – and the skill of his craftsmen (some of whom were surely Greek).

MESOPOTAMIA (left)
Enamelled vase, *c.* 700 BC
The vase perhaps reveals, when set beside an early Greek vase, how much the rising Aegean civilization owed to its Asian links – a whole formal vocabulary.

IRAN (right)
Ewer, 6th/7th century AD
The superb metalwork of the Sassanians often has early Persian motifs – deliberately revived.

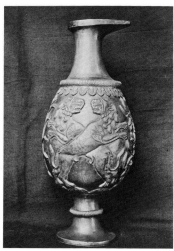

The Lion Hunt Reliefs from Nineveh

KHORSABAD (below)
*Lamassu, c.*710 BC
Colossal winged figures
stood in pairs flanking
the entrance to Assyrian
palaces, benevolent spirits
opposing evil. There are
parallels in Hittite art.

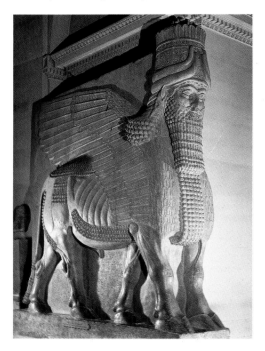

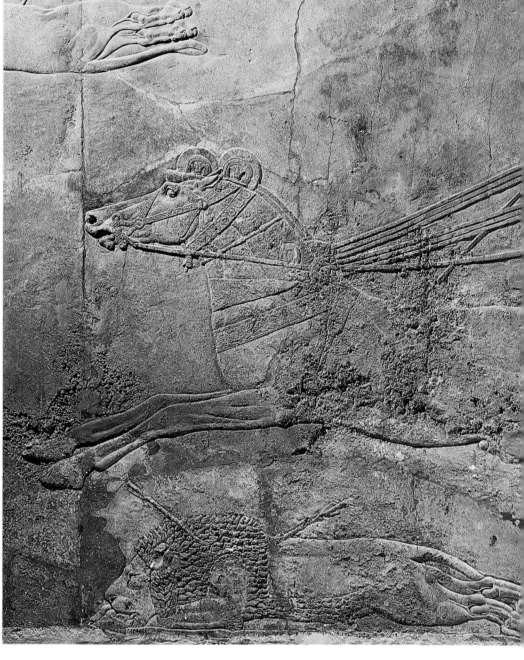

NIMRUD (below)
Bird-headed god,
*c.*865-860 BC
Nimrud, the old capital,
has yielded some of the
earliest Assyrian reliefs
– imposing, but modelled
schematically compared to
the later Nineveh reliefs.
The stylized tree reads as
virtually a grammar of
architectural ornament.

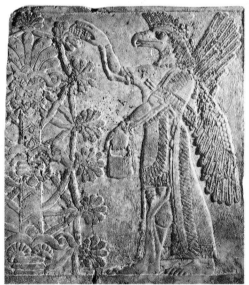

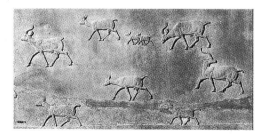

NINEVEH (above)
A herd of gazelles,
*c.*645-640 BC
Mostly the highly finished
but repetitive forms tread
the ground undeviatingly;
these gazelles range the
slab with unusual freedom.

The ascendancy of the Assyrians, first over the Mesopotamian area and eventually extending even into Syria, Urartu (Armenia) and Egypt, where they sacked Thebes, began about 1500 BC and ended suddenly with the destruction of their capital at Nineveh in northern Meso-potamia in 612 BC. Their art, like that of their predecessors, was chiefly devoted to the exal-tation of an absolute monarch, but the As-syrians, unlike the southern Mesopotamian peoples, had access to plentiful stone, and their most characteristic, and durable, medium was stone carved in low relief. Assyrian relief sculpture reached its greatest accomplishment in the decoration of the palace at Nineveh of King Assurbanipal (ruled 668-627 BC), not very many years before the whole Empire was overwhelmed by the assault of the Medes.

The reliefs at Nineveh are thought to have lined the approaches to the focus of the palace, the throne room, and to have amounted alto-gether to a length of more than 100 metres (350ft). Men and animals are represented in a continuous processional frieze. This serial arrangement of profile figures along a ground-line goes back very much earlier, not least to the finely modelled cylinder seals that are virtually all that survives of early Assyrian art; it seems almost an instinctive vision, and its principles were applied even to sculpture in the round, for instance to the colossal winged bulls with human heads that guarded the portals of Assyrian palaces, notably at Khorsabad. (Each was provided with five legs rather than four; they were conceived as being seen either from the front or from the side.)

Both the subject matter and the artistic conventions of the carvings at Nineveh had

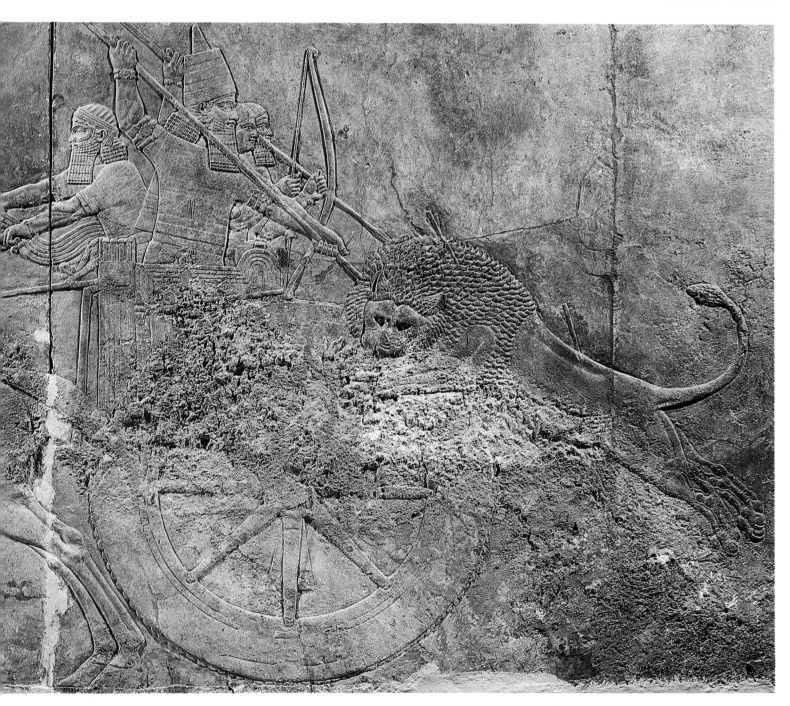

been established earlier, notably at the magnificent palace built by Assurnasirpal II (ruled 883-859 BC) at Nimrud. Here stood bird-headed gods, and kings and attendants larger than life, awe-inspiring in their hieratic rigidity of pose, gesture and costume, and the inhumanity of their expression. Commentaries in cuneiform script were often inscribed across the middle of the friezes; narrative scenes, on themes of royal conquest and triumph, whether over enemies or beasts of prey, supplemented the long rows of figures. Earlier reliefs are quite highly stylized, men and animals alike stiffly articulated. In the Nineveh reliefs the human figures, though richly detailed, are still conventionally handled, but the treatment of the animals has become vividly, sometimes movingly naturalistic. It is as though the artists were moved with some

compassion for the stricken beasts, which they never show for the human victims in the panoramic views, swarming with detail, of armies routed and massacred, cities besieged and stormed. The slaying of lions, however, was virtually a ritual, reserved for the king only, and a symbolic demonstration of his power, brought to ceremonial climax by the pouring of libations over the dead animal.

Figures are seen from the side, though occasionally their shoulders are swivelled; there is no hint of foreshortening. Battles, sieges and hunts, however, are often shown in vistas, mostly with the subject matter mounted up line above line, but sometimes in diagrammatic plan, or bird's-eye view. And landscape effects, remarkable illusions of space or depth, are sometimes created by a sensitive disposition of animals on an empty background.

NINEVEH (above)
A lion springing at King Assurbanipal, c.645-640 BC
Such is the finesse, that electric potency emerges within stylized convention.

NIMRUD (below)
Cooks in a fortified camp, c.858-824 BC
The Assyrians put figures in a landscape, but never attempted naturalistic space.

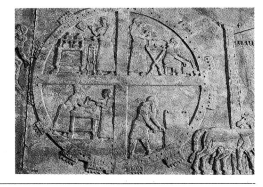

Cycladic, Minoan and Mycenaean Art

Somewhere about 2700 BC – about the time when the great pyramids were being built in the Old Kingdom of Egypt – an independent Bronze-Age culture flourished in the group of small islands in the eastern Aegean named the Cyclades. Little is known about it; it was preliterate, and the only witness of its existence is a quantity of objects made on the islands. Most famous are the little marble figures like quintessential dolls, smooth, formal, elegant abstractions of the human figure, delightful to a twentieth-century taste accustomed to the work of a Brancusi. Their original effect, however, was not so pure, as traces of colour indicate that they were once polychrome.

Near the end of the third millennium BC, a remarkably sophisticated, apparently unwarlike civilization began to evolve on the island of Crete, just south of the Cyclades. Called Minoan (from a legendary king, Minos), its culture depended on a highly organized economic and administrative structure at the centre of a prosperous trading network across the whole eastern Mediterranean. It developed, too, its own system of writing ("Linear A", still undeciphered, and not Greek), but almost all we know about its history rests on the

evidence that archaeologists have laid bare in the twentieth century. It was centred on several royal palaces; the most famous, Knossos, was excavated by Sir Arthur Evans at the beginning of this century, and has been reconstructed on its ruins, perhaps too much so. By about 1800 BC pottery with painted abstract decoration of great vitality, yet with a precise control in the balance of the pattern, was being produced. By 1600 BC the feeling for curvilinear design was yielding to representational forms, and by then human and animal imagery was taking varied and extremely accomplished shape in other media.

The Minoans seem to have had no interest in large-scale sculpture, but smaller-scale examples survive in abundance. The fullest evidence of the range and development of the Cretan figurative style is found in a profusion of seals for containers and in numerous stone vases, such as the "Harvesters' Vase" (see vol. 1 p. 42). The seals are in various materials, the best usually engraved in a hard, semi-precious stone such as agate. Highly stylized, but very various in their activity, these figures or animals retain an individual vitality unlike anything Greek or Egyptian.

Many small figurines in the round also exist, connected presumably with religious rites. They are in terracotta, in a material loosely known as "faience", occasionally in ivory, and from perhaps about 1600 BC in bronze. Generally, the modelling of the terracotta figurines is relatively crude and rough; the bronzes are often more vital, of a higher quality, even though they must have been worked, in the wax from which they were cast, with much the same freedom as the terracottas. Important in Minoan imagery is a form of bull sport, presumably of religious significance, but involving daring feats of acrobatics rather than the blood and swords of modern bullfighting.

Minoan history was interrupted, apparently by an earthquake, about 1700 BC. In the subsequent rebuilding of the palaces on a grander scale the art of wall-painting was developed, in a true fresco technique, the colour worked directly on to the wet plaster. The surviving examples (fragmentary, though in many cases now linked up by restoration) date from between 1600 and 1400 BC, and show the same delight in movement and relative naturalism as other Minoan art. The famous head of a girl, christened "*La Parisienne*", has

THE CYCLADES (right)
"Fiddle" figurine,
c. 2800-2500 BC
Such long-necked females, nicknamed "fiddle" after their violin shape, were an early form of Cycladic idol. Emery from Naxos was used to round and polish the small rectangular block.

THE CYCLADES (left)
Female figure, c. 2300 BC
The commonest Cycladic type represents a woman with her arms clutching her body under the breasts. Ranging from 30cm (1ft) high to life-size (rarely), these can justly be called idols, in contrast to such talismans as the "*Venus of Willendorf*" (see p. 12).

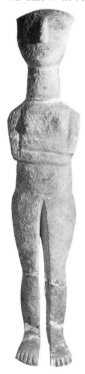

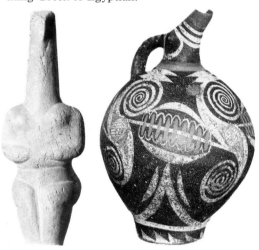

MINOAN CRETE (left)
Jug, *c.* 1850-1700 BC
The terracotta jug itself is a rather sophisticated object, and the bold, free spirals and the clam-like figure unite satisfactorily with its bulbous shape. It was found in the palace at Phaistos, and dates from before the first of the earthquakes by which Minoan history is charted.

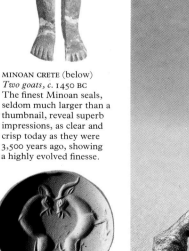

MINOAN CRETE (below)
Two goats, c. 1450 BC
The finest Minoan seals, seldom much larger than a thumbnail, reveal superb impressions, as clear and crisp today as they were 3,500 years ago, showing a highly evolved finesse.

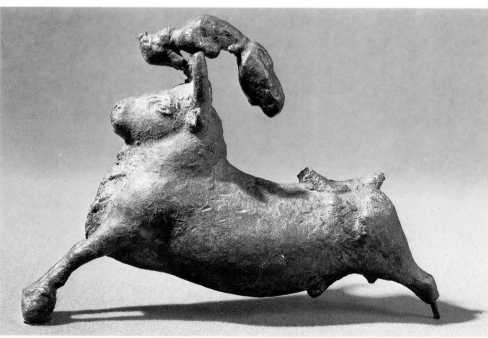

KNOSSOS, CRETE (above)
"*Snake Goddess*",
c. 1600 BC
In Greek cult snakes were attributes of underworld deities, and this figurine must be an earth goddess. And yet there is nothing sinister about her, though a bird of prey perches on her head. She displays her breasts – symbols of her fertility – as if she were a Rococo courtesan.

KNOSSOS, CRETE (left)
An acrobat leaping over a bull, c. 1600 BC
Parts of the acrobat's tautly springing body are unfortunately missing; his feet rest on the bull's back, and his arms are locked round its horns as he does a somersault. This is one of the finest surviving Minoan bronzes, cast solid by the lost-wax method.

KNOSSOS, CRETE
Bull's head *rhyton*, or shaped sacrificial vessel, *c.* 1500 BC
The engraved and painted head is stone, with gilt wooden horns, rock crystal eyes and, encircling the nostrils, inlaid shells. Its naturalism is vivid. The Minoan cult of the bull suggests that the Greek myth of the Minotaur retains a grain of history.

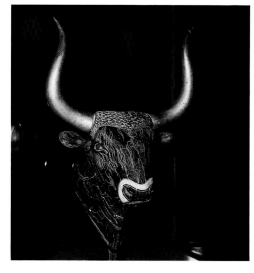

a startlingly modern, impressionistic chic. Recent excavations on the neighbouring island of Thera (modern Santorini) have revealed, marvellously preserved under the volcanic ash, extensive fragments, including what has been claimed as the earliest true landscape of the European tradition.

About 1500 BC, there began a cross-fertilization between the Minoan culture and that of the Greek mainland, especially, to judge by what has survived, with the city of Mycenae, after which the whole civilization is named. Mycenae was excavated in 1876 by the German archaeologist Schliemann, and his finds there and at Troy gave historical substance (though a limited one) to heroic Homeric myth, which scholars had been coming to believe was pure fiction.

Greece had earlier been inhabited by warriors who left little trace of any settled civilization; by about 1550-1450 BC, however, a certain luxury of life is attested by finds in the so-called "shaft-graves" at Mycenae. In these were found objects that must be of Cretan workmanship alongside work in gold, such as the famous gold face masks, of local origin. Then, about 1450 BC, a natural catastrophe

reduced much of Crete to rubble, and the Mycenaeans seem to have taken over the island – tablets from this period, in "Linear B", are in a language of Greek character. Knossos seems finally to have been destroyed not long after 1400 BC, when the leadership of the Aegean passed definitely to mainland Greece.

The Mycenaean version, or adaptation, of Minoan culture flourished most successfully between about 1500 and 1400 BC. In non-Minoan fashion, it expressed itself in terms of violence and of gold. The beautifully modelled bulls on some gold cups are aggressive, while much of the finest ornament was applied to weapons. In fresco and in pottery decoration, the Mycenaean style was much more formal, hieratic and unemotional than the Minoan. But the peak of Mycenaean power came later, between about 1400 and 1200 BC, when its influence was felt throughout the eastern littoral of the Mediterranean, and its art found its most characteristic expression in formidable, rather brutal architecture. Mycenae itself was then destroyed, possibly by Dorian invaders coming south, and the ensuing obscurity lasted until about 800 BC; only then does the tradition of European art begin to take shape.

KNOSSOS, CRETE (right)
"*La Parisienne*", fragment of a fresco, *c.* 1600 BC
The lady was once part of a group of men and women who seem to be toasting one another, presumably in a religious ceremony.

THERA (below)
An interior: *Rocks and lilies*, *c.* 1500 BC
There is much still to be excavated in Thera, but it has already revealed an archaeological wealth in its buried rooms. Thera was a province of the Minoan civilization, without the huge palace complexes of Crete itself, but its relics are often better preserved.

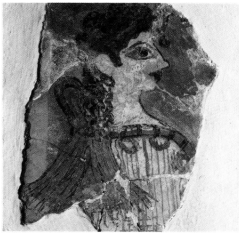

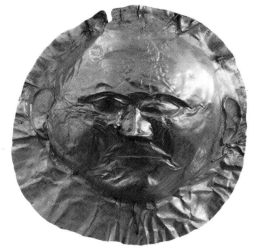

MYCENAE (above)
Gold face mask, *c.* 1500 BC
Gold seems never to have been used by the Minoans; the Mycenaeans imported it, probably from Egypt. Numerous stern, hieratic masks such as this have been found in graves, and suggest a society ruled by despotic warrior chieftains, models for Homer's Agamemnon, "king of men".

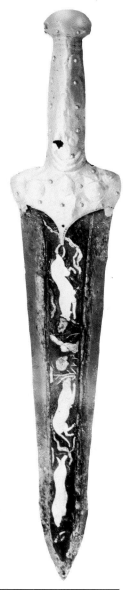

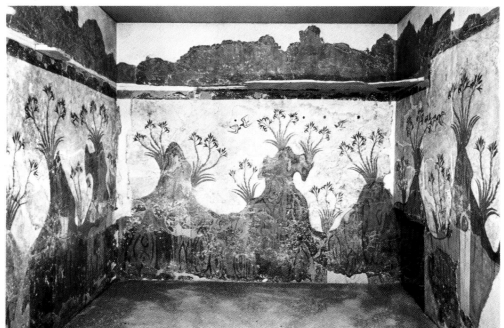

MYCENAE (right)
Decorated bronze dagger: *Leaping lions*, *c.* 1500 BC
The rapacious lions are clearly hunting amid the scraps of landscape. They are again of gold, inlaid on a bronze blade about 20cm (8in) long. Even in the jewellery found along with daggers, masks, cups in Mycenaean graves, there is little that is feminine.

Archaic Greek and Etruscan Art

When the Mycenaean culture disintegrated about 1100 BC, conditions in Greece were too unsettled to allow art to develop. It took some three centuries for a shifting, warring society of small kingdoms to stabilize itself in a system of city states. Iron was being worked for tools and weapons; an alphabet evolved; gradually there grew up a rich and complex religious outlook and a sense of national and cultural identity – Hellas.

With the development of commerce and crafts, exploratory traders ranged throughout the Mediterranean and into the Black Sea, and slowly Greek outposts, virtually colonies, were established throughout the region. Not only the Aegean islands but southern Italy and the whole coastal area of modern Turkey became Hellene. Meanwhile, during the seventh and sixth centuries BC, kingships yielded to oligarchies; the first philosophers propounded rational explanations of the world; the first written codes of law were drafted. But it was probably no later than the eighth century BC that the epic poems associated with the name of Homer – still one of the supreme achievements of the human imagination – were organized in their lasting form.

The visual arts were not so precocious. By the tenth century BC, however, some accomplished pottery was being produced, especially in Athens: its style of simple, often very precise, linear decoration is now known as "Protogeometric", and gradually evolved into the full, highly elaborate patternings of the mature "Geometric" of the ninth and eighth centuries BC. These vases are often very large, as tall as a man, and were used as grave markers; the whole surface might be girt with symmetrically balanced and ordered bands of linear decoration – meanders, zigzags, triangles – but in the early eighth century BC figurative elements began to intrude amongst them. First animals, then humans appeared – highly schematized, but foreshadowing that enduring fascination with "man, the measure of all things", that was to characterize Classical and Hellenistic Greek art, persist through the Roman period, and again become dominant in Renaissance Europe. By the end of the eighth century an influence from the east was reflected in vases from Corinth, and the subject matter was increasingly enriched.

In sculpture, during the Geometric period, small schematic figurines in bronze and ter-

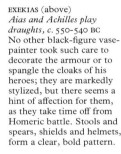

ATHENS (right)
Protogeometric vase,
10th century BC
Earlier decoration had been freehand; a compass was used for these circles.

ATHENS (below)
Geometric vase, c. 750 BC
Amid the typically Greek friezes of meander (or fret pattern) and of animals, a corpse rests on a bier and mourners tear their hair.

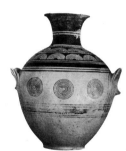

CORINTH (below)
Stoppered *oinochoe*, or wine cruet, 7th century BC
There is a simple, sturdy delicacy about this little object; and Corinthian pots were widely exported. The cruet, found in Syracuse, is in the early, so-called "Proto-", Corinthian style; the animals were inspired by Asian ornament (see p. 29), but are incorporated with an assured restraint.

EXEKIAS (above)
Aias and Achilles play draughts, c. 550-540 BC
No other black-figure vase-painter took such care to decorate the armour or to spangle the cloaks of his heroes; they are markedly stylized, but there seems a hint of affection for them, as they take time off from Homeric battle. Stools and spears, shields and helmets, form a clear, bold pattern.

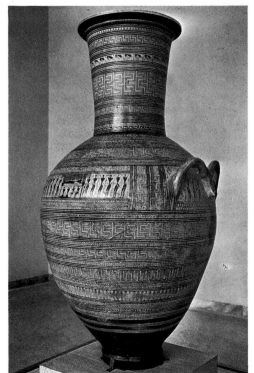

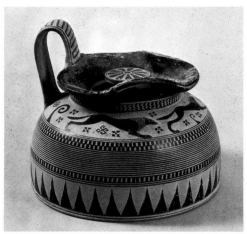

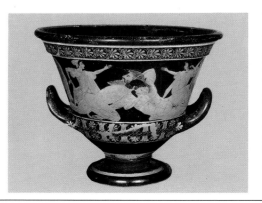

EUPHRONIOS (right)
Herakles strangling Antaios,
c. 510-500 BC
The red-figure technique

allowed finer detail, a freer, more naturalistic line, but artists remained conscious of pattern and symmetry.

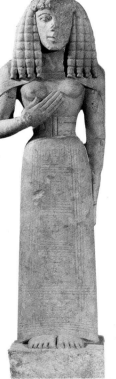

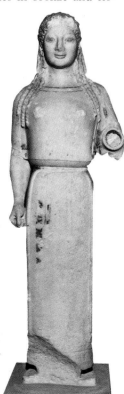

UNKNOWN GREEK SCULPTOR
"The Lady of Auxerre",
c. 630 BC
The lady is about 60cm (2ft) high; she stands at the head of the tradition of *Kouroi* and *Korai* in Greek sculpture. Her limestone figure has waist and bust, but, except in thin lines at the shoulders and the feet, the drapery is not distinct from the body. There is no more than a schematic sense of volume. With her triangular face and wig-like hair, she represents the so-called "Daedalic" style.

ATHENS, ACROPOLIS
"The Peplos Kore",
c. 540-530 BC
The *peplos* from which the statue takes its name is the Greek female robe – still smooth, without the carved folds that will soon appear. A little colour is preserved; exactly the same pattern recurs on women's drapery on numerous vases. She is more rounded than *"The Lady of Auxerre"*, and her missing arm once protruded. It was a piece attached – itself a sign of freedom from the block.

racotta were produced. It was about the mid-seventh century BC that contact with Egypt inspired a decisive step towards the great Greek tradition of monumental marble statuary. There is still a pronounced oriental, perhaps Mesopotamian, feeling in the four-square statuette known as "*The Lady of Auxerre*" of about 630 BC. The great series of *Kouroi* (boys) and *Korai* (girls) – statues of naked youths and draped women – start slightly later. They are life-size, and carved in that lucent marble in which Greece and her islands are so rich. Initially the *Kouroi* have a standard pose following Egyptian example very closely, but essentially Greek is the complete nakedness, and the emphasis on the body led to an astonishingly swift development towards a brilliant virtuosity in naturalistic representation. The early *Kouroi* are still tightly conditioned by the squared block of stone from which they are cut, and invite only two views, frontal or profile; facial expressions are fixed in the famous, enigmatic "Archaic smile". The latest, those dating from the beginning of the fifth century, show the same basic pose anatomically fully coherent, and the movement of the body implicitly indicated. Their female counterparts, though draped, show a comparable development.

In the Archaic period the Greek stone temple developed its essential form, providing scope for both painted and sculptural decoration, though the painting has now all disappeared. The sculpture on the pediments, and the reliefs on the rectangular panels (metopes) or friezes that banded the buildings above the columns, sometimes included narrative action. Carved with sharp but exquisite precision, in shallow or deep relief, or almost fully in the round, the figures would have responded dramatically in the bright Aegean sun; their original effect, further enriched by colour, was far removed from their usual bland, monochrome appearance in museums.

During the late seventh and sixth centuries BC Athens regained from Corinth its pre-eminence in vase-painting. Individual artists emerged, and potters and painters sometimes signed their work. Athenian painters at first used the same black-figure technique as the Corinthians – painting the figures in black silhouette over the red Attic clay with details incised – but about 530 BC they invented the red-figure technique, in which the figures are left unpainted ("reserved") on the clay, defined sharply against the painted ground. The red-figure technique permitted a great advance in subtlety and vitality: internal definition and expression could be achieved by drawing instead of scratching. The subjects were still mainly from heroic mythology, but representations of athletes, of drinking and feasting, courtship, weddings, funerals and everyday scenes – almost genre – increased.

The artefacts of the mysterious Etruscan civilization, dominant in central Italy from about the eighth to the second century BC, were predominantly Greek-inspired, although politically Etruria seems to have been fiercely hostile to Greece, and the Etruscans interpreted Greek themes with independence. The free-standing sculpture that adorned temple roofs has a slightly sinister vigour and expression alien to Greek art, while the carousing reclining couples on their tombs seem to welcome eternity with a toast, as if it were the culminating course in life's banquet. Life's pleasures are often celebrated in the painted decorations, in a comparable style (see further p. 44), of numerous surviving tombs, and the Etruscans were also skilled metalworkers.

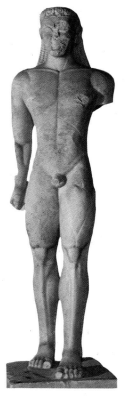

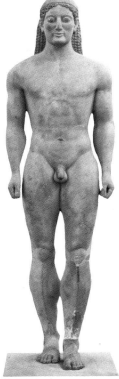

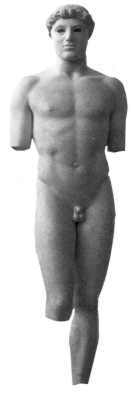

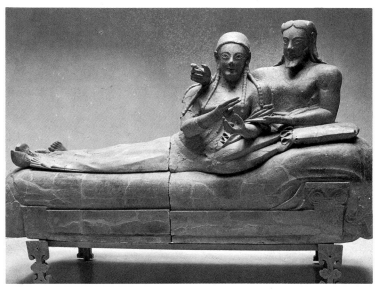

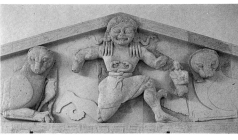

SOUNIUM, ATTICA
Kouros, c. 600-580 BC
Left foot advanced, arms close to the body, hands clenched – the pose could be Egyptian; so could the broad shoulders and thin waist, and the scale – the figure is well over life-size. The treatment of the anatomy, however, is distinctly Greek, though the sculptor has done little more than modify the surface. The tool he mainly used was a point or punch, rather than a chisel, and it was a long, laborious process.

ANAVYSOS, ATTICA
Kouros, c. 540-515 BC
There is no change in pose, but relaxation has set in: rounded contours begin to replace the sharp planes and linear anatomy of the earlier *Kouroi* – though the bones of the calves are cut to a fine edge. On the base an inscription once read: "Stop and grieve at the tomb of Kroisos, slain by wild Ares (god of war) in the front rank of battle". *Kouroi* were often used as grave markers, though they were not of course portraits.

ATHENS, ACROPOLIS
"*The Kritios Boy*",
c. 490-480 BC
When they came to rebuild the Acropolis after it had been burnt by the Persians in 480 BC, the Athenians shovelled its defiled and broken statuary into the new foundations. Exposed by modern archaeology, far more Archaic sculpture has survived than Classical. The *Kouros* is hardly still Archaic: the limbs are fully modelled and articulated, with the left hip raised as the right leg goes forward.

CERVETERI, ETRURIA
(above) A sarcophagus,
c. 550-520 BC
The life-size terracottas gesticulate animatedly, even if their bodies and faces are types, directly comparable to Archaic Greek funerary sculpture.

VEII, ETRURIA (right)
"*The Apollo of Veii*",
c. 500 BC
Once adorning the roof of a temple, and in terracotta, the god moves more freely than Greek *Kouroi*. There is also less concern for anatomical proportions.

CORCYRA, TEMPLE OF ARTEMIS
West pediment, detail:
A gorgon and two lions,
c. 600-580 BC

The enormous gorgon is a splendid figure of fright; but there is no unity of scale, or even of subject.

The Artemisium Zeus/Poseidon

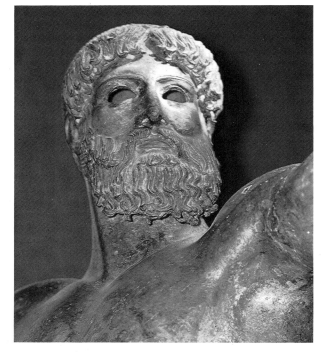

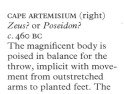

AFTER KRITIOS AND
NESIOTES (below)
Harmodios and Aristogeiton,
original 477-476 BC
The violent action of the
limbs is followed through
into the trunk muscles of
the martyrs for democracy.

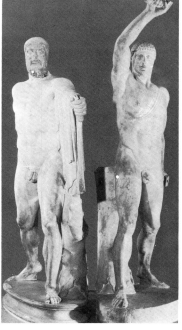

CAPE ARTEMISIUM (right)
Zeus? or *Poseidon?*
c. 460 BC
The magnificent body is
poised in balance for the
throw, implicit with movement from outstretched
arms to planted feet. The
head (detail, left) is a
naturalistic, if superhuman,
mask of imposing energy.
The view intended seems
to be the profile (unlike
Myron's *"Diskobolos"*, see
over), yet the musculature
is harmonious all round.

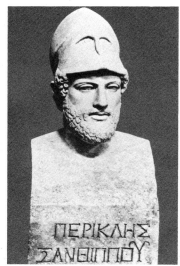

AFTER KRESILAS (left)
Perikles,
original c. 429 BC?
Phidias was prosecuted, it
is said, for incorporating a
portrait of Perikles in a
relief for the Parthenon.
Though the story is not
now usually believed, it
is some indication perhaps
that the concept, at least,
of portraiture was born.
Kresilas' statue is often
dated c. 440 BC, but then
Perikles was still alive.

AFTER AN ATHENIAN
SCULPTOR (below)
Anakreon,
original c. 450 BC
The posture suggested to
a Roman visitor to Athens
"a man singing when he is
drunk" – admittedly wine
and love were this sixth-
century poet's main themes.

In 1928 a slightly more than life-size bronze
statue was yielded up by the sea off Cape
Artemisium on the island of Euboea, close to
the scene of a second Greek victory over the
Persian fleet in the year after Salamis, 479 BC.
Since the style of the statue indicates a date of
about 470-450 BC, and since after their victory
the Greeks honoured Poseidon, god of the sea,
as Saviour, Poseidon seems to some an apt
identification. However, others disagree, and
it is just as likely that the bronze was on its way
as booty some centuries later from a quite
different location to Rome, or to Egypt, when
the ship carrying it was sunk by one of the
vicious Aegean storms. In that case the statue
might well represent Zeus, poised to launch a
thunderbolt; Poseidon is perhaps less likely to
be letting go in quite this way with his trident.

Whichever god it shows, this is unquestionably one of the most magnificent of all
surviving Greek heroic statues, and almost
incredibly well preserved (the eyes, once inlaid, are lost). Well over two metres (6½ft) high,
with an arm-span rather wider than that, it
correlates the most closely observed and accurately rendered movement of muscle and
limb in a majestic unity.

Its sculptor is unknown. Various names
have been suggested, including that of Onatas,
recorded in Aegina as a sculptor in metal, but
since there is no known work by him for
comparison, this is pure surmise. Yet in its
muscular power, the suggested movement, the
expressive head, the *Zeus/Poseidon* clearly differs from contemporary Athenian work. It is in
the so-called "Severe" style that precedes the
mature Classical age, and, technically, it is a
feat of astonishing refinement and virtuosity,
in a medium then only newly exploited. To
cast sculpture on such a scale sophisticated
smelting ovens with shaft furnaces must have
been developed; the *Zeus/Poseidon* is already
more advanced in technique than the equally
famous Delphi *Charioteer*, made perhaps a
decade or so earlier. The *Zeus/Poseidon* was
probably modelled in clay and wax and cast by
the lost-wax process. The *Charioteer* has much
thicker metal walls, and originated perhaps in
a carved wooden model, while projecting elements were worked independently and then
soldered on. The *Zeus/Poseidon* is in one piece.

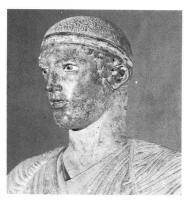

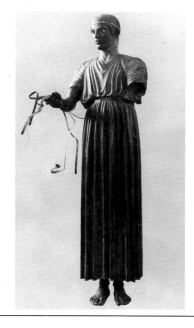

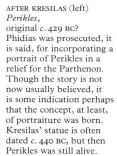

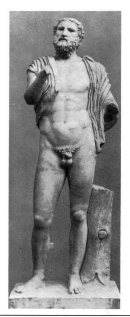

DELPHI (right)
A charioteer, fragment
of a group, c. 475-470 BC
The detail still tends to
be linear; the feeling for
volume is not quite ripe.
But the head (detail, above)
has the "eternal springtime"
that Winckelmann found to
dwell in Greek sculpture.

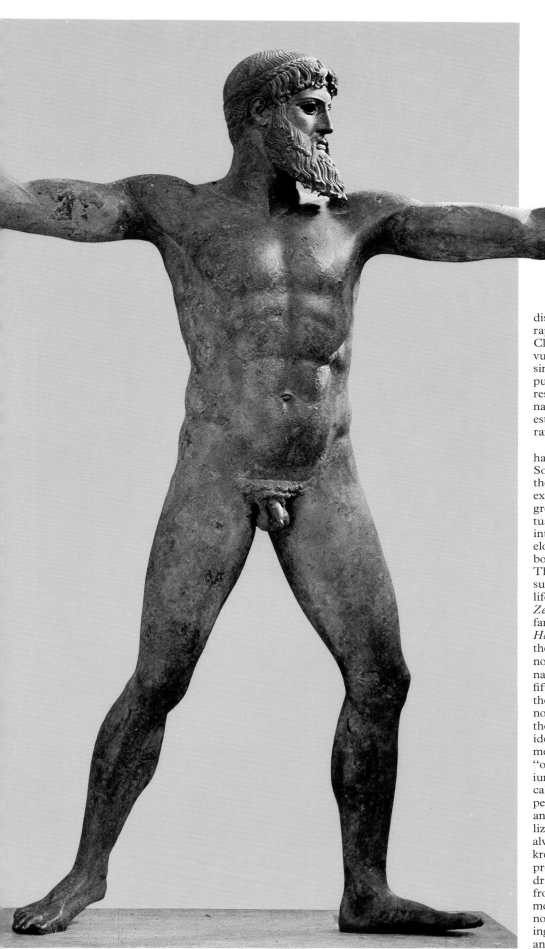

For monumental, free-standing statuary, as distinct from architectural sculpture, bronze rapidly became the prime medium in the Classical age. Bronze, however, is much more vulnerable than stone, being valuable and simple to melt down and recycle for other purposes; the loss has been enormous. As a result it is difficult to appreciate the original nature of the Greek achievement, and to estimate how the Artemisium *Zeus/Poseidon* ranked for quality amongst its lost peers.

The *Charioteer*, unlike the *Zeus/Poseidon*, has preserved its inlaid enamel and onyx eyes. So still in poise, yet intense in concentration, the Delphi *Charioteer* was originally part of an extraordinarily ambitious bronze chariot group with four horses, offered to the sanctuary by a victor in the Pythian Games. It was intended to be seen from below, and the elongation of the lower part of the driver's body would have been hidden by the chariot. The sites of the gods' temples became rich with such offerings, but civic statuary also proliferated, and the striding pose of the *Zeus/Poseidon* is anticipated notably in the famous group by Kritios and Nesiotes of *Harmodios and Aristogeiton*, lovers who slew the tyrant Hipparchos in 514 BC. These were not literal portraits; but the trend towards naturalism crystallized in the second half of the fifth century BC in an interest in the individual; the sculptor Kresilas made a bronze *Perikles*, now known in various Roman marble copies of the head alone, in which the features are still idealized, but the strange shape of the helmeted head corresponds to reports of the "onion-shaped" deformity of Perikles' cranium. Not only statesmen, soldiers and political heroes were honoured with public statues, perhaps always posthumously, but poets, too, and the characterization, though still generalized, was clearly vivid and lively – and not always flattering, as a statue of the poet Anakreon recorded in a Roman copy shows. The props and struts of the copy demonstrate the drawbacks imposed by the transposition – from the bronze original to the less versatile medium of marble – quite apart from the normal tendency, endemic in the act of copying, to blur detail, dilute the concentration, and lose altogether the quality of the surface.

Classical Greek Art

When at the beginning of the fifth century BC the Greek cities of Ionia, under Persian domination, revolted, some of the mainland cities, notably Athens, sent help to their kinsmen. The subsequent punitive expedition by the Persians in 490 BC was routed by the famous Athenian victory at Marathon, but the renewed, much more powerful invasion by Xerxes in 480 BC defeated the Spartans at Thermopylae, took Athens and sacked the city's sacred shrines on the Acropolis, before the Greeks drove the Persians off, first by a brilliant naval victory and then by one on land.

During the following years Greek culture, above all that of Athens, found with astonishing speed and certainty its maturity; this is the classic century of Greek art, the century of the great tragedians Aischylos, Sophokles and Euripides; of Aristophanes' comic masterpieces; of the founding fathers of modern history, Herodotos and Thoukydides, and of moral philosophy, Sokrates and Plato. Amid the violent internecine strife of the leading states, in mid-century, under the leadership of the aristocrat Perikles (c. 490-429 BC) there was established in Athens the classic ideal of democracy, its ceremonial and spiritual centre the Acropolis, on which Perikles initiated a vast building programme. Here the Parthenon was built from about 447 to 432 BC under the overall direction of Phidias (died c. 432 BC), Perikles' appointed master of the works and the first impresario of the arts in history. The Parthenon sculpture has long been accepted as the masterpiece of Classical Greek art.

The earlier emergence of the Classical style from the Archaic can be seen in the superb fragments that survive from the Temple of Zeus at Olympia, and which once decorated the pediments and the panels known as metopes. They feature mythological stories: on the metopes, the Labours of Hercules; on one pediment a magnificent Apollo towering in a brawl between Lapiths and Centaurs. The mastery of anatomy is matched by the ability to present both expressive movement in the battling figures and, in the *Apollo*, the serene dignity of divine authority, dispensing order. Within the temple was later placed a colossal gold and ivory (chryselephantine) statue by Phidias of *Zeus*; had this survived it might have seemed barbaric rather than classical to modern eyes; it is a reminder that early Greek sculpture was not pristine white, but poly-

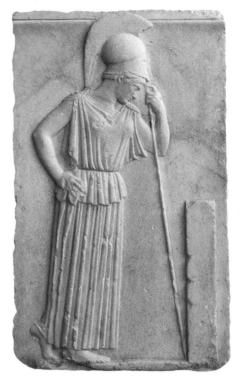

ATHENS, THE ACROPOLIS (above) *"Mourning Athene"* c. 470-450 BC
Such votive reliefs, and the similar grave stelae or markers, were the modest commissions of ordinary people. Their understatement is famous: they speak volumes without comment. The style is pure, simple, direct – inscrutably clear.

AFTER MYRON (below) *"Diskobolos"* (The discus thrower), original c. 450 BC
The original was bronze, the copy is marble. If the changing contours do not draw the viewer round the form as multiple-viewpoint Renaissance sculptures do, the complementary torsions of the body unfold with a stupendous elasticity. The statue does not correspond with a photograph taken of a discus thrower: it is a summary of his action.

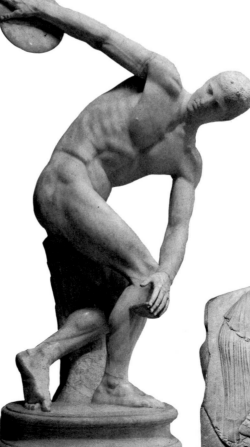

OLYMPIA (right) *Zeus carries off Ganymede*, c. 470 BC
Movement is mastered: the god strides with convincing purpose, but there is trace still of Archaic stylization in the hair. The colours are bright and flat, unmodelled.

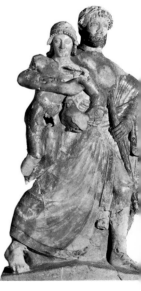

UNKNOWN ARTIST (below) *"The Ludovisi Throne"*, detail: *The birth of Aphrodite*, c. 470-460 BC
The altar-like block was unearthed in Rome, and was probably carved by a Greek settled in Italy from imported Parian marble. Folds in Aphrodite's dress reveal the form beneath, as the robes of Archaic *Korai* do not, and their textures are clearly differentiated. Typically for this date, the symmetry is insistent.

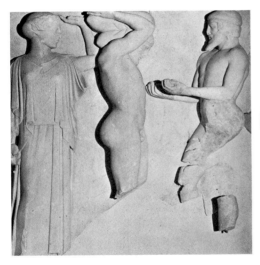

OLYMPIA, TEMPLE OF ZEUS (above) A metope: *Herakles' twelfth Labour*, 465-457 BC
While Atlas returns with the golden apples of the Hesperides, Athene helps Herakles fulfil his part of the bargain, to take the world from Atlas' shoulders. The static composition fills out the nearly square field.

(below) The west pediment, detail: *Apollo, Lapiths and centaurs*, 465-457 BC
The impassive "Archaic smile" has faded: emotion – surprise, gloom, delight – is expressed not only by gesture but in the faces. Differentiations of age are clear, and figures may sit or recline, twist or engage.

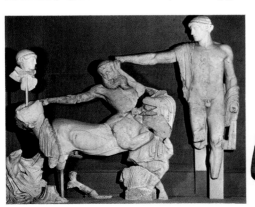

chrome – to which a remarkable terracotta fragment of *Zeus carrying off Ganymede*, also from Olympia, is vivid witness. It is also sometimes forgotten that the ancients themselves believed that the finest Classical work was in bronze (see preceding page).

In the early Classical period the names and personalities of individual artists begin to emerge, although their work is known, if at all, almost entirely through the medium of later Roman copies. Kalamis, Pythagoras (not the philosopher), Myron, were recognized as outstanding in their time, but only Myron can be connected with confidence with surviving copies. The most famous of these is the "*Diskobolos*" (The discus thrower) of about 450 BC, witness not only to the expanding range of poses explored by sculptors, but to their ability to translate the implications of movement into harmonious form. For the first time, there seems no obvious viewpoint; the statue is seen in the round, from any and all angles. The distance between images such as this and the Archaic style of 50 years earlier is startling. The interest in realism slowly increases; on female figures the drapery begins to flow and cling more naturally.

In the second half of the fifth century the style associated with Phidias is dominant. Though nothing now exists that can be confidently ascribed to his own hand, the Parthenon sculptures (superbly coherent in style, though clearly worked on by many different hands) must reflect his vision. Their plenitude was extraordinary: 92 metopes above the colonnade with figures in high relief – mythological combat-scenes on different themes, probably alluding implicitly to Athenian victories over the Persians. Then a continuous frieze, once some 155 metres (500ft) long, set high up inside the colonnade, in very shallow relief – a Panathenaic procession, circling about its focus, the colossal chryselephantine *Athene* by Phidias that once stood within the shrine. Here the sense of forward motion through an implied depth is of great vigour and variety: monotony is skilfully avoided, while in the best-preserved portions the unparalleled precision and delicacy of finish can still be gauged. The third area for sculpture was provided by the pediments: the surviving figures, fully carved in the round, are still monumentally expressive in their majesty, in the fluid movement of their draperies. Plut-

arch, writing some 500 years later, commented with astonishment on the freshness and vitality of the Parthenon sculptures; nearly 2,000 years on again, they seem even more astonishing.

The Phidian style, characterized by serenity and majesty of conception, is discernible elsewhere, in statues – almost all copies – and on grave reliefs. Other names have survived – Kresilas, and Polykleitos, sculptor of athletes and author of a canon of figural proportions. Other temples were built on the Acropolis – the famous caryatids of the Erechtheion are superb amalgams of strength and grace, but a variant, more delicate, light-hearted style appears on the little temple of Athene Nike, making great play with light and airy drapery over the naked body; the *Nike* (Victory) of about 420 BC from Olympia, by Paionios, has a similar sensuousness, an almost weightless effect – the goddess alighting from flight.

In the fifth century BC mural-painting certainly flourished, but we can only infer its quality (see p. 44). Vase-painting continued unabated: scores of individual painters have been identified, developing towards the end of the century a taste for large showy pieces with increased use of colour.

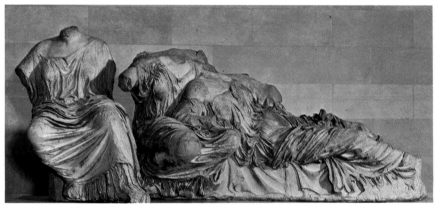

ATHENS, THE PARTHENON
(above) The east pediment, detail: *Aphrodite and two other goddesses*, 438-432 BC
Time has chipped off not only heads and limbs, but also the rich fluting of the drapery – out of the spare formal perfection of the Olympia style has emerged a sensuous, full mastery of medium and expression.

(below) The frieze, detail: *Horsemen in the Panathenaic procession*, c. 440 BC
Illusionistic modelling suggests the fully three-dimensional form within a very shallow relief – a technique quite new. The horsemen are by no means portraits; even if the event is real, not mythological, it is utterly generalized.

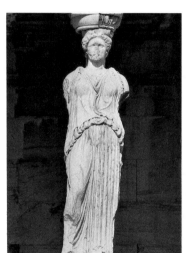

ATHENS, THE ERECHTHEION
(right) A caryatid, c. 409 BC
Caryatids, female figures serving as columns, were an eastern invention, according to Herodotos. Carved only a few years before Athens' humbling defeat by Sparta, the Erechtheion caryatids are a final legacy of the Phidian style – patterns of the classical figure. Each stands tensely, the weight evenly balanced, passing through the figure visibly. Uniquely, Roman copies at Tivoli can be tested against these originals; the carving, the transitions from plane to plane, are less delicate.

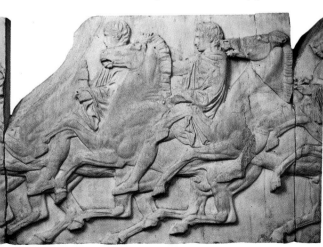

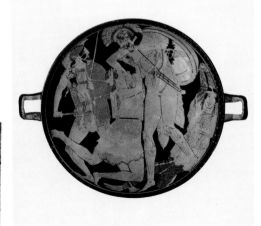

THE PENTHESILEA PAINTER
(above) *Greeks and Amazons, Achilles killing Penthesilea?* c. 455 BC
The foreshortened forms fitted artfully into the field, the precious, decorative effect, perhaps indicate that in both painting and sculpture there was a trend towards surface enrichment.

PAIONIOS (right)
Nike (Victory), c. 420 BC
Nike, originally accoutred in glittering bronze, was placed probably atop a tall column, high in the sun. In the fragments the imposing train of her draperies can still be inferred; and the round of her wind-pressed body is still appreciable.

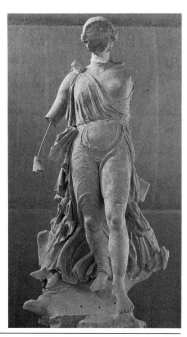

Fourth-Century Greek Art

In the early fourth century BC the Greek city states continued their struggles for advantage and supremacy – Thebes temporarily obtained hegemony – but in the second half of the century a new power emerged in what had been considered the barbarian north – Macedonia. In 338 BC Philip II of Macedon conquered the mainland to the south, and for the first time Greece was, despite itself, united. Then his son, Alexander the Great, one of the most remarkable characters in history, had by 323 BC, before his death aged only 33, conquered the entire Persian Empire, extending Greek influence from the Danube to the Nile, from the Mediterranean to beyond the Indus.

The fourth century saw important artistic innovations and experiments, still within the framework of the Classical aesthetic. The general trend was to modulate the idealism of the fifth century towards a greater naturalism. Following precedents such as Myron's *"Diskobolos"* (see preceding page), figure compositions were modelled more and more in the round, articulated by contrasting directions of gaze and gesture. Their poses offered the spectator a variety of different viewpoints, none of them complete in itself, not only suggesting movement in the sculpture, but also impelling the spectator himself to move. Not only is detail – the texture of flesh, the play of muscle, the cling and flow of drapery – more minutely and naturalistically observed, but the interpretation of individual character becomes more emotionally expressive, with an attempt to convey a passing mood in the features. Naturalistic portraiture, though adumbrated in the fifth century (see pp. 36-37), was first fully established in our sense in the statues that ornamented the colossal tomb of Mausolos at Halicarnassus of about 353 BC, where enormous quantities of sculpture were deployed; the Mausoleon was one of the Seven Wonders of the ancient world, and its name has passed into the European languages.

By mid-century, three outstanding artists in sculpture were established – Skopas, Praxiteles and the younger and apparently immensely long-lived Lysippos. Their names have become legendary; though again the attribution of any surviving work remains speculative, a fairly distinctive style is associated with each of them. Skopas was one of the four sculptors recorded working at Halicarnassus, and he also worked on the Temple of Athene Alea at Tegea and that of Artemis at Ephesus (another of the Seven Wonders). Battered though the surviving fragments from these sites are, they agree with ancient accounts of Skopas as a sculptor of drama and passion, of expressive and moody figures with deep-set eyes.

Praxiteles, with Phidias, was celebrated by ancient writers as supreme. A characteristic of the style associated with him is the "Praxitelean curve" – the rhythm of a nude treated with an overt sensuality based on a very subtle understanding of anatomy. His most famous work, *"The Cnidian Aphrodite"*, survives only in copies; it is the first life-size free-standing female nude in Greek art. Of his other statues, the *Hermes with the infant Dionysos*, excavated in 1877 at Olympia, is in quality by far the finest surviving work associated with him. The beautifully modulated balance of the torso is caught with impeccable accuracy.

Praxiteles worked both in marble and in bronze, and, though the ancients appear to have preferred him in marble, metalworking had become very sophisticated. This is borne out not least by the evidence of Greek coinage, setting a standard which has never been sur-

HALICARNASSUS,
THE MAUSOLEON
(right) A frieze, detail:
Greeks and Amazons,
c. 353 BC
Of the three friezes which decorated the monument, this is the best preserved, and is attributed to Skopas. The figures form a pattern of intersecting diagonals which carry the eye along.

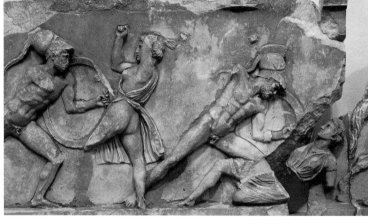

(below) *"Mausolos"*
The features are oriental, not of a Greek type, and so perhaps from life. Though probably not a portrait of the Carian satrap himself, but of a member of his family, the swathed figure is alert and individual.

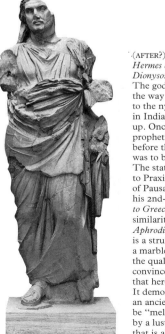

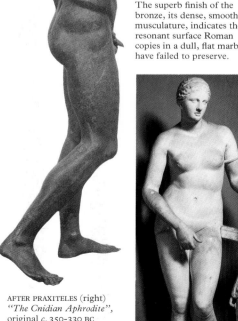

UNKNOWN ARTIST (left)
"The Anticythera Youth",
c. 350-330 BC
The rather traditional pose and proportions suggest a conservative sculptor, not one of the more famous artists active in the century. The superb finish of the bronze, its dense, smooth musculature, indicates the resonant surface Roman copies in a dull, flat marble have failed to preserve.

·(AFTER?) PRAXITELES (right)
Hermes and the infant Dionysos, *c.* 350-330 BC
The god is just pausing on the way to deliver the child to the nymphs on Mt Nysa, in India, who will bring him up. Once Hermes dangled a prophetic bunch of grapes before the child (Dionysos was to be the god of wine). The statue is attributed to Praxiteles on the basis of Pausanias' description in his 2nd-century BC *Guide to Greece*, and of its close similarity to *"The Cnidian Aphrodite"*. Although there is a strut (implying that it is a marble copy of a bronze), the quality of the carving convinces many scholars that here is an original. It demonstrates the beauty an ancient critic found to be "melting" – compounded by a lustre in the marble that is almost subcutaneous.

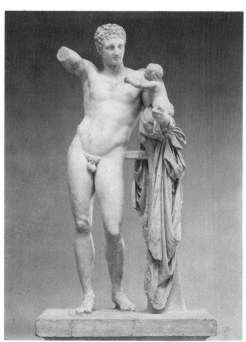

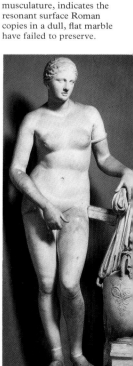

AFTER PRAXITELES (right)
"The Cnidian Aphrodite",
original *c.* 350-330 BC
In the twist of the body there is more movement than in the 5th century; the goddess is entering her bath. She was placed in a shrine so that she could be seen from four sides – each was equally admired.

AFTER LYSIPPOS? (below)
Alexander the Great
("The Azara Herm"),
original *c.* 325 BC
The bust's simplicity and non-committal calm is in marked contrast to the panegyrics of Alexander's historians, or to the legends Islam later wove about him.

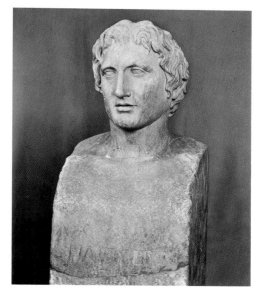

passed: superbly struck examples were being made even in the fifth century, for example the ten-drachma pieces struck in Syracuse (the richest of the western Greek cities) with noble profiles of the city's local goddess, Arethousa. The best of the few large-scale bronzes that have survived cannot easily be linked with a known artist: "*The Anticythera Youth*", recovered from the sea near Anticythera, is of superb quality, its physical perfection suggesting also spiritual serenity.

The third great sculptor, Lysippos, seems to have been active by 370 and still active about 312, suggesting a career comparable with Titian's in length and variety of achievement. At the height of his career he was appointed official portraitist to Alexander the Great, of whom the most sympathetic interpretation recorded in a Roman copy is perhaps that in the Louvre, which can be associated with Lysippos: it has features of a handsome majesty, with a certain brooding melancholy. In Lysippos' celebrated "*Apoxyomenos*" (Youth scraping down) the proportions of the counterpoised body are more elongated, more elegant than earlier, and the head is smaller – exemplifying the so-called Lysippan canon of pro-

portion, which superseded the Polykleitan. There is here, too, a suggestion of melancholy, and again in the massively sensual "*Farnese Hercules*", the archetypal image of heroic, superhuman physical strength, but shown in lassitude. This was an image destined to be repeated in countless copies after the Renaissance, like "*The Apollo Belvedere*", associated with Leochares, a contemporary of Lysippos who also worked for Alexander.

The ideal serenity of such images as these contrasts vividly with the increasing emphasis on naturalistic portraits in the round, with emphatic modelling in the features. A comparable interest, persisting well into Hellenistic times, is evident in many small terracotta figures, some distinctly genre in mood – from comic actors to exquisitely modelled female figurines. Many of these retain a delicate pastel colour, and the really grievous loss from the fourth century is the painting. Though the continuing development of vase-painting is attested by thousands of surviving examples, the visual evidence for mural and panel painting is available only in diluted copies (see p. 44), although recently discoveries have been made at Leucadia and Vergina in Macedonia.

SYRACUSE (below)
Ten-drachma piece,
obverse: *Arethousa*,
c. 479 BC
The nymph Arethousa was a spring on the island of Ortygia, near Syracuse. This coin was the first in a series struck by the city to celebrate its victories.

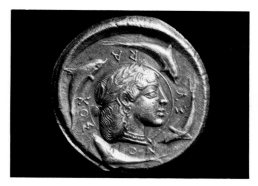

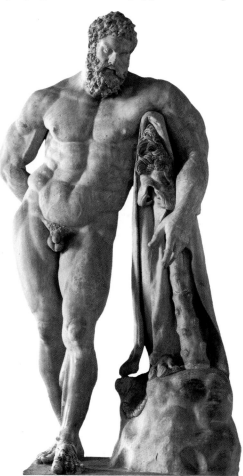

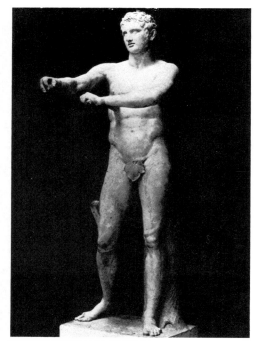

AFTER LYSIPPOS (left)
"*Apoxyomenos*" (Youth scraping down), original *c.* 325-300 BC
Strongly individual, yet quite novel in the way the pose reaches out into space, the figure is quick with life, in a moment of repose after strenuous exercise.

UNKNOWN ARTIST (right)
Comic actors, *c.* 350 BC
Clay figures survive from the 4th century and later in a range of subjects never touched in bronze or stone. They reveal everyday life: the man is shown with the padded jacket and phallus worn in Greek comedy.

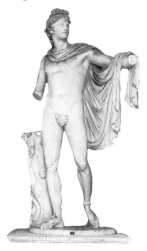

AFTER LYSIPPOS? (left)
"*The Farnese Hercules*",
original *c.* 350-300 BC
The 3rd-century AD copy is inscribed with the name of Glykon, but the figure is closely related to a coin from Sicyon, which is likely to have been based on the famous bronze *Herakles* by Lysippos recorded there.

AFTER LEOCHARES? (right)
"*The Apollo Belvedere*",
original 4th century BC
Apollo had a bow in his left hand and a laurel branch in his right, signifying his role as avenger, purifier, healer. Renaissance copies appear from the 1490s; it became for a long time the classic standard of male beauty.

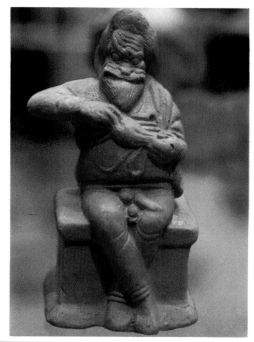

Hellenistic Art

By the end of the fourth century BC, after the death of Alexander the Great, Greek culture was pervasive throughout the Mediterranean area. Individual centres grew up far from Athens, the original pace-setter: the splendour of the new royal cities of the Macedonian dynasts who had divided Alexander's Empire between them outshone the relatively impoverished (and still generally bickering) city states of mainland Greece. Alexandria in Egypt, Antioch, Pergamum and Miletus in Asia Minor – these became the modern wonders of the ancient world.

A coherent account of the development and interaction of art and artists in the eastern Mediterranean during the long period known as Hellenistic (from about 323 to 31 BC) has yet to be established. The chronological development is often highly speculative, since at many different points in time and space there were contrary currents, and recurrent references to earlier styles – to the fourth, fifth or even the sixth century. Broadly, as the style of the fourth century had been an expansion of that of the fifth, so in the following 300 years artists exploited the new freedoms signalled especially by Lysippos. They readily extended the fourth-century delight in naturalism to themes far removed from the idealized heroics of Classical sculpture: figures of all ages and moods became subjects for sculpture – a drunken satyr, an old woman, a fisherman, a boy removing a thorn from his foot (the type known as a *spinario*), a black, a barbarian, a battered and brutalized pugilist. The treatment was extremely realistic; genre was extended even to caricature, in statues ranging from small terracottas to life-size bronzes. The Hellenistic style was fluent and lively, irregular, often asymmetrical; it gave full play to technical virtuosity, in rendering movement, in showing vivid emotion in pose, gesture and facial expression.

The aspect of Hellenistic style known as "sober" or "simple", or "closed-form" or "centripetal", was developed notably in the relatively conservative workshops of Athens in the third century BC. The famous statue of the orator Demosthenes by Polyeuktos is an admirable example. Copies of the lost bronze original of 280 BC show a balanced, self-contained composition of great dignity, yet the posthumous head (Demosthenes died in 322) is highly individual and movingly expresses a

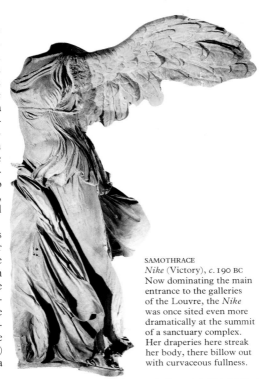

SAMOTHRACE
Nike (Victory), *c.* 190 BC
Now dominating the main entrance to the galleries of the Louvre, the *Nike* was once sited even more dramatically at the summit of a sanctuary complex. Her draperies here streak her body, there billow out with curvaceous fullness.

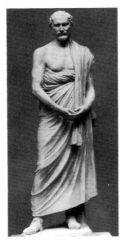

AFTER POLYEUKTOS (left)
Demosthenes,
original *c.* 280 BC
The true subject seems to be not so much the man, as Demosthenes the idealized champion of Athenian freedom (since lost) against Philip II of Macedon. Comparable interpretative statues were made of past tragedians and philosophers.

PERGAMUM (right)
The Altar of Zeus, outer frieze, east side, detail: *The battle of the gods and giants, c.* 180 BC
The head of Alkyoneus (on the left, embroiled with a serpent-limbed giant, but supported by Athene) is cut deeply, almost searingly.

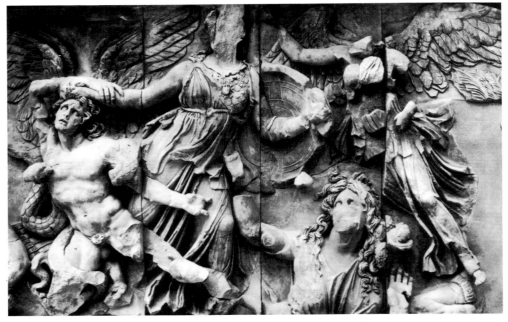

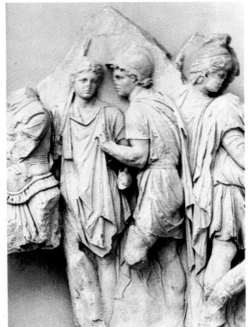

PERGAMUM (left)
The Altar of Zeus, inner frieze, detail: *Telephos and companions, c.* 165-150 BC
By choosing the story of Telephos, Herakles' son, who founded a dynasty in Mysia, Eumenes II (197-159 BC) was advertising his claim to divine descent.

AFTER A PERGAMENE SCULPTOR (right)
A dying Gaul,
original *c.* 200 BC
Shaggy hair and the torque around the neck denote a Gaul, shown in his agony with a new sympathy. The original was probably one of several in a sanctuary built to celebrate a victory over the Gauls in 228 BC.

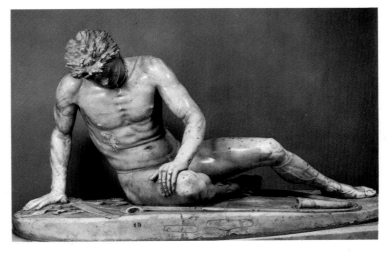

melancholic, almost introspective concentration. It is but one of many vividly particular Hellenistic portraits, reflecting an increasing fascination with individual psychology – the face observed as "the index of the mind".

The most remarkable monument at the opposite pole of the Hellenistic style – the style which has come to be known, by analogy with the work of seventeenth-century masters such as Bernini, as "Hellenistic Baroque" – is the colossal altar of Zeus from Pergamum, under construction from about 180 to 150 BC. The kings of Pergamum were the bulwark of Hellenic civilization against threats from the east, and the altar celebrates Pergamene triumph over barbarians. A whole school of sculptors flourished at Pergamum: their style is vigorous and dramatic, whether expressed in free-standing statuary – the famous studies of vanquished and dying Gauls (known from Roman copies) – or in deep-cut friezes – the originals now in Berlin. After the Parthenon frieze, these are the most ambitious and extensive examples of Greek monumental sculpture that survive. In the external frieze, showing *The battle of the gods and the giants*, running round the base of colonnade rather than above

it, great play is made with the contrast of light and shade, to convey a whirling violence of movement, powerful musculature and emphatic gestures, and at points the figures burst the constraint of the frieze and spill on to the altar steps. The rather later internal frieze seems in contrast to mark the beginning of a classicizing reaction – the relief is shallower, the figures more restrained and linear. This is one of the earliest examples in Greek art of continuous narrative, and foreshadows later, Roman, developments in relief sculpture.

The best-known original single piece in the "Baroque" style is surely the *Nike* (Victory) from Samothrace (an island in the north-east Aegean) of about 190 BC, now in the Louvre. It probably echoes the Classical *Nike* at Olympia (see p. 39), but this winged goddess alighting from the skies in the prow of a ship surpasses her predecessor, seeming almost to quiver against the sea-wind.

The sustained demand throughout the Hellenistic period for female nudes was answered by statuary which, at its best, combines the repose of the Classical tradition with a gentle, rounded sensuality of very subtle charm. "*The Aphrodite of Cyrene*" of the late second or early

first century BC is an exquisite example, a most human goddess arisen from the sea. More famous, and endlessly copied, is "*The Medici Venus*". More contrived, more consciously graceful, and the best known of all is "*The Venus de Milo*", from the island of Melos, now in the Louvre. She was once thought to be fourth-century, and she is indeed in the Praxitelean tradition, but the subtly complex turn of body, the sensuousness of the flesh, the slipping draperies are certainly Hellenistic.

The function of art shifted radically during this period. Monumental sculpture was no longer dedicated primarily to the service of an austere religion, but rather to the glorification of autocratic dynasties, as at Pergamum, and was increasingly employed for the decoration of palaces. The fashion of collecting – connoisseurship in the modern sense – was also established, and the collector's range was not necessarily confined to minor decorative works of art (though statuettes, cameos, engraved gems and seals, small bronzes, goldsmiths' work all proliferated) but extended to full-scale statues and to paintings. King Ptolemy III, for instance, had a vast collection of paintings in Alexandria.

AFTER AN UNKNOWN SCULPTOR (below)
"*The Aphrodite of Cyrene*", original *c.* 100 BC?
Such statues (or copies of statues) were widely used by the Romans to adorn their baths and gardens. This is a delicious, very chaste image of nubility.

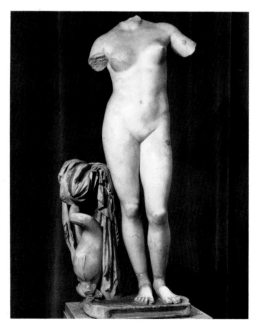

AFTER AN UNKNOWN SCULPTOR (left)
"*The Medici Venus*", original *c.* 150-100 BC?
The very conscious gesture of modesty adds to Venus' sensuality: she has become a more explicit image of sexual love than "*The Cnidian Aphrodite*" (see preceding page) on which her movement was based. Her posture recurs again and again in Renaissance art: she was a particularly suitable *Eve*. This statue is inscribed as the work of Kleomenes, member of an Athenian studio virtually mass-producing sculptural copies destined for Rome.

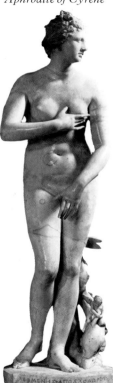

POMPEII (below)
Silenos, undated
This little bronze, a copy of a Hellenistic original, sways under the burden of the candelabrum it once supported. Silenos was a member of Dionysos' train, as his snake, and wreath of grapes and ivy, proclaim. He is wittily conceived, and beautifully finished.

AGASANDROS OR ALEXANDROS (left)
"*The Venus de Milo*", late 2nd or 1st century BC
The name of the sculptor, otherwise unknown, cannot be read fully on the plinth. The proportions of Venus' breasts and upper torso, and her head, are Classical, but the full, matronly hips, tilted in a gently swaying movement, are Hellenistic.

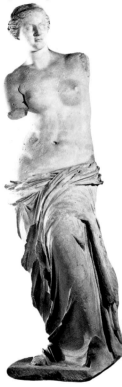

AFTER AN UNKNOWN SCULPTOR (below)
Antiochos III of Syria, original *c.* 200-150 BC
Antiochos' bid to revive Alexander the Great's Empire brought the new power of Rome into Greek view for the first time. Antiochos extended his control as far as India in the east, then turned to the west. There his opponents sought the help of Rome, which decisively defeated Antiochos, after he had disregarded the advice of the Carthaginian general Hannibal. The door was open for Rome to conquer Greece, and for Greek culture to conquer Rome.

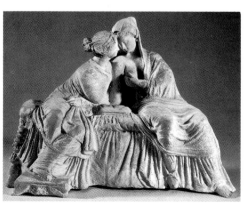

MYRINA (left)
Two women gossiping, *c.* 100 BC
Traces of paint remain: the couch was red, the pleats blue, the women's flesh was pink. An older woman giving advice to a young bride is perhaps shown. Myrina in Asia Minor was a source of numerous terracotta figurines of the type first associated with Tanagra in Greece proper, but it gradually developed its own distinctive forms. In mood and style, this little pottery ornament is a parallel to Rococo pieces.

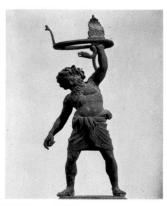

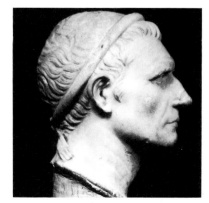

The Lost Riches of Classical Painting

Painting was no less important in ancient Greece than sculpture, but very few originals have survived except in one branch of the art – vase-painting. Not a single mural or panel painting by any of the artists so abundantly praised by classical writers exists in the original, and their nature and quality can be inferred only from literary sources or second-hand versions directly copied from, or distinctly influenced by, early masterpieces.

In the late Archaic period, mural painting seems to have corresponded closely to the style evident in vase-painting: it was essentially two-dimensional, linear, with a limited colour range. The murals in a Greek tomb at Paestum in Italy, of about 480 BC, are no doubt fairly typical, although this is provincial work, and how far it is representative of the best quality cannot be known. In the mid-fifth century, however, chroniclers record a startling progress, both in technique and in the range of effects gained – an increased realism, a sense of movement, a stronger appeal to the emotions. The important advance was the first understanding of foreshortening – but not perspective; at this time the more distant figures were placed above the nearer ones, but still on the same scale and the same plane. The media used were fresco – applying colour to the wet plaster – and an egg-based tempera applied on a dry surface; encaustic, in which the paint was held in warm wax, seems not to have become usual until Roman times.

In the mid-fifth century the most famous artists were Polygnotos, whose murals seem to have reinterpreted the old myths with much the same freedom and pungency as the great contemporary tragedians, and Apollodoros, who invented a primitive chiaroscuro. Apollodoros' pupil, Zeuxis, who is said to have specialized in easel-paintings, rationalized his master's use of shading into a developed system, and became, judging by the famous story that birds alighted to eat the grapes he had painted, the first master of *trompe-l'oeil*. In about 420 BC Agatharchos is reported to have introduced perspective effects in stage scenery. Parrhasios is said to have been the supreme master of that elegant line we can still admire in red-figure vase-painting.

It became increasingly difficult for vase-painters to reconcile the new naturalism with the limitations imposed by the curved shape of their pots, especially since the beauty of their art was dependent on a formal, linear pattern that could marry effortlessly into the surface of the clay. A three-dimensional effect inevitably broke into the harmony. Some delicate late fifth-century white-ground *lekythoi* (oil or perfume containers) show a quite fresh freedom, but there was a marked decline in the quality of vase-painting from about 400 BC.

The fourth century was regarded by later critics as the Golden Age of classical painting. Its most prominent master was the famous Apelles, court painter to Philip II of Macedon and to his son, Alexander the Great; second only to Apelles was Nikias. Apelles apparently excelled all in the brilliance of his colour, in the elegance of his composition and in his handling of light. He is said to have written a treatise, as many Greek architects and sculptors also did (all are now lost), and perhaps in it explained his use of colour. It seems that Classical and some fourth-century painters deliberately avoided the use of green and blue, possibly because it upset their careful modelling in light and dark. Later painters sometimes imitated them to obtain a "Classical" look, and the absence of blue often indicates a later copy of an early original.

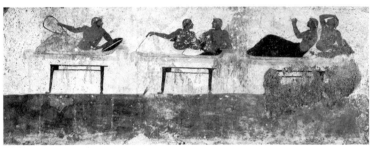

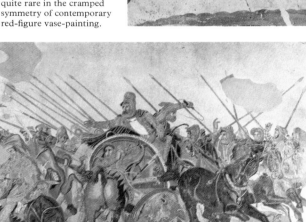

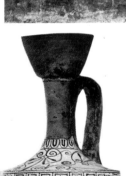

PAESTUM (above)
A banquet, c. 480 BC
The view is limited to the profile, except where the torsos twist – and even here there is no foreshortening. Between this and Egyptian or Assyrian art (see p. 30) there is no yawning divide.

PAESTUM (right)
A diver, c. 480 BC
Here there is a sense of space and scale implicit in the landscape, and a hint of movement and freshness quite rare in the cramped symmetry of contemporary red-figure vase-painting.

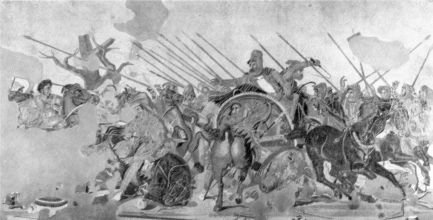

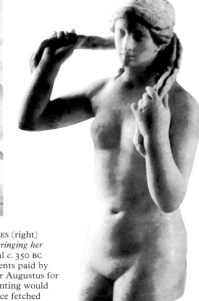

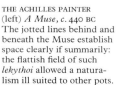

THE ACHILLES PAINTER
(left) *A Muse, c.* 440 BC
The jotted lines behind and beneath the Muse establish space clearly if summarily: the flattish field of such *lekythoi* allowed a naturalism ill suited to other pots.

AFTER PHILOXENOS? (above)
The Alexander mosaic:
Alexander meets Darios in battle, original *c.* 300 BC
The composition is densely peopled and animated, and organized both in depth and across the surface, so that the two monarchs confront one another dramatically. The expressions of their faces are equally dramatic. There is a sure mastery of light and shade, within a restricted colour scheme (no blue or green).

AFTER APELLES (right)
Aphrodite wringing her hair, original *c.* 350 BC
The 100 talents paid by the Emperor Augustus for Apelles' painting would rival the price fetched by a Rembrandt today.

The masterpieces of the fifth and fourth centuries BC were in some cases described in detail by writers (Botticelli, among others, used literary sources to attempt reconstructions in the Renaissance). Closer reflections seem to have been preserved in the volcanic ash that destroyed Herculaneum and Pompeii, and originals are also known by transposition to other media. One was sculpture: a statuette now in Philadelphia seems to derive from Apelles' most famous painting, "*Aphrodite Anadyomene*", showing the goddess standing in water wringing out her hair. Another was mosaic: the famous Alexander mosaic from Pompeii, made in about 90 BC, is associated with an original of about 300 BC by Philoxenos, and probably conveys something of the essence of the style of Apelles' time. Painted copies from Pompeii include one small but majestic *Zeus*, believed to relate to an Apelles painting described by Pliny; and a *Perseus and Andromeda* may be related to one by Nikias. Very recently, original fourth-century murals (not shown) have come to light in Macedonia.

By the end of the fourth century most of the principles and techniques that the Renaissance was to re-establish were known and exploited, with the notable exceptions of mathematical perspective and the potential of oil as a vehicle for colour. Following the establishment of the Hellenistic kingdoms across the eastern littoral of the Mediterranean, Greek art, or art inspired by Greek art, was widely propagated in several separate schools. Hellenistic survivors are far rarer and so that much more difficult to date; as in sculpture (or poetry), painting constantly referred to the art of the past. Its subject matter also expanded from predominantly mythological or historical events to genre – two famous mosaics in Pompeii by Dioskourides, themselves of about 100 BC, but held to reflect late third-century BC paintings, are an example. Still life is also found, and studies of animals, fish and birds. Landscape appears to develop as a distinct branch of art in the second century BC. The luxurious and various decoration of the houses of Herculaneum and Pompeii, dating from the first century BC and the first century AD, probably reflects quite accurately the range available: much of it depends on Greek originals, and even after Rome had become the dominant power in the Mediterranean, the Greek tradition was sustained, often by migrant Greeks.

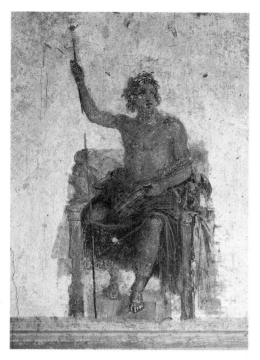

AFTER APELLES? (above)
Zeus, original *c.* 350 BC
Apelles was famed for his skill in portraiture, and painted, according to Pliny, an image of Alexander the Great as Zeus so lifelike it seemed three-dimensional. Naturalism was Pliny's chief criterion of quality.

AFTER NIKIAS? (below)
Perseus and Andromeda, original *c.* 350 BC
Though the composition is probably based on Nikias, the faces are unheroic, and the general effect is stolid. The Apelles copy (above) has at least some presence; this has none.

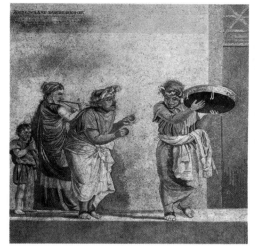

DIOSKOURIDES (above)
Street musicians, c. 100 BC
These strolling players, followers of the cult of Cybele, are remarkably vivacious, and the mosaic manages to convey a real impression of sunlight and the open air. It is signed in Greek by its immigrant maker; but it was perhaps not his own composition.

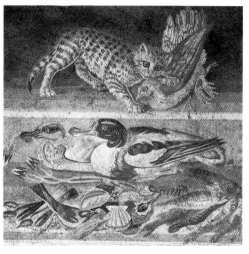

POMPEII (above)
A cat with a bird; ducks and fish, original *c.* 250 BC
As in the Alexander mosaic, the colours are limited to those four (red, yellow, black and white) cited by Pliny as in vogue with some famous painters of the 5th and 4th centuries BC – their use here indicates that the mosaicist imitated an earlier model. The quality is good: the cat almost bristles; the mullet gasp.

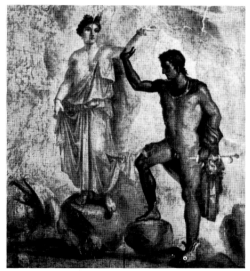

ROME, ESQUILINE
(right) *Odysseus enters Hades*, original *c.* 150 BC
This most lyrical painting is probably a copy of a Hellenistic landscape of about 150 BC. The treatment of light is especially effective; it enters Hades, with Odysseus, from the left, illuminating a broad sweep, in which the artist has placed his figures. The brushwork is swift, even "impressionistic" – which seems to be a later, Roman, technique (the Apelles copy is a better example).

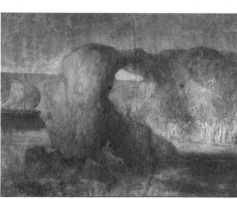

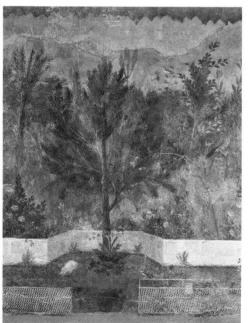

ROME (left)
The garden painting in the House of Livia at Prima Porta, detail, *c.* AD 25
A gentle woodland scene is represented in a profusion of foliage and birds seen here and there amongst the trees. These are set back behind the fence in clear perspective; there are subtle changes of tone between close and distant objects, but neither the scale nor the viewpoint is consistent.

Roman Art 1: Late Republic and Early Empire

Rome was founded, according to legend, by Romulus and Remus on April 21, 753 BC, and the date at least seems approximately accurate. Roman dominance over Italy came gradually: the regions to the north, including Etruria, succumbed in the fourth century BC, those to the south, including eventually the Greek cities there, in the third. During the second century BC Roman power expanded outside the confines of the Italian peninsula until it encompassed most of the Mediterranean seaboard, progressively extending to reach its furthest limits about AD 100, in the reign of the Emperor Trajan. Then the Roman Empire embraced the whole Mediterranean, and from Britain in the west to Mesopotamia in the east.

Roman art comprises three main strands – the native, so-called "Italic" of the region; the Etruscan, a culture that developed earlier and faster than the Roman although it was soon absorbed into it; and above all the Hellenic. The Greek influence came not only direct, but also filtered through the Etruscans; and especially after the Roman conquest of Greece it was to be decisive. After the Sack of Syracuse, from 212 BC onwards, ship-load upon ship-load of Greek artistic treasure was transported

as booty to Rome; Greek artists likewise migrated. In Rome, in Greece, in Hellenistic outposts (notably at Aphrodisias in Asia Minor), Greek workshops were busily employed, reproducing copies or variants of earlier masterpieces. Thus the dating and place of origin of one of the most celebrated compositions of antiquity, the *Laocoön*, is not untypically obscure. Certainly carved by three sculptors from Rhodes, Hagesandros, Polydoros and Athenodoros, it is equally certainly in the vigorous Hellenistic, specifically Pergamene,

"Baroque" manner, but it has been dated variously from the second century BC to the first century AD. But when it was rediscovered, in 1506, it was in Rome. Rome is the channel through which the Greek tradition was passed to the West.

Yet in Roman use the Greek tradition could entirely alter its character. The status of art and artists in Rome was quite different: art was anonymous, its makers mere instruments of the patrons who commissioned it, and, as artisans, of no social consequence. Art was

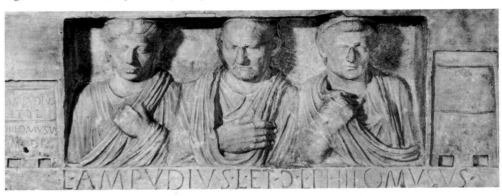

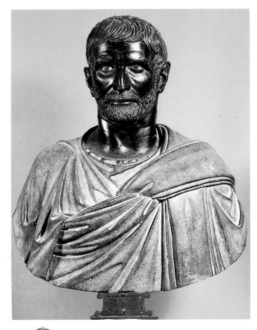

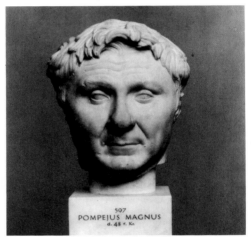

ROME (left)
"*The Capitoline Brutus*", 3rd century BC
Lucius Junius Brutus was the semi-legendary founder of the Roman Republic; the "portrait" shows a hero.

ROME (above)
Pompey (Pompeius Magnus), *c.* 50 BC?
The head is a subtle blend of native Roman, individual portraiture with the smooth harmony of Greek tradition.

ROME (above)
Ampudius, his wife and daughter, 1st century BC
Whatever his origins, the cornmerchant Ampudius was a Roman citizen: the toga he wears is proof. He, like so many Romans, had his very literal likeness planted outside his tomb.

ROME (below)
Augustus, after 27 BC
Augustus was depicted – naked, in armour or, here, in a toga as an officiating priest – in guises and poses derived from Greek prototypes. The head is youthful even in statues made when Augustus was more than 70.

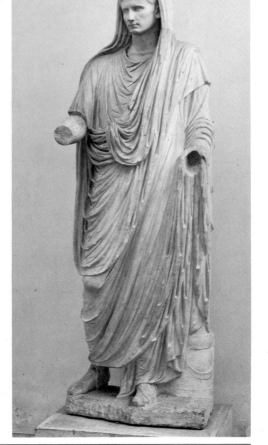

HAGESANDROS, POLYDOROS AND ATHENODOROS (right)
Laocoön, 1st century AD?
Apollo sent the serpents to slay Laocoön and his sons for voicing suspicions of the Trojan Horse. Writhing expressively, their figures became an object lesson for 16th-century artists.

APOLLONIOS (left)
"*The Belvedere Torso*", *c.* 100 BC
The famous torso, which, like the *Laocoön,* is clearly Hellenistic in the energy of its tensed musculature, was also made for Rome, or soon found its way there, and was found in the 1490s: it surely influenced Michelangelo's Sistine nudes (see p. 134), and much of his statuary.

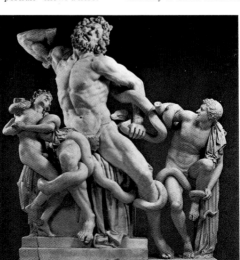

functional: in a highly material and prosperous urban society, it was an adjunct of luxury and a status symbol; or it extolled the glory of the state, the fame of family, the renown of national or civic heroes – propaganda art.

Portraiture became extremely important. There survives from as early as the third century BC an intense and sharply individual bronze bust known as "*The Capitoline Brutus*", which may be Roman or Etruscan. It was the Etruscans who invented the bust form, with its concentration on the head; the Greeks, though their interest in the head as the mirror of the mind is clear from Hellenistic times, did not sever it from the body. The Romans themselves had an ancient, rather macabre tradition recorded by Pliny: "In the halls of our ancestors, wax models of faces were displayed to furnish likenesses in funeral processions – so that at a funeral the entire clan was present". There is an extraordinary statue (not shown) illustrating this practice, a life-size figure of a patrician carrying two such heads of his ancestors, embodying the enduring virtue of the family or clan.

Countless funerary slabs in high relief show an uncompromising realism – with faces presumably taken directly from death masks. They cover a wide range, so that for the first time a comprehensive portrait of the individuals making up a society can be seen, from Emperor to tradesman. Yet a suaver, generalizing Hellenistic strain can also be discerned in the late Republic, for instance in a bust of Pompey (if it is contemporary). This is in fact the earliest certainly identifiable likeness of a major Roman historical figure.

Already in the first century BC such famous generals of the Republic as Pompey were honoured as near-divinities, and their statues erected in public places. When Octavian established himself as the Emperor Augustus, a deliberately idealizing style of portraiture, harking back to a precedent first set by Alexander the Great, was applied to present the supreme ruler, now a god, for adulation and adoration. Statues of Augustus were produced in various modes, and countless repetitions exported all over the Empire: they acted as proxy for Augustus himself, manifesting his authority in substantial form wherever Roman power was established. The official, propaganda aspect of early imperial art is most splendidly illustrated by the Ara Pacis Augustae

(the Altar of Augustan Peace), commissioned in 13 BC. When the processions on its side walls are compared to the friezes of the Parthenon (see p. 39), the specificity of the Roman mind is clear: a particular event is recorded, and the figures are thought to be portraits. The dignity and majesty of the Augustan age is reflected also in other media, for instance in the flawless virtuosity of the cameo known as the Gemma Augustea, where the Emperor presides serenely alongside the goddess Roma.

Augustus' successors appear in their portraits in a comparably cool and relatively idealized style, though the image of Nero is distinctly and uncharmingly taurine. But with the Flavian Emperors, starting with the forthright soldier Vespasian (AD 69-79), the Italic tradition seems to revive, and an individual, even unsophisticated character, bourgeois rather than aristocratic, is depicted convincingly in his busts. The propaganda reliefs take on a franker narrative interest, as on the Arch of Titus (Vespasian's successor). In painting, the acclimatization of the Hellenistic style is copiously illustrated in the domestic interiors of Pompeii and Herculaneum, and typically vivid painted portraits survive.

ROME (right)
The Altar of Augustan Peace, detail, 13-09 BC
In the unstated, consciously cool and static majesty of the processional reliefs, the influence of Greek Classical art is strong – Roman "Neoclassicism". Other, allegorical, reliefs are Hellenistic in style.

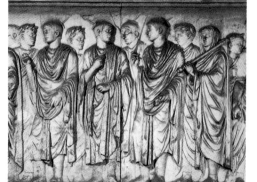

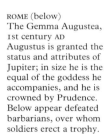

ROME (below)
The Arch of Titus:
Triumph with the spoils of Jerusalem, c. AD 81
The deep relief, the lively

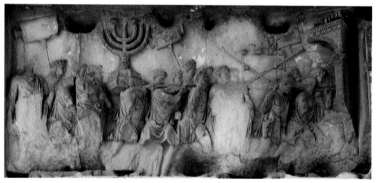

and varied poses, the foreshortened candelabrum of the Temple in Jerusalem – an accomplished narrative technique is now applied

to real events. The Flavian Emperors propagated its use: the finest achievement of this kind would be Trajan's Column (see over).

ROME (above)
Gold coin, obverse: *Nero, c.* AD 60-68
The Emperor's portrait was usually idealized, but the artistic Nero preferred a more individual image, of Hellenistic influence. He wears long-curled hair in the Greek fashion; his philhellenism annoyed his senators quite considerably.

ROME (below)
The Gemma Augustea, 1st century AD
Augustus is granted the status and attributes of Jupiter; in size he is the equal of the goddess he accompanies, and he is crowned by Prudence. Below appear defeated barbarians, over whom soldiers erect a trophy.

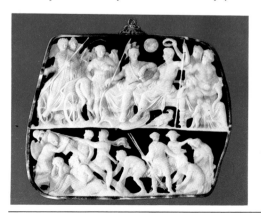

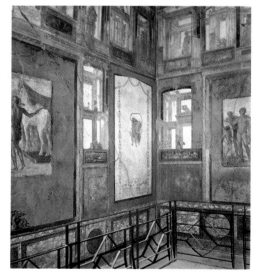

POMPEII
Paquius Proculus and his wife, before AD 79
The dark, distinctively southern features of the

couple are vividly rendered. The wax-based medium is found again in the equally individual, later portraits from Fayoum (see p. 62).

POMPEII
A room in "the House of the Vettii", before AD 79
The sophistication of the decorative scheme typifies a

late stage of wall-painting; murals featured in Greek domestic interiors but the *trompe-l'oeils* are probably a later, Roman invention.

47

Trajan's Column, Rome

In the reign of Trajan (AD 98-117) the Roman Empire pushed outwards to its furthest boundaries, an achievement copiously commemorated by monuments, not only in Rome – where Trajan's Forum, the grandest of all the imperial fora, was built, and in it Trajan's Column, an extraordinarily original conception – but elsewhere, for instance at Benevento in southern Italy, where one of the most splendid triumphal arches is preserved.

Temporary honorific arches were customarily erected on the route of generals returning in triumph from successful campaigns: the marble versions translated these into permanent form. One early survivor is the Arch of Titus in Rome, with vivid reliefs inside the arch (see preceding page) deeply cut – exploiting effects of light and shade – and using an appreciable, if unsystematic, perspective. Trajan's Arch at Benevento is the first known to have been decorated with figure sculpture and friezes over both main faces, merging with the architecture in a unified, harmonious composition of rich complexity; but the carving, though again in high relief, is more stately than that of the Arch of Titus, and its content more pacific, depicting the Emperor as a statesman rather than a general.

On Trajan's Column, however, the narrative relief is applied in a new way on a vast scale to spectacular effect. Thirty-eight metres (125ft) high, the Column was dedicated in 113. The marble low relief that winds unbroken up its shaft and retails the course of the Emperor's campaigns against the Dacians (in modern Romania) in 101 and 105-06 is some 200 metres (650ft) long. Its survival for nearly 2,000 years is due partially to its adaptation to Christian purposes: it was originally crowned by a colossal bronze-gilt statue of the Emperor, replaced in the sixteenth century by a *St Peter*.

Characteristically for Roman art, the artist responsible for the Column's conception is unknown; there must have been a team of sculptors working on it, and the quality of the carving is uneven, but the whole, in its magisterial sweep and impetus, clearly reflects the guidance of one remarkable controlling intelligence. This might have been the architect of the Forum itself, the Syrian Greek, Apol-

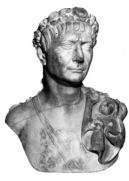

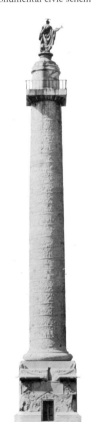

lodoros of Damascus, but that is only conjecture. The Column was sited originally between two new libraries (one Latin, one Greek; now vanished), from the top of which the details of the uppermost parts of the frieze were perhaps more legible (as they were not to be again until binoculars and the photographic zoom lens).

The handling of the subject matter is likewise novel, although reference to battle and victory, to the humiliation of barbarian enemies and to Roman triumph, was not of course new. Processional friezes go back to the Parthenon, and the *Telephos* frieze at Pergamum (see p. 42) shows the beginnings of storytelling in marble relief. A continuous historical narrative had not, however, been attempted before. Trajan's Column is the first visual documentary, a remote harbinger of the medium of film; although Roman scrolls with continuous illustration exist, those that survive are all later than the Column. The relief is shallower than on Trajan's Arch at Benevento, no doubt to help sustain the uninterrupted flow of the story; it was moreover originally heightened with colour. Individual figures are clearly differentiated one from another, and shown on a rather larger scale then either architectural or landscape elements, or their horses; the figure of Trajan himself, emphasized as hero, recurs on a still larger scale. Though consistency of scale had never been a canon of Greek or Roman art, the enlargement for emphasis of the important figures is significant for the future. The story proceeds in two parts, corresponding to the two campaigns, each ending with the submission of the Dacians. The most dramatically effective are the last scenes of all – the march on Sarmizegethusa, the siege, the firing of the city by the defeated Dacians, the pursuit of their ruler, Decebalus, finally his suicide. There are some 2,500 individual figures in all, together with their armour, equipment and all their military paraphernalia, depicted in great detail, making an unparalleled account of the Roman Army in the field. Often, too, the individual participants take on character: they register in facial expression as well as gesture the agony of battle, the pain of their wounds, the misery of their captivity.

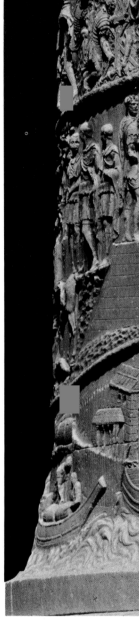

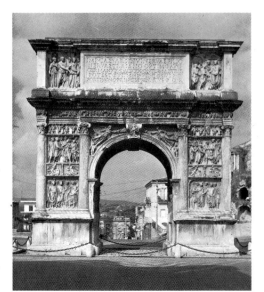

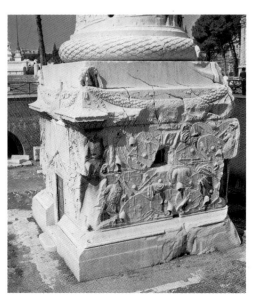

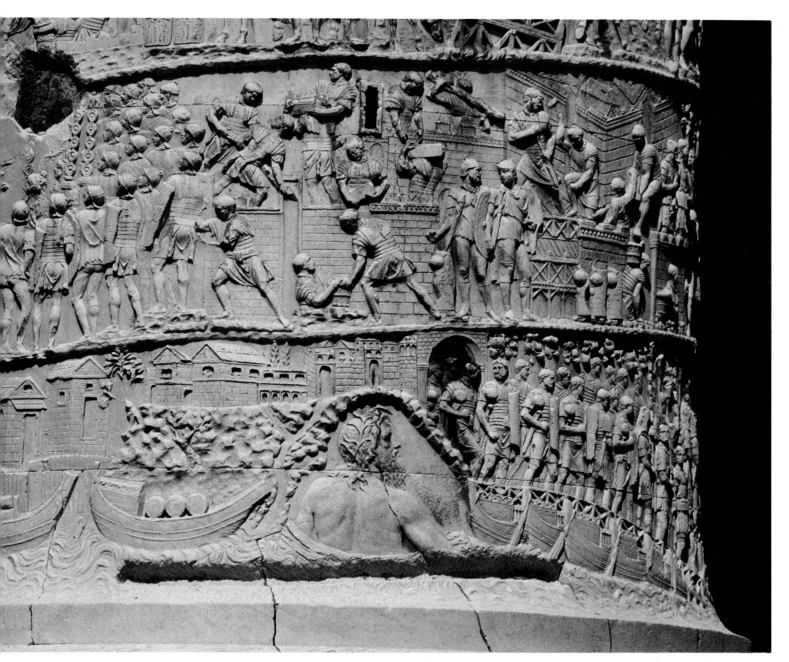

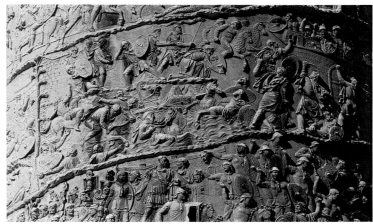

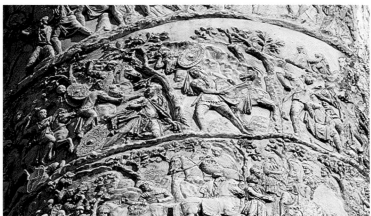

The siege of Sarmizegethusa
The cavalry charge, soldiers swim the river and all make ready to scale the Dacian walls, in a dramatic rush of action reproducing all the gore and confusion of battle. The composition is always vivid, changing its character with the action.

Decebalus' suicide
The agony of defeat, the tragedy of the individual, are recognized no less than the joy of triumph. Gesture and expression reveal the Dacian leader as a hero: he may be the enemy, and doomed to defeat, but he is given an epic role to play.

Roman Art 2: The Hadrianic Period

The reign of Hadrian (AD 117-38) has been called the Golden Age of the Roman Empire, expanded to its furthest extent, consolidated briefly in relative peace and in unheard-of prosperity. Of Spanish origin, Hadrian was a tireless traveller, personally fascinated by the Greek tradition of art (he was nicknamed *graeculus*). He commissioned spectacular architecture, for instance the dome of the Pantheon in Rome and his so-called Villa, his country residence at Tivoli, a huge conglomeration of gardens, baths, temples, pavilions and palaces, liberally adorned with sculpture. Here the generous eclecticism of Hadrian's taste brought together a host of ancient masterpieces – from copies of the famous caryatids from the Erechtheion in Athens to Egyptian gods, from Egypt.

The revival of Grecian taste stimulated a renewed interest in nude sculpture in the round, above all in statues of Hadrian's favourite Antinoüs, drowned in the Nile and subsequently deified by the Emperor. These echo Hellenistic types, but also show innovations in the use of the drill that can be seen again in imperial portraiture, which, though still idealized, took on a new vividness, es-pecially in the treatment of the eyes and hair. Eyes were given increased definition and expression by drilling out the pupils, hair was more variously and energetically shaped, and the beard reappeared. Highlights were created, "colouristic" effects achieved.

The fashion, begun in Trajan's reign, for burying instead of cremating the dead became widespread in Hadrian's time: the container for the body, the sarcophagus, often carved in elaborate relief, is the medium in which the progress of Roman imagery and style can best be studied and analysed in all its rich variety. Thousands of sarcophagi were produced all over the Empire in the following centuries, most notably outside Rome, in Athens and Anatolia. The carving developed from primarily decorative patterns of swags and garlands to figured reliefs depicting mythological incidents, battles, and extending even to subjects of everyday life. An outstanding, if unusually elaborate, early example is the Velletri sarcophagus: the figures illustrate a number of themes common in Roman funerary symbolism. Hercules' Labours symbolize the triumph of life: his descent into hell and return spells out the hope of rebirth, an extension of an interest in the individual personality for which the change from cremation to burial is doubtless also evidence.

Signs of disintegrating confidence appear even in Hadrian's time, but the old order was maintained for a time in the reign of that intriguing personality Marcus Aurelius (161-80). Known as "the philosopher Emperor", an intellectual, he was, however, embroiled in recurrent and major military crises. His victories were celebrated, following Trajan's example, by triumphal arches, now lost, and a spectacular Column, less well preserved than Trajan's. The relief is more deeply cut, but the narrative is jerky, repetitious, and less compelling. Of much better quality is his famous equestrian statue of bronze, originally gilded, in the Campidoglio in Rome, the best surviving equestrian monument from antiquity, the ancestor of the Renaissance masterpieces by Donatello and Verrocchio and of countless later images of mounted rulers and generals throughout the world. In fact the output of statuary in the Roman Empire was prodigious, and though a remarkable amount in stone survives (usually in part rather than in whole), staggering numbers have been lost – there are

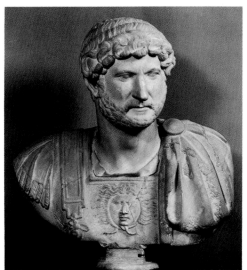

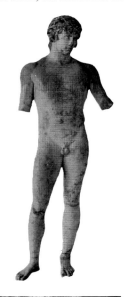

ROME (left)
Hadrian, c. 117-38
Inscribed in Hadrian's vast mausoleum, now the Castel S. Angelo by the Vatican, is the timid little verse: "Gentle little wee tramp soul, the body's guest and friend, where are you off to? Somewhere tiny, dank, bare and wan." The late Roman era seems to begin with Hadrian: outwardly so prosperous, it has been called "an age of anxiety".

DELPHI (right)
Antinoüs, c. 130
Hadrian's appreciation of Greek art is reflected in the marked idealization of his Bithynian love – though the image is still sensual; the head shows the use of a drill. The type was much copied in the Renaissance.

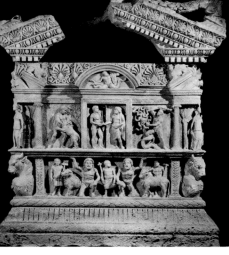

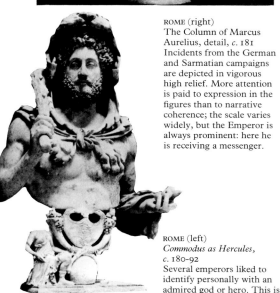

ROME (right)
The Column of Marcus Aurelius, detail, *c.* 181
Incidents from the German and Sarmatian campaigns are depicted in vigorous high relief. More attention is paid to expression in the figures than to narrative coherence; the scale varies widely, but the Emperor is always prominent: here he is receiving a messenger.

ROME (left)
Commodus as Hercules, *c.* 180-92
Several emperors liked to identify personally with an admired god or hero. This is near to caricature, almost Rococo in its hyperbole.

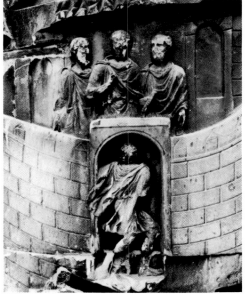

ROME (above)
The Velletri sarcophagus, early 2nd century?
Complex and crowded in its mythology – showing the increasing catholicity of Roman art and religion – the elaborate ornament and arcades of the sarcophagus may reflect the appearance of Roman theatre scenery. The crudely carved figures suggest Eastern influence.

ROME (below)
The Ludovisi sarcophagus: *Romans fight Germans,* mid-3rd century
The concern is entirely for movement, not only in the twisting bodies extruding every tiny space but also in their hair and drapery; the deep cutting throws up dramatic shadows. Reliefs such as these were emulated by the young Michelangelo.

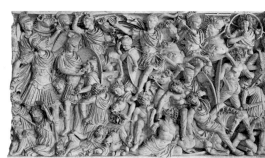

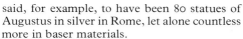

ROME (below)
Marcus Aurelius, c. 161-80
Probably once surmounting a triumphal arch now lost, the statue was preserved thanks to the Christian

misapprehension that it represented Constantine. Though the horse (as was usual) is small in relation to its rider, the anatomy is accurate and lively.

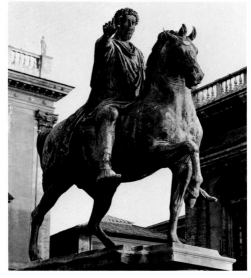

said, for example, to have been 80 statues of Augustus in silver in Rome, let alone countless more in baser materials.

The craftsmanship of late imperial portrait busts could reach a high pitch, conveying character and mood with great virtuosity – most remarkably in the notorious bust of Commodus (180-92), decked incongruously with the attributes of Hercules. The quality of reliefs on sarcophagi varied enormously, but they, too, could be superb, as on the Ludovisi sarcophagus. Here interest in the representation of space and coherent clarity of composition yields to an almost savage relish in a highly realistic welter of battling bodies, carved with masterly skill. A feeling close to compassion can be apparent in that ever recurring theme of Roman art, the conquered barbarian depicted in his human suffering.

During the third and the fourth centuries AD the formal values of Hellenistic art were gradually eroded. An early but significant stage in this process was reached in the grandest of all triumphal arches, that erected in the province of Tripolitania, in north Africa, at Leptis Magna in 203 by Septimius Severus. The reliefs are in varying styles and of varying

quality. The technique known as "negative relief" was extensively used, that is, undercutting with the drill around the figures, rather than modelling them in rounded form. This produces a strong but flattening contrast between light and dark; and the figures, often in stiff frontal poses, seem rigid and hieratic. Many of the artists engaged came from the East, but the old Greek vision, even the ability to carve in its terms, seems to have been lost.

By the time of Severus, the Emperor cult of the Roman West was merging with traditions of idolatry from the East: in reliefs this tells in the exaggerated scale of the principal figure, and in an ever-increasing emphasis on frontality. In portraiture there was considerable variety in style: for example, while Septimius Severus appeared in the guise of his patron deity, the god Serapis, Alexander Severus (222-35) opted for an image almost republican in its simple directness – though it has also a certain remote aloofness. Through it all the Roman genius for realism recurs in images of often superbly unflattering "verism": the formidable bust of Philip the Arab (244-49) conveys a sense of massive, crude physical power, undermined by psychological unease.

ROME (left)
Septimius Severus as Serapis, c. 200
This north African-born Emperor identified himself with an Egyptian deity; he sports here four ringlets, an attribute of Serapis.

LEPTIS MAGNA (right)
The Arch of Septimius Severus, detail: *Triumphal procession, c.* 202
Influences from Egypt and Syria consort in a style far removed from that of the Arch of Titus (see p. 47).

EGYPT (below)
Septimius Severus and his family, c. 199-201
Septimius' son Geta was erased from this stiff, even sanctimonious image after his brother and joint heir Caracalla had slain him.

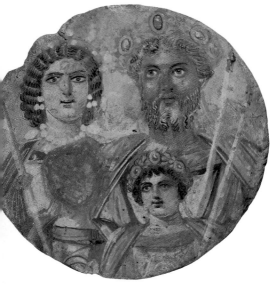

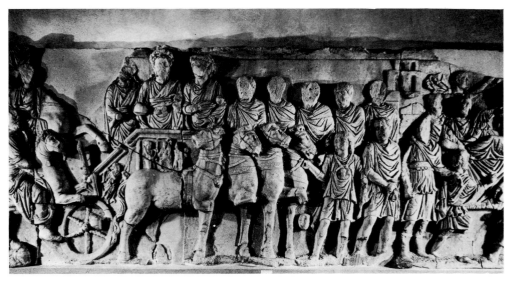

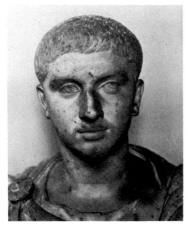

ROME (left)
Alexander Severus, c. 222-35
The full lips, irregular nose and sly eyes suggest a genuine likeness. The Emperor probably wished to propagate a virtuous image in choosing for his bust a republican style.

ROME (right)
Philip the Arab, c. 244-49
The millenary of Rome was celebrated during Philip's reign; but it is difficult not to read decadence into his unprepossessing bust. He gained the *imperium* by murder; so, too, he lost it.

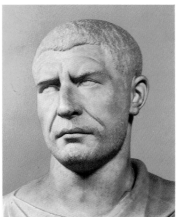

Late Antique and Early Christian Art

When, in AD 313, the Edict of Milan established freedom of worship for all religions, and Christianity became legal, the Roman Empire was already showing signs of fragmentation. It was held together, under the Emperors Diocletian (284-305) and Constantine the Great (306-37), by military strength and thoroughly autocratic government. However, in 330 Constantine removed the capital from Rome to Byzantium, and by the end of the century the Empire was finally split into eastern and western portions under separate Emperors.

In art, a withdrawal from naturalism is intermittently evident even in the third century. Its causes are difficult to trace and no doubt various – perhaps the upsurge of popular traditions in the provinces, even within Italy itself; the mood of spiritual crisis that seems to have infected the whole Empire. It was not brought about by the rise of Christianity, as the famous group of *Tetrarchs* embracing, now outside S. Marco in Venice, is proof: the tetrarchy, the quadripartite division of imperial rule, was established by the Christian persecutor Diocletian. Diocletian may be one of the four here, but if so he is indistinguishable from his colleagues. The ex-

pressionless figures carved in the obdurate but prestigious medium of red porphyry have the stiff articulation of puppets, and yet the image has a mysterious potency. In the images of Constantine, the earlier personality cult endures, or revives, but a surer individual characterization is married into a hieratic symbol of majesty – as in one of the most compelling portraits to survive from antiquity, the colossal 2.5 metres (8ft) high head from a statue of Constantine once towering in a basilica in Rome. Dominatingly frontal in pose, it is enlivened by the gaze, over and away from the spectator, of deeply-cut eyes, hugely enlarged in relation to the other features. This emphasis on "the windows of the soul", to express an inner being, is already obvious in many late Roman portraits and will become increasingly marked in Christian figurative art.

In the great triumphal arch set up in Rome by Constantine in about 312-15, the contrast between the old and the new styles is explicit. The arch was the first monument in which earlier reliefs were "cannibalized" – pieces taken from Trajan's forum and elsewhere were incorporated with contemporary work. What seems to be an eclectic appreciation of the

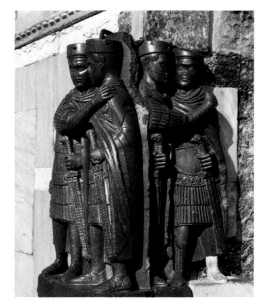

UNKNOWN ARTIST
The Tetrarchs, c. 303
Each Emperor clasps his deputy with his right arm and grasps his sword with his left. Each is identical, a symbol of an idea of unity rather than a real ruler.

ROME (right)
The Emperor Constantine,
c. 313
When Nero raised such a colossus, representing himself as the sun-god, he was decried as egomanic. Constantine's even larger statue of himself passed as nothing inappropriate, and its surviving head is indicative of the changed times. The late imperial period was one of renewed, pompous grandeur. (The fleck of stone in the pupil gives added vigour, like a glint of light, to the eye.)

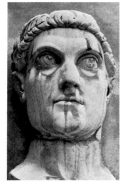

ROME (right)
The Arch of Constantine,
c. 312-15
Constantine's triumphal arch, commemorating his victory over Maxentius in 312, stands beside the Colosseum where, shortly before, Christians had been martyred. The thin frieze (detail, below) representing a *largitio,* or distribution of imperial largesse, shows a row of squat figures, much like the *Tetrarchs.* They line up like place-cards – token presences each in a ritual station.

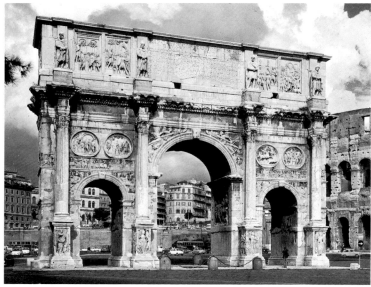

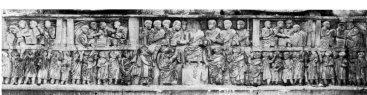

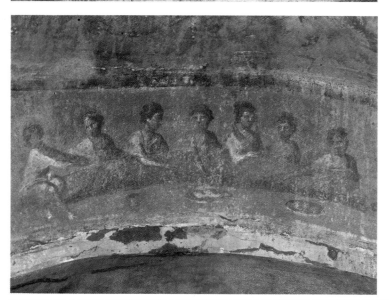

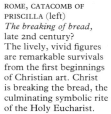

ROME, CATACOMB OF
PRISCILLA (left)
The breaking of bread,
late 2nd century?
The lively, vivid figures are remarkable survivals from the first beginnings of Christian art. Christ is breaking the bread, the culminating symbolic rite of the Holy Eucharist.

ROME, CATACOMB IN THE
VIA LATINA (right)
Hercules and the Hydra,
4th century
The rather crudely daubed hero joins in combat with a vague many-headed snake. Six Labours of Hercules appear among the biblical and mythological scenes in tunnels where both pagan and Christian buried their dead. Hercules probably has allegorical significance, be it pagan or Christian.

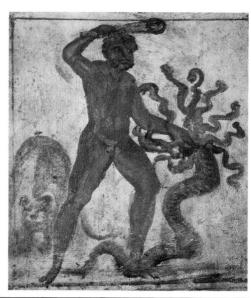

earlier art is combined with indifference to its tradition. Roundels of about AD 120, mythological subjects handled with great freedom of movement, are set just above a squad of strictly frontal figures rigidly aligned as if for inspection and drill; the bodies are barely formed, the heads large in proportion; there is no longer any sense of depth. The Hellenic feeling for the unity and physical harmony of the human body and spirit has vanished. For the Greeks, divinity had materialized in the form of the ideally perfect human body; Christian eyes were to be fixed on the hereafter rather than on human proportions.

In the beginning, however, Christians depended on traditional styles and even imagery. They had no other sources on which to draw. In three centuries, Roman art, like the Roman way of life, had spread throughout the Empire; much was exported from Rome, but local workshops also were active. There were inevitably marked regional developments in style: in the west, in Spain, Gaul or Britain, the Roman manner penetrated very thoroughly, even though it was often expressed with a provincial accent – coarser, clumsier, with its principles not always fully understood. In the east, however, the sophisticated traditions of older civilizations proved more resistant.

For the immediate followers of Christ in the first century AD, the visual arts had little relevance: there were no formal churches, no sites for art. The earliest known church dates from about 230. The earliest Christian art belonged instead to the burial places, the catacombs just outside Rome, cut long and deep into the rock and in use between about 200 and 400, after which they became shrines for veneration. Many painted decorations survive on the walls: space was limited, and techniques and artistic ability are usually of a very impoverished order, but the evolution of a Christian iconography in its formative stages can be followed. The subjects chosen often relate to the salvation of the soul, or to divine intervention on behalf of humans; miracles and episodes in the life of Christ also appear, as in *The breaking of bread* in the Catacomb of Priscilla. Pagan and Christian imagery commingle, not too surprisingly – Rome's ability to acclimatize and incorporate alien beliefs into its own culture was almost inexhaustible. Thus Christ may be equated with Orpheus, descending into hell to save a soul, or purely pagan symbolism may occur alongside Christian imagery. So Hercules may be Hercules, or he may be the good man who achieved immortality through his labours. The visual character of Christ himself is unsettled, and he is often represented as a beardless youth, interchangeable with Apollo or the sun-god. One of the essential Christian symbols, the Cross, does not appear at first, as in Rome its associations with common criminal executions seem to have been too strong.

Under Constantine, the official status of Christianity made the erection of churches both practicable and necessary, to house a now well-established and elaborate ritual of worship. Early Christian churches did not exploit sculpture, though the craft continued in the decoration of sarcophagi, and developed most notably in miniature form, on ivory reliefs; the wooden relief panels from S. Sabina in Rome (about 432), showing parallel incidents from the Old and New Testaments, are rare survivals. The traditional Roman craft of mosaic, practised all through the Empire as both floor and wall decoration, was soon applied with enthusiasm to Christian themes; fresco was also used, but has virtually all perished.

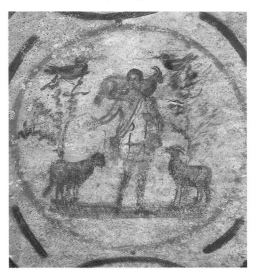

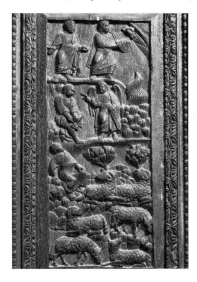

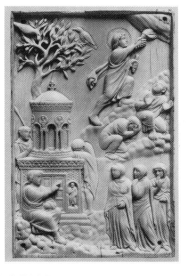

ROME, CATACOMB OF PRISCILLA (left)
The Good Shepherd, c. 250-300
Christ had said: "I am the good shepherd", and so he was often shown in early Christian art. Not only in style but in its attributes this figure is derived from pagan sources; it is small, hardly more than a graffito.

ROME, S. SABINA (right)
Panel of a door: *Moses and the burning bush,* c. 432
Since the story is new, it is told simply and directly, without virtuosity. Moses is shown tending his sheep, then removing his shoes at the direction of an angel; there is the burning bush; then in the upper register he communes with God.

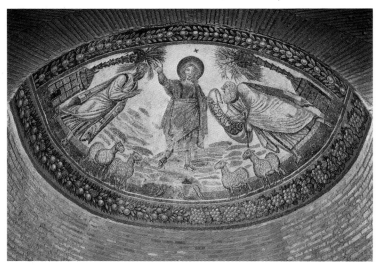

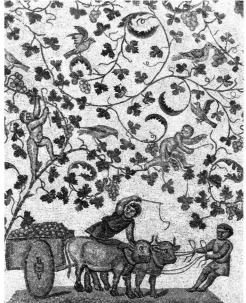

ROME, S. COSTANZA
An apse: *Christ gives the law to SS. Peter and Paul,* 5th century

Christ is youthful, haloed, and radiantly steps from the clouds to deliver his salutation like an Emperor.

Christ will later be shown bearded, but the tradition that St Paul was bald is already established.

UNKNOWN ARTIST (above)
The three Marys at the Tomb; the Ascension, late 4th or early 5th century
Though the simple, blunt forms are much like those of the S. Sabina doors (and similar doors front the finely detailed tomb), there is more indication of what the participants feel; Christ performs a bold, rushing movement; and the carving is of good quality. The compression of space, the varying scales, these are already medieval.

ROME, S. COSTANZA
(left) Detail of the vault of the ambulatory: *Putti harvesting grapes,* c. 350
In the rich mosaics of the round church, a mausoleum for Constantine's daughter, purely decorative, secular scenes occur alongside the religious subjects in the apses and (once) the dome.

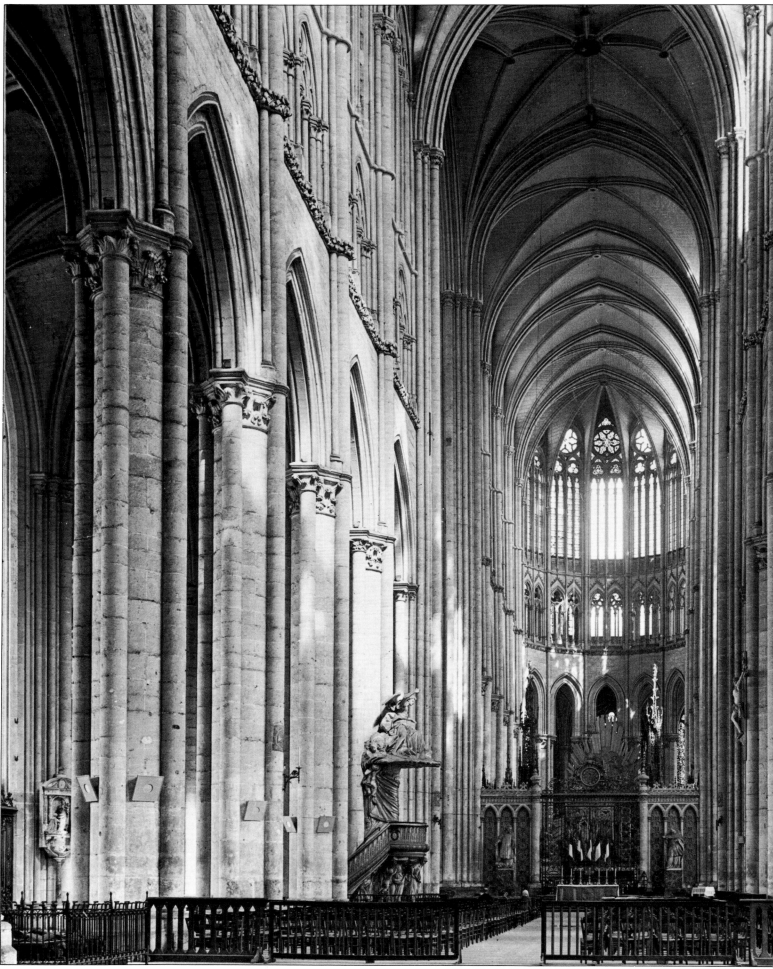

MEDIEVAL AND EARLY RENAISSANCE ART

The Middle Ages were so called because they intervened between the grandeur of Rome and the renewed ability of the Renaissance to emulate the Greek and Roman achievement. The term stretches to include virtually a millennium, from the fifth century AD to the fifteenth, when the men of the Renaissance became the first to invent a period identity for themselves. These were centuries marked by disruption and fragmentation, opening in chaos as the "barbarians" struck wherever Roman civilization was established. Though the newly accredited official religion, Christianity, found a secure haven in the East, in Byzantium, it was not until around 800 that Charlemagne revived aspirations of a European political and religious unity in the Holy Roman Empire.

To those looking back, the Middle Ages for a long time seemed a vast span of cultural debasement, and medieval art the product of ignorance; the name of its most daring and brilliantly innovative style, the Gothic, was originally synonymous with barbaric. As more sympathetic historical research and analysis focused on the period, however, scholars came to see it as transitional – rather than as catastrophic – and in many ways progressive. An interest in the Antique never entirely disappeared, while great positive foundations have survived from the Middle Ages, not least

the universities. The Renaissance itself was transitional, attempting the reconciliation of religious and secular enquiry and beliefs, of pre-Christian and Christian thought.

None the less, most medieval art is very different in form and spirit from classical or Renaissance art, and the difference lies essentially in its other worldliness; for the medieval artist the human body was no longer a subject for celebration in naturalistic form but a means of expressing spiritual realities. This is nowhere more clearly seen than in the mosaics of Byzantium – remote, hieratic and awe-inspiring. Art was for the glorification of God, and though great artistic personalities did exist in this period (Gislebertus is one whose name has survived), the individuality of the artist begins to be stressed only towards the end of the Middle Ages. A great deal of artists' work was carried out in collaboration – most notably in the Romanesque and Gothic cathedrals, in which painters, glass-workers, embroiderers, metalworkers all combined with the architects to create a splendour in which, as voices in a paean of praise, individual contributions are subsumed into a greater whole. With the Renaissance, we see the component parts beginning to separate out as "works of art". In particular, the detached easel-painting, soon to assume a dominant role in European art, comes into fashion.

AMIENS, FRANCE (left)
Interior view, facing east, of the Cathedral, begun 1220

URBINO, ITALY (right)
The courtyard of the Ducal Palace, 1465-69

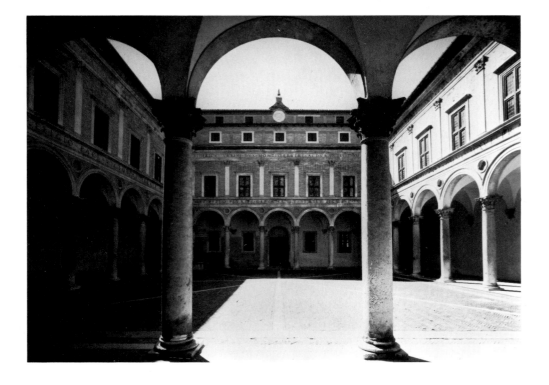

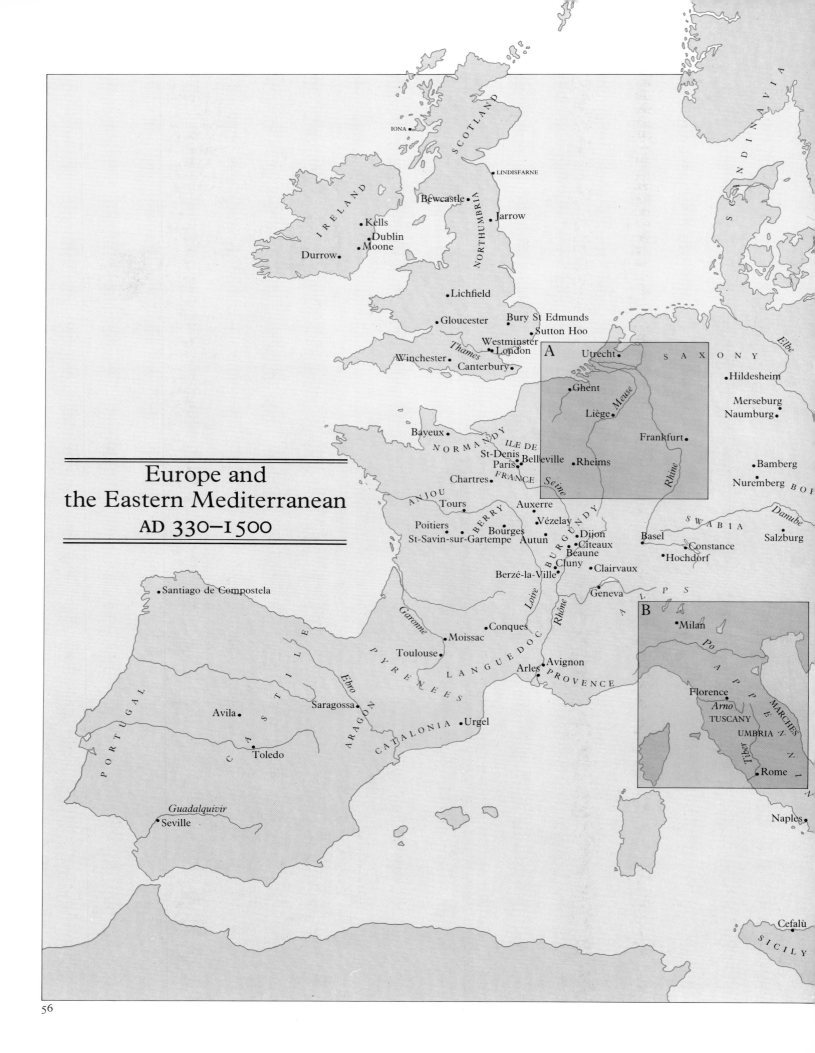

Europe and
the Eastern Mediterranean
AD 330–1500

IONA

SCOTLAND

LINDISFARNE

IRELAND

Bewcastle

NORTHUMBRIA

Jarrow

Kells

Dublin

Moone

Durrow

Lichfield

Gloucester

Bury St Edmunds

Sutton Hoo

Westminster

Thames

London

Winchester

Canterbury

SCANDINAVIA

Elbe

A

Utrecht

SAXONY

Hildesheim

Ghent

Meuse

Merseburg

Liège

Naumburg

Frankfurt

Bayeux

NORMANDY

ILE DE

St-Denis

Belleville

Rheims

Rhine

Bamberg

Paris

FRANCE

Seine

Nuremberg

BOH

Chartres

ANJOU

Tours

BERRY

Auxerre

SWABIA

Danube

Poitiers

Bourges

Vézelay

BURGUNDY

Dijon

Basel

Salzburg

St-Savin-sur-Gartempe

Autun

Cîteaux

Constance

Beaune

Hochdorf

Berzé-la-Ville

Cluny

Clairvaux

Santiago de Compostela

Geneva

A L P S

B

Garonne

Milan

Po

Conques

A P P E

Moissac

PYRENEES

Toulouse

LANGUEDOC

Arles

Avignon

PROVENCE

Florence

MARCHES

Arno

Ebro

ARAGON

CATALONIA

Urgel

TUSCANY

UMBRIA

Z

Saragossa

PORTUGAL

Avila

C A S T I L E

Tiber

N I

Rome

Toledo

Guadalquivir

Seville

Naples

Cefalù

SICILY

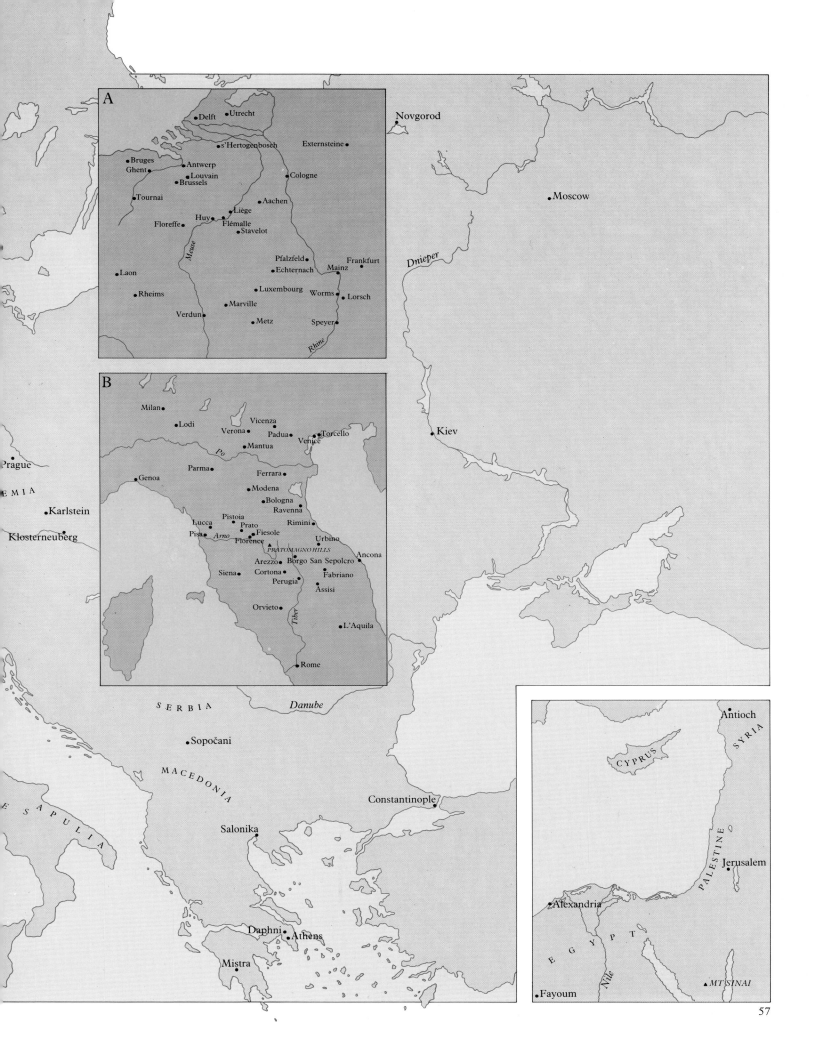

A

Delft
Utrecht
s'Hertogenbosch
Externsteine
Novgorod
Bruges
Antwerp
Ghent
Louvain
Cologne
Brussels
Tournai
Aachen
Moscow
Liège
Floreffe
Huy
Flémalle
Stavelot
Meuse
Pfalzfeld
Frankfurt
Echternach
Mainz
Dnieper
Laon
Luxembourg
Worms
Lorsch
Rheims
Marville
Verdun
Metz
Speyer
Rhine

B

Milan
Lodi
Vicenza
Verona
Padua
Torcello
Mantua
Venice
Kiev
Po
Parma
Ferrara
Prague
Genoa
Modena
Bologna
B E M I A
Ravenna
Karlstein
Pistoia
Rimini
Lucca
Prato
Klosterneuberg
Pisa
Arno
Fiesole
Florence
Urbino
PRATOMAGNO HILLS
Ancona
Arezzo
Borgo San Sepolcro
Siena
Cortona
Fabriano
Perugia
Assisi
Orvieto
Tiber
L'Aquila
Rome

SERBIA
Danube

Sopočani

MACEDONIA

Constantinople

E SAPULIA

Salonika

Antioch
SYRIA
CYPRUS
PALESTINE
Jerusalem

Daphni
Athens
Alexandria
Mistra
E G Y P T
Nile
Fayoum
MT SINAI

57

Byzantine Art 1: Justinian

In AD 330 the Emperor Constantine, having reunited the Roman Empire under his single rule, transferred its capital from Rome in the West to Byzantium in the East. He consolidated imperial power by embracing Christianity as the official religion, and the old Greek city of Byzantium on the shores of the Bosphorus, renamed Constantinople, and dedicated as a Christian city to the Virgin, became the hub of the Byzantine civilization which was to persist through many vicissitudes for over a thousand years, until the Turkish conquest of 1453, when Constantinople became Istanbul and the capital of the Ottoman Empire. By then the Renaissance had already broken in the West.

From early Christian adaptations of the late Roman styles the Byzantines developed a new visual language, expressing the ritual and dogma of the united Church and state. Early on variants flourished in Alexandria and Antioch, but increasingly the imperial bureaucracy undertook the major commissions, and artists were sent out to the regions requiring them from the metropolis. Established in Constantinople, the Byzantine style eventually spread far beyond the capital, round the Mediterranean to southern Italy, up through the Balkans and into Russia.

Rome, sacked by the Visigoths in 410, was sacked again by the Vandals in 455, and by the end of the century Theodoric the Great had imposed the rule of the Ostrogoths on Italy. However, in the sixth century the Emperor Justinian (reigned 527-65) re-established imperial order from Constantinople, taking over the Ostrogothic capital, Ravenna, as his western administrative centre. Justinian was a superb organizer, and one of the most remarkable patrons of art in history. He built and rebuilt on a huge scale throughout the Empire: his greatest work, the church of Hagia Sophia in Constantinople, employed nearly 10,000 workmen and was decorated with the richest materials the Empire could provide. Though it still stands gloriously, hardly any of the earliest mosaics remain, and it is at Ravenna that the most spectacular witness of Byzantine art in the sixth century survives – though the apse mosaic in SS. Cosma e Damiano in Rome, about 530, is an impressive reminder of the continued activity of the popes.

At Ravenna, within the dry brick exterior of S. Vitale, the worshipper is dazzled by a highly

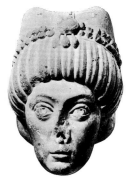

RAVENNA, S. VITALE
The Empress Theodora,
detail, before 547
Mosaic is composed of
thousands of minute cubes
of coloured glass or stone
set in plaster; it is very
durable. A rigid design
suits it; the sense of life
and movement comes from
the light, when it catches
on the unevenly set facets.

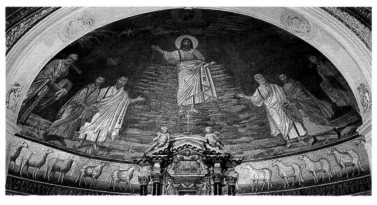

ROME, SS. COSMA E DAMIANO
(above) *Christ with saints,*
c. 530
Pope Felix IV appears
as the patron on the left.
The saints are SS. Peter
and Paul, SS. Cosmas and
Damian. There is still a
factualness about them in
contrast to the more other-
worldly *Justinian* (below).

RAVENNA, S. VITALE
(below) *The Emperor*
Justinian, before 547
On Justinian's left is
Archbishop Maximian,
on his right perhaps his
general Belisarius. The
Emperor has a halo, as
God's representative –
in modified form, the
emperor cult persisted.

RAVENNA, S. VITALE
(right) View of the
apse, before 547
In contrast to Western
practice, the Byzantines
conceived church and
decoration as a unity.
Following late Roman
tradition, they built in
brick, not stone, and then
transformed its surface.

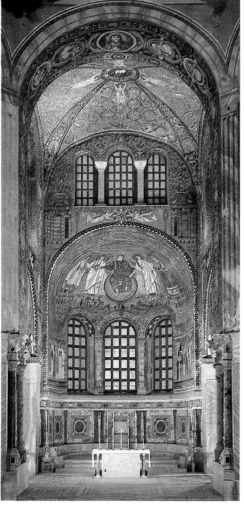

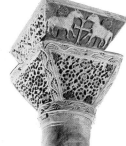

RAVENNA, S. VITALE
(above) Capital in the
apse, before 535
There is no trace of the
old classical orders –
Doric, Ionic, Corinthian.
The motif, horses or cattle
beside the Tree of Life,
is oriental, though the
tree has been displaced
by a Christian Cross.

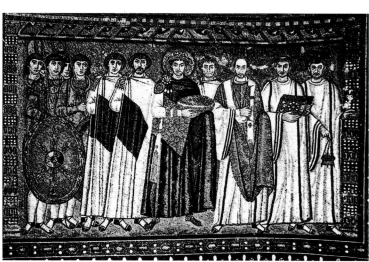

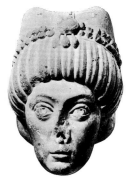

RAVENNA
Theodora? c. 530
Long-standing doubts
about the propriety of
images are reflected in
the rarity of Byzantine
sculpture in the round:
the Bible explicitly con-
demned "graven images".
The head is so idealized
it is hardly still a portrait.

controlled explosion of colour blazoned across glittering gold. Mosaic and beautifully grained marble cover almost all wall surfaces, virtually obliterating the architecture that bears them. The gold, flooding the background, suggests an infinity taken out of mortal time, on which the supernatural images float. In the apse, wrapped in their own remote mystery, Christ and saints preside unimpassioned. Nevertheless, in two flanking panels of mosaic, one showing the Emperor Justinian with his retinue and the other, opposite, his wife Theodora with her ladies, there persists a clear attempt at naturalistic portraiture, especially in the faces of Justinian and Theodora. Even so, their bodies seem to float rather than stand within the tubular folds of their draperies.

In S. Vitale, and in Byzantine art generally, sculpture in the round plays a minimal part. However, the marble capitals (dating from before Justinian's time) are carved with surprising delicacy with purely oriental, highly stylized vine-scrolls and inscrutable animals. A rare example of Byzantine figurative sculpture is an impressive head, perhaps that of Theodora, in which the Roman tradition of naturalistic portraiture lingers.

In the East, Justinian's most important surviving work is in the church, a little later than S. Vitale, at St Catherine's Monastery on Mount Sinai. There, in the great *Transfiguration* in the apse, the figures are again vital, substantial presences, suspended weightlessly in a golden empyrean. The contours, however, are freer, less rigid, than at S. Vitale, and the limbs of the figures are strangely articulated – almost an assemblage of component parts. This was to become a characteristic and persistent trait in the Byzantine style.

Elsewhere (notably at Salonika) there were other local variations of style in mosaic. Relatively little remains in the cheaper form of fresco, and still less in manuscript illumination. A very few sixth-century manuscripts, on a purple-tinted vellum, show a comparable development from classical conventions towards an austere formality, though pen and ink tend to produce greater freedom in structure and gesture. In the famous *Rabula Gospel* of 586 from Syria, the glowing intensity of the dense imagery may even bring to mind the work of Rouault in the twentieth century.

Ivory panels carved in relief have also survived, usually covers for consular diptychs.

These diptychs consisted of two ivory plaques, tied together, with records of the departing consul's office listed on their inner surfaces. The carvings on the outside, representing religious or imperial themes, have the clarity and detachment characteristic of the finest mosaics, and are splendidly assured.

In the eighth and ninth centuries the development of the Byzantine style was catastrophically interrupted in all media. Art was not merely stopped in its tracks: there was a thorough, wide-ranging destruction of existing images throughout the Byzantine regions. Figurative art had long been attacked on the grounds that the Bible condemned the worship of images; in about 725 the iconoclasts (those who would have religious images destroyed) won the day against the iconodules (those who believed they were justified) with the promulgation of the first of a number of imperial edicts against images. Complicated arguments raged over the issue, but iconoclasm was also an assertion of imperial authority over a Church thought to have grown too rich and too powerful. It was surely owing to the Church that some tradition of art did persist, to flower again when the ban was lifted in 843.

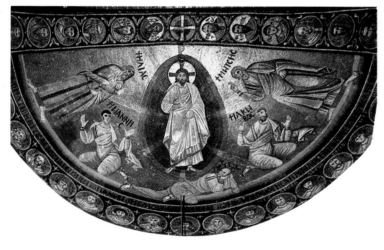

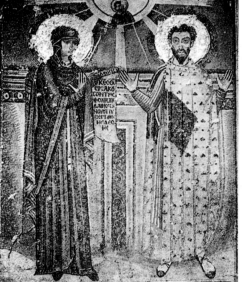

SALONIKA, ST DEMETRIOS (left) *St Demetrios and the Virgin*, late 6th or early 7th century
The insubstantial bodies and stylized, patterned robes are delineated almost entirely in straight lines. Though the craftsmanship is of a high standard, the figures lack the powerful presence of Constantinopolitan mosaic panels.

RAVENNA (below)
Archbishop Maximian's Throne, *c.* 550
The expense and craftsmanship of the Throne are remarkable; precious materials figured large in Byzantine art. In the decorative panels oriental motifs are conjoined with the profuse ornament of late classical art. Such non-representational art continued to flourish in the iconoclastic period.

MT SINAI, ST CATHERINE
The Transfiguration, *c.* 548-65
Justinian probably sent a team of mosaicists from the capital to decorate a strategically placed new centre of orthodoxy. Sects with heretical views on Christ's divinity were strong in Egypt, Syria and Palestine, and the Emperor was anxious to counter the threat with orthodox propaganda.

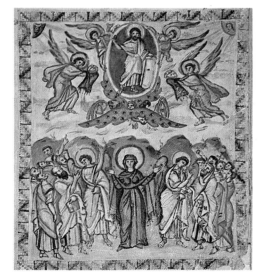

CONSTANTINOPLE (right)
The Barberini diptych: *The Emperor as defender of the faith*, 6th century
The Emperor on a rearing horse may be Justinian, or perhaps Anastasius. Earth personified supports his foot; below, Scythians and Indians pay tribute. The carving and design are precise, clear and certain.

SYRIA (left)
The Rabula Gospel: *The Ascension*, 586
Vigorously shaped in heavy outlines, the figures seem to echo the poses and symmetry of church mosaics, and the border even imitates mosaic. But the design is too crowded for a mosaic, and there is a suggestion of landscape, and much foreshortening.

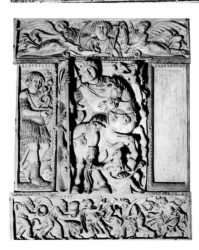

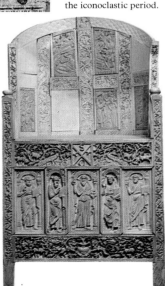

Byzantine Art 2: Revival and Diffusion

The end of iconoclasm – the destructive campaign against images and those who believed in them – came in 843. The revival of religious art that followed was based on clearly formulated principles: images were accepted as valuable not for worship, but as channels through which the faithful could direct their prayer and somehow anchor the presence of divinity within their daily lives. Art rarely had a didactic or narrative function, but was essentially impersonal, ceremonial and symbolic: it was an element in the performance of religious ritual. The disposition of images in churches was codified, rather as the liturgy was, and generally adhered to a set iconography: the great mosaic cycles were deployed about the Pantocrator (Christ in his role as ruler and judge) central in the main dome, and the Virgin and Child in the apse. Below, the main events of the Christian year – from Annunciation to Crucifixion and Resurrection – had their appointed places. Below again, hieratic figures of saints, martyrs and bishops were ranked in order.

The end of iconoclasm opened an era of great activity, the so-called Macedonian Renaissance. It lasted from 867, when Basil I, founder of the Macedonian dynasty, became absolute ruler of what was now a purely Greek monarchy, almost until 1204, when Constantinople was disastrously sacked. Churches were redecorated throughout the Empire, and especially its capital: in Hagia Sophia in Constantinople mosaics enormous in scale took up the old themes and stances, sometimes with great delicacy and refinement.

Despite the steady erosion of its territory, Byzantium was seen by Europe as the light of civilization, an almost legendary city of gold. Literature, scholarship and an elaborate etiquette surrounded the Macedonian court; the tenth-century Emperor Constantine VII Porphyrogenitos sculpted and himself illuminated the manuscripts he wrote. Though his power continued to diminish, the Emperor had enormous prestige, and the Byzantine style proved irresistible to the rest of Europe: even in regimes politically and militarily hostile to Constantinople Byzantine art was adopted and its craftsmen imported.

In Greece, the Church of the Dormition at Daphni, near Athens, of about 1100, preserves some of the finest mosaics of this period: there is a grave, classic sense of great delicacy in its *Crucifixion*, while the dome mosaic of *The Pantocrator* is one of the most formidable in any Byzantine church. In Venice, the huge expanses of S. Marco (begun 1063) were decorated by artists imported from the East, but their work was largely destroyed by fire in 1106, and later work by Venetian craftsmen is in a less pure style. In the cathedral on the nearby island of Torcello, however, *The Virgin and Child*, tall, lonely, and solitary as a spire against the vast gold space of the apse, is a twelfth-century survival. In Sicily, the first Norman king, Roger II (ruled 1130-54), was actively hostile to the Byzantine Empire yet he imported Greek artists, who created one of the finest mosaic cycles ever, in the apse and presbytery at Cefalù. The permeation of Byzantine art into Russia was initiated in 989 by the marriage of Vladimir of Kiev with the Byzantine princess Anna and his conversion to Eastern Christianity. Byzantine mosaicists were working in the Hagia Sophia at Kiev by the 1040s, and the Byzantine impact on Russian painting remained crucial long after the fall of Constantinople.

The secular paintings and mosaics of the Macedonian revival have rarely survived – their most spectacular manifestation was lost

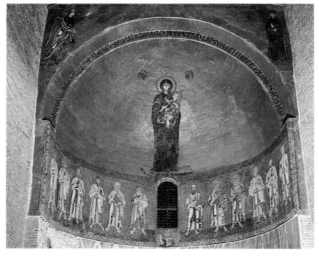

CONSTANTINOPLE, HAGIA SOPHIA (left)
The Virgin and Child enthroned, 867
The colossal, elongated Virgin dominates the main apse of the vast church. Chroniclers tell how lifelike she seemed, and how the populace was full of delight to see her – especially perhaps women, some of the staunchest opponents of iconoclasm.

TORCELLO CATHEDRAL (right) *The Virgin and Child*, 12th century
The Madonna's small head and elongated body enhance the striking effect of her isolation, as do the apostles, so much smaller below.

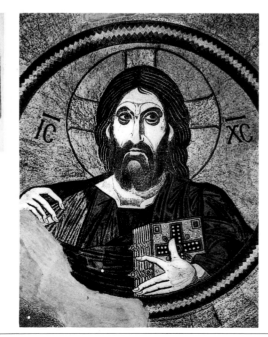

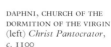

DAPHNI, CHURCH OF THE DORMITION OF THE VIRGIN (above) *The Crucifixion*, c. 1100
Though the rendering is austere and stylized, it has a lyric balance and a restrained tenderness prefiguring Duccio.

CEFALU CATHEDRAL (right)
View of the apse, c. 1148
The *Pantocrator* is here in the eastern apse, not in the central dome, the focus of the Orthodox church. The curvaceous, flowing outlines of the figures, and especially the device of modelling drapery in thin gold ray-like lines, were to persist in Italian painting, notably in Siena (see p. 79).

DAPHNI, CHURCH OF THE DORMITION OF THE VIRGIN (left) *Christ Pantocrator*, c. 1100
This awe-inspiring *Christ* bears little relation to the suffering Saviour shown crucified in the same church (far left). Looking down from the centre of the dome, the great head, with those curiously expressive hands, is indeed Christ the ruler of the world.

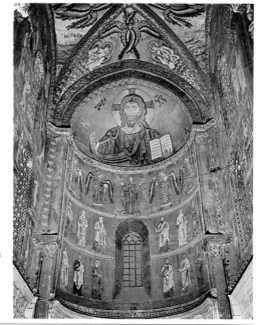

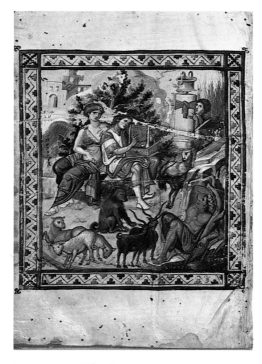

in the burning of the legendary Great Palace in Constantinople during the Sack of 1204. Such works retained much more clearly classical features – the ivory panels of the Veroli casket are an example – but such features are to be found, too, in religious manuscripts and in some ivory reliefs (sculpture in the round was forbidden as a concession to the iconoclasts). The Joshua Roll, though it celebrates the military prowess of an Old Testament hero, reflects the pattern of Roman narrative columns such as Trajan's at Rome; the famous Paris Psalter of about 950 is remarkably Roman both in feeling and iconography: in one illustration the young David as a musical shepherd is virtually indistinguishable from a pagan Orpheus, and is even attended by an allegorical nymph called Melody.

In 1204 Constantinople was sacked by Latin Crusaders, and Latins ruled the city until 1261, when the Byzantine emperors returned. In the interim craftsmen migrated elsewhere. In Macedonia and Serbia (now mainly Yugoslavia), fresco painting was already established, and the tradition continued steadily. Some 15 major fresco cycles survive, mostly by Greek artists. The fresco medium doubtless

encouraged a fluency of expression and an emotional feeling not often apparent in mosaic.

The last two centuries of Byzantium in its decay were troubled and torn with war, but surprisingly produced a third great artistic flowering. The fragmentary but still imposing *Deesis* in Hagia Sophia in Constantinople may have been constructed after the Latin domination, rather than during the twelfth century. It has a new tenderness and humanity which was continued – for instance in the superb early fourteenth-century cycle of the monastic church of Christ in Chora (see p. 64). In Russia, a distinctive style developed, reflected not only in masterpieces such as the icons of Rublev (see over), but also in the remarkably individual interpretations of traditional themes by Theophanes (Feofan) the Greek, a Byzantine emigrant, working in a dashing, almost impressionistic style in the 1370s in Novgorod. Though the central source of the Byzantine style was extinguished with the Turkish conquest of Constantinople in 1453, its influence continued in Russia and the Balkans, while in Italy the Byzantine strain (mingling with Gothic) persisted in the new art founded by Duccio and Giotto.

CONSTANTINOPLE (above)
The Paris Psalter:
David harping, c. 950
Byzantine art in its maturity was always open to the revival of classical or of earlier Byzantine styles. In this instance the reuse of a classical model is unusually obvious.

CONSTANTINOPLE (right)
The Joshua Roll: *The stoning of Achan*, c. 950
The long papyrus scroll was probably written and illustrated at the order of Emperor Porphyrogenitos. The Carolingian Utrecht Psalter (see p. 68), though in book form, must derive from a work such as this.

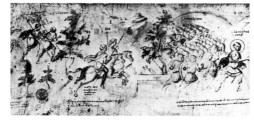

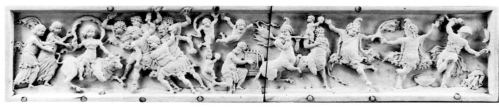

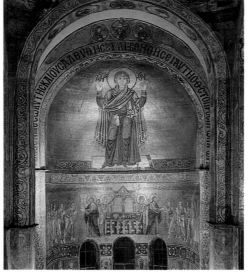

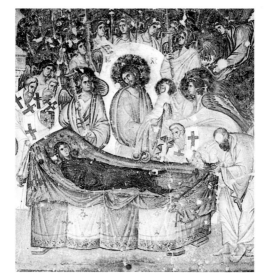

CONSTANTINOPLE (above)
The Veroli casket:
The rape of Europa, 10th or 11th century
The doll-like ivory figures enact an episode from classical mythology in classical groupings and in classical poses. The group of stone-throwers, inappropriate to the myth, is also in the Joshua Roll, and must be taken from the same classical source.

CONSTANTINOPLE, HAGIA SOPHIA (below)
The Deesis, c. 1261?
The Deesis consists of Christ shown between the Virgin and St John, who intercede with him on behalf of humanity. The mosaic was perhaps made as part of the reception for the Emperor, returning after the Latin rule. The figures are remote, more compassionate than stern.

KIEV, HAGIA SOPHIA (above)
View of the apse, 1042-46
Austere and monumental, these mosaics are the earliest example of Christian art in Russia. They show Byzantine art extremely pure and hieratic; the stylized figures are ordered in firm symmetry.

THEOPHANES (below)
The Holy Trinity, 1378
The three angels who visited Abraham came to symbolize the Trinity. The mannered but lively style of Theophanes took root and flourished for many decades in a native "Novgorod school".

SOPOCANI, YUGOSLAVIA
The dormition of the Virgin, detail, c. 1265
The Dormition is the Byzantine equivalent of the Western Assumption.

Surrounded by elders, Christ, glowing behind the dying Virgin's bed, holds in his arms the babe that is the Virgin's soul reborn into Heaven.

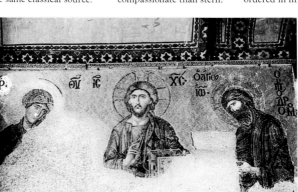

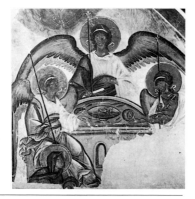

The Virgin of Vladimir

Icons, generally small and so easily transportable, are the best-known form of Byzantine art. A tradition persists that the first icon was painted by St Luke the Evangelist, showing the Virgin pointing to the Child on her left arm. However, no examples that date from before the sixth century are known. Icons became increasingly popular in Byzantium in the sixth and seventh centuries, to some degree precipitating the reaction of iconoclasm. Although the iconoclasts asserted that icons were being worshipped, their proper function was as an aid to meditation; through the visible image the believer could apprehend the invisible spirituality. Condensed into a small compass, they fulfilled and fulfil the same function in the home as the mosaic decorations of the churches – signalling the presence of divinity. The production of icons for the Orthodox Churches has never ceased.

Dating of icons is thus fairly speculative. The discovery at St Catherine's monastery on Mt Sinai of a number of icons that could be ordered chronologically with some certainty is recent. Many different styles are represented. An early *St Peter* has the frontal simplicity, the direct gaze from large wide-open eyes, that is found again and again in single-figure icons. It also has an almost suave elegance and dignity, allied with a painterly vigour that imparts a distinct tension to the figure. There is a similar emotional quality in a well-preserved *Madonna and saints*, despite its unblinking symmetry and rather coarser modelling. Both surely came from Constantinople.

Immediately after the iconoclastic period, devotional images in richer materials, in ivory, mosaic or even precious metals, may have been more popular than painted ones. From the twelfth century painted icons became more frequent, and one great masterpiece can be dated to 1131 or shortly before. Known as "*The Virgin of Vladimir*", it was sent to Russia soon after it had been painted in Constantinople. The Virgin still indicates the Child, as the embodiment of the divine in human form, but the tenderness of the pose, cheek against cheek, is eloquent of the new humanism.

From the twelfth century the subject matter of icons expanded considerably, though the long-established themes and formulae, important for the comfort of the faithful, were maintained. Heads of Christ, Virgins and patron saints continued, but scenes of action appeared – notably Annunciations and Crucifixions; later, for iconostases, or choir-screens, composite panels containing many narrative scenes were painted. Long after it had ceased in Constantinople with the Turkish conquest, production continued and developed in Greece and (with clearly discernible regional styles) in Russia, and in modern Yugoslavia, Romania and Bulgaria. In Russia individual masters emerged even before the fall of Constantinople. The most famous of them was the monk Andrei Rublev (*c.* 1370-1430), whose masterpiece, *The Holy Trinity*, is the finest of all Russian icons. He transcended the Byzantine formulae, and the mannerisms of the Novgorod school founded by the Byzantine refugee Theophanes the Greek; Rublev's icons are unique for their cool colours, soft shapes and quiet radiance.

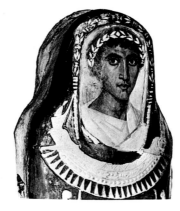

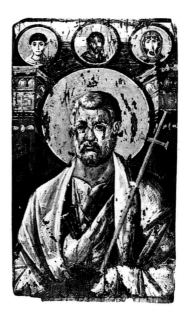

FAYOUM, EGYPT (left)
Artemidorus, portrait on a mummy-case, 2nd century AD
Fayoum has yielded some of the best-preserved painted portraits from classical times. Early icon painters were recognizably schooled in the same tradition: the hypnotic eyes of the icons are already found here, and the *St Peter* (right) was painted in the same technique, using encaustic paint – coloured wax applied while hot.

CONSTANTINOPLE (below)
The Madonna among saints, 6th century
SS. Theodore and George flank the Virgin, who seems withdrawn and preoccupied, and the archangels behind look fearfully up to God.

CONSTANTINOPLE (right)
St Peter, early 7th century
St Peter's pose and format, and the roundels up above, recall consular diptychs, perhaps deliberately. Note how freely the drapery is painted, with bold strokes.

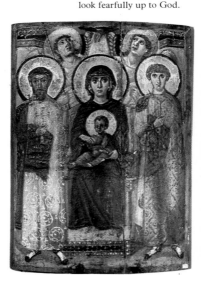

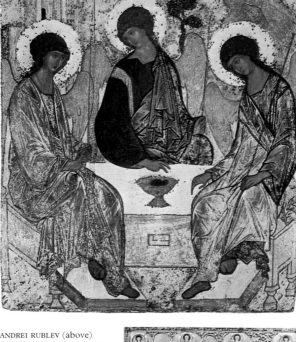

NOVGOROD SCHOOL (below)
The Presentation in the Temple, 16th century?
Typical of the Novgorod school are such tall, rather wooden figures, in cramped poses. The drawing is jerky and the drapery geometric.

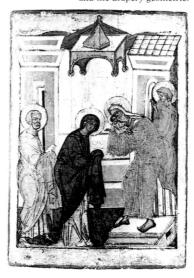

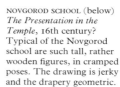

ANDREI RUBLEV (above)
The Holy Trinity, *c.* 1411
The three angels who were entertained by Abraham, as Genesis relates, became symbols of the Trinity in art. The firm and unifying symmetry of the meek but aristocratic figures is softened by the subtle play of shape and colour.

CONSTANTINOPLE (right)
St Michael, *c.* 950-1000
The Frankish Crusaders who sacked Constantinople in 1204 destroyed the city's treasures barbarously; the Venetians, equally piratical but more discriminating, preferred to loot. This icon in gold and silver, inset with jewels and enamels, was part of their booty.

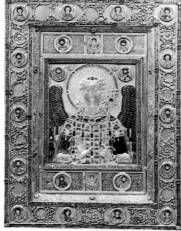

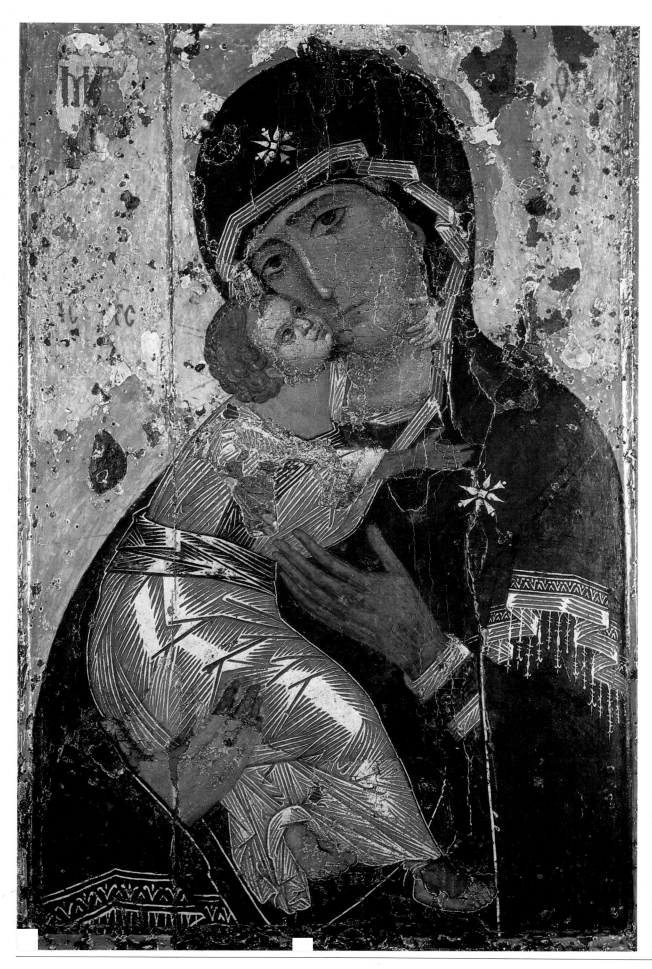

CONSTANTINOPLE
"The Virgin of Vladimir",
c. 1131
The icon has been care-
fully cleaned, but little of
the paint now left is
original – with the great
exception of the Virgin's
and Child's faces. Almost
all early icons have been
repainted not once but
several times. Because it
was abraded by a silver
cover, or *oklad*, the rest of
the icon was damaged too
badly to be restored.

Christ in Chora, Constantinople

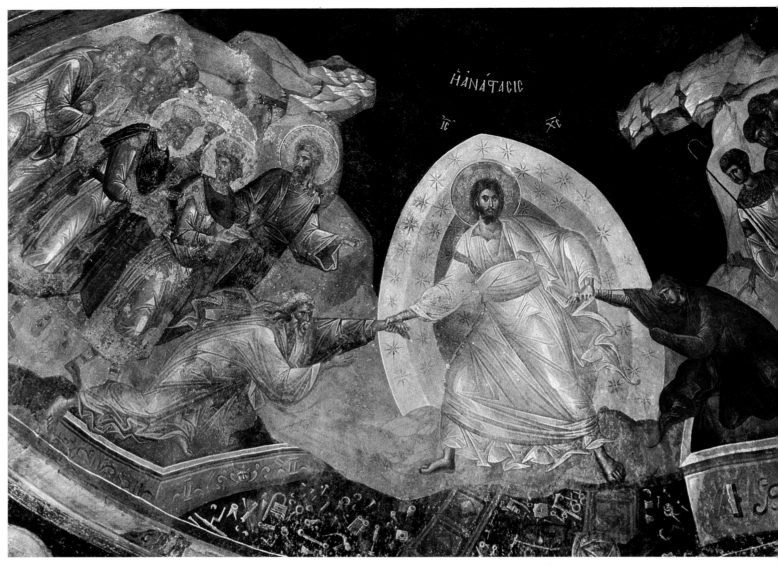

The Chora Monastery, now Kariye Camii, Istanbul (it was converted into a mosque by the Turks and is now a museum) is an outstanding witness to the magical quality of Byzantine art in its late flowering between the Latin occupation of Constantinople of 1204-61 and the Turkish conquest of 1453. Extraordinarily well preserved in many areas, its church was largely remodelled and entirely redecorated by a leading Byzantine statesman, Theodore Metochites, about 1315-21.

The impoverished Emperor was no longer the principal source of patronage; it was more than he could do to maintain and repair the great monuments of the past. New undertakings were on a small scale and were initiated by a few rich feudal families. Yet within the shrunken Byzantine territories, which had been Greek soil for 2,000 years, there was a marked pride in being Hellene, and the Palaeologan artistic revival went hand in hand with the renewed study of the Greek classics. Christ in Chora bears witness to the scholarly refinement of the last Byzantine aristocrats.

One mosaic portrays Metochites, the donor, presenting the church to Christ, but the theme of the decorations is the celebration of Christ and Mary, with incidents from their lives almost in counterpoint. The detail and elaboration of the narrative are rare elsewhere in Western art until considerably later. However, the decoration still serves the ceremonial function of all Byzantine religious art, and has a visionary quality, a dreamlike spirituality, in marked contrast to the monumental, substantial figures being painted (see pp. 82-83) by Giotto at almost exactly the same date. At Kariye Camii the figures and drapery are still subject to conventions nearly a thousand years old, but animated by a novel sprightly vigour.

A colossal *Christ Pantocrator* must have presided over the central dome (lost in its collapse) and the largest surviving mosaic (not shown) is damaged, though still of magisterial yet humane authority. It is a *Deesis*, which would usually show the Virgin and John the Baptist interceding with Christ on behalf of humanity, but John is here omitted because the theme of the church is the Virgin and Christ alone. The subsidiary narrative scenes are of a lively brilliance, at times almost merry, perhaps especially in the apocryphal scenes of the Virgin's childhood, where the artist's imagination might have freer play. Even in more orthodox episodes, or in scenes taken from the Gospels, the treatment is always inventive, full of movement and incident. *The miracle at Cana*, a Gospel story quite com-

monly represented, is entirely original, the artist having obviously become absorbed by the formal rhythms of the great oil jars, with the strange architectural shapes of the house adding a diminuendo above.

The chapel at the side of the main body of the church, probably a mortuary chapel with wall-tombs, was decorated at much the same time as the rest, but in fresco rather than in mosaic, and probably by a different artist or team of artists. It is of no less splendid quality, though different in theme to answer its special function. The subjects include a spectacular version of *The Last Judgment*, featuring the blessed and the damned, and including weird imagery – of the worm that corrupts all things corruptible and of the scroll of heaven. The lower ranges of the chapel are occupied by hieratic figures, including portraits of the dead, in draperies as stylized and mysterious as incantations. The dome is occupied by a more orthodox image of the Virgin with the Child (not shown), central with angels in the ribs radiating out from her, but the supreme image is the magnificent *Anastasis*, or Resurrection, shown, as often in the East, in terms of Christ's descent into Limbo. With serene but irresistible strength, he lifts Adam and Eve (and so, by extension, all of us) into eternal life.

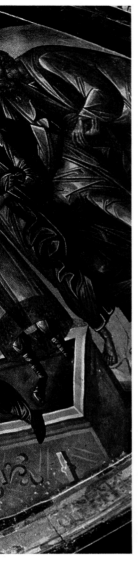

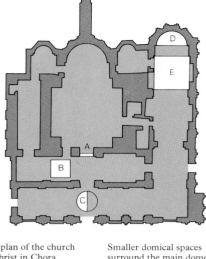

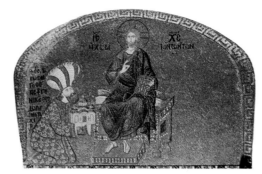

(left) *Theodore Metochites presenting the church to Christ*
Metochites (*c.* 1269-1332), a considerable philosopher and a poet, wears the official head-dress of the Grand Logothete, the controller of the imperial income. Exiled when Andronikos III ousted his master, Andronikos II, he returned in 1330 to become a monk in the monastery he patronized.

The plan of the church of Christ in Chora
The mosaic of Metochites with Christ (A) marks the entrance to the church proper, opening into the space beneath the central dome. Here was once a *Pantocrator*; in the apse ahead there is a *Deesis*.

Smaller domical spaces surround the main dome: the two scenes from the Virgin's life illustrated here are at (B). *The miracle at Cana* is at (C). Flanking the church is the mortuary chapel with an *Anastasis* (D) and a *Last Judgment* (E).

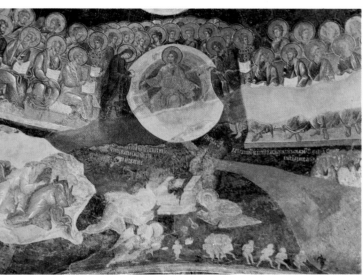

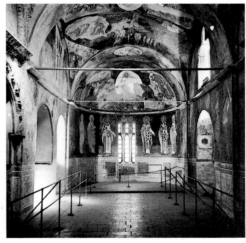

(above) *The Last Judgment*
Christ, enthroned on a rainbow, sits in judgment between the Virgin and St John the Baptist, with angels and apostles on either side. Beneath is the earth, where humanity crouches in prayer or in dread. The whole scene is strongly visionary, with the figures below forming abstract shapes, enclosed in strange, flaring membranes.

(below) *Scenes from the life of the Virgin*
Anna and Joachim embrace their daughter, and she is taken by Joachim to be blessed by the priests. Many such apocryphal but touching and human scenes were included in the huge cycle of the Virgin.

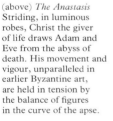

(above) *The Anastasis*
Striding, in luminous robes, Christ the giver of life draws Adam and Eve from the abyss of death. His movement and vigour, unparalleled in earlier Byzantine art, are held in tension by the balance of figures in the curve of the apse.

(above) The side-chapel of Christ in Chora
The Anastasis is in the conch of the apse at the east end. In the vault before it is *The Last Judgment*, and the rich profusion of frescos are all concerned with life after death. Interceding saints stand beneath.

(below) *The miracle at Cana*
The Virgin, St Peter and St John the Baptist are shown with Christ on the right, but the lively servants, and the jars into which they pour the water that will be changed into wine, have become the centre of the action.

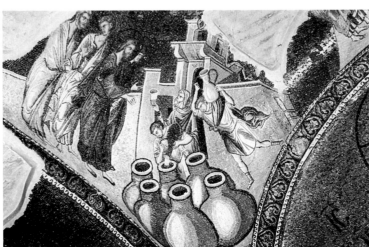

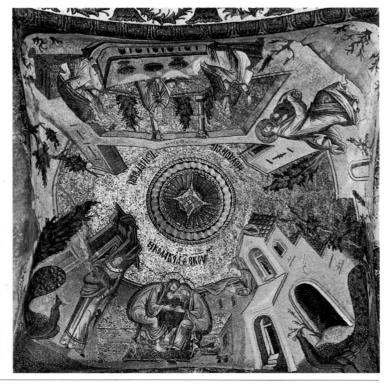

Celtic or Insular Art

The masterpieces of Celtic Christian art – stone crosses raised stark against northern skies, dazzling convoluted illuminations in manuscripts from Ireland and north Britain – have their ancestry in the artefacts of the prehistoric Indo-European tribes. In the centuries before the birth of Christ migratory races moved in successive waves from the north-east, settling the regions to the north of the classical Mediterranean from Mongolia to as far west as Ireland. The Greeks and Romans christened these restless tribes "barbarians": they were illiterate, they had no architecture, painting or sculpture. They nevertheless developed skilled techniques of metallurgy, and worked easily transportable objects – jewellery, helmets, harnesses – with dynamic, abstract or stylized designs. These were their currency; the tombs of their chieftains have revealed not only sophisticated native craftsmanship, but silver and bronze works of Mediterranean origin. Metalwork designs remained the pervasive influence in Celtic art.

The Celts, the tribes called Keltoi by Greeks and Galli by Romans, had established themselves in western Europe long before the rise of Rome. Those in northern Italy, Spain, France,

Germany and England were incorporated more or less permanently into the Roman Empire and, when the western Roman Empire fell apart, were embroiled in the disintegration and turmoil of the "Dark Ages", from the fifth to the eighth century. In Ireland, Scotland and northern Britain, however, the tribes had maintained their Celtic traditions intact. Ireland was Christianized in the fifth century, and in the sixth century, while England was still pagan, monasteries in Ireland and north Britain were almost the sole Western strongholds of civilization and the written word.

Engraved, patterned stones are still to be found in astonishing numbers on monastic sites. From simple engraved monoliths they developed into elaborate sculpted crosses, six metres (20ft) high or more. The technique advanced from engraving to relief sculpture, and by the seventh century the regular and symmetrical cross-shape of the top of the stone shaft was standard. Their patterning remained Celtic, incorporating a whole range of geometric designs (deriving from metalwork), and especially interlace patterns. The interlace, that characteristic interweaving of ribbon-like or lace-like tendrils – perhaps a remote echo of

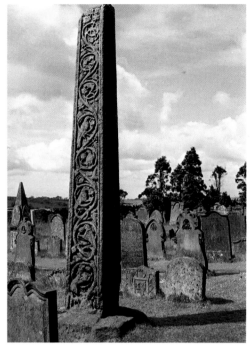

BEWCASTLE, ENGLAND (above) High Cross, late 7th century AD
The sandstone Cross lacks its head, which was probably much like that of Moone. Its sides are carved in low relief with interlace inhabited by animals and birds – the most characteristic and enduring Celtic motif. The Cross gives no clue to its artist or patron.

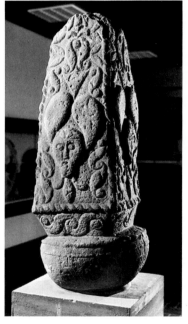

PFALZFELD, GERMANY (left) Carved stone, 4th century BC
The stone was carved in the Rhineland for a heathen purpose that is obscure. On each side is a human head with large, projecting eyes and with converging lobes for hair. Primitive monoliths like this one are the ancestors of the Christian crosses.

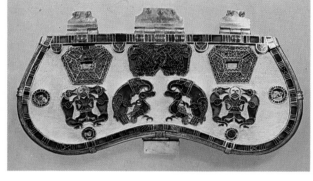

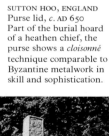

SUTTON HOO, ENGLAND Purse lid, c. AD 650
Part of the burial hoard of a heathen chief, the purse shows a *cloisonné* technique comparable to Byzantine metalwork in skill and sophistication.

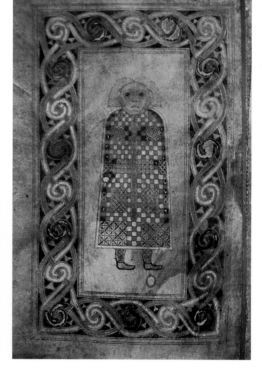

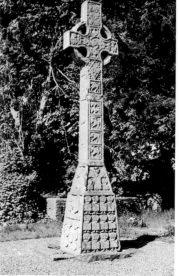

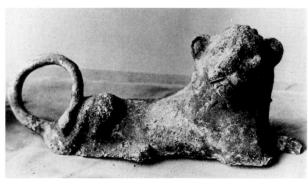

HOCHDORF, GERMANY
Lion, ornament from a bronze vessel, c. 500 BC
The lion, from a tomb of a Celtic chief found near Ludwigsburg in 1978, may be Etruscan. It is witness to an established trade between the Celts and the Mediterranean – which, however, left few marks on Celtic art.

MOONE, IRELAND (left) High Cross, 9th century AD
The imposing granite Cross shows biblical scenes, with cipher-like figures in a repetitive and symmetrical design. The flat relief recalls the intaglio designs found in Celtic metalwork.

IRELAND
The Book of Durrow: *St Matthew, c.* AD 680
The page is only 16.5 cm (6½in) high. The emphatic, sharp contours of the figure and frame are a sure sign of metalwork derivation. The stocky, block-like figure is like those at Moone.

running water – often involves in its strands stylized animals and in some examples, for instance the ninth-century Cross at Moone in County Kildare, is combined with figurative sculpture. Sometimes the figurative sculpture is even relatively realistic.

This same tradition of interlace ornament and stylized figurative imagery is repeated in the manuscript illuminations produced in Ireland and north Britain, which became celebrated throughout Christian Europe. The crucial texts for the maintenance of the Christian faith were the Gospels – in the beginning was the Word. In the illustration of the Gospel books artists adapted the styles and motifs of their illiterate, heathen predecessors to serve a new belief, and in so doing revitalized them. This is immediately visible in one of the earliest books to be preserved from the great Irish centres, the seventh-century Book of Durrow. In the Durrow manuscript, Celtic interlace, abstract and figurative, is superbly organized in rhythmic line and clear colour.

The usual scheme of decoration included a large decorated initial to mark the opening of each Gospel, sometimes with an elaborately decorated facing page – the so-called "carpet pages". Normally their design is woven symmetrically about the central motif of a cross, but it can be elaborated unrecognizably into a tightly knotted mesh. There may also be a page with the symbol or portrait of the relevant Evangelist: the Durrow *St Matthew*, chequered, flat and frontal as a playing card, but with his feet proceeding eagerly to the right, is an early, undeveloped example, memorable in its simplicity. Later the Evangelist is more usually represented seated full-length, frontal, with the book held up in his hands, or seated at a desk or lectern writing.

England had lapsed into paganism with the Anglo-Saxon invasions of the fifth to sixth centuries, but was converted in the early seventh century. Thereafter, until the Viking invasions in the ninth century, superb manuscripts were produced in the British Isles. The Lindisfarne Gospels of the 690s develop the possibilities of complex ornament still further, introducing new colours and exploiting linear rhythms with great virtuosity. Of the superb manuscripts surviving from the eighth and ninth centuries, the most spectacular is the Book of Kells, made in the remote monastery on the island of Iona, perhaps about 800. In this the decoration is richer, more pervasive, and denser in its interlaces than anywhere else. There are more than 400 decorative initials through the manuscript, no two identical, all elaborated with fantastic exuberance and apparent freedom. The freedom, however, is an illusion, as the compositions are carefully articulated and structured. The most famous of all, the Incarnation initial, XPI, roves with glints of gold through spirals and roundels and interlacings including human heads as well as animal motifs. Left centre, near the bottom, there is a charming study, almost a genre scene, of cat and mouse. This large and luxurious manuscript exemplifies Insular illumination in the splendour of what has been called its "baroque" phase. New decorative elements, more usually found on stone crosses than in manuscripts, are introduced, and also – in the Evangelist portraits – quotations from early Christian and Byzantine manuscripts.

The Book of Kells is contemporary with the first manuscripts of the Carolingian revival, which not only made use of Insular scholarship, but also was alive to the decorative possibilities so brilliantly exploited by the Celts, though its art developed on different lines.

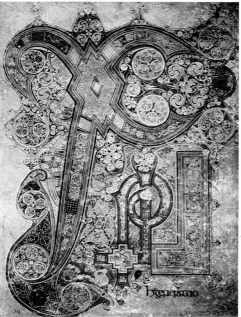

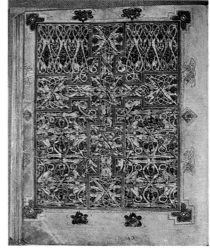

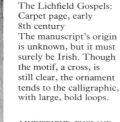

IONA, SCOTLAND
(left) The Book of Kells:
*St John, c.*800
The Kells Gospels are
twice the size of those
of Durrow, but the size
of the figure is much the
same, and the greater
space is used for enriched
ornament. The style of
the figure is entirely
different, and reflects
Mediterranean influence.

(below) The Book of Kells:
The Incarnation Initial,
*c.*800
XPI, the Greek letters
CH, R and I, start the first
word of St Matthew's
Gospel, "Christ". The
flamboyant convolutions
are a dazzling expression
of the value of the Word.

IRELAND (left)
The Lichfield Gospels:
Carpet page, early
8th century
The manuscript's origin
is unknown, but it must
surely be Irish. Though
the motif, a cross, is
still clear, the ornament
tends to the calligraphic,
with large, bold loops.

LINDISFARNE, ENGLAND
(below) The Lindisfarne
Gospels: Carpet page,
*c.*690
The artist was Bishop
Eadfrith of Lindisfarne:
the illumination of the
Gospels was no menial
task. The design is hard
and clear, transferring
into the book the values
of precious metalwork.

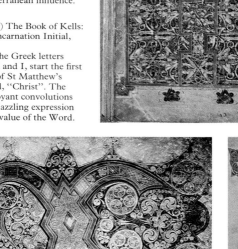

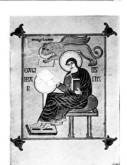

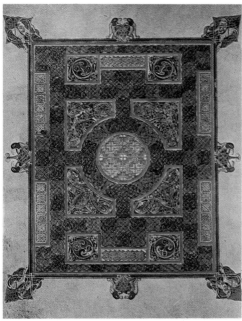

JARROW, ENGLAND
The Codex Amiatinus:
*Ezra restoring a damaged
Bible, c.*690
This is not an image of
a contemporary scribe in
the guise of a prophet:
the pose and furniture
are a literal copy of a
6th-century manuscript
illuminated in Rome.

LINDISFARNE, ENGLAND
The Lindisfarne Gospels:
*St Mark, c.*690
The pose is exactly the
same as that of Ezra in
the Codex Amiatinus
(above left), reversed.
Celtic taste transforms
the motif by introducing
sharp lines, patterning
and flattening the figure.

Carolingian and Ottonian Art

Western Europe emerged from the chaos of the "Dark Ages" when the Frankish kings, in collaboration with the papacy, gained sufficient strength to stabilize and consolidate the huge territories they owned. The process was symbolically sealed on Christmas Day 800 with the coronation of Charlemagne as Holy Roman Emperor.

Charlemagne's ambition was to re-create the Roman Empire from his capital at Aachen (Aix-la-Chapelle). With an eye to the Byzantine imperial bureaucracy of educated administrators, he sought a renaissance of learning and art – a *renovatio*, as it was called at the time. Aachen was to reproduce visually the semi-legendary ideal of early Christian Rome: Charlemagne imported massive bronze Roman sculptures from Italy, and wished to be buried in a classical sarcophagus. He took a personal interest in the written word, the primary medium for the propagation of learning, and the script evolved in his time, subsequently refined by humanist scholars of the fifteenth century, is the basis of the lower-case type in which this book is printed. With the help of abbot scholars, such as Alcuin from Northumbria and Theodulf from Spain, he set up a network of centres of learning in monasteries across present France and Germany, where, under imperial auspices, the masterpieces of Carolingian art were produced.

Charlemagne was not unaffected by the iconoclastic dispute that rent the Byzantine Empire to the east, but, though he pronounced against the worship of images, he accepted the didactic uses of art. The range of subject matter in his time was limited, confined to illustrations to the Bible and the lives of saints, but secular learning was soon also encouraged. Unfortunately almost all the wall-paintings that once helped instruct the people in the Christian faith have vanished – none survive in the important centres – but illuminated manuscripts give some indication of what the large-scale works were like. Aachen and each manuscript centre developed distinctive styles, though all, to a varying extent, borrow from Mediterranean art, and are essentially figurative, though they use the decorative idiom of Celtic traditions in the borders and frames.

The Godescalc Evangelistary of 781-83, written in gold and silver on a purple parchment, sets a luxurious standard. The modelling of the monumental seated *Christ in*

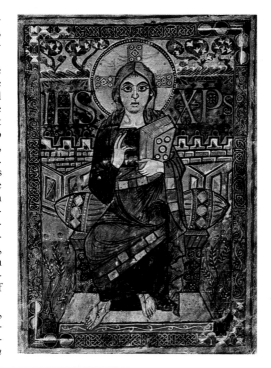

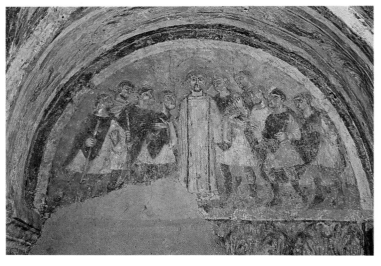

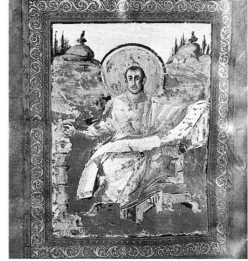

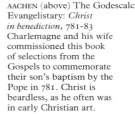

AUXERRE, ST GERMAIN (above) *St Stephen preaching*, begun 851
The insistent symmetry, and the heavy modelling of basic facial features, suggest a mosaic model, although these are also characteristics of Carolingian manuscripts.

RHEIMS (below) The Utrecht Psalter: Psalm 108, c. 816-35
The fresh and expressive narrative has been seen as an early manifestation of a specifically northern spirit. The manuscript, which by the 10th century was in England, markedly influenced Anglo-Saxon illumination, and it was copied by Romanesque artists. In the copies, however, the scenes are individually framed, and the classical conception of illusionistic space, still understood here, was lost or abandoned.

RHEIMS (below) The Ebbo Gospels: *St Mark*, c. 816-35
The Evangelist's pose, despite his frenzy, is classical, like those of the Coronation Gospels. Ebbo, Archbishop of Rheims, who ordered the book, had been librarian to Charlemagne's son and heir, Louis the Pious.

(left) The Coronation Gospels: *St John*, c. 795-810
The freely dabbed landscape is an obviously classical feature; so is the suggestion of space within the frame. Later Carolingian artists betray their models less patently, except in secular texts.

(below) The Lorsch Gospels: *Christ between angels*, early 9th century
The style, scheme and iconography are directly related to such works as Maximian's Throne (see p. 59). Christ treads upon beasts symbolizing evil.

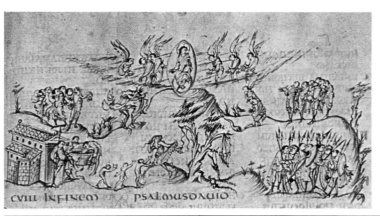

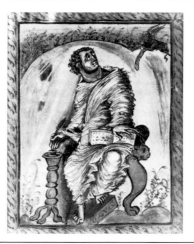

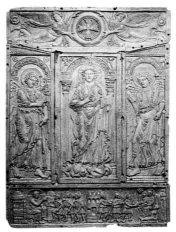

benediction is clearly indebted to Byzantine models, less clearly to classical ones. In the Coronation Gospels (*c.* 795-810), the debt to Roman precedent is beyond doubt (though significantly the Evangelists are shown writing – in Roman times this would have been a menial chore performed by slaves). In the scriptorium at Rheims, about 816 to 835, there developed one of the most remarkable of all medieval styles: the liveliness of the Utrecht Psalter comes as a shock after its austere predecessors, and the scenes are quite freely dispersed through the text, unhampered by any framing. The most striking manuscript in this style is the Ebbo Gospels, in which the figures of the Evangelists are seized with a divine, mystic fury, a quaking or shaking that infects their very garments. This is almost Expressionist art, unparalleled until El Greco.

At Metz, Tours and elsewhere, other magnificent manuscripts were produced, and also carved ivories, generally book-covers, such as the famous covers of the Lorsch Gospels, which are closely related in style to the manuscript paintings. The fine metalwork, in which the regions round the Rhine were to excel for centuries, has now mostly vanished. The ninth-century gold altar in S. Ambrogio in Milan, which may possibly be connected with the Rheims workshops, can give at least an idea of the sumptuous craftsmanship which once decorated the Carolingian centres.

Under Charlemagne's heirs the Empire was dislocated, and by the end of the ninth century had fallen apart under threats from all sides (Vikings from the north, Muslims and Hungarians from the east). However, in 955 Otto the Great was victorious over the Hungarians, heralding a rebirth of the Empire. Ottonian rule aimed to restore the power and splendour of the Carolingian epoch, but its art developed largely independently of the court, in the fiefs of the increasingly powerful bishops and abbots. The styles depended on Carolingian models, and also harked back directly to early Christian examples, but the strongest influence on them was from contemporary Byzantium, as, for instance, in the Speyer Gospels from the Echternach school, showing an increased emphasis on the human figure.

Not only ivories, but also a few larger, spectacular pieces of Ottonian sculpture survive. The most famous are the great eleventh-century bronze doors at Hildesheim, commissioned by Bishop Bernward. Nearly five metres (16ft) high, in two wings, each apparently cast in one piece, they are startling evidence that the knowledge of lost-wax casting had continued since Roman times; in design they are the ancestors of Ghiberti's doors at Florence (see p. 100). On the left wing are eight scenes from Genesis, on the right a corresponding eight from the New Testament. The little figures in the various incidents are full of movement and poignancy. Bernward also commissioned a bronze column, more than three metres (12ft) high, with a continuous spiral relief illustrating the life of Christ; it was clearly inspired by Trajan's Column in Rome.

Perhaps the most impressive surviving Ottonian sculpture is the Crucifix (969-76) of Archbishop Gero. Christ's head is a reliquary, still containing its valuable relic, still venerated in Cologne Cathedral. Carved in wood and painted, it combines painful realism with austere stylization – the heavy sag of the body from the arms of the Cross, the features drawn down in defeat, contrast with the still folds of the loincloth. It looks forward to the masterpieces of Romanesque sculpture.

MILAN, S. AMBROGIO
(right) The Golden Altar of St Ambrose, central panel: *Christ in majesty with the Evangelists and the apostles, c.* 824-59
The sketchy but fluent modelling has parallels in Carolingian ivories. In Ottonian works such as Bernward's at Hildesheim (though there the medium is bronze) the modelling is harder, more patterned.

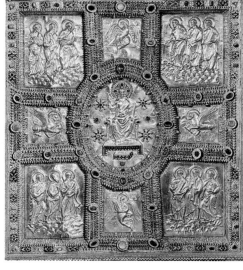

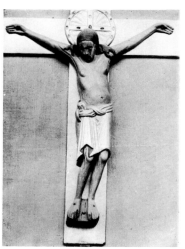

HILDESHEIM CATHEDRAL
(left) The bronze doors, detail: *The Nativity* and *The Adoration of the Magi,* 1015
Archbishop Bernward, who had visited Rome, took a personal interest in the Hildesheim workshop. In particular the low-relief backgrounds reveal the stylization that would be typical of Romanesque (see over); the background of *The Nativity* represents no space or structure, but is highly decorative.

COLOGNE CATHEDRAL (below)
Gero's Crucifix, 969-76
Many of the devices used here, such as the huge, emotive eye-sockets, could be paralleled in 12th-century Romanesque sculpture in Germany (such as the famous reliefs at Externsteine). A style has emerged that is fully independent of Byzantine or Roman models.

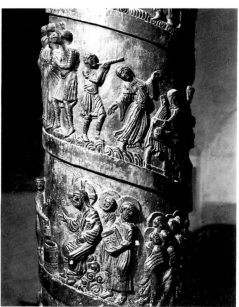

HILDESHEIM CATHEDRAL
(left) Bernward's Column, *c.* 1010
In bronze, and on a much smaller scale, Bernward's Column describes the triumph of Christ just as Roman columns had recorded the feats of emperors. The figures, modelled with patterned incisions, are often splendidly animated.

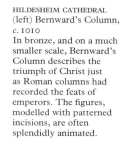

ECHTERNACH (right)
The Speyer Gospels: *St Mark,* 1045-46
The conventions of the drapery and setting are Byzantine, but rendered strikingly monumental. This was an influential product of Echternach.

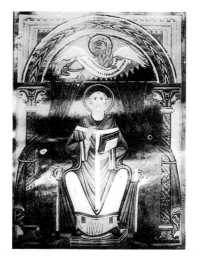

Romanesque Sculpture

The more settled conditions of the eleventh and twelfth centuries permitted the prosperous development of the Church, and particularly of certain monastic orders, notably the Benedictine order of Cluny. In the words of the Cluniac chronicler Radulphus Glaber, "the whole earth ... was clothing itself everywhere in the white robe of churches". The tremendous expansion of building bore with it a profusion of painting and sculpture, especially stone sculpture, relatively neglected since Roman times. Europe was free from invasion; this was the period of the first Crusades, and of movement not only eastwards, towards Jerusalem, but westwards, on pilgrimage to the magnetic shrine of Santiago de Compostela in northern Spain, and to and fro throughout western and southern Europe. Craftsmen migrated from place to place; they were more frequently than before professional laymen rather than monks, and are sometimes known to us by name. Small wonder that Romanesque art (Romanesque was coined as an architectural term, implying a dependence on Roman building techniques that was ended by Gothic) embraces a considerable variety of styles, reflecting regional differences, cross-fertilizations and the varying impact of Carolingian and Ottonian, Byzantine, Islamic and also classical Roman influences.

Romanesque sculpture is most commonly carved in relief, and stone sculpture is usually, but not always, an integral part of the architecture of the church to which it belongs. North of Italy, the finest work is found in the portals of churches, and on the capitals of their piers. In France, particularly, the areas round the door – jambs, lintel and semicircular tympanum above – were elaborately carved: in the tympana the great stylized *Last Judgments* inspire awe, but the jambs and capitals often revel in a relative naturalism, or at least in a humane, affectionate mood.

Some elements of Romanesque are apparent in Ottonian art, but its finest flowering was in France, particularly around the abbey of Cluny in Burgundy, and in Languedoc, strategically placed on the pilgrimage routes towards Compostela. In St Sernin in Toulouse, a marble relief of 1094-96, showing *Christ in majesty*, reads like an enlargement of a Carolingian work in ivory or metal: it is uncompromisingly frontal and severe. The colossal tympanum at Conques, another Lan-

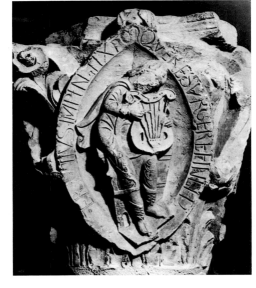

CLUNY, ST PIERRE
The third tone of plainsong, 1088-95
The monks at Cluny often spent 10 or 12 hours a day in choir: cosmic "fours" – the 4 Rivers of Paradise, the 4 chief senses – figurated on the apse capitals included musical octaves.

TOULOUSE, ST SERNIN
(right) *Christ in majesty*, 1094-96
Unlike mature Romanesque sculpture, the image does not "grow" out of the architecture. In style and iconography – in the surrounding mandorla and Evangelist symbols – it depends on Carolingian art.

MOISSAC ABBEY (below)
St Peter, c. 1100
In the early work in the cloister the sculptors drew on many models: *St Peter* resembles certain decorated initials in manuscripts from Moissac, but other details are of Roman or Islamic inspiration.

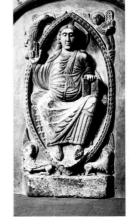

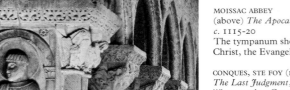

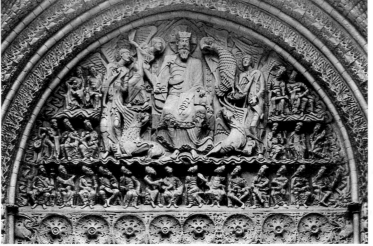

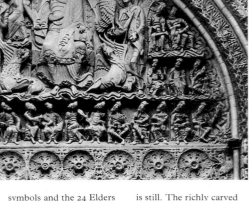

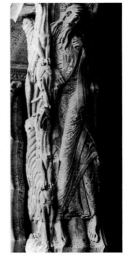

MOISSAC ABBEY
(above) *The Apocalypse*, c. 1115-20
The tympanum shows Christ, the Evangelist symbols and the 24 Elders described by St John. The Elders perch agitatedly on their seats: only the strangely elongated Christ is still. The richly carved whole, including arch, lintel and its supporting pillar with a prophet, is incomparably imposing.

(above) *Jeremiah?*
The prophet represents a peak, both of restless distortion and of sculptural and architectural unity.

CONQUES, STE FOY (right)
The Last Judgment, c. 1135
The portal at Conques, one of the finest and best-preserved pilgrimage churches in France, has the largest tympanum of all. The figures have the same hard, stylized clarity as those at Moissac, but are serene by comparison. The clear framework and ordered calm on the left-hand side, Paradise, is effectively contrasted with the chaos and confusion of Hell on the other.

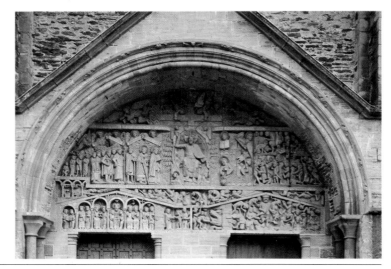

guedoc pilgrimage church, carved only about 40 years later, retains the hieratic element, but is vastly more ambitious and impressive. A similar astonishing development in style can be seen within the confines of the abbey of Moissac, near Toulouse, between about 1100 and 1125. A relief in the cloister shows *St Peter* as rigidly formal as the St Sernin *Christ*. The portal, with *The Apocalypse* in the tympanum, was carved only about 20 years later, and is crowded, busy, almost seething; the prophet, perhaps Jeremiah, carved into the stone strut supporting the lintel, is everything the cloister reliefs are not. His immensely elongated figure is swept sinuously into the undulations of the pillar, hair and beard flowing in unison with the drapery. The undulating rhythm is a feature of Islamic architecture; the emotional intensity seems Spanish. Although the figure is entirely unnaturalistic, and its crossed legs are an anatomical impossibility, the expression of the face is humane and gentle.

Moissac was one of the hundreds of abbeys following the discipline of the great abbey of St Pierre at Cluny in Burgundy. Its vast church was destroyed after the French Revolution, but the fragments that remain include capitals

that accurately reproduced classical Corinthian capitals, though many of them quite happily incorporated little figurative scenes as well: some of these, such as the musicians with instruments illustrating the eight tones of Gregorian plainsong, look almost like genre scenes. The great tympanum of the west façade of Cluny has been lost, but echoes of what must have been a masterpiece survive in the portals of Autun and Vézelay (see over).

Further north, the regional variation of Romanesque known as Mosan, of the river Meuse district, is represented by a fundamentally different masterpiece, the brass font made by Renier de Huy about 1110 for the church of Notre Dame des Fonts. Its technical accomplishment is as remarkable as its sophisticated style, free from the squeezed distortions of Romanesque art elsewhere. It is both sure and free, naturalistic and classical – Romanized rather than Romanesque. Renier must have looked long and hard at antique sculpture; he could certainly have seen sarcophagi, probably triumphal arches with reliefs, and even free-standing classical statues in bronze or stone.

In Britain, there was nothing comparable to the great portals of the French churches,

though sculpture reflects influences from all over the Continent. An impressive survivor is a gilt-bronze candlestick from St Peter's, Gloucester, closely related to German metalwork. German metalwork was widely known and esteemed, and of considerable variety, in silver and gold with enamel insertions, as well as in bronze. The distinguished bronze tomb-cover of Rudolf of Swabia, who died in 1080, is the oldest tomb-figure in Europe.

In Italy, classical influence was always stronger, and more importance was given to the figure in the round. In the north sculptors were clearly also aware of the achievements of Burgundy and Languedoc. Individual artists emerge, such as Wiligelmo, who signed his work in Modena, and Niccolò, who worked in Ferrara, but seems to have journeyed twice to Toulouse. The church of S. Zeno at Verona preserves panelled bronze doors of about 1135-40, in the pattern of the doors at Hildesheim. In the south, in works such as the Archbishop's Throne at Bari, in Apulia, of about 1098, the persistence of the classical tradition is evident, and the supporting "Atlas figures" even suggest the work of Nicola Pisano (see p. 80) in the Gothic period.

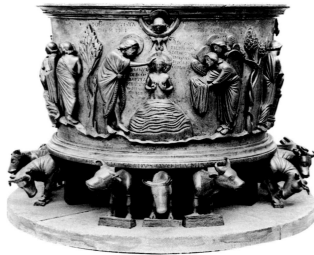

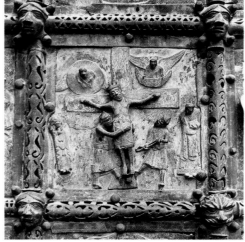

VERONA, S. ZENO (left)
The bronze doors, detail: *The Crucifixion*, c. 1140
Compared to Ottonian work, especially the doors of Hildesheim, the figures are crudely modelled, and often grotesque. The technique is less sophisticated. However, the awkward poses make up for their lack of finesse by their liveliness. The borders are of German inspiration; the grotesque heads can be paralleled in the Romanesque art of any country.

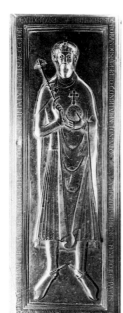

RENIER DE HUY (above)
The brass font: *The baptism of Christ*, c. 1110
The style is remarkably classical: observe, for instance, the figure with his back turned on the left; generally, how drapery is used to model the form beneath. The font was cast in one piece, except for the oxen, representing apostles.

GLOUCESTER ABBEY (left)
The Gloucester candlestick, c. 1110
The hollow shaft is alive with beasts, foliage and figures, some of them with religious meaning but most ornamental. Though its origins were in metalwork, such interlace is better known in Celtic or Anglo-Saxon manuscripts, even Romanesque ones. In type and shape the candlestick follows Ottonian example.

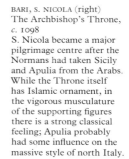

MERSEBURG CATHEDRAL (left) *Rudolf of Swabia*, after 1080
This is the earliest known example of what became the standard type of tomb for centuries to come. It is not a portrait; the head, in higher relief than the rest, is a mask, and the rest of the body, too, is quite highly stylized.

BARI, S. NICOLA (right)
The Archbishop's Throne, c. 1098
S. Nicola became a major pilgrimage centre after the Normans had taken Sicily and Apulia from the Arabs. While the Throne itself has Islamic ornament, in the vigorous musculature of the supporting figures there is a strong classical feeling; Apulia probably had some influence on the massive style of north Italy.

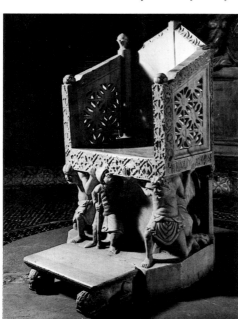

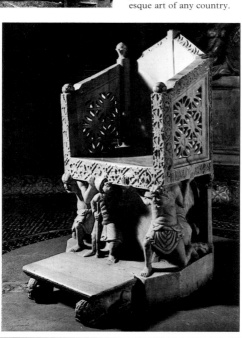

Gislebertus: The Sculpture at Autun

Central in the great tympanum of the west façade of Autun Cathedral is Christ seated in majesty, presiding with extended hands over the Last Judgment. Central again, just beneath Christ's feet, is the prominent and unabashed claim of individual proprietorship: GISLEBERTUS M(AGISTER) HOC FECIT: Master Gislebertus made this.

This inscription, and the work it signs, is almost all that is known of Gislebertus. It is clear that the source of inspiration for Autun, both the building and its sculptures, was Cluny, and a few fragments from the great abbey church have been attributed to Gislebertus on grounds of style. Autun, dedicated to Lazarus, was closely linked to the church at Vézelay, dedicated to Mary Magdalen, in legend his sister, and certain capitals at Vézelay also bear the marks of Gislebertus' style. Gislebertus was called to Autun soon after 1120, and had made all the carvings in the church by about 1135. His work there is truly unique: though he must have had assistants, his workshop was completely dominated by his personality – style, technique and quality are throughout remarkably consistent; and no other decorative scheme survives from the Middle Ages on such a scale, with such unity of style and conception, and yet so rich in subject matter and formal invention.

Gislebertus started, like the builders, at the east end, and finished with the huge portal at the west. Inside the church he carved capitals of great variety – biblical scenes, moralizing allegories warning of the consequences of sin, and many purely decorative capitals, often with beautifully composed foliage. His iconography clearly stemmed from Cluny, but he usually reorganized the subject to suit his personal, expressive style, and he seems occasionally to have borrowed his imagery from "mystery" plays enacting religious stories. The programme also included a second major portal in the north transept, which has been mostly lost; one remarkable fragment is from the lintel, showing *Eve* naked, lying prone, toying pensively, sensuously with the apple.

The great west tympanum and lintel were carved in the workshop on 29 pieces of limestone, and subsequently assembled above the doorway. The relief is fairly deep, but with

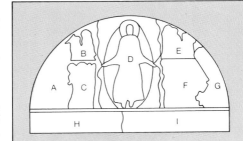

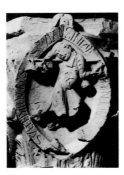

CLUNY, ST PIERRE (above)
The fourth tone of music, 1088-95
The tones of music were part of a complex scheme of "fours" – Gospels, ages etc – in the apse at Cluny. Gislebertus' use of this unusual motif is evidence that he was trained there.

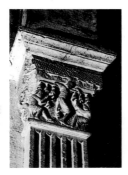

AUTUN, ST LAZARE (below)
The fourth tone of music, c. 1125
Gislebertus' *Tone* appears entirely by itself at Autun and there are more than four bells. It looks as if he used the motif solely because the composition happened to appeal to him.

subtle variations in its depth, so that there is a harmonious balance between the colossal Christ and the numerous small-scale figures. The composition is crowded, but divided into ranges simply and legibly. Heaven is above, with the Virgin Mary and others; on the left, the chosen, led to Heaven by St Peter; on the right, the damned, with St Michael and a devil supervising the Psychostasis – the weighing of souls in a pair of scales. On the lintel below, the elect are on the left, the doomed are deployed in a frieze of despair on the right. The surrounding arch has 31 roundels monitoring the seasons of the year and the Zodiac.

The central Christ, some three metres (10ft) high, is both awesome and serene. His anatomy, like that of the major supporting characters, is physically impossible, and disposed according to the needs of the linear rhythms of the design. The drapery falls in a quite distinctive way in shallow scallops, like marks of the tide in sand, which combine an earlier convention, showing drapery in groups of small parallel lines, and the plate-like drapery characteristic of the Cluny workshop. These arbitrary, unnaturalistic features stress Christ's supernatural independence of earthly norms.

Autun and Vézelay are the most impressive survivors of Romanesque art in Burgundy. The tympanum of the central portal at Vézelay is in a more agitated, dynamic style; the linear whorls and waves of the drapery create extraordinary tensions and movement. After the middle of the century, Burgundian sculpture went abruptly into decline, and for the next major sculptural commission in Burgundy, at Dijon, the sculptors turned for their inspiration to the Ile-de-France, to Gothic.

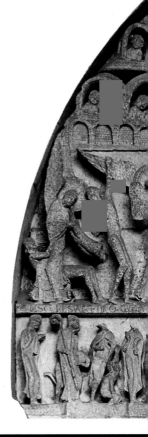

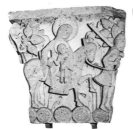

AUTUN, ST LAZARE
The Flight into Egypt, c. 1125-35
Sword on shoulder and panting a little, Joseph leads the donkey, while Mother and Child hold each other tight. Its wheels may represent those on the wooden donkeys used in religious processions; Gislebertus' personal imagery may have its origin in festivals or plays.

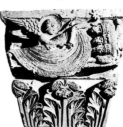

AUTUN, ST LAZARE
The dream of the Magi, c. 1125-35
Seldom is naivety quite so affecting. No doubt there was nothing strange in the Middle Ages in three Magi sharing a bed, but the composition is so conceived and handled that the angel interrupting the great decorative sweep of their blanket is both sweet and purposeful.

AUTUN, ST LAZARE (right)
Eve, fragment of the north transept lintel, before 1132
After the destruction of the portal *Eve* was used as a building block and so survived. There is no more sensuous nude in medieval art. Stretching forward to whisper seduction to the *Adam* once on the lintel opposite her, she is rather more than 1m (4ft) long, and was originally painted. Perhaps the composition was dictated rather more by the shape of the blocks making it up than was the later west tympanum.

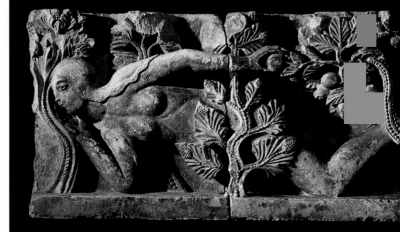

AUTUN, ST LAZARE
The west tympanum and
lintel: *The Last Judgment,*
c. 1135
Gislebertus' tympanum
follows the Cluniac
formula, but is enlivened
by details, especially along
the lintel, and refinements
that are entirely his own.
The smaller figures are
more rounded, in higher
relief than the larger ones;
Christ is in the flattest
relief of all. The diagram
(right) shows the number
and jointing of the stones
making up the tympanum;
their quantity, and the way
the composition continues
across the limits of the
blocks, are unusual. The
sense of an individual
artistic personality emerges
at Autun as it seldom does
elsewhere in medieval art.

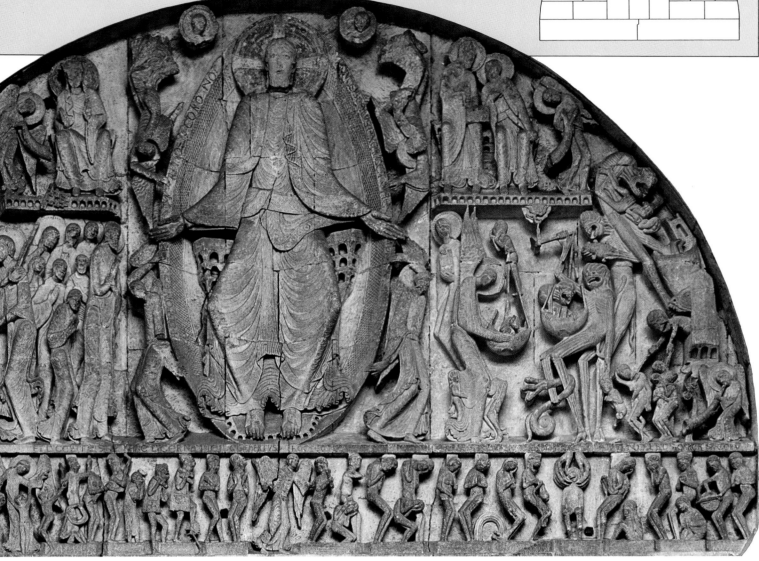

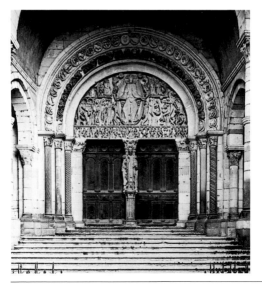

AUTUN, ST LAZARE (left)
The west portal, *c.* 1135
The outer porch is a later
addition. All three arches
of the portal were once
decorated, but the inner
one was destroyed in the
18th century when every-
thing was plastered over
to hide these works of
"the age of superstition".

VEZELAY, STE MADELEINE
(right) The tympanum of
the central west narthex
portal: *The mission to the*
apostles, c. 1130
Christ's blood streams
from his hands on to the
apostles in an infusion of
grace – perhaps reflecting
the missionary zeal of Peter
the Venerable, Abbot of
Cluny. The strange crea-
tures may be inhabitants
of the unexplored world.

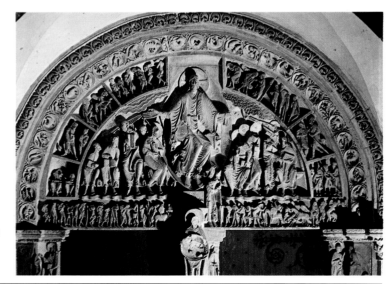

Romanesque Painting

Many Romanesque churches that are now stark, simple and empty once glowed and vibrated with colour. Damp, Puritan disapproval or unappreciative indifference have destroyed their mural paintings, and their church furniture has been discarded or looted. In France, however, a few murals survive to convey a glimpse of the original appearance of Romanesque interiors, in a style close enough to that of the sculpture to suggest what that, too, looked like when paint still adhered to its surface. Medieval artists were versatile, working with equal skill in different media – sculpture, metalwork, large-scale painting or miniature illumination – and ideas originating in one medium travelled rapidly to another.

The vanished abbey of St Pierre at Cluny once had spectacular murals, which were surely of the first quality and as influential as its sculpture. Its great Abbot Hugh, in his old age, furbished the little priory of Berzé-la-Ville nearby as a quiet retreat, and fortunately parts of its lavish decoration survive to illustrate the Cluny style forcefully. The composition and detailed drapery of its *Christ in majesty* prove that it followed the Carolingian tradition, modified by influences from the

Byzantine style practised in Italy. The other important surviving example of Romanesque painting in France is near Poitiers, at St-Savin-sur-Gartempe: here the four distinct cycles include 30 Old Testament illustrations, painted with imaginative freedom on a grand scale; their iconography and style point back to the fantasy and leaping rhythms of Anglo-Saxon manuscripts of the tenth century.

Before the Norman conquest of 1066 an insular style of great originality and splendid vitality had developed in England, to which the illuminators of the Romanesque period often referred. Its figures were characterized by agitated drapery and gestures (stemming ultimately from the Carolingian school of Rheims, which had produced the Utrecht Psalter). Large, very inventive decorated initials continued the complex linear patterns and interlace of the Celtic tradition, usually enlivened by animal grotesques (compare the Gloucester candlestick, p. 71). Under the Normans, notably at Winchester and Canterbury, sumptuous manuscripts were produced to stock the libraries of the proliferating monasteries. Their influence spread as far south as Cîteaux in Burgundy, where the Englishman

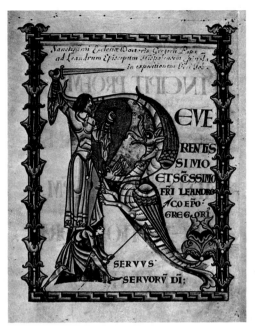

CITEAUX (above)
St George, initial of a manuscript, before 1111
As Romanesque sculpture seems often to be shaped by the space it has to fill, so these figures are formed by the shape of the initial R, and decorate the page rather than reproduce the saint's likely mode of battle.

ST-SAVIN-SUR-GARTEMPE (below) *Scene from the life of St Savin, c.* 1100
The lively narrative – every figure is drawn as if in motion, eyes and hands are expressive – is like that of the Bayeux Tapestry. This scene is from the crypt; the entire barrel vault of the nave was also painted.

BERZE-LA-VILLE (right)
The apse: *Christ in majesty with apostles*, before 1109?
Though the details of the drapery consist of parallel, V-shaped or zigzag lines, there is a sense of the form beneath – as in Byzantine art. There the patterning is seldom so pronounced. The mural is clearly akin to the Cluniac tympana at Vézelay or Autun.

MASTER HUGO (below)
The Bury Bible: *Moses expounding the law, c.* 1130-40
The striking colours and the new vocabulary of the drapery patterning had a wide influence on mural and manuscript painting. The abstract stylization of the rocks (?) (lower panel) is typically Romanesque.

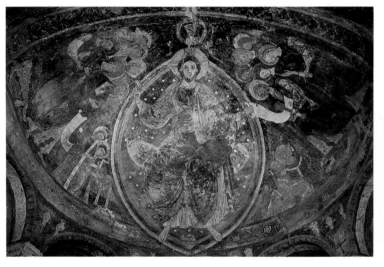

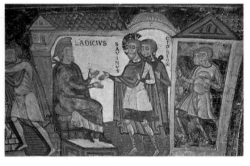

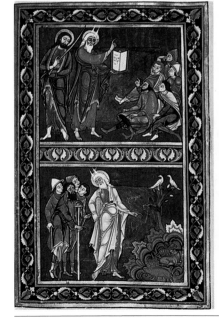

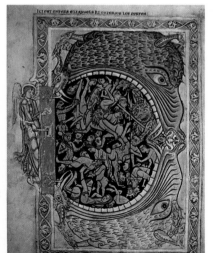

WINCHESTER (left)
The Winchester Psalter: *The mouth of Hell, c.* 1150
The artist must have been struck by an image of St Michael locking the door of Hell in a manuscript (the New Minster Register) produced in his monastery more than 100 years earlier. He made out of it a superb pattern, moral and story.

FLANDERS (right)
The Stavelot Bible: *Christ in majesty*, 1097
This is Mosan work: the strong sense of Christ's bodily structure relates the painting to Renier de Huy's font (see p. 71). Similar Byzantine sources, differently interpreted, lie behind this and the Berzé-la-Ville *Christ*.

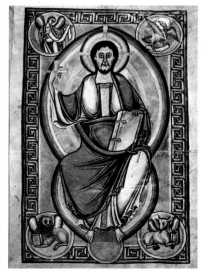

Stephen Harding was Abbot from 1108.

The middle of the twelfth century marks the decline of Cluniac power and patronage, and the simultaneous rise of the Cistercians, taking their name from Cîteaux. The Cistercians, in reaction to the musical, literary and artistic devotions of Cluny, retrenched the rule of St Benedict, and called for monks, with the help of lay-brothers, to work on the land. St Bernard of Clairvaux, Harding's successor, fiercely condemned the fantasy and luxuriance of Cluniac church decoration, even though the spreading tide of the Cistercians did not everywhere practise his rigid austerity. Before St Bernard's ban on art of 1134, Cistercian painting had a rare quality of simple humanity.

By the twelfth century, delight in "historiated" or "inhabited" initials, displaying ingenuity and fantastical wit, had become widespread. The interchange of manuscripts was commonplace, and a great variety of styles and manners flourished, absorbing and re-interpreting with confidence older elements or other regional traditions. A feeling for the monumental was always present, as in the superb hieratic *Christ in majesty* in the Stavelot Bible, written at a monastery near Liège.

Mosan (district of the Meuse) painting was hardly less important or accomplished than its sculpture. The maturity of Romanesque painting in England is seen in the Bury Bible of about 1130-40, illuminated by Master Hugo, a "freelance" craftsman who also cast bronze doors and bells, painted murals and carved wood for the appreciative monks of Bury St Edmunds. Characteristically Romanesque in the Bury Bible is the emphasis on hardened contours; the figures are shaped and structured – regardless of anatomy – by the patterns of their draperies; the colours are rich, glowing and enamel-like; there is absolute control of the overall surface design.

In Italy, where Byzantine influences were dominant, there were also strong reminiscences of Roman or early Christian art, from which the new styles of the thirteenth century, notably Giotto's, would develop (see p. 78). In Spain, the style of manuscript illumination and mural painting was markedly individual. The "Beatus" Apocalypse of St-Saver, a commentary on the Revelations of St John by a Spanish monk, Beatus of Liebana, was illuminated for the Gascon abbey of St-Saver in the mid-eleventh century by a Spaniard named

Stephanus Garcia, and was highly influential in France. Its colours are harsh, almost clanging; its fantastic beasts are deployed across the compartmented field of the page with rigidly controlled violence. The Church, while aggressively challenging Islam in Spain, was never impervious to influences from it. Forceful murals and altar frontals painted in Catalonia have a glaring intensity coupled with a strong tendency to geometrical abstraction.

Early in the Romanesque period there was no great emphasis on narrative, although, later, rich narrative sequences illustrated luxurious Psalters and Bibles, or filled the walls of churches (the earliest extant stained glass, so important for the future, is of the mid-twelfth century). However, the most famous surviving narrative is neither religious nor painted, and quite early: the Bayeux Tapestry (it is in fact embroidery) is a vivid secular history of the Norman conquest of England. It was made perhaps in Canterbury about 1080 for Odo, Bishop of Bayeux, and shows the Anglo-Saxon gift for telling a clear, strong story; it has much in common with eleventh-century English illumination. It retains the irrepressible appeal of a strip cartoon.

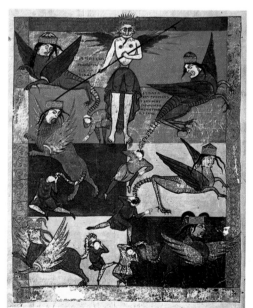

MEUSE DISTRICT (left)
The Floreffe Bible:
The Crucifixion; the sacrifice of Isaac, c. 1155
The figures are compact and simplified, related to metalwork. They lack the distortion, if also the animation, of Romanesque elsewhere, and anticipate in this Gothic humanization.

CITEAUX (right)
The Tree of Jesse, from a manuscript margin, *c. 1130*
The image of the Tree of Jesse, Christ's lineage as explained in St Luke's Gospel, was a Romanesque invention. The Virgin's pose is Byzantine, but her meekness is Cistercian.

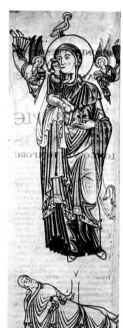

STEPHANUS GARCIA (left)
The St-Saver Apocalypse:
The torture of souls,
mid-11th century
The firm contours, the areas of arbitrary colour in the field or ground, the elimination even of any suggestion of space, these are Romanesque features.

CANTERBURY? (right)
The Bayeux Tapestry: *King Edward of England, c. 1080*
The embroidery is more than 70m (230ft) long, but only 50cm (20in) high. This is the opening scene: the king sits as kings sat in Ottonian manuscripts, though the animals of the borders are refugees from manuscript initials.

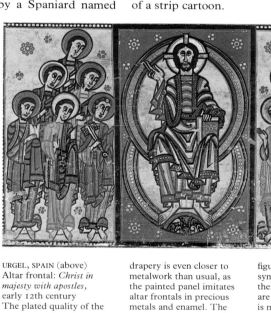

URGEL, SPAIN (above)
Altar frontal: *Christ in majesty with apostles*, early 12th century
The plated quality of the drapery is even closer to metalwork than usual, as the painted panel imitates altar frontals in precious metals and enamel. The figures are grouped into symmetrical shapes, but their faces, eyes and hands are expressive. Great play is made with the haloes.

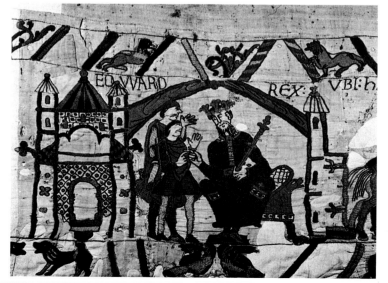

Gothic Art in Northern Europe

The shift from Romanesque to Gothic in the twelfth century is gradual, and first and most clearly apparent in architecture. The styles and technique of Gothic building, announced in Abbot Suger's famous church at St-Denis, outside Paris, in 1137-44, rapidly developed and spread throughout France and then elsewhere: it became established in England after 1174, and imitations of French High Gothic appear in Spain and Germany in the thirteenth century. In Italy Gothic had some impact, but fundamentally was resisted (see p. 80). Gothic was primarily a French style, originating in an area not previously distinguished for art – the Ile-de-France, the personal domain of the French kings and the heart of the slowly emerging French nation. The centre of this area, Paris, became a capital city in this period, and a focal point of European culture.

The best known Gothic art is both complementary and integral to the architecture. The devices of the pointed arch, the ribbed vault and the flying buttress made it possible to erect churches of a kind never seen before, soaring to incredible heights that seemed to deny their physical structure. Solid walls were opened out in huge windows, and stained glass effectually replaced mural painting in church decoration. The glass soon became totally dominant: in the Sainte Chapelle in Paris the walls seem to have disappeared in a flood of coloured light. Such translucent curtains of brilliantly coloured glass, dominating a huge enclosed space, enriching and almost dissolving the architecture in heavenly light, are amongst the most breathtaking effects in all medieval art.

In counterpoint to the heightened spirituality of Gothic art, there was an increasing interest in the natural world and in humanity, which found its expression in the proliferating sculpture on the portals of the great cathedrals. The trend is clear at Chartres. The figures of the early Royal Portal of the west front are still fully part of their columns, almost three-dimensional but closely related to the structure of the doorway. In their cool elegance they are unearthly: the sheer fall of drapery emphasizes their elongation and they float rather than stand on pointed-down toes. The later figures of the much larger and more complex transept portals are far more naturalistic, more relaxed in pose and gesture, and have their feet solidly on *terra firma*. At Rheims, there is a clear

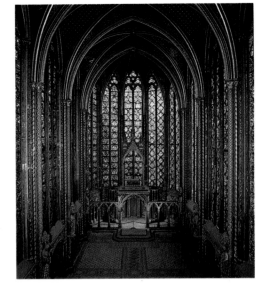

PARIS, SAINTE CHAPELLE
Interior looking east,
1243-48
The chapel was built to
house relics bought by
Louis IX, among them
the Crown of Thorns. It
is walled in stained glass
framed in delicate tracery,
and gloriously decorated.

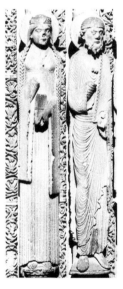 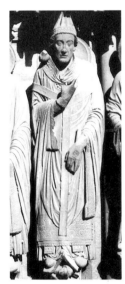 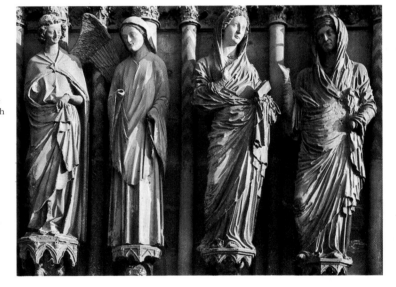

CHARTRES CATHEDRAL
(far left) Detail of west
portal figures, *c.* 1150
(left) Detail of south portal
figures, *c.* 1215-20
The west portal *Kings* and
Queens are rigidly pinned
to their columns, benign
but impassive, and hardly
human. The transept *Saints*
are much more natural, with
more varied gestures, and
more expressive faces.

RHEIMS CATHEDRAL (right)
The Annunciation and *The
Visitation*, *c.* 1230-40
Gothic drapery is seldom
so rich as in the two right-
hand figures – there are
few parallels for such close
imitation of classical sculpture. The left-hand figures
are in a smoother, more
obviously Gothic style.
There is a frieze of very
lifelike foliage behind.

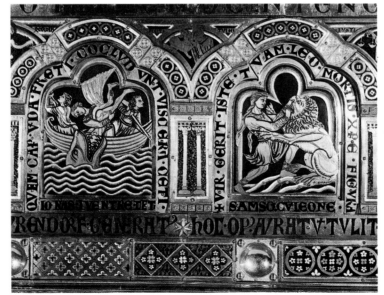

NICHOLAS OF VERDUN
(left) The Klosterneuberg
Altar: two of the 45 enamel
plaques with biblical
scenes, completed 1181
Whether Nicholas' easy,
expressive style stemmed
from classical or Byzantine
sources, it was a distinctly
new venture. In its flowing
naturalism it moved
clearly towards Gothic.

BAMBERG CATHEDRAL
(right) "*The Bamberg
Rider*", *c.* 1236?
Secular representations,
of historical figures or
contemporary potentates,
became more frequent in
the 13th century, both in
France and Germany. The
enigmatic *Rider*, in his
relaxed and naturalistic
pose, recalls the Roman
bronze equestrian statue
in type but not in style; the
style comes from Rheims.

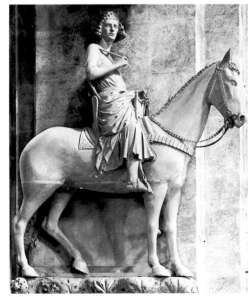

classical influence as well, and the decorated portals are sumptuously developed across the whole west front, extending upwards to a gallery of kings above the rose-window; there are statues of angels on the buttresses, corbels sculpted with heads, gargoyles – the vast body of the cathedral is said to carry about 2,000 pieces of stone sculpture in all.

The iconography of such vast sculptural programmes was carefully worked out, and closely related to theological teaching of the time. There was a gradual movement in the Gothic period towards a gentler, more merciful Christianity, and the changed mood was reflected in the great Gothic portal schemes by the prominent place given to the Virgin, invested with tenderness and grace. In the new universities a humanistic attitude emerged; the search for truth was renewed, which sent scholars back to ancient texts, to Aristotle and Plato. The interest in classical texts runs parallel to a classical current in the arts, and in this the Romanesque font of the Mosan master Renier of Huy had anticipated certain aspects of Gothic. At the end of the twelfth century a great artist from the same region, Nicholas of Verdun (active 1181-1205) introduced a clas-

sicizing style which was widely influential on sculpture, stained glass and manuscript illumination in both France and Germany.

In England, the dominant influence on sculpture was French, but its disposition on church façades and the decorative emphasis of church interiors was quite different. In Germany, the urge to realism produced sculpture of an unprecedented earthly presence: the series of imaginary portraits of the church's founders carved about 1245 by an unknown sculptor in the cathedral of Naumburg in Saxony is a striking example. A similar vivid impact is made by "The Bamberg Rider", an equestrian statue of classical inspiration, introduced via Rheims. Funeral effigies, once rigidly formal and impersonal, became increasingly lifelike, in bronze – the serene figure of Eleanor of Castile in Westminster Abbey (not shown) – or in stone – the tomb-plate of King Philippe IV le Bel of France in St-Denis. These are not yet literal likenesses, but are much more than stereotypes.

Lay patrons and craftsmen were increasingly involved in the arts in the Gothic period. Craftsmen's guilds began to be established in the twelfth century, and the centres of artistic

activity were no longer the monasteries but the cities and towns. Artists travelled, often quite extensively: recurrence of identical designs in places as far apart as Sicily and England can be explained only by good international contacts, and by the circulation of pattern books.

There was no revolution in manuscript painting, as there was in architecture. Gothic illumination remained rooted in the tradition of Carolingian and Ottonian art, but the growing taste for naturalism is often apparent – there is at least one drawing from the life in the work of the English chronicler and illuminator Matthew Paris (took vows 1217; died 1259). Matthew's more formal productions follow long-standing tradition, though there is a softness in his drawing style that derives from France. The most important development was the emergence of elegant and sophisticated court styles under royal patronage in Paris. Personal devotional books became increasingly popular, and those produced in the workshop of Master Honoré (died before 1318) in the reign of Philippe IV le Bel look forward in format and mood to the lavish examples in the "International Gothic" style prevailing at the end of the fourteenth century.

RHEIMS CATHEDRAL (right)
The west façade, begun
c. 1225
Rheims is a culmination of the steady development of portals from the 11th century. The rose-window dominates; the centre gable with *The coronation of the Virgin* shows the later trend to decorativeness.

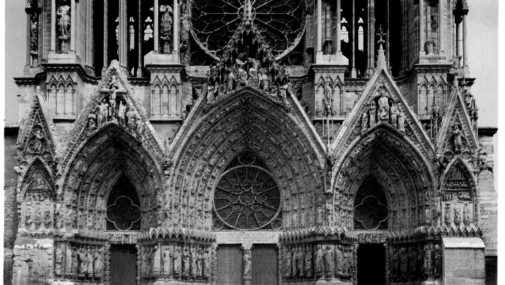

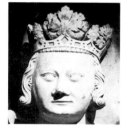

ST-DENIS (above)
Philippe IV, begun 1327
The king's marble face is of an idealized gentleness, with a trace of a smile.

MATTHEW PARIS (below)
The Virgin and Child, frontispiece to *A History of the English*, c. 1250
The monk Matthew, who dedicates his manuscript to the Virgin, illuminated his own history with lively tinted outline drawings.

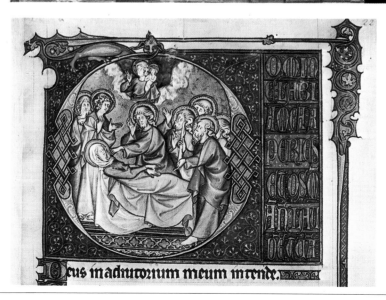

NAUMBURG CATHEDRAL
(above) *Eckhart* and *Uta*,
c. 1250
Uta draws her cloak up to her cheek, and Eckhart adjusts his sleeve. The two stone figures, life-size and coloured, have a striking stolid naturalism, influenced by Rheims.

MASTER HONORÉ (right)
The death of the Virgin, from the Nuremberg Book of Hours, c. 1290?
The heavy frame of the delicately painted scene is characteristically Parisian. Honoré's type of page, its sprays of foliage linking text and picture, became usual in the 14th century.

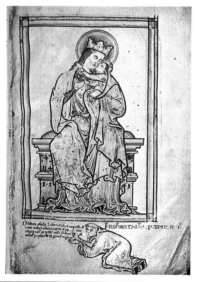

The Genesis of Italian Painting

In the second half of the thirteenth century a revolution of critical importance took place in Italian painting – a new naturalism emerged, in which can be seen the first stirrings of the Renaissance. The change took place in Italy partly because there the tradition of wall decoration in fresco or mosaic had persisted from the time of the Roman Empire, despite a succession of destructive calamities. In the north, by the end of the thirteenth century, this tradition had almost been lost, mainly because Gothic architects had eroded the available wall space in favour of windows.

However, in the same period, altarpieces appear – the earliest examples of what was to prove the dominant format of Western painting, the easel-painting. Their appearance was perhaps prompted by a change in the liturgy, as priests had begun some time before to conduct the service from in front of the altar rather than behind it, but also coincides with a new religious feeling. Now Christ on the Cross was no longer seen with eyes open, in awesome divinity, but with head drooping and eyes closed, in suffering humanity. Emphasis on the Last Judgment was yielding to the theme of the Virgin and Child, images of compassion, in-

tercession and hope. The moving spirit of the new feeling in Italy was St Francis of Assisi, preaching simplicity and humanity, and a more direct approach to God. A fresco in the great church built at Assisi in honour of St Francis commemorates his institution of the custom of making a crib, which serves now as it did then to explain mysteries in human, homely terms. This, to a varying extent, is what both altarpieces and frescos, very often commissioned for the numerous, newly built Franciscan churches, were now to do.

In the thirteenth century the dominant all-pervading style in Italy was Byzantine, its strongest centres Venice and Sicily. In Rome, however, examples of early Christian art, still close to its sources in the painting of antiquity, were plentiful. One of the most important was the fifth-century frescos in S. Paolo fuori le Mura, which were repainted in the late 1270s

by Cavallini (and destroyed by fire in 1823). Meanwhile, in the merchant city-states of Tuscany and north Italy, trade expanded contacts with the north, and the influence of French Gothic art began to be felt. In Tuscan Pisa, well before the end of the thirteenth century, the sculptor Nicola Pisano had achieved a remarkable synthesis of Gothic elegance and fluency with the solidity and realism of antique tradition (see over). By the time he died, before 1284, two painters who in part herald the achievement of their younger contemporary Giotto are already recorded at work in Rome, Pietro Cavallini (active 1273-1308) and Cimabue (active c. 1272-1302).

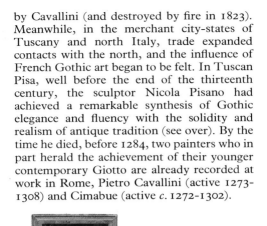

CIMABUE
Crucifix, c. 1285
Taking up a pose first explored by sculptors, Cimabue brings both pathos and grace to his figure of Christ. He relies for his effect on decorative line (as in the body's silhouette or in the loincloth) but tries to make the figure less flat, more solid and lifelike in detail.

GIOTTO? (below)
St Francis makes the first crib, c. 1290-1300
The sanctuary where St Francis places the crib is screened off. Above the screen a Crucifix like Cimabue's (right) faces the nave; in Byzantine churches there was a similar arrangement.

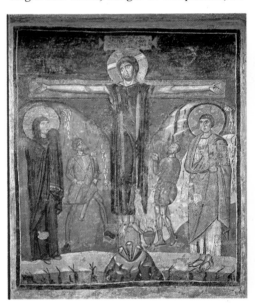

ROME, S. MARIA ANTIQUA (above) *The Crucifixion*, 8th century
In Rome the unbroken succession of popes kept alive the memory of early Christian art; here, even though the iconography is Byzantine (Christ wears a robe, for instance), some of the modelling and drapery recall classical painting.

COPPO DI MARCOVALDO (right) *The Madonna and Child*, 1261
The image is Byzantine, but is signed and dated, and larger than a typical icon. The gilt lines and sharp angles of the life-size Madonna's robes are richly decorative, and beneath them there is a sense of rounded form. (The face is repainted.)

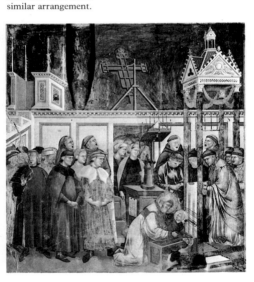

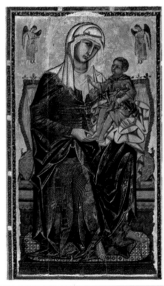

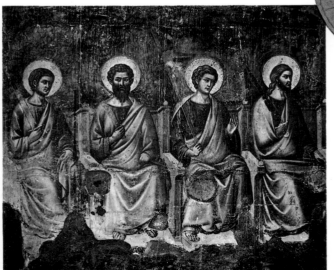

CAVALLINI (left)
Four apostles, detail of *The Last Judgment*, c. 1293
The seated saints have an imposing and convincing solidity. Cavallini is free of the linearity so strong in Cimabue, and his figures anticipate Giotto's in sculptural modelling. But he has not yet mastered the difficulty of presenting a figure in consistent foreshortening – the head (above) of an apostle is a composite view: the right-hand ear is seen in profile. But the head has power.

Cavallini, working in Rome in both fresco and mosaic on a very large scale, was not so much an innovator as a very sophisticated practitioner of the "Greek" or Byzantine style. Most of his work has perished, but the fragments of *The Last Judgment* (*c*.1293) in S. Cecilia in Trastevere, Rome, show an awareness of the way in which light can be made to model form almost sculpturally, to achieve not only realism but a monumental gravity recalling some classical sculpture. At the same time Cavallini relaxes the rigidity of the Byzantine style; he has a stronger sense of the space figures occupy, he attempts foreshortening and his touch is relatively gentle and free.

Cimabue, too, worked briefly in Rome, but the single work beyond doubt by him is in Pisa, and he is essentially an artist of Florence and its school. He is cited by his contemporary Dante in *The Divine Comedy* as the outstanding artist of his generation, and was diagnosed as the great pioneer by Vasari, who placed his life first in his (the first) history of art. We know now that earlier Italian painters had already begun to humanize the Byzantine vision, notably in Siena Coppo di Marcovaldo (active 1260-76) and Guido da Siena; but Cimabue's name is the one that has survived to attract to itself works of high quality that are due probably to a variety of hands. The colossal Crucifixes associated with him, especially that in S. Croce, Florence (severely damaged in the floods of 1966), show a clear movement towards a more naturalistic treatment of the human figure. The most famous work attributed to him, the four metres (13ft) high "*S. Trinita Madonna*" in the Uffizi Gallery, Florence, has a new sensitivity, an increased tenderness.

"*The S. Trinita Madonna*" hangs in one room in the Uffizi with two other large altarpieces; clearly it has much more in common with one, "*The Rucellai Madonna*", than the other, Giotto's "*Ognissanti Madonna*". Vasari attributed "*The Rucellai Madonna*" to Cimabue. However, it is now usually identified as the altarpiece commissioned in 1285 for S.

Maria Novella, Florence, from the greatest of the Sienese painters, Duccio di Buoninsegna (active 1278-1318). One great masterpiece is certainly Duccio's own work, the colossal *Maestà* (The Virgin in majesty), painted in 1308-11 for the high altar of Siena Cathedral.

In terms of style Duccio's achievement in the *Maestà* was to modulate the Byzantine tradition into "Latin" Gothic. From the Byzantine come elements in the characterization and poses of his people, and the delicate linear gold rays of the draperies. But the Byzantine now kindles into movement, and in the small panels Duccio and his close followers show a consummate mastery in the art of story-telling – his people are vigorous, their action and interaction subtly ordered and compelling. His interiors and landscapes are not literally drawn, his use of light is not consistent, but in narrative terms the panels are marvellously coherent. In his delight in line and colour, as in his almost miniature scale, Duccio's style is very close in feeling to that of the French Gothic illuminators – yet within this small scale, in the scene, for instance, of the Crucifixion, in the centre of the rear face, he can achieve the most solemn monumentality.

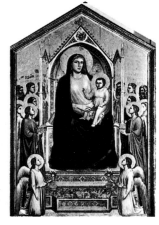

CIMABUE (left)
"*The S. Trinita Madonna*", *c*.1280
The Madonna's shrouded, soft, rounded face and gold-striated draperies are Byzantine, but the panel's gabled shape, the throne's elaborate architecture and the layering of the angels framing her are Italian.

DUCCIO (right)
"*The Rucellai Madonna*", 1285
By showing the Madonna from the side, Duccio makes her less hieratic – a real figure, understood to be occupying space, and gentle in contour and colour.

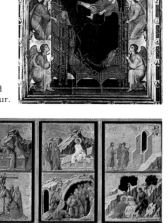

GIOTTO (left)
"*The Ognissanti Madonna*", *c*.1305-10?
The Madonna occupies space like a statue, in fact much like Tino di Camaino's stone *Madonna* (see over). She is charged with monumental solidity, but the delicacy and grace and the human tension between Mother and Child achieved by Duccio (far left) has been foregone.

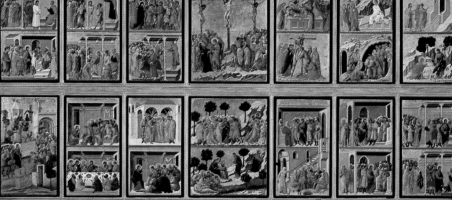

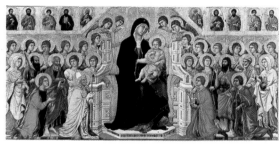

DUCCIO
The *Maestà*, rear face: *Scenes from the life of Christ*, 1308-11
The sequence starts at the bottom left (indicated by the larger panel). The figure groupings and the colours are so exquisitely calculated that, despite the small scale, the main

characters and meaning of the story emerge instantly and effectively. In *Christ's arrest* (right), Christ is picked out by the deep colours of his robe and its gold hem, and St Peter, cutting off a soldier's ear, is in green set against the red tints of the crowd. The slight interval and sharp

juxtaposition of feet pointing opposite ways masterfully express the apostles' flight. For its time, the landscape (and that of *The Agony in the Garden*) was ambitious: Duccio attempted to set out an organized space more complex than Giotto's bare stage (see pp. 82-83).

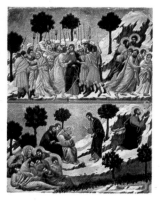

DUCCIO (above)
The *Maestà*, front face: *The Virgin in majesty*
Some 4m (13ft) wide, free-standing, painted on both sides (many panels are now dispersed) the finished *Maestà* was borne in solemn procession from Duccio's workshop to Siena Cathedral to the music of trumpets. The Virgin's rich throne sets her back into space; she is notably more solid than "*The Rucellai Madonna*" of some 20 years earlier.

Italian Gothic Sculpture

Between Romanesque and the Renaissance comes Gothic, but "Gothic" is an uneasy term when applied to Italian art of the thirteenth and fourteenth centuries. In Italian architecture the only major building immediately recognizable to northern eyes as characteristically Gothic is the buttressed, soaring, pinnacled mass of Milan Cathedral, begun in 1387. In Italian painting and sculpture we find not only the local adaptation of French and German styles coming south, but the original innovations of Duccio and Giotto in painting, and in sculpture those of Nicola and Giovanni Pisano, father and son, from Pisa.

Pisa is now about 10 kilometres (six miles) from the sea; it once lay at the very mouth of the river Arno, and had developed into a flourishing maritime and merchant republic. It was rich enough in the twelfth century to undertake Pisa Cathedral and the Leaning Tower beside it, and proud enough to compare itself with the ancient Roman republic. In the thirteenth century it had one of the most advanced metalworking industries in Europe; better stone-cutting tools as well as the patronage of an intelligent community may have contributed to the Pisani's new realism.

Although Nicola Pisano (active c. 1258-84) had his origins, as his name indicates, in Pisa, he was brought up in the far south, in Apulia, where the Emperor Frederick II Hohenstaufen had deliberately fostered a classical revival at his court. Nicola's first known (though fully mature) work, the marble pulpit in the Baptistery at Pisa, displays clear borrowings from classical models (specifically from sarcophagi still preserved nearby), though the pulpit is an unmistakably Gothic conception. Signed and dated with proud clarity *Nicola Pisanus 1260*, it continues an Italian tradition of elaborate free-standing carved pulpits: in Italy, the northern fashion of using the portals of great churches to carry sculpture was rarely followed; the Christian mysteries were depicted instead on carved pulpits or on church doors. Here Nicola surpasses his predecessors in the management of crowded figures, merged into broad narrative panels instead of being tightly compartmented in the Romanesque manner. The sense of depth and space, in which the figures seem to move and use their limbs, is quite new. In this emulation of classical form, Nicola Pisano was, like Giotto, an example to the Renaissance.

Nicola's second great pulpit (1265-68) was carved for Siena Cathedral. Here the northern influence is more marked: the movement is both more animated and more fluent, though the figures are still classical in feeling. Already working with him on the pulpit were two assistants who were to become as famous as he, his son Giovanni (active c. 1265-1314) and Arnolfo di Cambio (died 1302?). Giovanni was his father's chief assistant, perhaps even equal collaborator, in Nicola's last major project, an elaborate fountain in Perugia, finished in 1278: characteristically medieval in its encyclopaedic profusion, it has relief panels carved with even greater confidence and freedom than the pulpits. On his pulpit at Pistoia, Giovanni Pisano described himself unabashedly as "born of Nicola, but blessed with greater science", and he was clearly of a tempestuous pride and independence more usually associated with artists of the Renaissance. The pride was matched with genius, energy and versatility. He was also an architect, and from 1284 worked on a design for Siena Cathedral that approximated the French style, involving figure sculpture in the façade; but instead of subordinating the sculpture, he

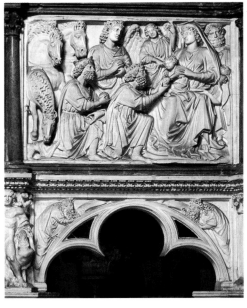

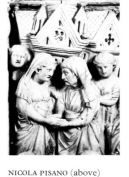

NICOLA PISANO (above)
The Visitation, detail of the Siena Cathedral pulpit, 1265-68
Here Nicola carved more deeply and sharply than at Pisa, developing a more dramatic style that was to be followed by his son and assistant Giovanni (right) – compare the women's faces.

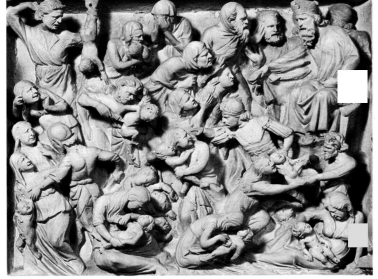

GIOVANNI PISANO (above)
The Massacre of the Innocents, detail of the Pistoia pulpit, 1301
The action seems to swarm over the panel, and yet the deeply undercut figures are grouped by emphatic diagonals swinging the eye across, up and down the composition. The faces are masks denoting grief, fury and terror.

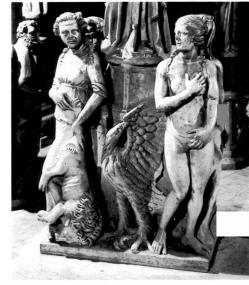

NICOLA PISANO (above)
The Adoration of the Magi, detail of the Pisa Baptistery pulpit, 1260
A Gothic trefoil arch supports a relief panel full of classical echoes; beside the arch *Fortitude* is naked like a Hercules.

PISA, CAMPO SANTO (below)
Phaedra, detail of a sarcophagus, 3rd century
Nicola has borrowed for his Virgin the pose and the matronly dignity of a Roman Phaedra. He lets her drapery, however, fall in Gothic V-shaped folds.

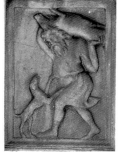

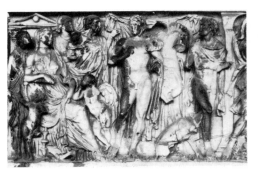

NICOLA PISANO (above)
December, detail from the Great Fountain, Perugia, 1278
The squat figures in the 50 panels set round the fountain are no longer monumental; they have an ease and vigour (though weathered) more akin to French Gothic sculpture.

GIOVANNI PISANO (right)
Temperance and *Chastity*, detail from the base of the Pisa Cathedral pulpit, 1302-10
Naked Chastity reproduces a standard pose of Venus. The carving here is tight, more rigid than at Pistoia. Long inscriptions sing Giovanni's achievements.

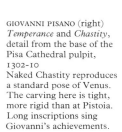

animated it dramatically so that the architecture became almost a backcloth. The figures, of prophets and wise men of antiquity, are now heavily weathered; the technical virtuosity of Giovanni's chisel has to be seen in his pulpits, at Pistoia (finished 1301), and in the cathedral at Pisa (1302-10). Here, although classical models, especially at Pisa, are used for some individual figures, there seem to be positive echoes of French Gothic sculpture, but Giovanni is not known to have visited the north, and the impact could have come through imported ivories and manuscripts. However, even in the panel at Pistoia of *The Massacre of the Innocents*, a relief composition of turbulent complexity scarcely matched before Michelangelo, Giovanni's style is always subservient to and directed towards narrative ends, even if sometimes his search for vivid expression forces him into audacious distortions.

In his free-standing figures – in wood and ivory as well as marble – Giovanni achieved a remarkable synthesis of Gothic rhythm with classic monumentality. He could convey, in his *Madonnas* (for instance that in Giotto's Arena Chapel, see over), a most tender intimacy between Mother and Child and, in his Christ

figures, a sense of human anguish within divinity. His feeling for expressive movement took on three dimensions in his now fragmented tomb of Margaret of Luxembourg (1313), in which the dead woman was represented rising from the grave.

Nicola's other famous pupil, Arnolfo di Cambio, stayed closer to his more classicizing manner than did Giovanni, even increasing the monumental simplicity of his figures – as in his crib at S. Maria Maggiore, Rome. The new type of wall-tomb he introduced, for instance Cardinal de Braye's at Orvieto, set a fashion for more than a century, providing a new theme for elaborate sculpture.

The Pisano traditions were continued and adapted in the fourteenth century by sculptors such as Tino di Camaino (c. 1285-1337), working in Pisa, Siena, Florence and Naples, and Lorenzo Maitani (active c. 1302-30), designer of the façade of the cathedral at Orvieto. At Orvieto also worked another Pisano, Andrea (active from before 1330 to c. 1348; no connection with Nicola), but his masterpiece is the bronze doors, 1330-37, for the Baptistery at Florence, in which the figure style, dependent on Giovanni's, is as economic as Giotto's.

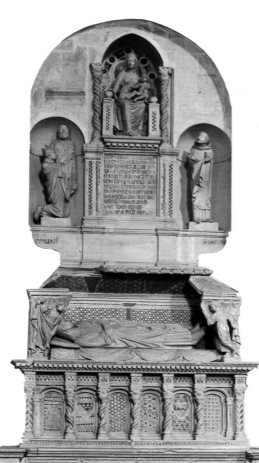

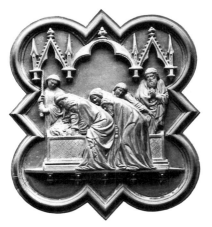

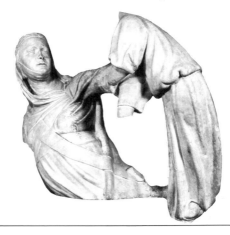

GIOVANNI PISANO (below) Fragments of the tomb of Margaret of Luxembourg, 1313
The Empress rises up to her salvation from death between two angels as the Virgin had done in French art – further evidence that Giovanni knew such art.

ARNOLFO DI CAMBIO (above) Detail of a crib: *The three Magi, c.* 1290 Arnolfo's heavy, solid figures (not as originally arranged) have much of the intimate appeal of Nicola's Perugia fountain reliefs: they are elegant as well as dignified.

ARNOLFO DI CAMBIO Tomb of Cardinal de Braye, after 1282 This is an early tomb on two levels: above, the Cardinal with two patron saints kneels before the Madonna; two angels close curtains in vivid motion on his dead body below.

ANDREA PISANO (above) *The death of St John the Baptist,* panel of the Florence Baptistery doors, 1330-37
The disposition and the anguish of the figures show the influence of Giotto's Bardi Chapel frescos of *St Francis* (see over).

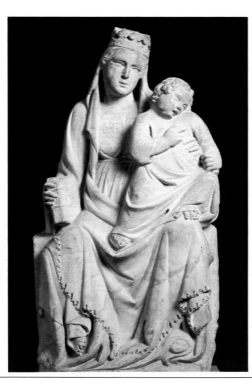

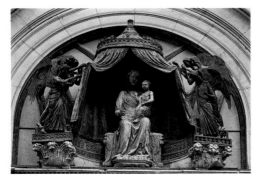

TINO DI CAMAINO (left) *The Madonna and Child,* 1321
The Madonna, originally seated above a tomb like Arnolfo's of Cardinal de Braye, has an appropriate classical dignity, but the Child moves from her in sturdily animated contrast.

MAITANI (above) The centrepiece of the façade of Orvieto Cathedral: *The Madonna enthroned,* 1330 Maitani's Madonna, beset with delicately agitated angels, has a slenderness and sweetness far removed from Tino di Camaino's.

Giotto di Bondone

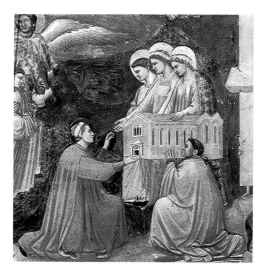

GIOTTO (above)
The Last Judgment in
the Arena Chapel, Padua,
detail: *Scrovegni presents
the chapel*, before 1306
The merchant Scrovegni
built the chapel to atone for
a rich man's sin, usury.

GIOTTO (below)
Crucifix, *c.* 1290-1300
Giotto's Christ, an early
work, is modelled more
softly than Cimabue's in
S. Croce (see p.78) and the
Byzantine prototypes from
which its design derives.

Giotto di Bondone (*c.*1267-1337) was described by Dante as the foremost painter of his
time, displacing the elder Cimabue in fickle
fame and fortune. Posterity, however, has seen
Giotto in stronger terms, as the revolutionary
who altered the course of painting in Europe,
striking out of the Gothic and Byzantine styles
towards the Renaissance. Though Giotto's
innovations are clearly definable there is, curiously, no documentary proof that he painted
the works attributed to him, and this despite
the fact that more is known about Giotto the
man – his travels, business interests, connections and family life – than is known about
any previous Western artist.

Giotto was a citizen of Florence, though he
also worked, probably or certainly, in Assisi,
Rome, Padua, Milan and Naples. Robert of
Anjou, King of Naples, called him his "close
and faithful friend". His art and evident
business acumen made him sufficiently prosperous to marry twice, support eight children
and provide handsome marriage settlements
for two daughters. His workshop flourished:
three paintings signed by him survive, but they
are almost certainly the work of his assistants,
signed by Giotto almost as a brand-name.

Comparison with the work of his predecessors, even with Cimabue, makes Giotto's
innovations obvious. The great painted Crucifix ascribed to Giotto in S. Maria Novella in
Florence shows Christ sagging painfully with
the weight of a real human body, seen in depth
against the surface of the Cross. Earlier Crucifixes, by Cimabue for instance (see p. 78), are
by contrast ceremonial portrayals, in which
the physical meaning of Christ's sacrifice is
subordinate to ritual decoration. Giotto's
"*Ognissanti Madonna*" – solid, monumental,
clearly positioned in space and gravity-bound
– makes Duccio's slightly earlier "*Rucellai
Madonna*" (see p. 79) seem a floating dream.

Giotto's style is, however, closely anticipated in the fresco cycle of the life of St Francis
in the Upper Church of S. Francesco in Assisi.
This fact has made the authorship of these
paintings one of the most extensively argued
controversies of Italian art. Who painted here?
Was it an unknown artist who taught Giotto
the principles of composition that are more
fully developed in the Arena Chapel in Padua?
Or was it, as many believe, the young Giotto,
here forging his style for the first time?

All are agreed in assigning to Giotto the

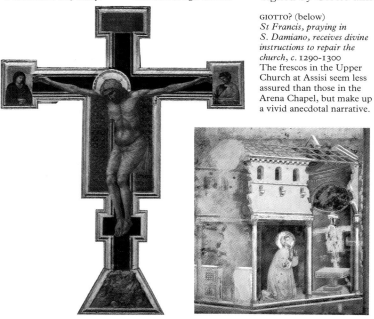

GIOTTO? (below)
*St Francis, praying in
S. Damiano, receives divine
instructions to repair the
church, c.* 1290-1300
The frescos in the Upper
Church at Assisi seem less
assured than those in the
Arena Chapel, but make up
a vivid anecdotal narrative.

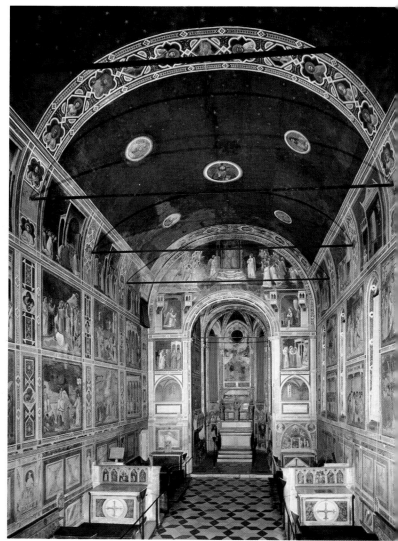

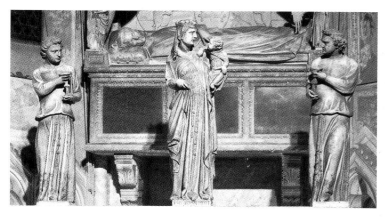

GIOVANNI PISANO
*The Madonna and Child and
two angels, c* 1302-10
Presiding over the altar
of the Arena Chapel, the

free-standing statues are
both sombre and gentle;
Mother and Child are in
mood intimate rather than
majestic. In their gravity

Giotto's figures emulate
contemporary sculpture;
in their expressive force
they rival specifically
Giovanni Pisano's range.

decoration (and possibly the architectural design) of the Arena Chapel in Padua, commissioned by the wealthy merchant Enrico Scrovegni and completed by 1306. It was a private oratory dedicated to the Virgin, and its sidewalls were decorated with the story of the life of the Virgin (and her parents) and of Christ; Giovanni Pisano sculpted a *Madonna* for the altar. To the east the angel announces her destiny to Mary across the space of the arch, and to the west is the Last Judgment – the beginning and the end of the Christian drama. Each scene of the narrative is complete in itself, yet each is organically related to the others. Giotto's analysis, reducing each episode to its dramatic essentials and presenting it in a form that satisfies both visually and psychologically, has lost none of its force today. At the beginning of the fourteenth century his approach was revolutionary.

In the opening scene, *The expulsion of Joachim from the temple*, the temple is indicated by its essentials – a tabernacle, a pulpit, an enclosing wall indicating the shelter of a sanctuary, a priest blessing a kneeling young man. Joachim, Mary's father, the elderly haloed figure on the right, is almost being pushed

from the temple by the priest into the void outside – the misery of his situation is expressed not only by the priest's action and Joachim's whole appearance, but also by the arrangement of the composition. The difference in scale between the figures and their settings, the representation of a scene not by its optical appearance but by a summary of the objects it contains, are medieval, and the narrative technique can be paralleled in Duccio's *Maestà* (see p.79). Giotto, however, has introduced a new structural logic and rationally (if not scientifically – that was a fifteenth-century achievement) defined the stage on which his figures enact their play. These figures are often starkly simplified, but there is a credible weight beneath the heavy folds of their draperies – even though Vasari's comment that Giotto deserved "to be called the pupil of Nature and of no other" may now seem a little surprising. Giotto's co-ordination of convincing objects and convincing space into an effective two-dimensional pattern anticipated Renaissance ideals, yet it is perhaps Giotto's feeling for the human figure and the passion it can express that makes his art still so strikingly effective today.

Two other major surviving works generally held to be Giotto's were painted ten or more years later; they are *The life of St Francis* in the Bardi Chapel in S. Croce, Florence, painted perhaps about 1316-20, and *The life of St John the Baptist* in the Peruzzi Chapel in the same church, painted perhaps in the mid-1320s. These scenes, less well preserved than those at Padua, are placed in much larger panels, oblong rather than squarish, and the narrative is generally more fluid and relaxed, with more realistic settings and more habitable architecture, with the narrow stage used in the Arena Chapel opened out. Giotto's followers further elaborated his settings and refined his perspective, but seldom matched his psychological portrayal of the human figure.

In 1329 Giotto was painting in Naples for Robert of Anjou, but hardly a trace remains of his extensive work there. He was appointed architect to Florence Cathedral in 1335 and began its campanile. For the last two years of life he was working in Milan and is believed to have died at the age of 70 in 1337. He soon became a figure not only of history but of legend, and for a time his name served virtually as a synonym for "painter".

GIOTTO
The Arena Chapel, Padua: (left) interior looking east, dedicated in 1306
The frescos narrate the lives of Mary and Christ in three horizontal bands, reading to the right and from top to bottom, then culminating in *The Last Judgment* on the west wall. *The expulsion of Joachim* (right) begins the cycle.

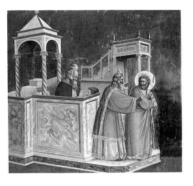

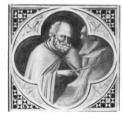

Between the framed scenes are Old Testament scenes or symbols presaging the events of each panel: Moses (above) is placed beside the *Feast at Cana* (right) since in striking a rock to draw water for the Israelites he had prefigured Christ turning water into wine. Much of the undiminished power of Giotto's frescos derives from his economy: observe the firm, bold outlines with which the actions of Christ's humiliators are depicted in *The mocking of Christ* (right). The chapel was clearly built to be decorated and the heavy painted framing provides an architectural division of the box-like, simple structure. The blue of the ceiling seems also part of the original design.

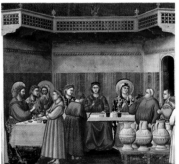

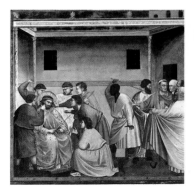

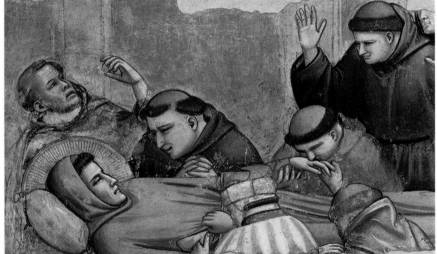

GIOTTO (above)
The death of St Francis, detail from the Bardi Chapel, S. Croce, *c.* 1320
Giotto's mature style is evident in the Franciscan church in Florence where

he painted four chapels (the frescos in two are lost). Vasari tells us it was Giotto who painted "with great effect the tears of a number of friars lamenting the death of the saint".

GIOTTO (below)
The dance of Salome, detail from the Peruzzi Chapel, S. Croce, *c.* 1325
In his later work Giotto made use of more elaborate architectural settings.

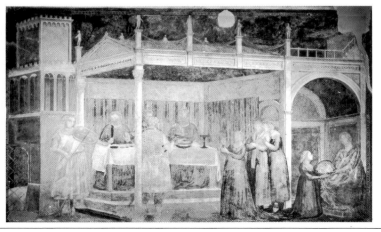

Italian Gothic Painting

The conception of Giotto as the founding figure of Western art emerges in the writings of fourteenth-century humanists such as Boccaccio. However, the idea was firmly and definitively stated only in the sixteenth century by the adopted Florentine painter Vasari. For all Giotto's immense influence, his contemporaries and successors in the fourteenth century did not see his work as breaking away in a new direction they were compelled to follow. The leading school of painting in the first half of the century was not really in Florence, but in Siena. It was Sienese painting, still rooted in the Byzantine tradition – enlivened, in Duccio's work, by the elegance of Gothic – that exerted the greater influence, not only in the courts and city-states of Italy, but further north, in the courts of France.

The most seductive interpreter of Duccio's style was Simone Martini (*c.* 1285-1344), who was certainly in Duccio's circle, and may have been his pupil. Simone's work has impressive variety, but is characterized by his delight in sinuous line and clear colour, already to be seen in his first known work, a large *Maestà* (Madonna in majesty) of 1315 (reworked 1321). One of a series of important commissions for the Sienese Town Hall (see over), it is very close, in composition and style, to the front face of Duccio's great *Maestà* (see p. 79), but there are hints in the fresco of Simone's innovative talent. In his *St Louis* altarpiece, painted in Naples in 1317, the image of the saint is severely frontal, icon-like, though offset by the movement of the drapery, the sumptuous colour and the detail of the decoration; but the kneeling figure of the donor, Robert of Anjou, is very individual, and the little scenes at the bottom constituting the predella have a coherent unity of perspective never before attempted. Simone's fresco of the military commander Guidoriccio da Fogliano, painted in 1328 (and sited opposite his 1315 *Maestà*) is the first such "history" painting.

Simone's masterpiece – signed by himself and by his brother-in-law Lippo Memmi – is the brilliant and dramatic 1333 *Annunciation*, originally an altarpiece for Siena Cathedral. Set against a field of matt and burnished gold, the angel, swirling in an arabesque of white and gold draperies, fretting his wings, kneels before the Virgin: she shrinks from his awesome message, creating a space between them that almost vibrates. Simone, like nearly every great artist of the time, had worked at Assisi, and something of the massive Giottesque manner of frescos is reflected in his later works; but in the exquisite lyric grace of *The Annunciation* there is no trace of that, but rather an affinity with certain French manuscript illuminations. In 1340/41 he went to France, to the papal court at Avignon; there he met and befriended the great humanist Petrarch, and there he died.

The impact of Giotto on two, perhaps slightly younger, contemporaries of Simone in Siena, the Lorenzetti brothers, Ambrogio and Pietro (both active *c.* 1319-48?), was more marked. Pietro worked in Assisi as well as in Siena; Ambrogio had close connections with Florence. They have clearly distinct artistic personalities, and apparently worked together on only one project, a fresco, now lost, in 1335. Pietro's first documented work, *The Virgin and saints* of 1320 at Arezzo, shows in its little upper *Annunciation* skilful experimentation with the perspective. In Pietro's latest dated work, *The birth of the Virgin* of 1342, this interest in perspective is developed in an interior which has a thorough logic unknown to Giotto. The analysis of three-dimensional

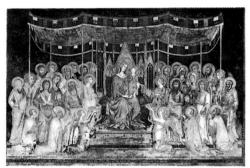

SIMONE MARTINI (above) *Maestà* (The Madonna in majesty), 1315-21 The Madonna, as Queen of Heaven, sits under a canopy. Beneath it the reverent figures stand one behind another, in greater depth and variety of pose than in Duccio's *Maestà*.

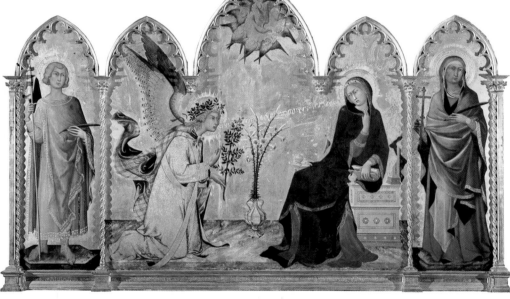

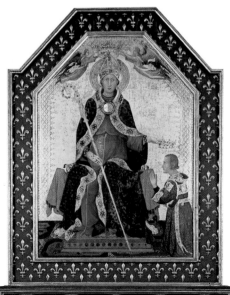

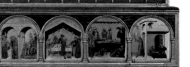

SIMONE MARTINI (left) *St Louis*, 1317 To support his claim to the throne of Naples, Robert of Anjou had the artist paint his canonized great uncle, Louis IX, crowning him as he knelt.

SIMONE MARTINI (above) *The Annunciation*, 1333 Here Simone has wholeheartedly embraced Gothic rhythms – even the format of the picture echoes the typical portal scheme of a French cathedral façade.

SIMONE MARTINI (below) *Guidoriccio da Fogliano*, 1328 The Sienese general rides between two towns he has wrested from the Florentines; the Sienese siege-camp is shown on the right. One of the first equestrian portraits since antiquity, it must echo the Roman idea of triumphal procession. Guidoriccio is both magnificent in his pageantry and hauntingly forlorn against a black sky.

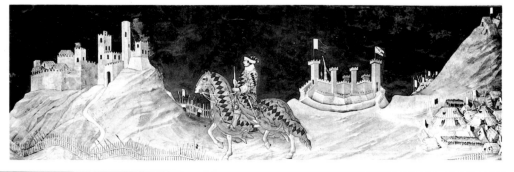

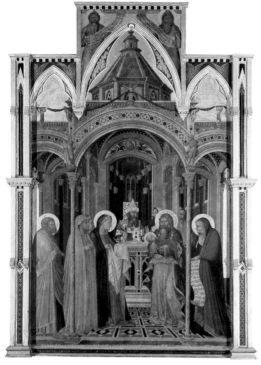

space is equally ambitious in Ambrogio's *Presentation in the Temple*, and the figures, in their simplicity of contour and mass, recall not only Giotto but Nicola Pisano; Ambrogio may even have used Roman or Romanesque sources, as he surely did for his *Good Commune* (see over).

In Florence, none of Giotto's immediate followers was comparable in stature to him or to the great Sienese. The epithet "Giotteschi" (little Giottos) applied to them rather vaguely is, however, scarcely just, and they included some notable artists. The prolific Bernardo Daddi (active *c.* 1290-1348; not shown) offered a sweeter version of the style of Giotto and specialized in small portable altarpieces that became very popular. Taddeo Gaddi (*c.* 1300-*c.* 1366) is said to have been Giotto's godson and to have worked with him for 24 years. His best-known paintings are perhaps the lively frescos in the Baroncelli Chapel in S. Croce, Florence, in which he deployed Giotto's style in a more overtly decorative and animated narrative, packed with incident. Roughly contemporary was Maso di Banco, whose life is entirely obscure, but he was surely the greatest of Giotto's followers; his frescos of *The life of St Sylvester* in S. Croce, probably of the late

1330s, have a striking clarity and solidity, and show a profound grasp of Giotto's principles.

The Black Death, erupting in Tuscany in the middle of the century, inevitably had an effect on art. The population of Siena was halved, and the city never recovered its prominent position. The Franciscans' outgoing humanity was checked, and the bulk of patronage was undertaken under the auspices of the more didactic Dominicans. The Last Judgment or standing saints holding messages or symbols were more typical subjects than intimate scenes from the life of the Virgin set in a perspective interior. In the work of Orcagna (active 1343-68), the versatile dominant figure – painter, sculptor, architect and impresario – in Florentine art in the two decades following 1350, there is a clear tendency to revert to the other-worldly images of the earlier Byzantine tradition. However, the narrative techniques of the Giotto tradition were continued, in more crowded and fanciful designs, by artists such as Taddeo Gaddi's son Agnolo (active 1369-96; not shown). His graceful rhythms and brilliant colours usher in the Florentine version of the "International Gothic" style of the century's close.

AMBROGIO LORENZETTI (above) *The Presentation in the Temple*, 1342
The building is half interior, half exterior, the typical medieval formula, here at its most developed.

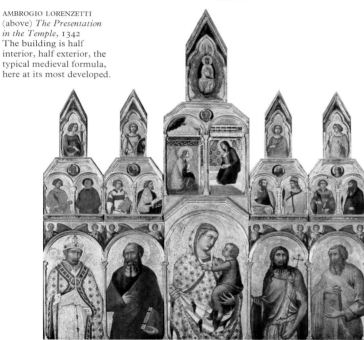

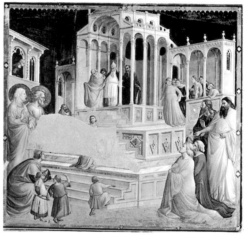

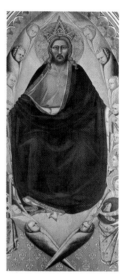

PIETRO LORENZETTI (above) *The Virgin and saints*, 1320
Pietro's figures differ from those by Simone; the central Virgin and Child have a solidity of form inspired by Giotto, but also a human tenderness that derives from Duccio.

PIETRO LORENZETTI (left) *The birth of the Virgin*, 1342
The room is like a three-dimensional stage, linked architecturally to the picture's frame. To the right, parallel lines in the coverlet pattern converge as they run into depth, and together with the floor tiles create a coherent space.

TADDEO GADDI (above) *The Presentation of the Virgin*, *c.*1332-38
Taddeo's repertoire of varied settings, displayed at their best in his *Life of the Virgin* frescos in S. Croce, was copied enthusiastically – this one reappears in French illuminated manuscripts.

MASO DI BANCO (below) *St Sylvester and the dragon*, late 1330s
St Sylvester is seen twice: calming a dragon, and resurrecting two Magi it had killed (seen alive and dead). Maso introduces more detail than Giotto had without prejudicing the narrative impact.

ORCAGNA (above) *The Redeemer*, detail of an altarpiece, 1354-57
Though massive in form, the remote, unsmiling figure of Christ reverts to icon-like immobility and staring-eyed intensity.

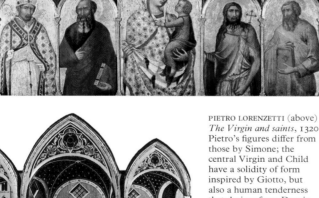

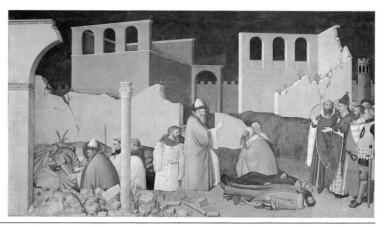

Ambrogio Lorenzetti: The Good Commune

The lively, independent mercantile republics of central Italy were growing both in size and prosperity during the thirteenth century. Among them, Siena is the most brilliant example of a community rebuilding and adorning its communal heart, the city. In Pisa, Florence, Siena and elsewhere the cathedrals were already well advanced; now the streets and squares were levelled and paved, and meeting places, halls and government buildings erected. Siena's new fabric was planned as the visible expression of the city's order and harmony – even as a mirror of the City of God described by the theologians. Its most significant enterprise was the Palazzo Pubblico, or Town Hall, begun in 1284 and largely completed by 1310; from 1315 the nine elected city consuls undertook to fill the huge bare walls of its interior with a remarkable series of frescos, expressing communal aspirations.

In 1315 Simone Martini was commissioned to paint a *Maestà* (see preceding page) in the room where the general council met: there the Madonna presided as patroness and divine ruler of the city, her message spelled out in an inscription. In the adjoining room where the Nine met, Ambrogio Lorenzetti was commissioned in 1338 to paint a series of frescos: on one wall, an allegory of Good Government, of Justice and the Common Good; on the second, an allegory of Tyranny; on the third wall, 12 metres (40ft) long, a vision of the city of Siena and its countryside enjoying the benefits of Good Government. The inclusion of Siena Cathedral, its campanile and the streets and houses around it, brought home the meaning of the allegory to the spectator personally.

The main allegory of Good Government on the north wall is expressed in solemn seated figures representing various virtues, moral, political and administrative. Each figure is named, and its significance spelled out in rhymed inscriptions. The enthroned figure on the left is Justice, linked by a cord to the largest figure on the right, Common Good, or Good Commune. The group of citizens below all face their elected choice, the Common Good; on the right, soldiers securely guard wrong-doers. On the opposite wall is the alternative, a group of vices about the throne of Tyranny – Cruelty, War, Treason and Division. The overall message is clear, an exhortation to the citizens and a call to unity; and it was urgent: the government of the Nine, though unusually durable, was constantly threatened by tension and violence between rival factions.

On the east wall the hieratic range of Virtues adjoins an astonishing city and landscape, unrolling beneath the hovering figure of Security. City and countryside are recorded with an attention to their physical reality in a way never attempted before, although two little panels ascribed to Ambrogio (the first pure landscapes in Western art?) foreshadow his achievement in the frescos. The peasants had carried out their same Monthly Labours on Cathedral portals; but they work now in a real landscape, indicated not by a token rock or tree but by an undulation of hills, winding roads, water and cultivation shaping the earth as it is still shaped about Siena today. The sky, however, is a grey-black blank.

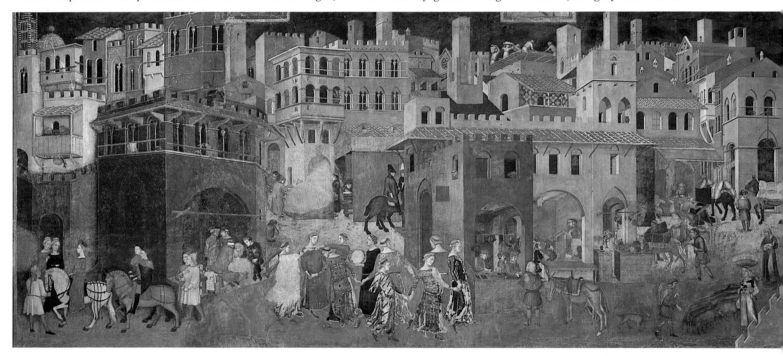

AMBROGIO LORENZETTI
(above) *The effects of Good Government on town and countryside*, 1338
Siena Cathedral is on the far left; other buildings, not identified, suggest real structures, with known Sienese features. Ordinary activities such as building a house and washing at a communal fountain are truthfully observed. This realism, so different from the conventions of previous painters, is apparent also in the landscape beside.

(right) *Allegory of Good Government*
The row of citizens pass a symbolic cord running from Justice on the left, with Concord beneath her, to Common Good, throned with sceptre on the right.

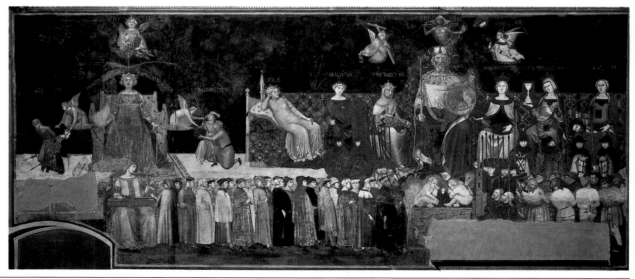

SIENA (below)
Winged Victory, 2nd century?
Known to have been in Siena in Ambrogio's day, the Roman arch relief may have inspired his figure of Security, guarding the landscape in *The effects of Good Government*. The original has a suppleness Ambrogio does not match.

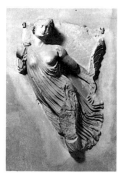

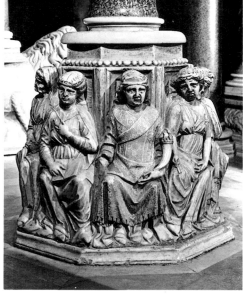

NICOLA PISANO (left)
The Liberal Arts, detail of the Siena Cathedral pulpit, 1265-68
Nicola's matrons were prominent monuments in the heart of the city.

AMBROGIO LORENZETTI (below) *Grammar*
The influence of Pisani sculpture on Ambrogio is apparent in the drapery and mass of *Grammar*, shown teaching a child, but is less so in figures that are not allegorical.

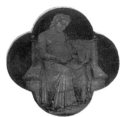

The reality rendered has been carefully interpreted. Central in the city dance maidens, the focus and symbol of the harmony of the whole: the light radiates from them to left and right, the buildings recede obliquely from them, and the scale of the figures behind them diminishes. This compositional unity had its counterpart in the deliberate disorganization of *The effects of Bad Government* (much damaged; not shown) where there was no clear focus of attention, and no coherent light.

A whole summary of medieval thought is completed in the medallions that border the frescos; these include symbols of the Liberal Arts and Sciences, the seasons and the planets. In representing these allegorical figures, Ambrogio was clearly stimulated both by contemporary sculpture and by antiquity.

A decade later Siena was to be overwhelmed by a disaster of which the Palazzo Pubblico programme had taken no account – the Black Death, which perhaps killed both Ambrogio and his brother Pietro about 1348, and, in a sense, served to delay the Renaissance.

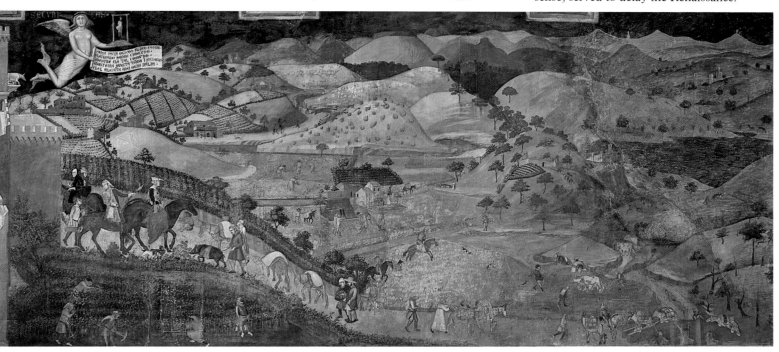

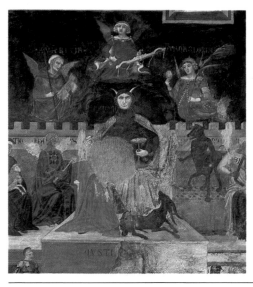

AMBROGIO LORENZETTI (left) *Allegory of Bad Government*, detail
This fragment from the now badly damaged fresco shows horned Tyranny, negative counterpart to the Common Good, with some of her cohorts.

AMBROGIO LORENZETTI? (right) *Landscape*, c.1335?
This, and another similar panel, are probably the two earliest pure landscapes in Italian art. In its uniform bird's-eye view this differs from the very much larger Palazzo Pubblico landscape, which is seen from a view much closer to eye-level. Had Ambrogio seen a Roman landscape fresco that no longer survives?

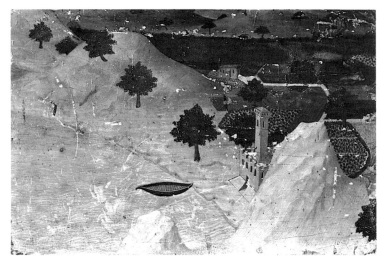

Netherlandish Art 1: Sluter and the van Eycks

In the fifteenth century, both north and south of the Alps, artists succeeded in transcribing the facts and details of the natural world convincingly, in wood or stone, in tempera or in oils. An interest in decorative detail develops into a determination to render nature objectively and with consistency. The things shown have an importance of their own: they are no longer secondary to the demands of pattern or to the need to project sacred figures in hieratic form. The flat surfaces of paintings are given a luminous depth. However, particularly in the north, symbolic meanings are hidden in the naturalistic forms. Plants, fruits, furniture and buildings, carefully reproduced in a real world, in real space, are invested with religious significance.

The Netherlands, the vital centre of realism in the north, passed in 1387 under the control of Duke Philip the Bold of Burgundy, but the Netherlandish cities, rich in the trade of cloth, wool and linen, retained their own local government. When in 1420 Duke Philip the Good of Burgundy moved his court north from Dijon to Bruges, Netherlandish artists, enjoying twin sources of patronage – pious, prosperous merchants and what was briefly the

most splendid court in Europe – came into their own in their own region.

The pioneers of the new realism had worked in Dijon, at the Chartreuse de Champmol, a Carthusian monastery patronized by Philip the Bold, between about 1394 and 1404. The painter Melchior Broederlam (active 1381-1409) is at first glance essentially of the International Gothic – elegant, dreamy, clearly aware of Italian example, particularly Duccio and the Lorenzetti – but his figures have an earthy solidity that is specifically northern. The revolutionary innovator was a sculptor, Claus Sluter (died c. 1406), Broederlam's exact contemporary at Champmol. In his work uncompromising realism is injected into the Gothic world, with scarcely any concession to rhythmic pattern and ornament. In the characterization of his figures he anticipates the psychological approach of Donatello (see p. 102) working 20 years later in Florence: the more than life-size prophets on his Well of Moses at Champmol have a similar presence and emotional intensity, and, as in Donatello, the bold, freely handled draperies are outward elements of an inner drama. Some of the mourning figures about Sluter's tomb of Philip

the Bold, once also at Champmol, are invisible within their hooded draperies, and the heavy robes themselves become images of grief.

The first painter of the new realism clearly emulated the dense solidity of such sculpture as Sluter's. This master, the Master of the Mérode altarpiece, also called the "Master of Flémalle", is generally but still not universally identified as Robert Campin of Tournai (c. 1378-1444). In the work associated with him, the sharply defined bulk and mass of the figures and draperies have lost all trace of the aristocratic delicacy of International Gothic. In the Mérode altarpiece, for the first time the Annunciation, a supernatural happening, is set within a homely contemporary interior. The whole vision is related to the daily experience of the ordinary man. The angel may have wings, but neither he nor the Virgin is haloed.

Campin's *Annunciation* was painted about 1425; by then his slightly younger but far more famous and securely identified contemporary, Jan van Eyck (c. 1385-1441) was fully active, while by 1426 Jan's mysterious brother, Hubert, was already dead. Jan was the appointed court painter to Duke Philip the Good, and seems to have had a close, personal relation-

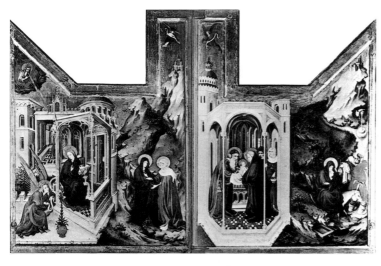

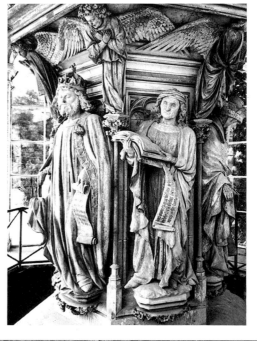

BROEDERLAM (left)
Scenes from the life of Mary, c. 1394-99
The sharply receding architectural boxes are composite interior-exteriors: the formula is still that of Ambrogio Lorenzetti's *Presentation* (see p. 85). What is new is the symbolism residing in apparently ordinary objects: the three windows by God the Father in *The Annunciation* signify the Trinity; the domed tower and walled garden are symbols of chastity; and there is much more.

SLUTER (right)
The Well of Moses, detail: *David* and *Jeremiah*, 1395-1403
The prophets and kings predicting the Passion once stood beneath a Crucifix, now lost; and Jeremiah once had metal spectacles. What remains is still powerfully realistic, rich in human feeling.

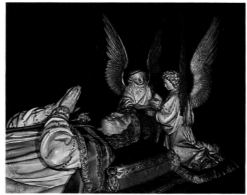

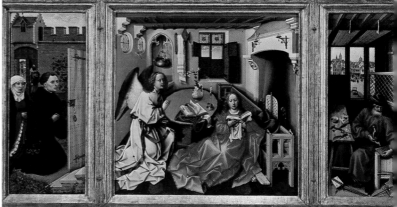

SLUTER
The tomb of Duke Philip the Bold, details: (above) *Mourners*; (above right) *Duke Philip*, 1385-1405
Sluter first worked on the tomb as an assistant to Jean de Marville (died 1389), and took over at his death. The mourners – the Duke's

vassals, officers and relations in funeral robes – are entirely his work, and strongly individualized. The Well of Moses, also in stone, was originally no less richly and vividly painted. Sluter's realism had wide influence; Gerhaerts (see p. 158) took up his mantle.

CAMPIN? (right)
The Mérode altarpiece: *The Annunciation*, c. 1425
The Virgin and angel seem somewhat clumsy, almost plebeian, though the room is comfortably furnished. The presence of objects – the shadows they cast, the stuff they are made of – is crucial to Campin.

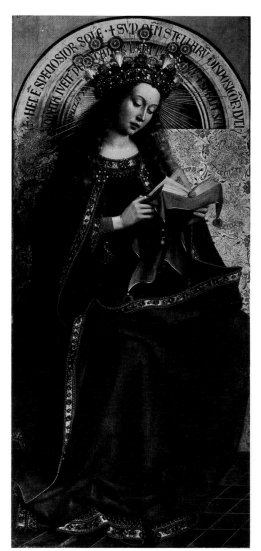

ship with his patron, travelling to Spain and Portugal on diplomatic missions. He clearly enjoyed a status and respect, and probably an income, previously not granted to artists.

Any approach to the van Eycks must centre on their huge altarpiece at Ghent. Its inscription, crediting Hubert with its inception and Jan with its completion (in 1432), is one of the very rare pieces of evidence that Hubert existed and was a painter, though distinguishing Hubert's work from Jan's remains highly speculative. The altarpiece is both large and complex. On the outside of the wings when closed there is an *Annunciation* and below it portraits of the donors, with their patron saints, represented as monochrome statues in niches; when opened, the central theme is revealed as *The adoration of the Lamb*. Though the altarpiece as a whole has many puzzling, even contradictory elements (which the dual authorship may explain), the overall impression of rich and vivid colour, the exactitude with which the appearance of the visible world is tirelessly rendered, the conviction with which the religious theme is translated into physical terms – these qualities make it a landmark in the history of Western art.

Of Jan's own undisputed work, *The Madonna with Canon van der Paele* (1436) represents his style at its most pure. Virgin, saints, and the minutely scrutinized head of the aged donor, solid as a weather-ravaged rock, are presented with a positively ruthless objectivity and completeness: they are held together by the unifying fall of light in a stillness and silence that is almost like a *trompe-l'oeil* waxwork. Though the command of perspective is intuitive and empirical rather than geometrically based as it was to be in Italy (see p. 104), it was quite convincing enough to convey the illusion of distance and depth as never before – whether internal, as here, or external, as in the extraordinary view through the arched window over a great estuary in *The Madonna with Chancellor Rolin*. There, even though the recession of the middle ground is not quite logical, the union of the figures with the setting is complete. Virgin and Child are no less physically present than the great Burgundian official acknowledging their divinity, perhaps not all that humbly – they seem to be visiting him, not he them. Not the least of van Eyck's achievements was the establishment of the modern portrait in its own right.

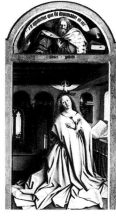

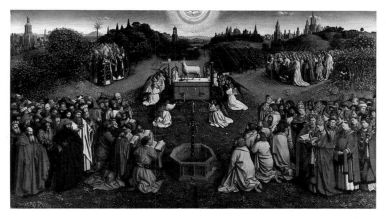

THE BOUCICAUT MASTER (below) *The Visitation*, c. 1405
The Book of Hours from which this page comes, and the man who painted it, take their name from its owner, a commander under the French king. The sky and hills show aerial perspective, the changing light and colour suggesting distance.

JAN AND HUBERT VAN EYCK (above)
The Ghent altarpiece open, detail: *The Virgin*, c. 1426-32
The contrast between the van Eycks and, for instance, Campin or the International Gothic Boucicaut Master is startling; though their aims are similar, the others lack the van Eycks' technique.

JAN AND HUBERT VAN EYCK (above)
The Ghent altarpiece closed, detail: *The Virgin Annunciate*
The round, Romanesque arches symbolize the old order; the trefoil, Gothic windows stand for the new, borne in by Christ's birth.

JAN AND HUBERT VAN EYCK (above)
The Ghent altarpiece open, central panel: *The adoration of the Lamb*
Saints, prophets, virgins foregather to adore. The individual heads, the grass spread with flowers like a tapestry, the glow of light on the horizon are notable.

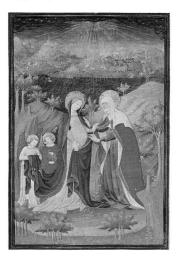

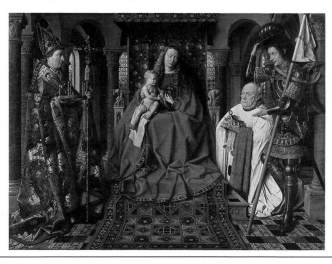

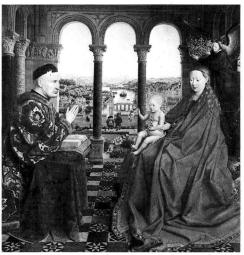

JAN VAN EYCK (left)
The Madonna with Canon van der Paele, 1436
In the wealth of minutely rendered detail – of the architecture, draperies, throne or carpet – there is a carefully calculated, often obscure, symbolism. The light is all-pervasive.

JAN VAN EYCK (above)
The Madonna with Chancellor Rolin, c. 1435
Jan must have refined the use of oils as a vehicle for the pigment, so that he could build the painting up slowly in thin glazes, to achieve subtle modelling and atmospheric luminosity.

Jan van Eyck: The Arnolfini Marriage

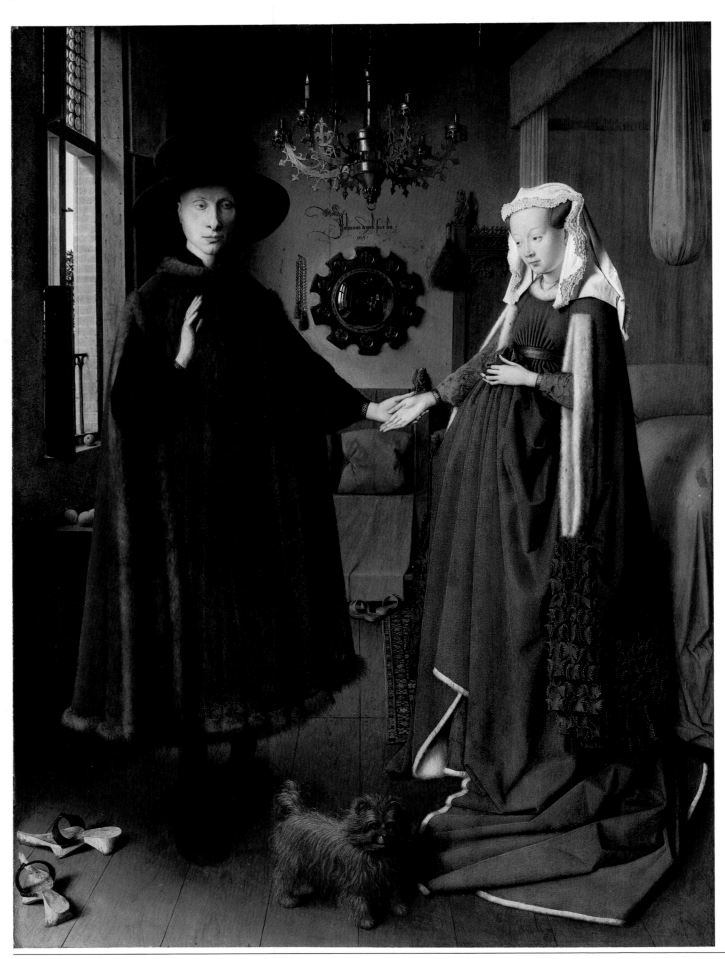

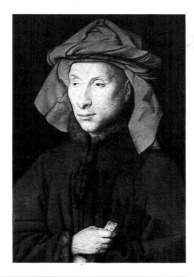

JAN VAN EYCK (right)
Giovanni Arnolfini,
*c.*1437
Arnolfini's modest but
warm attire (van Eyck
superbly conveys the
texture of heavy wool)
marks him as a prosperous
bourgeois merchant. He
had court connections,
through which he must
have met and become
friendly with van Eyck.
He became a counsellor
to the Duke of Burgundy,
and advanced him money.
(It is generally accepted
that the sitter here and in
the *Marriage* is Giovanni
Arnolfini, but this is not
absolutely certain.)

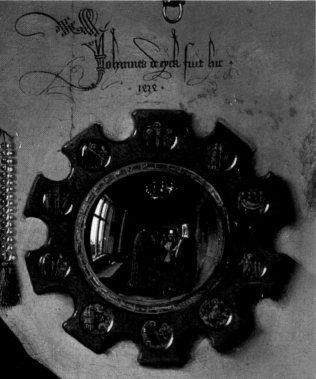

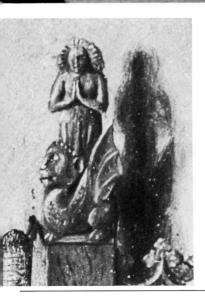

JAN VAN EYCK
(opposite page) "*The
Arnolfini Marriage*", and
details: (above) the mirror;
(left) *St Margaret*, 1434
St Margaret was said
to have escaped from the
belly of a dragon: hence
her role as patron saint
of childbirth. (Giovanna
is quite possibly pregnant.)
The ten roundels of the
mirror show scenes from
Christ's Passion, solem-
nizing the oath-taking.
The mirror indicates
things existing outside
the picture's limits, and
in the 17th century, when
van Eyck's picture was in
Madrid, Velazquez saw
and used the device in his
"*Las Meninas*" (see p. 210)
– complicating further
van Eyck's metaphysics
of illusion and reality.

Within a room of some luxury, Giovanni di
Arrigo Arnolfini and Giovanna Cenami stand
side by side. Her right hand rests on his left,
and his right hand is raised as if to confirm a
vow. They are being betrothed, or perhaps
married. The year is 1434.

It seems that the painter Jan van Eyck, a
friend of Giovanni Arnolfini, a silk merchant
from Lucca in Tuscany who had settled in
Bruges, attended, and recorded the event with
documentary, even legal precision. The signature, *Johannes de Eyck fuit hic 1434* (Jan van
Eyck was here 1434) is written in a careful
Gothic script, as though he were inscribing his
name as an official witness to the ceremony,
and it is placed above a mirror in which two
figures are reflected, one presumably the painter, the other a second witness. It is as if the
picture were painted for posterity, as if the
artist knew full well that in 1534 or 1634 he
would not be there, but others would be.

The painting is not, however, a literal record
of a real event, for it is rich in symbolism,
unobtrusive but explicit, though more readily
understood by his contemporaries than by us.
Many details illuminate the significance of the
event, the married state as a continuing human
sacrament. The candle, lit in full daylight, was
not only a necessary prop in the ceremony of
oath-taking, but was a "marriage-candle", a
flame emblematic of the ardour of newly-weds.
The dog was a symbol of marital faith. The
fruit on the window-sill and the crystal beads
beside the mirror are taken over from the
symbolism surrounding the Virgin Mary. The
little figure carved above the back of the chair
is St Margaret, patron saint of childbirth.

This little painting, about 80 × 60 centimetres (32 × 23½ in), has become one of the
most famous masterpieces of Western art, a
celebration of a human relationship as vital
today as it was five and a half centuries ago. It
was then astonishingly original – in presenting
full-length portraits confronting the onlooker;
in siting them in a domestic interior without a
religious context; in introducing narrative, and
even genre, elements into a double portrait.
For the picture is also an inventory of objects
lovingly described – the discarded shoes, the
little dog, the fruit; the planked floor, the
grandly intricate brass candelabra; the rich
texture and glowing colours of materials. All
these, ranged in immutable order, comple-
menting the calmly tender central figures and
extending their symmetry, are fused into the
serene composition of the whole by that pervasive light, welling from the window.

The picture is the summit, but not the
whole, of van Eyck's revolutionary achievement in portraiture. His single portraits reveal
a human approach that is quite new; with
modestly posed head and shoulders, the sitters
are seen for themselves and themselves alone.
Their faces (that of the *Man in a turban* may be
van Eyck's own) are intensely scrutinized –
one, at least, preceded by a silverpoint drawing
of vivid delicacy, certainly from the life – but
again the inventory of detail is modelled into
harmony, each item precisely related to the
others. The secret is the accuracy with which
the light is realized, with a subtlety and
flexibility which the refinement of the oil
medium allowed for the first time.

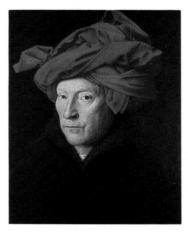

JAN VAN EYCK
A man in a turban
(Self-portrait?), 1433
The day, month and year
are written on the frame,
with van Eyck's motto
"Als Ich Kan" – as I
can (but not as I would).
He seems conscious
that his art will outlive
him – reviving a theme
of classical poets.

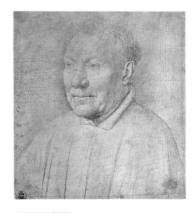

JAN VAN EYCK
(above and below)
Cardinal Albergati,
*c.*1432
The study for the oil
portrait is a drawing
in silverpoint, that is,
using silver wire on
paper specially prepared
to take its impression.
Notes for the colours are
on the drawing; has the
oil been slightly idealized?

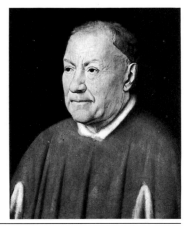

Netherlandish Art 2: Rogier van der Weyden

The dominant figure in Netherlandish painting in the middle years of the fifteenth century was Rogier van der Weyden (1399/1400-64). He was most probably the "Rogelet" (little Roger) documented in Robert Campin's workshop in 1427, for his work certainly reflects Campin's style, though it draws also on Jan van Eyck's. He soon settled in Brussels, and in 1435 was appointed city painter. He visited Ferrara in Italy about 1450, and his works became widely known throughout Europe in his own lifetime. Many exist in several versions – witness both to his popularity and to the assistance of a large workshop.

Rogier van der Weyden's work is characterized by an intense emotionalism, expressed in flowing and dynamic line, which is alien to both Campin and van Eyck. It has been seen as a reversion to Gothic; certainly his calculated appeal to the emotions is paralleled in German art, which persisted into the fifteenth and even the sixteenth century in a recognizably medieval, late Gothic tradition. Rogier, however, whole-heartedly embraced the realism of Campin and van Eyck, and if his grieving figures weep tears, the tears glisten naturalistically. Rogier's vision, like Campin's, expresses the religious sentiment of the ordinary man, but sharpened and deepened by the *devotio moderna*, a spiritual revival initiated in the Netherlands and strong also in Germany. Its textbook was *The Imitation of Christ*, a manual of meditation first appearing in 1418, ascribed to Thomas à Kempis.

Van der Weyden's art is in many ways a critical revision of the work of his two great elder contemporaries. His early *St Luke painting the Virgin* was consciously based on Jan van Eyck's *Madonna with Chancellor Rolin* (see p. 91) – two figures are again placed in a room overlooking a river, and even van Eyck's two little figures peering over the balustrade reappear. In contrast to van Eyck, Rogier introduces an emotional relationship between his two main characters, creating a gently curving movement echoing from one to the other. Both figures are seen with an involved and tender humanity, far from the objective detachment of Jan's descriptions. The Virgin suckling a child is entirely a mother; the Child crisps fingers and toes with pleasure. Beside the fantastic detail of van Eyck's landscape, van der Weyden's view seems fairly summary,

VAN DER WEYDEN (below)
St Luke painting the Virgin, c. 1434-35?
St Luke's pose looks better suited to an angel in an *Annunciation*, and not very appropriate for drawing. The Madonna is in type like Campin's but the handling is softer more like Jan van Eyck's.

VAN DER WEYDEN (right)
The Deposition, c. 1435
The actors are set out like sculptures on a stage (such life-size tableaux were not unusual), yet overriding a sense of weight or solidity in the figures there is a dominant, dynamic line. The emotion is tragic, yet tenderly resigned.

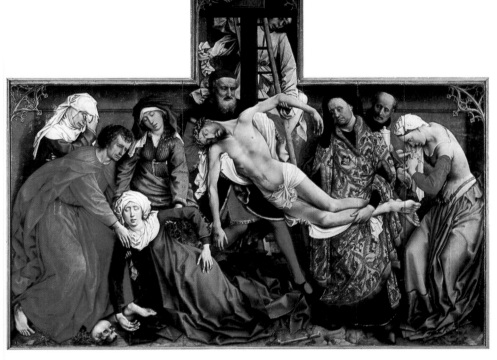

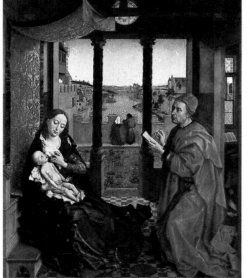

VAN DER WEYDEN (below)
The Last Judgment, c. 1450?
In contrast to the Ghent altarpiece, the single subject continues over the panel divisions. All detail has been pared away. St Michael with the scales advances irresistibly, cleaving Saved from Damned.

AFTER CAMPIN (right)
The Deposition, central panel, c. 1430-35?
Campin's composition no longer exists in its original huge scale, but the impression it made is recorded. Van der Weyden reversed Christ's position, flattened out the figures and characteristically concentrated the effect.

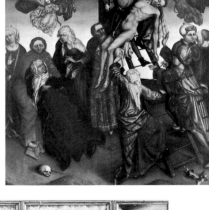

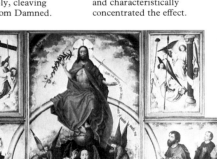

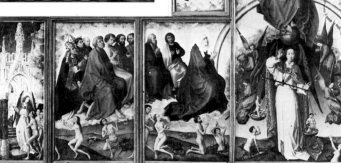

and the two little figures are made more strongly the focus of attention.

Perhaps van der Weyden's best-known masterpiece is his *Deposition* in Madrid. For this the starting point was surely a famous huge *Deposition* by Campin, of which a fragment survives, ıt which is known in full only in a small copy. From Campin Rogier took over the scale – his figures are almost life-size – the use of a gold background and, above all, the frieze-like disposition and sharp, sculptural definition of the figures. Campin's composition has been superbly simplified – the expressive curving diagonals of the dead Christ and his fainting Mother are held in balance by the central stark vertical of the Cross behind and by the protective sway of the figures at each side. Colour is used to heighten the tragedy: on the left it is in a sombre key, then breaks into agitation in the gold and red of the stricken Nicodemus and the multicoloured garb of Mary Magdalen on the right.

Van der Weyden's enormous *Last Judgment* at Beaune seems a response to the challenge of the van Eycks' Ghent altarpiece. Rogier succeeds in treating a similar compositional problem with much greater unity and monu-mental effect. This suggests an Italian in-fluence, although it was probably begun before Rogier went to Italy; such an influence is specifically visible in his *Madonna and saints* at Frankfurt, arranged like a *sacra conversazione* (see p. 107) of Italian tradition, uniting saints and Virgin in a tiered semicircle. An *Entomb-ment* (not shown) in Florence is clearly connected with a similar subject by Fra Angelico.

In his portraiture, van der Weyden continued the themes established by van Eyck, but was again more sculptural in feeling: the planes of his faces are more sharply cut by light focused from the side or front, rather than diffused from slightly behind the sitter. There is, too, a greater decorative feeling, as in the transparent linen head-dress of the woman in the portrait in Washington. His people are still, tinged with a pensive melancholy.

The two other important artists active in the mid-fifteenth century were Petrus Christus (died 1472/3) in Bruges and Dirk Bouts (died 1475), working mainly, it seems, in Louvain. Christus was the painter nearest in style and talent to van Eyck, but his drawing is less decisive and he tends to simplify that all-embracing, all-accounting vision. His portrait of Edward Grimston (1446) is a charming but relatively generalized account of the sitter's likeness; it is novel in setting a head and shoulders against an interior. His *St Eligius with two lovers* (1449), a visual inventory of a goldsmith's shop, is much in the spirit of van Eyck, but, while it has again a novel element – a hint of genre story-telling – it is weaker in drawing and rather cluttered in composition.

Bouts' style seems nearer in feeling to that of Rogier van der Weyden, though lacking his dramatic intensity. His use of colour was highly individual, while his delight in land-scape was stronger than Rogier's. His master-piece, *The Last Supper* (1464-68), illustrating the institution of the Eucharist, is drawn out with solemn precision in true geometrical perspective, with Christ, mild and patient, exactly central. The elongated proportions of the figures are typical of Bouts, and will recur in the work of his followers, such as Justus of Ghent. Bouts' little *Young man* of 1462 has a similar modest, calm and reserved quality, extending the innovation of Christus' *Grim-ston* to show a landscape glimpsed through a window; but the modelling and lighting of the face is far subtler and more minute.

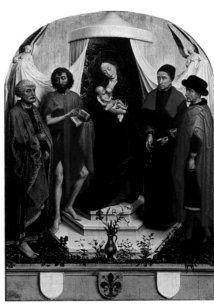

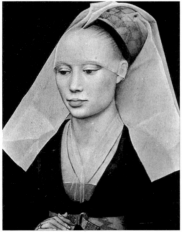

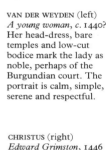

VAN DER WEYDEN (left)
A young woman, c. 1440?
Her head-dress, bare temples and low-cut bodice mark the lady as noble, perhaps of the Burgundian court. The portrait is calm, simple, serene and respectful.

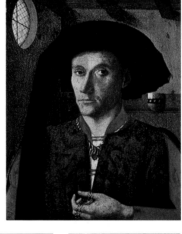

CHRISTUS (right)
Edward Grimston, 1446
In the manner of van Eyck, there is an attempt to trace the fall of light from the window on to the sitter. The device of placing in the hand a symbol of accomplishment or rank is persistent in 15th-century portraits.

VAN DER WEYDEN (left)
The Madonna and saints,
c. 1450
Cosmas and Damian, the Medici patron saints, appear on the right, and the arms of Florence beneath: this was surely an Italian commission.

BOUTS (right)
The Last Supper, central panel, 1464-68
Bouts was commissioned by the Confraternity of the Holy Sacrament in Louvain – hence this subject. The emotion is quiet, like the quietness during the Elevation of the Host in the Mass.

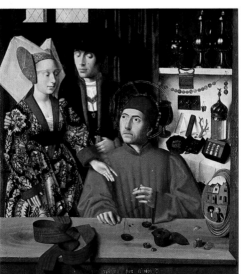

CHRISTUS (left)
St Eligius and two lovers, 1449
Objects are rendered as scrupulously as Jan van Eyck's – even pedantically – and surely have symbolic significance (now obscure); the couple have come to the saint to buy a ring.

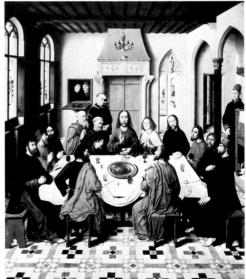

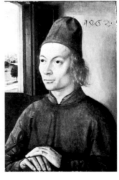

BOUTS (above)
A young man, 1462
The pose has an engaging touch of awkwardness or uncertainty. The hands rest as if upon the edge of the frame, a typical illusionistic device.

Netherlandish Art 3, and its Diffusion

The legacies of Robert Campin, Jan van Eyck and Rogier van der Weyden were taken up and amalgamated by Hugo van der Goes, in his brief but fruitful career in Ghent between about 1464 and 1482. In 1482 he died in a monastery, an insane melancholic, and the legend is recorded by a contemporary that he was driven mad by his inability to match the perfection of the van Eycks' Ghent altarpiece, although his own contribution established him securely as one of the greatest masters of early Netherlandish painting.

His Monforte altarpiece, probably of the early 1470s, shows Hugo fully mature. It is perhaps the most relaxed of his major works, painted with superb delicacy in very rich colours. His masterpiece is the Portinari altar-piece (finished before 1476), showing *The Adoration of the shepherds*. Here the colour is more subdued, and the mood is full of awe and even disquiet. The painting is very large, some six metres (19ft) wide including the wings, and full of minutely observed detail – examine the variety of texture of the garments, the still life and the modelling of the figures, faces and – Hugo's speciality – hands. The gentle hills and chill winter trees and sky in the right-hand wing constitute the most beautiful landscape painted in the north in the entire fifteenth century. Despite the naturalism, older traditions are drawn upon – the disparity of scale between the figures; the Gothic angels in elaborate fluttering robes, which contrast with the still birds in the bare trees; above all, the pervasive symbolism. The flowers, the birds, the colours of the draperies, the corn-sheaf, Joseph's discarded gloves and shoes – almost every detail hints at an episode in the Old Testament or in Christ's life to come. All these, but especially the figures, have an extra-ordinarily intense, or charged, presence, and in what is probably Hugo's last major work, *The death of the Virgin*, the undertones of anxiety in the Portinari altarpiece have sharpened to utter psychological disorientation.

The second major centre of art in the latter half of the century was Bruges. There Hans Memlinc (c. 1430/40-94) became the most successful and prolific painter, working primarily for a prosperous merchant clientèle. He was born in Germany, and is believed to have

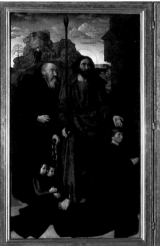

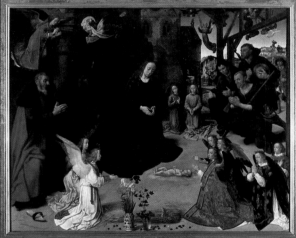

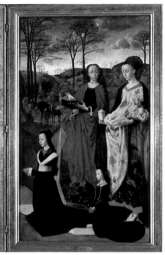

VAN DER GOES (right)
The Portinari altarpiece:
The Adoration of the shepherds, c. 1474-76
The figures seem heavy with the sorrows awaiting Christ and his Mother. The Child is tiny and isolated; the spacing of the figures is oddly unsettling. The earthy naturalism of the shepherds particularly impressed the Florentines when the altarpiece was installed in the city in 1483, and Ghirlandaio copied them in one of his frescos. The violets strewn in the foreground are among many details invested with symbolic meaning: they were associated with Lent, when they flower, and thus with Christ's Passion.

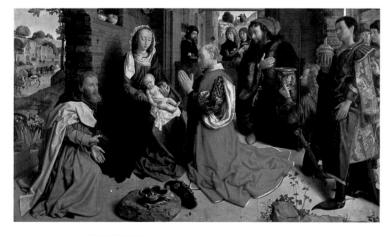

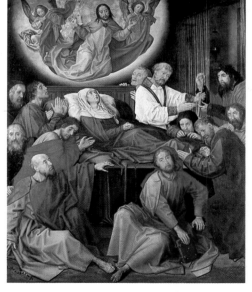

VAN DER GOES (left)
The Monforte altarpiece:
The Adoration of the Magi,
early 1470s
The setting is a ruined Romanesque building, rather than the decrepit stable favoured by Campin. This is Eyckian symbolism: Romanesque architecture symbolizes the old order (and ruined, its passing); Gothic symbolizes the new. The superbly painted land-scapes are an advance even on the aerial perspective of Jan van Eyck. The top of the picture, where angels once hovered, is missing.

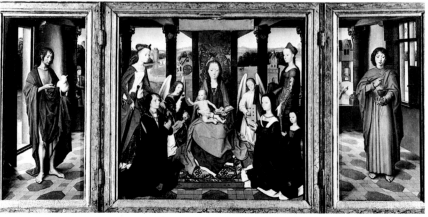

MEMLINC (left)
The Donne triptych:
The Virgin and Child with saints and donors, c. 1480
Memlinc's understatement has been little understood: this used to be thought an early work. In fact it shows his bland, undramatic style in its maturity. Sir John Donne, who ordered the work, travelled from England to Bruges on several occasions.

VAN DER GOES (above)
The death of the Virgin,
c. 1480
The apostle in the fore-ground, staring wildly out of the picture with his head-dress askew, is extra-ordinarily expressive of a world gone awry. Each apostle is an isolated individual, unable to offer his neighbour comfort. The colours have become strange, and ring harshly.

started in van der Weyden's workshop. In contrast to van der Goes, his style is almost bland, but consistently and flawlessly proficient, maintained by a large and well-run workshop. Memlinc's unobtrusive artistic personality has led to an undue depreciation of his achievement. The Donne triptych (probably of about 1480) is typical: calm and meditative, Madonna, saints and kneeling donors are all upright and symmetrical; there is a hint of music from one attendant angel, and the orderly countryside rolls away beyond. But his portraits are his most characteristic contribution: more than 25 are known. Often forming one half of a diptych, adoring a *Madonna* on the other half, they have always an air of composed contemplation, like lesser saints in their niches. They are unidealized, though the sitters are seen no doubt "at their best".

The diffusion of the Netherlandish vision through Western Europe in the fifteenth century was almost as pervasive as the Italian was to be in the sixteenth. Jan van Eyck, van der Weyden and van der Goes were all patronized by members of the Italian merchant community in the trade centres of Flanders, and their works were known and valued in Italy. A

friend and associate of van der Goes, Justus of Ghent (active *c.* 1460- after 1475) migrated to Italy, to work for Federigo da Montefeltro at Urbino; such immigrants disseminated Netherlandish oil techniques. In the 1470s Federigo seems also to have employed the Spaniard Pedro Berruguete (active 1474-1503: the portrait of Federigo attributed to him is reproduced on p.112). Netherlandish influence was particularly strong in central Spain, coalescing with the native taste in a distinctive Hispano-Flemish style. In England, by the end of the century, a pale imitation of Netherlandish painting was dominant; but in Germany the vigorous realism of the Netherlands took firmer root and was practised by individual artists of great quality.

In the middle Rhine area, Stephan Lochner (active 1442-51), who is said to have trained with Campin, was the leading painter. Lochner acknowledges Netherlandish perspective and naturalistic characterization, yet is very sweet in colour and softly delicate in his draperies, and still often uses the Gothic convention of the gold background. But very Eyckian indeed was Konrad Witz (*c.* 1400-47), working in the upper Rhine area, Basel and

Geneva. His *Miraculous draught of fish* is set in a closely observed Geneva lakescape with a fascinating and meticulous rendering of reflection and even refraction in water.

In France, the disruption of the Hundred Years War inhibited patronage, but there emerged nevertheless in Charles VII's court one major artist, Jean Fouquet (*c.* 1420-81). He was in Rome between 1443 and 1447, and knew the work of early Renaissance masters such as Fra Angelico as well as he knew the realism of the north. His figures, in settings of classical architecture, are singularly pure and monumental, and drawn with wonderful mastery. He also illuminated manuscripts, in which he made remarkable experiments with perspective. In the south, at René of Anjou's court in Provence, Netherlandish influence was also felt, and the illuminator of *Le Livre du Cuer d'Amour Espris* (The Book of Heart Smitten by Love, completed *c.*1465) applied Netherlandish techniques to scenes of allegorical romance with highly original results.

However, the most haunting image in French art of the period is on a traditional theme: "*The Avignon Pietà*" of about 1460 is at once harsh, austere and strikingly tender.

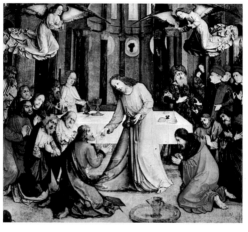

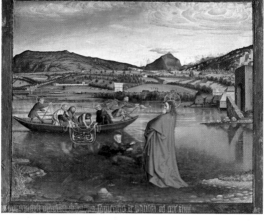

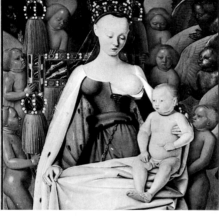

JUSTUS OF GHENT (above)
The Institution of the Eucharist, 1473-75
The elongated figures can be paralleled in van der Goes' and others' work, but may reflect Italian influence. Federigo da Montefeltro (with broken nose) appears on the right, copied from a medal(?).

LOCHNER (right)
The Adoration of the shepherds, 1445
The sweetness in the face of the Virgin, and in the animals and the angels, is typical of Lochner's brand of unworldly mysticism. All God's creatures seem gentle and lovable.

THE MASTER OF THE CUER D'AMOUR ESPRIS (right)
How Hope rescued Heart from the water, *c.*1465
The *Cuer d'Amour* is a typically Gothic romance, but its illustrations are in the latest realistic style – observe the variety of trees round the Black Knight.

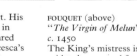

WITZ (above)
The miraculous draught of fish, *c.* 1444
Witz's lake is perhaps the first topographical land-

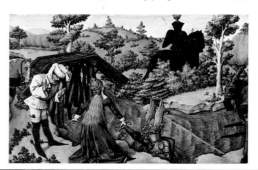

scape in Western art. His observation of light in water can be compared to Piero della Francesca's *Baptism* (see p. 110).

AVIGNON SCHOOL (right)
"*The Avignon Pietà*", *c.*1460
That delight in rendering the texture of things, so typical of Netherlandish art, has been put aside; instead the figures are like painted wooden sculptures. They are posed life-size on a shallow stage in strikingly expressive silhouettes.

FOUQUET (above)
"*The Virgin of Melun*", *c.* 1450
The King's mistress is said to have posed for

the Madonna, though she seems built out of spheres; Fouquet must have learnt his obsession with three-dimensional form in Italy.

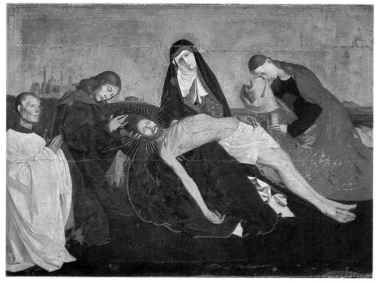

Bosch: The Garden of Earthly Delights

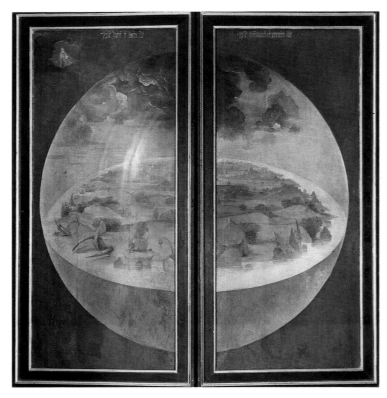

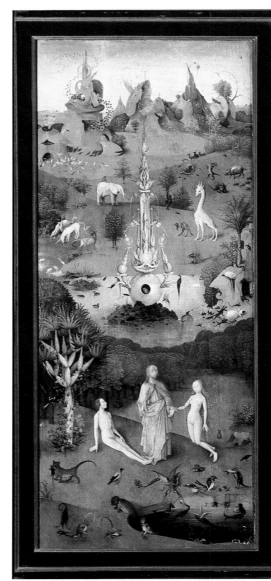

BOSCH (left and right)
The Garden of Earthly Delights, c. 1505-10

(left) with the wings closed: *The creation of the world* The world is housed in a crystal orb, like those often shown held by God the Father. He looks down on the third day from the top left: there are as yet no animals, only strange vegetable and mineral forms presaging those so weirdly and profusely developed in the interior of the triptych.

(right) with the wings open, left panel: *The creation of Eve*; middle panel: *The Garden of Earthly Delights*; right panel: *Hell* The central panel at first glance appears innocuous enough: a light green landscape, nudes disporting, pinks and blues, touches of scarlet. At a closer view, it resolves into separate groups and zones, into a weird motley of animal, technological, humanoid and architectural apparitions, and the nature of the Delight becomes ambiguous and disquieting.

The Garden of Earthly Delights by Jerome ("Hieronymus") Bosch (active *c.* 1470-1516) is in many ways the last fling of the Gothic Middle Ages. It is a huge triptych, more than two metres (7ft) high, painted, incredibly enough, about 1505-10, when in Italy the High Renaissance had already begun. Bosch, however, seems indifferent to the rationalism and realism of north or of south; instead, the symbolism underlying so much Netherlandish art – Jan van Eyck's work, or Hugo van der Goes' Portinari altarpiece – seems in the *Garden of Delights* to have run riot, and become entirely detached from reality. Its grotesque and fantastic elements are akin to the *drôleries* in the initials or margins of illuminated manuscripts, or to the gargoyles of Gothic cathedrals. But its pessimism, and love-hate obsession with the world of the senses turned sinful and terrifying, are representative of a deep-seated strain in the Christian outlook. In his own day Bosch's work was widely disseminated in engravings.

When closed, the two wings of the triptych show in bird's-eye view *The creation of the world.* They open to show, on the left, Adam waking to see (with pronounced interest) the newly created Eve; in the middle, the Garden of Delights, with a lake at the top with a bulb-based fantasy in the middle, which some have seen as a parody of the Fountain of Life at the centre of the van Eycks' Ghent altarpiece; on the right, Hell with no hint of Heaven. Even in Adam's Garden of Paradise, a cat is disposing of a mouse, and the ritual frolics of the Garden of Delights itself are unremittingly ominous.

The meaning of it all is by no means clear. Some of the symbolism seems fairly intelligible even now – for instance, the recurring giant soft fruits, strawberries, raspberries, as a symbol of carnal appetite – and other details presumably had particular associations for

Bosch's contemporaries. But though scholars have succeeded in penetrating the meaning of many objects in earlier Netherlandish painting, in the *Garden of Delights* the profusion of people, animals and things – real, legendary or the product of the artist's own fertile imagination – is baffling. The suggestion that the *Garden of Delights* is the visual manifesto of an heretical creed has been abandoned, not least because one of Bosch's greatest admirers was the ultra-Catholic Philip II of Spain. Psychoanalytical interpretation might seem more appropriate, but has not yielded definite results. Bosch's imagery had an immediate appeal to the Surrealists and their followers, but their hindsight is of little help in determining what meaning it had for Bosch.

However, virtually all we know of the man himself is the unsettling impact of his imagery. He worked in his native town of s'Hertogenbosch (Bois-le-Duc) apparently quite prosperously and comfortably: unlike van der Goes he was not an unusual citizen. Bosch's other compositions are not so unusual, though still unorthodox. In such paintings as *The Crowning with thorns* the evil physiognomies, exaggerating the earthiness of peasants' faces in earlier Netherlandish painting, are even comparable with some of Leonardo da Vinci's caricatures. There are hints of Bosch's strangeness in the usually charming paintings of Geertgen tot Sint Jans (Little Gerald of the Order of St John; active *c.* 1480-90) or in those of the so-called Master of the Virgo inter Virgines (active *c.* 1470-1500). Certain of Bosch's effects – notably the landscape elements in his work – are echoed in the work of Patinir or Metsys (see p. 160) and even the magic of Bruegel, though different, is not unrelated. However, the twentieth century's interest in Bosch is perhaps chiefly a reflection of its own interest in the Unconscious.

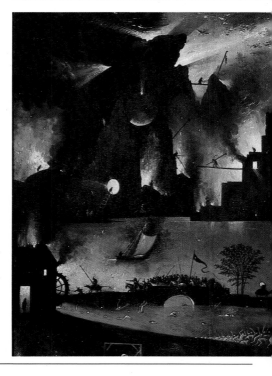

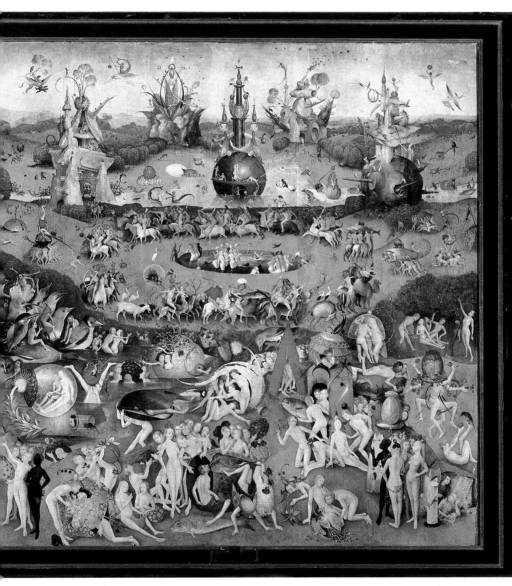

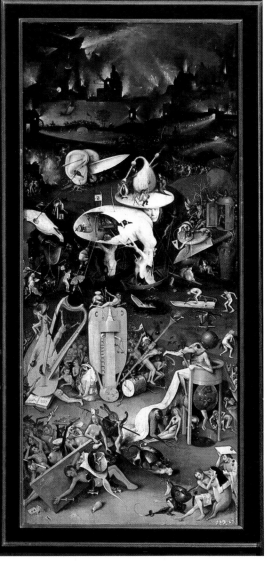

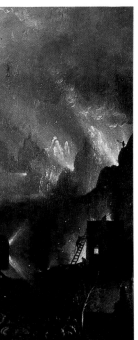

BOSCH (left)
The Garden of Earthly Delights, right panel, detail
In the rest of the painting the subject matter is extraordinary, but the technique conventional, even archaic. Such a sinister night, lit by terrifying eruptions, had not been seen before, and inspired imitations.

GEERTGEN TOT SINT JANS (below) *Christ as the Man of Sorrows*, c. 1490
Geertgen is perhaps better known for painting one of the earliest night-scenes, a touching *Nativity*. But here his theme of man's inhumanity is a parallel to the gloomy expectations of Bosch, and cries penitence.

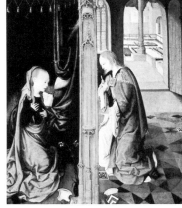

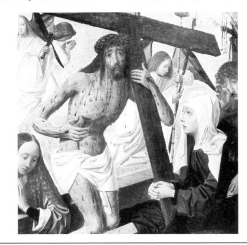

THE MASTER OF THE VIRGO INTER VIRGINES (above)
The Annunciation, c. 1495
This anonymous master painted probably in Delft. His figures are somewhat wooden and his pictures joyless, though sometimes harshly expressive. It is this pessimism that offers some parallel to Bosch.

BOSCH (below)
The Crowning with thorns, undated
The tormentors represent the four "humours" – phlegmatic, melancholic, sanguine and choleric. The picture seems related to Geertgen's *Christ*, but the symbolism and the enigma are peculiar to Bosch.

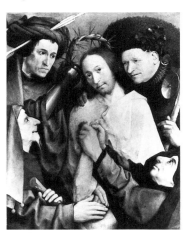

Donatello

Summing up the life and work of Donatello (1386-1466) a hundred years later, Vasari tells us that in Donatello the spirit of Michelangelo was pre-born. Certainly the similarities between the two Florentine sculptors are striking. Both were generous but formidable, not easily accessible personalities and dedicated artists, who early achieved a brilliant maturity. Both lived long lives, in which their search for emotional expression led them to remould and manipulate even to distortion the classical perfection of form they had recaptured.

Quite soon after he had completed his training under Ghiberti, some time after 1407, Donatello was producing works, rigorous in their nobility, that place him in the vanguard of the Renaissance. Already in his early figures he achieved profound psychological conviction, coupled with an unerring sense of theatre. His *St George* (c. 1415-17) is the second stride of Renaissance art after the 1401 competition for the bronze doors of Florence Baptistery. Originally helmeted and with a drawn sword in his hand, St George is a virile, handsome hero as naturalistic as any classical statue, but also alert; he does not move, but his face is so sharply formed, and his figure so sharply

outlined against his large niche, that he seems ready to move. So in the S. Croce *Annunciation*, also life-size, also quite early, a stage is set out for the figures, which are cut so deep and quick they seem to act. The stern prophets Donatello carved (1415-36) to be set high up on the campanile of Florence Cathedral are placed with foot overlapping the niche or looking down in a calculated relationship to the spectator; the heads are broadly and forcefully cut to register from below, but their somewhat severe presence is expressed chiefly by the weight of their deeply cut draperies, which are unprecedentedly monumental.

Even more than *St George* himself, the little relief on the base of the statue draws the attention of art historians, for though blurred by weathering it seems to demonstrate for the first time rationally calculated perspective. With it Donatello also created an entirely new concept in the art of relief carving, producing within an actual depth of millimetres the illusion of a large receding space. The perspective is more complex in his gilt-bronze *Feast of Herod* relief for the font of Siena Cathedral, which anticipates Alberti's 1435 account of single-vanishing-point perspective

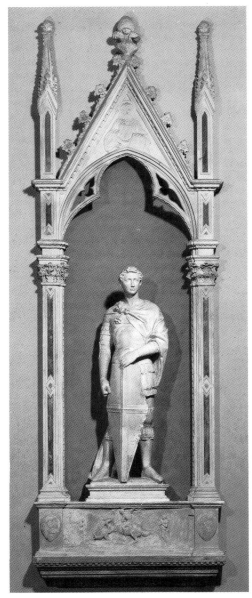

DONATELLO
St George, c. 1415-17
Standing in an unusually shallow niche outside Orsanmichele church, St George's life-size marble figure presents a striking silhouette, poised between defence and attack. On

the base, the relief with *St George and the dragon* is the first instance of *stiacciato*, the use of such low relief that the surface of the stone is drawn upon rather than carved – suggesting by pictorial means an atmospheric distance.

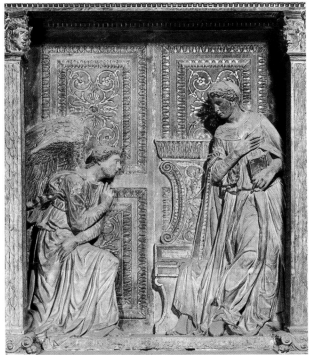

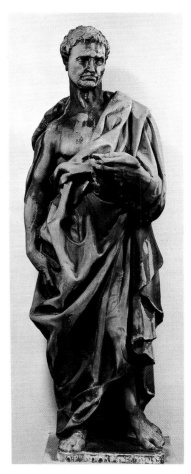

DONATELLO (below)
Jeremiah? 1423
Donatello's prophets for the campanile of Florence Cathedral are unsettling, unprepossessing figures, full of Old Testament fury. The unique drapery is not classical, nor Gothic.

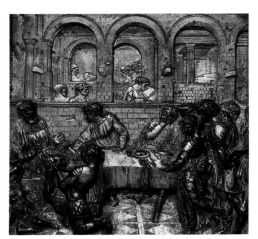

DONATELLO (left)
The feast of Herod, detail of the Siena Baptistery font, 1423-27
The architecture divides the action into three parts: while John the Baptist's head is brought in as if it were a dinner course in the rear, the musicians in the middle section are playing the accompaniment to the dance of Salome, who kicks back her foot on the right; on the left Herod and his fellow-revellers are polarized in shock as it arrives. Donatello makes calculated use of light and shade; the relief is below eye-level.

DONATELLO (above)
The Annunciation, c. 1430?
Carved in gilt *pietra dura* (grey sandstone), Mary and the angel are figures full of emotional insight: the timid, withdrawing Virgin suggests mingled humility and gratitude at God's awesome gift. But perhaps most striking at the time was the realism – Mary's twisting movement as she rises from her chair, the sensation of the angel's arrival. The whole makes a telling comparison with Simone Martini's Gothic, much more lyrical painting of the subject (see p.84).

by about a decade, but the technique is more traditional: the closer figures are in higher relief, the more distant ones in lower. Here the severe logic of the lines of sight, spelled out by the tiles of the floor, is used to contain in strong tension the explosion of horror of the figures starting back from St John's head proffered on the platter. The mathematician is revealed as a consummate master of narrative.

For the modelling of the *putti* (not shown) round this same font Donatello drew on antiquity, but surpassed it in the vivacity and unconstrained ease of the figures. Smooth and fluid modelling characterizes above all Donatello's *David*, justly one of the most famous sculptures of the Renaissance. It is a controversial work. It has been dated early, since in its sinuous elegance there seem traces of Gothic, and it has been dated late, because its sophisticated concept suggests the sort of humanist outlook that informed Botticelli's mythologies (see p. 118). However, here for the first time is revived the free-standing nude of classical times, and with superb effect – from every angle the body is expressive, the silhouette compact and beguiling, the limbs resting from an implicit movement.

In 1443, perhaps dissatisfied with the opportunities in Florence, Donatello took up a major commission in Padua – a life-size bronze equestrian statue of the army captain Gattamelata. The *Gattamelata* has a simple and austere dignity the equal of the antique *Marcus Aurelius* (see p. 51) in Rome, but it has also a certain introspective melancholy, a strangeness of atmosphere and proportion that grew more marked in Donatello's work as he grew older. In Donatello's second Paduan commission, seven almost life-size bronze statues in the round and 22 reliefs forming the great altar of the "Santo" (S. Antonio), the severe Madonna, rising and advancing to show the Child for worship, has many classical features, and a suavity and naturalism the equal of the best Hellenistic examples, but also an unclassical expressiveness that in Donatello's later work can become uncompromisingly harrowing.

An increasing restlessness characterizes Donatello's last years. He returned to Florence in 1454. From 1457 he was in Siena, preparing bronze doors for the Cathedral, a project which came to nothing. After 1461 he was back in Florence. Either then or before he carved the startlingly harsh *Mary Magdalen* in wood

for the Florence Baptistery. Painted wood was the usual medium of northern Gothic sculptors, and the anguish of the aged Magdalen's parched flesh and toothless grimace seems to reject Renaissance humanism. It must have been carved during one of the brief but violent religious reactions that shook Florence intermittently in the later fifteenth century, but the work is also highly personal; a similar desolation pervades Donatello's last work, the bronze reliefs for two pulpits in the church of S. Lorenzo. The subjects of these are well-known ones, but the design and imagery are quite out of the ordinary, with a forcefulness of expression, a spirituality barely emerging from despair, that rank them among the most sublime achievements of Western sculpture.

The influence of Donatello recurs again and again in the fifteenth century – not only in sculpture but also in painting (see pp. 105, 107) and (probably) in drawing, and not only in Florence but also in Siena and in Padua and northern Italy (see p. 120); only Michelangelo, however, equalled the majesty and anguish of his last visions – though certain Mannerists, such as the painter Rosso Fiorentino, seem to relive some of their torment.

DONATELLO (below) Reconstruction of the high altar, S. Antonio, Padua, 1446-54; (right) the central statue, *The Madonna and Child* The altar was dismantled then wrongly reassembled. A sculptural version of the *sacra conversazione* theme, the Madonna in silent conversation with saints, Donatello's altar brought the Florentine Renaissance to northern Italy, and had (especially its reliefs, see p. 120) immense influence, notably on Mantegna.

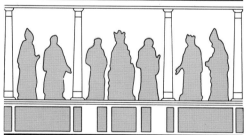

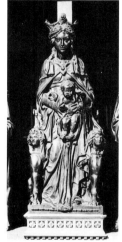

DONATELLO (right) *Gattamelata*, 1443-48 In his statue of Erasmo da Narni, the Venetian soldier known by his nickname, "the honeyed cat", Donatello transformed a traditional funerary portrait into an idealized image such as Roman antiquity had used to honour its emperors.

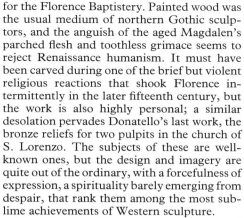

DONATELLO (below) *Lamentation on the dead Christ*, detail of one of the pulpits in S. Lorenzo, Florence, *c.* 1465 The effect is disjointed, unruly and intensely emotional – no sculptor had treated the subject with such violent movement and fury before.

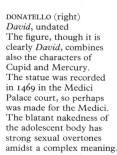

DONATELLO (left) *Mary Magdalen, c.* 1456? This mystic, introverted image reflects the free approach in Donatello's late sculpture, which has much of the extemporized quality of clay models – a forceful, raw and always personal expressiveness.

DONATELLO (right) *David*, undated The figure, though it is clearly *David*, combines also the characters of Cupid and Mercury. The statue was recorded in 1469 in the Medici Palace court, so perhaps was made for the Medici. The blatant nakedness of the adolescent body has strong sexual overtones amidst a complex meaning.

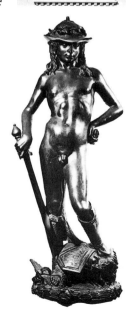

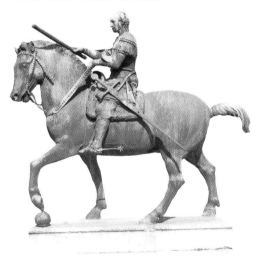

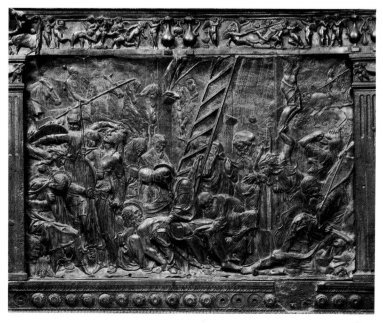

Masaccio: The Holy Trinity

Masaccio (1401-28?) probably completed his fresco *The Holy Trinity* in the north aisle of the church of S. Maria Novella in Florence at the age of 27, in the year when (so far as we know) he died. Who ordered this fresco and why is unclear, though the Lenzi family, corn chandlers, are believed to have been the donors. The fresco has been bruised by time, but five and a half centuries have not blurred its unmatched and magisterial statement of the fundamental principles of the early Renaissance.

The picture has a carefully organized perspective system on the lines first set out by Brunelleschi. The modelling and characterization of the figures have parallels in the sculpture of Donatello. But specifically Masaccio's is the exact control of directed light that unifies the whole, and the indivisible majesty of the conception. The composition is designed to be seen from eye-level as we stand in front of it. Nearest is the skeleton, stripped and stretched in its niche, with an inscription in Italian reading *I was once that which you are; and that which I am you will become.* Slightly above, and set back, kneeling outside the architectural frame, are the two donors in prayer. Above them again, and set back this time within the vault, the Virgin and St John attend the Cross planted on its outcrop of rock. The crucified Christ is supported by the outstretched hands of God the Father, looming majestic behind, who is the only figure seen foursquare in frontal view. Between the heads of Father and Son, in the image of a dove, hovers the Holy Spirit.

The perspective plotting is geometrically exact, the lines converge on a single vanishing point still visible to the searching eye, scored into the plaster beneath the paint. The architecture seems as real as the church in which it is painted – or, as Vasari put it, the painted chapel looks as if it opens through the wall. The classical detail – Corinthian pilasters that frame Ionic columns supporting a coffered vault – is worthy of Donatello or Brunelleschi, and the chamber so well planned in three dimensions that it could be built in stone.

In siting the Christian Passion within classical architecture, not against a Gothic gold background or in an insubstantial landscape, Masaccio suggests that its mystery is not only a matter of faith but is also penetrable by human reason. By his use of perspective, Masaccio anticipates the argument of Nicholas of Cusa, cleric, mystic, geometer and astronomer, that mathematics is the most certain of the sciences, a reflection on earth of heavenly light. The truths of mathematics are not subject to change; neither individual death nor the fall of empires can affect them; natural laws are the reflection or symbols of eternal laws, and it is within their logic that Masaccio's masterpiece is constructed.

Specifically invited into the picture by the Virgin's direct gaze and beckoning hand, the beholder becomes involved in the illusion, calculated to his own human measure, and appearing to his eyes exactly as does any earthly phenomenon. All, divine and human alike, living and dead, share here and now in an immutable eternity, through the mediation of Christ central on the Cross.

MASACCIO: *The Holy Trinity*, 1428

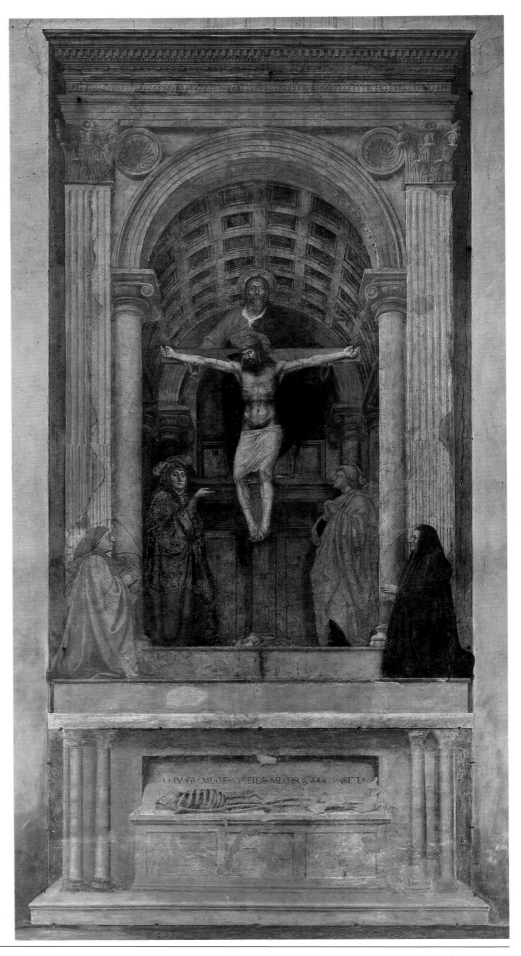

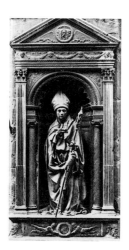

DONATELLO (left)
St Louis, c.1422-25
These classical columns
between pilasters were a
rare precedent for the
Trinity architecture. It
is known that Donatello
and Masaccio were friends,
since Donatello received
on Masaccio's behalf in
1426 money due to him
for his Pisa altarpiece.

BRUNELLESCHI? (below)
Crucifix, c.1412
It is rather appropriate
that the *Trinity* Christ
should have been based
on a work in the same
church by that pioneer
of Renaissance art in
Florence, Brunelleschi.

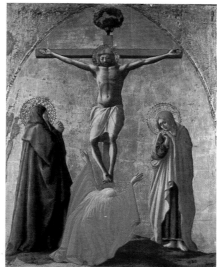

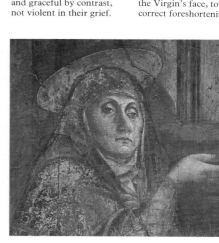

MASACCIO (above)
The Crucifixion, fragment
of the Pisa altarpiece, 1426
Christ's raised chest is
very forcefully modelled,
perhaps so as to stress his
asphyxiating agony. The
figures are strong, simple
shapes, highly expressive;
but note how solidly St
John's feet are planted.

LORENZO DI NICCOLO
GERINI (right)
The Holy Trinity, late
14th century
In other pictures of the
Trinity, God the Father is
shown enthroned; save for
Masaccio's this is the only
known example in which
He stands. Christ's Cross
rests on a rock with a skull,
Adam's skull; his blood
falling on it redeems the
human race. In Masaccio's
fresco the skull has been
replaced by a skeleton.

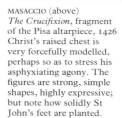

MASOLINO (above)
The Crucifixion, c.1428
Masolino's figures show
Masaccio's influence –
they often shared work
(see over) – but are gentle
and graceful by contrast,
not violent in their grief.

MASACCIO (below)
The Holy Trinity, detail
Geometrically calculated
parallelograms, scored in
the plaster, "squared up"
from cartoons, underlie
the Virgin's face, to ensure
correct foreshortening.

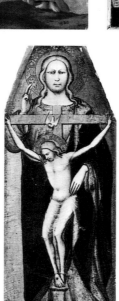

MASACCIO'S PERSPECTIVE
The left-hand diagram
reveals the logic of the
perspective Masaccio used:
seen here as it were side-
on, the figures are placed
back in explicitly defined
layers of depth. The line
(AA) marks the picture
plane, the window through
which the viewer sees the
illusion, standing a few
paces back. The floor of
the chapel is tilted down
out of sight, since it is
above the observer's viewpoint; the viewpoint is in
fact precisely level with
the top of the altar: the
skeleton under it is seen
from above. None of this,
however, is permitted to
interfere with the impact
of the figures, who are all
of the same size and who
all seem to press against
the picture plane. This
play of flat surface and
illusory space is typical
of early Renaissance art.

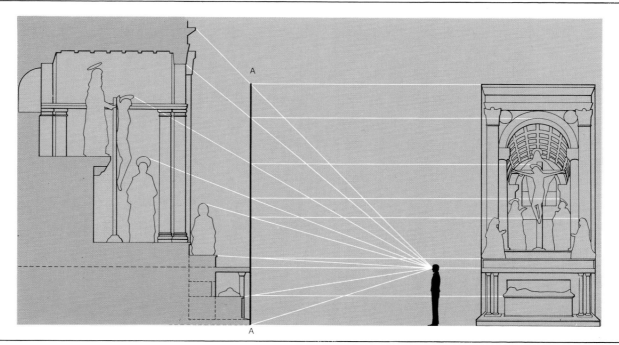

Italian Renaissance Painting 1

In three works, between 1424 and 1428, Masaccio established what we call Renaissance painting. He introduced into public art the experiments Brunelleschi had made a little earlier with geometrical perspective; he revived the sculptural modelling of Giotto, translating Donatello's stringent characterizations into paint; and he fixed and ennobled his grave figures in controlled and directed light. He was, in the words of the art historian Berenson, "Giotto born again, starting where death had cut short his advance".

Masaccio's three great works were *The Holy Trinity* (see preceding page); an altarpiece, now dismembered, painted in 1426 for the Carmelite church in Pisa; and frescos for the Brancacci family's chapel in S. Maria del Carmine, the Carmelite church in Florence. Here *The tribute money*, a rare subject, alludes perhaps to an episode in Florentine politics, the imposition of a property tax, which the rich Brancacci family is said to have opposed; and if so it can be dated 1427. Christ and his apostles stand – simple, substantial figures, tellingly present – in a real landscape, reflecting the profile of the Pratomagno hills east of Florence, and controlled within a Brunelleschian

perspective; in the expressiveness of their bodies and gestures, they reproduce not only Donatello's sculptural form, but also his sense of character in action.

Masaccio shared the commission with the older Masolino (1383/4-1447), and the contrast between their work illuminates vividly the dramatic step Masaccio had taken. In Masaccio's *Expulsion of Adam and Eve* the rejected couple express in every sinew of their massively modelled bodies their shame and anguish; in Masolino's *Fall of Man* there is linear elegance, a Gothic lyricism. Although Masolino was influenced by Masaccio, his Gothic training still tells in the softness and relative sweetness of form and character: the drama is absent.

Masaccio never effected a revolution in taste as Giotto had done, and his example, though instructive, was too vigorous and too demanding for his successors. Florentine patrons, chief among them the Medici, still found irresistible the elegant, decorative tradition to which Masolino belonged. After Cosimo de' Medici had manoeuvred his return from exile in 1434, the Medici family ruled the city like princes in all but name; like princes, they

favoured paintings closer in feeling to the International Gothic which flourished in the courts of northern Italy.

This can appear even in the work of Paolo Uccello (1396/7-1475), an eccentric figure, but one of genius. A dedicated mathematician, Uccello's application of theory in his painting often seems pedantic, and in his fresco *The Flood* (about 1445) perspective complexity conflicts strangely with the tremendous assurance of the great figure in the right foreground. There is again paradox in the large battle decorations he painted to embellish an apartment in the Medici Palace, celebrating a lucky Florentine victory over the Sienese in 1432. These have little sense of real war, rather the ring of medieval pageantry, and Uccello's obsession with perspective merges with a fascination for heraldic patterning. A different poetry is expressed in his very late work *The night hunt:* the perspective is employed more subtly, and the strange scene, its dusk echoing almost audibly with the cries of the hunt, is distinctly romantic in feeling – it owes something perhaps to Netherlandish painting.

Fra Filippo Lippi (1406-69) stands again apart. He was a monk, but was expelled from

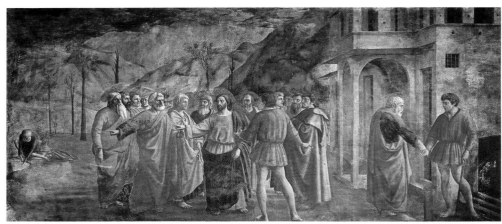

MASACCIO
(left) *The tribute money*, 1425-28; and (below) detail The taxman (the figure poised with his back to us) demands from Christ his shekel, which is found in the mouth of a fish caught by Peter on the left, and

paid over by him on the right. In each figure, the line from the weight-bearing foot to the head is perpendicular – hence its solid look. The heads are all based on classical heads, while Masaccio built his figures like Donatello's.

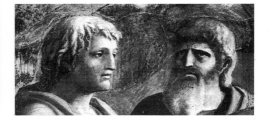

MASACCIO (below)
The expulsion of Adam and Eve, 1425-28
Though Masaccio learnt from classical art, there is nothing heroic in these figures; rather they show the influence of Giovanni Pisano's emotionalism.

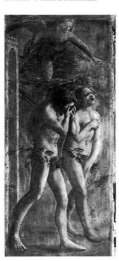

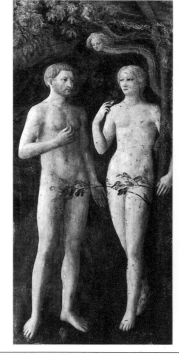

MASOLINO (left)
Adam and Eve under the Tree of Knowledge, 1425-28
Placed directly opposite Masaccio's *Expulsion* in the Brancacci Chapel, Masolino's work shows in contrast an interest not in the structure but in the surface of forms, though he, too, models by light and shade, much like Masaccio.

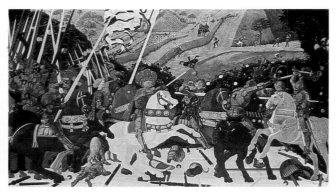

UCCELLO (above)
The Flood, c. 1445
This strange picture is a virtuoso performance in the use of perspective, and has two vanishing points. Wind blows through the draperies, as Alberti had recommended in his *On Painting* not long before.

UCCELLO (left)
The Battle of San Romano, c. 1455
Vasari relates that often Uccello sat up late into the night, and when called to bed by his wife, would cry: "Oh what a lovely thing is this perspective!"

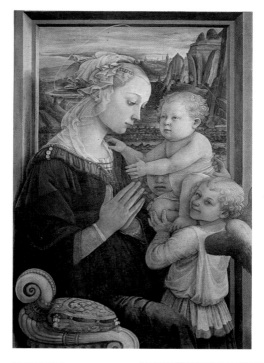

his order for abducting a nun – his patrons the Medici seem to have been indifferent to this peccadillo. The story goes that he was inspired to become a painter while watching Masaccio at work, and in his early paintings, such as his *Annunciation* of about 1440, his dependence on Masaccio is evident in the deep recession and unifying light. But the composition is somewhat illogical, while the drama so crucial in Masaccio gives way to a more static presentation, like a tableau – the kneeling angel is still, the Virgin rather acquiescent. But see the clear, sometimes rather arbitrary, play of colour, and the seductive charm of his flowing line: these are characteristic of Filippo Lippi. There are also elements probably due to Netherlandish example – the incidental domestic detail, the sweetness of expression in the faces and the delightful view through the arches into an enclosed garden. In Filippo's later work, recollections of Masaccio vanish. His delicate line conjures visions of rapt Madonnas, suffused with the radiance of early summer, which anticipate Botticelli. Yet in his frescos at Prato (between 1452 and 1464) the medium seems to have encouraged an epic grandeur not apparent in his altarpieces.

Domenico Veneziano (died 1461) came, if his name is an indication, from Venice, but was working in Florence by the late 1430s. His mastery was in the handling of light: his luminous colour, and the subtle way in which he modulated and reconciled light from different sources, infusing even the shadows, led Vasari to infer that he was already using northern oil techniques, though this is doubtful. Although his works are rare, his influence was far-reaching, most importantly on Piero della Francesca – who worked with him as a young man – but also on Filippo Lippi's son, Filippino Lippi. The signed St Lucy altarpiece, dating from about 1445, is Domenico's major surviving work; the delicate character of his figures acknowledges the Florentine ideals served by Filippo Lippi, but he also was aware of Masaccio and influenced by Donatello. This altarpiece has wonderful little predella panels, now scattered, of which the most delightful is *St John the Baptist in the desert*. St John is, surprisingly, nude (recalling most closely perhaps Ghiberti's sculpture), and seemingly pagan rather than Christian. There is no such ambivalence in the work, equally brilliant in light and colour, of the Blessed Fra Angelico.

FILIPPO LIPPI
The Madonna and Child with two angels, c. 1460
Filippo enshrines the enduring Florentine love of sweetness and charm; he was a prime inspiration for the Pre-Raphaelites.

FILIPPO LIPPI (right)
The Annunciation, c. 1440
Like much of Filippo's work, the altarpiece is exquisitely detailed, and the finesse of his finish was unrivalled. The arbitrary orange of the building placed at the vanishing point is a deliberate emphasis. The Virgin echoes Donatello's in S. Croce (see p. 102).

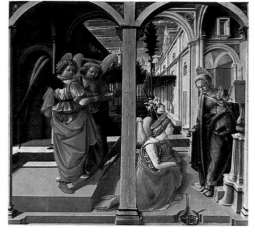

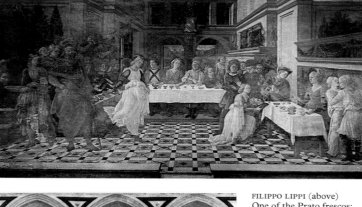

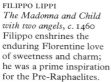

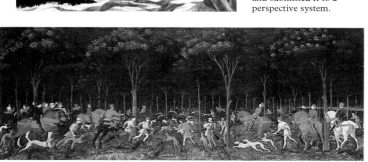
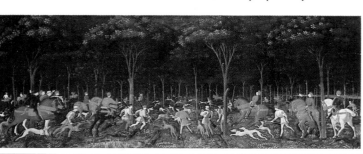

DOMENICO VENEZIANO (left)
St John the Baptist in the desert, c. 1445-48
The nude form almost has the look of bronze about it, so closely is it related to sculpture. Though they are stylized, the rocks behind enclose coherent space.

UCCELLO (below)
The night hunt, c. 1460
As in *The Battle of San Romano*, so here Uccello has taken a subject typical of International Gothic and submitted it to a perspective system.

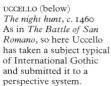

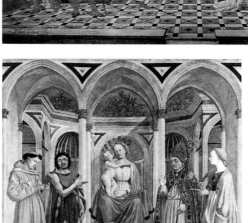

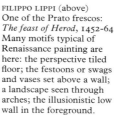

FILIPPO LIPPI (above)
One of the Prato frescos:
The feast of Herod, 1452-64
Many motifs typical of Renaissance painting are here: the perspective tiled floor; the festoons or swags and vases set above a wall; a landscape seen through arches; the illusionistic low wall in the foreground.

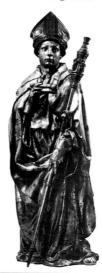

DOMENICO VENEZIANO (above) The St Lucy altarpiece, c. 1445-48
The Virgin and saints share one setting (even though the old divisions of Gothic altarpieces are recalled in the arcade) in complex perspective. Two sources of light cast differently slanting shades setting off the heads of both Virgin and Child.

DONATELLO (right)
St Louis, c. 1422-25
The gilt-bronze statue once stood in a niche in the wall of Orsanmichele. Forming half of the semicircle typical of the so-called *sacra conversazione*, St Lucy and St Zenobius, on the right of Domenico's picture, derive from it, the one in pose, the other in the fall of the drapery.

Fra Angelico: The San Marco Annunciation

Fra Angelico (born *c.* 1395 or 1400; died 1455) is quintessentially part of early Florentine Renaissance painting, and yet an individual and untypical personality. The critic Ruskin termed him "not an artist properly so-called but an inspired saint", but he was very much a professional, running a workshop, aware not only of his predecessors but of contemporary trends in art, and taking up commissions in Florence, Cortona, Orvieto and Rome (where he died). In early youth, however, he entered the Dominican monastery at Fiesole, just above Florence, and thereafter led the pious life of a friar.

The Observant Dominicans whom Fra Angelico joined were a reforming movement within the order, emphasizing the need for direct and simple preaching, and rejecting mystic emotionalism. Giovanni Dominici, former Prior of Angelico's convent, had stressed that, steeped in the study of the natural world and inspired by love, the mind of man could grasp the nature of the heavenly world. Fra Angelico's painting is correspondingly clear, direct and optimistic; the certainty of his line-drawing, the radiant light of his pictures and their lucid, shining colours all express this, and also convey irresistibly the painter's own sweetness of nature.

Even when Angelico's subject is high tragedy, the message is not of horror or grief – or even sadness. His *Deposition*, the dead body of Christ being taken down from the Cross, is a *magnificat*, a serene hymn of praise and thanksgiving. The format was not determined by Fra Angelico, but he was able to dispose his imagery very happily within its three divisions: in the centre the body of Christ is displayed with ceremonial gravity; on the left the holy women, with the shroud, are gathered about the kneeling Mary; on the right Florentine worthies in contemporary dress stand in contemplation. On the left, it has been said, the religion of the heart; on the right, that of the mind. To left and right recede landscapes of magical beauty, which have elements still of International Gothic – the flights of angels, the Jerusalem built rather fantastically in Florentine architecture – but they are handled with a sophistication hitherto unseen in Florentine painting. The broad treatment of the draperies, and the figures modelled by light, recall Masaccio (and also Giotto); the tender delicacy of Christ's nude body indicates awareness of Ghiberti's sculpture. The sense of ritual, the singing colours, the flood of heavenly light – these, however, are unmistakably Fra Angelico.

Masaccio had painted chiefly for the Carmelites, who even earlier than the Dominicans had realized the use of naturalism in stating their message with force and immediacy. It is not surprising to see Masaccio's influence already in Fra Angelico's early *Annunciation* for Cortona, although it is tempered by the gentler vision of Masolino. Here also is Brunelleschi's classicizing architecture and his perspective system, characteristically applied towards doctrinal ends: the recession leads from the Virgin, the new Eve, back to the little figures of Adam and the old Eve: Paradise lost is linked to hope of redemption. Fra Angelico's style is always governed by the doctrinal

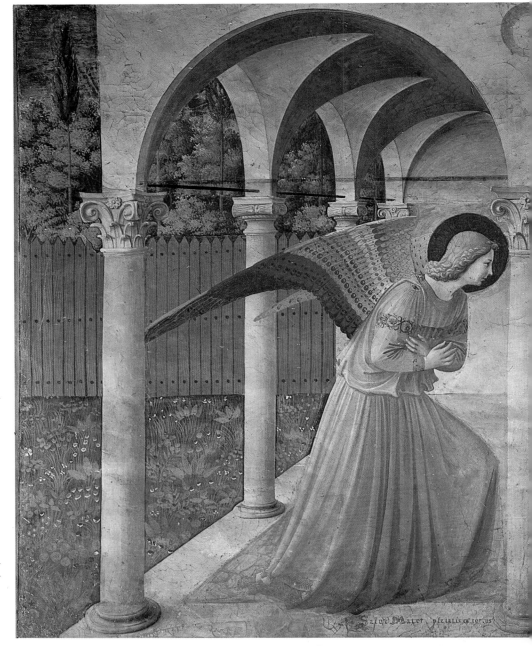

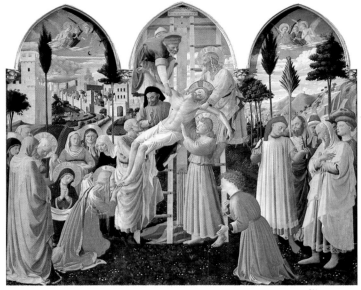

FRA ANGELICO
The Deposition, c. 1440?
Fra Angelico took over the commission from the Gothic master Lorenzo Monaco, who died in 1425, having already prepared the panels in their present shape, and partially painted the frame. Fra Angelico divided his composition according to the format, but joined the three panels in a single coherent space. St John, in blue beneath the Cross, closely resembles the St John painted by Masaccio in the *Tribute money*. Nicodemus, in the red cap on the right showing the crown of thorns and the nails, is said to be a portrait of Michelozzo, the architect who designed the new buildings at S. Marco.

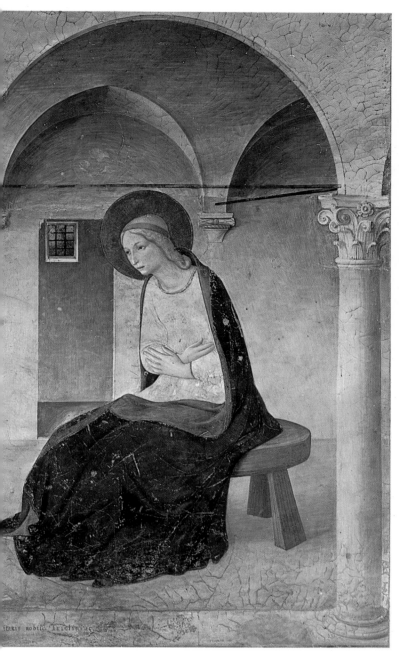

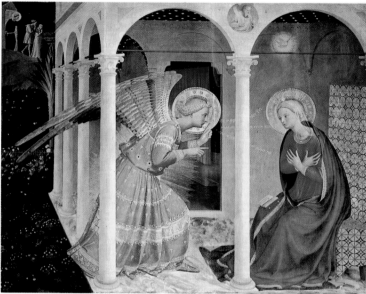

FRA ANGELICO (left)
The Annunciation, at the
top of the dormitory stairs
in S. Marco, *c.* 1450?

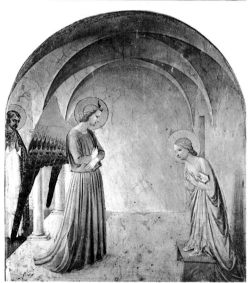

FRA ANGELICO
(above) *The Annunciation*,
for S. Domenico, Cortona,
c. 1428-32
The silhouettes of the
figures and the spatial
structure are subtly co-
ordinated, so that the tip
of the angel's wing is on
the picture's centre line.
In the left half, doom; in
the right half, hope of
redemption. This work
formed the basis for many
later *Annunciations*.

(right) *The Annunciation*,
in Cell 3 of the dormitory
of S. Marco, *c.* 1441
St Peter Martyr looks
on, motionless in prayer.
The corridor in which the
figures stand is closed; the
import is concentrated in
the pose and placing of the
Virgin and the angel.

function of his art. Its development can be
traced in two other *Annunciations*, both frescos
painted in the dormitory of the monastery at S.
Marco in Florence where the Fiesole Dominicans moved in about 1437.

Fra Angelico and his assistants painted the
chapels, refectory, cloisters and the cells of the
dormitory of the new premises. Each cell had
one window, and one fresco as a window on the
divine world. In these little chambers of utter
simplicity the paintings are entirely austere:
the *Annunciation* in cell 3 presents the scene in
its most essential terms, pared down from the
Cortona version. Fra Angelico's masterpiece,
the *Annunciation* at the head of the dormitory
stairs, was painted probably after he had been
in Rome, at the cultured court of Pope
Nicholas V. The Virgin's humility is both
plainer and more haunting than before; the
articulation of space is exquisite and yet grand.
The balance of shapes and structure in the
picture is delightful in purely abstract terms.

FRA ANGELICO (right)
*St Stephen preaching and
addressing the Jewish
council, c.* 1447-49
St Stephen's preaching
caused him to be
summoned before the
council, and his profession
of faith there caused him
to be stoned. The two
episodes form part of a
cycle of scenes from the
lives of SS. Stephen and
Lawrence, painted in
fresco in the private chapel
of Pope Nicholas V in the
Vatican. Their wealth of
detail and rich colouring
set them apart from Fra
Angelico's S. Marco
frescos – reflecting the
difference between the life
of humble monks and the
procedural pomp of the
papacy. The spatial clarity
and solid figures directly
recall the work of Masaccio.

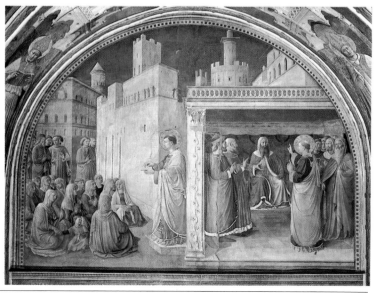

Italian Painting 2: Tuscany in Mid-Century

Line-drawing as the basis for design was to become increasingly dominant in Florentine art during the fifteenth century, and the fame of Florence, as the leading school of the arts in Italy, was centred on its *disegno*, its compositional draughtsmanship. We have already seen the emphasis on graceful contour in the later work of Filippo Lippi; his pupil, Botticelli, became the greatest master of sinuous line. Even in the clear light and colour of Fra Angelico, line is the controlling element, and in the work of his chief assistant and follower, Benozzo Gozzoli (*c.* 1421-97), the influence of Masaccio almost peters out, and line, not light, is used to detail his multitudinous figures.

Gozzoli, trained as a goldsmith, was a tireless painter of colourful pageantry. His greatest work was a lavish commission to fresco the walls of the private chapel of the Medici Palace, in 1459. By this time Cosimo de' Medici was aging, and the work was organized by his son Piero the Gouty, whose taste was more courtly than his father's, favouring the glittering and ornate. In Gozzoli's fresco, *The journey of the Magi*, an exotically costumed, animated procession winds its way round the walls of the room; guided by the star in the ceiling above, it travels through fantastic landscapes towards the altarpiece, a *Nativity* by Filippo Lippi. It is full of portraits from the life: included in the crowd are members of the Medici family. The approach and style recall Gentile da Fabriano and International Gothic. Gozzoli's second greatest work was a series of Old Testament frescos (damaged in World War II and now very faded) in the Campo Santo in Pisa – they, too, teem with figures, engaged in contemporary pursuits.

A much stronger artist, who acknowledged Masaccio at least in his method of modelling in light, was Andrea del Castagno (*c.* 1421-57). Such is the extraordinarily harsh vigour of his drawing, that his work seems sometimes a literal translation of Donatello's clear-cut sculpture into paint. The figures he painted between the ribs of the dome of the apse of S. Zaccaria during his sojourn (1441-42) in Venice are forced by an inner emotion into poses of great strain, but their vitality and strength derive from close anatomical study. Castagno's *Last Supper* in the monastery of S. Apollonia in Florence is an early example of illusionism, painted as if it were an extra bay on the end wall of the refectory. Castagno's

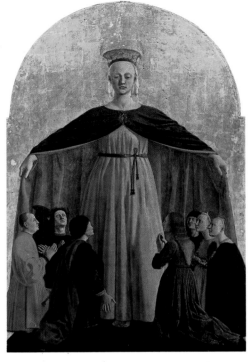

GOZZOLI (below)
Man treading grapes, detail of the Campo Santo frescos, 1468-97
The damaged frescos are now difficult to read, but even in their pristine state the crowded incidental detail must have swamped the biblical narrative.

PIERO DELLA FRANCESCA
The Compassionate Madonna, begun 1445
The frontal Madonna, a massive cylindrical form, imposingly solid against the unearthly gold ground, protectively encircles the human beings who invoke her (among them perhaps

Piero himself, at the back of the left-hand group). The abstract, geometrical quality of Piero's art transforms his compositions into devotional images of remarkable power; the Virgin's head has even been compared to African cultic masks.

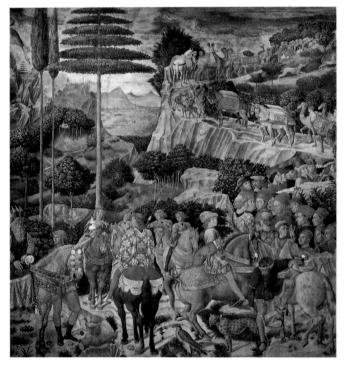

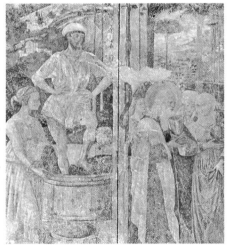

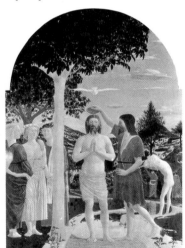

GOZZOLI (above)
The journey of the Magi, detail, 1459-61
The numerous animals leap, hop, sit and fly like those from International Gothic copybooks. But the figures, though decorative, are keenly observed, and the foreshortening is skilful.

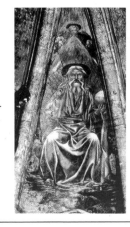

CASTAGNO (right)
God the Father, detail of S. Zaccaria apse, 1442
The turbulent grandeur of the drapery recalls the prophets for the campanile of Florence Cathedral by Donatello (see p. 102): this figure, too, is high up.

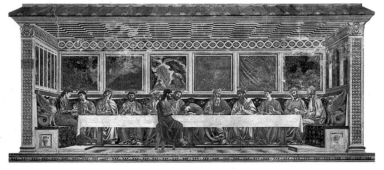

CASTAGNO (above)
The Last Supper, c. 1445-50
Andrea's archaeological

interest is displayed, for instance, in the griffins at each end of the bench: they were a popular motif in

antique furniture. Judas was always placed alone in front of the table until Leonardo (see p. 128).

PIERO DELLA FRANCESCA (above) *The baptism of Christ*, c. 1440-50
Here is a famous example of Piero's naturalism: the water of the river in which Christ stands is rendered as transparent in the foreground, then as opaque and reflecting in the background; the change comes just at Christ's feet, where tiny bubbles are visible in the original.

tautness of line and strained poses resemble the work of Antonio del Pollaiuolo a little later, but also anticipate Mantegna, who was to take further Castagno's interest in illusionism and in archaeological detail.

The greatest painter of the mid-fifteenth century was Piero della Francesca (1416?-92). Piero worked in his youth as the assistant of Domenico Veneziano in Florence, and his abiding interest in mathematics was no doubt formed there, but he worked mainly in provincial centres of southern Tuscany – Arezzo, his native Borgo San Sepolcro – in Urbino, in Ferrara and in Rome. In his own time he was famous, but by the seventeenth century he was almost forgotten, and the recognition of his true stature is fairly recent, fostered by a twentieth-century urge to discover abstract essentials even in the most naturalistic art.

An early work of Piero's is the monumental *Madonna della Misericordia* (The Compassionate Madonna) commissioned in 1445 for Borgo San Sepolcro. The almost palpable weight of the Madonna indicates that Piero had looked long and hard at Masaccio. The rigorous geometrical structure underpinning the composition is, however, alien to Masac-

cio, and the different scales of the figures and their setting, a gold background, are archaic: there is already here an other-worldly quality that inhabits all Piero's work. The characters' serene gravity, the relatively light tonality and the clear colour are found in another early work, *The baptism of Christ*. Here in the modelling there is much less contrast between light and shade; instead Piero's characteristic, almost shadowless, all-pervading light (developed in part from Domenico Veneziano) holds the action in a meditative, magic spell. Piero was to handle the modulation of tone and colour with a subtlety that has never been surpassed; his figures, though their shadowing is so slight, are nevertheless as solid as any ever painted. Piero wrote treatises on mathematics and on perspective in painting, but despite his fascination with geometry he was alive to the naturalism of Netherlandish painters, as his landscape backgrounds demonstrate (he may have met Rogier van der Weyden at Ferrara). In Piero's work the claims of line and colour, of naturalism and abstract construction are reconciled uniquely.

Some of Piero's greatest paintings were made for the court of Federigo da Montefeltro

at Urbino (see over). But the major commission of his career was the fresco cycle, *The history of the true Cross*, in the choir of S. Francesco at Arezzo, which occupied him from about 1452 for twelve years – Piero always painted with slow deliberation. The Cross, tangible proof of redemption, was perhaps the most prized of all sacred relics. The story is taken from the *Golden Legend*, a collection of lives of the saints, full of miracles and wonder-working, that remained popular from the Middle Ages to the Reformation. It is divided into ten episodes, starting with *The old age and death of Adam*, for a sprig of the Tree of the Knowledge grew into the wood of which the Cross was made. Subsequent scenes trace the history of the wood in the Old Testament and after the Crucifixion. The calculated perspective and precise use of line and pale colour convey, paradoxically, grandeur and mystery; the narrative and decorative functions of the whole are fulfilled and reconciled in perfect balance. In silence and simplicity Piero finds inexhaustible variety, regardless of scale – later in the majestic, mute triumph of *The Resurrection*, almost life-size, or in the tiny panel of *The Flagellation* at Urbino (see over).

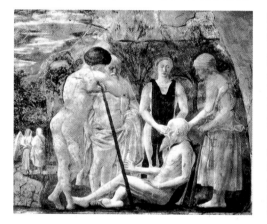

PIERO DELLA FRANCESCA
Details from the Arezzo frescos, *c.* 1452-64
(left) *The old age and death of Adam*
The hard consequence of the expulsion from Eden was eventual death. Adam's last moments are witnessed by the members of his family with restrained grief.

(below) *The victory over Khosroes*
The Persian king had removed the Cross from Jerusalem; the Emperor Heraclius here regains it, in frozen, eerie pageantry.

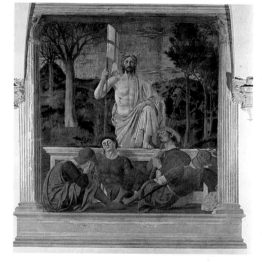

PIERO DELLA FRANCESCA
(left) *The Resurrection*, *c.* 1463
Christ holding a banner is a Byzantine image, a little archaic; but the sleeping soldiers are a brilliant essay in Renaissance foreshortening. Symbolic dead trees on the left sprout into new life on the right.

PIERO DELLA FRANCESCA
(below) Detail from the Arezzo frescos: *The Annunciation*
The first episode in Christ's life stands for its whole in the *History of the Cross* frescos, which omit the Passion. Architecture both symbolically divides human and divine spheres and plots out the space.

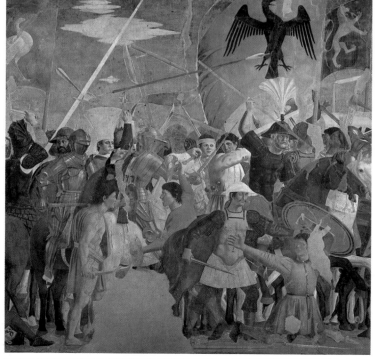

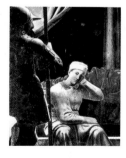

PIERO DELLA FRANCESCA
(above) Detail from the Arezzo frescos: *The dream of Constantine*
According to the legend, Constantine's dream of the Cross (shining from above) won the Roman Empire to Christianity. In this detail it can be observed how the gentle glow of light falling from above into the centre is carefully plotted as it creeps round the edges of the armour of the guard.

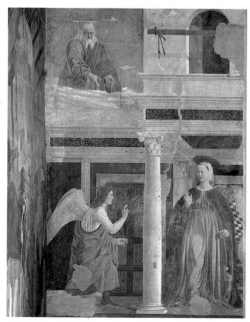

Piero della Francesca: The Flagellation

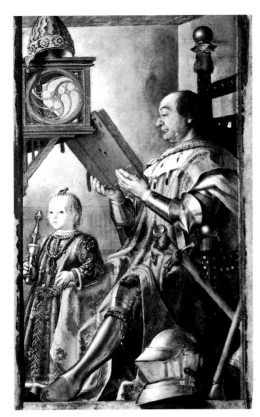

The dukes or despots ruling the local centres of power in northern and central Italy were always on the lookout for artists to adorn their courts and enhance their prestige. In the mid-fifteenth century they turned most commonly, as one might expect, to the Netherlands or to Florence. The Este in Ferrara briefly obtained Rogier van der Weyden about 1450; Sigismondo Malatesta, tyrant of Rimini, had a classical, humanist monument to himself, the Tempio Malatestiano, designed by Alberti, and his portrait painted by Piero della Francesca in 1451. Alberti moved on to build for the Gonzagas in Mantua; Piero went to Urbino, to the court of Federigo da Montefeltro. In Federigo's magnificent palace, denuded of most of its treasures in the sixteenth century, now resides one of Piero's finest paintings, the small panel of *The flagellation of Christ*.

Piero's picture is not a straightforward representation of an episode in Christ's Passion, since the Flagellation is relegated to a secondary position in the middle ground. Dominant are the three figures in the foreground, on whom the further meaning of the picture must depend, but their identification still poses puzzling questions. Though it no longer exists, in the nineteenth century a phrase from Psalm 2 was written beneath the picture – *Convenerunt in unum* (They met together). Those who met together were princes and kings of the earth, with the purpose of stirring up war against the Lord and his Christ. The Psalm is quoted in the Acts of the Apostles, where the princes are identified with Pontius Pilate, seated here in judgment, and Herod, perhaps the man in luminous grey who directs the flagellators. Grouped together by some com-

BERRUGUETE? (above) *Federigo da Montefeltro*, 1477
Soldier, diplomat, scholar and informed patron of the arts, Federigo, Duke of Urbino, was a Renaissance "complete man". He wears the Garter awarded by the King of England and the Ermine bestowed by the King of Naples; the mitre is from the Pope. His son Guidobaldo is beside him.

PIERO DELLA FRANCESCA (below) *Federigo da Montefeltro, c.*1472-73
On one panel of a diptych Federigo looks towards his wife, profiled on the other. Behind them atmospheric, panoramic views suggest that Piero learned from Netherlandish painters. On the back of the two panels Federigo and his wife are shown seated in allegorical triumphal cars.

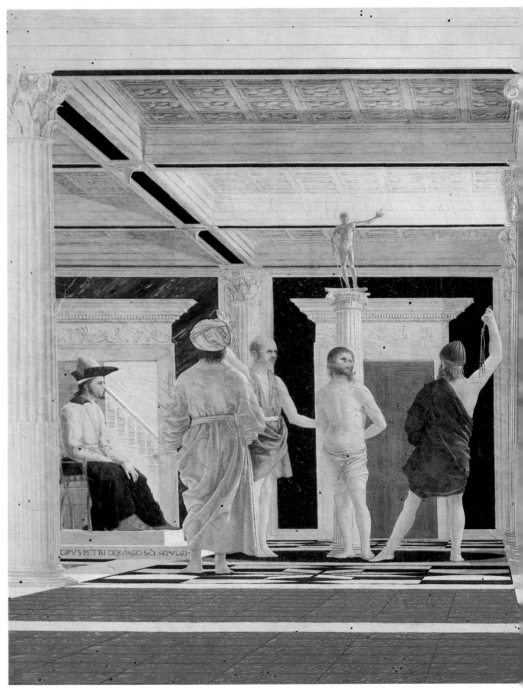

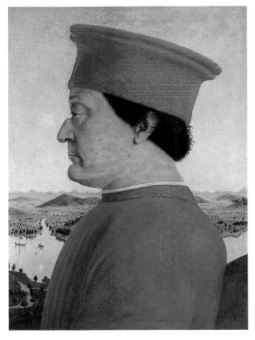

PIERO DELLA FRANCESCA (right) *The flagellation of Christ*, undated

pulsive force stronger than ordinary conversation, the three foreground figures may on one level represent the Old Testament, prefiguring the torment of Christ in the New.

The emphatic placement of the three figures, however, suggests also a topical reference, and the strong individuality of the two flanking figures makes it likely that they are also portraits – the man in profile on the right bears some resemblance to Ludovico Gonzaga of Mantua, who had close connections with the court of Urbino. The austerely beautiful youth, however, whose hair is as blond as a halo, framed by the laurel-tree behind, who stands in a pose so close to that of Christ, left foot forward, his hand at his waist, must be allegorical: it would be bold to represent even the most blameless youth as a larger reflection of Christ.

The picture is divided into two halves, into two theatres of being, by an elaborate perspectival system, mathematically so precise that the plan and elevation of the Hall on the left can be deduced exactly. The loggia, constructed with a perfect command of its classical elements, strongly recalls Alberti's architecture; the design is not perhaps arbitrary, but based on reports brought back from Jerusalem of the surviving buildings there, including Pilate's Judgment Hall. Alberti's Holy Sepulchre in the Rucellai Chapel in Florence, with which Piero's Hall has some details in common, was probably based on the Holy Sepulchre in Jerusalem. The area on the right, however, the real world contrasted to the divine one, is fragmentary in plan. The two areas are lit by different sources of light, but are linked indissolubly by the reiterated elements of the composition, by the harmony of colour, and by Piero della Francesca's extraordinary still and solemn mood. The timeless Christian Passion is reconciled with the topical likenesses of Piero's contemporaries in an immutable formal framework.

The *Flagellation* was painted for the appreciation of learned humanists – not least among them Federigo (who wrote superb Latin). Besides painters – not only Piero but the Netherlandish Justus of Ghent and the Spaniard Pedro Berruguete – visitors to Urbino included the leading intellectuals of the day, among them Alberti. It was in Urbino that Castiglione was to set his famous account of cultured courtly life, *The Book of the Courtier*, and in Urbino that Bramante, the High Renaissance architect of St Peter's, was trained, and the great Raphael born.

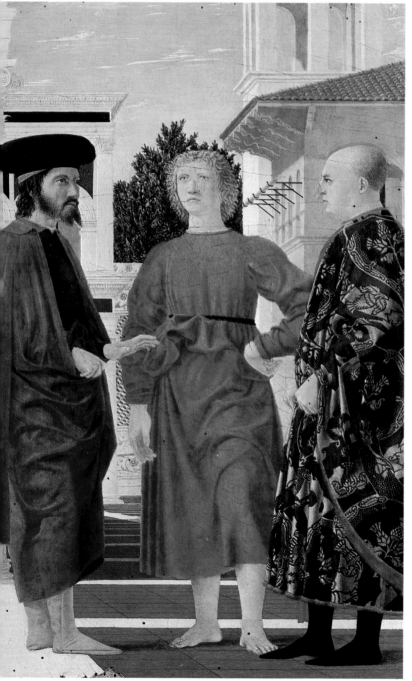

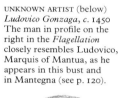

UNKNOWN ARTIST (below)
Ludovico Gonzaga, c. 1450
The man in profile on the right in the *Flagellation* closely resembles Ludovico, Marquis of Mantua, as he appears in this bust and in Mantegna (see p. 120).

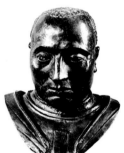

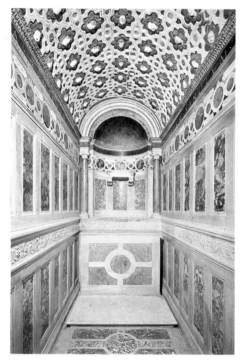

URBINO, DUCAL PALACE
(right) The *Cappella del Perdono*, 1468-72
The tiny remembrance chapel is comparable to Alberti's structure (below right). Perhaps like Piero's picture it served some private, learned piety with personal references.

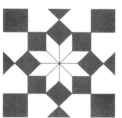

PIERO'S FLOOR PLAN (above)
This is a flagstone of the loggia of *The Flagellation*. The paving, and the whole ground plan of Piero's picture, can be precisely reconstructed – such is the complexity and accuracy of his perspective geometry.

ALBERTI (right)
The Holy Sepulchre in the Rucellai Chapel, Florence, 1467
Alberti's building and Piero's painting share the idiom of their classical ornament and the motif, perhaps symbolic, of a star.

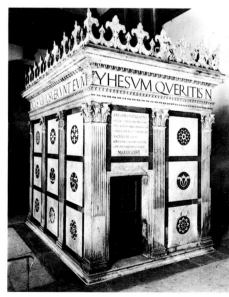

Italian Sculpture 2: New Modes and Types

That persistent Florentine feeling for sweetness and charm so evident in early Renaissance painting is also clear in contemporary sculpture. But if Donatello's harsher style had no immediate followers (save the painter Castagno), this was partly due to a change in the nature of patronage: about the time that Donatello left for Padua, in 1443, expensive public commissions, such as those that had filled the niches of Orsanmichele, died away. Sculptors were engaged mainly on tombs, pulpits and altar furniture, or modest domestic pieces, reliefs and portrait busts.

However, in this period of consolidation, some specifically Renaissance types and forms of sculpture appeared, such as portrait busts and classicizing tombs. Leonardo Bruni, author of a history of Florence and Chancellor of the city, died in 1444. His lavish state funeral commemorated as much his intellectual prowess as his political status, and consciously echoed Roman ceremonies. His tomb is a compound of Christian and classical elements, and looks backward to his earthly accomplishments rather more than it looks forward to his heavenly destiny. The commission went to Bernardino Rossellino (1409-64),

the fourth brother of a family of five masons. He also worked as a master-mason under Alberti, who may have provided the tomb's overall design. The effigy of Bruni itself is beautifully serene and dignified.

The fifth brother of the family, Antonio Rossellino (1427-79), used Bernardino's formula for his tomb (1460-66) in S. Miniato for James, Cardinal of Portugal, who died while visiting Florence. His version was affected by the fashion of the third quarter of the century for graceful movement, so the tomb is brought almost to life by flying angels and delicate drapery. Antonio also produced some remarkable busts. His bust of the physician Giovanni Chellini was probably based on a plaster cast taken from the life, but Antonio has so sensitively handled the texture and mass of the marble that it is more than a mere facsimile. This bust is not of the classical type, though the classical form also became popular; the relatively unsubtle, but powerful head of Piero de' Medici of about 1453 by Mino da Fiesole (1429-84) has conscious classical mannerisms.

The work of Desiderio da Settignano (c. 1430-64) is characteristic of the "soft" Florentine style. The angels on his tabernacle in S.

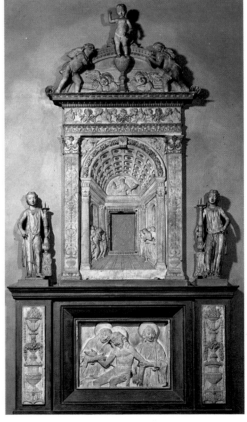

MINO DA FIESOLE
*Piero de' Medici, c.*1453
Piero the Gouty, Cosimo de' Medici's son and heir, enjoyed art and the society of humanists. He had "pictures, manuscripts, jewels, cameos, vases and rare books without equal

in Europe", as a contemporary reported. In Mino's bust the hair and eyes especially are deliberately classical, reflecting Piero's cultivated taste for the antique. He had perhaps less relish or aptitude for banking or politics.

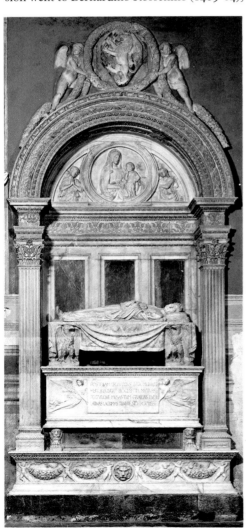

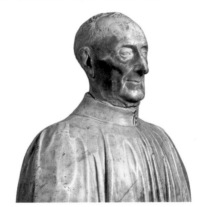

ANTONIO ROSSELLINO
Giovanni Chellini, 1456
Medieval busts much like this, but set on a pedestal, had contained sacred relics. This, however, is a secular, unidealized image of a distinguished doctor.

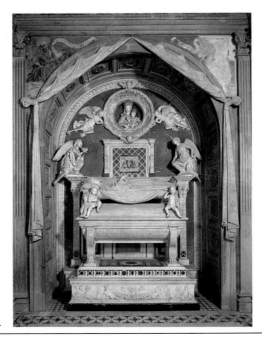

BERNARDINO ROSSELLINO
Leonardo Bruni, c. 1445-50
The Virgin and Child in a roundel above intercede for Bruni's soul. Otherwise his tomb, like a Roman emperor's triumphal arch, celebrates earthly prestige. The profuse classical ornament lends a rich grandeur.

ANTONIO ROSSELLINO (left)
The Cardinal of Portugal, 1460-66
Round the recumbent Cardinal there is a marked flurry of movement: foreshortened angels in relief bear the Madonna forward; free-standing angels spring from bended knee upwards towards her; two mobile *putti* shed tears beside the effigy.

DESIDERIO DA SETTIGNANO
Tabernacle in S. Lorenzo, *c.* 1460
The deep recession is achieved within a thin layer of marble. In their delicacy and finesse the vases and foliage flanking the tabernacle door (now missing) and *The lamentation over Christ* surpass their antique models, and even precedents by Donatello.

Lorenzo in Florence are the equivalent of the fragile grace of painters such as Filippo Lippi (see p. 107), and an extension of the sentiment of Luca della Robbia's *Madonnas*. The extraordinary subtlety with which Desiderio handled shallow depths of marble had its basis in Donatello's technique.

Movement, specifically the human body in movement, was the major preoccupation of Antonio del Pollaiuolo (1431/2-98). He was said to be the first artist to practise dissection, and the study of the muscular male nude is crucial in his painting and sculpture. In his paintings line defines the forms, in the Florentine manner, with the same vigour we have already seen in Donatello and Castagno. Correspondingly, his sculpture has hard, faceted planes and presents angular silhouettes. There is nevertheless a strange elegance in his work, both in his *Ten nudes fighting*, one of the earliest Italian engravings, and in his little bronze *Hercules and Antaeus*. This represents another Renaissance re-invention, the action group, often on a small scale, which has a dynamic movement inviting the viewer to inspect it from all round. In Pollaiuolo's *St Sebastian* of about 1475, the figures are again

showpieces of the human body in action, as Pollaiuolo makes evident in posing the archers on each side in identical attitudes, like two viewpoints of one statue.

Towards the end of the century an increasing gravity becomes apparent, especially in large-scale commissions carried out by Benedetto da Maiano and Andrea del Verrocchio (1435-88). Verrocchio was even more versatile than Pollaiuolo: he was goldsmith, painter, sculptor and impresario, the master of a large workshop (in which Leonardo da Vinci

VERROCCHIO (below)
Bartolommeo Colleoni, 1481-90
The horse is marching forward, and Colleoni frowns with menacing disdain. He dominates the square in which he stands, presenting a dramatic and peremptory silhouette.

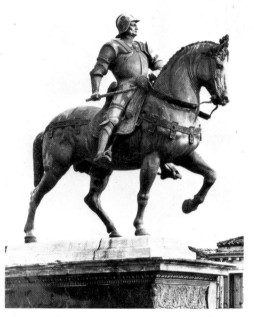

was to learn most of his many arts). His earlier work is in the softer tradition of Ghiberti and Desiderio, but there is a more vigorous drama in the life-size *Doubting of Thomas* (1465-83) for Orsanmichele. Even more theatrical was his colossal equestrian bronze of the Venetian general Bartolommeo Colleoni, cast after Verrocchio's death. Its ferocious realism makes a revealing contrast to the sober classicism of Donatello's *Gattamelata* (see p. 103). There is again a lighter, sweeter touch in Verrocchio's work for the Medici. His admirable little *Putto with a fish*, made to adorn a fountain, invites the spectator to move round it, as does Pollaiuolo's bronze.

The sculpture produced elsewhere in Italy was certainly competent, though still Gothic in feeling. One highly individual exception was the work of Agostino di Duccio (1418-81). He was born in Florence but trained perhaps by the Sienese della Quercia: he produced at Rimini and Perugia strange shallow reliefs (not shown) aswirl with drapery. An unknown collaborator with Agostino at Rimini, perhaps Matteo de' Pasti (active 1441-68), carved other reliefs there, remarkable in reproducing the form of Classical Greek sculpture.

VERROCCHIO (right)
Putto with a fish, c. 1470
The twisting and turning form, inviting the spectator to move round with it, was to be perfected by the great Mannerist Giambologna in the next century.

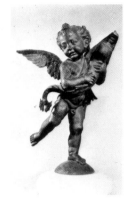

VERROCCHIO (below)
The doubting of Thomas, 1465
Thomas explores Christ's wound as if he already senses his divinity. The balanced movements of the figures hold the moment in moving, dramatic suspense.

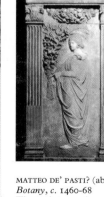

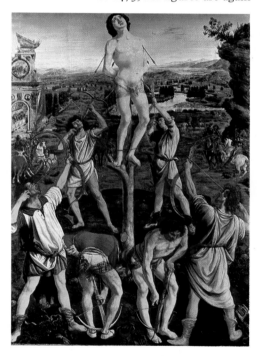

POLLAIUOLO (left)
St Sebastian, 1475
Florence and the river Arno are identifiable in the "portrait" landscape. The picture's pyramidal structure was becoming a common Renaissance compositional theme.

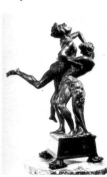

POLLAIUOLO (above)
Hercules and Antaeus, c. 1475-80
Lifted from his mother, the Earth, Antaeus lost his strength and so Hercules conquered him. This is a small version of a life-size painting by Antonio.

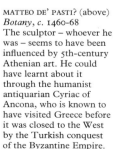

MATTEO DE' PASTI? (above)
Botany, c. 1460-68
The sculptor – whoever he was – seems to have been influenced by 5th-century Athenian art. He could have learnt about it through the humanist antiquarian Cyriac of Ancona, who is known to have visited Greece before it was closed to the West by the Turkish conquest of the Byzantine Empire.

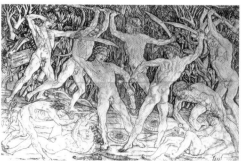

POLLAIUOLO
Ten nudes fighting, c. 1460
Uncommissioned and with no real subject, the engraving seems to have been a display piece, demonstrating Pollaiuolo's mastery of movement and anatomy. Engraving, a German invention, enabled an artist to disseminate his work more widely.

Italian Painting 3: Florence and Rome

Florence boomed in the fifteenth century, and, under the control of the Medici banking family, became a national and international centre of finance and commerce. Its prosperity reached its zenith under the leadership of Cosimo de' Medici, from 1434 to his death in 1464. Thereafter symptoms of decline appeared, and at the death of his grandson Lorenzo the Magnificent in 1492 the Medici dominance ended for the time being. There followed a long-threatened French invasion of Italy in 1494, almost welcomed as God's punishment by the fiercely radical Dominican priest Savonarola, whose anti-humanist influence held sway in Florence during the sorely troubled years 1494-98.

However, the artistic prestige of Florence continued supreme throughout the century, acknowledged all over Italy. Commercial contacts with the north promoted artistic interchange; and Florentine artists were gradually assimilating the lessons of Netherlandish naturalism. Works by Jan van Eyck, Rogier van der Weyden (who visited Italy in 1450) and Hugo van der Goes are recorded in Florence, and were much admired, especially Hugo's altarpiece (see p.96) commissioned by

Tommaso Portinari, the agent of the Medici bank in Bruges, and set up as a great spectacle in 1483 in the church of S. Maria Nuova.

Italian approval of the Florentine achievement was sealed when, in the early 1480s, Pope Sixtus IV commissioned Florentine artists to paint the walls of his newly built Sistine Chapel in the Vatican. The controlling artist was Perugino (c. 1445-1523), born in Umbria but trained in Florence, perhaps under Verrocchio; with him worked the Florentines Botticelli, Ghirlandaio and Cosimo Rosselli.

During the course of Perugino's long and prolific career he was a leader of fashion and

then, abruptly, old-fashioned. In the grace and harmonious proportions of his figures, in his mastery of perspective and feeling for space and symmetry, some of the key characteristics of the High Renaissance, which overtook him, are nevertheless clear. His achievement is underrated by comparison with Raphael, his pupil, who learned these qualities from him, and his deficiencies are overstressed. At his best he is an entrancing painter, as the most successful of his surviving frescos in the Sistine Chapel, *The giving of the Keys to St Peter*, demonstrates. (Three others were destroyed to make way for Michelangelo's *Last Judgment*.)

SIGNORELLI (right)
The Last Judgment,
detail: *The Saved*, 1499
It is often difficult to see in Signorelli's much more dramatic style that he was Piero della Francesca's pupil. His interest in the nude and harsh sculptural forms recall Pollaiuolo, but the sweeping drapery, the variety of gesture, the serried movement, are typical of the later second half of the 15th century.

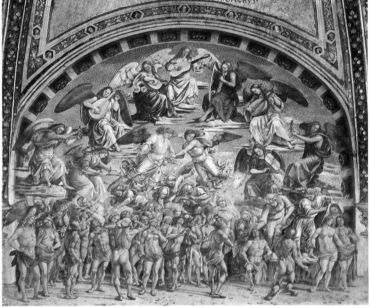

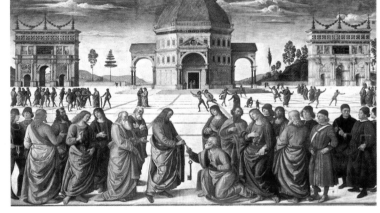

PERUGINO (above)
The giving of the Keys to St Peter, 1481-82
Perugino's skill was to tell a story clearly and simply, affectingly and gracefully, though later in life his invention failed. In the line of figures there is a lovely rhythm.

GHIRLANDAIO (below)
The birth of St John, 1485-90
The birth takes place in a well-to-do 15th-century Florentine private house, visited, it seems, by interested 15th-century neighbours: some are known portraits.

GHIRLANDAIO (right)
The calling of the first apostles, 1481-82
The freshness of the landscape, the vivacity of the loosely clustered crowd, these are the pleasing but perhaps rather shallow qualities of Ghirlandaio's work.

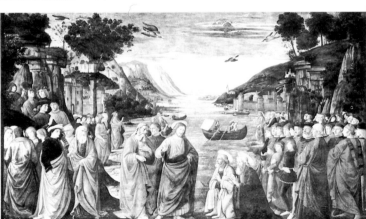

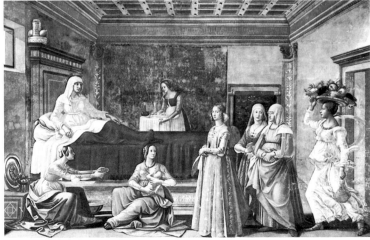

BOTTICELLI (right)
"*The Madonna of the Magnificat*", c. 1480-90
The circular or *tondo* frame permits a closed, harmonious composition, but it is difficult to fit upright figures within it. The rainbow, marking the Virgin as Queen of Heaven, is one device that binds them together. Graceful line describes the forms – the hallmark of the Florentine school and of Botticelli's work in particular. This, perhaps, is the most enchanting of all Botticelli's *Madonnas*.

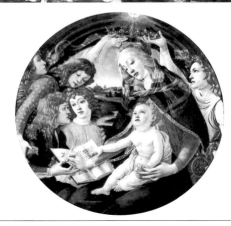

The contribution of Domenico Ghirlandaio (1449-94), *The calling of the first apostles*, is more essentially Florentine in style: in the density of the figures there is something of Masaccio, but rather more of the light, fluent line of Filippo Lippi. Ghirlandaio's shop in Florence was large and prolific, and the most popular with the general public. His major work, frescos (1485-90) in S. Maria Novella, have all the ingredients the public enjoyed – minute detail, inventoried with the delight of a Netherlandish painter; decorative motifs derived from classical antiquity; and gossipy references to contemporary persons.

If Ghirlandaio represents the established, perhaps rather backward-looking, style of the last years of the century, the Umbrian Luca Signorelli (active 1470-1523) anticipates in some respects the style of things to come. As Perugino later did, he acknowledged the influence of Leonardo; unlike Perugino, he could learn from the young Michelangelo, who admired Signorelli's work. He was employed in the Sistine Chapel, and by the Medici in Florence, but his greatest large-scale masterpiece is his work in fresco at Orvieto, with a *Last Judgment* teeming with struggling nudes.

The most remarkable talent working in the Sistine Chapel was Sandro Botticelli (*c.*1445-1510). He trained, probably, with Filippo Lippi in the 1460s, and his female faces retained elements of Filippo's characterization throughout his career. By about 1470 he had established his independence and originality, and was working for the Medici; it was for the Medici that he painted the allegorical scenes that now seem his greatest achievement (see over). His main output, however, was religious, and the many *Madonnas* produced by his workshop and probably also by imitators were especially popular. Botticelli's Sistine fresco, *The punishment of Corah*, shows an instinct for drama and a mastery of expressive gesture: his line could be both delicate and sinewy like Castagno's. His work of the 1490s, however, seems disturbed and strained, affected by the fevered emotionalism associated with the fanatic teaching of Savonarola. His late *Lamentations* are harsh and angular by comparison with earlier work, and make direct and fierce demands on the spectator. In "*The Mystic Nativity*" of 1500 (not shown) the joy of Christ's birth is undermined by little devils scuttling in the foreground.

Filippino Lippi (*c.* 1457-1504), the son of Filippo Lippi by the nun he abducted, was trained in Botticelli's studio and through Botticelli learned the sweetness and grace of his father's painting. *The vision of St Bernard* of about 1480 is impressively defined and detailed, seen life-size in hard, clear light and strong colours. However, Filippino also painted monumental frescos in churches in Rome and Florence, which are remarkably well organized and as dramatic as Botticelli's *Punishment of Corah*, with a still greater profusion of antique detail; his figures can be dynamic, very freely painted.

Netherlandish painting had a considerable impact on Florentine portraiture during the late fifteenth century, but naturalistic observation was seldom as unflinching as in Ghirlandaio's *Old man and his grandson*. Not only Ghirlandaio but also, for instance, Botticelli inserted portraits into their frescos, and Botticelli painted a considerable number of panel portraits, usually half-length, set against a plain background or against simple, almost geometric architecture. His sitters look out with the same pensive, haunting gaze as his invented characters.

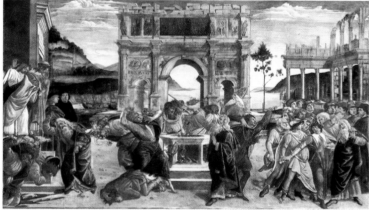

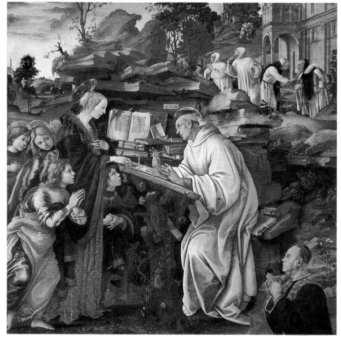

BOTTICELLI (above)
The punishment of Corah, 1481-82
Corah had usurped the priestly authority Moses had delegated to Aaron. In the centre, beneath a replica of the Arch of Constantine, Moses, rod in hand, invokes God's wrath: on the left the

earth opens up to swallow his opponent. Botticelli's fresco repeats again the tripartite division (set perhaps by Perugino) of all the Sistine Chapel works, and it, too, celebrates the divine constitution of the papacy – Moses and Aaron prefigure Christ and St Peter opposite.

BOTTICELLI (below left)
Lamentation over Christ, *c.* 1490-1500
The unremitting grief, the frenzied drapery, the claustrophobia induced by the bleak masonry all create disquiet. The gestures are strangely artificial. Van der Weyden was clearly an influence.

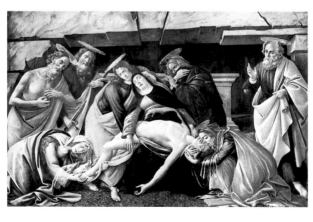

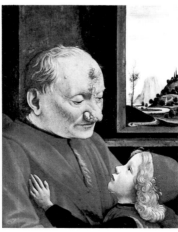

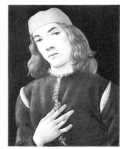

FILIPPINO LIPPI (above)
The vision of St Bernard, *c.* 1480
The elongated figures are drawn with a grace like Botticelli's; the lively angels move eagerly; the rich detail is delightful. St Bernard gazes on the attenuated Virgin with an almost agonized piety, and the donor below echoes him.

GHIRLANDAIO (left)
Old man and his grandson, undated
The old man is shown "warts and all", but also radiantly and tenderly – in a posthumous memorial?

BOTTICELLI (above)
*A young man, c.*1482?
Botticelli's portraits are conventional, without penetration or variation in pose. However, they have undeniable charm.

Botticelli: Primavera

Botticelli's *Primavera* and *Birth of Venus*, his two most famous mythological paintings, were probably commissioned by or for Lorenzo di Pierfrancesco de' Medici, who was the first cousin of Lorenzo the Magnificent, ruler of Florence. Both hung in the villa at Catello, outside Florence, which Lorenzo di Pierfrancesco had bought in 1477, but they were not necessarily painted as a pair: the *Primavera* is earlier, of about 1478, and *The birth of Venus* later, of perhaps 1482-84. The *Primavera* is the most enchanting visual celebration of spring ever made. Beyond that, its significance is obscure – which is perhaps one reason why it is so endlessly fascinating.

The main theme of the *Primavera* is chosen from Ovid, and is unfolded on the right: the wind-god Zephyr pursues the nymph Chloris, who, at his touch, is transformed into Flora. The central figure, modestly gowned but welcoming with an inclination of the head and hand, is marked out as Venus by the winged Cupid with drawn bow hovering above: she appears not only as Goddess of Love, but as the astrological symbol presiding over April. Her head and shoulders are haloed by a circle of light in the grove of golden-fruited trees: she is "Christianized", a pagan Venus become a source for good. To the left three Graces dance, emanations of Venus (singled out by Alberti in his treatise on painting as admirable subjects for the exercise of artistic skill). On the extreme left stands Mercury, but why he stands just as he does has yet to be convincingly explained.

The mood is festive, a kind of grave rapture, but no story binds the characters together. They are dispersed in solitary or self-sufficient groups, each one in pale introspection. The picture has little depth, instead a two-dimensional patterning which must have resembled most closely Netherlandish tapestries, much prized in Florence at the time. The figures are lucidly drawn and roundly modelled, but come from a dream: they tread weightlessly, leaving the flowers uncrushed beneath their feet. Unreal, elongated, they move to the sinuous rhythms of the picture like slender saplings to an eddying breeze.

In short, the picture is a deliberate reversion to some of the characteristics of International Gothic, disregarding the realism initiated by Masaccio. Although Ovid may have been one starting-point and a classical statue in Florence once identified as Flora another, the mood is more akin to medieval romance than to classical antiquity. Though the faces of his Venuses closely resemble those of his Madonnas, Botticelli's mythologies did not serve the devotional or narrative functions of his religious pictures. The style and subject of the *Primavera* answered the specifications of an intellectual and esoteric circle of humanists, humanists, however, of a quite different stamp from Alberti or Leonardo Bruni (see p. 114). A leading light in the Medici circle was Marsilio Ficino, versed in classical and medieval astrology, poetry, lore and symbolism, and in the abstruse flights of Neoplatonic philosophy. Possibly he conceived the *Primavera* for Lorenzo di Pierfrancesco's education (Lorenzo was only 15 in 1477) – as a homily of which the symbols, acting in some way like astrological

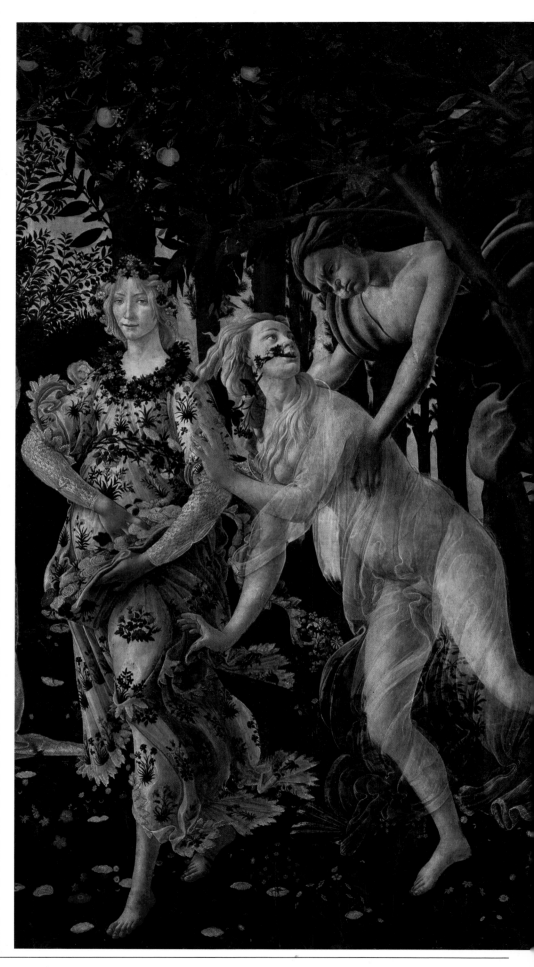

BOTTICELLI: (below) *Primavera*, c.1478; and (left) detail

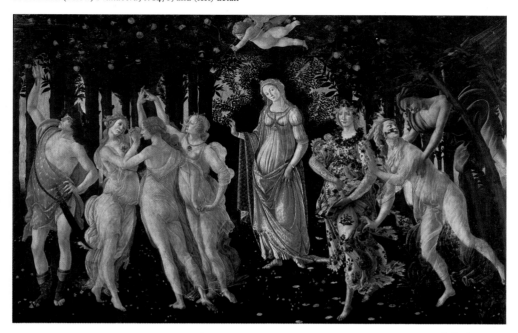

symbols, would exercise a benign influence on the young man. In 1478 Ficino wrote a letter to Lorenzo in which he asked him to meditate on Venus as *Humanitas*, in whom all virtues were compounded, and perhaps the Venus of Botticelli's painting is this same *Humanitas*.

This is one theory, advanced by the art historian Gombrich; another is that the painting was inspired by the poems of Poliziano, also a member of the Medici circle, and that the Venus of the *Primavera* signifies human love while the Venus of *The birth* signifies divine love, in an antithesis of a kind enjoyed by humanists. *The birth of Venus* is a more straightforward enactment of classical myth (or perhaps of the myth retold by Poliziano in a poem of about 1475), although it, too, may contain levels of significance, in a moral and philosophical allegory. Botticelli's *Mars and Venus*, painted for the Vespucci family, perhaps to commemorate a marriage, also has an allegory, of brute strength conquered by benign love. Again, though classical lovers are represented, the figures are not based on classical prototypes.

By 1500 Botticelli was hopelessly out of key with public (or private) taste. He was rediscovered only in the nineteenth century, when artists such as the Nazarenes and the Pre-Raphaelites responded eagerly to the delicacy and vitality, the apparent clarity and deeper mystery of Botticelli's paintings.

A strange, positively neurotic, loner in late fifteenth-century Florence may be mentioned here, Piero di Cosimo (1462-1521). He likewise painted mythological series for private patrons, apparently allegories of the primeval, savage state of man.

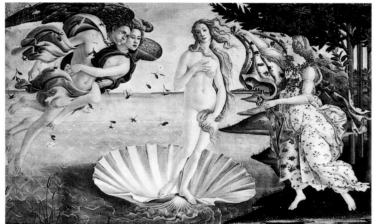

BOTTICELLI (below)
Mars and Venus, late 1480s
No known text describes the traditional lovers Mars and Venus in this way: it is Botticelli's or his patrons' interpretation. Its meaning could be both literary and astrological. There are wasps, *vespi* in Italian, buzzing by Mars' head, which allude to the patrons, the Vespucci.

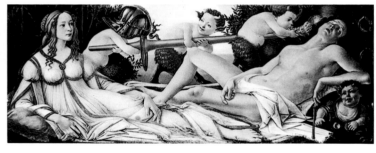

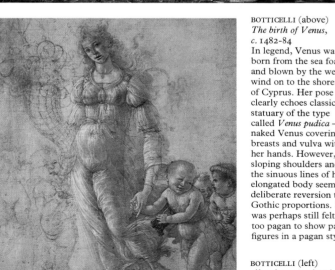

BOTTICELLI (above)
The birth of Venus,
c.1482-84
In legend, Venus was born from the sea foam and blown by the west wind on to the shores of Cyprus. Her pose clearly echoes classical statuary of the type called *Venus pudica* – naked Venus covering breasts and vulva with her hands. However, the sloping shoulders and the sinuous lines of her elongated body seem a deliberate reversion to Gothic proportions. It was perhaps still felt to be too pagan to show pagan figures in a pagan style.

BOTTICELLI (left)
Abundance, undated
Botticelli went over a first drawing in black chalk with a pen, introducing highlights with white body-colour. The animated calligraphy is even more pronounced than in his painting.

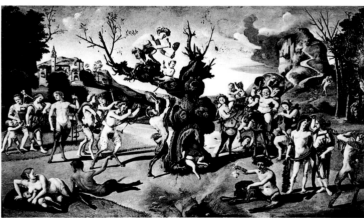

PIERO DI COSIMO
The discovery of honey,
c.1500
Piero, like Botticelli, also painted mythologies, but

very different in mood. They range from sinister, desolate and yet tender, all but surreal visions to almost comic fantasies.

The main theme or story here is that Bacchus, with the drunken Silenus on a donkey, discovers bees' honey for human use.

Renaissance Painting in North and Central Italy

Andrea Mantegna (c. 1430-1506) was the first Italian born and trained north of the Appennines to make an individual contribution to Renaissance art. His classicism was more extreme than any previous artist's – his settings are archaeological reconstructions – and his experiments in perspective illusionism were bolder than those even of the more mathematically inclined Florentines. He worked in a hard, dry, clear and conscientious style, sometimes unnaturally stony, as if his figures were sculptures; but his art was enlivened by sensitivity and delicacy of touch, and occasionally pierced by fierce emotion.

Mantegna acquired his intellectual love of antiquity in Padua, where the university was an established humanist centre. He was the adopted son and pupil of Francesco Squarcione (1397-1468; not shown), an obscure figure, an indifferent painter, an antiquarian and probable dealer in classical antiquities, an entrepreneur. Squarcione had been deeply impressed by Alberti's theories of painting, and must have passed these on to Mantegna, but Mantegna also gained his knowledge of perspective – and of quality in art – from Florentine artists who had come north – not only Donatello, but also Filippo Lippi, Castagno and Piero della Francesca. He formed his style, which was to change little, astonishingly rapidly: it was already set in his first commission, frescos for the Eremitani church in Padua (ruined in World War II), which he undertook at the tender age of 17. Their powerful perspective effects were clearly inspired by Donatello's reliefs for the high altar of S. Antonio nearby.

In 1454 Mantegna married the daughter of the Venetian painter Jacopo Bellini (see over), and in 1459 he was installed with his family in a house in Mantua as court painter to the Gonzaga dukes. Mantua, small but politically independent since 1328, became under the Gonzagas a centre of humanist learning – Ludovico Gonzaga, as we have seen (p. 112) was in close touch with Urbino. Mantegna subsequently visited Florence and Pisa and painted briefly in Rome (where none of his works survive) but Mantua was to be his base until his death. His most famous work, the frescos of the *Camera degli Sposi*, is in Mantua, in a corner room of the Ducal Palace.

The *Camera degli Sposi* is the most impressive secular decoration of the early Renaissance in all Italy. It was the first to cover walls and ceiling in a single perspective scheme – even co-ordinating the fall of light in the frescos with the light from the windows into the room – and the ancestor of the great illusionist decorations of the High Renaissance and of the Baroque. Central in the room, over the chimney-piece, is a family group – including the court dwarf – on a sort of terrace, revealed by curtains drawn back. The illusionism is sophisticated: one figure stands between the spectator and a pilaster (painted) with his feet on the chimney-piece (marble). On the adjacent wall scenes from Ludovico

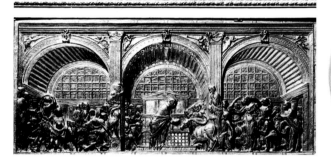

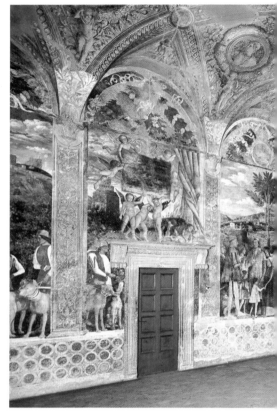

DONATELLO (above)
Relief from the Santo altar: *The miracle of the mule*, c. 1447
A mule led forward by St Anthony of Padua knelt before the Host, convincing a sceptic. The double grills across the arches are an example of the elaborate perspective that influenced Mantegna.

MANTEGNA? (above)
Self-portrait, c. 1490
Mantegna was very aware of his status as an artist. He is wreathed in laurel as the antique poets were; the bust is a prototype for the High Renaissance image of proud genius. (The bronze bust may be by one Gianmarco Cavalli, rather than by Mantegna.)

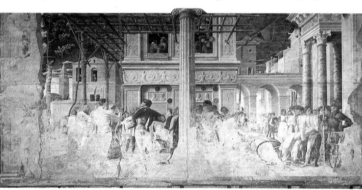

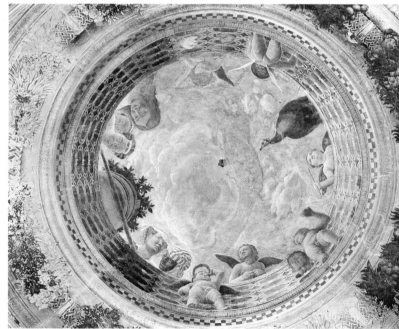

MANTEGNA
Fresco from the Eremitani: *The martyrdom of St Christopher*, 1448-51
A foreshortened column divides the two episodes. On the left, arrows shot at St Christopher fail miraculously to strike him; on the right the saint's giant body is dragged away, with his head on a platter once visible in the foreground. Mantegna's lifelong preoccupations are already clear – ambitious perspective and bold foreshortening; archaeological detail; firmly modelled, harshly lit, static forms; and colours veering from a clashing intensity to a virtual monochrome.

MANTEGNA (right)
The *Camera degli Sposi*, ceiling, c. 1474
Inspired, perhaps, by the similar *oculus* in the dome of the Pantheon in Rome, Mantegna's skyward peep is a first example of foreshortening from below, which Correggio (see p. 148) was to exploit in his aerial fantasies in nearby Parma some 40 years later.

Gonzaga's life open out over countryside, with the Duke and his small children welcoming home his son Francesco, who had newly been created a cardinal. The countryside, however, featuring Roman ruins and statuary and hilltop towns, is imaginary – Mantua is flat. Above, the room is opened to the elements by an illusionist circular opening inserted in the richly decorated vault. It is like an inverted well, to which *putti* cling, and smiling women looking down into the room seem about to push over into it a precariously balanced flower tub as a practical joke. The illusionism, when it was quite new, must have been even

more startling: the colour and the firmly painted portraits (the first family group in Italian art) would have been even more vivid.

Mantegna's next major work was a pageant sequence of nine huge canvases illustrating *The Triumph of Caesar*. Their original setting and function are unknown, though in 1501 they served as a backdrop to the performance of a Latin play. There was no doubt some suggestion that the Gonzagas were comparable with Caesar, but the sequence was the ideal commission for Mantegna, offering full scope to his antiquarian obsessions.

Mantegna also produced many altarpieces, often enlivening conventional themes by virtuoso effects of foreshortening, as in his *Dead Christ*, stretched out feet first on a table (reproduced on p. 182). There, and in his painting of *St Sebastian*, he introduces "cutoff" figures as an illusionistic device, like the foreshortening, to suggest the picture is larger, but hidden by the frame. The two figures in the *St Sebastian*, with their grotesque features, may show the influence of northern paintings or engravings; Mantegna himself made widely influential engravings, and was the first artist in Italy to produce them regularly.

The Gonzagas had links also with the ruling family in Ferrara, the Estes. Previously the Estes had imported Netherlandish artists or artists from the south, such as Piero della Francesca, but after the middle of the century a local school developed of high quality. Its finest painters, Cosimo Tura (*c.* 1431-95), Francesco del Cossa and Ercole de' Roberti, all reflect something of Mantegna's angular harshness, and, in varying degree, his interest in antiquity. Isabella d'Este was a passionate, and demanding, art-lover, determined to form a collection of all the best living painters in Italy: she ordered mythological works from Mantegna, Perugino and Giovanni Bellini.

Carlo Crivelli (1435/40-1495/1500) was a Venetian painter who worked mostly in the Marches, and was also strongly influenced by Mantegna in his figure drawing. He specialized in elaborate altarpieces rich with swags of fruit, peacocks and other such decorative detail, sometimes with raised *gesso* relief and studded with semi-precious jewels. Mantegna was as important for northern Italy as Masaccio had been for Florence – his influence, however, was most crucial and fertile in the art of his brother-in-law, Giovanni Bellini.

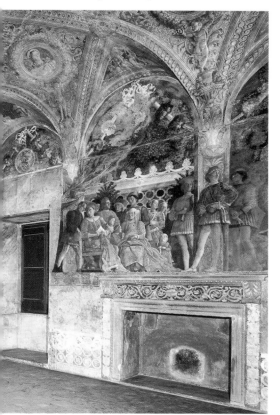

MANTEGNA (left)
The *Camera degli Sposi*, general view, *c.* 1474
The eye-level views on the left wall make an interesting comparison with Gozzoli's *Journey of the Magi* in the Medici Palace in Florence (see p. 110); the landscape is equally fanciful but evokes now a classical world. The harsh clarity of Mantegna's drawing, clear in the detail (right) of a lady-in-waiting and the court dwarf, is also comparable with that of contemporary Florentines, though it is more static, not concerned to show vigorous movement as was Pollaiuolo, for instance.

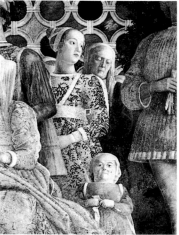

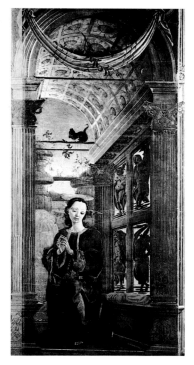

COSIMO TURA (right)
The *Virgin Annunciate*, 1469
Cosimo's intense, brittle figures have the same surface hardness as Mantegna's. His love of detail, not so archaeological as Mantegna's, is typical of north Italy.

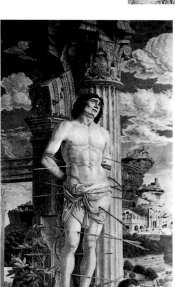

CRIVELLI (below)
Pietà, 1493
Crivelli's metallic hardness belies his Venetian origins; it is a legacy from Mantegna; so is his

accomplished illusionistic decoration – his delight in marbled surfaces and shining objects. With it he and others could achieve abrasive emotional effects.

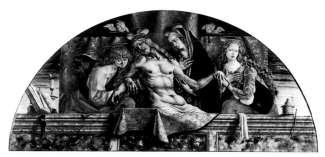

MANTEGNA (above)
The Triumph of Caesar, *c.* 1486-94
Mantegna's fascination for everything antique – buildings, sculpture, furniture, caparisons, utensils, costume, armour – has here full scope.

MANTEGNA (right)
St Sebastian, undated
Vasari was one who complained that Mantegna's figures "sometimes seem to be made of stone rather than flesh and blood". The stone foot beside the saint's seems a wry retort.

Renaissance Painting in Venice

During the Middle Ages, the political and cultural interests of the republic of Venice were more with Byzantium and the East than with the rest of Italy. "Queen of the Adriatic", Venice had already become in the thirteenth century a great naval and mercantile power, but had only gradually expanded her protection over the north-east mainland of Italy, into the Veneto. Apparently unmoved by Giotto's revolutionary work in Padua, virtually next door to Venice, Venetian art had continued largely Byzantine in feeling, and somewhat provincial in quality, until Gentile da Fabriano introduced the International Gothic about 1408. Thereafter a succession of distinguished visiting Florentines (Uccello, Lippi, Castagno) made some impact, but the crucial influence was Donatello, working in Padua in the 1440s. Mantegna, an apprentice in Padua at the time, had been profoundly impressed, and Mantegna's own example was followed for a time by the outstanding Venetian painter of the fifteenth century, Giovanni Bellini, who was his brother-in-law.

The Bellini family was the dominant artistic dynasty in Venice during most of the fifteenth century. The father, Jacopo (c. 1400-70/71)

had worked in Florence; he had been a pupil of Gentile da Fabriano, and his style was essentially a somewhat stiff but luminous version of International Gothic. Surviving notebooks show also a sensitive, if free, appreciation of classical art. Gentile (c. 1429/30?-1507) is believed to have been the elder of his two sons, and was for long the most famous, ennobled by the Emperor in 1469, and even working for the Sultan Mehmet II in Istanbul in 1479-81. His most remarkable surviving works are ceremonial pageant pictures, large-scale, and painted on canvas: these panoramas feature accurate portraits both of Venetian architecture and townscape (establishing a tradition that was to culminate in Canaletto), and of important citizens. Gentile's grouping, however, is formal and static; it was left to Vittore Carpaccio (c. 1450/55-1525/26), who probably started as his pupil, to transpose Gentile's skills – if not quite into movement, into poetic narrative packed with incident and detail from everyday life. Carpaccio's directness and his humanity make him one of the most accessible and loved of all Italian painters, but he was, too, a master of tone and light, clearly reflecting the influence of Giovanni Bellini.

Giovanni Bellini (c. 1430?-1516) is presumed the younger son of Jacopo. Uncertain though his birth date is, he must have been well into his eighties when he died. He continued working throughout his very long career, and was always astonishingly inventive and sensitive to the changing moods and discoveries of the passing years, so that right at the end of his life he was responding creatively to the innovations of his own pupils, Giorgione and Titian. He was one of the first artists to sign his work – or the products of his large and busy workshop – fairly consistently, although in his earlier years especially he rarely dated it, and his early development is difficult to reconstruct. A characteristic work, such as the *Pietà* in the Brera, Milan, perhaps of about 1470, clearly acknowledges the sculptural clarity of Mantegna; indeed the design is very close to a relief on Donatello's altar in Padua. But Giovanni's own tenderness is already distinct.

In 1475-76 the sojourn in Venice of an artist from Sicily, Antonello da Messina (c. 1430-79), seems to have had a fundamental impact on Venetian painting. The innovation that he demonstrated was (ironically, since he was a Sicilian) the Netherlandish technique of oil-

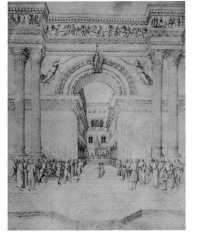

JACOPO BELLINI (left)
Christ before Pilate,
undated
Jacopo's two copybooks show both the influence of Pisanello and an interest in the Antique comparable to Mantegna's – though not classicizing in his sense. They are difficult to place.

GENTILE BELLINI (right)
Sultan Mehmet II, c. 1480
The temporary export of the city's painter (he was so appointed in 1474) to the Infidel is a sign of Venice's predominantly Eastward interests; her entry into the mainstream of Italian art coincides with a retraction of her power in the Levant.

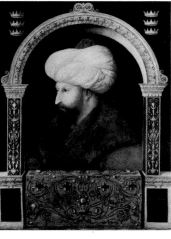

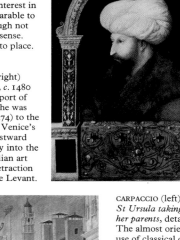

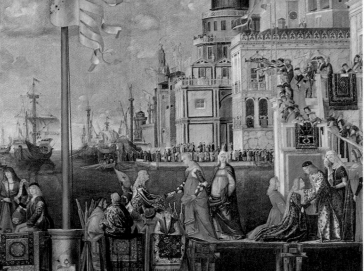

CARPACCIO (left)
St Ursula taking leave of her parents, detail, 1495
The almost orientalizing use of classical ornament, which is evident not only in Gentile's portrait (above) but even in Jacopo's sketch, has vanished (except for the occasional detail in the faithfully recorded architecture). Architecture, naval rig, dress, hangings, the whole splendour of the city is intimately notated, though the view is fictive. The assured perspective is the legacy of successive visiting mainland artists, from Pisanello onwards.

ANTONELLO DA MESSINA (right) *St Jerome in his study,* c. 1460
The detailed interior, with its five sources of light and enamel-smooth finish, was once attributed to Jan van Eyck, and may have been based on part of a triptych by him recorded in Naples.

GENTILE BELLINI (below)
The miracle at Ponte di Lorenzo, 1500
The series illustrated the miracles performed by a

fragment of the Cross: here the relic fell into a canal; a friar dived in after it; he could not swim, but the Cross kept him afloat.

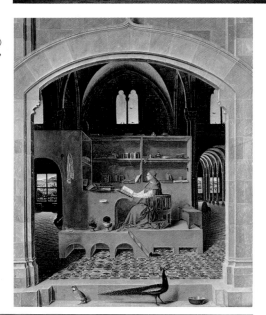

GIOVANNI BELLINI (below)
Doge Loredan, c.1502
Loredan had his portrait
prepared by his official
court painter not long
after taking office in 1501.
The Doge, the titular head
of the Venetian oligarchy,
was elected for life from
among the leading families.
In his palace almost every
important Venetian painter
executed large-scale works;
those of the 15th and early
16th centuries are lost, the
victims of successive fires.

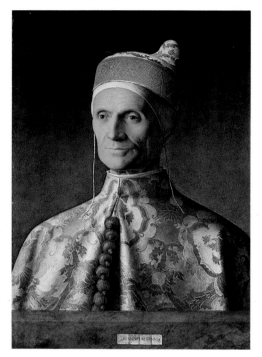

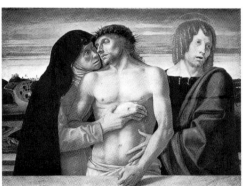

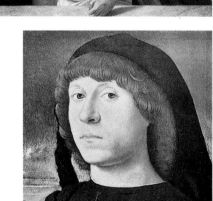

painting, which he had probably learnt from Netherlanders in Naples, rather than in the north. Although oil had been used in Italy, nothing like the range of Netherlandish techniques, especially in the rendering of pervasive and enveloping light, had been developed there. Antonello's *St Jerome in his study*, painted some years before his arrival in Venice, is very distinctly Eyckian both in the treatment and in the detail of its domestic interior. He also approached portraiture in a Netherlandish fashion: in marked contrast to the standard Italian formal portrait, the atmospheric portrait heads of his sitters, with their alert vitality and vivid eyes, are as individual and natural as Memlinc's. He has been called the first Italian painter to practise portraiture as an art form in its own right, and his impact on Giovanni Bellini's portraits is clear. Bellini's portrait masterpiece is considerably later, about 1502, *Doge Leonardo Loredan*: it is a superb synthesis of formal, hieratic clarity with the subtlest modelling – conveying both the magnificence of the office and the full humanity of its holder.

It was the flexibility and brilliance of the oil technique that made Bellini's later master-

pieces possible – *St Francis in ecstasy*, for instance, with its conjunction of figure and landscape that looks forward to the fusion that Giorgione and Titian were to achieve. *"The Sacred Allegory"*, perhaps of the mid-1490s, seems again to anticipate the work of his great pupils – here specifically the mood of enigmatic mystery that suffuses Giorgione's work. The subject of the picture is difficult to explain, though the Child on the cushion is surely Christ, and a recent title is *Meditation on the Incarnation*. Its landscape is both of this world and a symbol of another.

A deep and sincere religious faith lies behind Bellini's painting, and undoubtedly informs the lasting beauty of his religious works, not least his long series of *Madonnas* (see p. 138). In old age, however, he ventured on secular allegories (not shown) often now difficult to interpret – moved perhaps by the example of his pupils Giorgione and Titian, but no doubt also by humanist interests like those which had moved patrons such as the Medici in Florence rather earlier. The alertness of his response to new developments was inexhaustible: reactions to Dürer, as to Leonardo, have been convincingly traced in his last paintings.

GIOVANNI BELLINI (right)
St Francis in ecstasy,
c.1470-80
The Appennine Monte La
Verna with its birds and
beasts dominates the scene.
The saint received the
stigmata there in 1224.

GIOVANNI BELLINI (left)
The Brera *Pietà*, c. 1470
The expressions and hands
delineate in still silence
the precise configuration of
grief: it is a lamentation
to make an atheist weep.

GIOVANNI BELLINI (below)
"The Sacred Allegory",
c. 1490-1500
The smoky river probably
represents Lethe, the river
in which souls – the naked
babes – are purified before
passing into life – thus a
mixture of Christian belief
with an allegory by Plato.

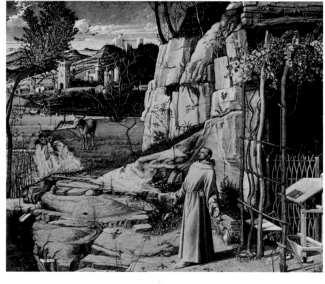

ANTONELLO DA MESSINA
A young man, 1478
The Italian practice had
been to present the sitter
in profile. Such a view as
this, in which, further, the
sitter looks straight at the
viewer, recalls van Eyck's
Man in a turban (see p. 93),
the first known example.

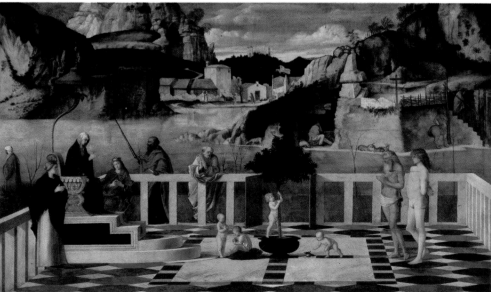

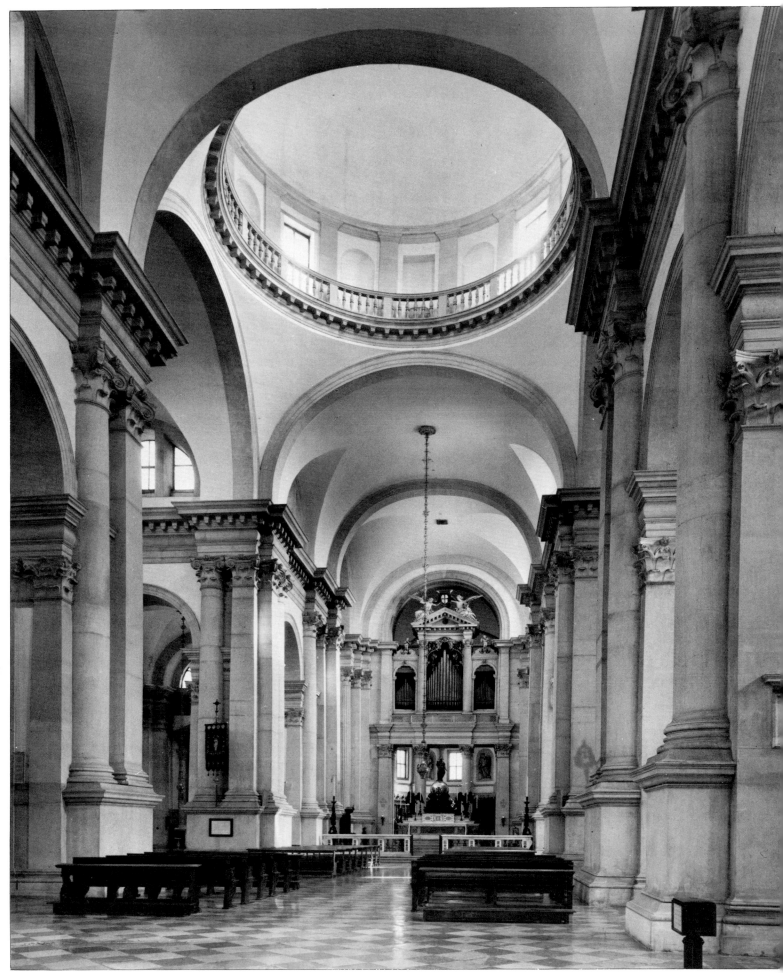

THE SIXTEENTH CENTURY

The concept of the artist as genius originated in sixteenth-century Italy and was applied to three men who were accorded an almost god-like stature – Leonardo, Michelangelo and Raphael. Both in their art, characterized by its mastery of rational design and structural harmony, and in their lives, they created an enduring model of humanist ideals. Yet their masterworks, and those of the other giants of the century, Dürer in Germany, Titian in Venice, Bruegel in the Netherlands, were produced against a background of increasing political and religious turmoil.

In the earliest decades of the century, the spiritual and political unity of the medieval world under the dual authority of the Pope and the Holy Roman Emperor was shown to be fragmented beyond repair. Political conflict between Pope and Emperor came to a head in 1527, when troops led by Emperor Charles V sacked Rome in retribution for Pope Clement VII's alliance with the rising power of France. A greater challenge not only to the Papacy but to the survival of religious art was the Reformation begun by Luther in 1517 under the protection of German principalities, leading as it did to civil war, persecution and, at times, to the pillaging of churches and destruction of images. It was only with the Council of Trent (1545-63) that the Catholic Church began to regain its spiritual confidence – a Counter-Reformation demanding a stricter code for its artists, including the restricted use of what had been a hallmark of Renaissance art, the nude.

Challenges to the authority of antiquity, tradition and the Bible came from other quarters, the astronomy of Copernicus for instance, the physics of Galileo, the altered world view initiated by the discovery of the New World and by the growth of sea trade with the East. Not only the sciences but all the arts were turned to new directions, to ends that were often distinctly secular. Yet the prototypes which were to influence Western art for nearly four centuries were produced under Church patronage. The Roman works of Raphael and Michelangelo for Popes Julius II and Leo X established Italian art as the guiding force for northern artists such as Dürer. The same works provided a point of departure for the development of Mannerism. Though many attempts have been made to show that this style was the outcome of a neurotic sensibility induced by the instability of the established Church and state, it may be understood simply as a "mannered" interpretation – which could be witty, erotic or grotesquely inflated – of the art of the High Renaissance.

Rome's major rival in the sixteenth century was Venice, whose long monopoly of trade with the East had been broken but whose civic wealth still permitted patronage of a most lavish kind. Contemporary writers who praised central Italian artists in terms of *disegno* (draughtsmanship) were sometimes by implication critical of the Venetian emphasis on *colore*, a freer handling of colour and paint and a more spontaneous and less intellectual approach. Yet it is the art of Venice, and the more isolated but great achievements of the north, together with the High Renaissance of Florence and Rome, that established the painting and sculpure of the sixteenth century as the touchstone of Western art.

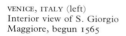

VENICE, ITALY (left)
Interior view of S. Giorgio
Maggiore, begun 1565

PRAGUE, BOHEMIA (right)
Vladislav Hall, Prague
Castle, begun 1487

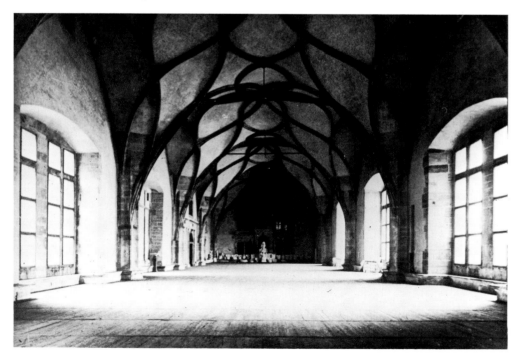

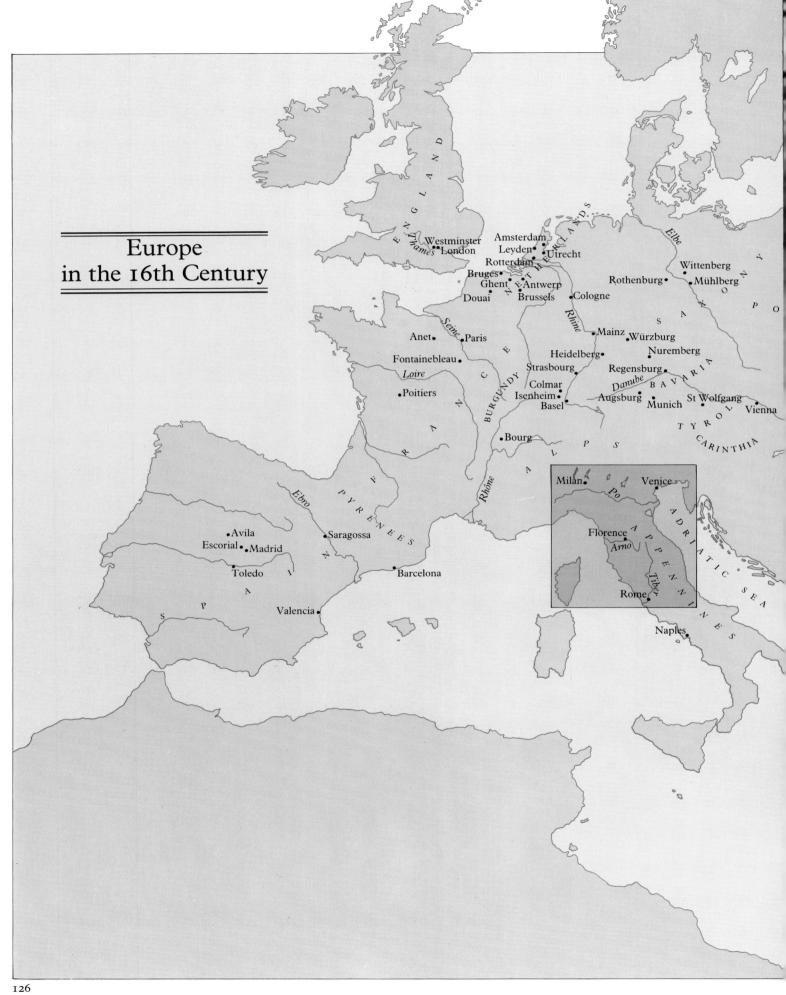

Europe
in the 16th Century

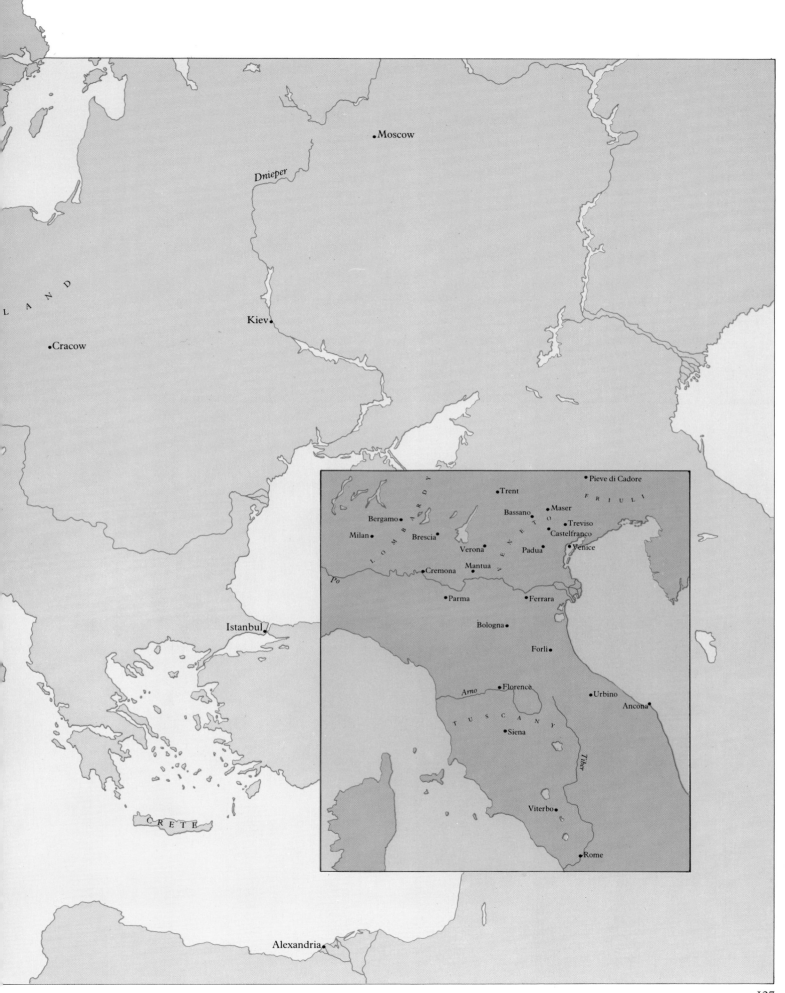

Moscow

Dnieper

Kiev

Cracow

L A N D

Istanbul

C R E T E

Alexandria

Pieve di Cadore

Trent

F R I U L I

Bassano
Maser

Bergamo
Treviso

L O M B A R D Y

Milan
Brescia
Castelfranco

Verona
Padua
Venice

V E N E T O

Cremona
Mantua

Po

Parma
Ferrara

Bologna

Forlì

Arno
Florence
Urbino
Ancona

T U S C A N Y

Siena

Tiber

Viterbo

Rome

The High Renaissance 1: Florence and Rome

It is still generally accepted that the High Renaissance was both a peak and a watershed in the history of European civilization, and that the Christian era can be divided essentially into pre-Renaissance and post-Renaissance, into medieval and modern. The early Renaissance had been a gradual revolution affecting not only the visual arts but literature, technology and the sciences as well; its consummation and climax, its point of no return, came in the brief moment of the High Renaissance in the early sixteenth century.

Vasari, in his *Lives of the Artists* (1550, revised 1568), formulated the art historical tradition that traces a path from Giotto, who began the break away from Byzantine and Gothic, through the early Renaissance and its prophets Masaccio and Donatello to the summits stormed by Michelangelo. The twentieth century has since discovered a fully realized perfection in Piero della Francesca, but perhaps the quintessential figure of the early Renaissance was Leon Battista Alberti. He was a poet, musician, scholar, mathematician and athlete, a painter, sculptor and architect – the prototype of the "universal man". His treatises conceived the arts as based on reason

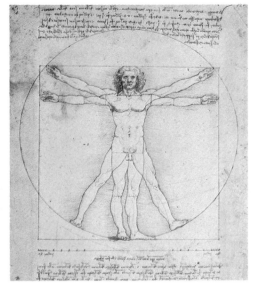

LEONARDO
"Vitruvian Man", c. 1490
The Roman architect Vitruvius had described how the human body could be the basis for a system of proportions. Leonardo's diagram reconciling circle and square is one image of High Renaissance harmony.

and human reality, and encouraged the scientific study of structure – whether in perspective or in anatomy – so that even religious themes were set forth in realistic terms. However, the attempt of the Dominican priest Savonarola, between 1494 and 1498, to build in Florence a new Jerusalem is a reflection of the continuity of religious belief and its prime claim.

Leonardo, Michelangelo and Raphael, the three great figures whose names often stand for the whole High Renaissance, are discussed in the following pages. They were all grounded in the Florentine tradition, but during the High Renaissance Rome became quite suddenly the main centre of the arts in Italy, barring only Venice. The ambitions of the fifteenth-century popes, such as Nicholas V, had been hampered by lack of political control, and, despite its classical sites and its libraries, Rome had been artistically provincial. Visiting artists, however, such as Fra Angelico, Piero della Francesca, his accomplished follower Melozzo da Forli (1438-94) and then many more, had painted there. By the beginning of the sixteenth century the papacy had established a temporal power, and Pope Julius II, elected in 1503, could dream of reviving the

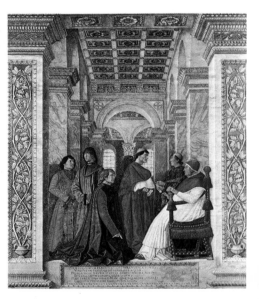

MELOZZO DA FORLI (left)
Sixtus IV ordering his nephew Palatina to reorganize the Vatican library, 1475-77
The crisp outlines and the relatively flat, unmodulated colour belong to the early Renaissance. The tallest cardinal near the centre is the future Pope Julius II.

PINTORICCHIO (right)
Susannah and the Elders, in the Borgia apartments in the Vatican, c. 1492-94
The gilt gesso relief was inspired by similar work in Nero's Golden House; so also was the elaborate geometric ceiling design. Pintoricchio's work was light, pretty and detailed.

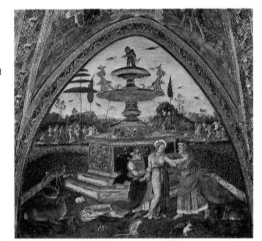

LEONARDO (below)
The Last Supper, c. 1495
It is said that even before Leonardo had finished it the painting had begun to decay. Leonardo departed from the usual fresco techniques to experiment with oil, probably because he wished to work up all the parts together, and so link the individual expressions and gestures of the apostles into one common drama. Vasari's anecdotes suggest that the artist spent rather more time pondering over the work than painting it; beautiful drawings survive to witness Leonardo's perfectionist preparation.

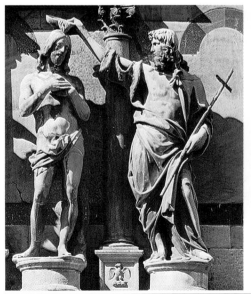

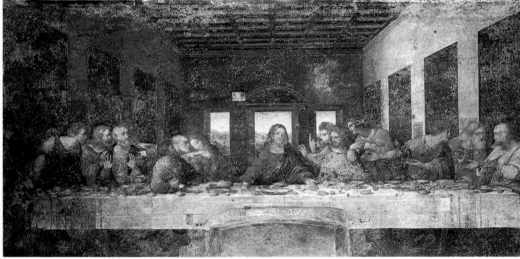

ANDREA SANSOVINO
(left) *The baptism of Christ*, 1502-05
The graceful, almost nude marble Christ stands in a classical *contrapposto* – the direction of the head balancing that of the legs – and conforms to a canon of classical proportions. Commissioned for Florence Baptistery and set above Ghiberti's Paradise doors, the group was left unfinished in 1505 when Sansovino was called to Rome. It was completed by Vincenzo Danti (1530-76).

prestige of ancient Rome, and began to rebuild St Peter's, the central church of Christendom, in monumental classical style.

Artists' study of the Antique had become more penetrating, and just at this time excavation yielded important examples of classical sculpture and painting – the *Laocoön*, "*The Torso Belvedere*", "*The Apollo Belvedere*" (see pp.41, 46) and the paintings and stuccowork of the Golden House of Nero. Though still of the early Renaissance, Pintoricchio (*c*.1454-1513), who had trained under Perugino a little earlier than Raphael, painted "grotesques" inspired by the remains of the Golden House for the apartments of Pope Alexander VI. These were a precedent for Raphael's Stanze (see p.137) and even for Michelangelo's Sistine Chapel ceiling (see p.134).

High Renaissance art is far from being all of a piece, and yet its qualities of grace, balance and restraint are quite distinct beside the generally hard and dry manner of the late fifteenth century. Artists not only emulated but surpassed antique models, as the early career of Michelangelo (see p.132) specifically demonstrates; but even the works of less titanic figures, such as *The baptism of Christ* by

Andrea Sansovino (*c*.1467-1529) for the Baptistery in Florence, display as confidently as Michelangelo's *David* the full assimilation of classical form. The High Renaissance occupied, however, an extremely brief period, coinciding roughly with the working career of Raphael, from his arrival in Florence in 1504 to his death in 1520. It was certainly over by 1527, which brought the shock of northern mercenaries sacking Rome. Yet it had been announced in *The Last Supper* painted in Milan by Leonardo in about 1495, and virtually from the beginning its classic resolutions of early Renaissance preoccupations suggest the fresh departures of the future.

The High Renaissance may be said to open with a flurry of activity just after the turn of the century in Florence, where Leonardo painted *The Battle of Anghiari*, known only through copies, and the *Mona Lisa* (see over), and also set forth crucial compositional problems – the pyramidal group and the *tondo*, or circular, form – explored by both Michelangelo and Raphael. Perhaps its most perfect resolution is Raphael's "*Madonna della Sedia*" (The Virgin enthroned) of 1516-17. Raphael's portrait of Baldassare Castiglione of about the same date,

which still reflects the *Mona Lisa*, also demonstrates the extremely rapid development that occurred within the High Renaissance. Leonardo, Michelangelo and Raphael may each exemplify that classic balance, restraint and harmony claimed as characteristic of the High Renaissance, but none of them can be contained within such a formula.

Briefly together in Florence, these three artists soon left for Rome but Fra Bartolommeo (1472/75-1517) and Andrea del Sarto (see p. 164) continued working there – painters of the first rank by the standards of any other age. At the same time in Venice the great masters Giovanni Bellini, Giorgione and the young Titian were demonstrating the triumph of colour in painting (see pp.138ff).

The High Renaissance established the fact in Italy that the artist was no longer an artisan but an independent creator, the equal of the poet, the intellectual and the humanist courtier – all of which he might be as well. His fame and distinction depended not only on his craft and skill but on his *invenzione* (invention, imagination), by which he was enabled to undertake and carry off stupendous projects. The concept of the artist as genius was born.

AFTER LEONARDO (below)
The Battle of Anghiari, detail, 1503-06
Leonardo's cartoon for a painting in the Town Hall to celebrate the victories of republican Florence is

now lost, but Rubens' copy of its central part reveals that it intended to convey swift, fierce movement in a complex, close-knit design, with a particular emphasis on the warriors' grimaces.

LEONARDO (left)
*The Virgin and Child with a cat, c.*1478-81
Leonardo's drawings show him "thinking on paper" as artists had never done before – this is not careful study but free experiment, an attempt to solve purely theoretical compositional problems in an early trial of the pyramidal theme.

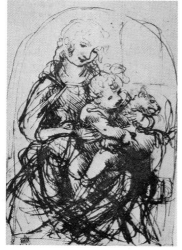

MICHELANGELO (right)
"*The Pitti Madonna*", 1504-05
Replying to the challenge of Leonardo's *Madonnas*, Michelangelo made three *tondi* between 1501 and 1505, two in marble, one a painting. Like Leonardo's, his poses are contrived and often sharply foreshortened.

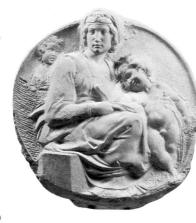

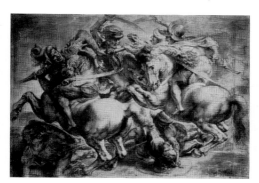

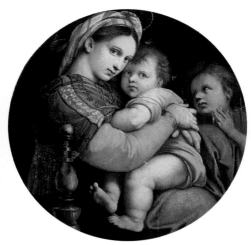

RAPHAEL
"*The Madonna della Sedia*" (The Virgin enthroned), *c*.1516-17
Raphael's composition is a perfect balance of curving forms in a round frame,

stabilized by the discreet upright of the throne arm. It is also an equilibrium of harmonious colours, not rich and glowing like those of the Venetians, but full and subtly satisfying.

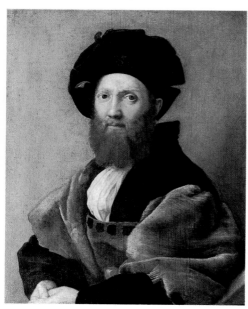

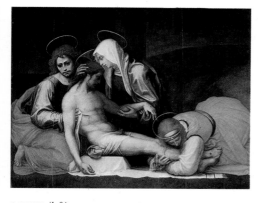

RAPHAEL (left)
*Baldassare Castiglione, c.*1516
The clear gaze and muted colours create warmth and an alert dignity without affectation, setting a new standard in portraiture. In his famous *Book of the Courtier* Castiglione hints at his esteem for Raphael beyond all other artists.

FRA BARTOLOMMEO
The Entombment, 1515
The refinement, softness and pure colours are typical of the Dominican's mature work. He was influenced by Leonardo, but his figures lack Leonardo's mystery, being more sculptural and monumental. There is an emotional strain, recalling Savonarola's preaching.

Leonardo da Vinci

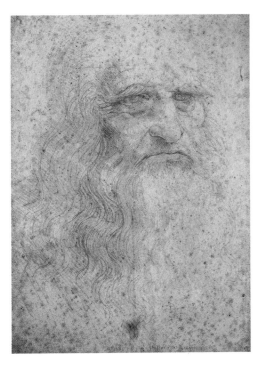

Leonardo da Vinci (1452-1519) was both prophet and arch-exponent of the High Renaissance. The oldest of its three supreme masters, he was nearly 50 when Michelangelo and the precocious Raphael entered their mature careers, but in his paintings of the 1480s and 1490s he had already absorbed and even surpassed the attainments of his contemporaries and, with an extraordinary intellectual grasp matched by an unfaltering skill of hand, he then passed far beyond them – indeed into fields apparently remote from art.

Leonardo's first master was Verrocchio (see p.115), in whose workshop he learned all the techniques the Florentine fifteenth century could teach him. His first known work, which he painted as an assistant, is the left-hand angel in Verrocchio's *Baptism* of about 1472. Verrocchio, it is said, was so impressed by the intimations of his pupil's genius that he gave up painting.

By 1472 Leonardo was enrolled in the Guild of Painters and was able to accept independent commissions. His concern to convey emotion through subtleties of expression meticulously observed is clearly evident in the early portrait, *Ginevra de' Benci*, perhaps of 1474. There is

again a strong sense of atmosphere in the unfinished *Adoration of the Magi* of 1481, in which many themes that will recur are seen for the first time – in particular his *sfumato* – no clear edge defines the contours – also the structure, created by the disposition and massing of the figures, linked by movement and gesture. The intensive preparation, the multiplication of preliminary sketches, was no less characteristic of Leonardo. Never before had so much of the artist's effort been devoted to the development of the idea, the process of invention. As a result the number of his drawings is immense but his pictures, though highly refined and novel, are relatively few, and often remained uncompleted.

By 1483 Leonardo was working for Lodovico Sforza il Moro in Milan. He seems to have announced himself primarily as a military engineer but also as an architect and sculptor. An equestrian statue got no further than a huge clay model, destroyed, for which, however, numerous drawings survive. *The Virgin of the rocks* was commissioned in 1483 (a second and later version was produced with an assistant's help). The pyramidal group of figures centred on the Madonna, set in a fantastic landscape

LEONARDO (above)
Self-portrait, c.1512
Vasari once described the artist, here aged about 60: "In appearance he was striking and handsome;

his magnificent presence brought comfort to the most troubled soul". He was a musician of famed skill, a lover of animals – "Nature's own miracle".

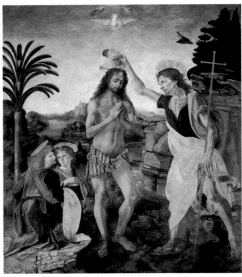

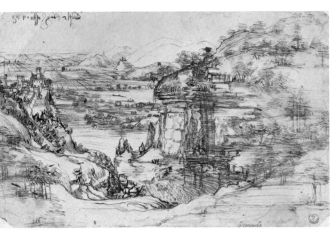

VERROCCHIO AND LEONARDO (above) *The baptism of Christ, c.1472*
The graceful angel kneeling in profile, and also his finely modelled robe, the tuft of grass beneath and the landscape above, are attributed to the young Leonardo. He adds to Florentine lucidity a new spiritual element in the pensive head. His master Verrocchio's work by contrast seems brittle, without fluidity or ease.

LEONARDO (left)
The Adoration of the Magi, 1481
Leonardo worked from dark to light, building up in oils – a new medium and a new technique in Italy. The almost monochrome underpaint reveals his methods. He created form by tonal blending "without lines or borders in the manner of smoke" – his famous *sfumato* technique. An elaborate perspective preparatory drawing has survived, but even there the mathematical grid is laden with creatures apparently of fantasy, full of inner life.

LEONARDO (below)
Ginevra de' Benci, c. 1474?
The background juniper, in Italian *ginepro*, is the emblem of the poetess. There is a suggestion of her veiled thoughts, of what Leonardo was to call the "motions of the mind"; a sombre, misty riverscape behind echoes the mystery of her heavy-lidded eyes.

LEONARDO (left)
Landscape, 1473
The pen-and-ink drawing of the Arno valley above Florence is Leonardo's earliest signed and dated work, with an inscription written from right to left. His interest in geography is apparent as well as his preoccupation with movement: lines suggest swaying trees, and the sweeping strokes foreshadow the pantheism of the later *Deluge* sketches.

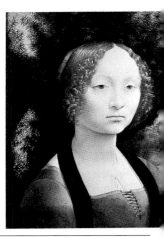

illumined by a mysterious twilight, was to prove a recurrent source of inspiration, especially for Fra Bartolommeo's and Raphael's *Madonnas*. Around 1495 Leonardo embarked on another famous project, *The Last Supper* (illustrated on preceding page): this, though now a ruin, was one of the most influential paintings of the Renaissance. It conveys the psychological drama of a moment of crisis – something never expressed in the more rigid treatment of the subject by earlier painters.

When Milan fell to the French in 1499 Leonardo returned to Florence via Mantua and Venice. Between 1500 and 1508 he produced three major works that have haunted the imagination of posterity – the now vanished fresco of *The Battle of Anghiari* in the Palazzo Vecchio, Florence; the *Mona Lisa*; and *The Virgin and Child with St Anne*. Copies of the central part of Leonardo's cartoon for the *Battle of Anghiari* survive (see preceding page); these, and preparatory studies, witness his concern both for anatomical accuracy and for expressiveness – in the warriors' faces and in the pent-up energy of the horses and men. The *Mona Lisa*, begun in 1503 and taken by Leonardo to France, has been claimed as the first modern portrait. The consummate technical skill with which tones and colour are merged into volume and the mysterious individuality evoked were unparalleled. The surviving versions of *The Virgin and Child with St Anne* are all unfinished, but they fully demonstrate Leonardo's search for complex and perfect balance in composition, and the unfailing ingenuity he brought to it, which amazed his contemporaries.

Leonardo's last years were restless. He produced fewer paintings but continued to be active in his many fields – in Milan again in 1508. Some sculptural projects are recorded, but no authenticated sculpture by Leonardo survives, and he never built a building, though from an early age he produced theoretical architectural plans and elevations. Then in 1513 he left for Rome, where he seems to have devoted himself chiefly to scientific experiments. His dissections, for instance, gave him an unprecedented grasp of anatomy, and led him to discuss the circulation of blood long before Harvey described its true workings. In 1516 he left for France, where he was the honoured guest of Francis I until his death at the age of 67 in 1519.

Vasari records Leonardo's intellectual curiosity, but his notebooks, virtually unknown to his contemporaries, have revealed to the modern world his astonishing observations and the full scope of his inventive genius. He was quite unlike his contemporaries in his relative indifference to the authority of classical scholarship, to philosophy and to poetry – he started always from what he saw – but he has become the archetype of "*l'uomo universale*", the universal man in whom all human knowledge was embodied. He also, like Michelangelo, provided a model for the concept of genius – not least by his fiercely independent, restless style of life; even by the fact that he was born illegitimate. Claiming the pre-eminence of his preferred art, painting, over the others, he argued that the painter's mind was endowed with a creative capacity which brought him closer to the mind of God. His reputation in his life-time was immense, and it was acknowledged visibly not only in the work of the foremost painters of the time in Florence – Fra Bartolommeo, Andrea del Sarto and, above all, Raphael – but also in Milan and northern Italy – by Correggio in Parma, and by Giorgione in Venice.

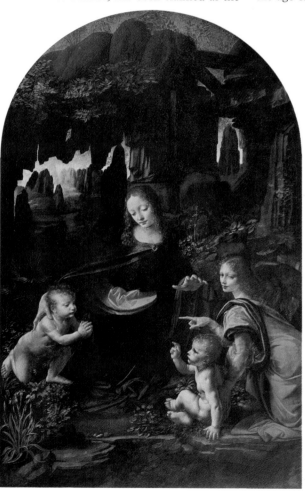

LEONARDO (above)
The Virgin of the rocks,
c. 1483-85
Strangeness – a nebulous metaphysical, even divine quality – is conveyed by the mysterious light and the quiet expressions of the Virgin and the angel.

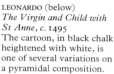

LEONARDO (right)
Flying machine, c. 1486-90
Years spent studying the flight of birds inspired Leonardo's anticipations of a helicopter. The attempt at flight is typical of his ambitiousness and absolute confidence in his powers.

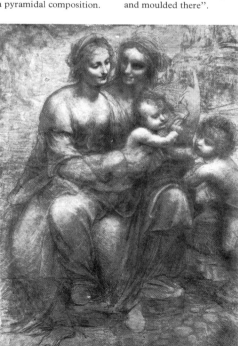

LEONARDO (below)
The Virgin and Child with St Anne, c. 1495
The cartoon, in black chalk heightened with white, is one of several variations on a pyramidal composition.

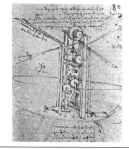

LEONARDO (right)
Anatomical drawing:
Sexual intercourse,
c. 1492-94
Dissections made possible a knowledge of anatomy unrivalled in Leonardo's time. Limitless curiosity and sure draughtsmanship yielded scores of studies. The script is in mirror-writing – an unusual but logical consequence of the artist's left-handedness.

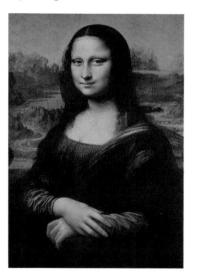

LEONARDO (right)
Mona Lisa, c. 1503-06
The critic Pater expressed a common awe: "All the thoughts and experiences of the world have etched and moulded there".

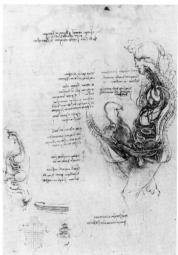

Michelangelo Buonarroti

Michelangelo Buonarroti (1475-1564) was the most sought-after artist in the sixteenth century, and for posterity the outstanding example of an artistic genius. His tumultuous career, with its perpetual struggles and its passionate commitment to art, was to become the master pattern for the Romantic artist.

In 1488, at the age of 13, Michelangelo was apprenticed as a painter to Domenico Ghirlandaio in Florence. He moved after less than a year to the somewhat mysterious "academy" set up in the Casino Mediceo by Lorenzo il Magnifico, where he could study "antique and good statues" and could meet the sophisticated humanists and *literati* of the Medici circle. The Neoplatonic thought current amongst them seems to underlie not only his poetry but much of his painting and sculpture as well.

Following Lorenzo's death, and the brief rule of the priest Savonarola, whose ascetic religion and republican ideals both influenced the young man deeply, Michelangelo left Florence in 1496 for Rome. His reputation, established by the sale of a *Sleeping Cupid* (now lost) as a genuine antique, was sealed by the Vatican *Pietà*, completed in 1499. In its exquisite finish, its flawless classicism, and its evocation of the human in the divine and the divine in the human, the *Pietà* is indeed a consummation of fifteenth-century art. The perfection of the two figures is informed both by an expert knowledge of anatomy (based on dissections) and by the Neoplatonic theory that the beauty of the body is an expression of its spirit.

Returning, famous, to Florence in 1501, Michelangelo was commissioned by the new republican government to carve a colossal *David*, symbol of resistance and independence. This was the first full statement of Michelangelo's heroic style, and of his inimitable and characteristic *terribilità* (awesomeness). He was also engaged to paint a fresco in the Palazzo Vecchio in rivalry to Leonardo, next to his *Battle of Anghiari* - The Battle of Cascina. The fresco was never painted but the cartoon (now lost), with its convulsive nude soldiers, fascinated artists in Florence.

In 1505 Michelangelo was summoned by the new Pope, Julius II, to Rome and entrusted with an immense sculptural project, the Pope's mausoleum. Although only three of the 40 life-size or larger figures of the early designs were executed – the formidable *Moses* and the unfinished "*Struggling slave*" and "*Dying*

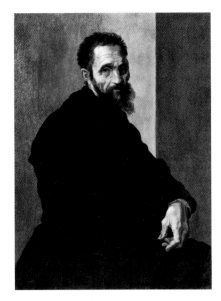

Michelangelo Buonarroti
The artist's troubled, even battered face reflects a lifelong struggle with colossal projects, and the sense of failure that recurs in his letters and poetry of often tormented piety. His hand is painted in the shape of the hand of his own *David*.

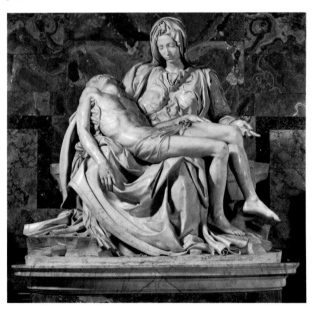

MICHELANGELO (above)
The Vatican *Pietà*, 1499
Christian emotion never has been more perfectly united with classical form. Michelangelo never reached such flawless finish again.

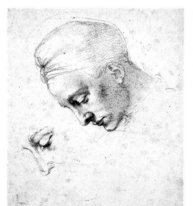

MICHELANGELO (right)
David, 1501-04
The more than life-size *David* is heroically clear-eyed, finely proportioned, and characteristically has both tension and languor.

MICHELANGELO (left)
Study for *Leda*, c. 1530?
The subject, the rape of Leda by Jupiter as a swan, could not be more sensual; and yet the head is so pure.

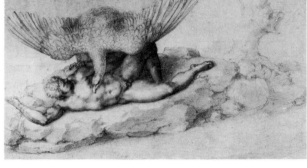

MICHELANGELO (left)
Tityus, 1532
The giant Tityus fed upon by a vulture was a symbol perhaps of the torture of sensual love – as opposed to heavenly love. It was drawn to give to one of his beloved.

MICHELANGELO (below)
"*Dying slave*", 1513-16
Probably once representing the grief of the world at the passing of Julius II, the suffering figure seems now to feel Michelangelo's and all human torment.

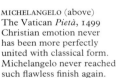

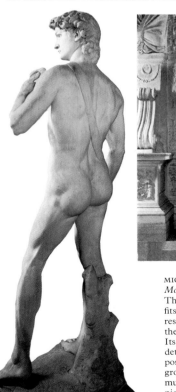

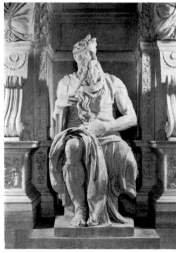

MICHELANGELO (above)
Moses, 1513-16
The severe, massive figure fits uneasily into its final resting place, a mockery of the original, grand scheme. Its strange proportions were determined by its intended position, high up from the ground. In concept, it owes much to Donatello, who had pioneered the Renaissance monumental seated figure.

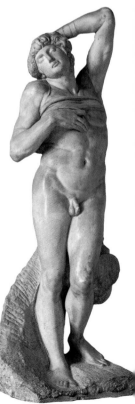

slave" – the commission dominated most of Michelangelo's life. In 1508 he was transferred by Julius to the Sistine Chapel ceiling, but the constantly aborted history of the tomb, "The Tragedy of the Tomb", ended only in 1547 – some 40 years and five revised contracts later. The final, disproportionately truncated version is in S. Pietro in Vincoli, Rome.

The Sistine Chapel ceiling (see over) was to prove Michelangelo's most celebrated work, but he was always to maintain that he was primarily a sculptor, and, contrary to Leonardo's view, affirmed the superiority of sculpture over painting "as the sun is to the moon". By sculpture, he said, he meant "taking away", that is, carving rather than modelling, as if releasing the image from within the stone. All through his career the unfinished creatures recur, struggling for freedom as if imprisoned in the stone – like man, according to Neoplatonic doctrine, imprisoned in his body.

After the death of Julius II in 1513, Michelangelo could work on the tomb undiverted for a while, but the new Pope, the Medici Leo X, soon engaged him on the façade of S. Lorenzo in Florence. Here was a still better opportunity to harmonize architecture and sculpture in one

design, but it, too, aborted, although Michelangelo was able to fulfil some of his architectural and sculptural ambitions in the Library and the New Sacristy, or Medici Chapel, of S. Lorenzo. The Medici Chapel fell not far short of being completed: two of the Medici tombs intended for the Chapel were installed, and for the third Michelangelo had carved his last great *Madonna* (unfinished; not shown) when he left Florence for ever in 1534.

Arrived in Rome, Michelangelo undertook for the new Pope, Paul III, *The Last Judgment* on the altar wall of the Sistine Chapel. Far from being an extension of the ceiling, this was an entirely novel statement. Between the two projects the stability of Italy had been shown to be pitiably fragile by the Sack of Rome in 1527; the buoyant Neoplatonic Christianity of the early humanists had been overtaken by papal impotence and error and the rise of Protestantism. The mood of *The Last Judgment* is sombre; the vengeful naked Christ is not a figure of consolation, and even the Saved struggle painfully towards Salvation. The colour likewise is sombre; the figures are thick-waisted and heavily muscular, and very forcefully modelled. Michelangelo's last paintings

were frescos in the Cappella Paolina just beside the Sistine Chapel, completed in 1550, when he was 75 years old; but *The conversion of Paul* and *The crucifixion of St Peter* are disturbing visions of undiminished dynamism.

Michelangelo's crowning achievement, however, was architectural – he was appointed architect to St Peter's in 1546. He continued in his last years to write poetry, renouncing in the moving late sonnets the world and even his art; he made remarkable drawings expressing his profound, now often pessimistic, religious feeling; and he carved the two extraordinary, haunting and pathetic late *Pietàs*, one *"The Rondanini Pietà"* in Milan, on which he was working six days before his death.

For his contemporaries the emotionally charged, heroic male nudes of the Sistine Chapel, or the spiralling, exquisitely contorted figures like the marble *Victory* (see p.164), were more significant, but it is Michelangelo's unfinished, unresolved creations that have especially interested the twentieth century. After Michelangelo, the aesthetic focus becomes not simply the created art object, but the inextricable relationship of the artist's personality and his work.

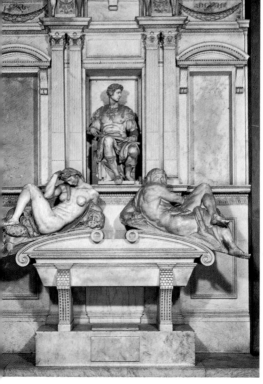

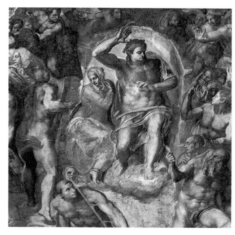

MICHELANGELO (right)
The Last Judgment, detail, on the altar wall of the Sistine Chapel, 1534-41
At the summit of a wall filled with struggling nude figures rising and falling (many have had the nudity overpainted), Christ curses the Damned. With his left hand he much less clearly beckons the Saved, and he seems also to point to his wounds as in the gesture of the Man of Sorrows. It is in strong contrast to the ceiling of 25 years earlier: the nudes have lost their beauty, but doubled their power, their *terribilità*. The great example of the Grand Manner, Vasari called it.

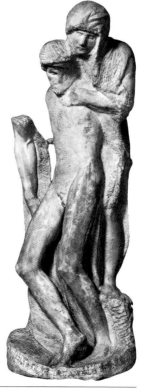

MICHELANGELO (below)
"The Rondanini Pietà", c. 1555-64
Mother and Son merge in a rough unfinished sculpture of a rarefied beauty and almost Expressionist power. Reworked and in process of transformation – the artist had destroyed one Christ – the attenuated new beginning has formal parallels in Western art no earlier than this century. Michelangelo was doggedly working on the stone within a few days of his death.

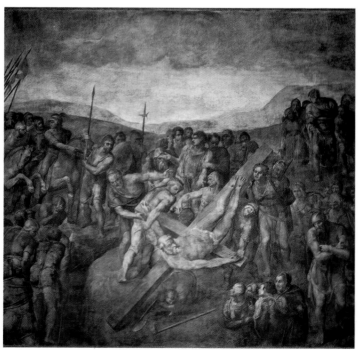

MICHELANGELO (above)
The tomb of Giuliano de' Medici in the Medici Chapel, S. Lorenzo, 1534
Giuliano, with head alert, ready to rise, embodies the Active Principle; on the opposite side (not shown) Lorenzo embodies the Contemplative Principle – a Neoplatonic allegory. The immensely powerful figures of Day and Night, precarious on their sarcophagus, seem to be alien beings of the Unconscious.

MICHELANGELO (right)
The crucifixion of St Peter, 1546-50
Upside down on the cross, St Peter twists round with disturbing contortionism to stare fiercely out at the spectator. He is surrounded by elemental forms that are no longer lit, as before, by potential divinity. The isolated groups cluster round an unsettling vortex, seeming to float without solid edges – as veiled as the unfinished sculptures.

Michelangelo: The Sistine Chapel Ceiling

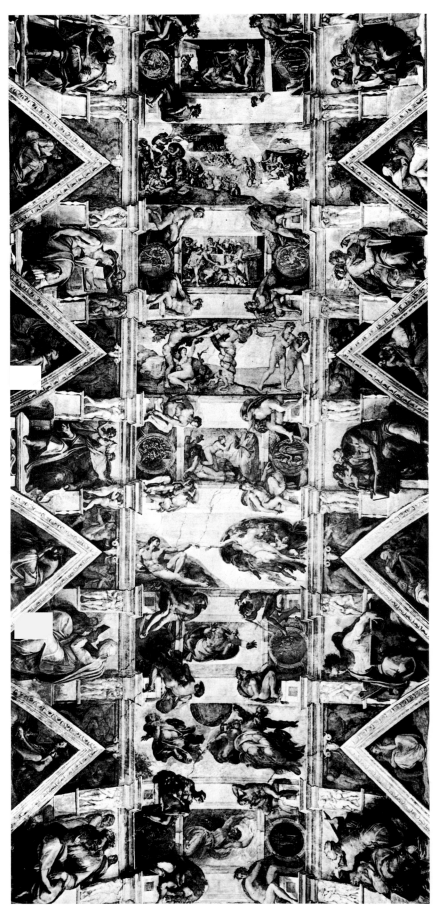

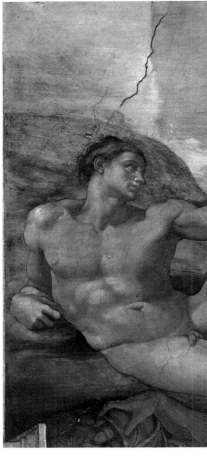

MICHELANGELO
(left) The Sistine Chapel ceiling, 1508-12
The narrative is contained within the long central strip of the barrel vault. It consists of nine scenes from Genesis, three for *The creation of the world*, three for *The creation of Adam* (detail, right), *The creation of Eve* and *The Fall*, and three for *The story of Noah*. The last scene, *The drunkenness of Noah*, above the entrance, shows man in weakness but implies his redemption. Along the sides are figures illustrating the indissoluble concordance of Old and New Testaments, the Old foreshadowing the New: *The ancestors of Christ* listed in St Matthew's Gospel, and pagan *Sybils* and Hebrew *Prophets*, who foretold Christ's coming, in the triangular spandrels of the vault. Separating the nine central scenes are the famous *Ignudi* (male nudes), whose meaning is unclear. Perhaps, though wingless, they are angels, but their vivid force far exceeds the needs of their function, to support fictive medallions and sprays of oak (emblem of Julius II's family); they culminate the Renaissance adaptation of classical modes to Christian use.

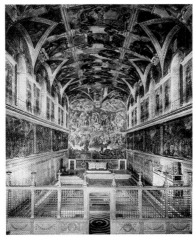

(left) The interior of the Sistine Chapel
When Michelangelo painted the ceiling there were two frescos and an altarpiece by Perugino at the end, and windows like those down the sides. These, and two lunettes of Michelangelo's own ceiling, were removed when he came to paint *The Last Judgment*. In 1519 tapestries by Raphael were hung round the lower walls.

(below) *The Libyan Sibyl*
The huge Sibyl, painted after the break of 1510, is in the more monumental, later style. Her figure is an idealization synthesizing the beauty of both sexes.

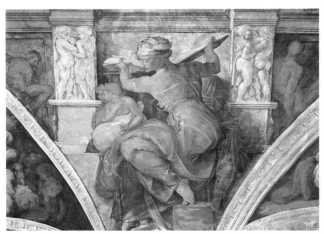

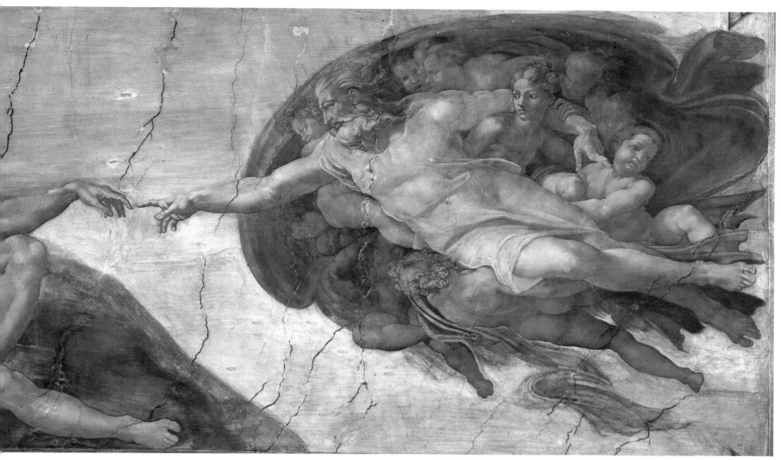

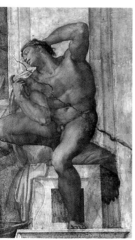

(left) *Ignudo*
The *Ignudi* can be interpreted as a series of formal variations on the classical *"Belvedere Torso"* (see p. 46). They are also an expression of Michelangelo's individual genius – almost art for art's sake; in this and in their strain, thrust and counter-thrust of pose, they were an inspiration for succeeding generations of Mannerist artists.

(below) *The prophet Jonah* Vasari called it the peak of genius in this supreme work that Michelangelo could paint on a forward-sloping surface a figure that apparently falls backwards.

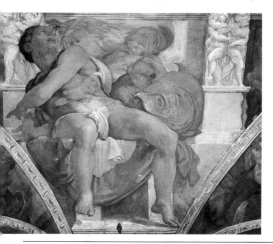

The Sistine Chapel in the Vatican, begun by Pope Sixtus IV in 1473, was and is a place of worship, but it is also the setting for certain extraordinary functions – notably the conclave of cardinals for the election of a new pope. The decorations of the 1480s – frescos by Perugino, Signorelli, Botticelli and others girdling the walls – had illustrated the basis of papal authority in the Old and New Testaments. When he commissioned Michelangelo to paint the ceiling in 1508 Pope Julius II probably wished to assert not only the Christian faith and his role as its leader, but also papal independence from such temporal powers as Louis XII of France, with whom he was embattled. Once entrusted to Michelangelo, however, the scheme became one primarily of Michelangelo's devising.

The commission to paint the ceiling came to Michelangelo at a point when he was obsessed with the design for Julius II's tomb, that is, with sculptural problems, and at first he seems to have fiercely resented the imposition. Julius II was an impatient and demanding patron, while Michelangelo's temperament was often neurotic or moody. In a poem written in 1510 Michelangelo bemoaned his lot – "I am not in a good place, and I'm no painter". But in the event the ceiling was to prove a more satisfactory project than the tomb.

The vast area of the Chapel ceiling, 38.5 × 14 metres (118 × 46 ft), took four years to paint, and was unveiled in part in August 1511 and completely on October 31 1512. It was Michelangelo's first major exercise in fresco, for the *Battle of Cascina* project had never passed the cartoon stage. After un-

satisfactory trials with assistants he locked himself away in the Chapel, and virtually single-handed, on dizzy scaffolding of his own design, worked slowly across the expanse of the ceiling, through the days and months, often in acute discomfort. It was an heroic feat never to be surpassed by himself or another.

The extraordinary programme of the ceiling evolved from very simple first ideas – figures of the twelve apostles in an ornamental setting. But once the project had seized hold of his imagination, Michelangelo emended and aggrandized the first conception beyond recognition, though he must have discussed his ideas with learned churchmen – the Vatican was certainly not lacking in theological expertise. Formally, the imagery used clearly reflects the sculptor's frustration: the figures of the *Sibyls* and *Prophets* are variations on the theme of the great statue *Moses* for the tomb of Julius II; the famous *Ignudi* (nudes) likewise take up the mood of the so-called *"Slaves"* intended for the tomb. Michelangelo's style evolved as he progressed from the entrance to the Chapel, with its complex *Story of Noah*, towards the altar wall, and, especially after the break of 1510 when the scaffolding was removed, he simplified the compositions and form, reduced the details, and made the images ever bolder and more dynamic. One of the first images Michelangelo painted when he resumed work in early 1511 was the most famous scene in the Chapel, its climax, *The creation of Adam*, with its electric charge passing from the outstretched hand of God to the hand of the awakening Adam – an unsurpassed image of the most profound human mystery.

Raphael

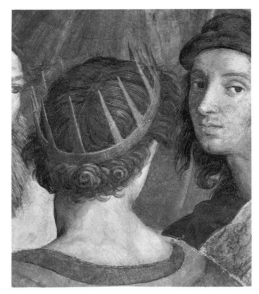

If the name of Raphael is synonymous with the "classical" in High Renaissance art, that is partly because his genius was essentially one of strengthening and refining rather than of revolutionary innovation. In his compliance with his patrons' wishes he resembled an early Renaissance artist more closely than Leonardo or Michelangelo, and in contrast to their moody and formidable personalities he was renowned for his affable and gracious charm.

Raffaello Sanzio (1483-1520) was born in Urbino, the son of a court painter, Giovanni Santi. He was working with Perugino at Perugia by 1500. His early independent work is closely related to Perugino's: elements of that grace that marks his whole career were due to Perugino, and the subtle elegance of his figures and the sweetness of his female faces. But he soon outstripped his master: in his early masterpiece, *The marriage of the Virgin*, so close to Perugino's fresco *Christ handing the Keys to St Peter* (see p. 116), his power of integrating graceful figures into a rhythmic, harmonious unity is already fully developed.

In 1504 Raphael arrived in Florence, where the work of Leonardo and Michelangelo came as a revelation to him. Leonardo's *Mona Lisa*

and *Battle of Anghiari* fresco influenced him crucially, yet Raphael proved, as he would time and time again, that his ability to adapt from others what was necessary to his own vision and to reject what was incompatible with it was faultless. Now began the series of *Madonnas*, whose charm, matchlessly evoking the divine within tender humanity, has captured popular imagination ever since. In composition, Raphael's early *Madonnas* relate closely to the pyramidal structures evolved by Leonardo (see p. 129), but the complexity and contrivance of Leonardo is resolved into a perfectly balanced harmony; the enigmatic expression of Leonardo's figures yields to an untroubled radiance; in place of fantastic lunar settings, a serenely placid landscape unfolds.

In his portraits, too, Raphael was influenced by Leonardo, but he retained his own clarity of definition and a strikingly direct apprehension of character. In the portrait of Agnolo Doni the half-length pose, the counterpoint between head and body and the expressive placing of the hands are clearly from Leonardo. There is some trace of Michelangelo in the works Raphael painted before he left Florence, but the full impact of Michelangelo came later.

RAPHAEL
Self-portrait, detail of *"The School of Athens"* Raphael looks out (from a group of astronomers) with

modesty and calm – clear, untroubled. His courtesy was a rival to his artistry: and both, in Vasari's words, "vanquished the world".

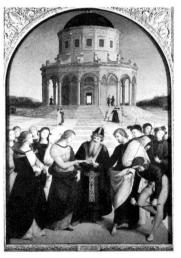

RAPHAEL (left)
Agnolo Doni, 1505
The main elements of the pose derive from the *Mona Lisa*, but the mood is now masculine, and is Raphael's – with almost no *sfumato*.

RAPHAEL (below)
"The Sistine Madonna", 1512
The grandest of Raphael's long series of Madonnas, the human yet visionary Virgin walks on air as if on

earth. Originally in the apse of S. Sisto in Rome (hence its name), the altarpiece perhaps deliberately rivalled Byzantine mosaics in the splendour of its colour, its composition, its presence.

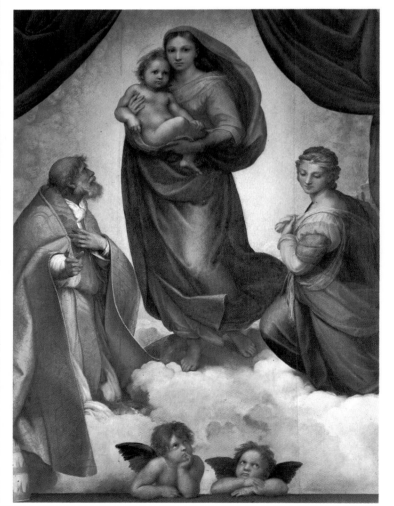

RAPHAEL (above)
The marriage of the Virgin, 1504
Firmly signed and dated by Raphael when he was 21, the picture demonstrates a reconciliation of abstract symmetry with the movement and drama of human life – one defining aspect of High Renaissance art. Figures, architecture and atmospheric perspective have poised, solid control.

RAPHAEL (right)
"La Belle Jardinière" (The Madonna and Child with St John), c. 1506
The Virgin's features still recall Perugino's *Virgins*; and the series of *Madonnas* Raphael made in Florence (being mostly small, for private devotion) have a domestic intimacy lost in the later ones in Rome. The physical movement of the figures is wonderfully united with the compositional lines of direction.

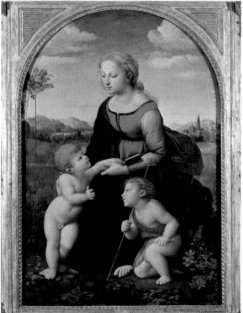

Within four years Raphael had achieved success in Florence and his fame had travelled. By the autumn of 1508 he was in Rome and was entrusted by Pope Julius II with the decoration of the Stanze, the new papal apartments, an enormous commission for the 26-year-old artist. It was nevertheless a triumph. The first room, the *Stanza della Segnatura*, was completed by 1511; its two larger frescos, *"The School of Athens"* and *"Disputa"* (Disputation over the Sacrament; not shown), are a consummation of High Renaissance principles. They stand for the intellectual reconciliation of Christianity and classical antiquity: the Eucharist, one of the central Christian mysteries, is represented on the one hand, on the other an encyclopaedic illustration of classical philosophy, centred on the figures of Plato and Aristotle. Both frescos are miracles of harmony, of movement within strict symmetry, of the marriage of the real and the ideal. In the later Stanze Raphael moved away from the serene perfection of the *Segnatura* and in a sense the climax of the High Renaissance had been reached and passed.

While Raphael was at work on the first Stanza, Michelangelo was locked from sight not far away painting the Sistine Chapel ceiling. It is in the later Stanze that the impact of his work is clearly felt, though Raphael could assimilate even Michelangelo's influence without in the least compromising his own genius. The dominant fresco of the second Stanza, *The expulsion of Heliodorus* (1511-13), is full of tempestuous movement – anticipating aspects of Mannerist, even of Baroque art. There are dramatic contrasts of light and dark, the colours are richer and stronger – perhaps Raphael had learnt something of Venetian colourism from Sebastian del Piombo (see p. 146), who had just arrived in Rome.

Enormous demands were now placed on Raphael, and much of his work, notably in the third Stanza, was carried out by assistants (led by Giulio Romano) following his designs. Many of his designs were engraved in his lifetime, and by this means his influence spread far beyond Rome. Under the new Pope, Leo X, he held an important position in the papal court, besides combining the careers of painter, architect and archaeologist: he initiated the first comprehensive survey of the antiquities of Rome. The High Renaissance obsession with the Antique governed several of Raphael's most important commissions – decorative schemes in the Vatican *Loggie* (not shown), inspired by the antique paintings discovered in the Golden House of Nero, and in the Villa Farnesina. In the Farnesina the fresco of *The triumph of Galatea*, entirely from Raphael's hand, is outstanding – effortlessly perfect, radiantly fresh. Its intricately balanced composition frames in Galatea the supreme example of the figure-of-eight pose.

From this intensely active period date some of Raphael's greatest masterpieces – *"The Sistine Madonna"*, with its exquisite simplicity of design and supremely idealized Mother and Child, painted with the softest *sfumato*; *"The Madonna della Sedia"* (The Madonna enthroned, see p. 129); several portraits, notably that of Castiglione (illustrated on p. 129). In the cartoons for the tapestries (not shown) ordered by Leo X for the Sistine Chapel, he achieved a classic majesty and grandeur yet more vigorous than before. When he died, suddenly, at the age of 37, he left unfinished one of his greatest easel-paintings, *The Transfiguration*. His death was felt as a public calamity; he had become the embodiment of an ideal which seemed to die with him.

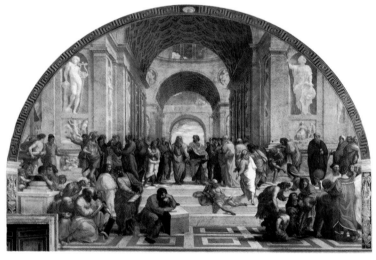

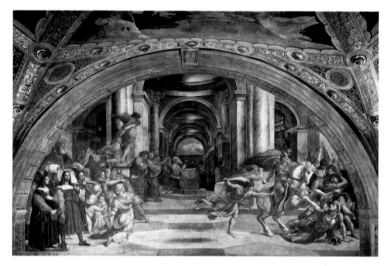

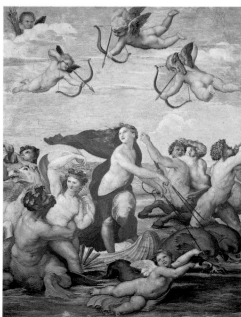

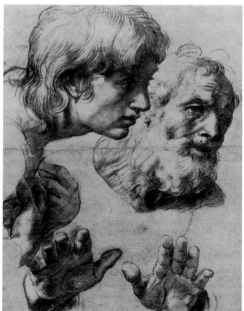

RAPHAEL (above)
"The School of Athens" in the *Stanza della Segnatura*, 1509-11
The perfect structure of reason built by the antique philosophers is symbolized by the architecture – which echoes the plans for the new St Peter's. This has been described as the first "history" painting, a model for countless subsequent "histories". Michelangelo must have influenced the seated foreground thinker.

RAPHAEL (right)
The triumph of Galatea, c.1513
Surrounding Galatea are riotous pagan creatures, tritons, hippocampi and cupids – classical but also sensual. Even the paddles on Galatea's shell-float are a recondite classical allusion, referring to the paddle-boats recorded in Roman reliefs.

RAPHAEL (above)
The expulsion of Heliodorus, 1511-13
Heliodorus, attempting to steal temple treasures, was thwarted by a miraculous horse and rider (which owe much to Leonardo's *Battle of Anghiari*). For Julius II, borne on a litter to the left, anyone who threatened papal temporal power was a Heliodorus. The effect is most dramatic upon entering the room – the fresco is revealed from left to right.

RAPHAEL (left)
Two apostles, study for *The Transfiguration*, 1520
The study for two figures looking on with amazed expressions reveals Raphael's superb draughtsmanship, and the care and discipline in all he undertook – his art was never "carried away". The proto-Mannerist work itself is shown on p. 164.

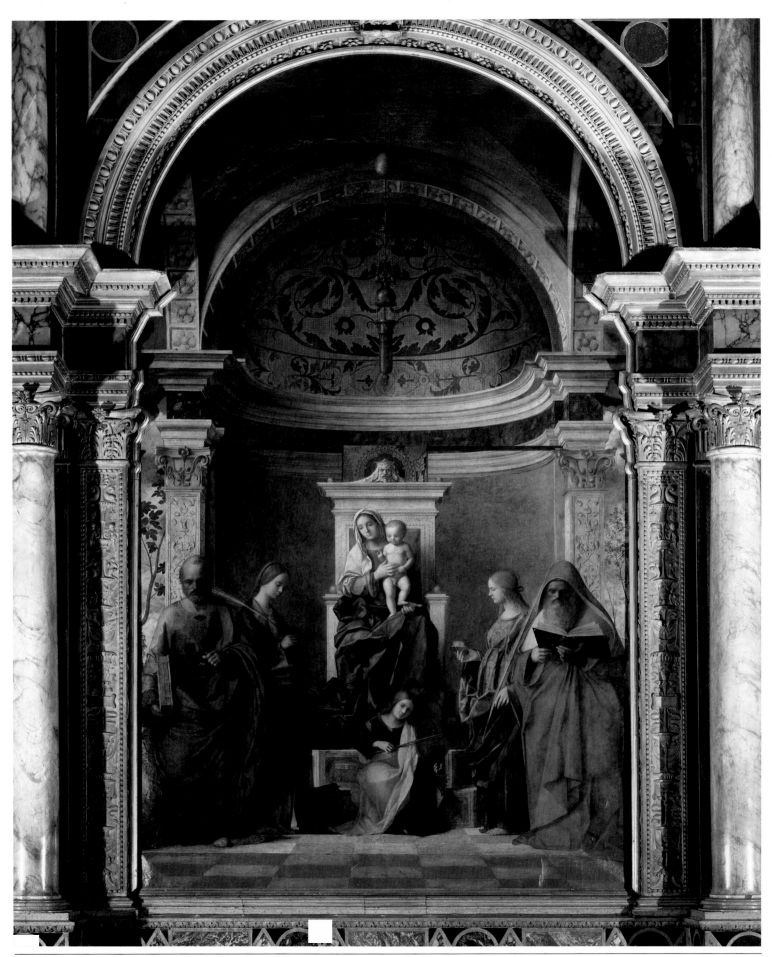

Giovanni Bellini's great altarpiece in S. Zaccaria in Venice was painted for that church in 1505; it is signed and dated IOANNES BELLINUS MCCCCCV, and has been there ever since. It represents *The Virgin and Child with saints*, and it is perhaps the most perfect realization of the *sacra conversazione* theme in all Western painting. In 1506, the year after it had been finished, the greatest artist of the Renaissance in northern Europe, Dürer, visited Bellini in Venice and noted: "He is very old, and is still the best in painting". Possibly Dürer was thinking of this painting when he wrote that; and this work of a man in his seventies was judged by the critic Ruskin to be one of the two best paintings in the world (the other was also by Bellini).

The S. Zaccaria altarpiece is the climax of a long series of meditations by Bellini on the theme of *The Virgin and Child*. Especially early on in Bellini's career his *Madonnas* were generally smallish panels intended for domestic devotion, continuing the tradition of Gentile da Fabriano and of Giovanni's father Jacopo. The earliest are still very much in the early fifteenth-century tradition, hieratic and quite austere, but very soon human tenderness between a flesh-and-blood mother and her child becomes apparent. The slightly melancholic mood could be that of a woman consumed with wonder at the miracle of birth, but also apprehensive, since the infant in her lap is a hostage to fortune; yet simultaneously the image is divine. Divinity is indicated not so much by the halo (not always present) or by the hands joined together in prayer, as by that heavenly radiance and solemnity with which Bellini imbued his women. Often, when the Child is recumbent, there is a haunting foreshadowing of the *Pietà*, of the dead Christ supported by his mother. Bellini developed and enriched the still charm of his *Madonnas* throughout his career, and in the very late ones, such as *"The Madonna of the Meadow"*, the image of the Madonna is merged convincingly into one of the most beautiful of Giovanni's landscapes, serene in the cool light of spring, with the little village clear-cut on the rise beyond. The Mother of God is brought into direct relationship with day-to-day life.

Bellini's sequence of more monumentally scaled *sacre conversazioni* began with one, now lost, painted about 1475, related to a famous one by Antonello da Messina painted in Venice about the same time. From the fragments of this work, and from Bellini's surviving S. Giobbe altarpiece of about 1490, it can be deduced that the architectural frame was conceived as integral with the painting, thus tying the image bodily into the structure and presence of the church as a whole. In the S. Giobbe altarpiece, the sense of space, the relative relaxation of the figures, the glowing, translucent colour all speak of Antonello's Netherlandish-oriented vision, and probably of his technique. The composition, however, is a little busy, even claustrophobic (it is the only one of Bellini's compositions entirely enclosed in an interior). The gain achieved through simplification in the S. Zaccaria altarpiece is subtle but substantial.

Here the five figures are almost life-size and the viewpoint is higher, the spectator closer, while there is a hint of landscape and open air at each side. The Virgin is seated, with the Child blessing, amongst attendant saints – St Peter with his key, St Catherine with her martyr's palm, St Lucy, and St Jerome with his open book. The draperies and the heads are softly modelled in the fall of a unifying light (the head of St Jerome, in its pensive meditation, seems already tinged by the mood of the young Giorgione, whose *"Castelfranco Madonna"* is thought to have been finished in the previous year). The colours glow in a rich harmony, and the serene symmetry and balance of proportions exist in a silence that somehow is full of music – the music indicated by the angel with the viol on the step of the Madonna's throne. The figures, as in most of Bellini's mature work, have an ample ease both monumental and peaceful.

Bellini's painting is already of the High Renaissance. The composition unites in harmony the primarily Florentine concern for the logical, even mathematical, control of space and proportion with the typically Netherlandish interest in the rendering of light, while there is more than a promise of the revolutionary colourism with which Bellini's pupils and followers were to startle the world.

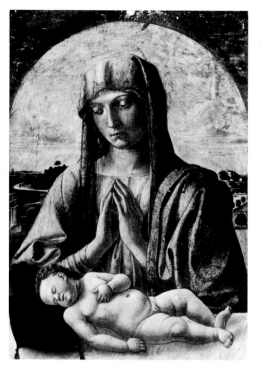

GIOVANNI BELLINI (above)
The Madonna and Child,
c. 1465-70
Giovanni's early *Virgins* often have a distinctly waxy texture; ideal images, they have a precisely sculptured form, an almost geometric neatness. The light is still hard and dry; the breath of air which relaxes his later work has not yet arrived.

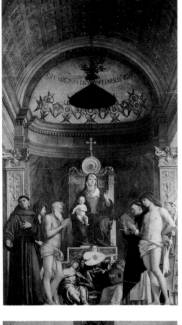

GIOVANNI BELLINI (right)
The S. Giobbe altarpiece,
c. 1490
The painted architecture correlated with the real altar, probably designed by the architect of S. Giobbe, one of the first Venetian Renaissance churches. The space is an extension of the spectator's world – and to be seen from below.

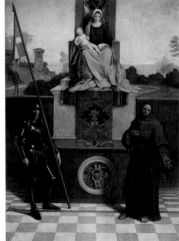

GIORGIONE (right)
"The Castelfranco Madonna", *c*. 1504
Giorgione's only altarpiece, painted for his native town of Castelfranco, is so dated because it seems similar to the S. Zaccaria altarpiece, and it seems to confirm that Giorgione at first worked in Bellini's studio. The strange proportions, however, with the Madonna so high, and the moodiness, are Giorgione's own (see over).

GIOVANNI BELLINI (above)
"The Madonna of the Meadow", *c*. 1501
The supernatural is hinted at both in symbolic details – the stork battling with the serpent, beneath the eagle in the dry tree; the monk in his white robe – and, above all, in the serene calm.

GIOVANNI BELLINI (left)
The S. Zaccaria altarpiece:
The Virgin and Child with saints, 1505

Giorgione: The Tempest

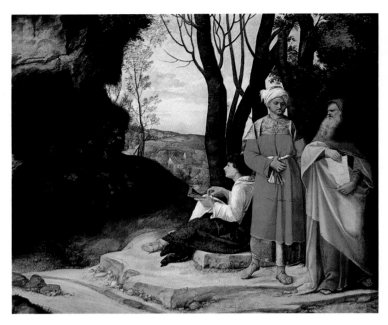

GIORGIONE (left)
"Laura", 1506
What exactly the laurels
signify is unknown. The
sitter's gaze is veiled and
introspective; the *sfumato*
also recalls Leonardo's
Mona Lisa. Is this woman
the one in the *Tempestà*?

GIORGIONE (below)
Venus, c. 1509-10?
A tiny cupid, later painted
out, played at Venus' feet.
She lies improbably but
convincingly in a superb
landscape (the picture is
perhaps in need of cleaning,
however). Titian reworked
the theme in his *"Venus
of Urbino"* (see p. 144).

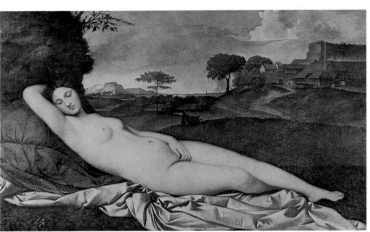

GIORGIONE (above)
"The Three Philosophers",
after 1505?
The enigmatic figures are
set before a mountain cave,
a dark chasm symbolizing
birth? Or the unknown? If
they were Magi, Christ's
birth could be meant. The
figures and landscape are
still reminiscent of Bellini,
but Bellini is always clear:
Giorgione escapes analysis.

The brevity and obscurity of the career of Giorgione (died 1510) are no index to his importance in the history of art. Although only some 20 paintings are generally associated with him, of which only about six are attributed without dispute, his originality was so potent that these few works have come to stand for an enduring quality of the Western imagination.

Surviving documentation on his life and work is sparse: the main reflection of his personality is that recorded in a brief *Life* by Vasari, who visited Venice about half a century after his death and talked with Giorgione's early collaborator, Titian, and others who may have known the young painter years before. Giorgione was clearly a phenomenon, of a kind new to Venice if not to humanist circles in Florence – a creature endowed with unusual physical beauty as well as grace and wit; gentle and courteous, "always a very amorous man"; a brilliant singer and lute-player. Not least, he had an instinctive gift for the visual arts. He was associated with the humanist circle of the poet Bembo, and with a sophisticated group of private patrons, for whom he painted generally small-scale pictures. Giorgione's only public commissions in Venice were paintings, now lost, in the Doge's Palace, and frescos, now something less than ghostly fragments, on the exterior of the Fondaco dei Tedeschi, the important trading centre (just by the Rialto Bridge) of the German community.

Significantly, Vasari, himself a master of esoteric allegory, was unable to understand the meaning of the figures on the Fondaco dei Tedeschi ("nor, for all my asking, have I found anyone who does"). A certain hermetic mystery is a characteristic of virtually all the paintings ascribed to Giorgione: his characters are engaged in some concern of unworldly significance, in a mood so intense that it verges on the mystical, which no prosaic explanation can ultimately elucidate. Beneath what Vasari called "a harmonized manner, and a certain brilliance of colour" there is an underlying tension, and in this, and in the softness and subtlety of his modelling, Vasari recognized the influence of Leonardo. The emotional

vibrancy of his colour, however, is Giorgione's own, although he could never have achieved it without earlier developments in the flexibility of the oil medium. Vasari observed that he worked directly from nature – and surely swiftly, directly on to the canvas, without the elaborate structural preliminaries that were a necessary part of Florentine *disegno*.

The famous *Tempest* is a key work among Giorgione's few paintings, and a turning-point in the history of art. It is confidently identified with a painting inventoried in 1530 as a "small landscape . . . with the storm, and the gipsy and the soldier". Significantly, hardly 25 years later the compiler of the list did not know what the subject of the painting was, and, significantly also, it is described as a "landscape". For the modern observer the picture must be primarily a meditation, a "mood painting" needing no explanation, exciting chiefly an emotional response. That the story, if any, was never specific seems indicated by the changes Giorgione made as he went along: X-rays have revealed that before the "soldier" existed there was another figure, a naked woman, seated by the river. The mood, however, reflects the recent humanist discovery of a lyrical pastoral world in the Latin and Greek poets. The Renaissance mind also delighted in symbolism and allegory: broken columns may stand for Fortitude, while the naked mother with the child at her breast is an image of Charity, a secularized echo of the Madonna. The male figure may be a soldier, and so personify Fortitude again: his breeches are like those of a German mercenary, but he appears to hold a staff rather than a lance. Pervading all is the

atmosphere created by the impending storm. It is extraordinarily real – the lightning is indicated not as a notional zigzag but as the retina flinches at it; the buildings of the town loom in the weird stillness of the thunder-light; the storm has not yet broken in on the enchanted, mute dialogue of the two figures.

Hints of Giorgione's achievements are to be found in Giovanni Bellini's work – the stillness and, more pertinently, the feeling for landscape (it is probable that Giorgione worked in Bellini's studio). But Giorgione united landscape and figures in one mysterious whole as Bellini never quite did, and he achieved a new harmony between man and Nature, in which one appears to reflect the mood of the other. A similar mystery and harmony of figures with landscape is achieved in the so-called *"Three philosophers"*. There is enigma even in Giorgione's portraiture, in the so-called *"Laura"* of 1506, his single firmly dated work, and in the strangely chaste sensuality of Giorgione's *Venus*, the "founding mother" of generations of recumbent nudes.

Giorgione was snatched to his death by plague in his early 30s, and the *Venus* is one of several paintings of his that are known to have been finished by other hands – the *Venus* by Titian. Giorgione's hold over Titian's imagination seems for a period to have been complete, and the famous *"Concert Champêtre"* in the Louvre (see over) is now more generally ascribed to Titian than to Giorgione. In this and in other works Titian realized again Giorgione's magical coherence of figures with landscape, that mysterious sense of music unheard – the essence of his enchanting vision.

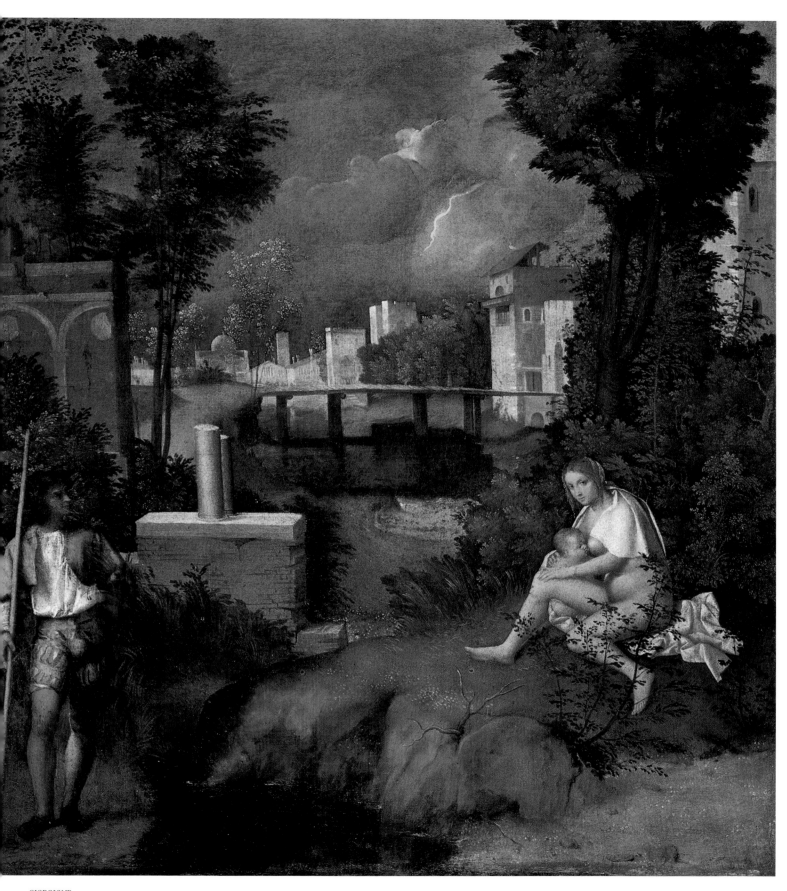

GIORGIONE
The tempest, 1st decade
of the 16th century

Titian

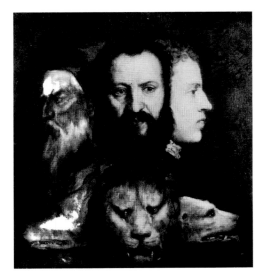

Titian (Tiziano Vecellio, died 1576) came to Venice from his native Pieve di Cadore in about 1500. The city was then at the height of its splendour, although in fact its long political, military and commercial decline had already set in. The Turkish wars, the jealous alliance of other Italian states against her and the pressures of the struggle between foreign powers that raged the length of the peninsula crucially weakened the city. The arts, however, remained resilient. By the mid-sixteenth century supremacy in painting had passed from Florence and Rome to Venice, and the prince of painting was, as a Venetian wrote in 1553, "our Titian, divine and without peer".

Titian's apprenticeship with Giovanni Bellini was followed by association with Giorgione. Even for some years after Giorgione's death in 1510, Titian's identification with Giorgione's style and vision was almost total: he completed several of Giorgione's pictures, and argument as to whether certain early works are in whole or in part by Titian or Giorgione still continues. Both *"Le Concert Champêtre"* (Pastoral music-making) and a *"Noli Me Tangere"* have been ascribed to Giorgione but are now usually accepted as

Titian's; in the latter the landscape is repeated from Giorgione's *Venus* (see preceding page), which had been completed by Titian himself a few years earlier. The idyllic mood and the tenderness are still close to Giorgione.

Soon, however, the titanic but infinitely flexible force of Titian's own genius emerged. With Giorgione's death, the departure of Sebastian del Piombo to Rome, and finally the death of Giovanni Bellini in 1516, Titian was unchallenged. He succeeded Bellini as painter to the city, with a secured income and public commissions. One of these, *The Assumption of the Virgin* for S. Maria dei Frari in Venice, was an astonishing and revolutionary work. It looks forward to Baroque in its dramatic, rushing movement, even in its calculated harmony with its setting, its shape and articulation repeating the forms of the windows, its brilliant colour taking up the rosy tints of the brickwork. *"The Pesaro Madonna"* in the same church is again a daring innovation, placing the Madonna asymmetrically as Bellini would never have dreamed of doing, and creating soaring space above her. The mythological pictures Titian painted between 1518 and 1523 (see over) were no less remarkable. Besides

TITIAN
An allegory of Prudence,
c. 1570
Titian himself, in profile on the left, represents Old Age in an allegory of experience and wisdom. He has shown himself fierce, sharp-featured; this agrees with reports of his character, and of his avarice and pride. Beneath, the dog, lion and wolf represent the attitudes of youth, prime and old age.

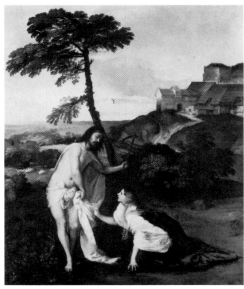

TITIAN (above)
"Noli Me Tangere"
(Christ with Mary Magdalen), c. 1512
Christ's pose is based on an engraving (1510) of a *Venus* by Raphael. Titian typically would use any source that seized his fancy.

TITIAN (below)
"Le Concert Champêtre"
(Pastoral music-making), c. 1510
If it is Titian's, this is his earliest mythology, before *Sacred and Profane Love* (see over) – an example for Watteau, and many others.

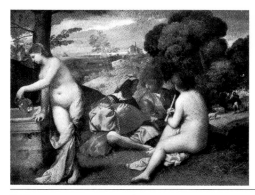

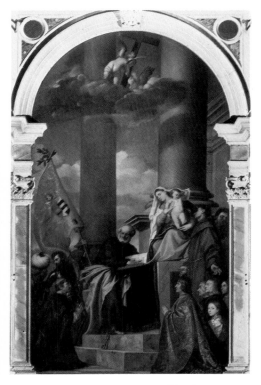

TITIAN (above)
The Assumption of the Virgin, 1516-18
The picture is divided into three zones, linked by the gestures of the figures, who are all impelled by a powerful upward motion. Its unprecedented movement, mastered with such control on such a scale, made Titian's reputation.

It has always remained in its original frame and in its original setting, the late Gothic church of S. Maria Gloriosa dei Frari (right).

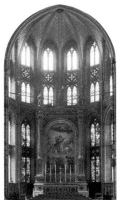

TITIAN (above)
"The Pesaro Madonna",
1519-26
The unusual asymmetrical arrangement of the figures was probably occasioned by the picture's situation, to one side of the church, where it would be seen obliquely. It inaugurated a new type of composition of crossed diagonals.

Venice, Titian's works went to Ferrara, Treviso, Brescia and Ancona, and his fame spread to Mantua and Urbino, and further.

In 1530, in Bologna, Titian entered into his long association with the greatest prince in the West, the Holy Roman Emperor Charles V. He became his court painter, portraying him in many guises – as wise ruler, relaxed gentleman or victorious commander – in portraits evoking an ideal of majesty, authority and power. In return he was ennobled, and a story even tells of the Emperor picking up the brush Titian had dropped. Later, Titian painted Charles' son Philip II of Spain, and Charles' great rival Francis I of France. Beside the work of northern European portraitists, Titian's powers of subtle organization and compositional harmony, together with his feeling for a grave and simple dignity, were outstanding. Meanwhile his services as a portraitist continued in demand among the aristocracy, intelligentsia and rich merchants of north and central Italy.

Titian, like Raphael, responded to all the needs of his patrons, although his portrait of the Farnese Pope, *Paul III with his nephews*, perhaps proved too revealing, for, unusually, it was not well received. Titian's versatility, his freshness of approach to each new project, the variety of his treatments, are astonishing. In portraiture he produced a stock of poses so comprehensive that his successors down to the Impressionists used his work as a source-book – most especially Rubens (who, for example, was inspired by *The girl in a fur wrap*), van Dyck, Reynolds and Rembrandt – and Rembrandt alone may be judged to have surpassed him. He introduced into portraiture procedures belonging to other kinds of painting, "history" painting or genre, showing his subjects now in excited motion, now in a dramatic pageant, now intimate and informal.

When Titian visited Rome in 1545-46, at Pope Paul III's invitation, Michelangelo was also in Rome, and the two greatest artists of the period met. Michelangelo admired Titian's work but with reservations: his handling and colour were praised, but his drawing, according to Florentine ideals of *disegno*, had to be condemned. Titian's method, modelling by tone and colour rather than by line or sculptural massing, was clearly opposed to the Florentine tradition, and his response, as if in declaration of independence, was to open up his own colouristic style – as his portrait of the Pope makes evident. His style and technique were already evolving from the more precise contours, modelling and finish of the early portraits to a much bolder, freer style with more highly charged brushwork; he handled the paint increasingly broadly, creating an effect almost like mosaic, with patches of colour. He always, however, built up in stages (unlike his Baroque successors), even though in old age he sometimes used the handles of the brushes or his fingers to move the paint. It was noted of his late work (as it was later of the Impressionists) that while the painting did not cohere if seen close up, when seen from the "proper" distance it became brilliantly clear.

For splendour of colour, the climax was reached in some of Titian's late mythologies painted for Philip II (see over). His last works became sometimes sombre in tone, but they are the most broadly painted, and the most emotional, of all. Such works as the *Pietà* Titian painted for his own tomb are profoundly expressive, highly personal. He died in 1576, aged perhaps 90. Rich in worldly goods and highly honoured in his own time, he had established a claim on immortality that few artists can match.

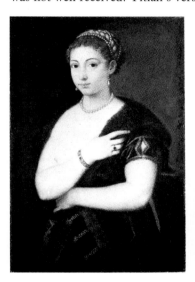

TITIAN (left)
The girl in a fur wrap, c. 1535
The sensuality of the half-naked girl is heightened by the soft richness of the fur. She was perhaps also the model for *"The Venus of Urbino"* (see over), too. Rubens adapted the pose and the fur for an equally sensuous portrait of his second wife (see p. 202).

TITIAN (right)
Pope Paul III and his nephews, 1546
It is difficult for 20th-century eyes not to read satire into this portrait; and it is supposed that it was unfinished because it annoyed the Pope. Put so baldly, this is wrong, and Titian's major concern is clearly to infuse into the portrait dramatic action.

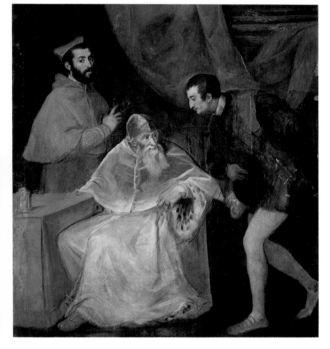

TITIAN (below)
"The Young Englishman", c. 1540
Implicit in the whole is the aristocratic bearing and gentility of the young man. The blacks glow with splendour, set off by the light of smouldering eyes.

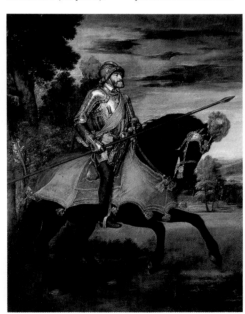

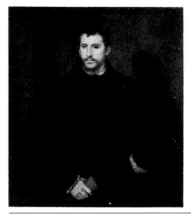

TITIAN (above)
Charles V at Mühlberg, 1548
The Emperor is portrayed as a knight of chivalric virtue, the defender of the Church, the mighty, noble and magnanimous victor. The composition became a basic formula of stately kinship, used by Rubens (see p. 202) and van Dyck.

TITIAN (right)
Pietà, 1576
The design is most unusual, sad, sombre, funereal, but animated by an impulsive movement and by a kind of warmth. At first the picture was based on Michelangelo's Vatican *Pietà* (see p. 132); then Titian extended it at the sides, adding the arm-flinging Mary Magdalen.

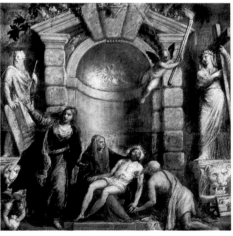

Titian: The Rape of Europa

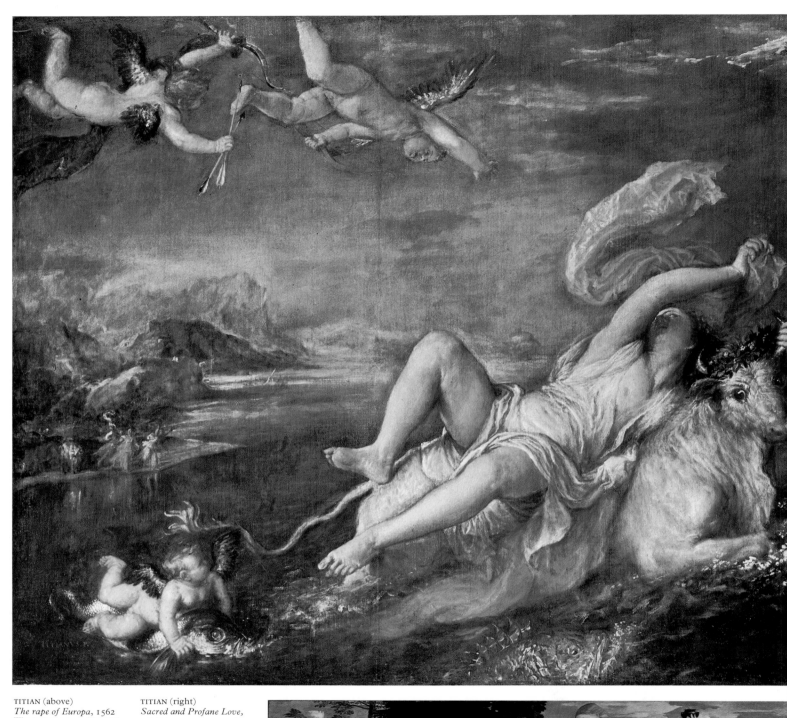

TITIAN (above)
The rape of Europa, 1562
The pagan sensuality of the
poesie Titian painted for
Philip II was surprisingly
contrary to the spirit of
the Counter-Reformation.
It was equally at odds with
the religious austerity and
melancholia that overtook
Philip II at the end of his
life. It is clear that Titian's
mythologies, especially the
poesie, in all their inventive
vigour and uninhibited but
controlled splendour, were
fired by personal passion –
as other works were not; in
contrast his religious works
can often seem superb
ceremonial formalities.

TITIAN (right)
Sacred and Profane Love,
c. 1514
The "meaning" of the two
Venuses has aroused much
learned argument. It is now
generally accepted that the
naked figure is celestial
Love, the divine Venus,
while the clothed woman is
earthly Venus, representing
the generative forces of
Nature. The sculpture on
the sarcophagus, the dis-
tinct landscapes and many
other quiet details, seem
to indicate an elaborate
humanist allegory. What
no one questions or denies
is the supreme beauty, the
elegiac mystery of the work.

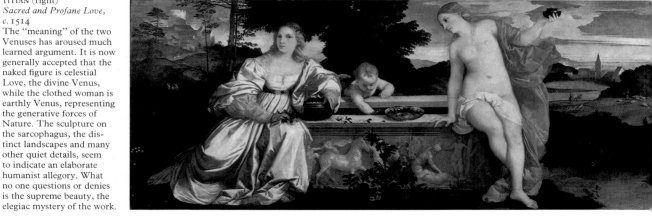

In his great series of mythological paintings, continuing throughout his career, Titian's dominant and ever-recurrent theme is the female nude. Although they often illustrate subjects from classical literature, especially Ovid, and adapt poses and motifs from classical sculpture, these paintings are sometimes so overtly erotic – though rendered with the greatest subtlety and skill – that they disturbed nineteenth-century critics, and their greatness has been fully acknowledged only recently.

One of Titian's most celebrated early essays in the theme is the *Sacred and Profane Love* of about 1514. Its dreaming landscape still echoes Giorgione's, but its celebration of the female figure is much more overtly sensual. Titian's famous *"Venus of Urbino"* of about 1538 has none of the delicate, vernal chastity of Giorgione's sleeping *Venus* (see p. 140) and in later variations he even introduces a male figure contemplating the naked Venus, in some of them a lute player – creating an additional dimension, joining the idea of music to the voluptuous visual harmony. The direct appeal to the senses, as distinct from the more intellectual approach of the Florentines, seems essential not only to Titian but to Venice.

Early in his career, between 1516 and 1523, Titian had painted a magnificent suite of three mythological subjects for Alfonso d'Este of Ferrara. But his greatest mythologies are the seven paintings painted in his old age for Philip II of Spain, called by Titian *poesie* (poetries). The commission probably came when artist met patron at the court of Philip's father, the Emperor Charles V, at Augsburg in 1550-51. Except for the unfinished *Death of Actaeon*, they had all been shipped to Spain by 1562.

The last to be shipped, *The rape of Europa*, is the most joyously sensual of them all. Jupiter, disguised as a white bull, has enticed the unsuspecting maiden Europa to climb on his back; Titian depicts the moment when Europa realizes that the bull has ceased its playful meander in the shallows of the tide, and is taking off for deep waters where she cannot escape. Her perilous, open-bodied pose, with one hand's grasp on a horn so inadequately securing her to her steed, is one of the most breathtaking in all Renaissance art; its inspiration goes back no doubt to the maenads' abandoned Dionysiac dance in reliefs of classical sarcophagi, but it conveys with remarkable naturalism both the ripeness and the frailty of human flesh. Even this picture has been read as tragic, but it is surely not: the lady is no doubt alarmed, reasonably enough, and her companions, gesturing far behind on the shore, are astonished, but ecstasy is promised by the volley of cupids above and the marine cupid riding the great gold fish. The picture has also been called "hilarious", but it is one of the greatest masterpieces of European painting, the dazzling climax of the optimistic side of Titian's late style. The splendour of its colour is matched by the subtlety of its handling – for example, in the play of tones of white in the woman, her draperies and the bull. The iridescence of sea, distant mountains and sky suggests not solid form, but its dissolution in veils of colour: such an illusion of space and atmosphere remained unparalleled until Watteau. Its virtuosity has never been surpassed.

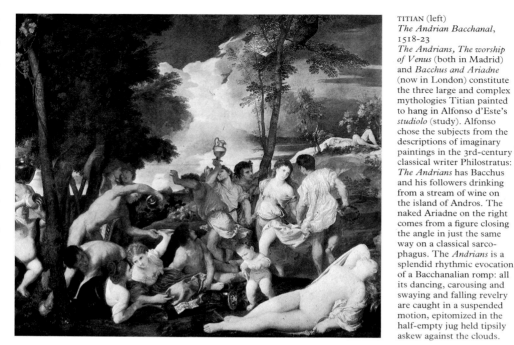

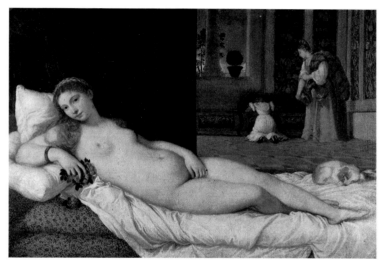

TITIAN (left)
The Andrian Bacchanal, 1518-23
The Andrians, *The worship of Venus* (both in Madrid) and *Bacchus and Ariadne* (now in London) constitute the three large and complex mythologies Titian painted to hang in Alfonso d'Este's *studiolo* (study). Alfonso chose the subjects from the descriptions of imaginary paintings in the 3rd-century classical writer Philostratus: *The Andrians* has Bacchus and his followers drinking from a stream of wine on the island of Andros. The naked Ariadne on the right comes from a figure closing the angle in just the same way on a classical sarcophagus. The *Andrians* is a splendid rhythmic evocation of a Bacchanalian romp: all its dancing, carousing and swaying and falling revelry are caught in a suspended motion, epitomized by the half-empty jug held tipsily askew against the clouds.

TITIAN (right)
"The Venus of Urbino", c. 1538
Unlike Giorgione's *Venus*, Titian's nude is aware of her own beauty and invites appraisal from admiring eyes. She is, of course, far more than a "pin-up", not only in the harmony and brilliance of the colours but also because there are allusions to marital love and fidelity. The little dog symbolizes faithfulness, and the chest being opened in the background perhaps contains a trousseau. The painting may specifically refer to the marriage of the Duke of Urbino, who bought the painting, and has lent it his name. But its eroticism is unexcused by a mythological setting.

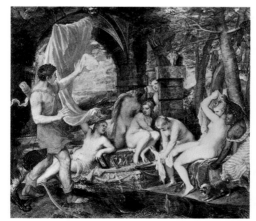

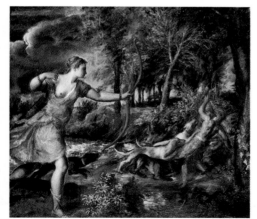

TITIAN
Diana and Actaeon, 1558
The *poesia* is based upon Ovid, who describes the hunter Actaeon surprising Diana and her nymphs bathing: he was punished by being transformed into a stag and killed by his own hounds. Titian's painting is an unabashedly erotic celebration of the female body, though hints of Actaeon's fate are clear – for example the little symbol of fidelity that yaps at his intrusion. Titian's play of white on black flesh, in Diana and her maid, has since held the Western imagination.

TITIAN
The death of Actaeon, after 1562
In most of the *poesie* for Philip II there are tragic overtones, though no other is so sombre as this, the last in the series, which Titian never dispatched. Its vibrant, brusque contours, the almost palpitating forms, offer a striking parallel to the contemporary late work of Michelangelo. The striding Diana avenges her discovery by Actaeon, who, transformed into an animal, in Titian's interpretation sinks into the landscape, and becomes one with it.

The High Renaissance 2: Venice

The dominance of the Bellini family in Venice, the spell cast by Giorgione in the first decade of the sixteenth century, then the long, almost imperial sway of the genius of Titian, tend to obscure the achievements of other artists in Venice and the neighbouring regions, though these are far from negligible.

Long before Titian's first visit to Rome the young Sebastiano del Piombo (c.1485-1547) played the part of Venetian ambassador in painting, bringing to Rome a richer use of colour, a sensual splendour, and something of Giorgione's strangeness of mood. Sebastiano worked on some of Giorgione's unfinished paintings, and is sometimes claimed as the sole author of paintings otherwise attributed to Giorgione. He left Venice for Rome in 1511: there his colours influenced Raphael, and Raphael in turn influenced him, but Michelangelo impressed him still more strongly, as Sebastiano's *Pietà* in Viterbo of about 1515 reveals – it is a formidable synthesis of rich Venetian colour with the monumentality of Michelangelo. Partly with Michelangelo's help, Sebastiano was successful in Rome; some of his best works are portraits, displaying individuality within a controlled grandeur.

In Venice itself, the able and sensitive Jacopo Palma il Vecchio (c.1480-1528) made an individual contribution. His early work reflects perhaps Carpaccio rather than Bellini, but he later established a kind of middle ground between Giorgione's mood of dream and the riper, hedonistic sumptuousness of Titian. Palma Vecchio may well have influenced Titian in his appreciation of a characteristically lush type of blonde feminine beauty. Towards the end of his career, he was clearly affected by the work of Lotto and by central Italian example (not only Raphael but even the cool distancing treatment of the early Mannerist painters). All this is brought into enchanting synthesis in what is perhaps his masterpiece, his *Venus and Cupid*: matching Giorgione or Titian in colour, it has a distinct lyricism, not least in the precise lines of Venus' nude figure. Palma Vecchio also painted religious works, especially *sacre conversazioni*, and romantic portraits of very high quality.

Although he was painting in the Vatican in Rome in 1509, Lorenzo Lotto (c.1480-1556) was certainly trained in the Venetian tradition, and spent most of his peripatetic career in the north. He was a prolific and inventive artist, but his work was variable in quality. His early style seems sometimes more fifteenth- than sixteenth-century, and his pictures usually have some strangeness, whether of proportion, pose or subject matter. Nevertheless his handling of paint, colour and light was both sensitive and original, especially in his smaller-scale pictures, and he soon took advantage of the discoveries of his contemporaries in north and central Italy; he sometimes, too, seems to echo Netherlandish or German example. His originality tells most strikingly in his portraiture, in which he was concerned with the psychology and personal aura of the sitter as no previous painter had been. His relative lack of success in Venice may have been due more to his temperament than to any want of talent.

Venetian demand for sculpture had been increasing, like that for painting, since the second half of the fifteenth century, but the results were not quite comparable in splendour. Donatello's decade in Padua, 1443-53, seems to have had greater impact on painters than on Venetian sculptors, although the tradition of bronze-casting Donatello established bore splendid fruit in the work of his pupil Bartolommeo Bellano, and Bellano's

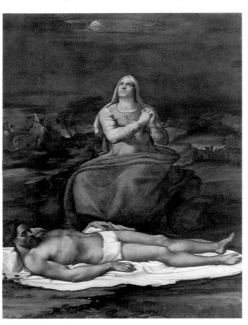

SEBASTIANO DEL PIOMBO (left) The Viterbo *Pietà*, c.1515
Michelangelo, according to Vasari, provided the design. Certainly the muscular sculptural forms, especially the masculine bulk of the Madonna, clearly show his influence. The colour seems applied to the surface rather than binding the picture into a whole; the effect, the menacing landscape, its lonely moon, is still successfully stupendous.

PALMA VECCHIO (below) *The three sisters*, c.1520-25
The title, recorded in 1525, suggests a triple portrait; the half-length format and impersonal features are typical of Palma's many portraits of Venetian beauties, though the sisters may in fact be the Three Graces. Palma Vecchio's ladies are less fleshy, more ornamental, than Titian's.

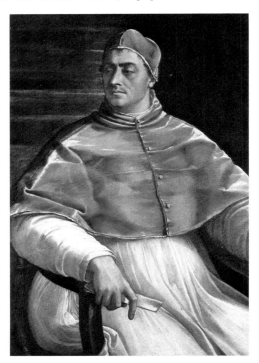

SEBASTIANO DEL PIOMBO (left) *Pope Clement VII*, 1526
After the death of Raphael, Sebastiano was the most fashionable portraitist in Rome. Here he adopted the pose in which Raphael had painted Pope Julius II (not shown), introducing a sharp haughtiness and a glittering sheen in the colours. On first coming to Rome Sebastiano must have felt acutely his lack of training in *disegno*, hence his frequent, sometimes urgent, pleas to his friend Michelangelo for drawings; but this portrait shows him to have mastered the principles of Florentine form.

PALMA VECCHIO (below) *Venus and Cupid*, c.1520
The blonde flesh of the recumbent nude (a type familiar from Giorgione and Titian) shines radiant against the intense blue of the sky; its sensuality, however, is offset by cool and impassive expression.

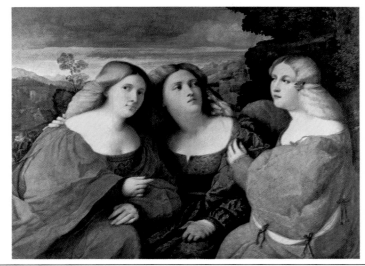

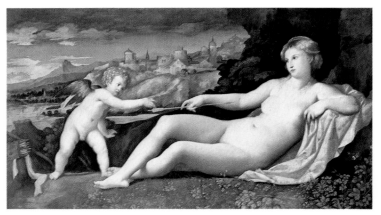

naturalism was refined by the greatest master of the bronze statuette, Riccio (Andrea Briosco, 1470-1532), who worked in Padua. His masterpiece is the great bronze Easter Candlestick in the "Santo" (S. Antonio), in which he characteristically handled Christian subjects as if they were episodes from classical mythology. His single figures are often frankly pagan, of an extraordinary technical brilliance and finish: his *Pan* at Oxford has been called the most beautiful bronze in the world. Riccio's numerous such ornaments for a scholar's study have an immensely inventive charm, and even his inkwells in the shape of frogs have an almost monumental dignity.

In Venice, the main field for monumental sculpture was tombs. After a somewhat uneasy irresolution between the claims of the Gothic and Renaissance styles, the Lombardo family, Pietro (*c.*1435-1515) and his sons Tullio (*c.* 1455-1532) and Antonio (died 1516), developed a purer classicizing style owing much to Mantegna, expressed in a series of very grand tombs, especially for the Doges. Tullio Lombardo seems to have been not only a man of considerable learning but a collector of classical statuary. Some of his figures closely reflect

antique prototypes. He had, however, an innate lyrical feeling, most poignant in his late work, for instance the *Bacchus and Ariadne* of the 1520s. The relative stability of Venice in the endless warring that convulsed most of Italy was certainly one reason why major commissions in sculpture continued there into the sixteenth century, while they fell away elsewhere; a telling symptom is the arrival in Venice of Jacopo Tatti, better known as Jacopo Sansovino (*c.*1486-1570), after the Sack of Rome in 1527.

Tatti had taken his name from his master in Rome, Andrea Sansovino (see p. 129), with whom he had worked in the Vatican, gaining first-hand knowledge of antique sculpture. In 1529 he became the official architect in Venice, and his reputation is founded mainly on his Library opposite the Doge's Palace in the Piazzetta. In sculpture, his formal classical style, tempered with an almost romantic eloquence, is splendidly displayed in statues on the façade of his own Loggietta in the Piazza S. Marco, which are rather more delicate than his best-known work, the colossal figures of *Mars* and *Neptune* on the stairs in the courtyard of the Doge's Palace (not shown).

RICCIO
Pan, 1st quarter of the 16th century
The base is not original: the figure once formed part of an inkwell. In its civilized subtlety it could as well stand for the High Renaissance as the marbles of Michelangelo. Pan listens for the voice of the mourning Echo.

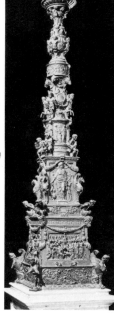

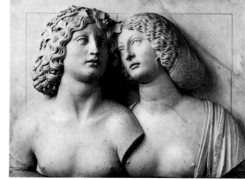

TULLIO LOMBARDO (right)
Bacchus and Ariadne,
c. 1520-30
Bacchus is identified by his vine-leaf fillet and androgynous pectorals. Such is the pastoral mood, the two seem like figures from an idyll by Titian translated into marble. The smooth flesh and patterned hair are much more refined and stylized than in any Roman tomb bust of this format, which also recalls half-lengths by Palma Vecchio. Here the lyrical mood, lacking in Tullio's dry earlier work, may have been induced by the court of the Gonzagas at Mantua, where he worked 1523-27.

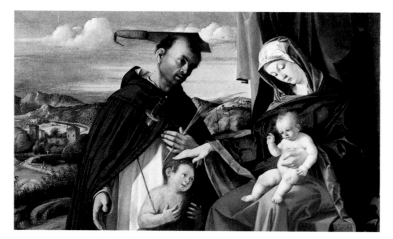

LOTTO (above)
The Madonna and Child with St John and St Peter Martyr, 1503
This is Lotto's earliest signed and dated work. The Madonna, in pose and in features, echoes Giovanni Bellini; so do the clear, glowing colours and detailed landscape.

LOTTO (right)
Andrea Odoni, 1527
The sitter, a well-known collector and antiquarian, is presented, unusually, in a horizontal format, with the choice pieces of his collection. Lotto knew Titian's portraiture, and achieved equally imposing results; though they lack perhaps the utter finality of Titian's impressions, his more theatrical productions have often greater power. He was always vivid in his presentation of character, and invented as many compositional solutions as he had sitters – varying setting, gesture, attributes.

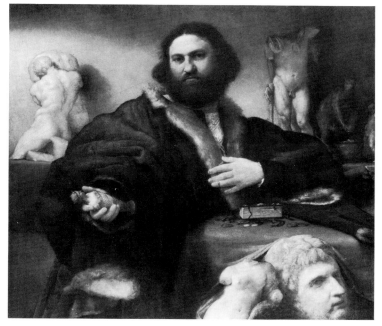

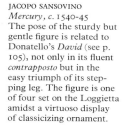

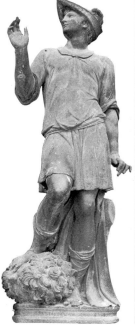

JACOPO SANSOVINO
Mercury, c. 1540-45
The pose of the sturdy but gentle figure is related to Donatello's *David* (see p. 105), not only in its fluent *contrapposto* but in the easy triumph of its stepping leg. The figure is one of four set on the Loggietta amidst a virtuoso display of classicizing ornament.

RICCIO (above)
The Easter Candlestick, 1507-15
The complex Candlestick is like an agglomeration of all Riccio's varied little bronzes in one setting; every detail is exquisitely worked; it is as rich as a wedding-cake. Its figures are *all'antica*, reflecting an interest typical of Padua.

The High Renaissance 3: North Italy

In the sixteenth century the smaller cities in northern Italy retained considerable independence of vision, though they acknowledged the triumphant advances of Venice and Rome. Original artists of high quality practised in Bergamo, Brescia, Ferrara and, most subtly and delightfully of all, in the city of Parma in the Po valley.

Why two very great painters, Correggio (Antonio Allegri, died 1534) and his younger contemporary Parmigianino (whose art is essential to Mannerism; see p. 165), should have emerged in this small provincial town has never been satisfactorily explained. Correggio is said to have trained at Mantua with Mantegna, but though his early illusionistic work clearly reflects Mantegna's example, Correggio's mature style is the very antithesis of Mantegna's austerity; he retained, however, an impeccable accuracy in drawing. Fundamental was the legacy of Leonardo, and his modulation of line by shadow, of shadow by reflected light, so that the spectator's eye almost caresses the form it follows. Correggio was also demonstrably aware of the classical High Renaissance in central Italy, and he was equally aware of Titian.

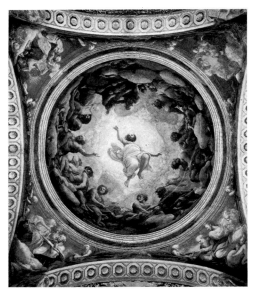

CORREGGIO
The vision of St. John on Patmos in S. Giovanni Evangelista, Parma, 1521
Christ and the apostles whom John sees are foreshortened from below – *di sotto in su*, first used by Mantegna in the *Camera degli Sposi* (see p. 120).

Nevertheless, Correggio's part in the High Renaissance may seem an odd accident of time, and almost all his major works anachronisms. His early fresco in the cupola of S. Giovanni Evangelista in Parma juggles illusion and reality, opening up a dizzying sky in a way that anticipates the effects of the Baroque. However, the idea comes from Mantegna, while some of the seated apostles are clearly related to Michelangelo's Sistine Chapel ceiling, and the violently foreshortened figure of Christ hurtling up into the empyrean owes much to Titian's *Assumption* in the Frari in Venice. Correggio's later frescos in the dome of the cathedral at Parma, with their fantastic tumultuous spirals of soaring figures, presage even more closely the development of ceiling painting by Lanfranco and Pietro da Cortona in the seventeenth century.

Correggio's altarpieces are also, in sentiment and structure, far removed from the monumental ideal and classic symmetry of many High Renaissance works. They have a melting tenderness that anticipates not so much the Baroque as the Rococo charm of Boucher or Clodion. In the *sacre conversazioni* the figures round the Christ Child can be as

CORREGGIO (below)
"La Notte" (The Adoration of the shepherds), *c.* 1527-30
The traditionally peaceful subject is transformed by the arrival of angels and by supernatural light emanating from the Child, which anticipates some of the

light and dark effects to be exploited in the later 16th century by Tintoretto and Bassano in Venice. The light is used to create a sense of the miraculous. Dawn streaking the distant sky and the dramatic diagonal recession can both be compared to Titian.

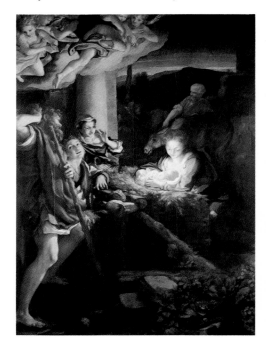

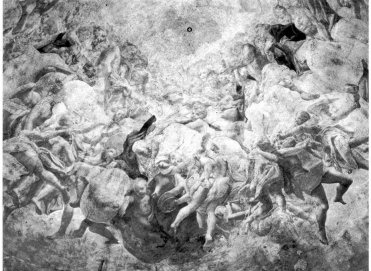

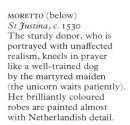

CORREGGIO (left)
The Assumption in the dome of Parma Cathedral, detail, 1526-30
Part of the fresco, a segment of the dome, is shown: the Virgin is borne aloft by a mass of angels in multicoloured clouds that seem almost to rotate. Her robe has now faded (Correggio touched up the fresco with tempera that has fallen off) but she is still visible as intended from the nave.

MORETTO (below)
St Justina, c. 1530
The sturdy donor, who is portrayed with unaffected realism, kneels in prayer like a well-trained dog by the martyred maiden (the unicorn waits patiently). Her brilliantly coloured robes are painted almost with Netherlandish detail.

CORREGGIO (right)
Danaë, c. 1531
The climax of Ovid's story, when Jupiter descends in a shower of gold on Danaë, was an uncommon subject, but was later painted also by Titian. Titian's version has greater psychological

drama; Correggio's view is more languid, more hazy, less intense. In contrast to Mannerist painting its lack of artificiality and straightforward simplicity were commended by Annibale Carraci (see p. 185) for revival and emulation.

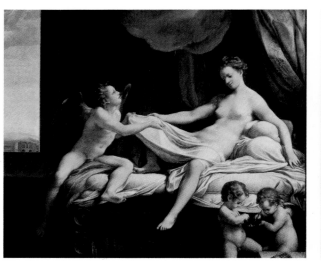

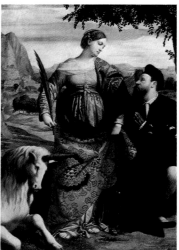

affectionate and intimate as a family doting over a christened baby. But the handling of the paint, especially the suggestion of the bloom of young life on the flesh, is uniquely Correggio's – in "La Notte" (The Adoration of the shepherds) it is supreme in the voluptuous hovering angels. Correggio applied a similar technique, perhaps more suitably, to a series of The loves of Jupiter for Federigo II Gonzaga, Duke of Mantua. Of these the Danaë has all the delicacy, lightness and felicity of the finest Rococo, even something of its frivolous eroticism. Although Correggio's impact on his contemporaries was limited, the independence of his vision remained fresh through the years, and subsequent critics more often than not ranked him second only to Raphael.

The towns of Bergamo and Brescia were both within Venetian territory, and as a result the influence of Venetian art was more insistent than for artists in Parma. Though there was no genius, no phenomenon like Correggio, there were considerable painters: Moretto (Alessandro Bonvicino, c. 1498-1554) painted large-scale decorative pageants and numerous altarpieces in Brescia. He responded in varying degree to Titian, but painted with an

engaging matter-of-factness – a directness that could be called provincial but which commands respect. His picture of St Justina shows a very human donor sharing the space with the unetherial saint. Moretto's interest in individual character served him especially well in his portraiture – he could capture not only the face but the idiosyncracies of his sitter's body. This aspect of his art was brought to an even sharper pitch by his acute and prolific pupil Giovanni Battista Moroni (c. 1525-78) from Bergamo. His work amounts to a gallery of entirely credible, realistic citizens from an unusually large social range portrayed with great informality. Lotto (see preceding page) also worked in Bergamo for a time, and in Brescia again there was Girolamo Savoldo (c. 1480/5-after 1548), perhaps an underestimated talent. He is recorded in Florence in 1508 and matriculated there. He delighted in rich textures shimmering in half light, brilliantly captured in his Mary Magdalen.

In Ferrara Dosso Dossi (Giovanni Luteri, c. 1490-1542) painted weirdly lit, romantic paintings, some of them recalling Ferrarese painting of the fifteenth century, but touched by the influence of Giorgione. Dosso's ex-

tremely opulent colour range may have been stimulated not only by Venetian works at the court of Ferrara but also by the rich collection of Netherlandish painting there. There is a powerful element of fantasy in his mythological and allegorical work, and poetry in the interplay of human figures with landscape. In his later works, however, he moved increasingly towards a rather conventional classicism, having spent some time in the vicinity of Rome, and been affected in the 1530s by the presence of Giuliano Romano in Mantua.

Pordenone (Giovanni Antonio de Sacchis, 1483/4-1539), born in the Friuli to the northeast of Venice, gravitated towards Venice and eventually settled there, but his Venetian frescos have almost entirely disappeared, and it is in Treviso and Cremona that his masterpieces survive. In Cremona he demonstrated an inventive and expressive style which reflects central Italian influence, especially Michelangelo's, with a kind of exaggerated sentiment which bears comparison with some of Sebastiano's religious dramas. In its fervour and energy Pordenone's work anticipates the greatest Venetian painter of the second half of the century, Tintoretto (see p. 170).

MORETTO (left)
A gentleman, 1526
This seems to be the first dated full-length standing portrait painted in Italy. But if Moretto introduced the type, Titian gave it its wide currency – perhaps never having come across Moretto's work, however.

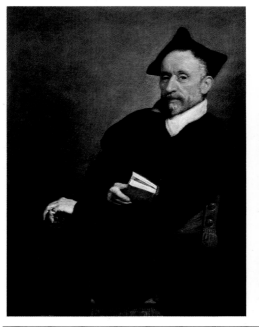

MORONI (below)
"Titian's Schoolmaster", undated
Moroni's portraits are unassumingly realistic, without heroic attributes, and with a clarity typical of Brescian painting. The elegance and ease of the picture, once attributed to Titian (hence its popular title) are rare in Moretto's religious work.

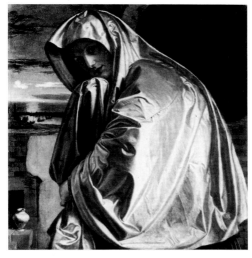

DOSSO DOSSI (below)
Alcina, c. 1523
Dense in strange detail, resplendent in colour, the picture may represent the sorceress Alcina from

Ariosto's *Orlando Furioso*, who transformed men into trees (visible in the top left corner). Dosso collaborated with Ariosto in devising entertainments at Ferrara.

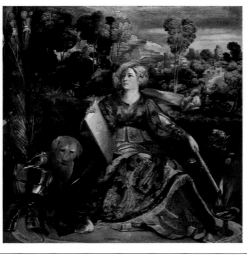

SAVOLDO (left)
Mary Magdalen, c. 1530?
The dawn sky and silvery highlights on the robes of the Magdalen approaching the tomb are meticulously observed by the Brescian painter. Its realistic force relates the painting to the northern Italian provinces

rather than to Venetian styles, though its virtuoso handling of light was surely influenced by Titian – Savoldo settled in Venice about 1520. This "cut-off" picture is known in several versions, but Savoldo's surviving works, typically on a small scale, are few.

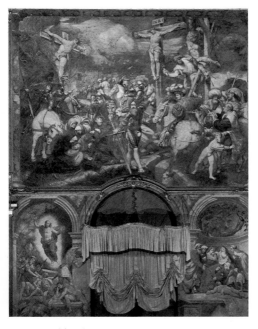

PORDENONE (above)
The Crucifixion, in Cremona Cathedral, 1520-21
Three scenes from Christ's Passion in the nave arcade culminate in the *Crucifixion* fresco at the western end. The illusion of a tableau on a stage seeming to open

out towards the onlooker reinforces the impression of violent drama, conveyed by the strenuous movement and bold gestures of almost every figure, and the deep chiaroscuro. Pordenone added *The Resurrection* and the *Pietà* beneath in 1522.

Dürer and Grünewald

In the Germanic territories of the Holy Roman Empire, under the rule of the first two Hapsburg Emperors, Maximilian and Charles V, the first half of the sixteenth century was a period of great economic growth matched by a swift cultural expansion. Great universities were flourishing at Heidelberg, Wittenberg, Vienna; Basel soon rivalled Venice as a centre for printing. The Reformation, gathering its impetus after Martin Luther had nailed his *95 Theses* on the door of the castle church at Wittenberg in 1517, did not at first stifle the magnificent outburst of creative activity, even though it was to split Europe in two, and to oppose Catholic and Protestant in often bloody violence. Maximilian, Charles V and his son Philip II of Spain were all informed, discriminating and active patrons of the arts, and Renaissance conceptions of princely splendour likewise impelled Francis I of France, Henry VIII of England, and German princelings to active patronage.

In south Germany, Nuremberg was a major trading centre between east and west, rich, beautiful, highly cosmopolitan, permeated by humanist ideas and learning from Italy. There was born Albrecht Dürer (1471-1528), son of a prosperous goldsmith. His early training was in drawing, woodcutting and printing, which were to remain his primary media throughout his career – he was the first truly major artist so to emphasize them. He was the first, and greatest, northern exponent of Renaissance ideals in the visual arts, although he never lost his northern individuality, and his obsession with line. He visited Venice twice, in 1494-95 and 1505-07; he travelled as far as Bologna, but perhaps never reached Florence or Rome. His fame was broadcast through his engravings, and artists in Italy were soon drawing on them for ideas. In Venice he knew and admired above all the aged Giovanni Bellini who, fascinated by Dürer's technique of drawing with the brush, reciprocated Dürer's esteem.

Dürer has been called "the Leonardo of the North", though his scientific investigations were limited compared with Leonardo's. Leonardo was never assailed by the religious anxieties that eventually converted Dürer to Protestantism, but in appetite for life, in fertility of invention and expression, they are comparable. Dürer's visual curiosity extended to the whole of nature – animals, people, costume; in extraordinarily vivid watercolours he noted effects of weather in topographical landscapes or the minute natural details of a piece of turf. Introvert no less than extrovert, he left the earliest sequence of self-portraits that qualify as deliberate autobiography. In the very grand *Self-portrait* of 1498, after his first Italian visit, he used an Italian formula, and, though the rhythms are linear, un-Italian, his pose might seem to derive from the *Mona Lisa* (see p. 131); however, this, one of the earliest portraits to show both hands of the sitter, predates Leonardo's masterpiece. It has been said that Dürer, in his absorption with himself in many guises – as a child of 13; totally naked; even as the Man of Sorrows – was his own *Mona Lisa*. Vanity is not absent. Though patronized by princes such as the Elector of Saxony from 1496 and granted a pension by the Emperor Maximilian himself in 1515, he seems never to have been quite content with his status, compared with the artist in Italy. So he wrote from Venice to a friend: "Here I am a gentleman, at home a parasite". Yet when he journeyed in the Netherlands in 1520 he was received as a great master.

Dürer's commissioned portraits show how skilfully he was able to incorporate Venetian

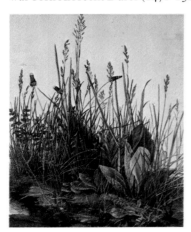

DÜRER (left)
The piece of turf, 1503
Dürer reproduces the wild profusion of grasses and flowers with loving care, all the more astonishing for its lack of precedent. Everything is green, and he differentiates the plants with the subtlest variations in tone.

DÜRER (right)
A young Venetian woman, 1505
Though only lightly painted and probably unfinished, the figure stands brightly out against the dark foil of the background. The sense of lively communication is typical of Dürer's portraits.

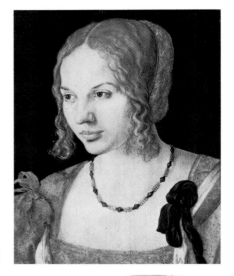

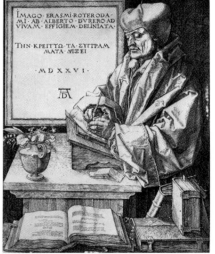

DÜRER (above)
Erasmus of Rotterdam, 1526
Dürer's largest portrait engraving is not entirely successful, judging by Holbein's portrait of the same sitter (see p. 157). It was probably based on a medal which Erasmus gave for the purpose, though in 1520 Dürer had met the scholar in person. Great care is taken for the light.

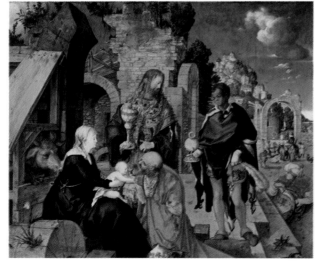

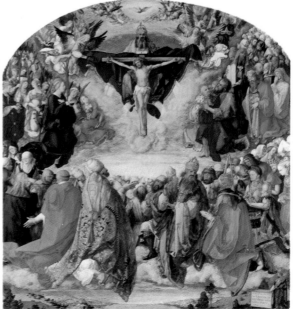

DÜRER (above)
The Adoration of the Magi, 1504
Dürer's starting point was northern, a scheme in essence like Hugo van der Goes' Monforte altarpiece (see p. 96). On to this he grafted Italianate gesture, grouping, colour, subsuming them into his own style. This is thought to be the central panel of a folding altarpiece, with lost wings.

DÜRER (left)
The Adoration of the Trinity, 1511
Especially the Virgin in *The Adoration of the Magi* was distinctively northern, in features, in proportions. In this vast, comprehensive statement Dürer achieves a more thoroughgoing blend, a magnificent synthesis of the northern and southern visions, orchestrating with Leonardo's coherence his huge crowd of individuals.

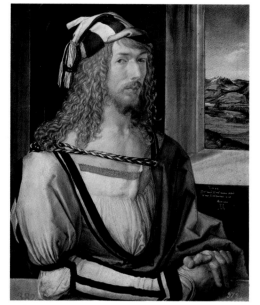

breadth of light and colour without sacrificing the precision of his drawing; he also made several magnificent portrait engravings. His paintings did not always match the achievement of his finest prints (see over), but the brilliance, the virtuosity of his *Adoration of the Magi* (1504) more than holds its own in the challenging context of the Uffizi. In *The Adoration of the Trinity*, 1511, he painted a grandiose vision of St Augustine's *City of God*, the Trinity suspended in the heavens amongst the airborne host of saints and martyrs, but with a delightfully detailed, tranquil landscape on earth beneath. The artist stands in one corner with a tablet proclaiming his authorship. Unquestionably, however, Dürer's supreme masterpiece in painting is the two great panels known as *"The Four Apostles"* (actually John and Peter, Mark and Paul).

In originality and in expression, Dürer is surpassed by his compatriot, generally known as Grünewald. His real name was Mathis Gothardt-Neithardt (*c.* 1475-1528). Though he was famous in his time, holding high office as painter, architect and engineer to the Prince-Bishop of Mainz, his life and his personality remain obscure. Said to have led "a

melancholy and secluded existence", he depicted only religious subjects, while just 30-odd drawings and a score of paintings survive. In them, the intensity of emotion, and the expressionist means of conveying it, shock the onlooker as does no other painting in Western art, not even by Goya, until the violent assault of the Expressionists in the twentieth century.

Grünewald's religious sympathies were apparently with the Reformers; they reflected anyway a profound and perhaps mystical spiritual commitment. His subjects mostly relate to Christ's Passion, and his work is summed up in one composite masterpiece (which includes nine of his 20 known paintings), the Isenheim altarpiece, a folding altarpiece with two sets of wings, completed in 1515 for the church of the hospital of St Anthony at Isenheim, near Colmar. The outer wings, when closed, reveal the famous *Crucifixion*, with a gigantic, lacerated corpse of Christ. These wings open to reveal an enchanting, lyrical celebration of *The Virgin and Child*, counterbalanced on the right by an extraordinary *Resurrection*. The kernel of the altarpiece is a wooden shrine with St Anthony enthroned, flanked with two further wings.

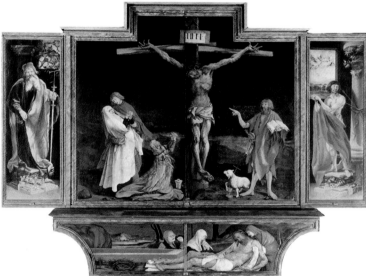

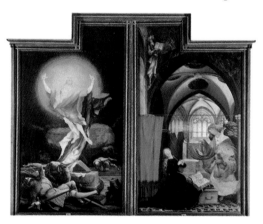

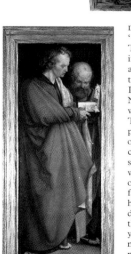

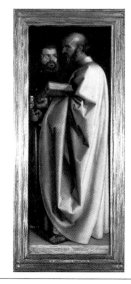

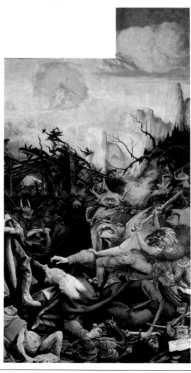

Dürer: The Four Horsemen of the Apocalypse

In the Book of Revelation, when the Lamb opened the first four seals of the prophecy of the Last Judgment, there rode forth four horsemen one after the other. One rider came with a bow, on a white horse, riding out to conquer; one with a great sword on a red horse, to unleash destruction; one with a pair of scales, on a black horse; and finally, Death on a pale horse, and Hell following with him, riding to kill in famine and pestilence.

Such movement, in almost audible thunder, had never been expressed in the woodcut medium before; in terms both of technique and of inspired imagination it has never been surpassed since. Much as Dürer loved experiment in all media, it was through prints, throughout his career, that he established his independence and broadcast his art. Through them, he could reach huge audiences, whether popular or sophisticated, literate or illiterate.

The Apocalypse appeared first in 1498, in a German edition and in a Latin one; a second issue in 1511 had a Latin text. The theme answered the mood of the times – a widespread religious disquiet which was to culminate in the Reformation and split of the Church. A prophecy, that the world would come to an end in the year 1500, was generally believed and, for some, the Pope was not Christ's representative on earth but the Anti-Christ of the Book of Revelation. The message, though, as set out by Dürer, was not entirely one of doom. In *The angels staying the four winds*, the elect are ordinary people with whom the reader could identify.

Dürer's book was the first published by an artist entirely under his own auspices. Earlier illuminated Apocalypses had generally been differently arranged – with full page illustrations distributed through the book, or smaller ones inserted in the text, or with pages consisting of tiers of images explained by captions. Dürer reserved the front of the page for the print, and had the text on the back. The subject matter, with its scope for visionary fantasy, obviously fired his imagination, but the medium, while it encourages expression in linear terms, allows little tonal modulation and is inherently a vehicle for bold, not very subtle, effect. Earlier artists had relied on colour to complete the effect; Dürer achieved a satisfying equivalent of colour in black and white.

Dürer continued to use woodcut, and developed his technique to a remarkable pitch of virtuosity, as in *"The Great Passion"* and *The life of the Virgin*, published also as books, in 1511. In copper engraving, however, he achieved a mastery of modulation in tone which really does make colour superfluous. In the famous print of *Adam and Eve*, 1504, this is applied to Italianate and classical themes. Nevertheless, his northern naturalism is vividly present in the drawing of flora and fauna, for all that these, too, have symbolic meaning. Both his mastery of technique and the richness of his learning, combined with an endlessly fertile invention, reached their peak in the three great single plates of 1513-14, *The knight, Death and the devil* (not shown), *St Jerome* (not shown), and *Melancholia I*. These, with their fantastic wealth of detail brought together in consummately harmonious compositions, can be read almost as humanist tracts. The *Knight* is an allegory of the Christian warrior, *St Jerome* of a Christian scholar, and *Melancholia* a meditation on the process of creation, full of recondite allusion.

Dürer also engraved several portraits (see preceding page) and illustrated three theoretical works, including the important *Four Books on Human Proportion* (1528).

DURER (right)
The Apocalypse: *The angels staying the four winds*, 1498
When the seals had been broken and the horsemen had ridden out, spreading terror, four angels were deputed to hold back the winds while the elect were marked with God's seal – interpreted as the Host.

DURER (below)
"The Great Passion": *Christ carrying the Cross*, 1511
Dürer believed one of the chief functions of art was to represent the Passion. The figure of Christ, the movement of his head, is expressive and pitiable.

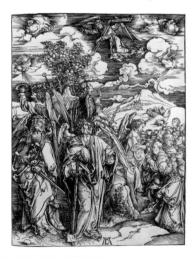

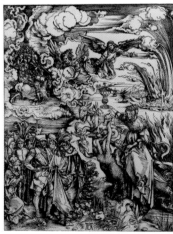

DURER (left)
The Apocalypse: *The Whore of Babylon*, 1498
The Whore is an exact copy of a drawing of a Venetian lady Dürer made in 1495. She sits on a beast with seven heads and ten horns, and conversing with her are the kings of the earth and also merchants – all the rich, powerful and worldly. Their oncoming destruction is apparent behind them, in the exploding sky.

DURER (below)
Adam and Eve, 1504
Both figures are based on antique sculptures – Adam on *"The Apollo Belvedere"* (see p. 41), Eve rather freely on a *Venus* – and are constructed according to canons of proportion. Every detail has meaning: the branch Adam holds may refer to the Tree of Life; the four animals may represent the four humours in their original harmony.

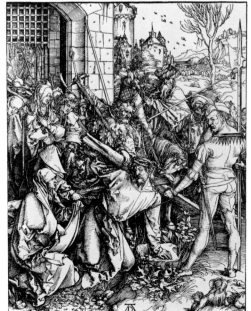

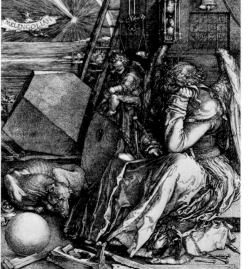

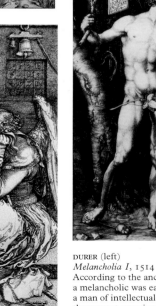

DURER (left)
Melancholia I, 1514
According to the ancients, a melancholic was earnest, a man of intellectual bent; the present meaning of the word came later. The print encompasses this duality: the Comet of Saturn is in the sky: a planet thought to have a depressing effect on the intellect, Saturn was also associated with mathematics, taken as the basis of all learning – hence the mathematical accessories.

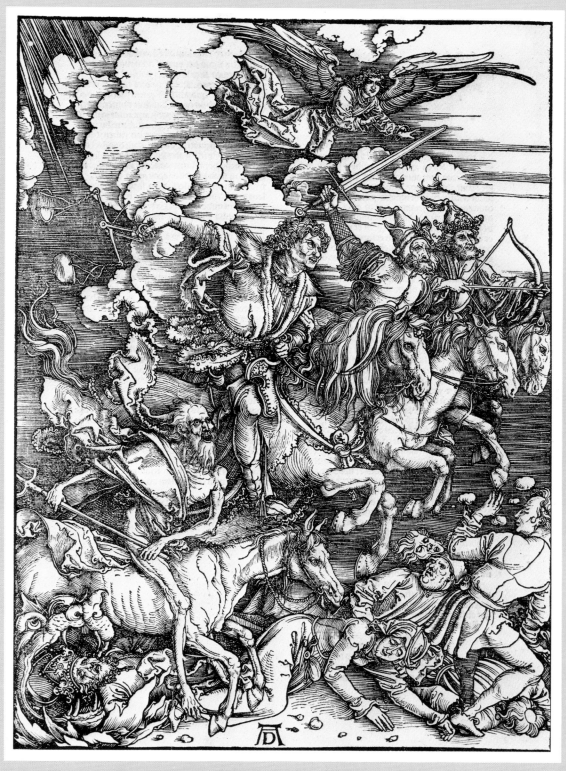

DURER
The Apocalypse: *The four horsemen*, 1498
Dürer condenses the text of the Revelation of St John in all the Apocalypse woodcuts, but nowhere with such effect as in *The horsemen*. Disregarding the mass of humanity under their hoofs, all four stare out into the distance, forming a chain across the sheet, which contributes to the sense of movement in the whole. This is reinforced by the contrast of light and dark, and the linear agitation of the fluttering saddle-cloths and other garments. Earlier German art had nothing to compare with Dürer's impression of pandemonium. The seething line is typical of Dürer's early woodcuts; the absence of colour signals its great technical accomplishment.

Painting in Germany before the Reformation

Germany, a congeries of more than 100 autonomous political units under the nominal rule of the Holy Roman Emperor – some 30 principates ruled by Electors; some 50 ecclesiastical territories ruled by Prince-Bishops; some 60 self-governing towns – was flourishing vigorously in the years before the turmoils of the Reformation. Its industries were expanding and prospering; the Fuggers, bankers in Augsburg, had destroyed the monopoly of the Italian finance houses, and the northern humanists had assimilated and were even advancing upon the achievements of Italian letters. The new universities and the printed word consolidated the spread of learning, and, in the sphere of art, the printed image – woodcuts and metal engravings – intensified and accelerated the influence of new styles and novel imagery. Through engravings, the art of the Italian Renaissance became the common heritage of all Europe.

The traffic was by no means all one way. The best known and most prolific of the Italian engravers, Marcantonio Raimondi (c. 1480-1527/34; not shown) had forged Dürer prints in Venice before moving to Rome and becoming the chief disseminator of Raphael and of the works of antiquity. As a boy in Florence Michelangelo had copied an engraving of *The temptation of St Anthony* by Martin Schongauer (died 1491), one of the first artists to raise engraving beyond the level of the popular print. Trained as a goldsmith, Schongauer worked in Colmar, where Dürer arrived too late to study with him in 1492. Schongauer's painting was fairly traditional; his engravings, however, had an original dramatic force and attracted wide attention. Dürer, as we have seen, subsequently developed both the technique and the potential audience of prints.

Dürer's genius, so copious in invention, so brilliant in technique, tends to overshadow all others of his generation in Germany – with the exception of Grünewald. But admirable talents existed besides these two, such as Lucas Cranach the Elder (1472-1553), who spent most of his life in Wittenberg, where he was court painter to the Elector. He was a friend of Luther – he produced the most famous portrait by which posterity knows him – and an early adherent of the Reformed faith, though he continued to work occasionally on Catholic religious commissions. At the outset of his career, in Vienna about 1500, his landscape

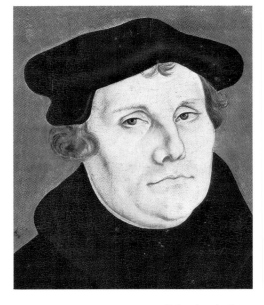

CRANACH
Martin Luther, 1521
Cranach painted several portraits of Luther as a new religious hero in the early 1520s. At that time a division of Christendom was not yet irrevocable.

SCHONGAUER (right)
"Noli Me Tangere"
(Christ with Mary Magdalen), after 1471
The basis of Schongauer's style was Rogier van der Weyden, reworked in his own softer idiom, recalling Lochner; but this is drawn with the hard outlines of an engraving. There is no chiaroscuro in the mass of meticulous, linear detail.

SCHONGAUER (below)
The temptation of St Anthony, c. 1470
Engravings and woodcuts were at first run off in large quantities and sold at religious festivals and fairs. *St Anthony* is above all didactic, a fearsome warning against the sins of the flesh. While there is sculptural modelling, the saint and demons drawn in such exuberant detail float free in a nebulous space, unnaturalistically.

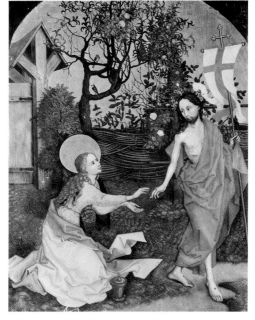

CRANACH (right)
Adam and Eve, 1526
Cranach's insistence on an unfashionably Gothic style may signify his wish to adhere to northern values, free from Italian decadence.

PACHER (below)
The Four Doctors of the Church, c. 1483
Four doves in virtuoso foreshortening swoop over (from left to right) SS. Jerome, Augustine, Gregory and Ambrose. The harsh modelling of the faces, the perspective and the cut-off figure of Trajan in the foreground repentant before St Gregory (in a dream) recall Mantegna; but the nervous, sinuous poses and contorted hands, not to mention the rich canopies, are Gothic. The modelling of the faces can also be compared with Pacher's painted sculpture; this is anyway a synthesis of outstanding success.

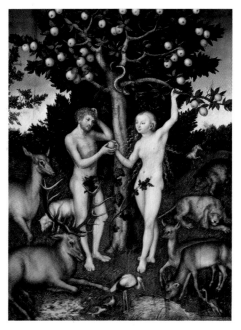

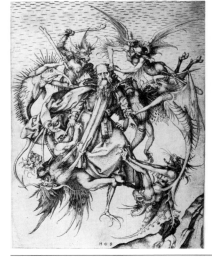

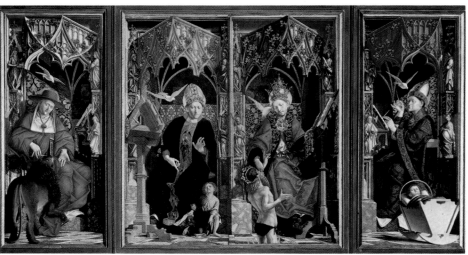

settings had parallels with the "Danube school", and his early portraits have a genial amplitude matching Dürer's. Later, in Wittenberg, aided by a large workshop that included his two sons, he began the prolific production of the kind of painting most generally associated with his name – nudes in landscapes, with biblical or mythological titles (virtually interchangeable) – *Adam and Eve, Apollo and Diana*, and so on. Hints of Dürer or of classical antiquity sometimes emerge, but his personal brand of erotic imagery, slightly fey, sinuous and at the same time somehow angular, with his figures looking a little like actors in an amateur charade, is unmistakable. His later portraits became comparatively formal; he was apparently responsible for the first life-size full-length portraits, heralding centuries of state effigies. His printmaking technique is coarse beside Dürer's, but he was the leading image-maker for the Reformation.

Cranach was, perhaps deliberately, a belated Gothic painter, and other artists continued or developed late Gothic traditions more or less unadulterated. The Austrian Michael Pacher (active *c.* 1465-98) remained relatively immune to Italian influence as a

sculptor (see p. 158); as a painter, he transposed Mantegna's perspective effects and rich classical detail into a superb Gothic equivalent. Several artists in Cologne maintained a fifteenth-century idiom well into the sixteenth century: the most accomplished of them, the Master of the St Bartholomew altarpiece (active *c.* 1470-1510), had been trained in the Netherlands and practised a charming version of the style of Rogier van der Weyden. A number of painters, who are known for convenience under the label "the Danube school", though they did not cohere as a group, shared an obsession with the wooded scenery of the Tyrolean region and developed an original vision of landscape, unparalleled in Italy. In power of imagination, the finest of them was Albrecht Altdorfer (*c.* 1480-1538), working in Regensburg in Bavaria. The twentieth century might read his work as "mood landscape"; obviously related to the watercolours Dürer had made on his trips to Italy, it even anticipates some of the effects of Ruisdael and nineteenth-century Romantic landscapists. In his little *St George and the dragon*, the landscape is the focus of interest; saint and dragon are entirely subservient. Altdorfer's masterpiece, how-

ever, is surely his *Battle of Alexander and Darius on the Issus*, with its dizzy illusion of sky and earth as tumultuously involved in the conflict as the multitudinous armies.

Hans Burgkmair (1473-1531), the major artist resident in Augsburg at the beginning of the sixteenth century, shows the impact of his visit to north Italy about 1505 very obviously; he was a prolific portraitist and painter of altarpieces, but also a virtuoso in the technique of the chiaroscuro woodcut, and his image of *Hans Baumgartner*, 1512, is one of the finest woodcut portraits ever made. Hans Baldung Grien (1484/5-1545), who had likewise visited Italy, settled in Strasbourg in 1509; working in many media, he came nearest to Dürer (whom he had known in Nuremberg) in talent and versatility. His most original works, however, were mythological or allegorical paintings, idiosyncratic in their range of colour, which sometimes achieve a macabre intensity. The characterization of his nudes owes something to Cranach, but their structure is more classical. Yet the complete reconciliation of the Italian Renaissance with northern line was not to be achieved until the next generation, by Hans Holbein the Younger.

ALTDORFER (below)
The battle of Alexander and Darius on the Issus, 1529
The concave roll of the land, bringing the horizon up the picture towards the spectator, is unorthodox, though the bird's-eye view can be paralleled in Bosch

or Patenier. The cartouche, and inscriptions within the painting, display a chief interest in the numerical odds against Alexander and the number of dead: painted for a duke of Bavaria, it is a precursor of the scenarios of classical history that lent lustre to Baroque palaces.

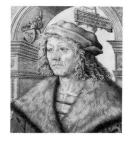

BURGKMAIR (left)
Hans Baumgartner, 1512
The classical arch framing the background – perhaps, too, his melancholy gaze – serves to indicate that the sitter is a scholar and a humanist. The modelling is bold and free but the detail is of great finesse; the print was made from three blocks, each one inked in a different shade of violet.

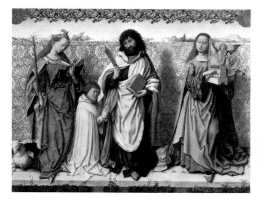

THE MASTER OF THE ST BARTHOLOMEW ALTARPIECE (above) The St Bartholomew altarpiece, central panel, *c.* 1505-10
St Bartholomew is in the

centre. The figures are fine examples of the late Gothic style – attenuated, with fragile, twisting fingers, heart-shaped faces and richly embroidered robes.

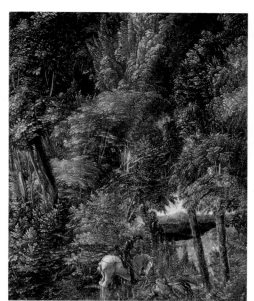

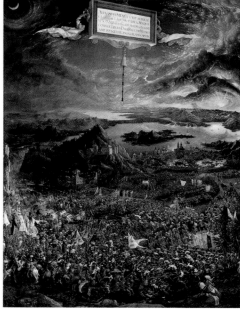

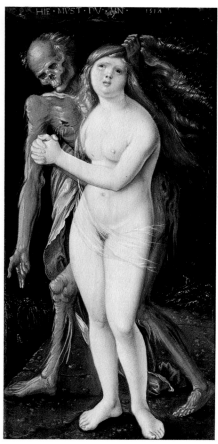

ALTDORFER (left)
St George and the dragon, 1510
There are no arbitrary crags, no orderly lines of hills and trees receding to the horizon – the usual landscape conventions are gone. Instead, glimmers of light seep through the trees that bristle over the panel (the painting is in fact on parchment, pasted on to wood, so like a miniature).

BALDUNG GRIEN (right)
Death and the Maiden, 1517
Baldung Grien returned to this theme several times, progressively refining and simplifying the image to a horrid immediacy – placing the Maiden's sensuous pale purity against Death's dark, scrawny, protoplasmic decay. The theme of lurking death had been banished in Italy by the Renaissance, but in the north kept its fervour.

Holbein: The Ambassadors

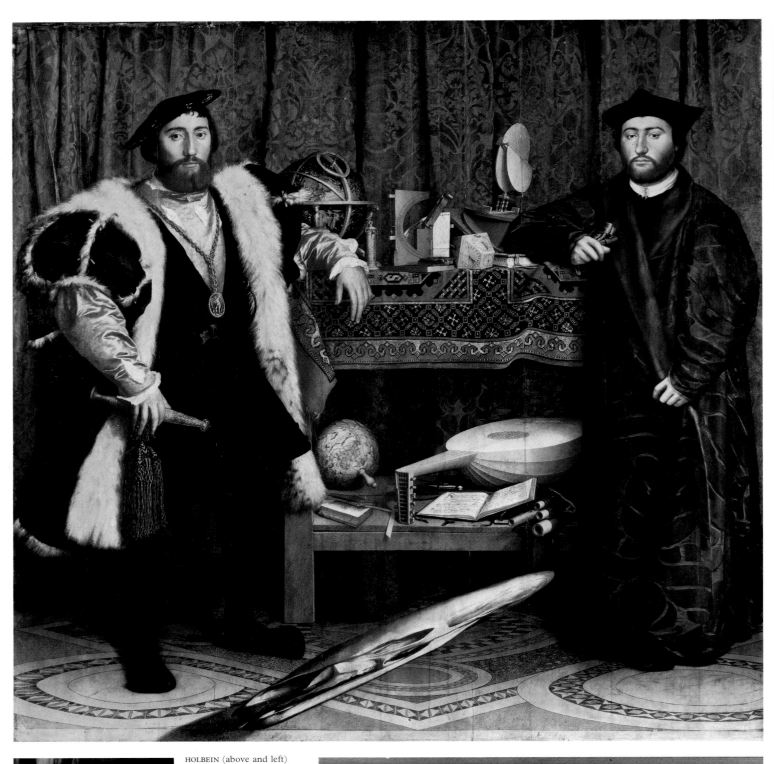

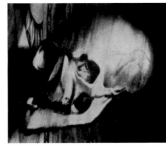

HOLBEIN (above and left)
"*The Ambassadors*", 1533
This is one of the earliest
portraits to show two men
full-length, life-size. They
are as close to real life
as the artist could make
them – illusionistic in every
particular, the picture is a
replica of an instant. It
was perhaps placed (at the
top of a great stair?) where
it could be seen either from
straight on or obliquely –
the angle at which the skull
takes on its true shape
(detail, left). When it is so
seen, the two men blur, and
eternal death overtakes all.

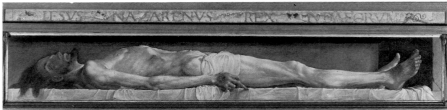

HOLBEIN (above)
The dead Christ, 1521
Though clearly influenced
by Grünewald's *Christ*
in the predella panel of the
Isenheim altarpiece (see p.

151), Holbein depicts the
body of Christ rigid in
death with an exactitude
that deprives the image of
all spiritual comfort: the
tomb imprisons the body

in its *rigor mortis*. Before
this painting, Dostoevsky
cried: "This picture could
rob a man of his faith". It
perhaps belonged to a lost
altar with *The Deposition*.

The men represented are French, Jean de Dinteville and Georges de Selve, Bishop of Lavaur, but Hans Holbein the Younger (1497/8-1543) painted their portrait in 1533 in London, where Dinteville was on a diplomatic mission to Henry VIII of England. Shown life-size, full-length, the two are depicted with exact realism down to the details of their very opulent costumes. The green damask curtain behind and the inlaid marble floor (based on one in Westminster Abbey) are equally scrupulously portrayed, while in the centre, on a two-tiered table, is displayed an elaborate still life – on top, instruments of science and astronomy; below, more earthly interests – a terrestrial globe, an arithmetical textbook, a lute, but also an open hymnal (the text is Luther's revised version). The composition seems to be a Reformed version of the traditional *sacra conversazione*, in which the still life, rather than the Madonna, is the focus of the two figures' intellectual and spiritual commitment. At the same time, in their paired placement, and impassive stillness, the figures are like "supporters" in a massive coat of arms.

Closer inspection, however, reveals an underlying disquiet: the minute badge in Dinteville's cap is a skull; a small crucifix is almost hidden away at the top left; a string of the lute is broken. Most strikingly, but also most enigmatically, the yellowish smear tilted across the foreground reveals itself when seen at an acute angle from the left below (or from the right above) as a skull, distorted by a mathematically exact trick of perspective. And the central still life is also a vanity, a *memento mori*. Dinteville's age is given, on his dagger, as 29; Selve's, on his book, as 25; dials indicate the time to be 10.30 am, the date April 11th; the two men are in the prime of life and health, of material and intellectual accomplishment. But the reality of the stated moment, the instantaneity, is undermined by the omens of mortality, above all by the added dimension of the distorted skull, which the sitters cannot see, and all their science cannot understand. This ambiguous picture, realized with scientific precision and consummate art, combining monumental realism with complex symbolism, is one of the most ambitious and successful achievements of Renaissance art.

Holbein's own name is, literally, a synonym for a skull, and his obsession with human mortality lasted throughout his career, from even earlier than his woodcut designs for a *Dance of Death* (not shown) about 1525. He was born in Augsburg and trained by his father Hans the Elder; he was fully established in Basel by 1520, and there came to know, through the printer Frobenius, a remarkable humanist circle including Erasmus. His early work reflects many influences and was in many media – portraits, designs for engravings, altarpieces, large-scale mural decorations – but common to all was his astonishing technical virtuosity. His *Dead Christ*, in its starkness, may be influenced by Grünewald's expressionism, but its detached, exact observation has a very different effect. A probable visit (or visits) to northern Italy was more fundamental; some paintings seem to acknowledge Leonardo's example very closely, but in his *Madonna and Child with the Meyer family* he

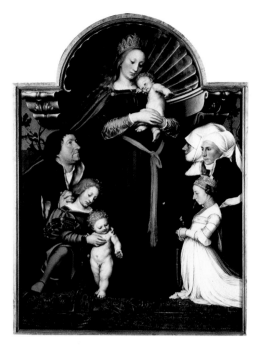

HOLBEIN (above)
The Virgin and Child with the Meyer family, c. 1528
Between 1528 and the death of Meyer in 1531, a portrait of the patron's second wife was added. The Virgin with her lively Child perhaps reflects local sculpture.

HOLBEIN (below)
Sir Thomas More, 1527
Holbein developed to a perfect realism the type of humanist portrait Massys (see p.160) had taken up. The expressive, sensitively modelled hands are typical of Holbein's minute skill.

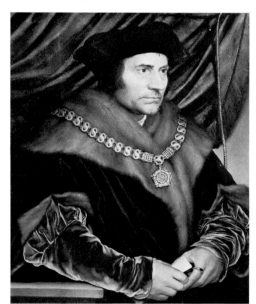

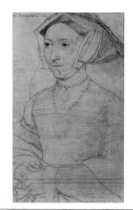

HOLBEIN (left)
Jane Seymour, preliminary drawing, c. 1535
Apart from a few details of dress, the finished portrait closely copies the drawing, indicating that, for Holbein, the basis of art lay above all in precision of outline.

HOLBEIN (right)
Henry VIII, 1542
In an image originated by Holbein, and repeated endlessly by copyists, the figure of the King already shows signs of an advanced obesity, skilfully hidden under a bell-shaped surcoat.

fused the principles of both Leonardo and Raphael with northern literalness into a magisterially monumental image. No one, not even Dürer, had achieved such a synthesis.

After an initial visit to London (1526-28) he finally settled there in 1532, and from about 1536 until his premature death from the plague in 1543 he was court painter to Henry VIII. His personality and his personal convictions remain elusive, but he was clearly sympathetic to the Reformation, even though the shrinking of religious patronage in the Reformed climate of Basel was certainly a strong reason for his move to England. On his first visit, he became attached to the circle of Sir Thomas More, Erasmus' humanist friend: his portrait of More is one of the most gravely humane portraits of the whole Renaissance, and his group of More's family – now lost, but known from a preliminary drawing (not shown) sent to Erasmus – was one of the first "conversation pieces". Like "*The Ambassadors*", it turns a traditional religious format to secular ends.

Soon after his arrival in London for the second time, Holbein painted some superb portraits of members of the German Steelyard, a merchant community. His painted portraits depended on studies from the life made with the aid of some form of perspective aid, such as a *camera obscura*, but the resultant drawings, of which a series has miraculously survived, show no trace of mechanical dependence; they include some of the most delicate but sure reflections of the human face ever made, captured within a contour line quick with life. Holbein established a tradition and standard of quality in miniature to which English practitioners constantly referred, especially the greatest Elizabethan miniaturist, Nicholas Hilliard (see p.206). From his drawings Holbein could project the images without any loss of quality to any scale – he is most famous for his awesome straddling life-size image of the King. In his state portraiture the static, linear quality became more marked, and he achieved images of cool, aloof splendour that were perhaps matched but not surpassed by Bronzino.

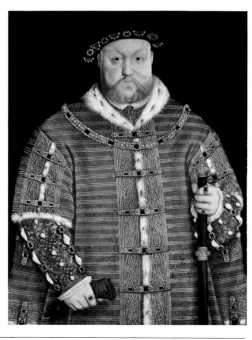

Sculpture in Germany: Late Gothic and Italianate

In the half-century before the Reformation the German-speaking lands produced remarkable sculpture in considerable quantity. Despite sculptors' increasing awareness of the achievements of Italian masters, through prints and also through first-hand reports by visitors to Italy, sculpture north of the Alps always preserved an individual flavour, and the influence of Claus Sluter was enduring. Sculpture was chiefly employed upon altarpieces, and generally conceived within the late Gothic tradition – in intricate, busy, tightly boxed set pieces, with elaborate fretted and pinnacled canopies; free-standing figures were rare, with the exception of the Virgin and Child. There was, however, a tendency towards heightened realism and expressive handling.

One of the first to adopt a more naturalistic style, emulating Sluter, was Nicolaus Gerhaerts (active 1462-73), who may have come from Leyden in the Netherlands, but whose known work is all in Germany – he seems to have ended up in the 1470s at the court of Emperor Frederick III in Vienna. His ability to draw out the character of a figure in stone – witness the atmospheric individuality of his so-called *Self-portrait* (c. 1467) at Strasbourg –

had a wide influence on German sculptors of the next generation. Michael Pacher, active slightly later in the Tyrol, produced one of the earliest surviving and best-preserved late Gothic altarpieces (the losses, dismemberments and discolorations have been enormous) for the isolated pilgrimage church of St Wolfgang. Typical is its towering magnificence, interlocking with the architecture of the choir, though Pacher's lavish use of gold is unusual. Pacher also painted (see p.154).

Pacher's near-contemporary Veit Stoss (c. 1450-1533) was one of the first to follow Gerhaerts' lead, and to move away from the Gothic spectacular towards a greater emphasis on the individual figure. He left his native town near Nuremberg in 1477, and for 20 years worked in Poland, where his principal commission was the altarpiece at St Mary's, Cracow. This, unlike Pacher's masterpiece, has a relatively simple structure – no spires, no surmounting crucifix, no flanking figures or panel paintings. The central scene is bounded by a great arch that lets air into the whole, though most of the figures are still densely massed along the bottom. On his return to Nuremberg in 1496, Stoss achieved an almost

classical clarity of form – his *St Roch* (not shown) in a church in Florence was admired by Vasari as "a miracle in wood" – then moved about 1507 to an even more emotionally charged expression – though still monumental – which perhaps finds its closest parallel in High Baroque sculpture.

Towards the end of his career Stoss had left his sculpture unpainted, but the first German sculptor known to have delivered his work bare, "true to its materials", is Tilman Riemenschneider (died 1531). Riemenschneider worked very successfully, with a large workshop, at Würzburg, where he was somewhat detached from the mainstream. He delighted still in the elaborate traceries of late Gothic, but experimented with unusual shapes and convolutions, and broke with tradition in designing altarpieces without hinging wings. His sculpture shows the most sensitive and delicate sureness in controlling form and expression.

Stoss was not the only master to practise with great virtuosity in Nuremberg. The stonecarver Adam Kraft (c. 1460-1508) produced vividly naturalistic figures still in a recognizably Gothic context, as in his Tabernacle at St Lorenz in Nuremberg. This is an

GERHAERTS (below)
"Self-portrait", c. 1467
The figure seems to feel some private emotion; face, hands, pose and garments together express an inner drama – just like Sluter's *pleurants* (see p. 90). The figure was probably once placed high up, and leaned illusionistically on a sill.

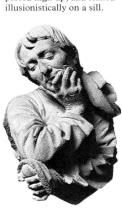

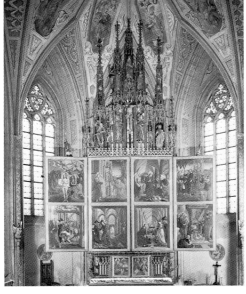

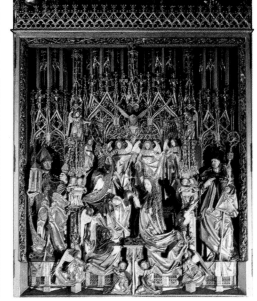

PACHER
The high altar of St Wolfgang: (far left) with the outer wings open; (left) with the inner wings open, the central tableau: *The coronation of the Virgin*, c. 1471-81
Sculptures and paintings, overlapping and alternating, make up a carefully wrought harmony, linking together the parts of the altar, and the altar to the architecture. There is clear evidence of Italian influence (notably Mantegna's) in the painting (not by Pacher's own hand), but none in the sculpture, unless it is in the skilful grouping of *The coronation*. This, revealed behind the massive wings, seems to be perfumed in rich gold; yet the complex intricacy of the drapery, and above all the canopy, is offset by a simple realism in the faces of the saints, the Virgin, even God.

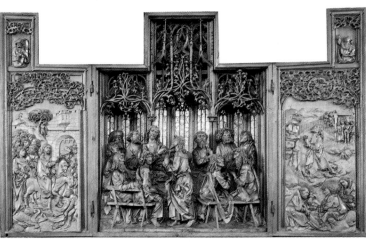

STOSS (right)
The high altar at St Mary's, Cracow: *The death of the Virgin*, 1477-89
The blue background and dividing bands of tracery serve to set out action and figures more clearly. Here the language of gesture and drapery has been recharged; over the Virgin in the altar's centre a towering apostle reaches out wringing hands.

RIEMENSCHNEIDER (left)
The altar at St Jakob, Rothenburg: *The Entry into Jerusalem; the Last Supper; the Agony in the garden*, 1501-05
Riemenschneider's figures have a dreamy quietude, for all the cracking bustle of drapery. He delights in the limewood's worked surface.

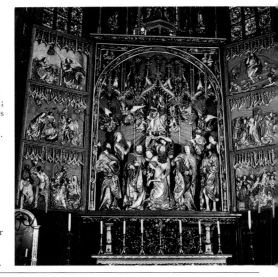

enormous free-standing shrine housing several ranks of life-size figures, arranged in almost conversational groups and seeming to overflow into the church. The Vischer family of bronze-workers, headed by Peter the Elder (*c.*1460-1529), worked on the Shrine of St Sebaldus from 1488 to 1519, in which time what had begun as a Gothic project much like Adam Kraft's had been combined with sometimes pronouncedly Italianate features. Peter the Elder had a collection of "old Frankish" art – perhaps including Gallo-Roman pieces – and he sent his two sons, Peter and Hermann, who assisted him, to be trained in Italy.

The demand for elaborately carved altar-pieces fell away sharply during the 1520s – due not so much to Italian influence as to the impact of the Reformation. A more secular mode became fashionable. In Augsburg, the great banking dynasty of the Fuggers commissioned Sebastian Loscher (*c.* 1480/5-1548) to decorate their private chapel. Loscher had had first-hand experience of Italian sculpture, and his *putti* once ornamenting the choir-stalls have no religious connotation and are entirely up to date with the High Renaissance. Elsewhere Conrad Meit (died 1550/1), who came

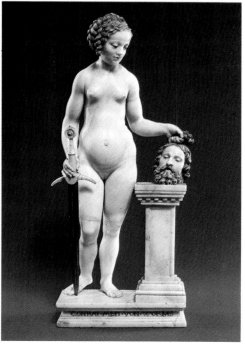

from the Middle Rhine region but worked for 20 years for the Regent of the Netherlands, produced small bronze and alabaster figures, precious, sensual, and closely observed. His little *Judith with the head of Holofernes*, an ornament for the cabinet or *studiolo* of a sophisticated patron, bears comparison with anything of its kind in Italy. Meit also worked in a monumental vein, on the spectacular effigies of the Regent's family at Notre-Dame-de-Brou at Bourg (not shown). These were stone figures smoothly and gently rendered with little detail and no agitation, though richly dressed and adorned with jewellery.

The full adoption of Italian principles can be seen in the work of Peter Flötner (*c.*1495-1546), working in Nuremberg. His master-piece, the bronze Apollo Fountain of 1532, is conceived without any trace of Gothic – or of Mannerism. It is very pure and classical, the delicate, superbly balanced and finished form contrasting with the elaborate movement of detail in the pedestal. However, the greatest sculptor of the mid-sixteenth century, though born in the north, in Flanders, did not work there: Giambologna became the supreme Mannerist virtuoso in Italy (see p.168).

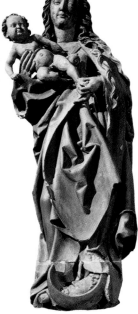

STOSS (above)
The Virgin and Child,
*c.*1520
It seems right to call the work of Stoss' last years "personal"; though he was widely honoured, he was un-settled, quarrelsome, lonely. The Virgin's draperies loop, cascade, twist, crumple and swirl upwards to the energetic, wriggling Child.

THE VISCHER FAMILY
(right) The Shrine of St Sebaldus, 1488-1519
The standard of finish and unity of style are unusually high; and the clarity of the complex whole remarkable. The Italianate figures – sphinxes, mermaids, *putti* – are most in evidence in the lower parts of the Shrine.

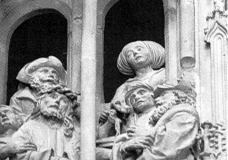

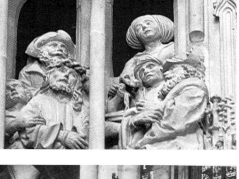

MEIT (above)
Judith with the head of Holofernes, 1510-15
The modelling is firm and economic; colour is used sparingly; the glow of the alabaster is made to suggest the bloom of nubile flesh. The Italianate style has conquered, and is mastered.

KRAFT (left)
The Tabernacle at St Lorenz, detail, 1493-96
The whole structure is a towering Gothic complexity, in which the life-size figures are realistically carved.

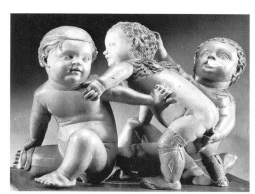

LOSCHER (above)
Fragments from the Fugger chapel in Augsburg: *Putti*, 1515
Not only the forms but the sculptural principles are Italianate: these figures are in interacting movement, recalling *The three Graces*. Apparently, however, there is nothing comparable in Italy at this date to this complex of free-standing babes playing in space – though it is suggested in the work of Donatello.

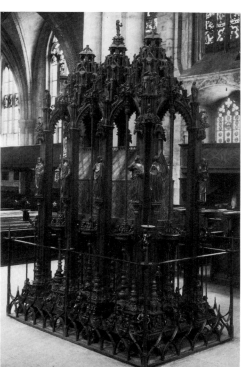

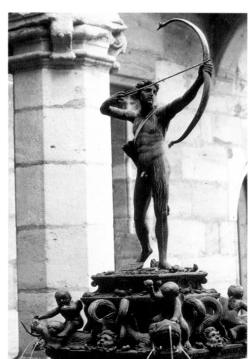

FLOTNER (left)
The Apollo Fountain, 1532
Before this work Flötner had visited Italy twice. He was himself an engraver and woodcutter, and here the design is taken from an engraving, one by Jacopo de' Barbari (died 1516?), one of the first Italian artists to seek and find patronage in the north.

Netherlandish and French Painting

By the end of the fifteenth century in the Netherlands the impetus of original exploration and invention stemming from the work of the van Eycks, van der Weyden and van der Goes faded, and the new generation turned to the all-pervading example of Italian art. Just as the great northern humanists, Erasmus or Thomas More, drew on Renaissance learning, so, too, the artists drew on Italian motifs and the Italian revival of classical antiquity. The "Italian journey" became almost obligatory.

However, among the many artists imitating, borrowing from or creating in the manner of Renaissance art, no genius emerged of the stature of a Dürer or a Holbein, who could integrate a full understanding of its underlying principles with the native northern tradition. Jan Gossaert, known as Mabuse (c. 1478-1533), who worked in Antwerp and for Burgundian patrons, started in a tradition close to Hugo van der Goes, but after an Italian journey in 1508 he began to feature Italianate motifs – classical architecture, classicizing poses – amidst his always teeming detail. He is said to have been the first artist in the Netherlands to paint classical subjects with nude figures. Something of the charm of his earlier

style is carried over into later works such as the Malvagna triptych, but here the Italianate music-making *putti* consort rather oddly with the sweetly Netherlandish Virgin, and even more oddly with the elaborate intricacies of the Gothic shrine in which she sits. Mabuse was perhaps most successful in his portraiture, which is direct and charming.

His main rival in Flanders was Bernard van Orley (c. 1488-1541), who worked prolifically in Brussels for the Regents of the Netherlands, producing altarpieces, portraits and designs for tapestries and stained glass. He is supposed to have visited Italy, and he certainly responded to the Italian-oriented, sophisticated taste of his patrons, but again his unpretentious portraits are his best work.

Quentin Massys (1464/5-1530) in Antwerp is the most sympathetic and sensitive artist of this generation in the Netherlands. Italian impact is once again strong (though it is not certain that Massys ever went to Italy) and the influence of Leonardo is apparent, especially in his altarpieces. But he also developed a vivid portraiture that is almost genre – or vice versa. His enchanting study of *A banker and his wife* (1514) is probably genre, with moralizing

intent. The still life is described with a loving finesse, down to the convex mirror, which is presumably symbolic. The whole picture has the conviction of a real event, and seems as much a portrait as his *Egidius* of 1517. Here the scholar is shown in his setting (the idea derives doubtless from traditional representations of St Jerome in his study) – a marvellously alert and human likeness. Joos van Cleve (c. 1490-1540; not shown), Massys' contemporary in Antwerp, was in demand for a more formal and official style, in state portraiture.

In his altarpieces, Massys sometimes collaborated with Joachim Patenier (c. 1485-1524), who painted the landscapes. He was a master of the bird's-eye-view panorama, and one of the first to practise landscape for its own sake – the biblical figures are important, but are usually so small as to be almost invisible. Visionary crags and mountains characterize not only Patenier's but most Netherlandish landscape backgrounds until the dawn of the great naturalistic era of the seventeenth century – with the great exception of Bruegel (see over), who stands virtually alone in the Netherlands in the next generation.

The most vigorous painting in the sixteenth

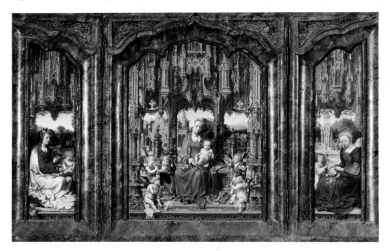

MABUSE (left)
The Malvagna triptych:
The Virgin and Child, and saints, 1510-15
Transalpine Europe had always had closer links with northern Italy than with Tuscany or Rome, and even though Mabuse painted this after he had accompanied a Burgundian embassy to the Pope, Ferrarese painting seems his chief inspiration.

VAN ORLEY (right)
Georges de Zelle, 1519
The Brussels physician was about to marry. The linked hands, of the sitter and on the panel behind, signify union; the N is his wife's initial; the monogram abbreviates "eternity".

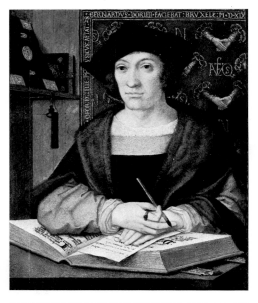

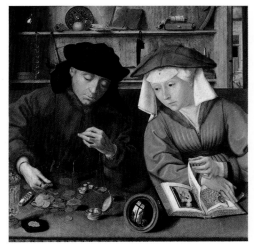

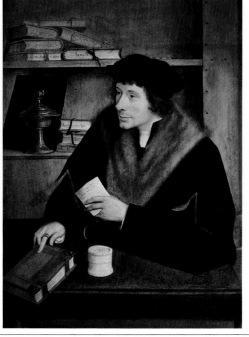

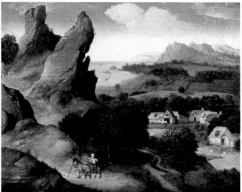

MASSYS (above)
A banker and his wife, 1514
The wife is distracted from her devotional book by the clink and glitter of the coins her husband counts; other details, too (of which the symbolism is now obscure), set spiritual against earthly treasure. Significantly for the future, Massys introduces a new psychological realism (in Christus' comparable *St Eligius* (see p. 95) there is nothing of the kind).

MASSYS (left)
Egidius (Peter Giles), 1517
Egidius was on one half, Erasmus on the other, of a diptych commissioned as a gift for Thomas More, their friend and fellow-humanist.

PATENIER (above)
The Flight into Egypt, undated
The Holy Family escape Herod's ire along a snaky path in (despite its artificial crags) a homely landscape.

century was in Flanders rather than in Holland: activity shifted from Bruges and Ghent to Antwerp, expanding as its deep-water port responded to commerce from the New World, and Brussels. A very puritan version of Protestantism had taken hold in Holland, and the outlook for religious art was bleak (indeed there was iconoclasm). Jan van Scorel (1495-1562) produced sophisticated, cosmopolitan work in Utrecht from 1524, after travels that had taken him to Nuremberg (where he met Dürer), Carinthia, Venice and Jerusalem before an extensive stay in Rome. His first-hand knowledge of Italian art was wider than that of any contemporary. He developed a rapid, fluent technique, with a delicate feeling for light and glowing colour. The delightful *Mary Magdalen* in Amsterdam shows him at his best, entirely himself, having absorbed the experience of his travels into his own vision. In other examples his differing references jostle less happily. Van Scorel's portraits are again his most satisfactory work: he could be both sensitive and very tender. A follower of his, Marten van Heemskerck (1498-1574), spent several years in Rome, and is important not only as a leading exponent of later, northern

Mannerism but also as a topographical recorder of sixteenth-century Rome.

Lucas van Leyden (1494-1533), based in that city, was a remarkably sensitive and delicate colourist, and possibly the first artist in the Netherlands to produce self-portraits. But his greatest achievement was in printmaking: in his engravings he followed very much in Dürer's footsteps, and could rival him in virtuosity. His genre scenes not only provided a starting-point for seventeenth-century Dutch and Flemish genre, but may also have been drawn upon by Caravaggio.

In France, that great patron Francis I attracted to Fontainebleau not only Italian but also Netherlandish artists (including Joos van Cleve), and the next generation of native French painters (the so-called second school of Fontainebleau) mingled the elegance of one tradition with the detailed realism of the other, though the sculptors reflected predominantly Italian example (see p. 167). The best fusion was achieved by François Clouet (c. 1510?-72), the scion of a long dynasty of artists, and an unattributed *Three minions* shows the blend of Netherlandish and Italian elements assimilated into a highly polished Mannerism.

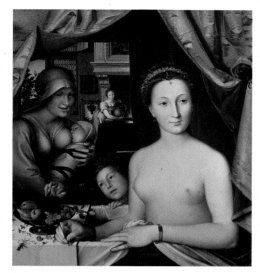

CLOUET
A lady in her bath, c. 1550?
The Italian influence on Netherlandish portraiture was in turn absorbed by the French court painters. According to tradition,

Diane de Poitiers, mistress to two French kings, was the sitter. The scheme – a nude in a definite context, now obscure – is much like that of Titian's "*Venus of Urbino*" (see p. 145).

MASSYS AND PATENIER
(right) *The Crucifixion; saints and donors, c.* 1520-30
Massys and his workshop, deliberately reverting to native tradition, have here "modernized" Campin and van der Weyden, and the figures' archaic gestures stand out vividly against Patenier's richly rolling panorama. Massys' sons continued his production.

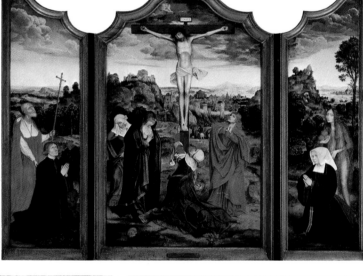

VAN SCOREL (below)
Mary Magdalen, c. 1540
More a portrait with the attributes of a saint than a devotional image, van Scorel's picture shows the impact of his travels. Against a Mediterranean sky the Magdalen wears a striped silk mantle and pearls such as a Venetian courtesan might display.

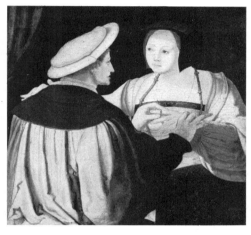

VAN LEYDEN (above)
The engagement, c. 1520-30
Dramatic frontal lighting and strong horizontal axes set up an almost abstract pattern of light and dark areas, indicating a graphic bias. This is very early for pure genre subjects.

FONTAINEBLEAU SCHOOL
(below) *Three minions, c.* 1580-89
The impeccably groomed courtiers of Henri III exemplify the very high finish and rather mannered sophistication of the second school of Fontainebleau.

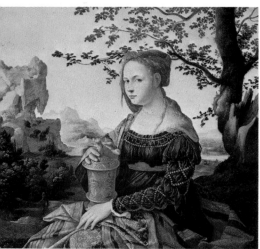

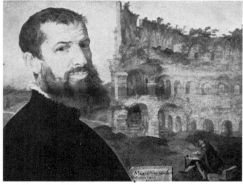

VAN HEEMSKERCK
Self-portrait beside the Colosseum, 1533
The artist turns proudly to the spectator in a vivid

image of the relationship of northern artists to Rome, then and for years to come. He recorded buildings and statuary, old and also new.

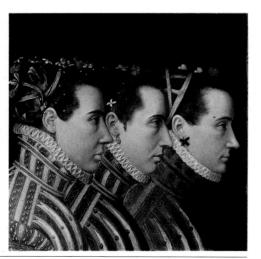

Bruegel: August, or the Corn Harvest

Pieter Bruegel (*c.* 1525-69) worked in Antwerp and then in Brussels, but early in his career travelled extensively in France and Italy, between about 1551 and 1553. Unlike almost all his northern contemporaries, he took from Italian art virtually none of the surface trimmings, though he surely developed in Italy his sense of space, his organization of majestic compositions in depth and the density of his human figures – though very different in effect, his broadly conceived peasant figures have a physical gravity like those of Giotto. From his journey through the Alps, however, he drew one enduring inspiration – mountains: views from the heights are recurrent in his work.

The most important early influence on Bruegel in Flanders was clearly the work of Bosch. This is apparent not only in the many designs that he made for engravings, but also even in quite late paintings. Many of his pictures illustrate proverbs and parables, most of them depicting humans as creatures of appetite subservient to the whims of nature or to their own folly. Bruegel's religious subjects are usually set in a contemporary context, almost submerged in the ebb and flow of everyday life about them; so in *The procession to Calvary* the spectator has to search amongst the teeming throng across the panoramic landscape, to discern Christ. Nor are his religious characters idealized: indeed, in the London *Adoration of the Magi*, not only Joseph but the three kings are portrayed much like the shepherds and attendant soldiers – in fairly brutish terms. Bruegel's grimmest works, such as *The triumph of Death* (not shown) with its serried legions of skeletons, date from around 1562, during the Spanish persecution of a large Protestant minority in Antwerp. Bruegel removed that same year to Brussels, but his own

BRUEGEL (right)
August (The corn harvest), 1565
This is probably the first picture in the history of art to transcribe the heat of high summer into paint. A group of peasants take a midday break in the shade of a tree, eating, drinking – one is sprawled in sleep. Others are still at work, scything, stacking the corn, carrying sheaves. Through trees on the brow of the slope is glimpsed the village church; in the valley below, close to a farm, other small figures are at work in the fields. Beyond, the landscape melts shimmering away for miles; land and the watery expanse of the estuary merge in haze into the opaque sky. The working figures move with a torpid sluggishness. A man arriving from a path through the dense, shoulder-high corn, bearing liquid refreshment – the sweat that trickles down his chest is not visible but it seems to be there. The extraordinary colours, the dominating hot yellow and green, reverberate through the picture.

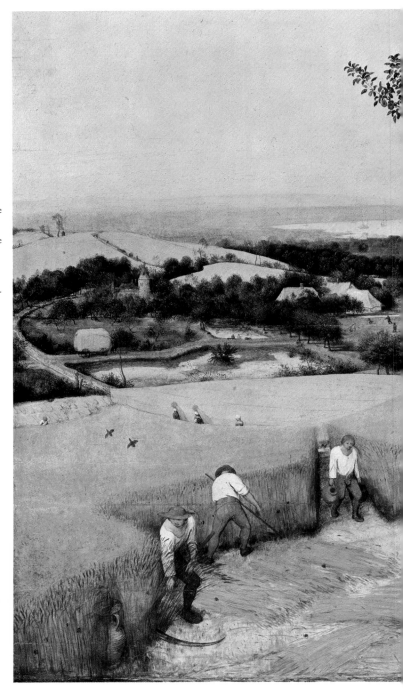

BRUEGEL (below)
January (The hunters in the snow), 1565
If *August* is heat itself, then *January*, in its whites, greys and blacks, is the very rigour of iron winter.

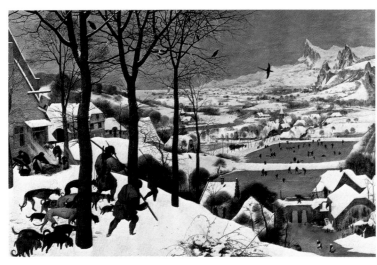

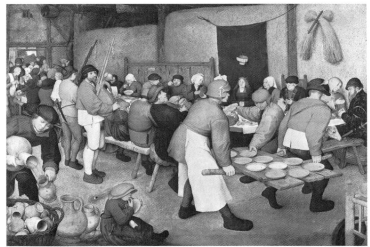

AERTSEN (left)
Christ in the house of Martha and Mary, 1559
Interposing huge piles of food and flowers between the observer and the central scene, Aertsen anticipated pure still life, seen for itself.

BRUEGEL (right)
The peasant wedding, c. 1567
Drawings of peasants from the life underlie the incisive characterization and detail.

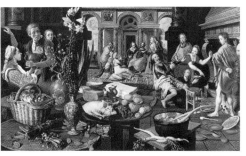

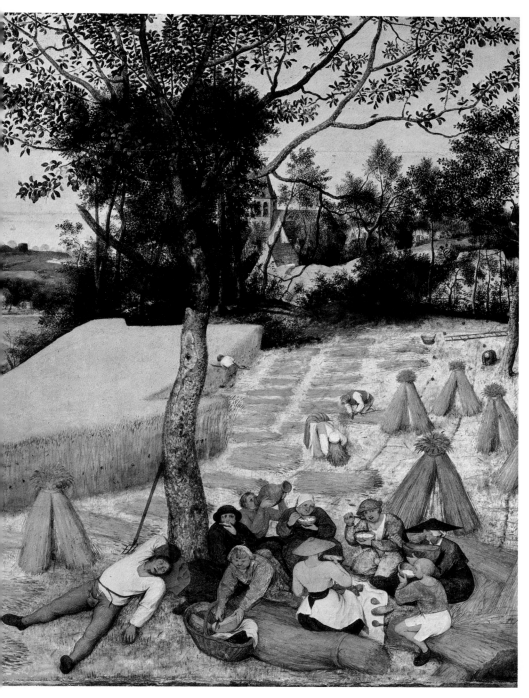

political or religious convictions are not clear; in Brussels the Spanish President of the Council of State, Cardinal Granvella, was an important patron. Despite his nickname, "Peasant Bruegel", Bruegel was a man of culture and discrimination, and a close friend of the great geographer Ortelius.

Quintessential in Bruegel's work is his "close-up" masterpiece of peasant life, *The peasant wedding*. Here composition, wit, and acute observation are superbly fused. Echoes of religious themes may linger – the Feast at Cana, even the Last Supper – but Bruegel's work is entirely of this world. His supreme achievement is *The Months of the Year*, a series painted in 1565 for the villa in Brussels of his patron Niclaes Jonghelinck; there are five survivors, astonishing in their range of mood, of which the most famous are *August* (*The corn harvest*) and *January* (*The hunters in the snow*). Their predecessors are the brilliant miniatures of the changing months by the Limbourgs, in which any religious significance was already peripheral, though the theme of annual rebirth and change always had astrological relevance and allegorical undertones of good and evil, light and dark, life and death. Bruegel's peasants, however, squat, tenacious and unlovely, work the world for survival. Food, its getting and its consuming, is one of Bruegel's preoccupations; no one has surpassed the sensitivity and skill with which he evokes the beauty of the earth that provides. His true subject is Nature herself, with man an integral part of her growth, decay and rebirth.

Bruegel's compositions were repeated by his son Pieter II, but the only painter to deal with similar subjects with originality and more than average competence was Pieter Aertsen (1508-75), working in Antwerp and Amsterdam.

BRUEGEL (below)
The Adoration of the Magi, 1564
There are perhaps traces of Schongauer and of Italian influence in the grouping of figures, but the grimacing onlookers themselves are a clear reference back to those of Bosch (see p. 99). The view of humanity is not kind; nor is it didactically moralistic; Bruegel's realism can be monumental, serene.

BRUEGEL (right)
The procession to Calvary, 1564
The crowded panorama is full of telling episodes condemning human folly – the moralism of Bruegel's engravings transferred to a religious setting. As an example of hypocrisy, his wife attempts to detain Simon of Cyrene, called to assist the fallen Christ, although a crucifix hangs at her belt. There are also topical references, and the Roman soldiers wear the uniform of the "Habits Rouges" who kept order in Flanders for the Spanish. *The triumph of Death* is in composition quite similar, teeming with corpses hung in attitudes of agony.

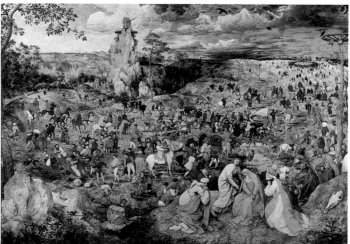

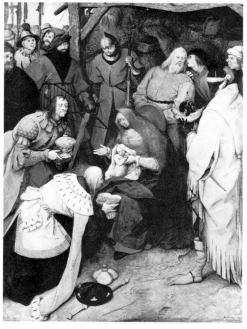

Mannerist Painting in Italy 1

"Mannerism" is a term that has been used in such varying senses through the centuries that it would seem best, in the interest of clarity, to abandon it altogether. However, it has become part of the language of the history of art, and is unavoidable. The first modern systematic historian of art, Giorgio Vasari, was himself a successful painter, and a Mannerist one, so that his application of the word was inevitably approving. For Vasari, the Italian *maniera* meant roughly "style". For later historians, *maniera* and its translation, Mannerism, came to signify rather "stylishness" or "stylization", and Mannerism was denigrated as affected, perverse, decadent – a degeneration from High Renaissance classicism; generally, the term was used to categorize artists who were felt to imitate the manner, especially of Michelangelo, without catching anything of the spirit – artists, that is, who were indeed insincerely mannered. In the last 50 years the term has gradually lost its pejorative force, and is now applied especially to Italian painting and sculpture of the period between about 1520 and 1600, or between the climax of the High Renaissance and the beginning of Baroque. It is seen as a phase of art that is valid

and needs no special justification. If argument continues about its terminal dates, about what qualities in a given work of art are Mannerist and what are not, some broad generalizations can be offered with fair confidence.

In Italy, the characteristic tendency of Mannerism was to refine even further the technical virtuosity, the elegance, that had been so consummately balanced with both monumental and human values in the High Renaissance. These gave way to an emphasis on serpentine line (the so-called *figura serpentinata* of Michelangelo); on attenuated forms; on the bizarre contrast of poses and colours; and even to strange, sometimes morbid or pornographic torsions and tensions. Nature seems to yield to artifice. Some seeds of Mannerism are almost evident in the last work of Raphael, as in certain aspects of Michelangelo's style, while the move away from the classic stability of Renaissance art into more shifting realms may reflect the political unsettlement that culminated, in Italy, in the Sack of Rome in 1527, and, in the north, in the Reformation.

However, the forcing-house of Mannerism was not only Rome but Florence, which was still nominally republican, but had in fact been

in the hands of the Medici dynasty since 1512. Michelangelo was working in Florence for the Medici from 1516 and there, too, that marvellously gifted painter Andrea del Sarto (1486-1530) was active. His masterpieces, such as "*The Madonna of the Harpies*", 1517, may at first glance compel comparison with Raphael's *Madonnas* – not only for their classicism but also in sheer quality – yet his handling of light, mysterious instead of calm and even, is emotive as Raphael's never was. Del Sarto's pupils included the brilliant Pontormo, Vasari, Salviati and possibly Rosso Fiorentino.

In Rome, Giulio Romano (1499?-1546), Raphael's chief and most gifted assistant, had completed Raphael's *Transfiguration* and other works, and his own style (influenced now by Michelangelo) became increasingly dramatic. Accused of making pornographic prints, he fled from Rome to Mantua in 1524, and there, in the Palazzo del Tè, he produced for Federigo II Gonzaga startlingly violent and illusionistic Mannerist decorations – especially the *Sala dei Giganti* (The Hall of the Giants).

The movement away from classical harmony is to be seen even before Raphael's death. Del Sarto's pupil Jacopo Carucci da

RAPHAEL (below)
The Transfiguration, 1520
The central message is the contrast between heavenly peace and earthly sorrow, as in Titian's *Assumption* (see p. 142), which is also separated into two distinct realms. Hence Raphael chooses to juxtapose the Transfiguration with the healing of an epileptic youth (which follows the Transfiguration in Mark's Gospel, but is not linked with it in a narrative sense). The brittle draperies, the hard colours, the virtuosity of the dramatically lit, gesticulating figures in the lower part, particularly the serpentine movement of the frenzied youth, are distinctly Mannerist in flavour.

MICHELANGELO (left)
Victory, c.1530?
The figure's pose, for all its contortions and spirals, has an effortless quality typical of Mannerism. The victim's features resemble Michelangelo's own – possibly the first of those ironic self-portraits appearing in his later works.

ANDREA DEL SARTO (below)
"*The Madonna of the Harpies*", 1517
The attendant saints glance up at the onlooker, as if no barrier exists between their world and his. Raphael's "*Madonna della Sedia*" (see p. 129) communicates in a similar way; Mannerists sought also directness.

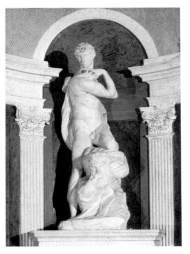

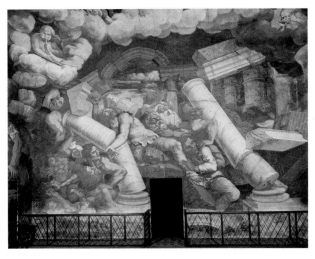

GIULIO ROMANO (above)
The *Sala dei Giganti* (The Giants' Hall), detail, 1534
The room is constructed in the shape of a beehive and the visitor is entirely surrounded by the illusion. There was once also a fireplace of real crushed rocks, fusing illusion with reality.

PONTORMO (below)
Joseph in Egypt, c.1515
There is obvious tension between the abundance of elegant forms and the narrative content, and this, combined with the glowing, unreal colour, imparts to the work a febrile quality, typical of early Mannerism.

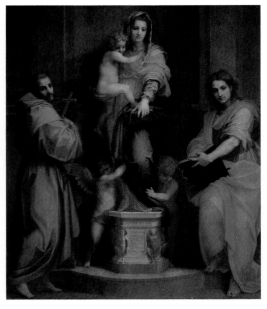

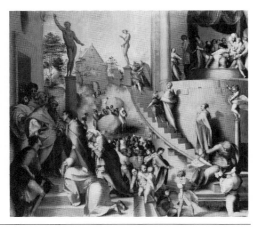

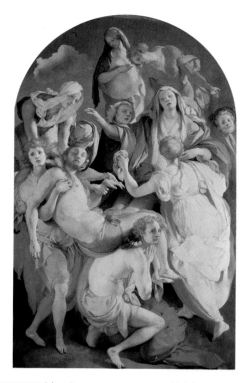

Pontormo (1494-1557), one of several painters commissioned about 1515 to paint a decorative "programme" for a Florentine bedroom, painted a most unorthodox *Joseph in Egypt*, with freaks of perspective and proportion, flights of stairs going nowhere, statues more lifelike than the human beings. Pontormo's later works are almost hallucinatory. In his *Deposition* in S. Felicità in Florence, the body of Christ follows that of Michelangelo's Vatican *Pietà* (see p.132), but the figures have little physical weight, and stand on no real ground and in no real space. The colours are high in key and clear, with little light and shade; the draperies seem to have an independent life of their own; the bodies are elongated – in some cases, Pontormo even quotes figures from Dürer. The unease of his art was matched by a neurotic, hypochondriac temperament vividly reflected in his surviving journal, a sensibility he seemed to find reflected in his sitters.

Pontormo's friend and contemporary Giovanni Battista Rosso Fiorentino (1495-1540) also painted a *Deposition*, some years earlier than Pontormo's, in 1521, and no less extraordinary. Cross and ladders form an almost geometric framework, across which the figures, with strange grimaces and emphatic gestures, are arranged in a bizarre conjunction of nakedness and independent draperies. As in Pontormo's version, the scene has no grounding in any earthly reality. Rosso also worked in Rome, but in 1530 he was summoned by Francis I to France (see over).

Mannerism had its effect elsewhere in Italy, most singularly in Siena, on Domenico Beccafumi (*c.* 1486-1551). His religious paintings have a high-keyed emotional quality, and often flame-bright colours in which something of the earlier Sienese colourist tradition persists. In the north, Parmigianino (Francesco Mazzola, 1503-40), having returned in 1531 to his home town of Parma after some years in Rome, there took the early Mannerist style to its most extreme pitch. Parmigianino, like Pontormo, was an irrational and neurotic personality, but a brilliant draughtsman; he was also an engraver and his work became widely known through engravings. The most famous example of the extreme attenuation of his style is "*The Madonna with the Long Neck*" of about 1535, notable not only for its expressive distortion of perspective and proportions, but also for the strange conceit of a topless pillar.

PONTORMO (above)
*The Deposition, c.*1526-28
In contrast to his *Joseph in Egypt*, Pontormo resolves the conflict between form and content: the emotion is at a high pitch without detracting from the beauty and grace of the whole.

PONTORMO (right)
*The halberdier, c.*1529-30
In 1529-30, 5,000 citizens rose to defend Florence against the expelled Medici. Elegant, poised, removed, this archetypal Mannerist portrait perhaps represents one of these militiamen.

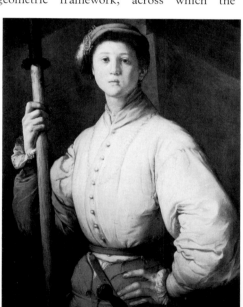

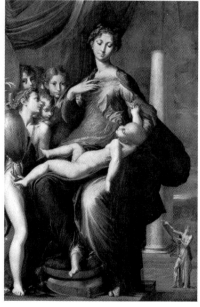

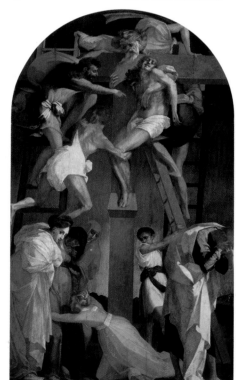

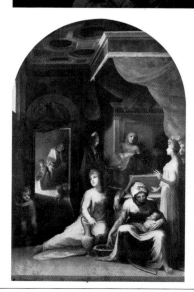

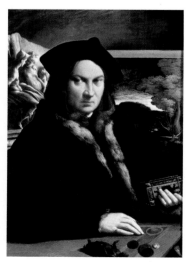

ROSSO (above)
The Deposition, 1521
The scene is lit as if by a flash of lightning, fiercely delineating the hard-edged forms which characterize Rosso's work throughout his career.

BECCAFUMI (right)
*The birth of the Virgin, c.*1543
The light is lively, the colours are rich but sombre; the Mannerism of this late work is less strident, and more intimate in mood.

PARMIGIANINO (above)
"*The Madonna of the Long Neck*", *c.* 1535
No Mannerist work goes further in the distortion of form: the Madonna's seated pose is improbable; the Infant has the proportions of a seven-year-old child. The result is both precious and monumental.

PARMIGIANINO (left)
"*The Priest*", *c.* 1523
This earliest surviving portrait by Parmigianino earned its title because of the shape of the sitter's hat. His attributes are hardly priestly, however – a relief of Mars and Venus, medals, a figurine, a richly bound book – these indicate, if esoterically, a humanist.

Mannerism 2: The Medici and the French Kings

In 1530 Medici rule was re-established in Florence and Alessandro de' Medici named the first Duke of Tuscany. After his assassination in 1537 Cosimo I consolidated the regime, which provided a degree of stability in Florence for the next two centuries. Cosimo's court painter and the quintessential artist of High Mannerism in Florence was Agnolo Bronzino (1503-72). A pupil of Pontormo, he developed from his master's troubled and troubling style into the coolest and most immaculate technician of the sixteenth century. His flawless polish and emotional detachment were unsuited to religious subjects, and his major exercises in that field, even at their best, as in Eleanora of Toledo's Chapel, remain unstirring, mere exercises. His style suited allegories better: the most famous of them, usually known as *Venus, Cupid, Folly and Time*, is almost certainly identical with a painting of 1545 sent to Francis I of France by Duke Cosimo as a present. The subject is obscure, and in some points open to contradictory interpretations – thus, is the figure of bald, bearded old Time, top right, in collaboration with Truth, top left, opening or closing the curtain between them? An alter-

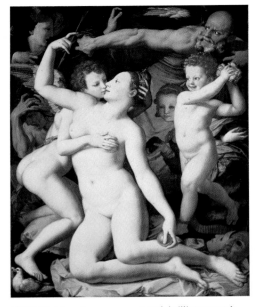

BRONZINO (above)
Venus, Cupid, Folly and Time, c. 1545
The colour is polished to a cool, brilliant enamel; the flesh is pale ivory or marble, the hair metallic, the eroticism disquieting.

native title is *The exposure of Luxury*, but, if intended as censure, in effect it suggests rather a celebration. Certainly pornography has often been proffered under the pretence of condemning itself; and Cupid's embrace of his mother is more than merely filial.

It was in court portraiture that Bronzino's style was most aptly and effectively engaged. In the creation of images of absolute autocracy in human form he has never been surpassed. Even in his portraits of lesser persons, he projects characters of ineffably detached superiority: communication with the onlooker is non-existent; the sitter is there for admiration. In the state portraiture of *Eleanora of Toledo and her son Giovanni*, of about 1546, the sitters' aloof detachment has become absolute; the figures are as still, cold and glazed as waxworks; in the magnificence of their costume, described with an exact refinement, they are effigies of their own status.

The two other leading exponents of the high Mannerist style were Salviati and Vasari, old friends and both former pupils of Andrea del Sarto. Francesco de' Rossi Salviati (1510-63) was a restless, peripatetic character who developed a very elaborate decorative style with a

BRONZINO (right)
Chapel of Eleanora of Toledo, Palazzo Vecchio, detail: *The crossing of the Red Sea*, 1542-44
The impact is chiefly in the posturing figures; the whole reads like an inexhaustible catalogue of Mannerist *contrapposto* and *figura serpentinata*.

SALVIATI (below)
Frescos in the Palazzo Sacchetti, detail: *Bathsheba going to David*, c. 1552-54
The muscular proportions of Bathsheba suggest the influence of Michelangelo's *Last Judgment* (see p. 133) combined with a brilliant flare of colour beloved of the high Mannerists.

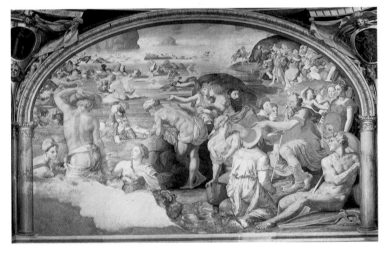

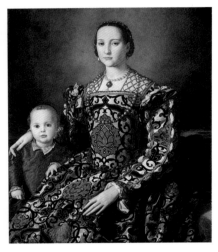

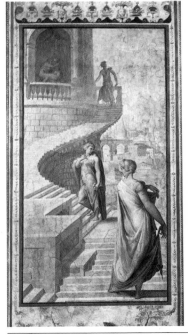

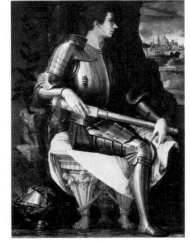

VASARI (above)
Alessandro de' Medici, c. 1533
Michelangelo's *Giuliano de' Medici* (see p. 131) was the model for the arrogant, dissolute Duke's portrait.

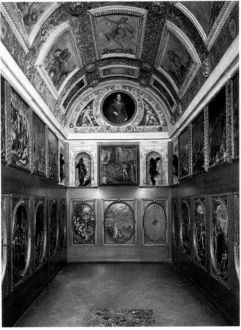

BRONZINO (above)
Eleanora of Toledo, c. 1546?
Redolent of the consciously aristocratic atmosphere of Cosimo's court, the portrait of the Duchess, daughter of the Spanish viceroy in Naples, has the effect of a still life, compounded by a slight unease – a symptom of the insecurity of Medici rule only 10 years after the infamous assassination of Alessandro by his cousin, the enigmatic Lorenzino.

VASARI (left)
Cosimo I's *studiolo* in the Palazzo Vecchio, 1570-73
The most perfect of high Mannerist "conceits", the decoration has the effect of an encrusted jewel-box, a storehouse of precious objects. Executed under Vasari's eye by a number of assistants, individual elements in the decoration suggest the younger artists, at least, were developing towards a more sober style.

consummate technique. He worked not only in Florence and Rome, but also in Venice and, briefly, at the French court. The clear influence of Parmigianino in his work suggests that he must also have visited Parma. His latest frescos, in Rome, are perhaps the most extravagant of all Mannerist fantasies. Bathsheba winding her way up the improbable aerial stairs towards David's embrace (from the *David* series in the Palazzo Sacchetti, 1552-54) has the febrile elegance of a dream interpreted in ballet; while in Salviati's celebrations of the Farnese dynasty in the Palazzo Farnese (not shown) in Rome the ambivalent play of illusion and reality is worked out with an unsurpassed ingenuity and virtuosity.

The reputation of Giorgio Vasari (1511-74) as a painter was established by a portrait of Alessandro de' Medici; he recorded that in his attempts to paint the armour "bright, shining and natural" he almost went out of his mind. Under Duke Cosimo, Vasari became the leading impresario of art in Florence, with a large studio executing, with varying degrees of quality, complex Mannerist decorations in Florence and Rome. He was a leading spirit in the Florentine Academy of Art, which held its first session in 1562, and the first architect of the grand-ducal Uffizi, now the great picture gallery. But it is above all for his diligent *Lives of the Most Excellent Painters, Sculptors and Architects*, first published in 1550 and expanded in 1568, that he is now honoured; in that work he set the dominant pattern of art-historical writing for centuries.

Italian Mannerism was transplanted into France by Francis I, whose costly attempts to maintain control over Lombardy did not abate his taste for the quality of culture and life he had found in Italy, and who decided that Italian artists were necessary to create in France the setting for the new princely dominance to which he aspired. In 1530, he imported Rosso (see preceding page), and a succession of others, some of whom stayed, others not. If he failed with Michelangelo, Francis did entice the aged Leonardo, but only to die there, and also Primaticcio, Niccolò dell' Abbate, the architect Serlio, Andrea del Sarto and Cellini. The focus of the King's attention was the decoration of the château-palace of Fontainebleau. Here, from 1532, Rosso, followed by Francesco Primaticcio (1504/5-70), attempted a fusion of stucco reliefs and paintings, moving in a coherent rhythm through the long stretch of the Galerie François I. The very elongated, often languid figures are developments of the style of late Raphael via Parmigianino, and in due course the rich elaboration and fantasy of Fontainebleau was to be echoed back in Italy in late Mannerist works such as the Sala Regia (not shown) in the Vatican, executed under the direction of Perino del Vaga (1500/1-45).

Native French painters and sculptors could not be unaffected by the Italian implantation, and, under Francis' successor Henri II, carried on their tradition – the so-called "second school of Fontainebleau" (see also p. 161). The sculptors showed a better grasp of Italianate form; they were indebted especially to Benvenuto Cellini, who made two famous surviving works for Francis I, a gold salt-cellar (see over) and the more than life-size bronze relief *"The Nymph of Fontainebleau"*. She is small-headed and enormously long-limbed, whereas Jean Goujon (died 1568) and Germain Pilon (1527-90) tended to be less extreme: Goujon's reliefs for his Fountain of the Innocents are in comparison highly classicizing. Pilon included in his funerary monuments sculptures of sometimes remarkably intense realism.

ROSSO AND PRIMATICCIO (right) The Gallery of Francis I, 1530-40
Long galleries were alien to Italian architectural tradition, and their chief drawback is, they cannot be viewed as a whole. The problem is solved here by setting up an undulating rhythm between the flat paintings and the posturing sculptures, which leads the eye down the gallery.

PRIMATICCIO (below)
Room of the Duchesse d'Etampes, Fontainebleau, detail, *c.* 1541-45
After Rosso's death, Primaticcio assumed his role as chief decorator to the French King. Even Rosso's forms seem sturdy by comparison with these rarefied figures, whose long limbs and small heads recall Cellini's *Nymph*.

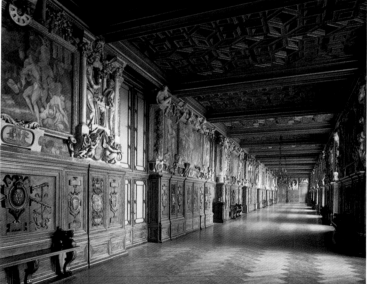

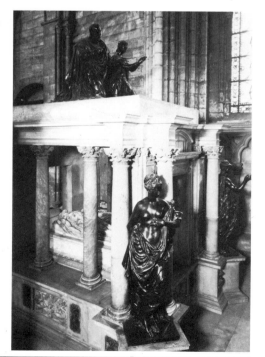

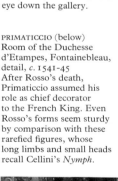

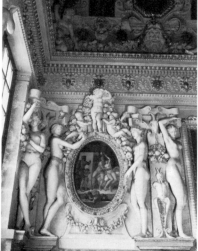

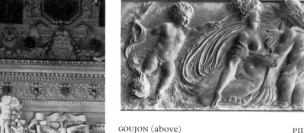

CELLINI (above)
"The Nymph of Fontaine-bleau", 1540-43
Despite the elongation of her limbs, the nymph has a monumental quality, on a foil of intricate, natural detail. She was designed to surmount the entrance of the Château of Anet, a gem amidst the block-like forms of the classical gateway.

GOUJON (above)
Panel from the Fountain of the Innocents: *Nymphs and tritons*, 1547-49
The figures, though placed against a sweep of draperies closely resembling those in Cellini's *Nymph*, have a more natural appearance. Goujon was at his best in relief, which provided scope for his feeling for surface. The movement is disciplined by French sobriety.

PILON (right)
The tomb of Henri II and Catherine de Médicis, 1563-70
The tomb was designed by Primaticcio, while Pilon executed the sculpture. The traditional realism of the kneeling statues and the effigies below is combined with attention to detail and a new sense of freedom in the poses, deriving from Cellini.

Mannerist Sculpture in Italy

The patronage of the Medici dukes of Tuscany in the last three-quarters of the sixteenth century was even more conspicuous in sculpture than in painting, not least because sculpture, deployed in an almost compulsive fashion for elaborate garden schemes and in public places, contributed spectacularly to the splendour and prestige of their dynasty. The Piazza della Signoria, the focus of civic Florence, was given final form, more or less as it is today, by the Medici. In style, the impetus came from Michelangelo, present in Florence between 1516 and 1534, and especially from the abiding example of his work in the Medici Chapel.

The irascible Baccio Bandinelli (1493-1560; not shown) rather undeservedly enjoyed a virtual monopoly of public commissions in Florence for some 20 years after Michelangelo had finally left the city. His pre-eminence came abruptly to an end in 1555, when Bartolommeo Ammanati (1511-92) returned to Florence from Rome and quickly secured a number of large commissions, among them the Fountain of Neptune (or del Gigante) in the Piazza Signoria. The chief interest of this imposing structure lies in the bronze marine gods and nymphs disposed around the basin;

the large marble block set aside for the giant central figure was defaced by Bandinelli when he heard that what he regarded as his commission was to be awarded instead by competition. Bandinelli also had a very public quarrel with the irrepressible Benvenuto Cellini (1500-71). Cellini's enduring, boastfully rumbustious *Autobiography* – illuminating about artistic life and practice of the time as well as about the variety of his own amorous activities – tends to overshadow his quality as a sculptor. His early work in Rome (where he lived through the Sack of 1527, which he vividly describes) was mainly as a goldsmith, and his sole surviving major work in gold, probably the most important piece of goldsmith's work that has come down from the Renaissance, is the famous salt-cellar he made for Francis I of France, where he was working between 1540 and 1545 (see preceding page). In Florence, his most significant commission, his masterpiece on a monumental scale, was the bronze *Perseus* holding aloft the severed head of Medusa, finished in 1554 and set up in the Loggia dei Lanzi. The composition is based on a type of Etruscan statuette, although the inclusion of Medusa's decapitated corpse suggests deliberate rivalry

with Donatello's *Judith* murdering Holofernes nearby. The grace, the macabre elegance, the precious detailing are entirely Mannerist.

A younger contemporary of Cellini, Giambologna or Giovanni da Bologna (1529-1608) was born Jean de Boulogne in Douai on the Flemish border. After two years in Rome, 1554-56, he stopped off, on his way back to Flanders, in Florence, where he remained until his death, as chief sculptor to the Medici and master of a large and flourishing workshop. His output was prodigious, and most variously inventive. He worked with equal virtuosity in stone or bronze, and excelled as much in the creation of fountains for the Medici formal gardens as in the production of small-scale bronzes. His bronze *Mercury* in flight is unsurpassed in its effect of weightlessness in movement. While Michelangelo's ideal beauty had been a nude of predominantly masculine character, Giambologna's *Mercury* is much lighter and more feminine, almost androgynous. Another such masterpiece is the *Apollo* cast for the *studiolo* of Francesco de' Medici (see preceding page). Giambologna's designs, and his own and his many talented pupils' variants on them, were turned out in

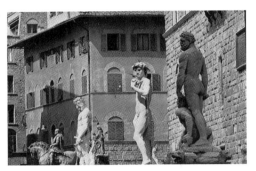

FLORENCE (above)
The Piazza Signoria seen from the Loggia dei Lanzi Here are Bandinelli's harsh *Hercules and Cacus*; a copy of Michelangelo's *David*; Ammanati's Fountain of Neptune; Donatello's rather dwarfed *Judith*; and Giambologna's *Duke Cosimo I*.

AMMANATI (below)
The Fountain of Neptune, detail: *A nereid*, 1571-75 Behind the nymph rises the outsize marble figure of Neptune: she is quite out of scale. The scheme is full of arcane allusions, indeed rather overloaded, but technically is superb.

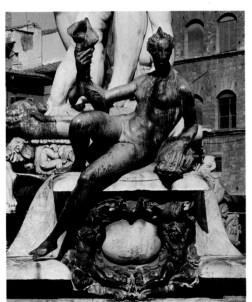

CELLINI (below)
Perseus, finished 1554 The muscular figure pays respect to Michelangelo; the pose, with its powerful, clearly defined profiles, recalls Verrocchio's work,

for instance the vigorous silhouette of the equestrian *Colleoni* (see p. 115). This was Cellini's first foray into life-size sculpture; its encrusted detail recalls his goldsmith's training.

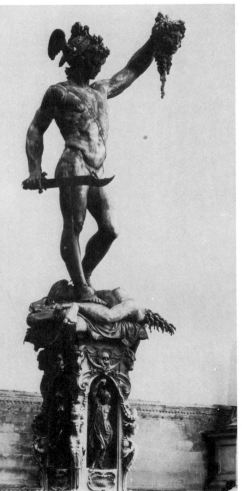

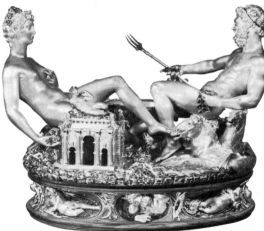

CELLINI (above)
The salt-cellar of Francis I, *c.* 1540 The two figures represent Earth and Neptune, and in style reflect Rosso's and Primaticcio's sculptures in stucco at Fontainebleau (see preceding page). The intense approach to form, with extreme elongation of limbs and a sense of poise, rather than physical movement, is characteristic of Cellini's exquisite work.

GIAMBOLOGNA (right)
Mercury, *c.* 1564 The figure, up on tiptoe, seems scarcely to rest on a puff of air from the mouth of the *putto's* head that is its sole support. In its high finish, suave elegance and rhythmic *contrapposto*, Mannerist principles are displayed at their purest. Yet in its open movement, its involvement in the space surrounding it, *Mercury* also presages the Baroque.

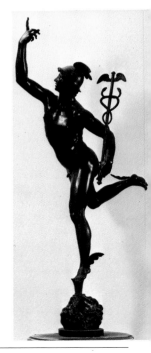

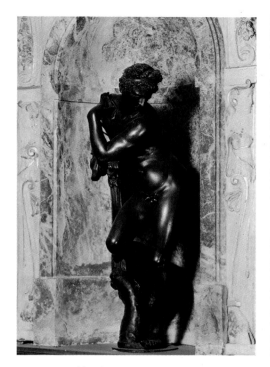

profusion by his studio; bronzes were favourite gifts of the Medici to other princes throughout Europe, and Giambologna's style became very widely disseminated.

On a large scale, Giambologna's range extended to such monumentally virile work as the equestrian statue of Duke Cosimo I, depicted as the founder of the Medici dynasty: gravely idealized, referring back again to the Roman statue of *Marcus Aurelius* (see p. 51), it soon superseded the *tours-de-force* of Donatello or Verrocchio as the pattern from which countless formal equestrian statues all over Europe were to derive. Earlier, in 1583, Francesco de' Medici had had Giambologna's colossal marble group, *The rape of the Sabine*, set up in the Loggia dei Lanzi. Originally the subject was not specific, but identification became necessary when it was set up in a public place, so Giambologna christened it. Beside Cellini's *Perseus*, across the Piazza from Michelangelo's *David*, the statue reads as the ultimate definition of Mannerist principles. A scene of extreme violence is controlled in a virtuoso display of supreme technical skill; the spiralling structure of intertwining bodies, the father defeated between the legs of the tri-

umphant Roman abductor of his daughter, offers no single viewing point to the spectator, but keeps him moving round it, one view dissolving into the next as he traces out the apparently effortless serpentine movement. As an "all-round" statue, it is perhaps the first truly modern sculpture.

Florentine sculpture, or Venetian (where the graceful monumentality of Sansovino's classicism was maintained), seems to have been little affected by the political and religious ferment of the Reformation and Counter-Reformation, or by the consequent artistic policies of the Catholic Church approved by the Council of Trent in 1563. That was more apparent in Rome, where tombs and chapels were encumbered with ponderous, usually prosaic marble, or in Spain. The Mannerist emphasis on grace, elegance, wit and sheer, even perverse, ingenuity was not easily adapted to religious purposes, though Cellini toyed with a religious vocation at the end of his life. But Giambologna's studio produced some exquisite small-scale crucifixes, while in his latest works, such as *Hercules and the centaur* of 1600, the trend towards the vigorous realism of Baroque is clear to see.

GIAMBOLOGNA (above)
Apollo, 1570-73
Both taut, contorted and easy, languid, flowing, the *Apollo* is constructed with a strong vertical on one side – the tree-trunk, lyre and Apollo's forearm – and on the other, swelling curves. It is the finest of the bronze statuettes that grace the tiny *studiolo* of Francesco de' Medici.

GIAMBOLOGNA (right)
Duke Cosimo I, 1587-95
Giambologna took on the task of sculpting the first equestrian monument to be made in Florence with even more than his usual care, and the result certainly surpasses all precedents in the smoothness of its line, its sense of gravity, its high-stepping movement.

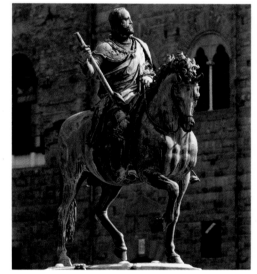

GIAMBOLOGNA (left)
Hercules and the centaur, 1594-1600
The subject had interested Giambologna for more than 20 years; as early as 1576 he had made a silver cast. His studio produced quite a number of statuettes on the theme. These, however, delight in the artificial contortions of consciously virtuoso variations; here the grace and "difficulty" of the form take second place. The demands of the action come first, indeed break the complex harmony up, dislocating its lines. The physical stresses are portrayed with consummate skill: the centaur twists all the way beneath Hercules' left arm, while his bucking legs and wildly spiralling tail intimate the violence of his effort, and his distress.

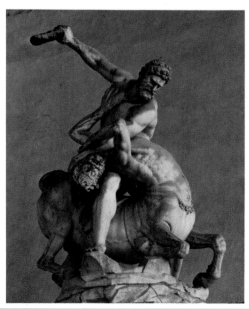

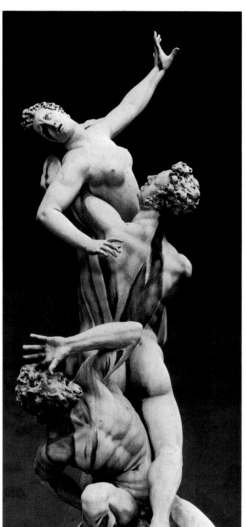

GIAMBOLOGNA
(left and below)
The rape of the Sabine, 1579-83
Giambologna clearly saw this group as a challenge to his virtuosity; no other sculptor had succeeded in integrating three figures into such a coherent spiral. Others had succeeded with two; and the prototype was Michelangelo's *Victory* (see p. 164), the classic demonstration of serpentine form. But the interaction of the figures is not only formal, gesture echoing to gesture, but psychological – glance leads on to glance, culminating expressively in the appeal of the woman to the unanswering heavens.

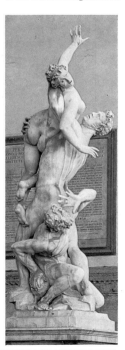

Painting in Venice: Tintoretto and Veronese

When the plague took Titian in 1576, he was so aged that legend had it he was 99 years old. His figure presided over Venetian painting during most of the sixteenth century, and all his younger colleagues referred to him in their work. But they were also affected by the heady currents of Mannerism emanating from Florence and Rome, which had indeed, briefly in the 1540s, affected Titian himself. And just as Titian's later work reflected the anxiety and spiritual disquiet of the Catholic Church faced with the Reformation, so the profoundly religious Tintoretto responded with an art of great emotional intensity.

Tintoretto (Jacopo Robusti, 1518-94) is reputed to have had written up on his studio wall: "Titian's colour, Michelangelo's line". Venetian colour, Mannerist line might be an accurate description of his sources, but his own synthesis has not much to do with either Titian or Michelangelo. Tintoretto seems to have been virtually self-taught. He evolved his own compositional technique, dependent not only on a large repertoire of study drawings but also on preliminary studies of figures modelled in wax: these he arranged experimentally in special boxes until he found the most dramatic viewpoint and the most effective lighting. The result was his idiosyncratic presentation of space seen down dizzy diagonals from unorthodox angles. Enormously prolific, employing a large team of assistants, he worked at speed (Ruskin, whose opinion of Tintoretto shifted from profound admiration to an uneasy disapproval, likened his brush to a broom) but with an expressive vigour that achieved a wonderfully pervasive rhythm. He tended to use the sombre ground colours on his canvas for the darks in his painting, working the design over them in lighter colours in broad strokes, "tuning" the whole finally with highlights – a technique that often gives his work an incandescent, unearthly radiance.

Tintoretto is sometimes categorized as a Mannerist painter, but he differs sharply from the Mannerists, especially in the violence of his expression and in his free, "unfinished" handling. He always admired Michelangelo, however, though he seems to have known his work only through copies or casts. *St Mark freeing a Christian slave*, of 1548, an early work in his mature style, is very reminiscent in composition, in its violent foreshortenings, of Michelangelo's almost contemporary *Conversion of St Paul* (see p.182). Its opulent colour

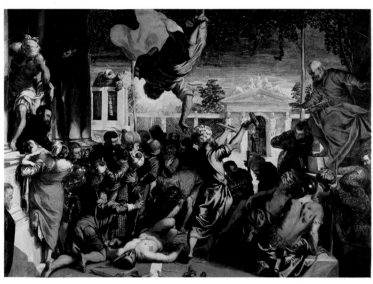

TINTORETTO (above)
St Mark frees a Christian slave, 1548
As the slave's bonds fall away, astonishment at the miracle ripples outwards in shots and glimmers of colour along the rhythmic line of arrested gestures. Chiaroscuro binds in the figures and unifies them all.

TINTORETTO (right)
The finding of the body of St Mark, 1562
Here the colour is muted, the funereal chiaroscuro flickers with livid light, the setting is eccentric. Both these *St Mark* scenes were part of a series for the Scuola di San Marco (St Mark's Confraternity).

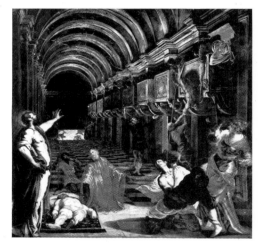

TINTORETTO (below)
The Last Supper, 1592-94
A turbulent atmosphere moves like heavy incense through the huge canvas, submerging the gestures of figures in movement or conversation; the heads gleam like spiritual coals. Only the long table, and the incidental genre and still life, provide a solid, earthly foundation for the mystery in the last of Tintoretto's many versions of the theme.

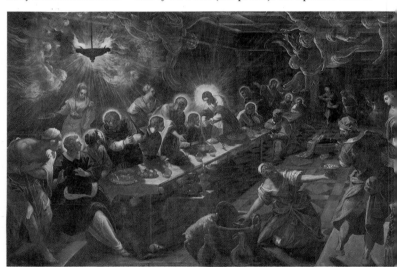

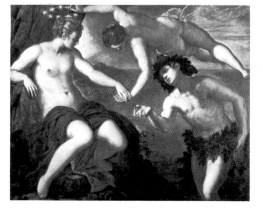

TINTORETTO (left)
Bacchus and Ariadne, 1578
The landscape evaporates into brown and blue mist, and the solid, monumental nudes float in an arabesque. This was one of a series for the Doge's Palace.

TINTORETTO (right)
Susannah and the Elders, c.1557
The voluptuous *Susannah* glows blonde in the dusky light of the summer garden. The contorted pose and exaggerated prominence of the nearest Elder is not Mannerist indulgence; it points up his voyeurism.

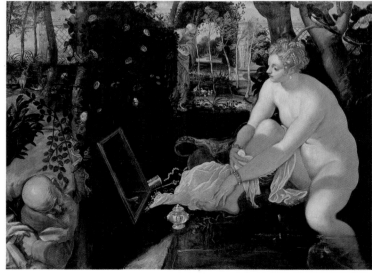

was later toned down, while the emphasis on dramatic contrast of light and shade, and on extraordinary recession into space, increased. In *The finding of the body of St Mark*, 1562, illustrating the Venetian theft of the body of their patron saint from Alexandria, the fantastic burial vault is lit only by the macabre slit of the opening at its far end and by the incandescent apparition of the saint on the left. In the late *Last Supper* of 1592-94, contrasting so strongly with traditional horizontal compositions, Tintoretto's revelation of miracle reaches a climax of drama. Over the diagonal thrust of the long table, the vertiginous tilt of the floor, Christ rises to break bread, which is his Body. Like the Christ here, other figures in Tintoretto's work seem to echo Byzantine motifs, and the glimmering light of his atmospherics may also owe something to the effect of the mosaics in the darkness of S. Marco. These Byzantine effects are paralleled by El Greco, while the movement, emotion and treatment of space foreshadow the imminent Baroque.

Tintoretto's work was not confined to religious subjects. His *Susannah* may be nominally a biblical story, but its impact is sensual and secular. His *Bacchus and Ariadne* is classi-

cal mythology treated with a grave, grandly lyrical pleasure worthy of Titian's great *poesie*, and it is not far in feeling from Tintoretto's great rival, Veronese. Tintoretto was also a prolific portrait painter, though his characterization is often relatively superficial. Yet a few late portraits (see over), mostly of aged men, have a troubling, sombre intensity.

Jacopo Bassano (1517/8?-92), chief among a family of painters taking their name from Bassano, a town in the foothills north-east of Venice, was the closest of the Venetians to Florentine Mannerism, at one stage of his career; later his most characteristic works came nearer again to Titian and to Tintoretto. These were virtually genre scenes with biblical incidents and titles; *The Adoration of the shepherds* (1568), a key-piece in his development, sustains a delicate balance between the religious subject (with that sturdy aerial dance of *putto*-like angels above) and the peasant characterizations of the shepherds below.

Tintoretto's opposite and rival was Paolo Veronese (Paolo Caliari, 1528-88). His pictures seem to come from a different world, and his temperament was certainly very different, but also he was more profoundly impressed by

Titian's early work than was Tintoretto. Veronese is most famous as a painter of vast opulent pageant paintings, celebrating the pleasures of the senses, the nobility of civilized life in Venice, untroubled by any more significant theme. He was also a great portrait painter, conveying the material luxury of aristocratic status, rather than the working of the mind or spirit, within the rich flesh, furs and silks of his sitters. His wealth of contemporary detail often came near to submerging his subject, and the Inquisition accused him of irreverence in his elegantly accoutred spectacular of what appeared to be a *Last Supper*; he made it acceptable by changing the title to *The feast in the house of Levi. Mars and Venus united by Love* is a typically sumptuous example of his mythological pictures. His greatest decorative commission was to fresco the Villa Maser for the highly cultivated and sophisticated Barbaro family, in which he collaborated with the great architect Palladio to re-create something of the Augustan atmosphere of Horace's poetic retreat in the Sabine hills. Yet it was Tintoretto, not Veronese, who was to create, in the Scuola di San Rocco, the Venetian counterpart to Michelangelo's Sistine Chapel ceiling.

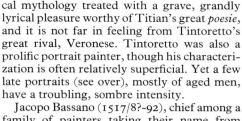

BASSANO (below)
The Adoration of the shepherds, 1568
The Virgin is gracefully Mannerist (influenced, it seems, by Parmigianino); but the solid, earthy, genre figures such as the kneeling shepherd and his dirty bare feet will reappear almost unchanged in Caravaggio's work. Bassano also painted night scenes, and religious landscapes anticipating Annibale Carracci's.

VERONESE (right)
The feast in the house of Levi, 1573
Since it was commissioned for a convent refectory, it is hardly surprising that the Inquisition objected to Veronese's patrician gala. His great achievement was to organize his teeming detail into an effortless, cool, fully legible grandeur. The figures are nearly life-scale, and Veronese painted even larger feasts.

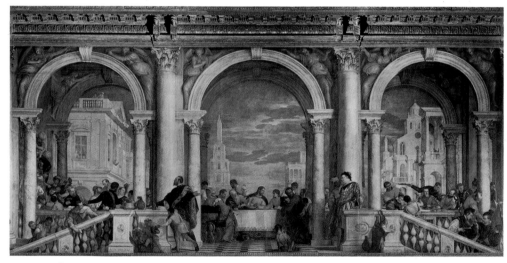

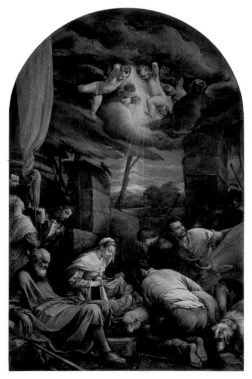

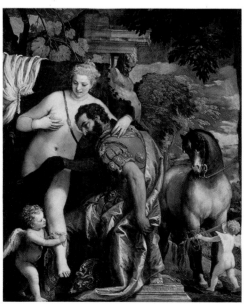

VERONESE (left)
Mars and Venus united by Love, c. 1580
Landscape, architecture, the splendid horse form a dark, cool backdrop, and Mars succumbs in tawny gold and shot purple to Venus' suffused, radiant flesh. The composition is broad and grand, utterly unaffected by a Mannerist interest in effects: it is sublimely decorative.

VERONESE (below)
A fresco from the Villa Maser, detail: *Giustiniana Barbaro and her nurse*, c. 1561
Veronese's illusionistic frescos at the Barbaro villa included not only *trompe-l'oeil* figures – initiating a Venetian tradition culminating in Tiepolo – but also landscapes of an enchantingly atmospheric delicacy.

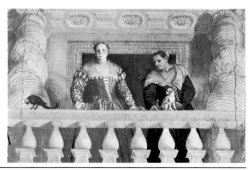

Tintoretto: The Scuola di San Rocco Crucifixion

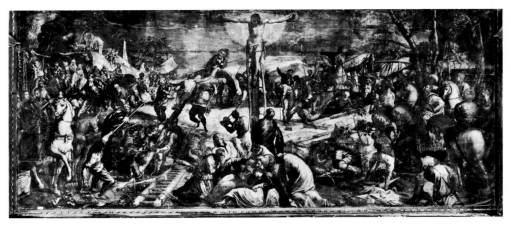

Between 1564 and 1587 Tintoretto virtually took over the building in which the Scuola, or Confraternity, of San Rocco was housed, and decorated its two storeys, both the walls and the ceilings, not with frescos but with canvases, many of them large, some huge – *The Crucifixion*, the largest of them all, is some 12.25 metres (40ft) across.

The Venetian Scuole were charitable organizations, rather like clubs or unions, each linked with a particular saint, and each with a strong *esprit de corps* motivating artistic patronage, often on a large scale. The Scuola di San Rocco, of comparatively recent foundation, in 1564 invited a number of painters, including Veronese and Tintoretto, to submit sketches in competition for the decoration of the smaller hall in its upper storey, the Council Chamber. Tintoretto assured himself of the commission by a trick: instead of a small sketch, he installed a full-scale painting surreptitiously *in situ*, which he then revealed to the astonished committee. He clinched the commission by suggesting that he present the painting to the Confraternity free – an offer which could not be refused, apparently, according to the Scuola's constitution.

The first phase involved the decoration of the Council Chamber only, but included *The Crucifixion*, 1565, and *The road to Calvary*, 1566. The second phase (1575-81) decorated the larger, main hall on the same floor – 13 Old Testament scenes on the ceiling in concordance with New Testament ones on the walls. The final phase, 1583-87, in the Lower Hall, was devoted to scenes from the life of the Virgin. The canvases, virtually encrusting the walls and the heavily coffered ceilings, do not make up a formally coherent whole, though they are disposed symmetrically, but through them all pulses the uniting rhythm of Tintoretto's formidable, rushing style.

The huge panorama of the *Crucifixion* occupies the whole wall facing the door of the Council Chamber. The impact is overwhelming, as it is impossible to get back far enough to take in the whole composition at once. The stark austerity of its central focus – Christ suspended over the huddle of his shattered followers beneath him – contrasts with the radiance ebbing from the Cross itself out to the edges of the composition. There ordinary folk, some interested, some not, set a context of both immediacy and enduring relevance, an effect that the wide screen of the cinema has yet to surpass. In the larger halls, Tintoretto created a wholly new range of imagery to rekindle the traditional stories, but his strange lighting – or lightning – is the essential agent that lifts them into the highest realism of visionary art. It is sometimes complemented by an unreal, hallucinating space and a disdain of mere physical possibility, so far from Renaissance principles as to seem almost medieval in some elements. Yet Tintoretto's vision is not necessarily so stupendous: *The Flight into Egypt*, ghostly in the weird moonlight, is set in a lyrical, rural landscape, and the handling of the Holy Family shows a tenderness quite rare in Tintoretto. In *The temptation of Christ*, in contrast, the luscious image of seduction embodied in Satan has been compared in its imaginative power with Milton's Satan in *Paradise Lost*.

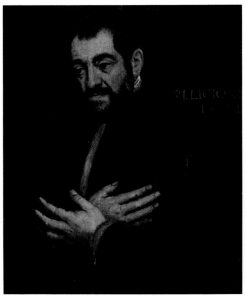

TINTORETTO (above)
Self-portrait, 1573
The humility of this *ex voto*, which hung to the right of the entrance to the Council Chamber in which *The Crucifixion* hangs, does not seem quite to dispel Tintoretto's reputation with his fellow-artists as a ruthless undercutter.

TINTORETTO (right)
The road to Calvary, 1566
The terrible lurching of the crosses and arduous ascent of the figures has the effect of forcing the spectator into the picture space, a characteristic of all Tintoretto's work. The *Calvary* is placed directly opposite *The Crucifixion*.

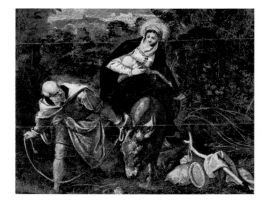

TINTORETTO (above)
The Flight into Egypt, detail, 1583-87
The Holy Family is placed before a wide landscape, sombre, but romantically echoing the tenderness of Mother and Child.

TINTORETTO (right)
The temptation of Christ, detail, 1579-81
Satan, whose demonic nature is hinted at only by the fire's reflection which reddens his cheeks, extends himself alluringly.

TINTORETTO (above)
The Crucifixion, 1565
The symmetry of the whole design is clear in reproduction, but, seen *in situ*, it is difficult to assimilate. "Surely no single picture in the world", wrote Henry James, "contains more of human life; there is everything in it, including the most exquisite beauty." Perhaps only Rembrandt equalled the cosmic power of this Christ (detail right), swaying forwards towards the onlooker vertiginously, both victim and redeemer: "And I, if I be lifted up, will draw all men unto me."

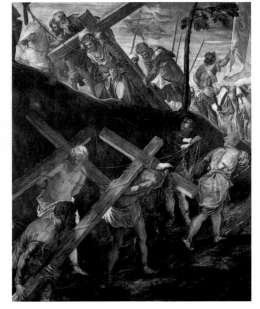

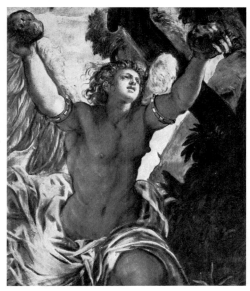

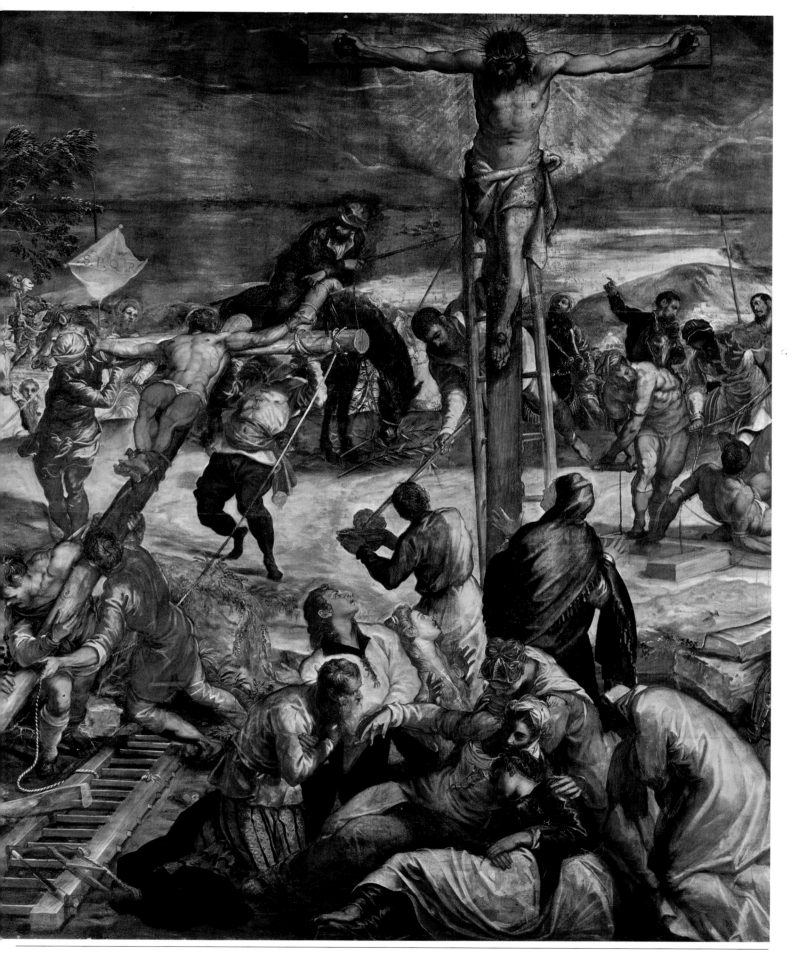

Art in Spain: El Greco

Spain was ruled during most of the sixteenth century by two monarchs, the Emperor Charles V from 1516 until his abdication in 1556, and his son Philip II from 1556 to 1598. Both sought to centralize monarchical power, and both virtually identified the crown with the Church. Charles V's vast inheritance involved Spain in the affairs of Italy (through Naples), the Netherlands and Germany, although influence on the arts in Spain came predominantly from Italy: Spanish artists went there for short or long spells, and Italian artists came to work, or even to settle, in Spain.

Although Philip II was interested in and informed about the arts, patronage in Spain came mainly from the Church. The Counter-Reformation in Spain developed along very pure lines, following the doctrines of the Council of Trent, and emphasizing in art especially those themes which Protestantism was challenging – the Immaculate Conception and the cult of the Virgin; the sacraments; the intercession of the saints. Protestantism never penetrated Spain, but the Counter-Reformation was very active. The Jesuit Order, a Spanish creation, was one expression of the nation's religious fervour, and the visionary poetry of St John of the Cross, the rhapsodies of St Theresa of Avila, were others.

There was considerable variety, almost a dichotomy, in Philip II's own patronage. For all his devout religiousness, he commissioned from Titian those voluptuous, profane *poesie* (see p. 144); he collected the work of Bosch; he aimed at a secular magnificence to reflect the wealth and worldly prestige of Spain, undeterred by continuous war and still unchallenged in her dominion of the New World, whence flowed in virtually unlimited bullion. To paint portraits Philip II employed not only Titian but also the Fleming Antonio Moro (Anthonis Mor, 1519-75), "the Bronzino of the North", who with admirable skill created polished, aloof Mannerist images of human authority. His designs, his tall, narrow poses, were to influence European state portraiture for three quarters of a century. Philip II also patronized the Italian Pompeo Leoni (1533-1608), who sculpted monumental bronzes of the Spanish royal family in the Escorial. But he never made use of El Greco, whose life and work remained centred on Toledo, the "Holy City" of Spain, the citadel of the Jesuits and the Inquisition. Though Toledo was also a cultural and commercial centre, at that time larger than Madrid, El Greco's patrons were primarily ecclesiastics.

El Greco (1541-1614), properly Domenikos Theotokopoulos, as he always signed himself, was born in Crete and trained and worked for some 12 years in Venice, where the paintings of Titian, Tintoretto and Bassano all influenced him; he then passed briefly to Rome, where he is said to have caused offence by suggesting he could improve on Michelangelo ("a good man, but he could not paint"); in about 1577, in obscure circumstances, he migrated to Spain, and lived in Toledo until his death.

El Greco's competence in the Venetian tradition is admirably illustrated by his portrait of Giulio Clovio, painted in Rome about 1570. There is little indication, however, of his mature style, a fusion of many strains – contact with Byzantine art in Crete and Venice; Tintoretto's energy; the elongated figures and acid colours of central Italian Mannerism; and also elements from Correggio and Michelangelo. In one of his many variations of *Christ driving the money-changers from the temple*, El Greco included, bottom right, portraits of his mentors, Titian, Michelangelo, Giulio Clovio

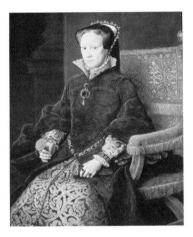

MORO (left)
Mary I of England, 1554
Rich jewels and brocades add lustre to the sombre formality of Philip II's wife, but Moro's precision is a little dour compared to Bronzino's lighter clarity.

LEONI (right)
The tomb of Charles V, detail, 1593-98
The life-size gilt-bronze figures have a ponderous, hieratic majesty, and are impressive technical feats. The tomb was an element in Philip II's project to create in the Escorial a grandiose setting for Hapsburg authority.

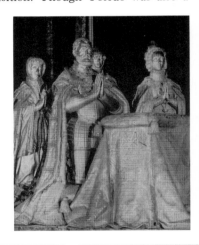

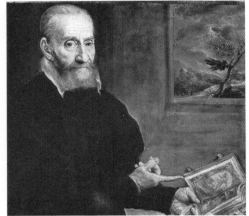

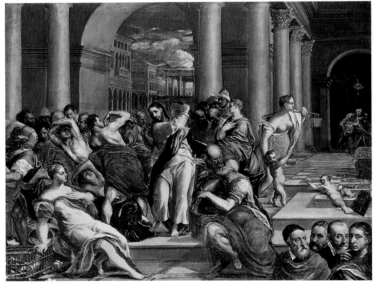

EL GRECO
Christ driving the money-changers from the temple, c. 1572
El Greco returned often to this theme and composition, seeking perhaps his own synthesis and revision of the achievements of his Italian predecessors. The figures are not so far from the Mannerist figures of such artists as Salviati; the architectural setting and the genre recall Veronese.

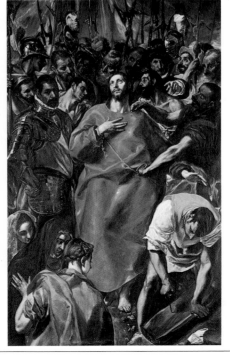

EL GRECO
Giulio Clovio, detail, c. 1570
In design – a half-length figure with a long, looming head in a dark surround – El Greco's portrait of his friend clearly depends on the example of Tintoretto. A renowned miniaturist – he points to his own work in his book – Clovio is our main source for El Greco's career before he left Italy.

EL GRECO (left)
"*El Espolio*" (The disrobing of Christ), 1577-79
Though trapped among crowded heads, a thicket of pikes, plucking hands, Christ is tall and broad in brilliant scarlet, a chord of triumphant colour amid the foreground yellows. A grandee in contemporary armour stands beside him, and the beholder himself closes the ring of figures. His eye is led inevitably to Christ's uplifted face, and its moist eyes, typical of Spanish religious feeling.

and (probably) Raphael. However, the essential impulse behind the extraordinary spirituality of his later style seems indicated in the story that a visitor to his studio in Rome, one brilliant spring day, found him working in a darkened room, for "daylight blinded the light within him". Increasingly he was to paint the visions of his inner eye.

One of his early commissions in Toledo was "*El Espolio*" (The disrobing of Christ), an unusual subject, though obviously suitable for its setting, the sacristy of the Cathedral. El Greco's seemingly quite original design, with its claustrophobic quality, baffled and shocked the authorities, who at first rejected it. The handling is Venetian, but, stylistically, its compression is like that of some Byzantine icons, and the huge *Burial of Count Orgaz* (1586) is reminiscent of a Byzantine *Dormition of the Virgin*. This was again an unusual subject, commemorating a miracle of 1323, when SS. Augustine and Stephen materialized to place the dead man, a benefactor, in his grave. Here the real cohabits with the supernatural, though the physical world is driven upwards by a mounting rhythm to be subsumed into the spiritual world. Increasingly, the narrative content disappeared from El Greco's imagery, and even his earthly figures became flickering and elongated, transubstantiated almost into flame; the paintings themselves became more vertical, and the colours incandescent. El Greco's art was highly personal, unique, but not narrow or provincial: a contemporary called him "a great philosopher ... he wrote on painting, sculpture and architecture". His writings are lost, but the inventory of his library reveals an interest in history, literature, theology and philosophy.

In later years his workshop (including his son) produced many repetitions of established themes, but in pictures like *The Immaculate Conception* in Toledo, entirely by his own hand, his later style reached a climax, in dazzling blues, reds and yellows, in the heavenward flare of the tapering figures. In portraits he could be just as emotional and spiritual, or he could retain the sense of the actual, though he imbued it with strange ambiguities. How indeed should the portrait of the enlightened and cultivated *Cardinal Fernando Nino de Guevara* be read? El Greco also produced rare landscapes – weirdly emotional views of Toledo. He had little apparent influence on Spanish Baroque, and was rediscovered only at the end of the nineteenth century (about the same time as Grünewald).

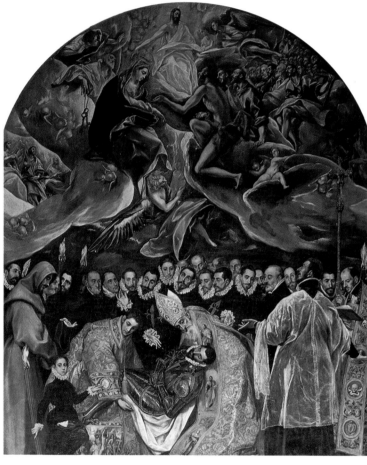

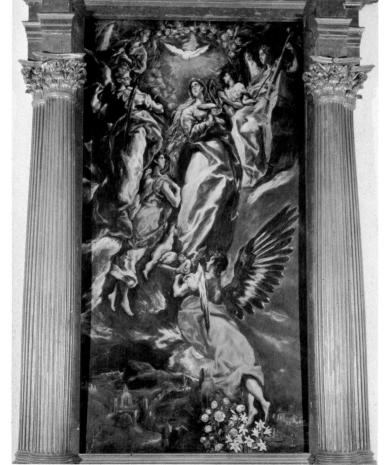

EL GRECO (left)
The burial of Count Orgaz, 1586
The strange mingling of earthly pomp with a supernatural vision is managed with remarkable coherence. The onlooker is beckoned almost imperiously into the painting by the boy; local dignitaries throng around the bending saints; then above the heavens open, to reveal the host on high.

EL GRECO (below)
Cardinal Fernando Nino de Guevara, c. 1600
He looks uncertain, as he grips the chair. But this is the Grand Inquisitor. He recalls Titian's rather odd *Pope Paul III* (see p.143).

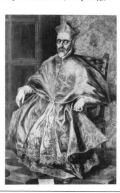

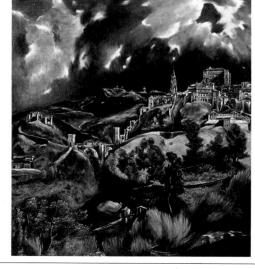

EL GRECO (left)
View of Toledo,
c. 1595-1600
The few, small, visionary landscapes of El Greco's late years – Toledo as a Jerusalem or a Sodom – are unique in their time.

EL GRECO
The Immaculate Conception,
c. 1607-13
The immensely attenuated figure of the Virgin is borne effortlessly upward by fluttering, immaterial angels, and all that ties it to the real world are the roses and lilies (symbolic or virginity), painted as if they were real flowers on the altar the picture backs. Hence again the onlooker is given an entry, a transition into the spiritual world.

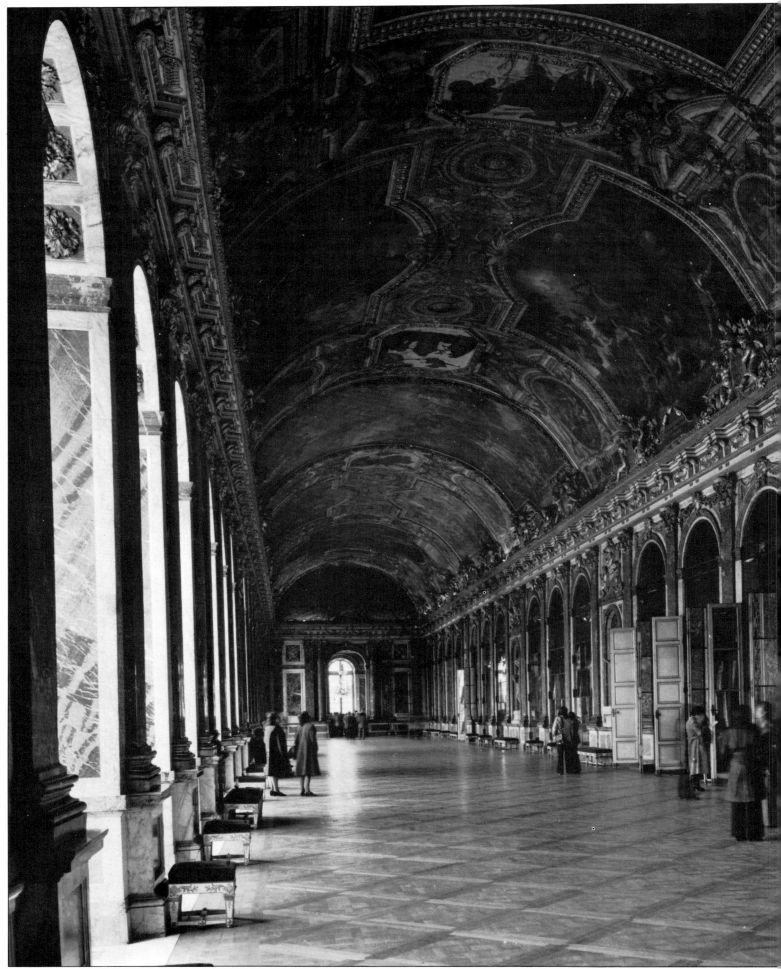

THE BAROQUE ERA

The division between the Renaissance and Baroque periods is a fairly recent convention of historians, and Baroque art represents an expansion and development of Renaissance art, rather than a radical transformation of its principles. Italy continued to be the goal and inspiration of many artists throughout Europe, not only because of the great monuments of the past, but also because artists such as Caravaggio, Annibale Carracci and Bernini had made Rome the most vital artistic centre in Europe. Louis XIV's summons of Bernini to Paris in 1665 and the rejection of the latter's plans for the Louvre are, however, events symbolic of the new order in which France was gradually to assume leadership artistically as well as politically. Baroque art was often used for propaganda purposes, whether for church or state, and Louis's enormous palace at Versailles is one of the most complete examples of the Baroque ideal of the union of all the arts, the *Gesamtkunstwerk*, the orchestration of architecture and landscape, painting and sculpture, furniture and metalwork into one splendid whole.

Though such unity is one characteristic of the Baroque, art also showed remarkable diversity during the seventeenth century and flourished in very different social and political circumstances. For both Spain and Holland this was a Golden Age in the arts, but whereas conditions in Spain represent a continuance of old values, with patronage almost entirely in the hands of the Church and court, in Holland art was no longer the preserve of the rich and powerful, but appealed also to the prosperous middle classes, who collected paintings suitable to the modest size and pretensions of their houses. Holland's Golden Age coincided with the birth of political independence and the growth of economic prosperity, but Spain at the same time was declining from its preeminent position in world affairs, and its great national school of painting and sculpture was perhaps a belated expression of its former glories. In terms of its importance for the future, the democratization of art in Holland is one of the most significant aspects of seventeenth-century culture. Virtually the whole fabric of Dutch life became the subject matter of artists, and genres such as landscape and still life were virtually instituted during this period. A great deal of space has been given to Dutch art, reflecting not merely the presence of some outstanding painters, but the extraordinary proliferation of minor masters of superb quality.

The change from Baroque to Rococo, the arrival of the eighteenth century, brought gradual modulations of mood and tempo. The scope of art remained essentially the same, though its scale was usually less grand, sited as much in the private house as in the palace, with the small porcelain figure perhaps more typical an expression of the taste of the time than the heroic marble statue. Secular art, and the portable easel-painting, continued to increase in importance, and showed unmistakably the impact of ideas of the Age of Enlightenment, and of the first seeds that would blossom, or erupt, in the French Revolution. In the nineteenth century there would be a definite change of direction – something much closer to a break in tradition.

VERSAILLES, FRANCE (left) The *Galerie des Glâces*, begun 1678

TWICKENHAM, ENGLAND (right) Strawberry Hill, begun 1747

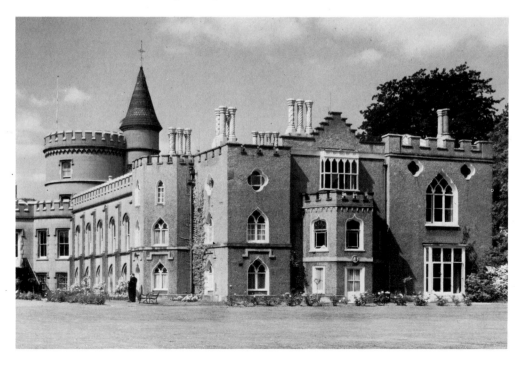

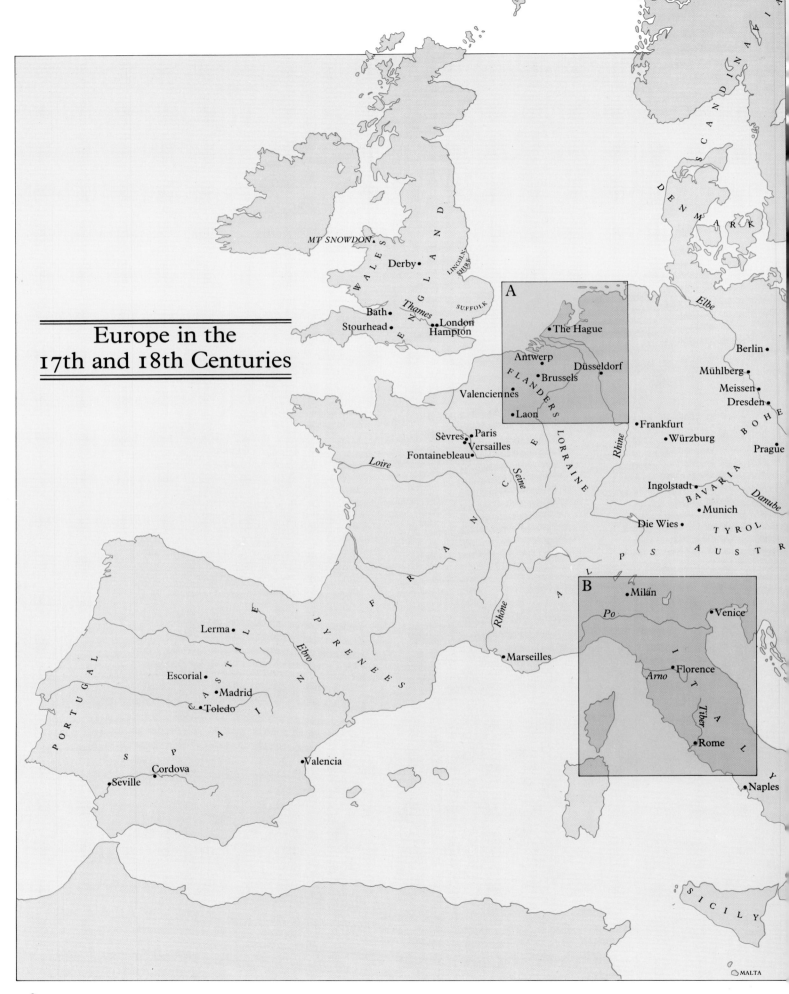

Europe in the
17th and 18th Centuries

MT SNOWDON

WALES

Derby

ENGLAND

LINCOLN SHIRE

SUFFOLK

Thames

Bath

Stourhead

London

Hampton

A

The Hague

Antwerp

Düsseldorf

FLANDERS

Brussels

Valenciennes

Laon

LORRAINE

Sèvres

Paris

Versailles

Fontainebleau

Loire

Seine

Rhine

Frankfurt

Würzburg

Prague

FRANCE

Ingolstadt

BAVARIA

Danube

Munich

Die Wies

TYROL

ALPS

AUSTR

Berlin

Mühlberg

Meissen

Dresden

BOHE

Elbe

SCANDINAVIA

DENMARK

B

Milán

Po

Venice

Arno

Florence

Tiber

Rome

ITALY

Naples

Rhône

Marseilles

PORTUGAL

Lerma

CASTILE

Escorial

Madrid

Toledo

SPAIN

Cordova

Seville

Ebro

PYRENEES

Valencia

SICILY

MALTA

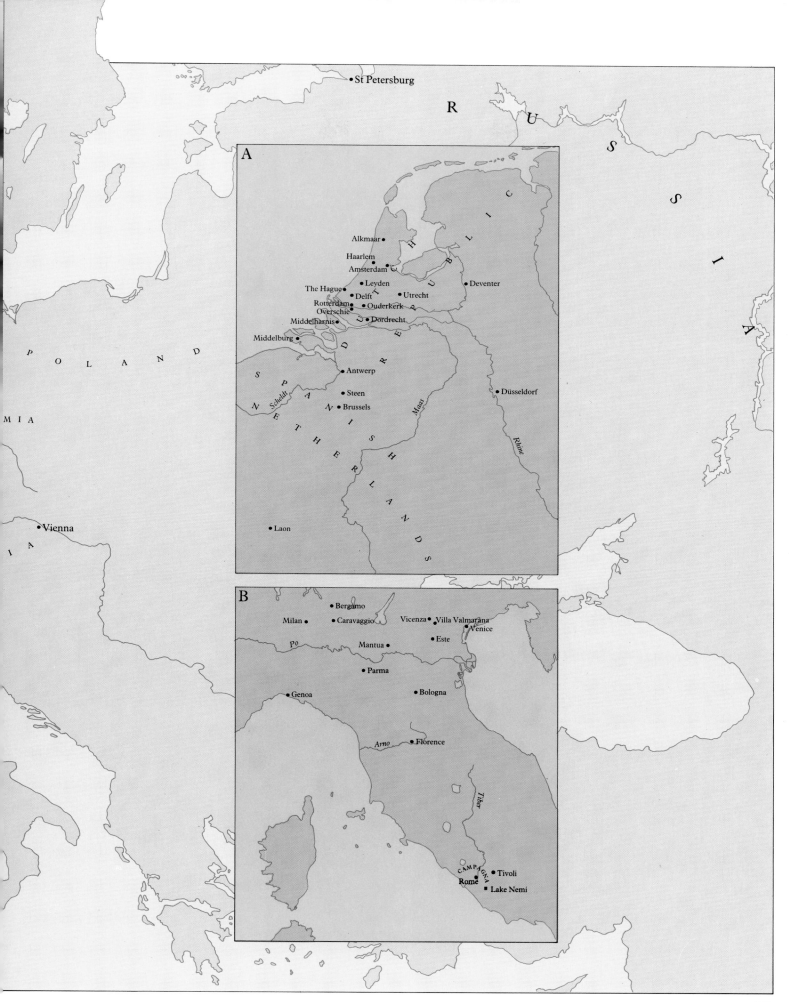

A

St Petersburg

RUSSIA

POLAND

Alkmaar
Haarlem
Amsterdam
Deventer
The Hague • Leyden
Delft • Utrecht
Rotterdam • Ouderkerk
Overschie
Middelharnis • Dordrecht
Middelburg •
Düsseldorf
Antwerp
Steen
Brussels

DUTCH REPUBLIC

SPANISH NETHERLANDS

Scheldt
Maas
Rhine

Vienna

MIA

IA

Laon

B

Bergamo
Milan • Caravaggio
Vicenza • Villa Valmarana
Venice
Po
Mantua • Este
Parma
Genoa • Bologna
Arno • Florence
Tiber
CAMPAGNA
Tivoli
Rome • Lake Nemi

Michelangelo da Caravaggio

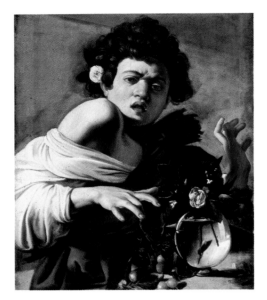

CARAVAGGIO
Boy bitten by a lizard,
c. 1596-1600
This subtly foreshortened
study of the physiognomy
of fright was perhaps not
ordered, but sold painted.
Caravaggio probably used
himself as a model, but
made the figure younger.

With Caravaggio (1571-1610), a new type of artist appeared on the European scene. It had been foreshadowed in Michelangelo, but the idea that artistic genius is autonomous, and almost necessarily in opposition to authority and convention, is embodied not only in Caravaggio's painting but in the drama of his brief and violent life.

He was born Michelangelo Merisi da Caravaggio – Caravaggio being the name of his native town near Milan. His earliest work was certainly northern Italian in feeling (derived ultimately from Giorgione), and continued so even after his arrival in Rome in about 1593. There he began by painting still lifes for the established late Mannerist painter Il Cavaliere d'Arpino, and still life plays a prominent part in most of his early work, both religious and genre. His genre scenes – not mere grotesques but situations observed with a novelist's eye – he probably sold on the open market, but he soon attracted the attention of wealthy patrons, men such as Cardinal del Monte, an important figure in the papal management of the Counter-Reformation, but a hedonist as well. For such patrons he painted not only religious works but also a series of Bacchic and narcissistic youths with unmistakably erotic overtones. In these early works the essentials of his revolutionary style are already clear – the realism of his characters; the sharply defined, rich and vivid colours, especially of stuffs; and the harsh light from a single source by which his compositions, for all their earthiness and detail, are consolidated into monumentality.

In his brief career in Rome – a mere 13 years – this epoch-making style was fully developed. So, too, was his picturesque and obstreperous personality. "He would swagger about . . . with his sword at his side, with a servant following him, from one ball court to another, ever ready to engage in a fight or an argument, with the result that it is most awkward to get on with him" – so noted a visiting painter from the north, van Mander. Before 1600 he received important commissions, but few of them were completed without major rows and rejections. His first public work, three pictures for the Contarelli Chapel in S. Luigi dei Francesi, Rome, was obtained through Cardinal del Monte. Painting here on a new scale, Caravaggio ran into technical difficulties, and there was considerable revision and repainting, while his original altarpiece for the Chapel, *St*

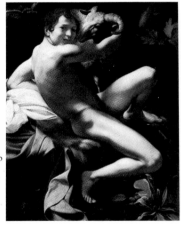

CARAVAGGIO (right)
St John the Baptist,
1597-98
This is primarily erotic,
a picture of a naked youth,
and the ostensible subject
can be identified only from
the ram, with a fleece worn
by John the Baptist in the
desert. Caravaggio often
used famous works as models
in his series of such youths:
here St John's pose recalls
Dawn on Michelangelo's tomb
of Lorenzo de'Medici (see p.
133). As in other early works,
the highly contrived design
and studied lighting effects
give the painting the air
of a virtuoso performance.

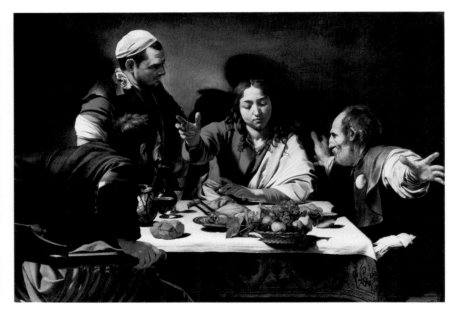

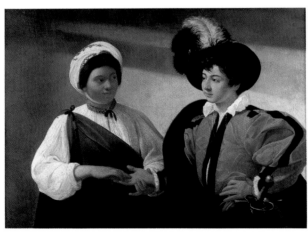

CARAVAGGIO (above)
The fortune teller,
c. 1594-95
Caravaggio's almost life-size genre subjects are few, but famous. Their direct and naturalistic approach was widely imitated, but their psychological sensitivity was seldom matched. Con-
temporaries described these genre works as being "in the manner of Giorgione". Caravaggio, from the north, owed much to northern masters such as Moretto of Brescia and Savoldo (see p. 149) and their followers, who could provide some precedent for his genre and his lighting.

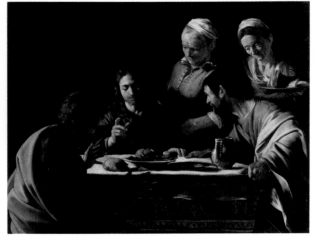

CARAVAGGIO (above)
The Supper at Emmaus,
c. 1596-1600
The moment is the sudden recognition by two pilgrims that the stranger who has joined them is the risen Christ. Caravaggio's own is the intensified drama, which includes even the basket of fruit that is about to fall from the table.

CARAVAGGIO (left)
The Supper at Emmaus,
c. 1605-06
The restrained, implosive tension of Caravaggio's later treatment contrasts with the drama of the first version. The shooting arm of the right-hand disciple, for instance, has been replaced by a clenched grip. The light picks out a few details with a greater calculation.

Matthew and the angel, was rejected by the clergy ostensibly because St Matthew looked too proletarian. The Chapel was completed only in 1602, after Caravaggio had undertaken new work in S. Maria del Popolo (see over).

The scale, force and revolutionary treatment of the famous *Calling of St Matthew* in the Contarelli Chapel shows his vision fully mature, even before he was 30. Matthew sits at the customs seat, amidst a group of gaudily plumaged, aggressively limbed layabouts, in a contemporary Roman tavern. Christ appears on the right, only his face and hand visible – the hand, beckoning and claiming Matthew, deliberately echoing the creative hand of God the Father in Michelangelo's Sistine ceiling. Matthew, interrupted, looks sharply up, his hand indicating as clearly as words: "What, me?" A comparable directness – an invitation almost to participate in the action – invigorates the first *Supper at Emmaus*: the disciple's hand, foreshortened violently, is flung almost out of the picture, as if to seize hold of the onlooker.

Several of Caravaggio's large altarpieces painted in Rome were fiercely criticized. In some the clergy objected to the naturalistic dirty linen and feet; everywhere to the lack of idealization; in *The death of the Virgin*, to the swollen Virgin herself, said to have been modelled on a drowned whore pulled out of the Tiber. Nevertheless, individual patrons, cardinals and lay aristocrats alike, recognized Caravaggio's genius and bought his work as eagerly as they bought the Carracci's (see p. 184), whose classicism seems radically opposed to it. But Caravaggio, the spontaneous innovator – he seems to have worked without drawings directly on to the canvas – was in fact on good terms with Annibale Carracci, and much of the power of his work stems from a profound assimilation of High Renaissance tradition, Roman and Venetian.

Caravaggio's career in Rome was punctuated by sharp and sometimes bloody clashes, documented in police files. He was imprisoned twice in 1605, and had also to leave Rome for a month after wounding a lawyer. In 1603 a resonant libel action had been brought against him by a fellow-painter, Giovanni Baglione (who later became Caravaggio's biographer). In May 1606 came the climax, when Caravaggio, enraged by an opponent in a game of tennis, stabbed and killed him. He fled to Naples, and then on to Malta in 1607. In Malta, his initial welcome, with commissions and installation as a Knight of the Order of St John, was followed, the next year, by an assault on a judge, imprisonment, escape and flight to Sicily. Thence back to Naples in 1609, where he was badly wounded, perhaps in a vendetta attack. He died in 1610 of malaria, aged 38.

His later works, religious compositions a little larger than life scale, are very dark and simplified in detail and in colour. Beside the clangour of his earlier works, they seem to be meditations in formidable silence, as if they were the work of a far older painter, brooding on the threshold of death.

Caravaggio's nature was not such as to form around him a faithful school of followers, but his spreading influence on European art is incalculable. In Italy, the Carracci pupils Reni and Guercino reflected him in various ways; on the Dutch Utrecht school his impact was decisive. These, however, adopted chiefly his method of lighting or superficial mannerisms. The essence of his vision was better understood by the more original artists of the age, by Ribera and Velazquez in Spain, by La Tour and the Le Nain brothers in France and – above all – by Rembrandt in Holland.

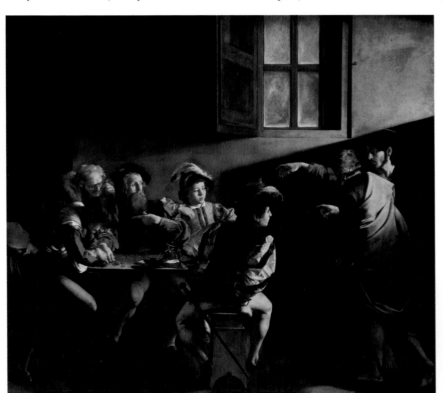

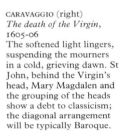

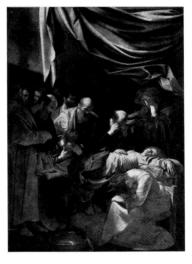

CARAVAGGIO (right)
The death of the Virgin, 1605-06
The softened light lingers, suspending the mourners in a cold, grieving dawn. St John, behind the Virgin's head, Mary Magdalen and the grouping of the heads show a debt to classicism; the diagonal arrangement will be typically Baroque.

CARAVAGGIO (below)
The Resurrection of Lazarus, 1609
The works Caravaggio painted after he had fled from Malta show signs of haste, and are not well preserved. But the pity and terror of their composition still shine through their blackened state.

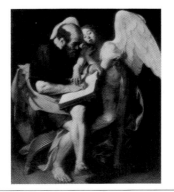

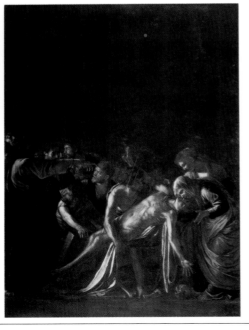

CARAVAGGIO (left)
St Matthew and the angel (1st version), *c.* 1599
Caravaggio's first public work was taken off the wall by the priests, who felt that "the figure ... did not look like a saint, sitting with crossed legs and with his feet crudely exposed to the people". But through this very indecorum the Christian message emerges clearly with new vigour. They may have objected really to the suggestive proximity of the angel.

CARAVAGGIO (above)
The calling of St Matthew, *c.* 1597-99
The principal of the Roman Academy, Zuccaro, could not understand the acclaim this picture instantly earned: in its realism he saw only imitation of Giorgione. In fact Caravaggio's sources for the Bohemian group were northern genre works: and here the psychological penetration of Caravaggio's genre is brilliantly adapted to the narrative purpose of this religious painting.

Caravaggio: The Conversion of St Paul

In July 1600 the papal treasurer Tiberio Cerasi acquired, for his resting place, a chapel in S. Maria del Popolo, Rome, and shortly afterwards commissioned the two outstanding (but very different) painters in Rome to decorate it: Annibale Carracci to paint the altarpiece and Michelangelo da Caravaggio to provide two paintings for the side-walls.

Caravaggio's subjects were the conversion of St Paul and the crucifixion of St Peter. His first versions were not satisfactory – whether to the client or to himself is not known; the second versions were paid for in November 1601. The Carracci altarpiece, *The Assumption of the Virgin*, had probably been finished before then, likewise the ceiling decoration, painted to Annibale's design by an assistant. The St Paul subject was already fairly popular, the St Peter one less so, but they are the two subjects of Michelangelo's last paintings, in the Cappella Paolina in the Vatican, which must have been in Caravaggio's mind, though his solutions are very different.

The large difference reflects not only Caravaggio's profoundly personal view of the world but also the shifting attitude, within the Catholic Church, to the function of religious painting and consequently its style. Faced with the division of Europe between primarily Protestant north and primarily Catholic south, the Catholic Church had reasserted its doctrines and against the Reformation proclaimed the Counter-Reformation: the rigour of the Inquisition was only one aspect of a movement of self-examination, of confirmation of faith and of positive propaganda. This new and active fervour was fuelled by direct and personal appeal to the faithful through the arts; Caravaggio strengthened the meaning of St Peter's martyrdom and St Paul's conversion by telling their stories in contemporary idiom and down-to-earth detail – even if the staider clergy felt he pushed realism too far.

The conversion of St Paul could represent a man tripped over backwards in a stable, but even before the viewer recognizes the subject he is aware of the electric potency of a supernatural event in this mundane image. Like Michelangelo, Caravaggio has chosen the moment when Saul was flung to the ground blinded, as if by lightning, and accused by God: "Saul, Saul, why persecutest thou me?" But there is in the Caravaggio none of the supporting cast of airborne Christ and angels present in the Michelangelo. The bucketing steed has become a rather heavy hack, and the agitated crowd is replaced by one solitary baffled groom, an old peasant with a varicose vein; these two have heard nothing. The source of light is not shown; but the violent, even awkward foreshortening of the figure hurled down expresses an impact of huge energy, and the outflung arms embroil the whole in the vortex of a blinding miracle.

For contemporaries, this must have been a stunning vision. Formally, Caravaggio has exploited already known methods – even more dramatic foreshortening occurs for example in Mantegna and Tintoretto. But the overall assault on the beholder's emotions in such concentration was unparalleled. The courtly elegance of the still prevailing Mannerist style seems both esoteric and effete in contrast.

CARAVAGGIO (below)
The crucifixion of St Peter, 1600-01
No earlier painter had made the focus of this subject so emphatically the action and effort of raising the cross. St Peter appears the more helpless – an ordinary, perplexed, suffering old man, though still robust and dignified. The composition seems more effective from an oblique viewpoint, from outside the chapel.

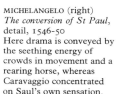

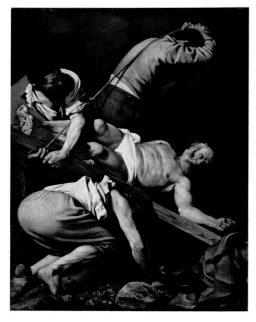

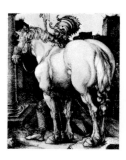

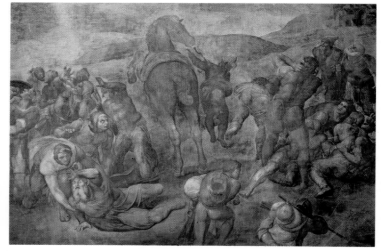

ANNIBALE CARRACCI (above) *The Assumption of the Virgin*, 1600-01
The Carracci altarpiece is flanked by the two Caravaggios; the artists worked in their studios probably without close knowledge of each other's designs. Neither was likely to compromise for the sake of the other, anyway, even though in many respects *in situ* their pictures clash. Annibale's forms are pale-coloured in a serene, diffuse light, against Caravaggio's luminous browns and blacks. Yet in both the figures are life-size, solidly modelled, and crowded against the frame.

MICHELANGELO (right)
The conversion of St Paul, detail, 1546-50
Here drama is conveyed by the seething energy of crowds in movement and a rearing horse, whereas Caravaggio concentrated on Saul's own sensation.

DURER (above)
"*The Large Horse*", 1505
Engravings by northern artists were an inspiration for Caravaggio's own vision of common-life realism. Dürer's stolid animal was perhaps the prototype of the nag in the *Conversion*.

MANTEGNA (right)
The dead Christ, c. 1490
Mantegna's picture is an early precedent for the use in the *Conversion* of extreme foreshortening for emotional effect.

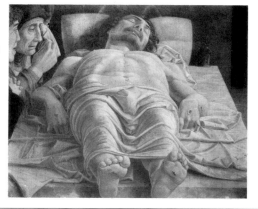

CARAVAGGIO (right)
The conversion of St Paul, 1600-01
The picture is a masterpiece of simple, forcefully stark, concentrated drama. The unbalanced composition, in which the massive, unmoved figure of the horse fills almost the entire canvas, makes all the more emphatic the prostrate Saul's shock. He falls back thunderstruck almost out of the picture frame, involving the viewer as a witness.

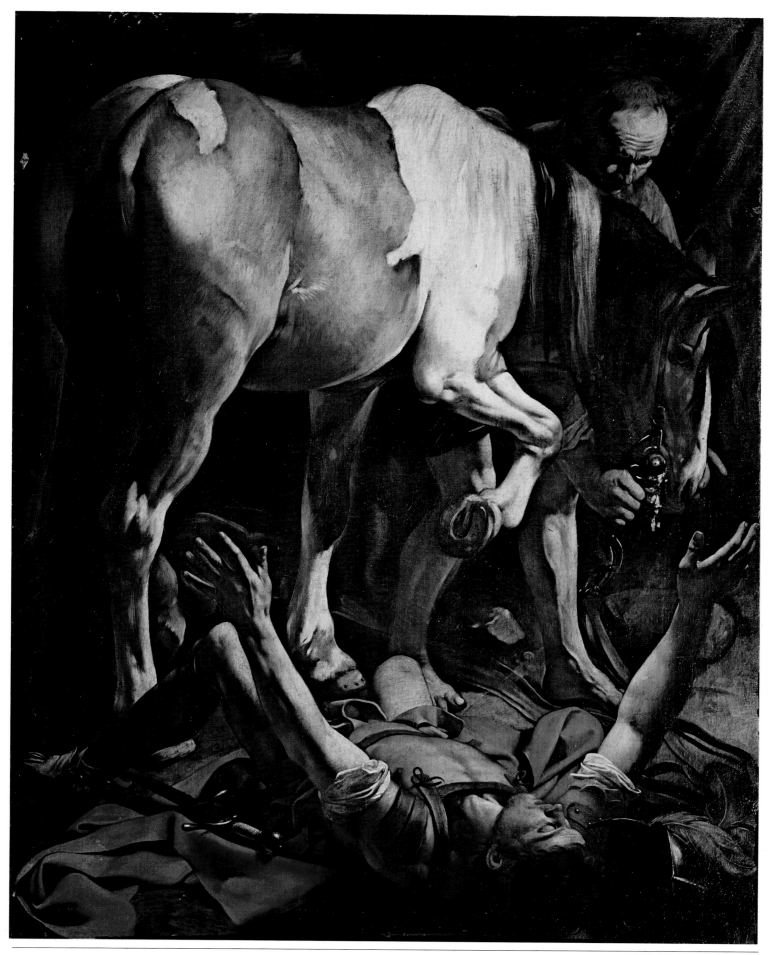

The Carracci and their Pupils

While Caravaggio's dramatic realism was to be one seminal constituent of Baroque painting, the vigorous and equally radical return to High Renaissance principles initiated by the Carracci family in Bologna was to be another – and in Italy the more important. The Carracci drew their inspiration not only from Raphael but also from the Venetians, excluding neither the grandeur of Michelangelo nor the tenderness of Correggio. Like Caravaggio, they were in reaction to the artificialities of the Mannerist style, but they attempted reform and, unlike Caravaggio, they wholeheartedly espoused the traditional practice of *disegno*, the elaborate analysis and resolution of a composition by means of drawings.

The Carracci designated their studio in Bologna a teaching academy about 1585. Their attempt to combine the best elements of previous masters produced a codification of "classicism", in which ideal forms, reprieved from Mannerist distortion, were clearly organized according to the demands of the subject, placed in correct perspective, structured by firm lines of direction and enlivened by resonant colour. Their "academic" programme inevitably repelled many critics of the nine-

teenth century, who saw the Carracci and those who followed them as deadhanded imitators, even plagiarists, boring offenders against the cardinal Romantic virtue of originality and the inspiration of genius. The renewed appreciation of their classical revival is comparatively recent.

The three Carracci were Ludovico (1555-1619) and his cousins, Agostino (1557-1602) and his younger brother Annibale (1560-1609). Though they shared much, they are clearly distinguishable artistic personalities. Agostino, the intellectual and the teacher, probably the principal motivator of the academy and a disseminator of Renaissance designs by able engravings after Old Masters, was less of a painter, though his altarpiece at Bologna, *The last communion of St Jerome*, was famous. The eldest, Ludovico, remained based all his life in Bologna. In his early work, full of colour and movement, a Venetian feeling predominates, but his later work is paler, more refined – sometimes sentimental.

Annibale was the major artist among the three. His fame during the seventeenth and eighteenth centuries rested on his decorations for the Farnese Palace in Rome (see over), and

ANNIBALE CARRACCI
Pietà, c. 1599-1600
Annibale Carracci and Caravaggio were both Counter-Reformation artists and sometimes had the same patrons: their works, otherwise distinct, share a clear, monumental

expression of immediate impact. Annibale's art intentionally reflects Raphael, Michelangelo and the Antique; this is a more softly idealized version of Sebastiano del Piombo's *Pietà* in Viterbo (see p.146).

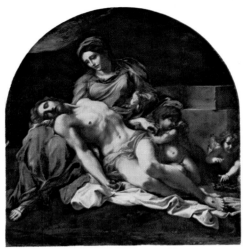

ANNIBALE CARRACCI (below)
The butcher's shop, c. 1582
Probably painted as a studio exercise, this is even more "low-life" than Caravaggio's genre scenes. Quite possibly it satirically represents the Carracci's own academy. For all their high ideals they did not lack humour.

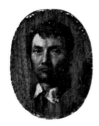

AGOSTINO CARRACCI?
(left) *Annibale Carracci*, late 1580s
In their different ways, the Carracci were as self-consciously artistic as Caravaggio: this portrait miniature has a certain romantic idealization. It seems also to presage Annibale's sad decline.

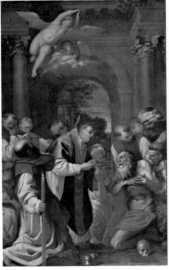
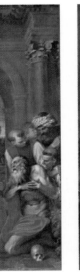

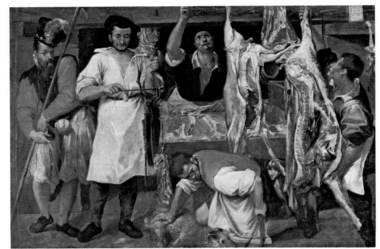

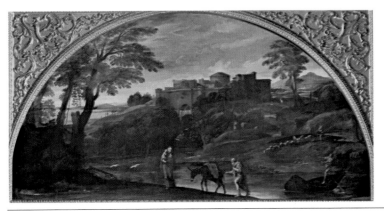

AGOSTINO CARRACCI
(above) *The last communion of St Jerome*, 1593-94
The firm verticals, the undulating, frieze-like horizontal grouping and the lines of direction forming a central triangle declare this work a classicist manifesto. It had wide influence, not least on Poussin.

ANNIBALE CARRACCI (left)
Landscape with the Flight into Egypt, c.1604
The landscapes painted by Annibale in Bologna show strong northern influence. In the later landscapes painted in Rome, such as this one, he evolved a lasting formula of "classical" landscape – a vista conjured along recessing diagonals of castles, trees, winding rivers and hilltop towns.

LUDOVICO CARRACCI
(above) *The Madonna and Child with saints*, c. 1590
The subject matter is clearly and hierarchically organized, composed with academic correctness but sweetened by a light touch and bright, gentle colours.

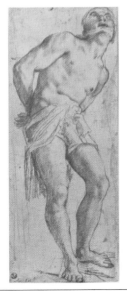

ANNIBALE CARRACCI (left)
A prisoner, early 1590s
This, one of the many fine drawings by the Carracci, is probably a copy after a *St Sebastian* by Titian; and it is also probably a preliminary drawing for an unfinished *Samson in prison*. The Carracci often adapted motifs in this way from Renaissance masters; their vigour and feeling were unimpaired by such deliberate eclecticism.

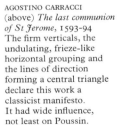

in the ninetenth century was denied on the same evidence. While his formal style shows a consistent development, the sensitivity of his technique was matched by a very flexible attitude to subject matter. Early on there were exercises in realistic genre, unprecedented in Italy, such as the life-size *Butcher's shop*; brisk drawings that are perhaps the earliest true caricatures; and many delightful "straight" portraits. Further, Annibale developed (from early experiments by Veronese or the Bassani) a new art of landscape; this was influenced when he was in Rome by Flemish artists resident there, and also by the fragments of antique frescos newly revealed. In Annibale's landscapes Nature, freshly observed and gravely ordered, reflects the solemnity of the events portrayed in it. Not only his pupil Domenichino but Claude and Poussin were to acknowledge Annibale's example in different ways in their own work.

Annibale had visited Venice and Parma (where he saw Correggio's work) in the mid-1580s. A remark from a letter of his, about Correggio, illustrates sharply a main and enduring concern in his own work. "I like this straightforwardness and this purity that is not reality and yet is lifelike and natural, not artificial or forced." In Bologna, he painted a series of large altarpieces, developing a sure ability in monumental composition, in the interrelating of large forms; he also acquired admirable fresco techniques in the decoration of various Bolognese houses. By 1595, when he was summoned to Rome, he was fully equipped for work in the Farnese Palace. The impact of Rome simplified his compositions and rendered his forms more massive – in this alone resembling Caravaggio's. His late work, overshadowed by attacks of melancholia, is darkly expressive and emotional.

Annibale brought from Bologna to work with him in Rome a sequence of superbly gifted younger artists, notably Domenichino (Domenico Zampieri, 1581-1641); Giovanni Lanfranco (1582-1647); and Guido Reni (1575-1642). Domenichino developed his own version of classicism, rather dry and correct but sometimes of great charm, as in his Raphaelesque *St Cecilia* cycle in S. Luigi dei Francesi, and he also carried on the Carracci interest in landscape. Lanfranco, who came originally from Parma, developed a much freer and more painterly style, which proved more popular and which his rival Domenichino was compelled to emulate. Lanfranco's *Virgin in glory* in the dome of S. Andrea della Valle, Rome, ascending like a paean to the open lantern, both followed up Correggio and indicated the way the High Baroque would explode masonry with simulated heavens.

Guido Reni's work shows both a slightly unexciting restraint and an ability to charm; his later work, such as *Atalanta and Hippomenes* (*c.* 1620), became subtly but markedly simplified. His studio's large output of cloying *Virgins* led to an unjust devaluation of his ability until recently.

The younger Guercino (Gianfrancesco Barbieri, 1591-1666) never worked with Annibale, but was much influenced by Ludovico: his early paintings in Bologna were attractively vivid, and soon reinforced by a rather Caravaggesque light and shade. In Rome, his *Aurora* of 1623, on the ceiling of the Casino Ludovisi, is a masterpiece of illusionist perspective. His boldness of conception was, however, to be followed up by others. His later work in fresco and oils is much more conventional, though the brilliance of his drawings was undimmed throughout his career.

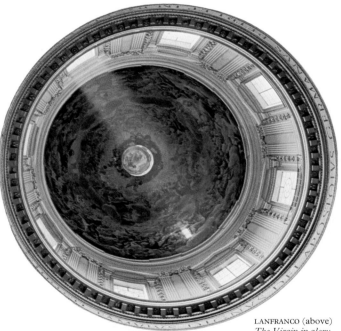

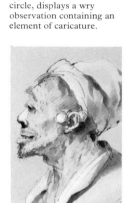

GUERCINO (below)
Profile head of a man,
after 1630
This sketch from the life, typical of the Carracci circle, displays a wry observation containing an element of caricature.

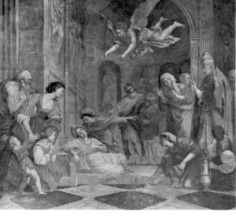

DOMENICHINO (above)
The martyrdom of St Cecilia, 1611-14
Eloquently posed figures clothed in harmonious, light colours act out an elegant classical drama. Such frescos may charm or may seem insipid; they influenced Poussin.

LANFRANCO (above)
The Virgin in glory,
1625-27
The groups of figures, on ascending layers of clouds, are illusionistically painted *di sotto in su* (foreshortened from below), not yet overflowing the vault as they were to do later, in the decorations of the developed High Baroque.

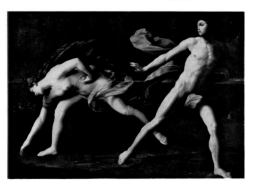

GUERCINO (right)
Aurora, 1621-23
The chariot and horses resemble a similar *Aurora* by Reni, but the addition of towering illusionistic piers – illusionistically ruined at one end – makes a more impressive ceiling.

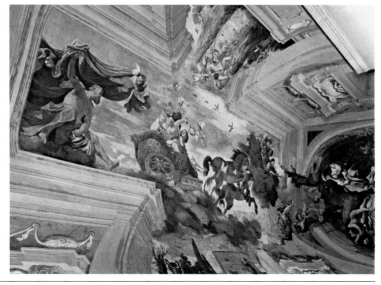

GUIDO RENI (above)
Atalanta and Hippomenes,
c. 1620
Hippomenes won his race against speedy Atalanta by dropping three golden apples, which she stopped to pick up. Their flowing movements are opposed in a softened chiaroscuro.

Annibale Carracci: The Farnese Gallery

The Gallery of the Palazzo Farnese is the last of the three great classic decorations in Rome, following Raphael's Stanze in the Vatican and Michelangelo's ceiling in the Sistine Chapel. The Palazzo is a building of much grandeur, the creation of a succession of famous architects, including Michelangelo and Giacomo della Porta, who built the Gallery, with its three tall windows overlooking the garden to the Tiber beyond, in 1573. The palace was the Rome headquarters of the great patrician dynasty of the Farnese, used by various members of the family, including the very young Cardinal Odoardo Farnese, who summoned Annibale Carracci from Bologna in 1595.

Annibale's first decorations were in Odoardo's study, the Camerino (1595-96, not shown). Painting began in the Gallery about 1597, and the frescos of the vault were finished in 1600. Annibale's brother Agostino played some part in these, but the overall design and the bulk of the work were Annibale's. The Gallery has noble dimensions – 20 metres (66 ft) long by 6.5 metres (21 ft) wide, its coved and vaulted ceiling ten metres (32 ft) high. Its function, which conditioned Annibale's design, was both for receptions and for the display of classical statuary in the Farnese collection (now in Naples).

The programme – subject matter and story-line – of the decoration was probably provided by Odoardo's learned librarian, Fulvio Orsini, in consultation with the painter. The preliminary workings were exhaustive, involving more than one thousand drawings. The theme – odd for a cardinal, however youthful, but natural enough for lay members of the family – is pagan, profane and erotic: scenes taken from classical mythology to illustrate the power of love, the exalted but very physical love of the gods – even if some discern a deeper Christian message of Divine Love pervading the whole. The scenes are not linked in any continuous narrative progression, but echo and respond to one another in form and composition.

The idea of opening up an enclosed space by means of illusionist painting was already well developed, and Annibale had several examples before him in Bologna. But he chose the system used by Raphael and Michelangelo, which was to build (or rather paint) a framework containing either paintings or illusory visions of the open sky above. However, the way in which illusionistic features are conjoined with real ones in the Gallery is much more complex than in earlier examples, and seen from a point central in the room, with one's back to the windows, the illusion of a picture gallery continuing above the cornice and carrying right across the vault is vivid – though the effect cannot be captured in photographs.

The colour is strong and lucent; the bodies of the participants are modelled densely, with a sculptural clarity, to answer the real antique marbles that once stood below. Their forms echo and restate precedents from the great masters of the Renaissance – the theme of the naked youths is obviously inspired by Michelangelo's Sistine *Ignudi* – and from classical antiquity. But their vitality springs from the fact that each is also studied from the life, and the central "framed painting", *The triumph of Bacchus and Ariadne*, which owes much to the study of reliefs on Roman sarcophagi, has a richness and fluency not to be found either in antiquity or in the High Renaissance. In the rhythm of this procession, at once measured and exuberant, both the classicism of Poussin and the surge of Rubens are heralded, and, although Annibale's compartmental solution for ceiling painting was not often followed, his mastery and delight in illusionism speak already of the High Baroque.

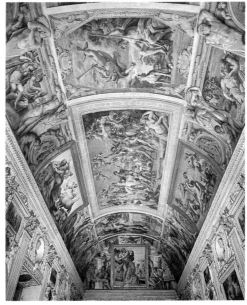

ANNIBALE CARRACCI (above) The Farnese Gallery: *The loves of the gods*, 1597-1600 Everything above the cornice is painted, even the frames of the pictures. At the end *Polyphemus* hurls a rock at Acis, whom he had caught in the arms of his love Galatea. Other panels illustrate similar stories, culled from Ovid.

(below) *View of the inner wall of the Farnese Gallery* The figures of the ceiling were a foil to the classical sculpture originally set in niches below, as Giovanni Volpato's engraving shows. Over the central door is Domenichino's *Virgin and unicorn*, painted, like the other wall panels, a little after the vault (c. 1604-08).

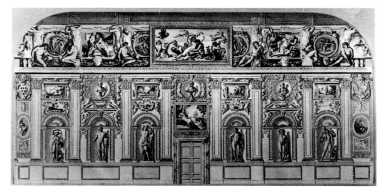

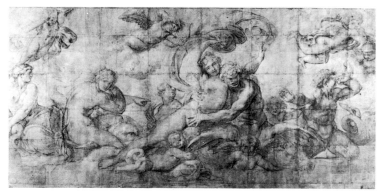

AGOSTINO CARRACCI Cartoon for *Glaucus and Scylla* on the inner wall of the Farnese Gallery, c. 1597-99 Though Annibale no doubt

sketched the preliminary design, the scale cartoon is the work of his brother and assistant Agostino. Conception and pose are magnificently robust, and

the triton blowing a conch in the (modified) painting probably inspired Bernini, who must have visited the Gallery; he used the motif in his *Neptune* (see over).

RAPHAEL (below) The ceiling of the Villa Farnesina *loggia*, detail: *The marriage of Cupid and Psyche*, 1518 Raphael's *loggie* in the Vatican and his ceiling in the Farnesina (across the Tiber from the Farnese Palace, and visible from its windows) were important precedents for Annibale, in both their style and their compartmental scheme. Raphael's vision of pagan deity, executed perhaps wholly by his assistants, clearly inspired Annibale.

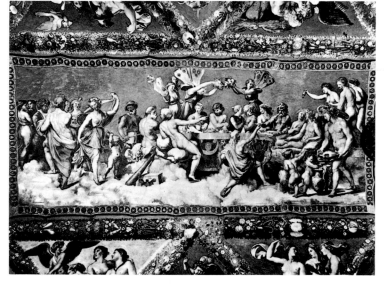

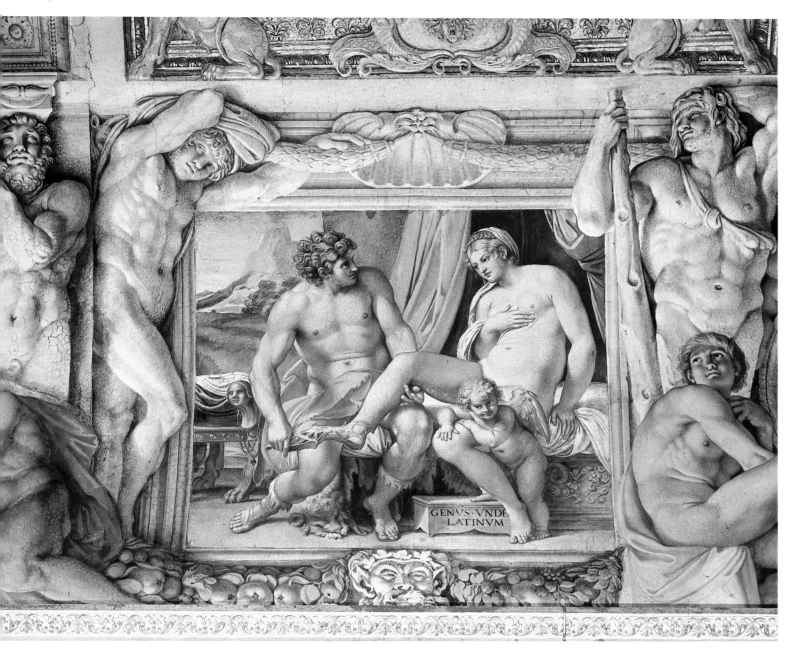

GENVS·VNDE LATINVM

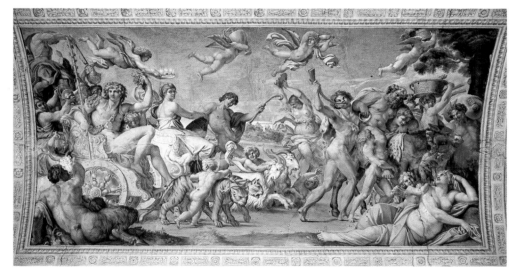

ANNIBALE CARRACCI (above)
The Farnese Gallery,
detail: *Venus and Anchises*,
1597-1600
From the union of Venus
and Anchises was born the
founder of Rome, Aeneas,
as the inscription on the
footstool, a quotation from
Virgil's *Aeneid*, indicates.
Surrounding the pair are
illusionistic stone "Atlas

figures" and busts called
"terms" – both classical
architectural ornaments.
In front of them, in vivid
contrast, are illusionistic
fleshy figures, based on the
Ignudi of Michelangelo's
Sistine ceiling. Further
details reproduce yet other
textures, and the illusion
of planes lapping and overlapping is very successful.

ANNIBALE CARRACCI (left)
*The triumph of Bacchus
and Ariadne*, 1597-1600
The *Triumph* is the centrepiece of the ceiling and
of the whole Gallery. The
idealized forms are derived
from Raphael, though their
heaviness and musculature

echo Michelangelo; the
reclining goddess filling
out the right-hand bottom
corner comes from Titian's
Andrians (see p. 145). This
classicist formula still has
energy, a disciplined richness and – despite lengthy
preparation – real warmth.

The High Baroque in Rome

"Baroque" is a description applied, often loosely, to most European art in the seventeenth century and on into the early eighteenth; but its variations, from Caravaggio to Poussin, from Rubens to Rembrandt, from its service to Catholicism to its use by the Protestant north, may seem at times to have little in common. If essentially it was a realist reaction against the artificiality of the Mannerist style, at the same time astonishing techniques of illusionism and exuberant movement were developed, especially in Rome.

Its greatest practitioners were all-rounders, to whom narrow specialization in any one art would have been an unacceptable limitation. It found its fullest expression in the persons of Bernini in Italy and Rubens (fundamentally influenced by his Italian stay) in the north: both supreme representatives of an aristocracy of genius, moving as equals amongst aristocrats of blood and rank. The latter, however, were also their patrons, and in Rome the period saw the sharpening of rivalries between the great family dynasties, Farnese, Borghese, Barberini, who were aware of the prestige and glamour that artists could provide for them. That awareness was to be brought to massive fruition in the absolutism of Louis XIV in France; employing armies of artists to celebrate at Versailles and elsewhere his invincible, all-conquering radiance, the Sun King needed (like Francis I shortly before) the best, wherever they might come from. He therefore brought to Paris in 1665 even Bernini, the maestro whose name is almost synonymous with the purest peak of the whole movement, the so-called High Baroque of Rome.

Son of a sculptor (Pietro) of considerable talent himself, Gianlorenzo Bernini (1598-1680) was a prodigy, enjoying papal patronage by the time he was 17. The reigning pope was Paul V, a Borghese, and before Bernini was 25 he had a series of remarkable sculptures behind him, all Borghese commissions. In them his development progressed rapidly, absorbing earlier influences (Michelangelo, Giambologna, the Antique) into a highly personal style, expressed with spectacular virtuosity. The fluent coherence of his *Neptune and triton* of 1620 is already far from Mannerist tension; in the *Apollo and Daphne* of 1622-24 he has abandoned the multiple viewpoint of Giambologna and the figures are presented in a limited view, as if they were figures in a painting. In the *Apollo* an appreciation of the Carracci, of Reni, even, in its vivid naturalism, of Caravaggio, is clear. His characters are seen at the most expressive moment – Daphne as she turns from woman to tree, then *David* (1623) at the moment of hurling the stone, compelling the spectator to complete the action with his own imagination, and so implicating him emotionally. So, too, in the portrait busts – often the most formal and pompous of modes – his sitters can be caught not only in movement but in speech to an unseen companion. In his bust of *Costanza Buonarelli* (c. 1635) – an intimate study of a friend, indeed mistress – he created a type of unpretentious, vividly naturalistic sculpted portraiture not to be found again till Houdon in the late eighteenth century.

In 1629 Bernini became architect to St Peter's, and from then on the great spectaculars, exploiting all kinds of techniques and materials, began. Between the Barberini Pope Urban VIII's death in 1644 and the election of Alexander VII in 1655 he was out of favour, though always busy, and his place at the Vatican was taken by Alessandro Algardi (1595-1654; not shown), an extremely pro-

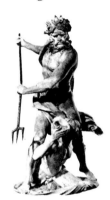

BERNINI (right)
Neptune and Triton, 1620
Bernini's art was founded from his earliest years on superb craftsmanship. He daringly contorts this single piece of marble to the limits of its strength, creating a rich variety of textures – in flying drapery, in straining musculature, or in Neptune's waterlogged, wind-blown hair.

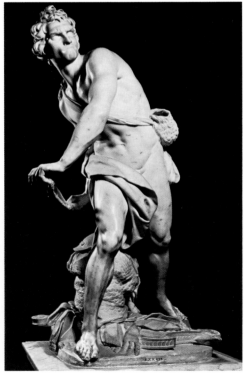

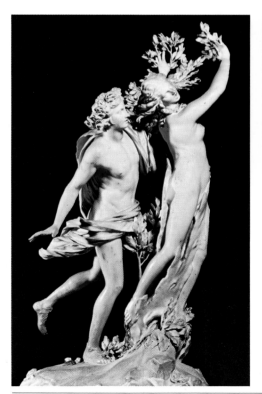

BERNINI (left)
Apollo and Daphne, 1622-24
The statue was originally set in a niche opposite the door to a room, to obtain impact upon entrance. Though his statues were never coloured, Bernini achieved an astonishing illusionism; nobody had previously represented Daphne's metamorphosis as such a convincingly organic process. The delicacy (for instance, of the leaves) and the contrast between flesh, bark, hair and drapery are amazing.

BERNINI (above)
David, 1623
The *David* shows the same interest in momentary facial expression, typical of the Baroque, as Caravaggio in his *Boy bitten by a lizard* (see p. 180) or Rembrandt in some early self-portraits (see p. 218). Commanding the viewer's gaze from a predetermined angle, *David* is conceived not simply as a work of art, but as an object dominating its surrounding space.

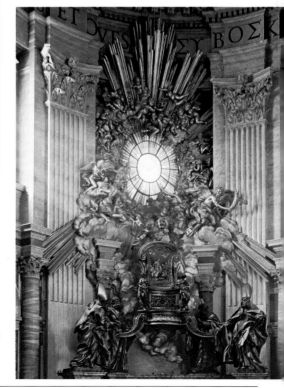

BERNINI (below)
Cathedra Petri (St Peter's Chair), 1656-66
Set beneath the dove of the Holy Spirit in the midst of gilded rays and a riot of angels, the huge papal throne closes the vista down the vast nave of St Peter's. The Four Doctors of the Church sustain the papal chair; their drapery is animated by a violent turbulence, as if the Holy Spirit were a wind rushing through the church, transporting the onlooker to another sphere. Using bronze, marble, stucco, stained glass and light itself, the *Cathedra* is architectural sculpture, both mystical and highly theatrical, propagandizing the awesome majesty of the pope's divine mission.

ficient but deliberately less exuberant sculptor. During this period Bernini's most complex display of bravura, the Cornaro Chapel, was completed (see over).

After 1655 he orchestrated his most important creation, the *Cathedra Petri*, his setting for St Peter's Chair in the apse of St Peter's – a sun-burst of imagery. His 1665 visit to France, to design an enlarged Louvre, was not a success – French taste resented the imposition of Italian forms – although from it came one of the most splendid of all royal busts, that of Louis XIV. His last years were busy with the creation of the great colonnade of St Peter's Piazza, but perhaps his most delightful contributions to the Roman scene were his fountains, such as *The four rivers* in the Piazza Navona, where he brought even water into play as an integral element of his sculptural vision. Bernini was always of boundless energy, not only sculptor and architect but dramatist, wit (terrible in his wrath), a brilliant painter and caricaturist (he executed several dashing self-portraits – though painting was for him more a private pleasure).

The leading painter of the High Baroque in Rome was Pietro da Cortona (1596-1669), a protégé of the Barberini. His early work, in the 1620s, develops the Bolognese traditions in easel-paintings and in fresco with a comparable range of religious and mythological subject matter. But these paintings, monumental in composition and gesture (almost matching Poussin), are free in movement and handling. In the 1630s he completed a most astonishing *tour de force* with his great allegorical ceiling in the Barberini Palace: extending the illusionistic examples set by artists such as Lanfranco and Guercino, he opened the space to the heavens with levitating figures apparently soaring not only up but down into the confines of the room itself. In Florence he carried out decorations of equal brilliance and meanwhile, as an architect, he designed churches in Rome of a remarkable individuality.

In Rome, Pietro's painting was not immediately influential, many patrons preferring the comparative sobriety of his classicizing rival, Andrea Sacchi (1599-1661; not shown), but its implications were to be developed further by Pozzo in the 1690s (see p. 234), and by the great Austrian and south German Rococo decorators of the eighteenth century.

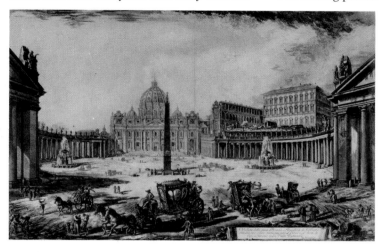

The Piazza and Basilica of St Peter's, Rome
Bernini began the great Piazza, his most famous work of architecture, in 1656 and completed it in 1667. It crowns and conjoins into coherence two centuries of building, and extends imposingly like two great arms to embrace the faithful. Its design is complex, but its effect simple and direct. The engraving is by Francesco Piranesi, 1772.

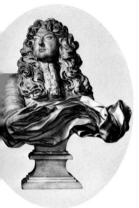

BERNINI (above)
Louis XIV, 1665
In old age Bernini's brilliance in handling textures was undiminished, exuberant, but also finely calculated in its effect – to create in marble an ideal of absolute monarchy.

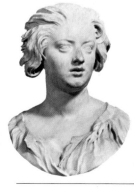

BERNINI (left)
Costanza Buonarelli, c. 1635
In the 1630s Bernini produced a series of portrait busts which for vividness can be compared only with rapid sketches. The surface is in fact painstakingly cut to serve an unusually precise and clearly conceived expression.

BERNINI (above)
The four rivers, detail, 1646-51
Bernini's picturesque allegory of the world's fresh water – the four rivers represent the four continents then known – is one of the landmarks of Rome, continuing the papal reorganization of the city round focal points. It complements the sculptural architecture of S. Agnese, by Francesco Borromini (1599-1667), behind.

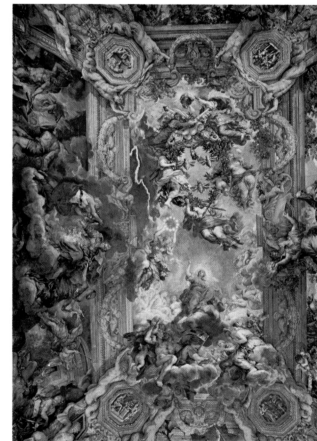

PIETRO DA CORTONA
Allegory of divine Providence and Barberini power, 1633-39
Pietro's ceiling is set in an architectural frame like that used by the Carracci in the Farnese Gallery, but is united in one composition, opens up greater illusionist space and is animated by upward and downward movement. Dominant is the figure of Providence, who gestures towards the wreath containing bees, the Barberini emblem.

Bernini: The Cornaro Chapel

The Cornaro Chapel, in S. Maria della Vittoria in Rome, is the fullest expression of the diverse talents of which Bernini's extraordinary genius was composed. Commissioned by the Venetian Cardinal Federigo Cornaro, it occupied some (but incredibly by no means all) of the energies of Bernini and his collaborators in the seven years between 1645 and 1652.

Its assorted elements – sculpture in various materials, painting and architecture – consort in inseparable concert; though music may seem to be the one form of art lacking, a musical analogy comes to mind. It is akin to a great concerto, in which the soloist is not only the conductor but also the composer and the producer of the whole spectacle. In fact the only part carried out by Bernini's own hand is the central group, St Theresa in her ecstasy (it is perhaps the most celebrated individual achievement in all Baroque sculpture). The rest, with that genius for delegation that also was Bernini's, was carried out by a team of collaborators, stuccoists, marble-cutters and painters, working faithfully to the master's carefully conceived design.

The whole is best seen, and designed to be seen, as a picture or scene on the stage, from a fixed point directly in front of the chapel. It consists of St Theresa's vision, the climax and centre of the action, attended and discussed by members of the Cornaro family in the "boxes" at the sides. The focus of light on St Theresa – real light, from a concealed window above, shafted down simulated light-rays of bronze behind – kindles her being in the moment of supreme ecstasy, expressed physically with such conviction that it seems almost sexual. It is in fact an exact translation into marble of the saint's account of her "transverberation", the vision of a smiling angel piercing her heart with a golden spear. "The sweetness caused by this intense pain is so extreme that one cannot possibly wish it to cease ... this is not a physical, but a spiritual pain, though the body has some share in it – even a considerable share." The effect of the swooning figure, the head fallen back with eyes blinded under half-closed lids, lips half-open – a spiritual orgasm – is strengthened by the brilliant agitation of the drapery, equally infected by the intensity of her agonized rapture. The whole composition is held in breathtaking balance by the dizzy equipoise of the two figures of saint and angel, almost in a rocking movement.

The vivid conviction of the whole springs from Bernini's personal identification with the beliefs of Counter-Reformation Catholicism in its maturity, especially as propagated by the Jesuit orders. The devout – and Bernini himself – practised the daily repetition of the spiritual exercises of the founder of the Jesuits, St Ignatius of Loyola, which were intended to intensify awareness of all-pervading, omnipotent Divine Love. Many of these exercises required their practitioners to imagine, as precisely and as physically, even as painfully as they could, the sufferings and experience of Christ and the saints. Art such as Bernini's, representing the saints in mystical ecstasy as an example to which the faithful could aspire in their own prayer, was similarly concerned to reveal spirituality through external means.

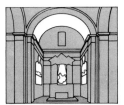

BERNINI
The Cornaro Chapel, S. Maria della Vittoria, 1647-52
The diagram (left) shows the architectural frame in which the Cornaro family, in "boxes" at the sides, witness St Theresa's ecstasy. She is placed at the centre over the altar, in a richly decorated open tabernacle – open both to the viewer in front and to the heavenly hosts above. St Theresa's ecstasy, her communion with an angel, is the Cornaros' vision, brought to the viewer in the church by courtesy of the Cornaro family. Shown below (marked white in the diagram) are the painted and stuccoed vault, the two "boxes", the tabernacle and also the skeletons inlaid in the floor before the altar.

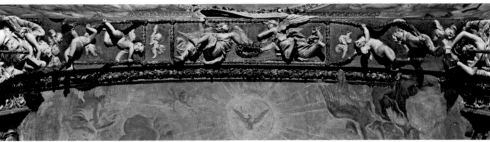

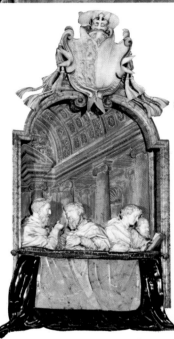

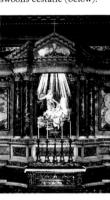

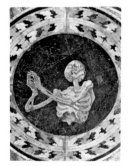

(above) The vault
The painting and stucco represent subject angels adoring the Holy Spirit. Thence the angel who strikes St Theresa has descended, blasting like a thunderbolt beneath which the pediment the saint swoons ecstatic (below).

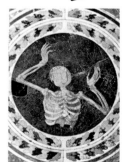

(above and above far right)
The Cornaro family
Federigo, the patron, is shown discreetly at the far (right-hand) end of the west "box". The others, deceased at the time of the commission, talk or read about St Theresa. The illusionistic reliefs behind them open space to the side like a transept, as if their Chapel were a self-contained church.

(left) *Skeletons*
Inlaid (intarsia) marble skeletons are placed left and right in the floor in front of the altar. A recurring feature, almost a signature, in Bernini's work, such skeletons perhaps symbolize both the ubiquity of death and its impotence (on the floor beneath the viewer's feet) against the power of faith (shown by the Cornaro).

The "supporting cast" for the *St Theresa* is composed of painting – the vault of the chapel's ceiling dissolved in a glory of cloud-borne heavenly hosts; of architecture, cunningly articulated to give the illusion of a larger space, to create a "stage" projecting, even bulging out, under the impact of the angel's arrival; of sculpture, in the watching figures and in the reliefs flanking the tabernacle; and of what are prosaically described as the "applied arts", here never more richly or ingeniously applied in variety of material and texture, providing chords of colour to sustain the lucent pallor of saint and angel – bronze, richly veined marble and marble intarsia (the skeletons inlaid in the pavements – here, as elsewhere in Bernini's imagery, not content to lie still but dancing almost a jig).

Orchestrated in superb harmony, the diverse elements in the Cornaro Chapel combine to produce the supreme synthesis of Bernini's sculptural career – a work that was to be a wonder of the world for a century and a half. Then for austere Neoclassic dogma it became more than suspect, notorious as the most outrageous example of Baroque excess, only to be reassessed and triumphantly reinstated for twentieth-century eyes.

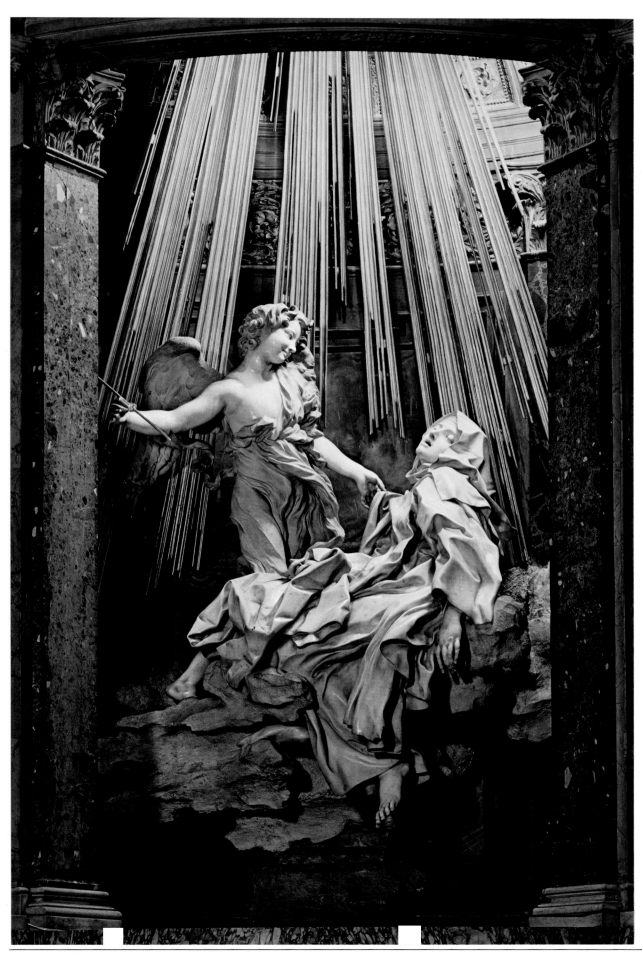

BERNINI
*Vision of the ecstasy of
St Theresa*, 1647-52
Bernini transmogrifies
glittering white marble to
express a purely psycho-
logical, indeed a mystical,
experience. St Theresa's
hanging foot and hand, her
entirely fluid and boneless
form, her ebbing drapery,
convey her utter surrender
to her transport. The little
angel's melting smile and
iron-tipped spear speak of
its bittersweet agony.
The climax of the Cornaro
Chapel's composition, St
Theresa is the kernel of its
message: through prayer
and faith real experience of
God in this life is possible.

French Art 1

Three strands can be distinguished within the texture of French art in the first half of the seventeenth century: the realistic; the classicizing; and, emerging at the beginning of the reign of the Sun King Louis XIV, the court Baroque. All reflect in some degree France's geographical position, between Italy and Flanders, but the influences she derived from the north had themselves been conditioned by exposure to Italy and its creative centre, Rome.

Thus the realistic strain, the art of the Le Nains or the very different art of Georges de La Tour, is typically northern – in the tradition of Bruegel – rather than Mediterranean, yet in style and approach derives in various degrees from Caravaggio. The three Le Nain brothers came from Laon, though they worked in Paris, and their art has a provincial feeling; it seems to have answered to a bourgeois taste rather than to a courtly one. The youngest, Mathieu (1607-77), fostered more social pretensions than the others as a master painter to the city of Paris, but his group portraits are reminiscent of the burgher groups so popular in Holland. Antoine, the eldest (c. 1588-1648), usually worked on a small scale (often on copper), but also produced many family

groups, sometimes set in domestic interiors, and some genre pictures. The borderlines, however, between the work of the three are still unclear, and they often collaborated.

The work associated with Louis (c. 1593-1648), the middle brother, is by far the most original. His usual subjects, low-life or peasant scenes often on quite a large scale, are the same as those of many Dutch painters, but akin most closely perhaps to the work of Il Bamboccio (Pieter van Laer, 1592-1642; not shown) who was one of the many Dutch artists working in Rome in the wake of Caravaggio, and who popularized scenes of beggars and brigands between 1627 and 1639. Louis, too, is supposed to have visited Rome, yet his characters are specifically and soberly French, and, peasants though they be, they have a classical quality in their statuesque grouping and in the enigmatic gravity of their demeanour; painted in subdued and often melancholic colours, greys, grey-browns and grey-greens, they compel with a strange, listening silence.

Georges de La Tour (1593-1652) was truly of the provinces, working in Lorraine all his life. The source of his style is Caravaggio transmitted through Dutch artists such as

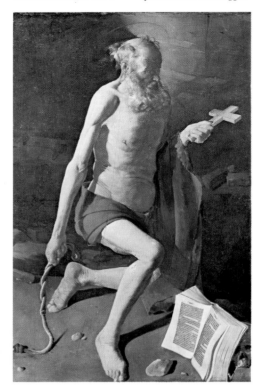

GEORGES DE LA TOUR (below) *St Jerome*, 1630s The single saint with still-life attributes was a favourite Caravaggesque type. The light and shade and sculptural realism are quite close to Caravaggio.

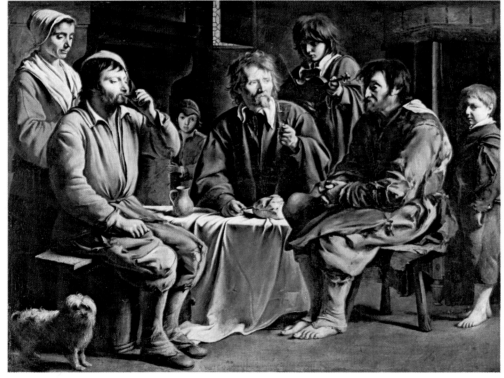

LOUIS LE NAIN (above) *The peasants' meal*, 1642 Louis's groups of patient peasants, whose air of melancholy is reinforced by the silvery colours, have no obvious parallel in contemporary art or literature, and it is not known who bought such works. The subject matter is genre, but the treatment is neither sentimental nor humorous; instead it is sober, factual, sincere.

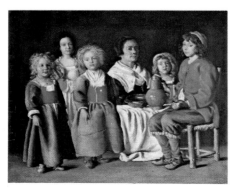

ANTOINE LE NAIN (left) *A woman and five children*, 1642 Antoine's paintings are distinctly more naive than his brothers'; the composition has not the same studied order, and is without the enigma of Louis's works or the worldliness of Mathieu's. His small, stiff and somewhat awkwardly constructed figures have much charm, like that of certain Dutch artists.

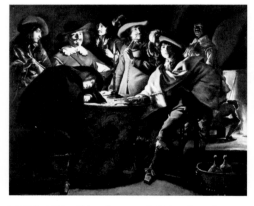

MATHIEU LE NAIN (above) *The guardroom*, 1643 The confident self-display of these Parisian officers recalls Dutch militia groups, and the Caravaggesque lighting the Utrecht school (see p. 213), but in composition this is more sophisticated.

THE LE NAIN BROTHERS (below) *The Adoration of the shepherds*, c. 1640 The Le Nains' religious works show that they were open to the influence of followers of the Carracci, such as Guercino. Here there are strong diagonals, counterpoised movement.

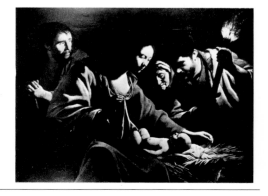

Honthorst or Terbrugghen (see p. 213). The early paintings concentrate on low-life genre, typically Caravaggesque subjects (even saints are shown very much as elderly peasants). In the 1630s he introduced into his paintings a lighted candle, naked or shielded, the single source of light; at the same time he simplified his forms, insisting less on detail, achieving in the single figure a classic monumentality – especially striking if, for instance, that figure is a serving-woman intent on crushing a flea.

La Tour's later paintings are mostly religious (connected possibly with a local Franciscan revival), but his people – even when mesmerized in contemplation and modelled almost without detail – remain of this earth. In his masterpiece, *The new-born child*, there is no explicit religious symbolism – simply a woman and her child and an attendant, observed in static calm in the warm, steady glow of the candle flame with utterly cool detachment – yet it is one of the fullest records of the miracle of birth, human or divine, ever painted. The quietism and intense serenity of La Tour's later work have answered some deep need of the twentieth century; like Vermeer, he remained unappreciated for centuries.

In the work of Philippe de Champaigne (1602-74), born a Fleming and trained in Brussels, French sobriety and control find alternative expression. His early work in Paris is a drier, more restrained version of Rubens or van Dyck, as in his portraits of his patron, Cardinal Richelieu. But after 1643, working for the Jansenists – a movement as near to Puritanism as was possible in the bosom of the Catholic Church – he developed a sober, realistic style of superbly proportioned portraiture. That, too, can be described as classic, with its effect of decorum and of dignity.

Champaigne's most famous painting, the *Ex voto* of 1662, represents his daughter, a nun, in beatific yet sober prayer. Afflicted by an apparently incurable paralysis, she was restored following a novena initiated by her prioress, beside her. A miracle is being celebrated, but the restrained composition is calm in its austere greys, blacks and browns. The two figures are disposed almost geometrically, and the only indication of supernatural intervention is the ray of light (that might be from some earthly window) falling between them.

As Champaigne adapted Flemish Baroque, so Simon Vouet (1590-1649) was the seminal figure who moderated Italian Baroque towards a compromise acceptable to French taste. In Italy for 14 years, from 1613 to 1627, he developed an eclectic style, but leaned more towards the classicizing manner of the Carracci than to the dramatic intensities and contrasts of Caravaggio; he was influenced by Guercino and perhaps especially by Reni. Back in France he had a very successful career, both with easel-paintings and with large decorative projects, threatened only by the arrival of Poussin in 1640. Vouet's work, comparable in colour to Champaigne's, is in structure a more fluid and expansive version of the classicism Poussin was formulating in Rome (see over). Vouet's influence was to be superseded in the later years of the century by that of Poussin, but Vouet had grasped both the rhetoric and the realism of Italian Baroque, and his restrained version of it indicated the direction to be taken towards the Grand Manner of the Sun King. In the same period, the great cardinal princes Richelieu and Mazarin were establishing the tradition of patronage which Colbert, Louis XIV's chief minister and factotum, was to consolidate under the directorship of Vouet's pupil, Lebrun.

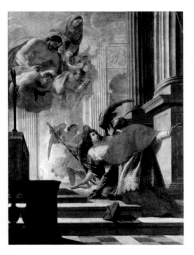

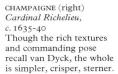

VOUET (left)
St Charles Borromeo,
late 1630s
On his return from Rome to France in 1627, Vouet opportunely introduced the new Baroque style of Italy – evident here in the firm modelling, insistent architectural background and strong diagonals.

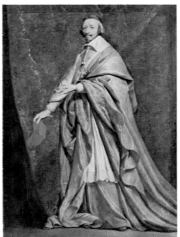

CHAMPAIGNE (right)
Cardinal Richelieu,
c. 1635-40
Though the rich textures and commanding pose recall van Dyck, the whole is simpler, crisper, sterner.

GEORGES DE LA TOUR (left)
A woman crushing a flea,
c. 1645
The light is used not so much to model in three dimensions as to delineate the forms sharply against a dull, darkling background. An almost sordid subject is treated with an abstract, transfiguring stillness.

GEORGES DE LA TOUR (right) *The new-born child*,
c. 1650
In La Tour's mature work the forms are severely simplified and reduced almost to silhouettes. The meticulously painted details and dry, wrinkled skin of the early *St Jerome* have gone: instead the forms are softly and very shallowly modelled, types not portraits. The result is to transform a homely moment into something permanent and universal.

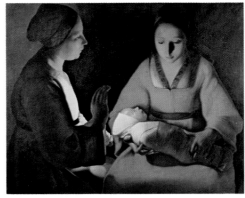

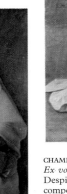

CHAMPAIGNE
Ex voto, 1662
Despite its bare, simple composition, the picture radiates a joyful piety. The inscription commemorates the sudden recovery of Champaigne's daughter "when the doctors had despaired, and Nature's jaws gaped". Missals and crucifixes, the hands and the daughter's eyes turned up to heaven, testify that it was all due to prayer.

Poussin: The Holy Family on the Steps

The classical strain in French art found its greatest exponent in Nicolas Poussin (1593/4-1665) – though Poussin's working life was spent almost entirely in Italy. For subsequent generations, not only in France, he gave classicism a definitive form – one that was at the same time so vital and rich in possibilities that Cézanne, prophet of the revolution in painting more than two hundred years later, sought "to do Poussin again, from nature", envying his perfect clarity of form and structure. Poussin sought the ideal synthesis of form and subject matter, of landscape with figures, of light with colour and mood, and in the noblest works of his maturity, between 1630 and 1660, achieved

it. In them he refined his early sensuousness, freely inspired by Giovanni Bellini, Giorgione and Titian, with a high seriousness, sobriety and linear perfection in the tradition especially of Raphael, from whom Poussin inherited the formal preoccupations of *The Holy Family on the steps* (1648) in particular.

Poussin's *Self-portrait* is sumptuous but severe, set against an almost abstract composition of rectangular picture frames. It is the portrait of a man who expressed visually a Stoic philosophy of self-control and self-sufficiency, perhaps more deeply than he transmitted the Christian faith or ethic. In seventeenth-century Rome, where he lived

from 1624, he found a learned and sensitive society that nourished the artistic expression of this temperament. A brief spell (1640-42) in Paris was unhappy; he worked habitually alone, painting what he wanted to paint, and he was ill at ease with the large-scale mural decoration and workshop management required of him at the French court.

Even in Rome, Poussin's cool severity, achieved by the rigorous elimination of all inessential detail, was in striking contrast to the emphatic art of his great Baroque contemporary, Bernini. The difference between Poussin and the swirling rhythms of the art being produced all around him seems extra-

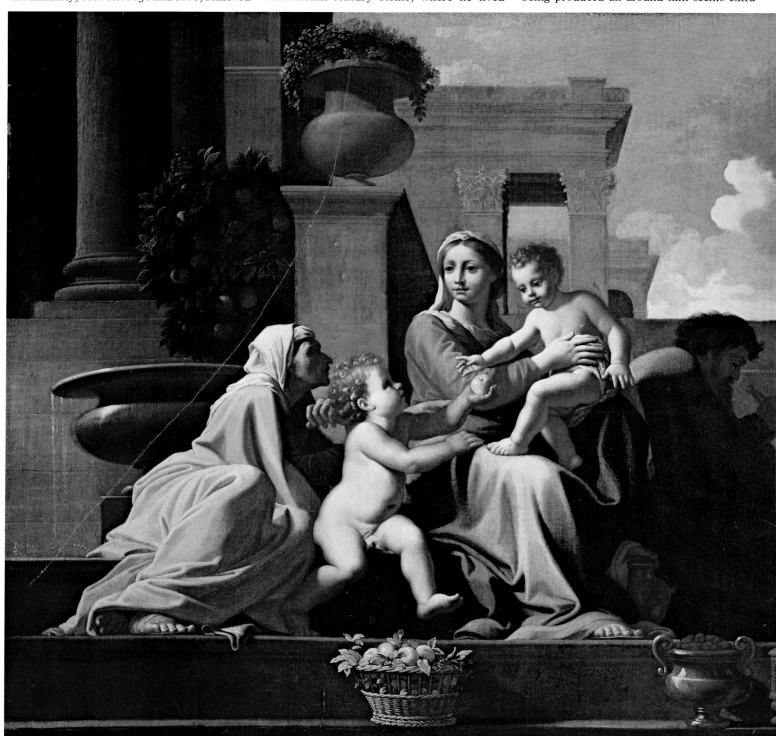

ordinary. Yet it was a logical enough development of that ordering of the picture space already achieved in the work of the Carracci and Domenichino. Although the theme of the *Holy Family* is entirely Christian, it has little in common with the propagandist emotionalism of the Counter-Reformation Baroque. Like Poussin's landscapes (see over) the *Holy Family* reads not as a mystical vision but as a superb effort of will, eye and intellect to extract an enduring order from the transitory world of life. Bernini realized Poussin's achievement when he tapped his forehead when looking at one of his paintings and said: "Signor Poussin is a painter who works up here."

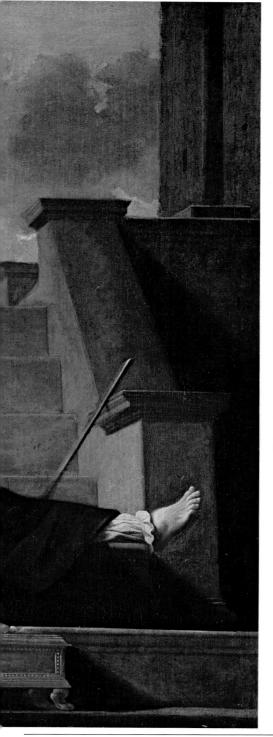

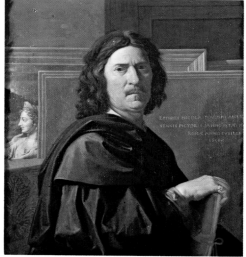

POUSSIN (above)
Self-portrait, 1649-50
Poussin painted only two, very similar, portraits, both of himself, as favours to friends. In recording his likeness he stated his principles, those of an austere and profoundly cultivated man, versed in the classics and in the Stoicism of Horace and Cicero. The female bust signifies Painting, her diadem Perspective.

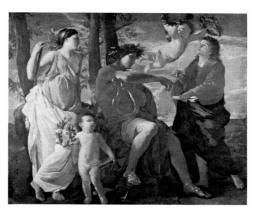

POUSSIN (above)
The poet's inspiration,
c. 1628-29
This early work shows the young Poussin's sensuous delight in Venetian colour and atmosphere. The poet, watched by the Muse of Epic, presents his work to the seated Apollo.

ROME, ESQUILINE (right)
"*The Aldobrandini
Marriage*", detail,
1st century BC
Found in a house on the Esquiline Hill, this is one of the few Roman frescos of the highest quality that survive. It inspired Poussin's general composition, and St Joseph's pose with outstretched foot seems a conscious reference to the reclining youth here. In Rome Poussin drew and studied classical remains avidly, so as to found his art on antique principles.

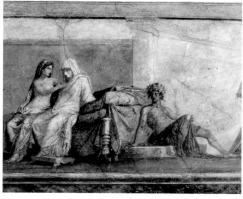

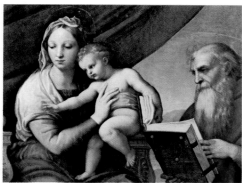

RAPHAEL (left)
"*The Madonna of the
Fish*", detail, c. 1513
Raphael's altarpiece was almost a proto-Baroque composition, not least in the use of a sweeping diagonal backdrop. It comes late in a series of Madonna compositions by Raphael, Leonardo and Michelangelo, to which Poussin's *Holy Family* is a deliberate coda. The pose of his Mother and Child is based on Raphael's; his Madonna's face has the same abstract purity.

POUSSIN (below)
Preparatory drawing for
The Holy Family, 1648
The figure group has been resolved almost in its final form, but the two middle background buildings that help to centralize the composition round the Virgin, and to suggest great depth, have not been determined. The way in which Poussin blocks out the figures in light and shade shows him thinking in sculptural terms, of solid forms displayed in an almost abstract harmony.

POUSSIN (left)
*The Holy Family on
the steps*, 1648
Though Poussin avoids Venetian colourism, the mask-like solidity of the Virgin's face recalls the *Madonnas* of Giovanni Bellini. Raphael, the Antique and Michelangelo all contibute to a work full of symbolic allusions to the Old and the New dispensations. There are few better examples, even in Poussin's varied range, of Baroque synthesis or of 17th-century classicism.

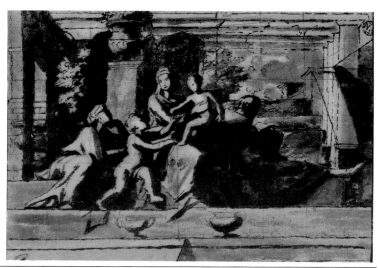

French Art 2: The Sun King

Louis XIV's reign of almost unparalleled stamina – 72 years long, from 1643 to 1715 – brought about the remodelling not only of French but of European court civilization. Palaces and their furniture were laid out and arranged so as to support and glorify the image of an absolute monarch. Well before the end of the century Rome had ceased to be the artistic centre of Europe, and the corridors and decoration of Versailles were to be emulated in England, Germany, Italy and Spain.

The arts were organized, almost industrialized, in the service of the Sun King by Colbert, one of the ablest administrators in history. The headquarters of artistic production were the Academy, founded in 1648; and Colbert's executive manager was Charles Lebrun (1619-90) who became Director of the Academy in 1663. Poussin, the greatest French painter of the century, lived in Rome, and his recall in 1640 had not been a success, but he had important French patrons, and it was Poussin's practice and principles that were to become the essential canons of the Academy's taste. However, Poussin became dogma only after a celebrated theoretical storm, the battle of the "Poussinistes" and the "Rubenistes":

Lebrun eventually gave judgment in 1672 in favour of antiquity and of Raphael, for the vigorous drawing and classical idealism of Poussin against the rhythms and colour and realism of Rubens and the Venetians; academicism was established.

Early on in his career Lebrun had been rivalled by Eustache Le Sueur (1616/17-55), a fellow pupil under Vouet. Although Le Sueur never visited Rome, he carried on the Rome-oriented vision of Vouet, notably in his decorative paintings for the Hôtel Lambert in Paris, and became influenced more and more by Poussin and Raphael. But the death of Le Sueur in 1655, following that of Vouet in 1648, left the field clear for Lebrun, whose organizational ability sometimes obscures the fact that he was a highly gifted painter. Lebrun was in Rome between 1642 and 1646, probably with Poussin but evidently also studying the great decorative schemes of painters such as Pietro da Cortona. In Paris, first the minister Fouquet recognized his abilities, and then Colbert saw in him the ideal instrument for his centralization of art in the service of the State, for "*la gloire de la France*". By 1664 he was first painter to the King and Director of the

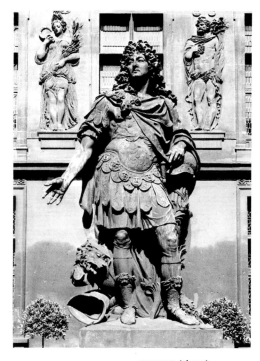

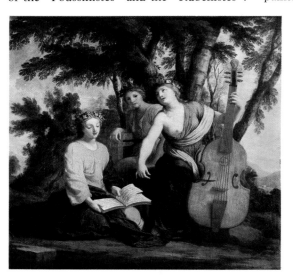

LE SUEUR (left)
The Muses, c. 1647-49
Le Sueur's pictures in the *Cabinet d'Amour* in the Hôtel Lambert introduce the type of chaste, blonde woman he derived from engravings after Raphael. In delicacy they compare with Poussin's early work.

LEBRUN (right)
Louis XIV adoring the risen Christ, 1674
Lebrun was often forced to deviate from his strictly classical theories by the task set him – to produce large-scale glorifications in which Baroque drama and gesture were invaluable. Forms and composition derive from Raphael's *Transfiguration* (see p. 164), but not the spirit.

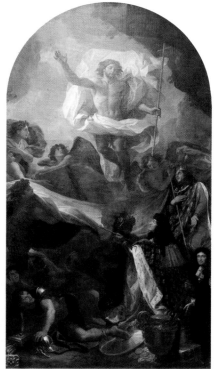

COYSEVOX (above)
Louis XIV, 1687-89
French court Baroque was founded on a vision of a new classical age – with the Sun King as Emperor and his court as a new Rome. Coysevox's statue for the Town Hall of Paris represents Louis dressed as for a Roman Triumph and in classical posture. In his portrait busts of his friends and fellow-artists, Coysevox struck a more informal mood.

SARRAZIN (below)
Caryatids on the Pavillon d'Horloge of the Louvre, 1641
As slaves supporting the roof of their conqueror's building, caryatids, too, had an imperial meaning. Sarrazin's females are as classical as Poussin's, and archaeologically more accurate than those of the artists he had met in Italy. They mark perhaps the first appearance of the classicism dominating the vast quantity of sculpture produced under Louis XIV.

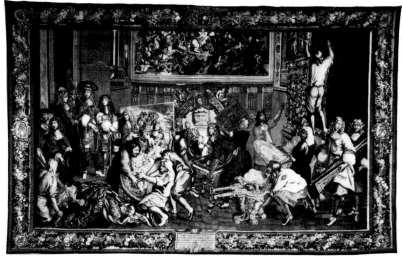

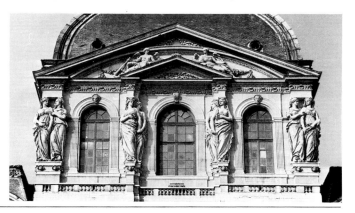

LEBRUN (above)
Louis XIV visiting the Gobelins factory, 1663-75
The tapestry gives an idea of the range of items made at Gobelins under the close direction of Lebrun. Above hangs Lebrun's cartoon for a tapestry of Alexander the Great, whose imperial virtues were understood as a prototype of Louis XIV's.

Gobelins tapestry factory; as Director of the Academy he codified its rules and practices, and wrote a treatise, *The Expression of the Passions*, a typically rational grammar of the irrational, which was an influential text-book for long after his death. His own painting was not entirely restrained by theory – a work such as his vision of *Louis XIV adoring the risen Christ* has both vigorous movement and a nice equation of the relative importance of the two main characters. However, his final importance in French art is certainly as a sort of team manager in the great decorative ensembles, especially Versailles, collaborating with architects and with sculptors to bring magnificently up to date the tradition of Fontainebleau.

Versailles and the palace pattern that it set offered numerous opportunities for the deployment of sculpture, not least in the vast formal gardens – 80 hectares (200 acres) at Versailles. The sculptors, responding to exactly the same taste as the painters, do not include, however, original masters of the order of the expatriate Poussin and Claude. Their outlook was established by Jacques Sarrazin (1588-1660), who indeed taught many of them. Sarrazin, during his long stay in Rome (some

20-odd years) worked with or for artists as diverse as Domenichino and Bernini, and he established himself in France as an extremely able and versatile technician, rather than an artist with a committed personal vision. With a large studio of assistants, he developed inevitably towards an ever more classicizing style. The Anguier brothers (François, 1604-69, and Michel, 1613-86), who had worked with Bernini's rival Algardi in Rome, were somewhat more individual, but the main ally of Lebrun in the extensive sculpture programme of Versailles was Sarrazin's pupil François Girardon (1628-1715). In his figural groups Girardon evolved a style based on Poussin's (and reflecting tacitly Poussin's method of constructing miniature groups of figures in wax as studies for his pictures). Pierre Puget (1620-94) had too individual a temperament to work successfully at Versailles; his works were classical enough, but too intense and perhaps too Italianate for most of the court. The impact of Bernini, even after his 1665 visit to Paris, was always muted in France, although the taste of the aging Louis XIV became increasingly florid, and sculptors such as Antoine Coysevox (1640-1720) pro-

vided a more full-blooded Baroque flourish in the last years of the century; Coysevox's *forte*, however, was perhaps his lively portrait busts.

In his last years, Lebrun yielded in favour to Pierre Mignard (1612-92; not shown), with a vivacious, colourful line in portraiture, kitting out his aristocratic sitters with allegorical attributes as Venus, Thetis and so on. Sébastien Bourdon (1616-71) developed in his portraits a very competent and elegant variation on van Dyck; his religious and mythological paintings were a softer version of Poussin, less rigorously ordered if more seductive in handling. Poussin and Rome, which he visited in 1634-37, were abiding inspirations, although Bourdon's work as a whole is not easily defined or consistent, and he also copied (perhaps fraudulently) both Claude and the Le Nains.

The splendour not only of the court but of the prosperous Parisian merchant class had its peony-like flowering in the parade-dress portraits of Nicolas de Largillière (see p. 242) and Hyacinthe Rigaud (1659-1743). Rigaud's *Louis XIV*, in full royal pomp and acres of ermine, was one of the most splendid (and influential) portrayals of royal absolutism, but loyal to the facts of an aged face amidst it all.

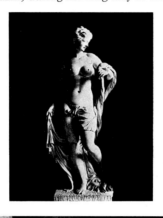

MICHEL ANGUIER (left)
Amphitrite, 1680
Anguier's figure is mildly Baroque: classically posed, but clothed in voluptuous flesh and lively drapery – signs of Algardi's tutelage.

GIRARDON (below)
Apollo tended by nymphs, 1666
The group was moved from its enclosed niche to this "picturesque" grotto in the late 18th century, and the original strict symmetry destroyed – the Sun King's rigorous formality had long ceased to be congenial.

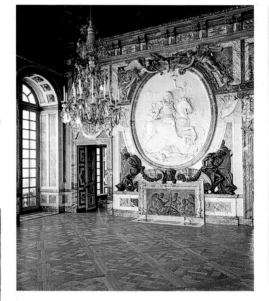

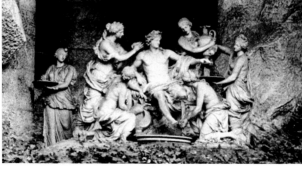

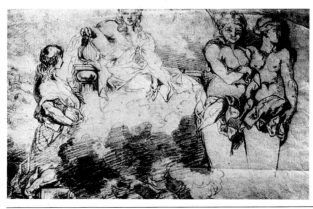

LEBRUN AND COYSEVOX (above) The *Salon de la Guerre* (Hall of War) at Versailles, 1681-83
The overall design is Lebrun's, the sculpture in bronze and stucco is Coysevox's. Within the scope of the roundel, *Louis XIV on horseback* caracolling over fallen enemies, there are fine, typically Baroque effects of movement both into and across the space.

BOURDON (left)
Mythological drawing, undated
Because he could work in almost any style and give it his personal flavour, Bourdon is difficult to classify. Yet he often enriched the classicism of the day with sensuality and poetic fantasy.

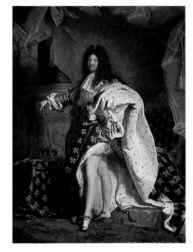

PUGET (above)
Milo of Crotona, 1683
In his marble of the legendary wrestler who was trapped in a tree trunk and devoured by wild beasts, Puget created a truly French form of Baroque: violent in movement and in expression of the victim's agony, yet classical in control and in purity of silhouette.

RIGAUD (left)
Louis XIV, 1701
Baroque motifs – swirling drapery, rich colour and swaggering figure – blend with a stiffness of pose and coldness of touch in Rigaud's state portraits. The affected, balletic placement of the feet was to become a regular feature of French art in the early 18th century.

Art in Flanders

Even before the death of Bruegel in 1569, the Netherlands had been rent by vicious fighting which continued for nearly 50 years. By the end of the sixteenth century, however, the territory had been divided into the Dutch Republic (including Holland) in the north and the Spanish Netherlands (including Flanders) in the south, and the art of the now quieted communities reached new heights.

Seventeenth-century painting in Flanders and in Holland is remarkable not only for its quality but also for its quantity, especially considering the smallness of each area; each was essentially different in character. The art of the fiercely independent Protestant Dutch was supported mainly by a prosperous merchant class, and much concerned with secular subjects; the art of Flanders, which remained under the Catholic Hapsburgs, was oriented to the court (both in Flanders and in Spain) and the Church of the Counter-Reformation. Flemish art reached its zenith rather earlier than Dutch art, but was shorter-lived, and did not produce so various and copious a harvest in almost every branch of art. In Flanders a single exuberant genius, Peter Paul Rubens (see over), was the presiding eminence and main

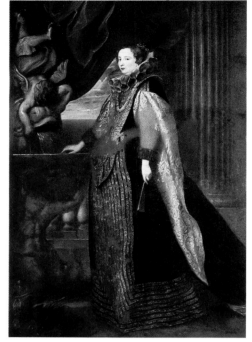

driving force, and on his death the decline of Flemish painting was almost instantaneous.

To some degree the earlier Netherlandish passion for naturalism, and the astute observation found in Bruegel's work, persisted. At the beginning of the seventeenth century, however, its best-known exponents worked abroad, providing specialist skills in still life or landscape for decorative projects in Italy – for instance the Bril brothers in Rome (see p. 196). The production of small genre and still-life paintings continued throughout the period in Flanders, but with few exceptions they do not compare in quality with the great output of religious and courtly painting.

Rubens' studio, the power-house of Flemish painting, was established in Antwerp by about 1612. His huge practice employed not only younger pupils and assistants, but distinguished artists of his own generation working in collaboration. Jan I Brueghel (1568-1625), younger son of Pieter Bruegel and known as "Velvet" Brueghel, specialized in still life and in extensive landscapes peopled with small genre or mythological figures. Jan seems a somewhat improbable ally for Rubens, and his collaboration, mainly in bowering Rubens'

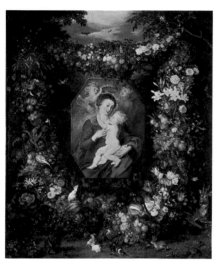

VAN DYCK (above)
Marquesa Caterina, c. 1625
The shimmering, tender Baroque style van Dyck evolved in his Genoese portraits depended on the use of crusts and glazes of pigment, which he learned from the great Venetian painters. Stately, refined, faithfully characterized, his portraiture soon rivalled Rubens' in its influence.

RUBENS AND "VELVET" BRUEGHEL (left)
The Virgin and Child in a garland, c. 1620
Brueghel's garland frames Rubens' Virgin, evoking a symbolic enclosed garden. His highly finished flowers contrast with Rubens' more broadly painted figures.

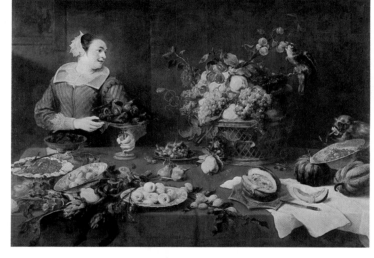

SNYDERS (above)
The fruit-seller, before 1636
Snyders was one of the first to concentrate on still-life and animal painting. He developed a particular interest in the handling of light reflected on objects, infusing fruit with a tempting succulence. He favoured quite large, complicated arrangements.

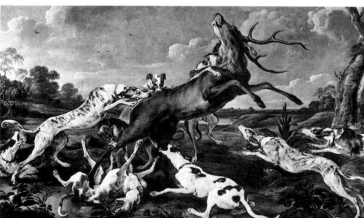

PAUL DE VOS
The stag hunt, c. 1630-40
Like Snyders, his teacher and brother-in-law, Paul de Vos was a specialist in both still lifes and hunting scenes. In both artists there was a development towards

greater drama and Baroque movement: in this late work the hounds arrow in on the upward-straining stag in a forceful composition made up of colliding diagonals. Rubens admired de Vos: he had four paintings by him.

CORNELIS DE VOS (right)
The artist and his family, 1621
Meticulous, factual portraiture made Cornelis very popular with burghers of Antwerp. His style depends on that of Rubens, also borrowing from the palette of the young van Dyck, but he lacks the sensitivity of either Rubens or van Dyck; beside them he seems rather linear and dry. He painted altarpieces, too, and some Baroque historical pictures in the manner of Rubens.

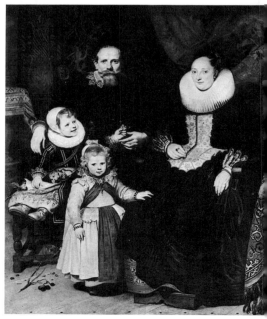

Madonnas with flowers, stemmed perhaps from close personal friendship rather than shared artistic feeling. Frans Snyders (1579-1657), having trained with Bruegel's elder son, Pieter the Younger, became closely linked with Rubens' studio after returning from Italy in 1609. A specialist in still life and animal and hunting scenes, he supplied these elements where needed in many of Rubens' compositions, and later in Jordaens'. The energy of Rubens' painting opened up Snyders' style and his scale; even his still lifes can be infused with violent movement, and are sometimes invaded by predatory animals which seem to have escaped from his vigorous and frequently ferocious hunting scenes. Closely linked to Snyders was his brother-in-law Paul de Vos (1596-1678), also an animal painter; Paul's brother Cornelis de Vos (1584-1651) was mainly occupied with relatively staid burgher portraits, but also worked for Rubens at times.

Rubens' studio was not so much a teaching academy as a production team, and his two most celebrated associates, Jacob Jordaens (1593-1678) and Anthony van Dyck (1599-1641), though of a younger generation, were not really pupils. Jordaens, who never visited Italy, was an Antwerp man and stayed there all his life, working with Rubens from about 1618 until the master's death, mainly as a figure painter. From his Mannerist beginnings he grew into a robust, Rubensian style and by about 1635 was developing it very much in his own way. Although on Rubens' death he took over the great artist's last commission, the extensive decorations of Philip IV's hunting lodge near Madrid, it was about then that he turned to Calvinism, and the most interesting works of his later career are his genre scenes.

Van Dyck, a precocious genius, was with Rubens little more than two years (about 1618-20), although the older master's style affected his own indelibly. By his twenty-first year he was already ripe for independence; a first foray into England in 1620-21 was followed by an extensive sojourn in Italy, mainly in Genoa but with trips through the rest of the country to study and copy the Venetian masters – Tintoretto, Veronese, above all his abiding inspiration, Titian. His livelihood derived in great part from portraiture, and in his series of court portraits of the Genoese aristocracy he established a style of characterization that was to persist all over Europe for more than two centuries: in his visions of tall and aloof, yet relaxed, elegance, he showed the most subtle ability to marry a precise physical likeness into compositions of fluent and elaborate Baroque splendour. His genius was, so to speak, the feminine aspect of Rubens': although, particularly in his early work, he could be so close to Rubens as to be confused with him, his more delicate sensibility soon became apparent – the moon to Rubens' sun. There was not room for both of them in Flanders, and after a brief second Flemish period (1628-32), he took up Charles I's invitation to come to London (see p.206), and remained based there until his premature death in 1641. He was certainly then investigating the possibilities of a return to Europe in the place of Rubens, who had died the year before.

Two outstanding painters who were not directly connected with Rubens were Adriaen Brouwer, who worked for much of his brief career in Haarlem (see p. 226), and David Teniers the Younger, whose genre paintings, for which he is best known, were much influenced by Brouwer. Teniers, however, was also court painter to Archduke Leopold Wilhelm, the Spanish Viceroy in Brussels.

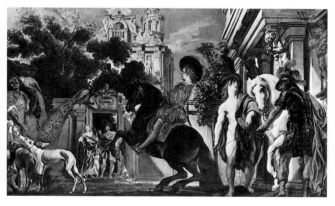

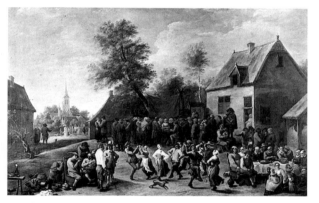

TENIERS (left)
The country fair, c. 1650
Teniers' best and most characteristic genre works are outdoor scenes filled with tiny figures carousing in a *kermis*, or festival. He produced at least a dozen variations on this scene, and many more like it.

TENIERS (below)
The picture gallery of the Archduke Leopold, c. 1650
The taste of the Archduke (seen in black) for Venetian painting is evident. Such crowded hanging was the norm until the 20th century.

JORDAENS (above)
The riding academy, c. 1635
Jordaens' oil-sketch of a rider with Mercury and Mars was one design for a series of tapestries. In scale and in allegorical content it was a typical courtly commission, like Rubens' Médicis cycle (see over).

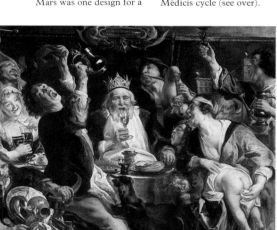

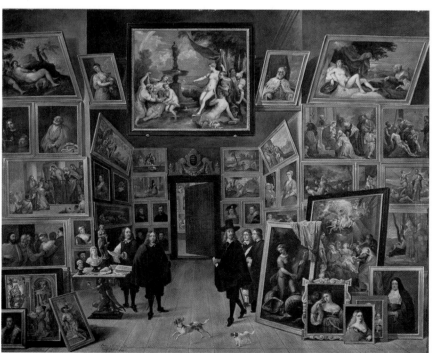

JORDAENS
The king drinks, c. 1645
The "king" was a figure of Flemish folklore, associated with the Epiphany and its feasting. Such an earthy subject was quite foreign to Rubens, although the rich fleshiness and even some of the facial types derive from him. Jordaens' bloated merriment seems a sort of genre pastiche of Rubens' voluptuous Bacchanalia.

Peter Paul Rubens

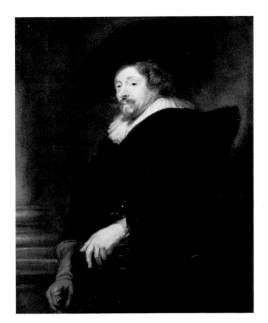

Self-portrait, c. 1639
Rubens was international
in scope as no artist had
been before him. He wrote:
"I regard all the world as
my country, and I believe I
should be welcome every-
where". A correspondent

of scholars and confidant
of crowned heads, he used
his status to propagate the
values of humanism, peace
and Italianate civilization.
A sensual appetite for life
was moderated by sincere
religious feeling in the
spirit of the Jesuit revival.

As Bernini is the supreme representative of
Baroque in Italy, so Peter Paul Rubens (1577-
1640) is the commanding figure of Baroque in
the north – indeed his influence was further-
reaching and more enduring than Bernini's.
Trained by Flemish Mannerists who are now
virtually forgotten, Rubens, more than most
artists of the past, developed his style by
assiduous copying: he set out for Italy in 1600,
and by the time of his return to Flanders in
1608 had absorbed, with remarkable industry,
both the heritage of the Antique and of the
Renaissance and the art of his contemporaries,
Caravaggio and the Carracci. Co-ordinating
northern and southern tradition, he emerged
in the first decade of the century with a new
vision, dazzling to patrons and artists alike.

The fame and prestige Rubens acquired in
his own lifetime was the equal of Titian's: he
was an artist prince, the peer of monarchs in
style, culture and deportment. His collection
of art rivalled that of the great patrons of the
time. He was both painter and supremely
efficient impresario; both polished courtier
and ambassador of peace between warring
states. The energy and exuberance of his art
resounded through the age and beyond it.

Rubens' crucial formative period began in
his twenty-third year, when he arrived in Italy.
He became painter to the Duke of Mantua, at
whose court he put the finishing touches to his
artistic education and courtiership (he had
already served as a page when an adolescent in
Antwerp). He visited Spain for the first time in
1603, and succeeded in fascinating the Duke of
Lerma, later to be Philip IV's Chancellor. His
equestrian portrait of Lerma, in which much
of his mature style is already clear, was inspired by Titian's portrait, still in Spain, of
Charles V at Mühlberg (see p. 143). With
Baroque illusionism, Lerma advances, life-
size and magnificent, out of the picture. Returning to Italy, Rubens continued to study –
especially Titian, Veronese and Tintoretto –
with detailed and critical care, building up a
reference library of hundreds of copies.

Back in Antwerp, he was appointed court
painter to the Archduke Albert and the Infanta
Isabella in 1609, and in the same year married
Isabella Brandt. Confidently launched on a
tide of enduring prosperity, Rubens built
himself a spectacular house and garden (still
to be seen in Antwerp) in the Italian style: he
pined for Italy and was already preparing *The*

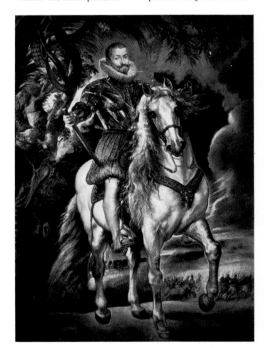

The Duke of Lerma, 1603
Rubens swivelled Titian's
profile equestrian portrait
of Charles V (see p. 143)
through 90° so that Lerma
seems to break through the
picture surface towards the
onlooker. The composition
is determined by diagonals
receding into depth and
by rhythmic curves. The
horse is a superb animal:
the English and the Dutch
depicted horses, but never
such splendid creatures as
Rubens' or van Dyck's.

*Self-portrait with
Isabella Brandt, c.*1609
Rubens' marriage portrait
is just the sort of picture
any gentleman in Antwerp
might have commissioned –
highly finished, proper and
discreet. He and Isabella sit
in a honeysuckle bower, a
symbol of their conjugal
bliss. The tenderness of the
portrait is restrained by a
poised elegance that is a
world away from the young
Rembrandt's *Self-portrait
with Saskia* (see p. 218).

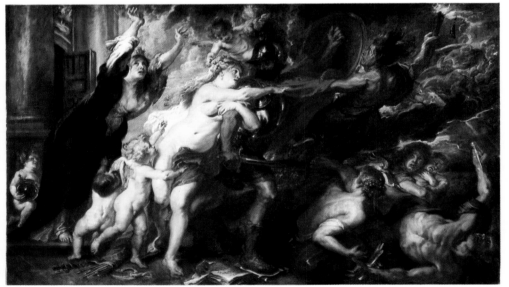

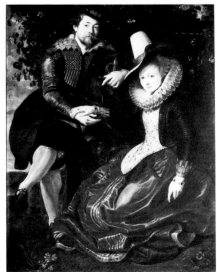

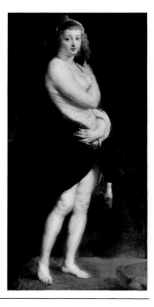

The horrors of war, 1638
Rubens himself explained
his allegory, painted for the
Duke of Tuscany: "That
lugubrious matron clad in
black (on the left) . . . is
unhappy Europe, afflicted
for so many years by rapine,
outrage and misery". In
vain Venus tries to restrain
Mars; in his train come
Pestilence and Famine.
Rubens' dynamic style can
carry off so large a theme.

*Hélène Fourment in a fur
wrap, c.* 1638
Of all Rubens' portraits of
his youthful second wife,
this is the most intimate –
playful, sensuous, erotic
– that classic gesture of
modesty, the arm across
the breasts, becomes here
a gesture of exposure.

Palaces of Genoa, published in 1622, as propaganda to displace the continuing Gothic style of architecture in the north. Even before the Archduke died in 1621, the Infanta came increasingly to rely on Rubens, as confidant and as adviser in her political difficulties.

After about 1615, Rubens' early vigorous but somewhat dark-toned style gave way to a clearer palette, and he achieved in such works as *The rape of the daughters of Leucippus* that radiance and abundance of colour that is the essence and delight of his painting. Numerous large and important commissions – notably *The descent from the Cross* (see over) and a series of 39 ceiling paintings (destroyed by fire in 1718) for the church of St Charles Borromeo – culminated in his best-known surviving series, *The life of Marie de Médicis*, for the Luxembourg Palace in Paris. On his journey to France he was already representing the Infanta Isabella; after a second visit to Spain in 1628, he visited England primarily as an ambassador charged to negotiate peace, but he also agreed to paint a series of canvases for the ceiling of the King's new Banqueting House.

The scale of his commissions, matching the scale of the Baroque palaces and churches for which they were destined, precluded the possibility that Rubens could carry them out single-handed. He had begun to organize his studio almost as soon as he had returned from Italy. He put together a team of collaborators – many of them already or later to be considerable painters in their own right – and determined his prices by the amount of his own work present in the finished object. Although he usually "pulled together" his assistants' work in the final stages, nowadays his preliminary drawings and oil-sketches sometimes seem more compelling than the finished works, which are highly contrived, though often freely and dashingly painted. In Rubens' day it was the other way round, however: the conventions of the courts and the ceremonial of the Counter-Reformation Church demanded pomp and circumstance, and a "suspension of disbelief" that people will usually only accord now to performances of Grand Opera. The speed and sureness with which he transcribed his first, free thoughts on to paper is amazing, and the small-scale oil-studies on panel, often virtually monochrome, in which he decided the balance of tones and established the dominant rhythms and accents of the final composition, have unprecedented vigour.

Rubens had been temporarily shattered by the death of Isabella Brandt in 1626, and the failure of his negotiations in England disillusioned him with statecraft. On his return to Antwerp he made repeated attempts to retire, so as to paint to please himself and to enjoy life with his second wife, Hélène Fourment. He painted Hélène frequently – in mythological or religious roles, or in frankly sensuous portraits (she was 16 when he married her in 1630, and he was 53). On his country estate, the Château de Steen, he painted boldly colouristic landscapes, glimpses of a wonderfully rich and varied nature, sometimes combined with visions of disporting nudes. Though he was wealthy enough not to need to sell another picture, he could never escape the embroilments of the Spanish court, and when he died in 1640 he was engaged on a series requiring 112 paintings for Philip IV's hunting lodge.

Rubens successfully disseminated his art by means of engravings, doing his best to control both their quality and his copyright. His heritage remained vital for two centuries to come, influencing artists as diverse as Watteau, Gainsborough, Delacroix and Renoir.

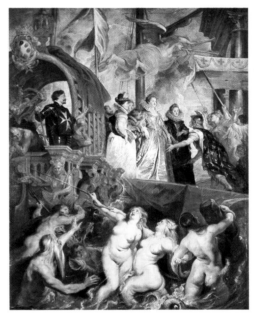

RUBENS (left)
The rape of the daughters of Leucippus, c.1618
The abduction by Castor and Pollux of Hilaria and her sister Phoebe calls out Rubens' full armoury: hard tawny muscles of men on opulent white female flesh; rearing horses; a gleaming cuirass. It is also a superb composition of interlocking curves, unfolding gestures.

RUBENS (below)
The Château de Steen, c.1636
Rubens' own mansion, the small castle surrounded by farms and orchards, is on the left, and it has been hazarded that the hunter in the foreground is a self-portrait. Rubens' lyrical landscapes lead the eye to and fro over a nature almost in movement. The lighting, and the sultry impasto of the sky, anticipate Turner.

RUBENS (left)
The Luxembourg Palace cycle: *Marie de Médicis lands at Marseilles,* 1622-25
The 24 paintings of the cycle describe the life of Marie, wife of Henri IV of France, in epic terms. By investing the prosaic events of Maria's career with dramatic splendour Rubens made his reputation as Europe's foremost court painter. Though he painted on groundwork provided by his assistants, Rubens' own bravura and spontaneity are unflaggingly displayed – a sign, among other things, of the efficiency with which he organized his studio. Fame sounds a clarion call as the Queen, arriving from Florence, is welcomed by the allegorical figure of France. Below, voluptuous naiads and hearty sea-gods rise up to celebrate it.

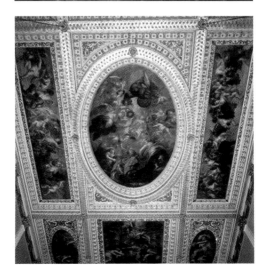

RUBENS (above)
The ceiling of the Banqueting House in London: *The apotheosis of James I,* 1629-34

The nine canvases of the ceiling uphold the divine right of monarchy in a scheme adapted from ceiling frescos in Italian churches.

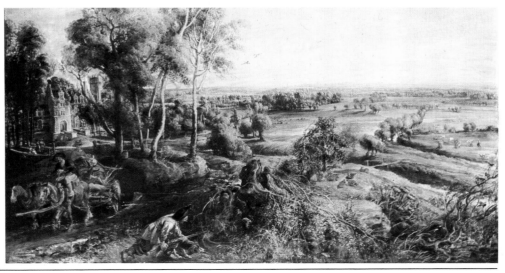

Rubens: The Descent from the Cross

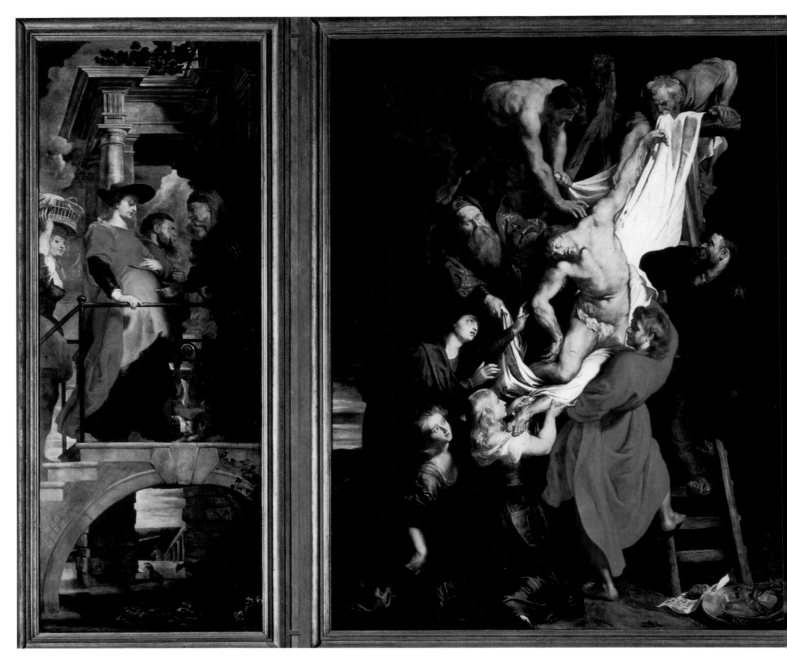

In the early phases of Rubens' career, after his return from Italy in 1608, two masterpieces are supreme. Both are large altarpieces, both now hanging in Antwerp Cathedral, but they were not painted as a pair. The first, *The raising of the Cross*, painted in 1610-11, was commissioned for the church of St Walburga in Antwerp, now demolished; the second, *The Descent from the Cross*, completed in 1614, was always intended for Antwerp Cathedral. Although Rubens had been appointed (in 1609) court painter to the Viceroys of the Netherlands, these commissions came not from that quarter, but from the merchant classes.

The Descent established Rubens then and there as the greatest painter in northern Europe but, though it was less well received, the muscular and emotional turmoil of *The raising* is closer to the subsequent trend of Rubens' work. In its original form, *The raising* had an old-fashioned, complex framework involving not only closing wings but predella

panels below, and God the Father with angels above. The central triptych, to which it was reduced in the eighteenth century, was far from old-fashioned. It was emphatically Baroque, and violent in action, treatment and expression – in the straining muscles of the men heaving up the Cross, in the deep, thrusting diagonals of the composition, in the anguish of the crucified figure. The two wings extend the action and the emotion: on the left, the Virgin and St John look on in a group of horrified women and children; on the right, a mounted Roman officer controls the preparations for the two thieves' execution. On the outer panels were four saints connected with the original church.

In contrast, *The Descent* appears calm and classical. Now the agony is past; the mood is of the most profound sorrow, almost elegiac in the superbly controlled decline of the dead Christ's body down the diagonal white fall of the winding-sheet, caressed by the eloquent

hands that guide it. The design is unforgettable, reused by Rembrandt and many others.

The subjects of the two wings are complementary in theme to the central panel, but do not extend the action as do those of *The raising*. *The Visitation* and *The Presentation in the Temple* on the inner surface of the wings, and a colossal *St Christopher* and a *Hermit* carrying a lantern, the light of the world, on the outer panels, are all linked by the Greek meaning of Christopher, "Christ-bearing", the patron saint of the commissioning guild.

The Descent from the Cross was a not uncommon subject both in northern and Italian painting, though Rubens' interpretation is influenced most clearly by the Italians – works by Caravaggio and the sixteenth-century painters Daniele da Volterra and Il Cigoli all provided ideas for Rubens' composition. Many of the working stages towards *The Descent from the Cross* survive, and illustrate Rubens' methods clearly – first drawings di-

RUBENS: (left) *The Descent from the Cross*, 1611-14

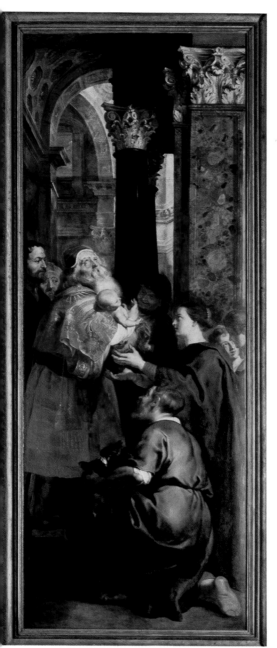

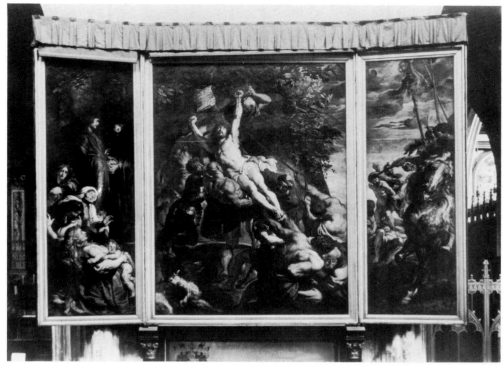

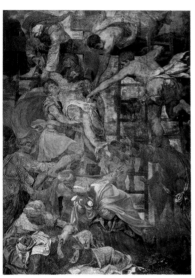

RUBENS (above)
The raising of the Cross,
1610-11
The realism of the action,
the lighting and the solidity
of the bodies show the
influence of Caravaggio,
but Rubens has introduced
passion and bravura, and
exaggerated everything –
the paint itself seems now
to shimmer and vibrate.

DANIELE DA VOLTERRA
(right) *The Descent from
the Cross*, begun 1541
The scale and spectacle
of Daniele's painting had
early showed the trend of
Counter-Reformation
taste. Rubens preserved
the strong diagonals, but
reworked the composition
to achieve greater unity
and dramatic coherence.

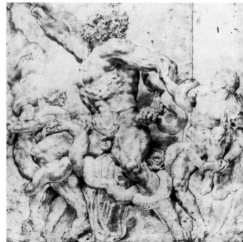

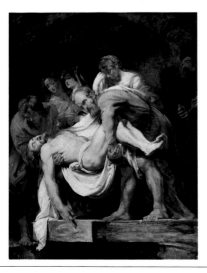

rected towards a resolution of the composition;
then an oil-study, sometimes very fully worked
out, as is that for *The Descent* (this was probably submitted to the client for preliminary approval); then a reference back to detailed chalk
studies from the life; and finally the execution
of the full-scale painting itself. The imagery is
rich in references not only to Italian masters
but also to classical motifs – St Christopher
clearly echoes "*The Farnese Hercules*" (see
p. 41) with his club, while the pose of the dead
Christ reflects closely (in reverse) that of the
late Hellenistic statue of *Laocoön*.

When Rubens' pictures were finished, the
studio often produced replicas, and through
engravings the design was broadcast to a far
wider audience. From an engraving of *The
Descent*, Gainsborough – to take an example –
made a free copy in oils, and then, fascinated
by its formal rhythms, transposed it into the
merry bucolic group on the cart in *The harvest
wagon* (not shown), one of his best landscapes.

RUBENS (above)
Drawing of the *Laocoön*,
c. 1606
Rubens' sketches of the
works of art he had seen
in Italy were an abiding
inspiration – he used them
rather as Rembrandt used
his hundreds of drawings
from the life. Rubens was
a superb draughtsman, and
often infused his drawings
with greater vividness than
the original (see p. 46) had.

RUBENS (right)
Copy after Caravaggio's
The Entombment, c. 1605,
reworked *c.* 1613
When he reworked the copy
of Caravaggio he had made
in Italy, Rubens probably
had in mind the design of
his own *Descent*. He has
heightened the luminosity
of Christ's white body, and
introduced more sorrowful
feeling into Caravaggio's
rather aggressive realism.

Art in England

English painting had its roots in the residence in London during the 1530s of the Swiss-German painter Hans Holbein the Younger. He founded no school, and after his death in 1543 inspired no successors in quite the same Renaissance tradition. To fill his place came painters such as Hans Eworth (c.1520- after 1573) from the Netherlands, who practised the international Mannerist style of court portraiture – after the example of Anthonis Mor (see p. 174) rather than that of Bronzino.

In the latter half of the sixteenth century, when, in Elizabeth I's reign, Protestantism was re-established, painting was virtually confined to portraiture. Its peculiarly English development was towards the stiff, linear and hieratic, and it reached its zenith in the miniatures of the native-born Nicholas Hilliard (1547-1619) and of his follower, the refugee French Huguenot Isaac Oliver (before 1568-1617; not shown). In miniatures of a jewel-like brilliance, Hilliard achieved a delightful balance between symbolism, allegory and individual characterization. On a larger scale, a pedestrian kind of formal portraiture – faces surmounting stiff, upright costumes, set in airless niches – persisted into the first quarter of the seventeenth century. Even the more naturalistic portraits by further Netherlandish immigrants were still very sober.

Charles I, who succeeded to the throne in 1625, changed all this. He had travelled in Europe, and was a sophisticated patron whose collection of Renaissance art, chosen largely by himself, rivalled anything in Europe. In 1630 he commissioned Rubens to decorate his classical Banqueting House, built eight years before. Failing to persuade Rubens to stay, Charles welcomed van Dyck (see p. 200) in 1632 like a prince – knighting him, bestowing gifts, a house, an income. Anthony van Dyck was crucial to Charles: his portraits were designed to support the King in his claim to be absolute monarch (a claim which he, unlike Louis XIV, failed to establish). Charles was celebrated in varying aspects of his kingly role: sumptuous in coronation robes; as the ideal gentleman engaged in country pursuits; as a knight and warrior, the chivalric defender of his people. Other artists painted Charles, too, but it is van Dyck's image of this melancholic, doomed King that is enshrined in history; no one else could conjure such romance and poetic elegance out of Charles' slightly unpre-

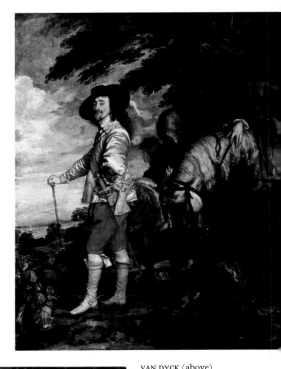

EWORTH (right)
Queen Mary I, 1554
Eworth's unpretentious but perfectly competent likeness typifies the state of English portraiture before van Dyck's arrival.

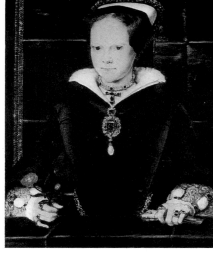

HILLIARD (below)
Young man in a garden,
c. 1588
The lovelorn youth – his condition is explained in an inscription – exhibits the elegant melancholy of an Elizabethan sonnet. Symbolic thorns and blossoms enclose his slender figure in delicate tracery.

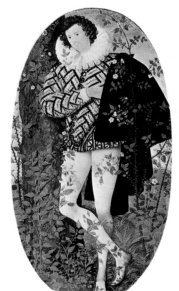

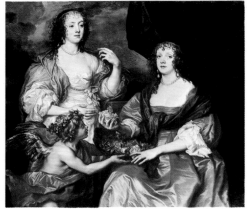

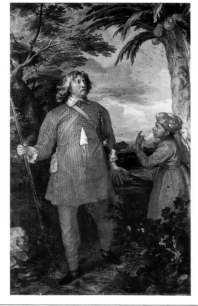

VAN DYCK (above)
Charles I hunting, c. 1638
In Protestant England van Dyck was unable to use allegorical personifications to indicate the qualities of his sitter. He managed, however, to suggest kingly ideals by subtler means.

VAN DYCK (left)
Lady Elizabeth Thimbleby and Dorothy, Viscountess Andover, c. 1637
Such languid elegance and sleepy *hauteur,* such a play of brilliant light upon the drapery – English artists were still recasting the spells of van Dyck's art in the early 20th century.

VAN DYCK (right)
Charles I on horseback,
c. 1638
Titian (see p. 143) and Rubens (see p. 202) had restated the theme of the equestrian ruler, and van Dyck portrayed Charles I in conscious emulation. The life-size picture was hung at the end of a long room, and created the impression of an extended vista into an ideal English park, with old English oaks, in which the King awaited the spectator's homage.

VAN DYCK (left)
William Fielding, Earl of Denbigh, c. 1633
Since van Dyck's portrait commemorated the Earl's return from India, he is shown wearing Indian silk pyjamas, attended by an oriental servant; he steps forward with the vigour of an explorer. The splendid costumes of van Dyck's sitters were often no more part of normal wear than the Earl's exotic garments.

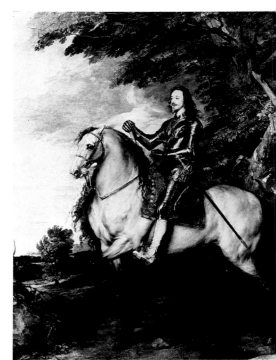

possessing figure. There is a story that van Dyck's portrait of Charles' head, painted to serve Bernini as a model for a bust, moved the devotedly royalist Italian to tears by its aura of tragedy to come – the King was executed by Parliament in 1649.

Meanwhile Charles' courtiers were dazzled by van Dyck's revelation of what the new Baroque vision could do for their prosaic persons. Employing his profound knowledge of his first master, Rubens, and of the great Italians, especially Titian, whose work he could study anew in Charles' collection, van Dyck achieved an easy fluency and rich brilliance hitherto unimagined in England. A breathing air floods the picture space; bodies formerly fixed in a rigid stance relax, caught in balance between one movement and the next; stiff Jacobean costume melts in coloured cascades of broken light, silks, soft leathers, satins. Van Dyck imported and established a tradition of portraiture that was to dominate English painting for more than two centuries. However, he also established Rubens' studio production methods, with assistants working not only on replicas but on first versions, so that the quality of his overall output is uneven.

Van Dyck died just before the outbreak of the Civil War that, in the 1640s, destroyed the royal autocracy and ultimately the King himself. The artistic patronage of the victorious rebels was minimal; Robert Walker (c.1605-after 1656; not shown), an indifferent artist, portrayed the Parliamentarians, using van Dyck's poses because, he said, being the best, they relieved him of the necessity of inventing new ones. However, in the work of William Dobson (1610-46), who painted the embattled Royalists, there can be seen a brief but remarkable native development of van Dyck's Baroque – a robust, individual vision that drew perhaps even more on Venetian painting. In the very English art of miniature a genius emerged, Samuel Cooper (1609-72), whose fascination with the idiosyncracies of the human face was reconciled to a strong decorative rhythm – "the van Dyck in little".

With the Restoration in 1660, the mantle of van Dyck passed to the Dutch-born Sir Peter Lely (1618-80) who, again with the aid of a highly organized studio, dominated the English scene until his death. His style developed van Dyck's in a more robust but less refined mode, admirably suited to the coarser, more self-indulgent manners and morals of the Restoration court, and to the well-fleshed attractions of Charles II's mistresses.

Lely was followed as court painter by the German immigrant Sir Godfrey Kneller (1646-1723), who painted the portraits of seven British monarchs (also of Louis XIV and of Peter the Great of Russia). His studio was still larger and more mechanized than Lely's, but at its best his own fluent and muscular brush could organize the wigs and draperies of the period into splendid ensembles, equal in quality to the portraits of Maratta in Rome or Largillière in France (see pp. 234 and 242).

In the second half of the century, a foundation for genre and landscape painting was laid. Francis Barlow (1626-1704), a naive but charming painter of wild life, was a native exception among immigrant Dutchmen painting landscapes and battles, most notably the van de Veldes (see p. 223), marine painters of seminal importance. Van Dyck towers over the age – "We shall all go to Heaven", Gainsborough was to say on his deathbed, "and van Dyck is of the company" – but these artists, too, were an important prelude to the Golden Age of English painting.

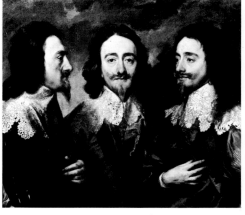

VAN DYCK (above)
Charles I from three angles, c.1636
Van Dyck succeeded in transfiguring Charles' features without altering their literal appearance. Even so, Charles' large nose is not so prominent in other portraits. Bernini's bust, for which van Dyck's picture was a guide, is lost.

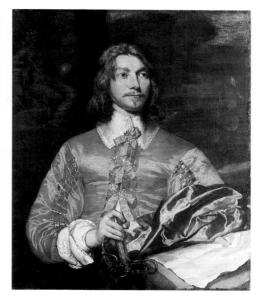

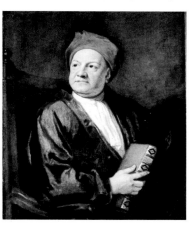

KNELLER (above)
Jacob Tonson, c.1717
Kneller's most famous works are his portraits of the members of the Kit-Cat club, the unofficial forum of Whig political and literary dissent. The portrait of Tonson, who commissioned the series, shows Kneller's splendid, sturdy grasp of character.

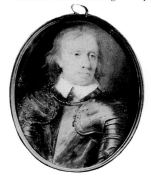

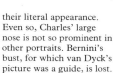

COOPER (above)
Oliver Cromwell, 1656
Having recorded Charles' vanquisher "warts and all" as he demanded, Cooper later painted miniatures of Charles II. His prices and international prestige were the equal of Lely's.

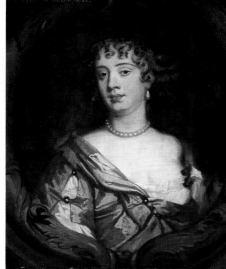

DOBSON (above)
A cavalier, c.1643
Dobson could hardly avoid the influence of van Dyck, but his portraits show an independent alertness, a forceful characterization and vivid colour contrasts new in English art. He was the most distinguished English painter between Hilliard and Hogarth.

LELY (left)
Anna, Countess of Shrewsbury, c.1670
The Countess was one of the more notorious of Charles II's mistresses. Lely's portraits, clearly deriving from van Dyck, are bolder, cruder, more direct. The textures of his draperies have none of the morning freshness of van Dyck's; they flicker with an afternoon light.

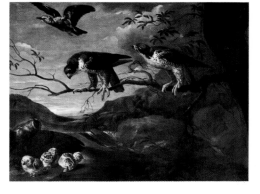

BARLOW (above)
Buzzards about to attack some owlets, undated
Barlow, known in his day as "the famous painter of fowls, beasts and birds", was the father of a long line of sporting painters.

Art in Spain

The flaming vision of El Greco has dazzled the imagination of posterity to the exclusion of all other late sixteenth-century painters in Spain, yet El Greco, for all his appeal to a mystic passion in the Spanish soul, was not only a foreigner but untypical. In the native character, the mystic strain was offset by a relish for physical detail, a delight in intense realism. The Church, in combative mood, took pride in the example of her visionaries and martyrs – but also in their sometimes hideously gory sufferings. Spanish dignity, her pride in her faith, her Empire and her nobility, so evident in the portraiture of the period, could easily erupt into sometimes ferocious passion.

By the time El Greco died, in 1614, Toledo had ceased to be the capital of Castile and Spain; the court was settled in Madrid, and other cities, too, had developed and prospered. Early in the century painting flourished especially in two centres, Valencia and Seville. Francisco Ribalta (1565-1628) in Valencia developed an early Spanish Baroque, influenced by Titian in technique but powered also by the enduring involvement of Spanish painters with the drama of light and shade first revealed by Caravaggio. Jusepe de Ribera

(1591-1652), believed to be Ribalta's pupil, settled in 1616 in Naples, then still a Spanish colony, where Caravaggio had been active only a short time before. His early work there is intensely Caravaggesque: sharply focused light lingers on vivid detail against a dark ground (hence the Spanish term, *tenebrismo*), and is used to portray with minute realism low-life and sometimes grotesque subjects (such as *The bearded woman* suckling her child).

The style of Ribera's middle maturity was more balanced, the contrasts of light and dark less fierce, but his painting lost nothing in immediacy. The predominance of martyr-

doms in his work tends to be exaggerated, but his most famous painting is *The martyrdom of St Bartholomew* of the 1630s, typifying the feeling aroused by the Counter-Reformation in Spain; the spectator is compelled into an emotional participation with the subject, by the coarse, heaving executioners, the sharply observed crowd, the tensions of the saint's naked body. All this is centred on the saint's heavenward gaze, appealing to God almost with despair. Later Ribera's colours lighten, and paintings such as *The mystic marriage of St Catherine* are suffused with a spirituality now of lyrical tenderness. Ribera was gifted with a

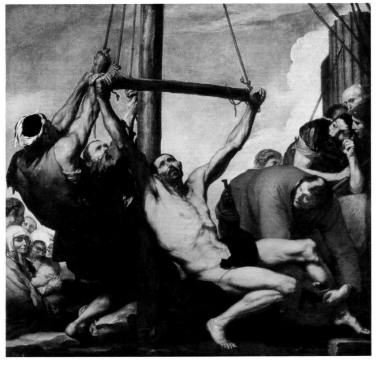

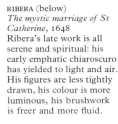

MENA (above)
Mary Magdalen, 1644
Mena excelled in carving grief or mystical passion with controlled intensity. The expressive head of his painted wood *Magdalen* is accentuated by her hand, so tautly spread, so penitent.

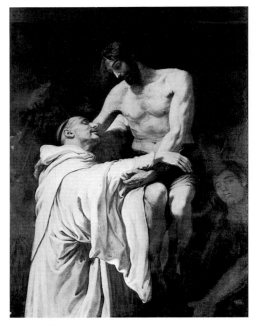

RIBALTA (above)
St Bernard embracing Christ, c. 1620-28
Ribalta was more than a mere *Caravaggisto*: he used Caravaggio's lighting to lend a sculptural monumentality to his figures. The composition is simple, the realism – despite the visionary content – strong.

RIBERA (right)
The bearded woman, 1631
The inscription hails a great wonder of Nature, and, though the subject is grotesque, the approach is respectful. Caravaggio had used strong chiaroscuro to dramatize action: the Spanish also employed it to add monumental force to entirely static subjects.

RIBERA (above)
The martyrdom of St Bartholomew, c. 1630
The flaying of the saint has not yet begun, but all its agony is already felt in the unbalanced distortion of his body and the efforts of his tormentors. In sheer violence Ribera passes both Caravaggio and Rubens.

RIBERA (below)
The mystic marriage of St Catherine, 1648
Ribera's late work is all serene and spiritual: his early emphatic chiaroscuro has yielded to light and air. His figures are less tightly drawn, his colour is more luminous, his brushwork is freer and more fluid.

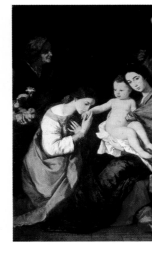

ZURBARAN
St Anthony of Padua with the infant Christ, 1650s
The soft atmospheric light, the delicate modelling, the

predominant browns and greys date the picture to the 1650s. The formidable simplicity of Zurbarán's art has lost its full starkness.

remarkable sureness of touch, and he developed a very swift technique, working directly on to the canvas – *alla prima*.

The most steadfast exponent of Spanish *tenebrismo* was Francisco Zurbarán (1598-1664). He spent most of his active life in Seville, where he early on established a friendship with Velazquez. His commissions came mostly from monks, and were on monastic themes: he responded with simple, imposing images – of monks in prayer or saints in adoration – boldly, powerfully, sculpturally modelled. Most stunning perhaps is the series he painted for the Convent of Guadalupe (1638-39, not shown); in a typically Spanish way his pictures express intense spiritual emotion in very physical terms, and are best compared to the polychrome wood sculptures of Zurbarán's contemporaries Martinez Montañés or Pedro de Mena (1627-88). Their theatrical realism was the sculptural equivalent of processions and festivals in which the sufferings of Christ or of martyrs were enthusiastically enacted, and their influence persisted for centuries in popular religious art.

Zurbarán's secular commissions were few, the most important being for ten great canvases on *The Labours of Hercules* from Philip IV, but a series of still lifes is attributed to him: these pots, dishes and fruit take on an almost sacred aura in the searching light that brings them into being out of the surrounding darkness. They recall similar elements in Velazquez's early work and represent at its best a continuing tradition in Spanish art.

Zurbarán was overshadowed towards the end of his life by Murillo, and his style softened slightly, perhaps under his influence. Bartolomé Esteban Murillo (1617/8-82) also worked almost entirely in Seville, at first in the dominant *tenebrismo*, but moving towards a much lighter, more open and freer style, modified again by Flemish and Venetian influence after study of the royal collections on a visit to Madrid in 1655. He not only painted religious subjects, but also developed a form of genre, carrying on the tradition of low-life pictures founded by northern artists working earlier in Rome. His many pictures of *Urchins*, usually ragged and poor, are characterized with a lively tenderness that captivated eighteenth- and nineteenth-century sensibilities, and made them some of the most highly priced paintings in the world – only to be dismissed (unjustly) by the twentieth century as sentimental. Sentiment indeed they have, but the masterly command of line, colour and composition is not weakened by coyness or mawkishness. Murillo's mature religious work shows great delicacy and fluency, and his many ethereal variations on the theme of *The Immaculate Conception* seem almost Rococo (the Spanish term is *estilo vaporoso*); they have also a sweetness which turned saccharine in the hands of innumerable copyists and imitators.

In 1660 Murillo founded, with others, the Seville Academy of Painting. Among his colleagues, Juan de Valdés Leal (1622-90) was perhaps the last of the great Spanish Baroque painters. He was trained in Cordova but was active most of his life in Seville. His early work is firmly in the *tenebrismo* tradition; in his mature style he deployed vigorous brushwork to achieve an intense emotional impact. His colour was often dramatic but sometimes very sombre, as was only fitting in his series on *Death and Judgment*. He sometimes verged on the grotesque, at the opposite pole to his colleague Murillo, and equally far removed from the magisterial control of the greatest Spanish painter of them all, Velazquez.

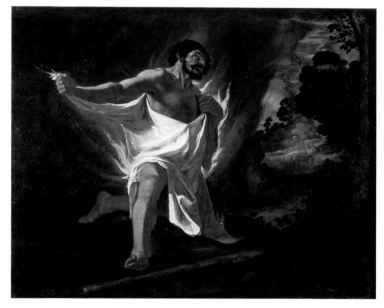

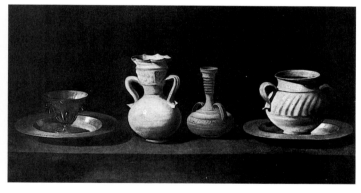

ZURBARAN? (above)
Still life, c. 1664?
Zurbarán seems the artist most likely to have painted such an austere, simple and yet mysterious evocation of quite ordinary objects. At Guadalupe he made still life an intense supplement to the mood of the narrative.

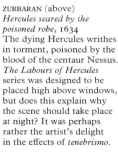

ZURBARAN (above)
Hercules seared by the poisoned robe, 1634
The dying Hercules writhes in torment, poisoned by the blood of the centaur Nessus. *The Labours of Hercules* series was designed to be placed high above windows, but does this explain why the scene should take place at night? It was perhaps rather the artist's delight in the effects of *tenebrismo*.

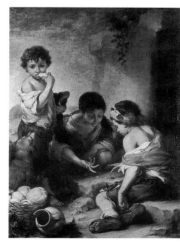

MURILLO (right)
Boys playing dice, undated
The frequency with which Murillo's engaging ragamuffins have been reproduced has lessened the impact of their exciting colour harmonies and finely modelled forms, painted in a deft *alla prima* technique.

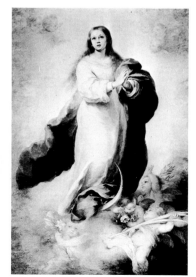

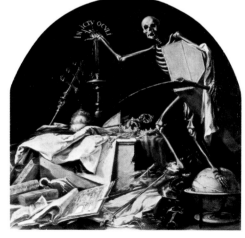

MURILLO (left)
The Immaculate Conception, c. 1655-60
The adolescent Virgin has a beauty at once serene and humble. The subtle drawing of her ascending figure, the rich broad blue of her mantle on its gently balanced diagonal, make this, among Murillo's many versions of the subject, one of the most attractive.

VALDES LEAL (above)
The triumph of Death, 1672
A quite unambiguous moral, gruesome chaos and violent religiosity pervade this whole allegorical series, painted for a hospital. Here Death extinguishes Life's flame. Mounds upon mounds of superbly painted still life describe the range of human activity to which Death puts a horrible end.

Velazquez: Las Meninas

Diego Rodríguez de Silva y Velásquez (1599-1660) was trained and began his independent career in Seville, painting mainly still lifes and scenes of peasants, who sometimes play a part in a religious story. His early works exhibit the Caravaggesque influence dominant in Spain, without the emphatic tonal contrasts of such *tenebrismo* painters as Zurbarán.

Almost abruptly, in 1623, he became court painter in Madrid, and thereafter until his death his prime concern was portraiture. He admired Rubens (who with characteristic generosity seems to have persuaded him to go to Italy in 1629-31), and was the exact contemporary of van Dyck and of Bernini, yet his portraiture in its sobriety is the antithesis of their Baroque rhetoric and elaboration. Velazquez extracted the essence of aristocracy – or, for that matter, of childhood or dwarfdom – in simplicity and dignity. He worked directly on to the canvas, usually, it seems, without preliminary drawings, realizing the physical form of his subject not so much in rhythmic line (as Rubens did) as by an immensely subtle tonal analysis in little touches – observe the smallness of the brushes on his palette in *"Las Meninas"*. His art is one of meditative observation rather than of overt expression or energetic composition – he admired Titian, but apparently actively disliked Raphael.

He himself summarized the complexity of his art in his famous *"Las Meninas"* (The maids of honour, finished in 1656). Here, seemingly, we have the painter at work in his studio, which has been invaded by the little Infanta (momentarily poised for admiration) with her suite – her attendant maids and her dwarf, who echoes the royal child so grotesquely, and a great dog. At the far end of the room, an enigmatic figure turned against a flare of light looks back as he mounts the stairs beyond an open door. Beside this figure are the framed images, shadowy and silvery, of the King and Queen, with two large paintings hung above. Each and every one is solidly there, established unerringly back from the foreground light into the shadowed depths of the great room, set in pyramid groupings interlocking across the surface. *"Las Meninas"* was once known as *The family*, and seems to be an assertion of the artist's pride and right of place in the royal hierarchy. But if you ask what is on the front of the huge canvas he is painting, or where the King and Queen in the mirror are standing, then the picture reveals ever richer ambiguities, in subject matter as in formal construction.

"Las Meninas" owes much to Velazquez's second stay in Italy, 1649-51, which forged his mature style. Freshly inspired by Venetian painting, he reached a new command of singing colour and a brilliant, liquid handling revealed in the portrait he made in Rome of Pope Innocent X (reproduced in vol. 3, p. 234) or in another set piece, probably painted before *"Las Meninas"*, *The tapestry weavers*, which again has layers of meaning.

Manet and the Impressionists would be fascinated by the way in which Velazquez could catch with unerring accuracy not the mere physical substance, say the hairs of a dog, literally recounted, but the essence of its appearance in light, its gleam in the eye.

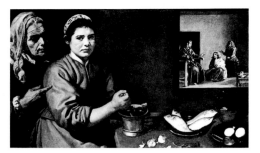

VELAZQUEZ (left)
Christ in the house of Martha and Mary, 1618
The figures and objects are observed with close intensity in strong light, but even in this early genre scene Velazquez was already conjuring with his subject matter, with small but vital ambiguities: is the background scene a picture on the wall or a glimpse through to a second room? The serious and enigmatic expression of the younger woman and the clear gesture of the older – echoing that of Martha in the scene behind – suggest that this is a meditation by two servants on a Gospel story intimately related to their calling. The objects may then take on symbolic meaning, and the work is deepened, enriched.

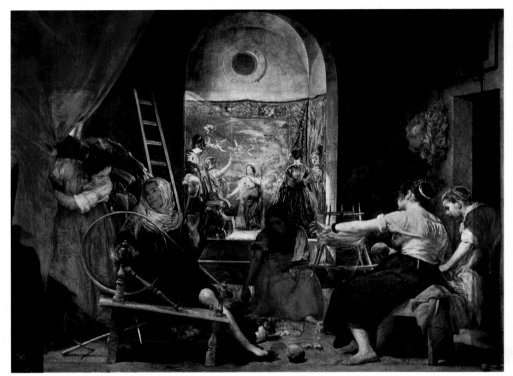

VELAZQUEZ (above)
The tapestry weavers, c. 1654
Beneath the realism of the picture (in his rendering of the spinning-wheel's blurred spokes Velazquez anticipates photography) there is a tacit reference to the myth of Arachne, who boasted her spinning was the equal even of the goddess Athena's. Note the interplay of separately lit spaces, and the movement.

VELAZQUEZ (below)
Philip IV, 1634-35
Like Rubens, like van Dyck, Velazquez based his royal portraits on Titian's prototypes – there were many Titians in the Spanish royal collection. Velazquez's less flamboyant portraiture expresses much the same ideal of a Baroque monarch as do his great contemporaries – splendour and decorum achieved with perfectly relaxed ease.

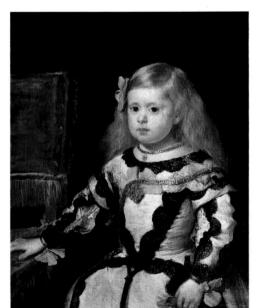

VELAZQUEZ (above)
The Infanta Margarita, c. 1656
The portrait of the little royal princess who is seen again in *"Las Meninas"*, painted at about the same time, shows a similar pose without repetition: the fall of light and the textures are observed entirely afresh. It is easy to see how much Velazquez could offer the Impressionists – the bold pattern, the liquid purity and truthfulness of colour.

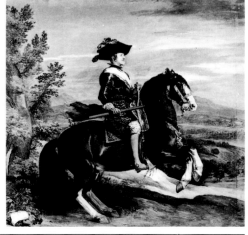

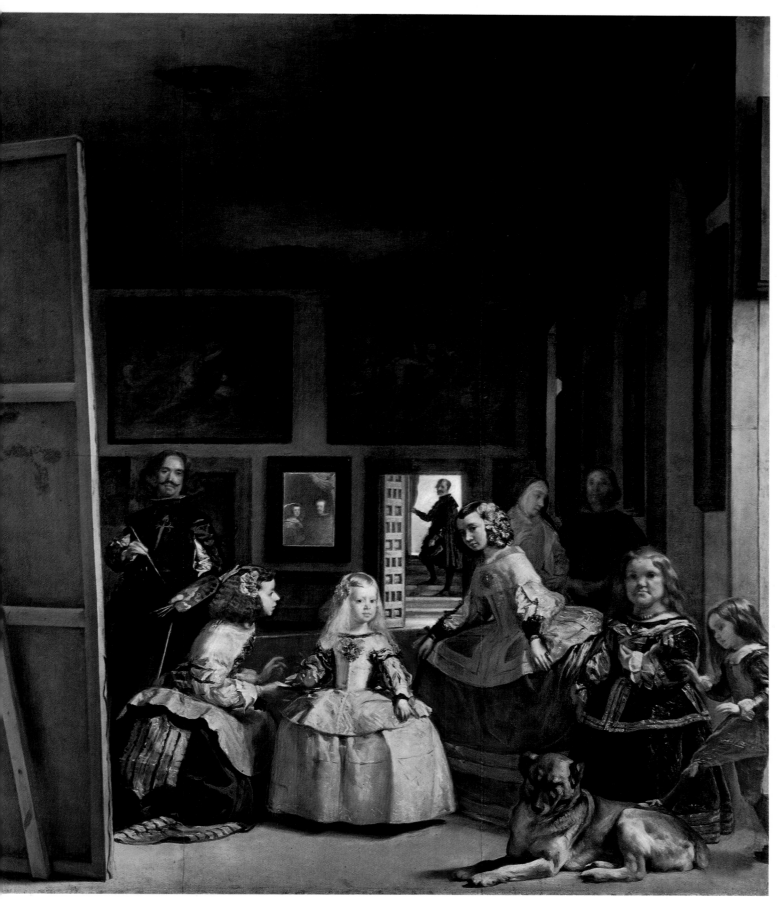

VELAZQUEZ: "*Las Meninas*" (The maids of honour), 1656

Art in the Dutch Republic

In 1555 the 17 provinces comprising the Netherlands had been made over by the Emperor Charles V to his son Philip II, King of Spain. Soon afterwards a bitter struggle for independence from Spanish dominion began, and by the Twelve Years Truce of 1609 the seven provinces that lay north of the great river estuaries (modern Holland) achieved their religious and political – Protestant and democratic – freedom. The other provinces, as Flanders, remained Catholic under the autocratic Spanish rule, and ultimately became modern Belgium. One painter stands for Flemish art in the seventeenth century – Rubens. He had a counterpart of equal if not greater stature in Holland – Rembrandt. Yet Rembrandt, though so universal a painter, cast no such spell over his contemporaries in Holland as Rubens did in Flanders. Although the art of both regions had its roots in early Netherlandish painting, the development of each was very different, and Dutch art was of astonishing variety.

Political and economic factors in Holland do not explain the sudden emergence of so many painters of the highest talent (and some of genius) but obviously they conditioned it in

some measure. The great achievements of Dutch art were not for court or Church, but for a primarily bourgeois and secular clientèle. Protestantism, especially the radical Calvinist kind predominant in Holland, permitted no images in churches; there was no hereditary aristocracy with great estates and palatial houses, and the patronage of the House of Orange at The Hague was relatively modest. The new patrons were the people, a phenomenon that astonished visitors to the country. "As for the art of painting", recorded an English traveller in Amsterdam in 1640, "and the affection of the people to Pictures, I think none other go beyond them ... all in general striving to adorn their houses, especially the outer or street room, with costly pieces. Butchers and bakers are not much inferior in their shops, which are fairly set forth: yea, many times, blacksmiths, cobblers etc. will have some picture or other by their forge and in their stall. Such is the general notion, inclination and delight that this country's natives have to painting."

Dutchmen earned the money to do this kind of shopping in a commercial boom supported by the great success of Dutch maritime en-

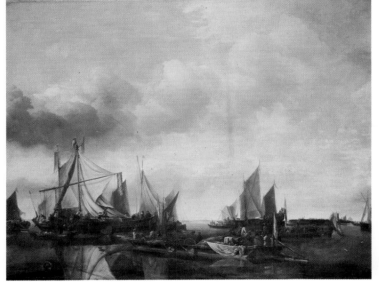

REMBRANDT
Two women teaching a child to walk, c. 1637
Realism is the keynote of Dutch art. While Rubens in Flanders founded his art on classical principles and ideal forms, Rembrandt in Holland refused to go south, or to compromise his own

vision for Italianate idiom. Rembrandt used sketches from the life almost as Rubens used a figure from a Renaissance masterpiece. Here Rembrandt catches in a few strokes the child's apprehension, and the two women's different attitudes, ages and physical strengths.

SAENREDAM (right)
St John's Church, Haarlem, 1645
Saenredam was a leading specialist in architectural painting (see p. 222). The north aisle in the picture shows the plain, bare walls typical of Dutch Protestant churches, in which art no longer had a place or function.

HOOGSTRATEN (below)
The slippers, c. 1660-75
Samuel van Hoogstraten (1627-78) had been a pupil of Rembrandt's, then spent a peripatetic career. This work shows clearly Delft influence – from Vermeer or Fabritius (see p. 228). His comfortable Dutch interior has two "cabinet" pictures, quite large of their kind. But he portrays more than a room: the slippers and keys hint at love and courting. Such symbolism is frequent in Dutch art.

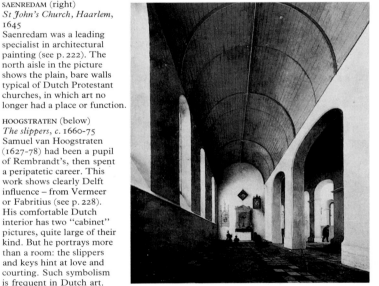

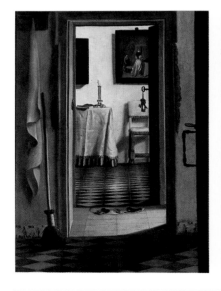

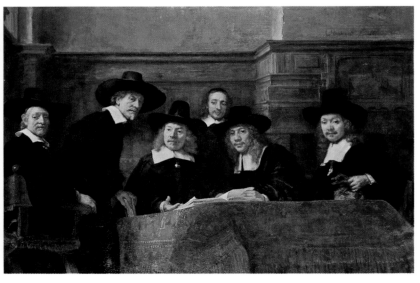

VAN DE CAPPELLE (above)
The large ferry, 1660s
Van de Cappelle's career underlines the bourgeois nature of art in Holland. He was by profession a dyer, and rich: he bought Rubens, van Dyck and Rembrandt. He painted as a hobby, and sketched for his paintings (see p. 223) from his pleasure yacht.

REMBRANDT (left)
The syndics of the Cloth Guild, 1662
The historian van Gelder commented that "five *staalmeesters*, of four different religious beliefs, in brotherly unity round a table, are a typical symbol of the power, commerce and tolerance" of the Dutch Republic. The painting is a masterpiece to rival any in the world.

deavour. As they bought for their own houses, they needed generally small-scale works; they preferred a subject matter that lay in the realm of everyday experience and reflected their own interests – those of a consumer society. They delighted in art as the "mirror of Nature" – that northern naturalism firmly established by the van Eycks and so despised by Michelangelo in Italy. They were answered by a brilliantly faithful portraiture – not only of themselves but of all aspects of life: the countryside; their streets and buildings; their ships and boats; their homes and all their contents; succulent inventories of fruit and meat; flowers, even utensils or articles of clothing; including also the *drôleries* of life, in scenes of taverns and brothels. The side of life not seen, as it had been in Bruegel, was work.

To meet the demand, artists became specialists, concentrating on one branch of art, often repeating their more successful compositions. A marketing system that was the forerunner of the modern art market emerged. Painters could sell at fairs or from their own studios, but the trade of picture-dealing was also established, many painters doubling as dealers. For many, painting was only one

means of livelihood, only one commercial outlet: the prolific landscapist van Goyen, for instance, speculated in the land he painted and (in the great tulip mania) in the tulips that grew on it; perhaps the favourite alternative occupation of artists was tavern-keeping. Many went bankrupt, though others prospered.

The two centres in which the Golden Age of Dutch painting was announced, in the first two decades of the seventeenth century, were Haarlem and Utrecht. At Haarlem local painters discerned with fresh eyes a local landscape as a subject worthy in its own right, and also the pictorial possibilities of the boisterous life of the taverns and brothels. These they exploited with a gusto of movement, a virtuosity of brushwork like that of Frans Hals, who portrayed the new patrons in the town – merchants, teachers and civic dignitaries.

Catholic Utrecht was different. Its artists were mainly oriented to Italy – the landscapists to its sunshine and to its classical associations, others, notably Gerrit van Honthorst (1590-1656) and Hendrick Terbrugghen (1588-1629; not shown), particularly to the discoveries of Caravaggio. They both went to Italy, and brought back a style delighting in the dramatic

effects of forced lighting, together with a fascination for the detail of rich materials and flesh, and for low-life subjects. Their interest in optical effects (Holland was the centre of scientific optical experiment at this time) was to be absorbed by Vermeer and refined from their often vulgar drama into the quiet silences of his unique world. Honthorst was really a cosmopolitan artist; he was a Catholic all his life (which was not in fact unusual in Holland or amongst painters there) and worked for Charles I in England before he became court painter to the House of Orange in The Hague. He specialized in quite sharply observed, rather stiff portraits, very far removed from the easy bravura of Hals or the psychological penetration of Rembrandt.

All Dutch towns of any size – Delft, Dordrecht, Alkmaar, Leyden, The Hague, Amsterdam – had their own painting industry. No one town was the capital of Dutch art. In each, strongly individual traditions and corporate prides persisted. Yet common to them all was fascination with the material substance of life; common to them also was an underlying affinity with the formal discoveries of the Baroque movement, stemming from Italy.

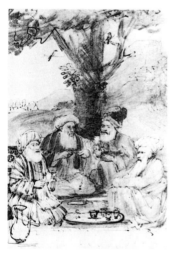

REMBRANDT (left)
Four orientals beneath a tree, c. 1655
The trade with the East that was an important part of Dutch prosperity also brought Mughal miniatures to Europe, and Rembrandt copied more than 20. This one formed the basis of his etching *Abraham entertaining the angels*, 1656.

LASTMAN (right)
Juno discovering Jupiter with Io, 1618
Jupiter had metamorphosed Io into a cow in an attempt to disguise his adultery. Lastman, one of the best exponents of the Italianate "history" painting favoured by court circles in Holland, was Rembrandt's teacher.

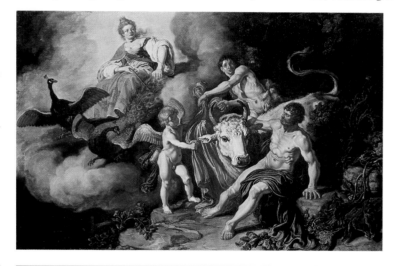

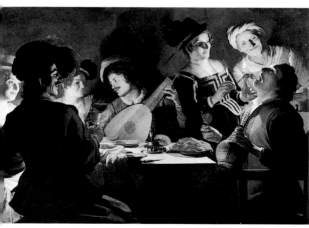

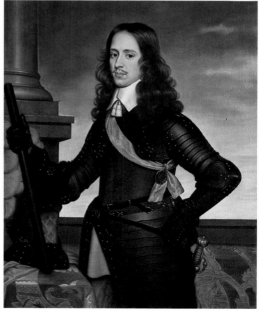

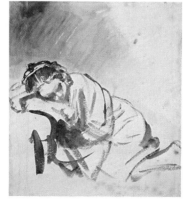

HONTHORST (above)
The banquet, 1620
This is one of the last pictures Honthorst painted in Italy, where he made his name painting night scenes. Silhouetting a figure in the foreground became a trick of the young Rembrandt.

HONTHORST (right)
William of Orange, after 1637
The pillar and the parapet are obvious props, and the whole approach is stolidly traditional. The absence of any drama was due as much to the patron as the artist.

REMBRANDT
A girl sleeping, c. 1656
The intimacy is very much Rembrandt's own, but the naturalism and spontaneity are features of Baroque art throughout Europe. The pose is from the life, and yet behind it is a profound knowledge of artistic tradition, both northern and southern.

Hals: A Banquet of the St George Civic Guard

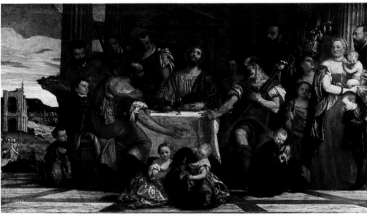

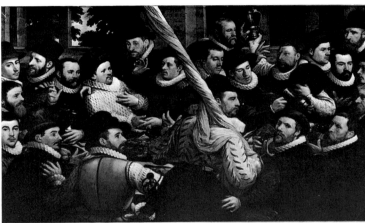

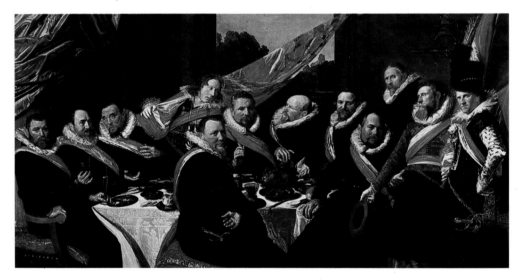

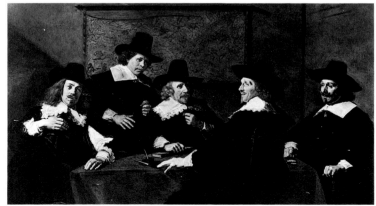

The work of Frans Hals (*c.* 1581/85-1666) is one of the inexplicable miracles of the great surge of Dutch painting in the seventeenth century. Hals was Flemish-born (which perhaps explains something of his bravura) but spent virtually his whole life in the small town of Haarlem, painting the locals. The sparse records of his career – a series of financial, domestic and legal disasters – indicate a failure to cope with life entirely at odds with the exultant vigour and spontaneity of his art.

Hals worked almost entirely in portraiture; even his genre subjects read as portraits. Hals – though it took centuries for this to be fully realized – turned mere likenesses into great pictures. His particular genius was not for "psychological insight" but the ability to capture the individual presence of his sitters and almost fling them alive on to the canvas. This he achieved by a swift, very free technique: working often with a restricted palette, he modelled, not by rounding off and smoothing out, but by a sequence of dabs, dashes and slashes that close-to can look haphazard, but then at a distance cohere into images vibrant with life. No drawings can be firmly attributed to him – he worked directly on to the canvas.

Hals' instantaneous technique and immediacy of effect make the unerring control and organization of his compositions all the more incredible. Everything is subordinate to the impact of the whole image. Consider the famous "*Laughing Cavalier*". What lingers in the memory is that not altogether explicit smile, yet the costume and all its detail is a marvel of laundering. Nowhere is Hals' spontaneous orchestration of detail better shown than in the great group portraits – Hals, as Vincent van Gogh remarked, "painted a whole glorious republic".

The group portrait of civic bodies was a Dutch speciality, beginning well back in the sixteenth century with stiff rows of individual heads. Cornelis van Haarlem (1562-1638) had succeeded in enlivening their composition, but it was Hals alone who could catch alive the brash, brilliant, vulgar ostentation of the Civic Guards at their junketing. The Civic Guards clung dearly to their memories of heroic resistance against the Spanish, but by 1616, when Hals painted his first group, their gatherings were more like the outings of a social club than military parades; although martial dress, banners and equipment were splendidly displayed, the main focus of their meetings was food and drink – consumed in indefinite banquets (the authorities tried to reduce them from a week to three days).

Hals painted the Company of St George at Haarlem three times, in 1616, in about 1627 and finally (not shown) in 1639. The 1627 composition is the most splendid: it is resolved into two groups, linked by the flash of the furled flag and by the marvellous invention of the genial and tipsy captain turning his glass upside down in the right centre. There is an explosion of colour against the purplish curtain in the background – a surf of blues, whites, reds, yellows and greens. Amidst it all each participant is sharply individual. It is a truly Baroque composition – the swirl, the emphatic diagonals; the direct technique, the colour and excitement; the naturalism and illusionism.

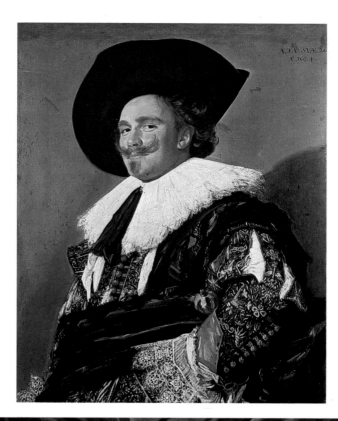

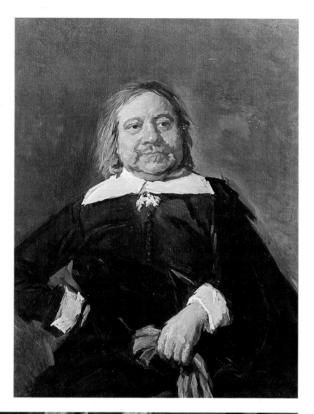

FRANS HALS (left)
"The Laughing Cavalier",
1624
Only Velazquez can rival
Hals for brushwork that
seems to live a life of its
own on the canvas. Yet
the figure is solid: the
elbow seems to jut out,
and the torso to pivot
against the background.

FRANS HALS (right)
Willem Croes, c. 1660
In his later paintings
Hals avoided complexity
of pose or brilliance of
colour, and the presence of
the sitter emerges the more
forcefully and frankly.

FRANS HALS (below)
*The banquet of the St
George Civic Guard,
c. 1627*
Each officer has more
character, and the whole
has a greater ease and
more natural variety than
had the earlier *St George*
group portrait. There the
interruption of the spec-
tator is clearly felt; here
there seems to be too much
din, the officers seem too
involved in their feasting
to pay much attention.

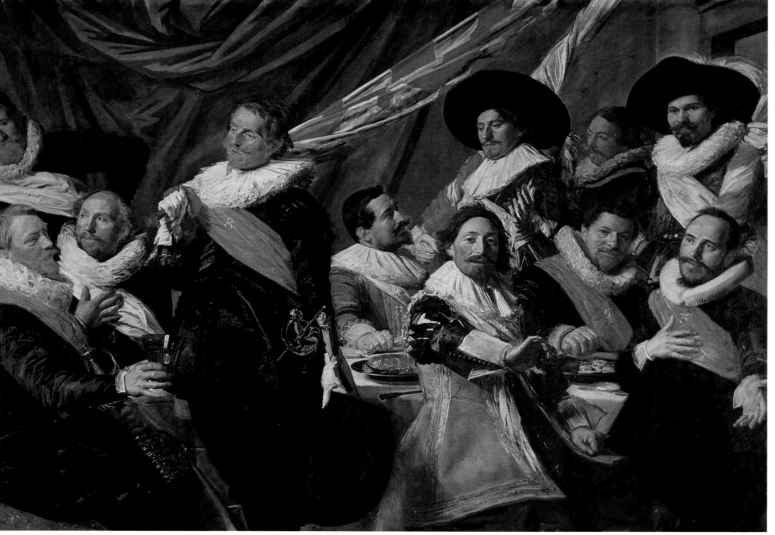

Rembrandt van Rijn

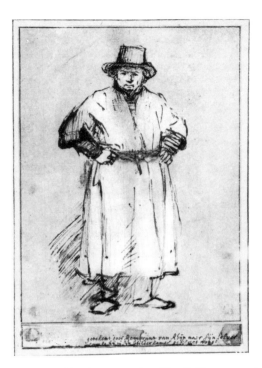

Rembrandt Harmensz. van Rijn (1606-69) is almost a separate dimension in Dutch art. His influence was felt in nearly every branch of it, and has recurred inexhaustibly in the history of art ever since. Though the broad outlines of his life are known, there are few informative details: Rembrandt himself, however, charted the moods of his career with extraordinary frankness in an unprecedented series of more than 100 *Self-portraits* (see over).

Rembrandt's early work in Leyden reflects his first master, the Amsterdam painter Pieter Lastman (see p. 213). Through him he learnt the general principles of Italian Baroque painting, especially of Caravaggio, and also of Elsheimer, which had been filtered back to Holland by the Utrecht painters. It was perhaps also Lastman who inspired the young artist to aim for the highest values in painting, attainable, according to the opinion of that time, only in "history" painting (that is, in epic, mythological or religious works). Although Rembrandt in particular was to demonstrate that these values could be revealed in any branch of art, his obsession with moral themes endured throughout his career.

His early work is dramatic, with stressed diagonals, sharp recessions, contrasts of light and shade (these are sometimes very fierce) and also hard, clear contours. His heroic characters, however, dressed in contemporary costume, sometimes as peasants, are even less idealized than Caravaggio's – even today some of his early pictures seem provocatively vulgar. For Rembrandt the Bible was a story of then, now and for ever: he was profoundly religious (in later life he became an adherent of a radical Protestant sect, the Mennonites) and his religion was profoundly rooted in real life. Rembrandt's insistence on truth – in nudes, genre, biblical scenes (often indistinguishable from genre scenes) and portraits – persisted throughout his life; his power to marry naturalism into majestic compositions of subtle design and sometimes transcendental power developed continuously. His naturalism was offset – maybe even deliberately counterpointed – by a delight in clothing groups or single figures in picturesque or romantic costume, or portraying them in dual roles, so that an epic subject, a saint or an historical figure, is also clearly a literal portrait.

By the 1630s, having moved to Amsterdam, the principal city of Holland, in 1631-32, Rem-

REMBRANDT (above)
*Self-portrait in studio attire, c.*1650-60
More than 50 pupils once in Rembrandt's studio have been identified by name; and they disseminated his style. His art was highly personal, but Rembrandt apparently needed constantly to teach.

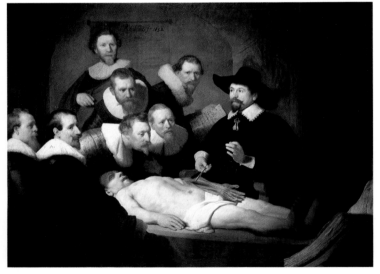

REMBRANDT (left)
The anatomy lesson of Dr Tulp, 1632
Hals' group portraits are clearly Baroque in an international sense, but *The anatomy lesson* is really not: it lacks a smoothly flowing or united composition: each figure is sharply individual and there is latent tension rather than overt violence. In the company's fascinated intentness on the corpse there is a palpable unease, almost an awareness of their own mortality. This is the first painting which Rembrandt signed with his full name, in keeping with its importance. Already the disposition of light and shade is masterly, and is a vital element of the drama. Yet the face of every man is also a precise portrait.

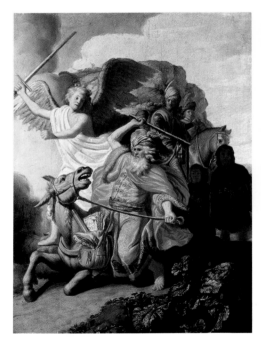

REMBRANDT (left)
Balaam, 1626
Balaam's ass halted at the sight of an angel Balaam could not see. Rembrandt's composition exaggerates an earlier one by Lastman. The richly cloaked Balaam typifies Rembrandt's love of ostentatious paintwork.

REMBRANDT (right)
The blinding of Samson, 1636
This is perhaps the most "Baroque" picture Rembrandt ever painted, probably emulating the searing drama of the Rubensian style favoured at courts. The horror is extreme, and so is the use of all the illusionistic, dramatic and violent devices dear to Baroque art. It may have been painted as a gift for Constantijn Huyghens: he greatly admired Rubens.

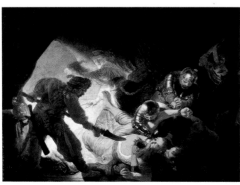

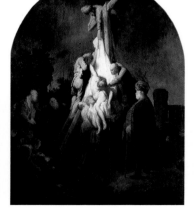

REMBRANDT (above)
The Descent from the Cross, 1633
The large costumed figure stresses the contemplative mood Rembrandt sought. He wrote that he wanted his series to express "the greatest and most natural emotion" – not movement.

REMBRANDT (above)
The return of the Prodigal Son, 1636
The etched line is febrile with the reunion's emotion.

brandt had refined the construction of his compositions, and especially his handling of the half-tones between the extremes of light and dark, and was now fully competent to organize paintings of a monumental scale. The first of his great group portraits, *The anatomy lesson of Dr Tulp*, 1632, no doubt established his reputation in Amsterdam, investing what might have been a formal group with high drama. The drama is higher still in his *Blinding of Samson*. The scope of his patronage was expanding, and, through the leading connoisseur Constantijn Huyghens, Rembrandt obtained a commission from the Stadtholder, the ruler of federal Holland, for five large *Passion* scenes. The *Passion* scenes are more characteristic of the mature Rembrandt: the mood is both dramatic and yet sombrely reflective – his *Descent from the Cross* shows an awareness of Rubens' composition in Antwerp (see p. 204) but is entirely Rembrandt's own in feeling. Christ is no elegant, ideal figure, but a broken wreck of human flesh.

Rembrandt's most famous work, *"The Night Watch"*, is also his largest – 3.5 × 4.5 metres (12 × 15 ft): finished in 1642, it marks both a climax and a turning point. Rembrandt transposed the traditional Dutch Civic Guard group into a "history" composition of stupendous drama, colour, tonal contrast and movement. Characteristically Rembrandt's is the inexplicable element, the incandescent figure of the little girl. The year 1642, however, marked the beginning of the decline of Rembrandt's financial and fashionable fortunes, and perhaps too of his personal confidence and happiness (his wife Saskia died in this year). The mood in his painting becomes ever more sombre, more searching; the paint itself both richer and more troubled; the psychological intensity of his images more impressive and haunting. The 1640s and 1650s were his most productive period for etchings – some, such as the famous Hundred-Guilder Print, as rich and complex as his major paintings – and for drawn, painted and etched landscapes (see p. 220); during the same period he made hundreds of direct and forceful drawings (usually in a thick reed-pen), tautly structured yet almost throbbing with life.

In his last two decades Rembrandt tended to simplify his compositions, rejecting his earlier highly-strung Baroque for a more classical, more stable and enduring structure. His use of paint and handling of light became ever richer and subtler. This light, charged with an intense spirituality, seems to come from within rather than from an external source. His portraits and self-portraits transcend the individual they so vividly and faithfully depict and become "intimations of the universal destiny of mankind". One of his greatest and most mysterious works, the picture known as *"The Jewish Bride"*, is conventional enough in theme – it is perhaps simply a wedding portrait of two ordinary people – but it celebrates marriage as a sacrament, a dedication in mutual love at once human and divine; formally it echoes traditional depictions of the biblical Jacob and Rachel.

Rembrandt taught pupils all through his working life, and many of them, while with him, responded to Rembrandt's vision with work of remarkable quality. Some, such as Ferdinand Bol, remained in some degree loyal to that vision throughout their careers, and Aert de Gelder, almost his last pupil, continued painting works of distinction in his style into the eighteenth century. His most able pupil was Carel Fabritius, the vital link between Rembrandt and Vermeer (see p. 228).

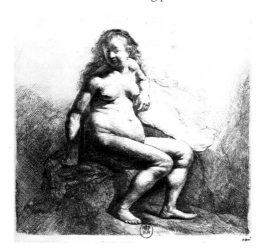

REMBRANDT (left)
Nude on a mound, 1631
In this early etching the contrasts of light and shade are heavy but the mature Rembrandt's transfiguring light is absent. The nude is a true "Venus with garter-marks": his art was always realistic, but later not so rebelliously unidealistic.

REMBRANDT (right)
"The Night Watch" (The Company of Frans Banning Cocq and Willem van Ruytenburch), 1642
A pupil wrote in 1678: "It is so painter-like in thought, so dashing in movement, and so powerful" that the pictures hanging beside it seem "like playing cards".

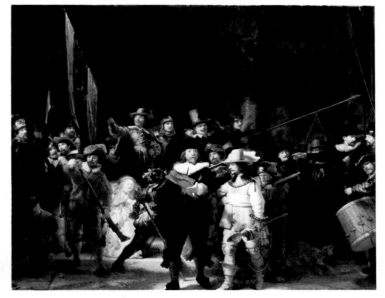

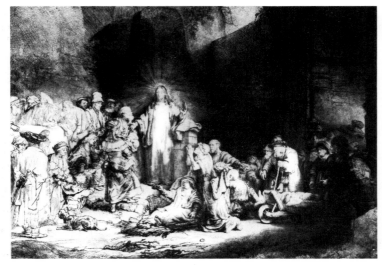

REMBRANDT (above)
The Hundred-Guilder
Print: *Christ healing the sick*, c. 1648-50
The etching, known by the very large price it fetched, is most carefully worked. Rembrandt made use both of drawings from life and of Renaissance sources – notably engravings after Leonardo's *Last Supper*.

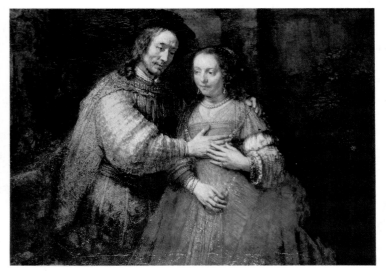

REMBRANDT (right)
"The Jewish Bride",
c. 1665
The silence seems to echo; the light seems spiritual, emanating from the figures.

Rembrandt: The Self-Portrait at Kenwood

The main course of Rembrandt's life is fairly clear – his birth in Leyden in 1606; his early success (with pupils even in his twenty-first year) in his home town; in the 1630s, fashionable prosperity in Amsterdam; then the decline in popularity, the death of his wife Saskia in 1642; financial mismanagement, culminating in bankruptcy and the enforced sale of his superb art collection in 1656/57; the deaths of his common-law wife Hendrickje Stoffels in 1663 and of his only son Titus in 1668; his own death in 1669.

The recorded facts reveal little about one of the greatest artists in history, rivalled in scope of imagination and universal appeal perhaps only by Shakespeare. But the skeleton provided by the documents is endowed with both flesh and spirit by the sequence of *Self-portraits* – more than 100 drawings, etchings or paintings, ranging from his beginnings as an artist to the last year of his life. They constitute the most remarkable autobiography ever painted, and culminate in the searching self-interrogations of Rembrandt's last decade: amongst these the three-quarter-length portrait at Kenwood, London, is one of the most impressive and haunting.

In almost all the late *Self-portraits*, the demand that the spectator identify with the artist is irresistible: he looks at himself, searching; you look at him; he looks at you. In some of these portraits, Rembrandt is very much the Protestant, holding his human identity clear of the dark as if by sheer will-power – alone with himself, uncertain perhaps if man is made in the image of God but determined to find out. The search for identity is there even in the earliest portraits, though these are often clearly studies, exercises in capturing momentary expression. The Dresden double portrait with Saskia, of his brash middle years in Amsterdam, is also a brash image, Rembrandt exultant at his fortune and rather vulgarly unconcerned with the dignity of his station (compare Rubens' similar portrait, p. 202). The element of role-playing, as in the London National Gallery portrait, where he is posed and clad like a Titian portrait then believed to represent the prince of poets, Ariosto, persists almost to the end. But in one of the last of all (also in the London National Gallery) Rembrandt, hands folded, quietly resigned on the threshold of death – but in his paint still vital with life – records simply himself.

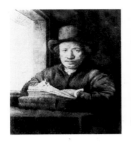

REMBRANDT (above)
Self-portrait drawing by a window, 1648
The pose and setting recall the many paintings and etchings Rembrandt made of scholars or of saints seated in a room by a window: in comparison and contrast the artist appears as an earnest, prosaic burgher – his hat completes the image.

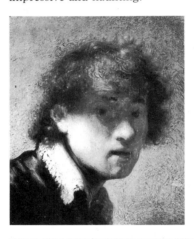

REMBRANDT (left)
Self-portrait in Munich, detail, c. 1629
Like Caravaggio (see p. 180) Rembrandt wants to catch a momentary start in paint, and exploits sharp contrasts of light and shade to do so – but also introduces mystery.

REMBRANDT (right)
Self-portrait in Berlin, detail, 1634
The somewhat mysterious drama of the portrait (left) is retained; there is now more of a swagger: the boisterous youth yields to a romantic, but hardly less truculent, young man.

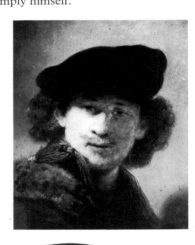

REMBRANDT (right)
Self-portrait at Kenwood, London, c. 1665
Against the predominant dark brown to red of the whole, the focus is on the lighter key of the face, the grey hair, the cap almost slashed on to the canvas. The face is old, seen without vanity or flattery. No one knows the meaning of the semicircles incised on the background: if they hint at a possible ideal order, the ruggedness of the face contradicts them sharply. There is paradox again in the rich fur of the robe and the workaday context. Tools of the trade are perfectly legible from a distance, but closely inspected become ambiguous. Seen closer still, they are like pure paint energized, and the hand holding them is just a brusque zigzag of paint dragged down, diminishing as the brush unloads. Rembrandt had no truck with the kind of art that conceals the art: he left his workings bare and one of his few remarks on record is a warning to connoisseurs not to expect high finish: "Don't poke your nose into the painting or the smell will kill you."

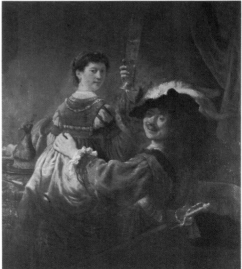

REMBRANDT
Self-portrait with Saskia, c. 1635
Of the bold self-conscious bravura there is no doubt; but beyond that the interpretations vary: is there some unease? What does Saskia think of it all? The still life and raised glass recall genre tavern scenes, with a moral undertone.

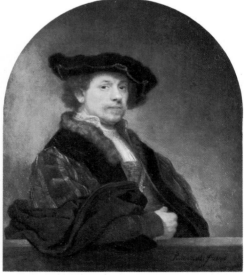

REMBRANDT
Self-portrait after Titian's "Ariosto", 1640
Both Titian's "*Ariosto*" and Raphael's *Castiglione* (see p. 129) had passed through the Amsterdam sale-rooms in 1639. The more mature Rembrandt's interest in Renaissance art was increasing, and was to be reflected in his painting.

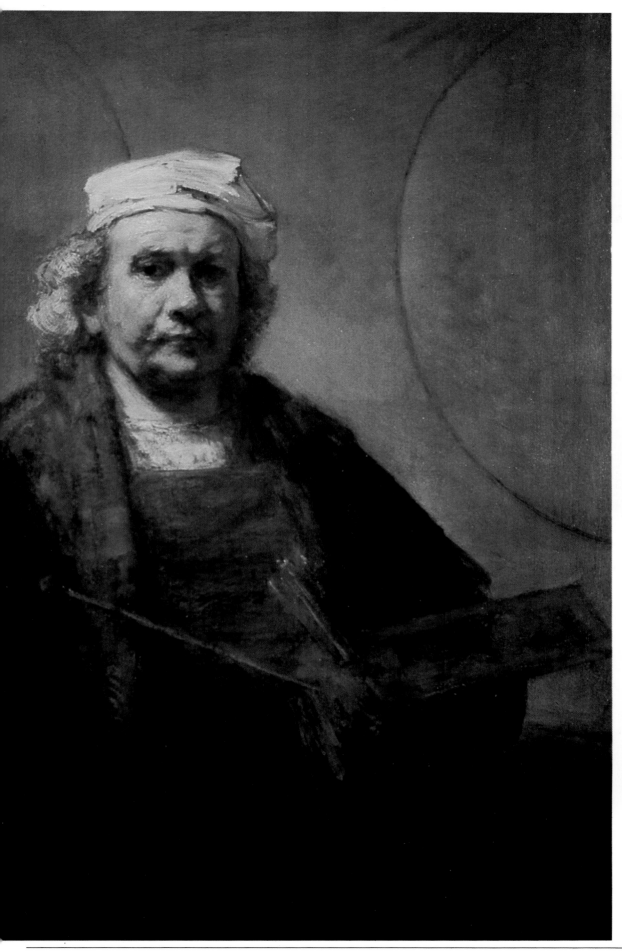

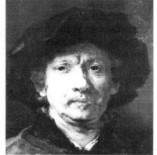

REMBRANDT
Self-portrait in Vienna,
detail, 1652
The later self-portraits
are mostly frontal – the
painter face to face with
himself. Rembrandt by this
time was painting probably
more for himself than for
clients or on commission.

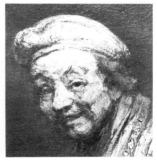

REMBRANDT
Self-portrait in Cologne,
detail, *c.* 1669
The image is undeniably
grotesque – Rembrandt as
a genre old man. However,
he peers from the shadows
with a bruised grin: the
vigour and freedom of
the impasto asserts life.

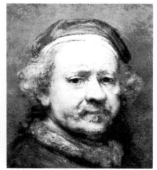

REMBRANDT
Self-portrait in London,
detail, 1669
The lonely suffering of
Rembrandt's last years
(with Hendrickje dead, his
son Titus dead, aged 27)
is never more than hinted
at even in his latest *Self-
portraits.* Their dignity is
powerful, utterly honest.

Dutch Landscape 1

"Landscape" was originally a Dutch word, established in the late sixteenth century. By then, the particular talents of Netherlandish, and especially Flemish, artists in the painting of earth and sky, woods and water were widely recognized, though the northern bent for landscape was much older than that: it had already been apparent in the miniature illuminations of the Limbourg brothers at the beginning of the fifteenth century, and in the sixteenth century in the panoramic settings of Bruegel's works. Until the seventeenth century, however, landscape had generally remained a setting or a stage for religious or mythological events; it was particularly the Dutch who found in the landscape itself a sufficient story-line, even a heroic quality.

The emergence of landscape painting in Holland was part of the general Protestant withdrawal from religious art: a changed clientèle demanded from artists a different subject matter and new aesthetic values. Pictures of the land, the fatherland for which they had fought, naturally appealed to a people that had just achieved its independence, and the countryside was an integral part of the daily life they loved to record in all its aspects,

capturing its reflection indoors, stabilizing its impermanence, in small easel-paintings.

Within the highly talented output of the early Dutch landscape artists, two main moods can be distinguished. One was more naturalistic – in extreme form, topography, mapping exactly the features of a given place at a given time; the other was an ideal vision. Even the most naturalistic landscapes, however, were all painted indoors, though built up on the basis of drawings sketched on the spot. Dutch ideal landscape, generally called Italianate, is suffused with nostalgia for a golden Mediterranean light and a climate in which a gentler way of life might flourish; it is parallel in form to, and partly dependent on, the work of Annibale Carracci, Domenichino and Claude

(see p. 196), though usually less dreamy and artificial, peopled with more homely figures.

The discovery of the local landscape was sparked off by a Flemish influx – refugees from the fighting that ended in the capitulation of Antwerp to the Spanish in 1585. It took shape – like many other forms of Dutch painting – in Haarlem, where in 1585 settled Gillis van Coninxloo (1544-1607). His work in Antwerp (and elsewhere) had been fully Mannerist, showing a relish for landscape but using it as a stage-set for his figures. He followed his predecessors in adopting a high viewpoint, sometimes even approaching a bird's-eye view, with much more land than sky. In his later work, the figures became less important, and were almost lost in the fantastic wooded scenes that he

CONINXLOO (below)
The forest, c. 1600
Coninxloo's pictures were popular as "poetic visions of the primeval wilderness". His figures are costumed, as if acting in a play; the landscape, too, is fanciful, but trees and shrubs are observed naturalistically, and there is a deliberate play of light and shade.

SEGHERS (right)
Landscape, c. 1630
Unlike artists such as Coninxloo, Seghers built up his landscapes in tonal masses. These tonal masses are the whole composition: in a sense, the landscape is neither real nor imaginary; it represents only a mood. His etchings have similar effects of light and dark.

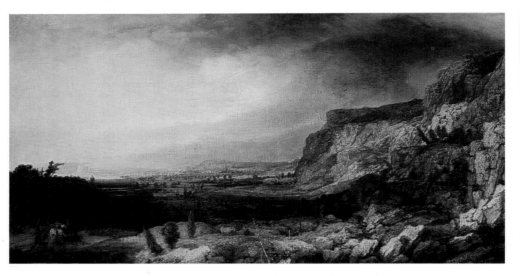

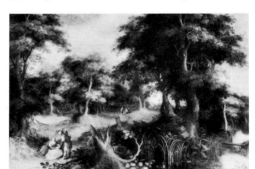

AVERCAMP (right)
Winter landscape, c. 1610
The high horizon is a sure mark of the picture's early date. The figures are disposed at careful intervals so as to lead the eye from detail to detail and back into space. Though the picture is thus artificially composed, the whites of ice and sky are convincingly wintry.

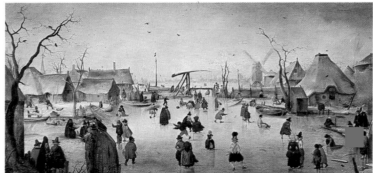

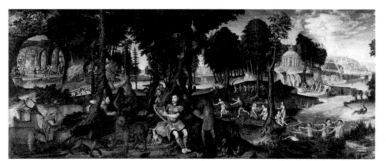

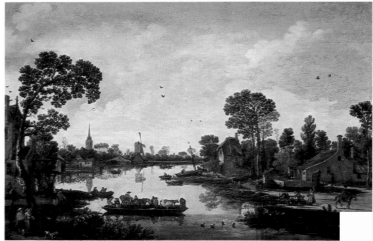

SAVERY (above)
Orpheus charming the animals, c. 1625
Savery's picture is more obviously Mannerist than Coninxloo's, though later. The trees, however, and the exotic animals are observed with even closer naturalism.

ESAIAS VAN DE VELDE (right)
The ferry-boat, 1622
Some of Esaias' landscapes are so full of figures and action that they could as well be called genre. Note that the tones lighten in the distance, as they do not in Avercamp's picture.

loved, though he kept to established conventions. His views were framed between two strong elements in the foreground (*repoussoirs*) and his colours proceeded in a standard formula from warmish browns in the foreground through shades of green into a bluish distance.

Coninxloo's followers included the Flemish-born Roelandt Savery (*c.*1576-1639) and David Vinckboons. The indigenous Dutch tradition, however, can be said to start with Hendrick Avercamp (1585-1634), probably a pupil of Coninxloo. Though still using many of the same conventions, Avercamp painted landscapes without a story, filled instead with the details of everyday life. He is most famous now for his winter landscapes, ice-covered rivers thronged with people, in which the hiss of skates on the ice and the voices sharp on the crisp air are almost audible. A far greater talent, indeed one of the original geniuses of the whole movement, was Hercules Seghers (1589/90-*c.*1635), who certainly trained under Coninxloo. He was born in Haarlem but worked also in Amsterdam and The Hague. His life is obscure – apparently much troubled – and his paintings are few. It was through his etchings, remarkable both in technique and imagery, that he was mainly known, although Rembrandt owned no fewer than eight of his paintings. Seghers' view of the world was grand yet desolate, with figures and buildings subordinate to a sweeping panorama of plains and arid mountains – brooding, often hostile, and charged with awe. Despite the vast distances they convey, his paintings are small in scale, and in a very restricted palette.

Esaias van de Velde (*c.*1591-1630), from Amsterdam, was perhaps also a pupil of Coninxloo. His vision seems to have been more generally influential and was certainly much less disturbing than Seghers'. He became the leader of the Haarlem landscapists, delighting in the detail of outdoor life as had Coninxloo, but lowering the viewpoint and the horizon, and developing a method of atmospheric, or tonal, recession. In paintings such as *The ferry-boat* he established the main themes to be developed by the next generation. Pieter van Laer, who painted street-scenes and beggars in Rome, where he was known as Bamboccio (see p. 192), was also a product of Haarlem.

The Italianate painters developed from the example of the long-lived, prolific and versatile Abraham Bloemaert (1564-1651; not shown) of Utrecht. His pupils, unlike him, all visited Italy, and came to see nature in terms of the sunny Roman Campagna, peopled with agreeably picturesque rustics and their animals. The likeness of the work of Jan Both (*c.*1618-52), of Cornelis van Poelenburgh (*c.*1586-1667) or of Breenbergh to Claude's is clear, though theirs lacks the variety and invention, and the superbly serene structure, of the Frenchman's art. The most successful of the Italianate landscapists was the prolific Nicolaes Berchem (1620-83); his work, devoid of the grandeur and heroics of Claude, was pleasurably and immediately digestible for generations of picture-lovers.

The Dutch landscapists who travelled to Italy had taken varying note of the miniatures of the German Elsheimer (see p. 196), but his work found a stronger echo in the painted landscapes of Rembrandt – almost doom-laden scenes (see p. 224) strongly influenced by Seghers. In his landscape etchings and drawings Rembrandt encompassed and surpassed the range of the specialists, above all in his elegiac meditations on the simplest of country views, transformed into breathing air by a miraculously economic use of line.

BOTH AND POELENBURGH (below) *Landscape with the Judgment of Paris*, undated The landscape is Both's, the figures Poelenburgh's. The landscape is constructed by means other than those of "native" landscape, though detail is no less naturalistic.

BERCHEM (right) *The crab-fishers*, undated There is no sense of the classical past in Berchem: even his ruins are haunted by cows, and picturesque rather than evocative. He could almost be described as a painter of rustic genre.

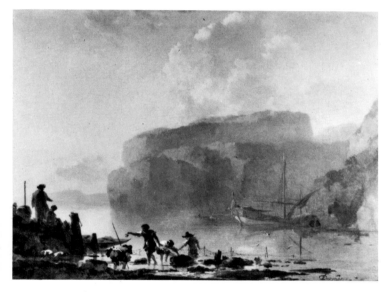

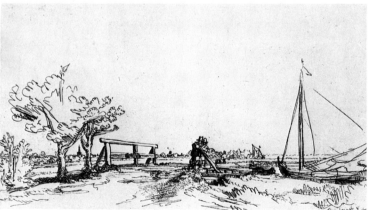

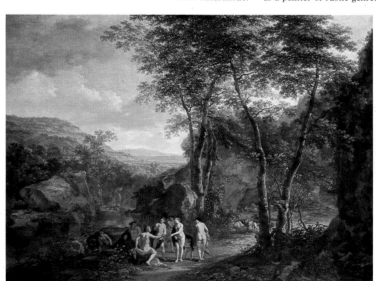

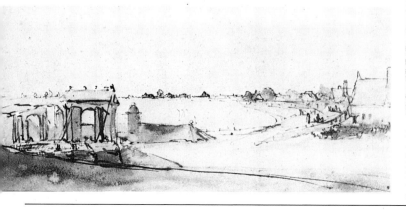

REMBRANDT (left) *Landscape with a village*, *c.*1650 Rembrandt's ink-and-wash landscapes are like van Goyen's compositions (see over) reduced to a skeleton.

REMBRANDT (above) *"Six's Bridge"*, 1645 The etching needle shapes one tree, then another; then the firm outline of a bridge rail; two little figures, a far horizon, the mast of a boat.

The assurance and exact power of Rembrandt's line are stupendous. Though the traditional title is wrong, this is a topographical view, and the bridge and village have been identified.

Dutch Landscape 2: "Classic"

In the wake of the pioneers of Dutch naturalistic landscape, Seghers or Esaias van de Velde, the discovery of the Dutch countryside really began – its endless flatness, laced with water; its endless skies for ever changing in wind, sun and cloud. The prolific painter and draughtsman Jan van Goyen (1596-1656) was the most remarkable figure of the first generation, based in The Hague from 1631 till his death, but an insatiable traveller.

Following van de Velde, who taught him for a time, he developed still further the emphasis on landscape. He lowered the horizon, so that the vista is observed generally from eye-level, and the elements in it are very much the commonplace ones that a Dutchman would see as he went about his ordinary business. Though held in tension by a system of shallow diagonals, his compositions seem indefinitely extensible on either side, and their flat horizontals are emphasized by the proportions of the picture, usually much wider than it is tall. His palette is almost monochrome, containing no more than browns, thin greens and muted yellows, and the grey tones of an overcast northern day. The cloud formations in the dominant sky are used to establish a mood. His

views are often identifiable, the silhouettes of known towns, churches and windmills fretting the far horizon. This delight in the portraiture of places was soon extended, in the work of other painters, to include meticulous records of streets and towns, the façades of buildings, the interiors of churches.

Salomon van Ruysdael (c. 1600-70), uncle of the more famous Jacob, a contemporary of van Goyen, spent a very successful career entirely in Haarlem. His paintings of the 1630s, especially his views over broad sheets of water, could easily be mistaken for van Goyen's. Gradually, however, his work became less austere, his palette richer, his subject matter somewhat more animated: both life and weather seem more cheerful, and there are sometimes quite colourful effects in the sky. Aert van der Neer (c. 1603-77) used again a restricted palette for his famous moonlight scenes (not shown); also working in Haarlem was the most remarkable of those artists who specialized in townscape or architectural painting, Pieter Saenredam (1597-1665). He painted little else other than the whitewashed interiors of churches, brimming with pale light through clear windows, empty and silent. The

diminutive figures exist, it seems, solely to establish the soaring scale of the vaulted roofs.

Between about 1640 and 1670 Dutch landscape reached its full maturity, its so-called "classic" phase as distinct from the "tonal" phase exemplified in van Goyen's and Seghers' paintings. The "classic" phase in its various moods consolidated the naturalistic discoveries of the "native" Dutch observers, such as van de Velde and van Goyen, with a truly Baroque strength and richness. Painters such as Berchem had been captivated by the reflection of Italian sunlight and the picturesque detail of the Mediterranean scene; artists such as Cuyp and Ruisdael were more deeply influenced by the Italianate tradition.

Aelbert Cuyp (1620-91) of Dordrecht painted sky, land and water suffused by a golden light much more Italian than Dutch, but the light grips and harmonizes the whole landscape: it is an integral, essential and extremely beautiful ·element in his achievement. He seems never to have gone to Italy, only to have studied its reflection lingering in the work of his contemporaries who had been there. Yet there is no greater master of sublime serenity in visionary landscape than Cuyp, besides

VAN GOYEN (below)
View of the village of Overschie, c. 1645
The details are just like those of Esaias van de Velde (see preceding page). But here the sensation of looking out over an artificially constructed stage has disappeared: diagonals (and the vertical spire) give the picture structure and, much more naturally, lend a subtler symmetry.

JACOB VAN RUISDAEL
(right) *View of Haarlem, 1660s*
The clouds are a powerful force, and strong contrasts of light and dark move over the face of the land.

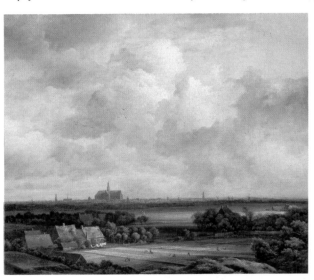

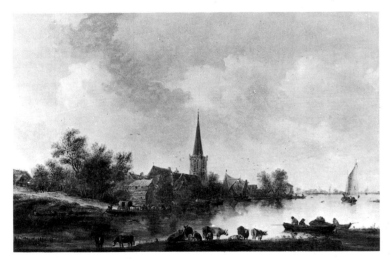

SAENREDAM (right)
St Bavo, Haarlem, 1660
The view shows the choir, wholly austere except for its patterned vaulting. The picture is quite small, and with virtually no colour; but the perspective, and the modelling of convex and concave surfaces, are extremely subtle; the tonal modulations of the airy space are exquisitely controlled. There is a quiet intimacy. Another view by Saenredam is reproduced on p. 212.

SALOMON VAN RUYSDAEL
(left) *View of a river, 1630s or early 1640s*
Salomon tended to paint a little more precisely than van Goyen, but could fix a gentle afternoon as freshly. He has none of the drama of his nephew Jacob (above). Note the subtle symmetry between the two uprights, the tree and the small sail.

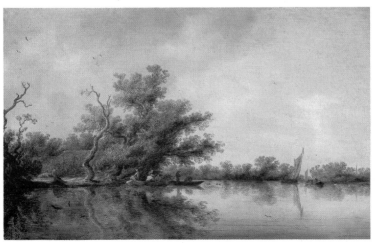

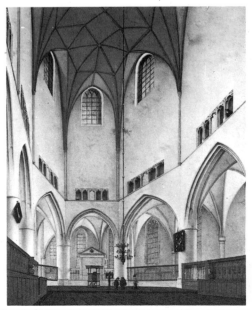

Claude himself. But while Claude peopled his Roman Campagna with figures from classical mythology, the Dutchman achieved a no less mysterious transcendence with a mundane cast of cows, horses and his stolid compatriots. The composition is usually anchored on the figures, human or animal, in silhouette at one side of the foreground; the landscape winds, often across water, back deep into the distance under a paradisal sky of late evening.

Cuyp's cows became, in the paintings of the young Paulus Potter (1625-54), the chief subject of the landscape, though the same cool golden light played about the variegated texture of their hides. Cuyp also loved to paint great sheets of water, with ships becalmed above their own reflections, and in this the Amsterdam painter Jan van de Cappelle (c. 1624-79) specialized. Van de Cappelle indeed could surpass even Cuyp in the magic of his dreams of sailing ships afloat like wraiths between sky and water, yet intricately and firmly structured by their lofty masts and sails and the dark horizontals of their hulls. Cuyp and van de Cappelle confined themselves to rivers or estuaries, but the two Willem van de Veldes went out to the open sea: Willem the

Younger (1633-1707) could achieve a majestic composition to rival in strength any by his contemporaries – as in his *Cannon shot*; later he and his father both migrated to England, and established marine painting there.

The greatest genius of Dutch landscape, unsurpassed in his power to endow it with heroic significance till then thought commensurable only with religious or epic painting, was Jacob van Ruisdael. His "tragic" work is considered, in relation to his famous *Jewish cemetery*, in the next pages. But his mood could also be gently pastoral, taking pleasure in the movement of the landscape, the changing pattern of sun and shadow. Ruisdael had no standard formulae: his trees are individuals; so, too, are his clouds; the humid air of Holland seems to move amongst them. In this his one-time pupil Meindert Hobbema (1638-1709) could rival him in strength, though Hobbema employed a limited range of compositional devices, and his work in mass can seem monotonous. Yet each one on inspection proves as sharply observed, as freshly painted, as Ruisdael's. His paintings as a whole show a much more cheerful and optimistic temper – Ruisdael with sunshine.

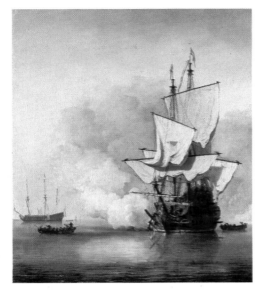

WILLEM VAN DE VELDE
THE YOUNGER
The cannon shot, c. 1660
In the "classic" phase of
Dutch landscape painting

the objects or elements in the picture were certainly naturalistic; but, more than that, they were dynamically organized to striking effect.

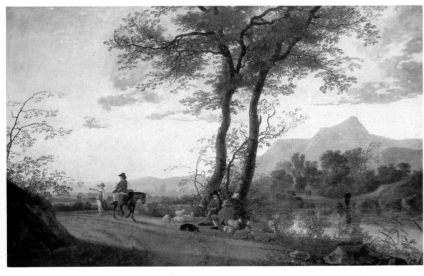

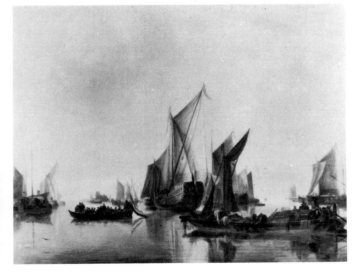

CUYP (above)
*View of a road near
a river*, mid-1650s
The colours are autumnal; it is peaceful early evening. If the light is Italianate, the structure – particularly the mountain on the right – is a development from Seghers' compositions.

POTTER (below)
Cows resting, 1649
Potter's light has not the quiet calm and airy repose of the great masters – his golden light is sometimes cloying. Yet he was both precocious and successful, and his smaller pictures are gloriously textured.

VAN DE CAPPELLE (above)
*View of the mouth of the
river Scheldt, c.* 1650?
In contrast to others, van de Cappelle favoured firm central motifs. The middle-ground boats are solid, but sky and water dissolve all around into a haze, being unbounded by any sharp horizon and unfixed by any foreground mass. Another scene by van de Cappelle is illustrated on p. 212.

HOBBEMA (left)
The avenue at Middelharnis,
1689
In the last three decades of the century, landscape – and other kinds of painting – declined in quality. Few artists kept that "classic" balance between naturalism and contrivance of Hobbema's late landscape.

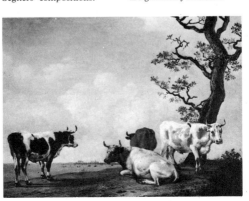

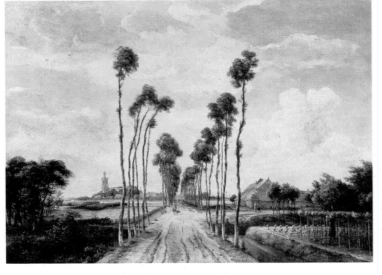

Ruisdael: The Jewish Cemetery

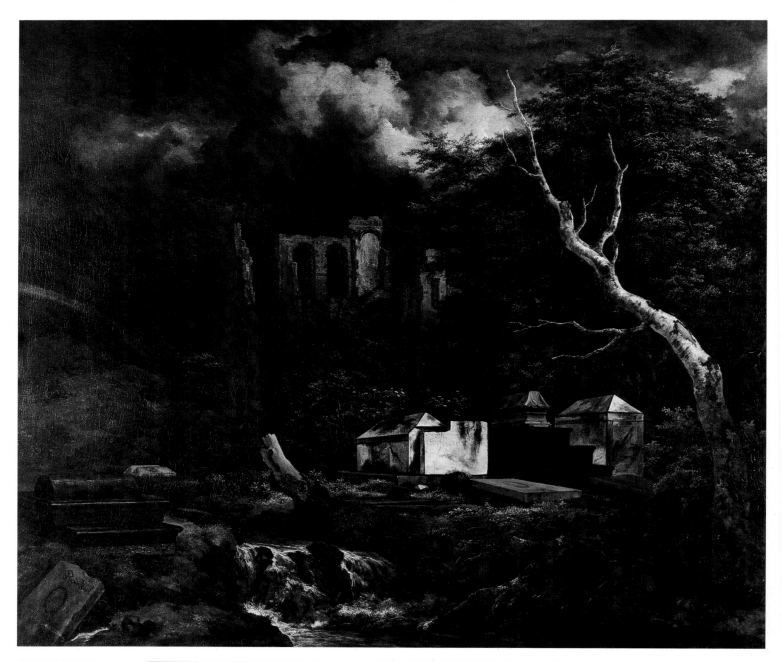

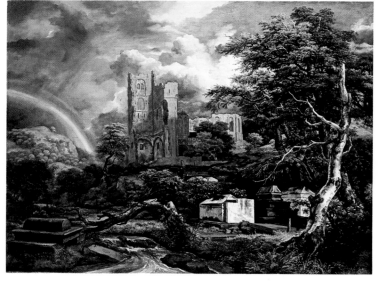

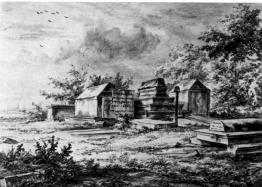

JACOB VAN RUISDAEL
(above) The Dresden
Jewish cemetery, 1660s
There are no figures, no
animals: the tombs are the
central characters; trees,
buildings, sky, a stream
and the changing light are
the supporting cast. Each is
charged with an animating,
transfiguring atmosphere.

JACOB VAN RUISDAEL
(right) The Detroit
Jewish cemetery, 1660s
In this version the mood
seems warmer: the trees,
for instance, are less stark;
the desertion is not quite so
absolute: there is a cottage
amid the ruins, and two
small, black-robed figures.

JACOB VAN RUISDAEL
*Tombs in the Jewish ceme-
tery at Ouderkerk, c.* 1660
The positions of the tombs
have been slightly altered
in the paintings, but they
retain their striking shapes.

So, too, the other elements
were no doubt closely based
on observation from life,
though even the drawing
has been organized into a
composition – the birds in
the sky, the placed trees.

The tragic drama of nature is felt in most of the paintings of Jacob van Ruisdael (1628/9-82), but only in the two versions of *The Jewish cemetery* is it so explicit, and the symbolism so overt. The strongest accents in the composition, in each case, are the tombs, painted "from the life", as is proved by two drawings and by the tombs themselves, still to be seen in the Jewish cemetery at Ouderkerk near Amsterdam. They catch the eye not only because of their near-central position, but because the light of the lowering sun picks them out and a tree almost points to them. Simultaneously amid the dark rain clouds kindles a rainbow – the age-old symbol of hope and Resurrection.

In both versions, the cluster of the tombs is identical, but otherwise the paintings vary considerably, in the whole and in the rest of the details. The surrounding landscapes, for all their vivid presence, are fantasies. Both versions are presumably of the 1660s, though which is the earlier is uncertain. The Dresden version is the more sombre, the rainbow more tentative, the ruined church a different building much further gone in decay, sunk deeper in oncoming night. (Note, however, how important in each version is the vertical accent of the ruined flank of the building, holding the light and stabilizing the whole composition.) As Constable was to observe, Ruisdael enveloped the most ordinary scenes with grandeur, and in his work as a whole – with its evocation of melancholy and its drama of light and shade – the Romantic movement would find a prophet of its own feelings towards Nature; Goethe, however, analysed a profounder poetry in this composition: "Even the tombs themselves, in their state of ruin, signify something more than the past: they are tombs of themselves".

Ruisdael developed that combination of realism and romanticism found in a greater or lesser degree in all his mature work from the example of his predecessors and contemporaries. His fascination with trees is reminiscent of the late Mannerist follower of Coninxloo, Savery; his ability to consolidate the facts of earth, foliage, water into classical compositions surely owed something to the Italian example filtered back to Holland chiefly by painters from Utrecht. His delight in mountainous spectacle, in crags and waterfalls alien to his native Dutch landscape, was formed perhaps by the Scandinavian visions of Allart van Everdingen (1621-75); in contrast, his panoramic sweeps of the true Dutch plains doubtless owed something to the great horizontal sweeps of Philips de Koninck (1619-88). Finally, his compulsive effect on the spectator's imagination demands comparison with Rembrandt. But, though in a few instances Ruisdael produced visions very close to some of Rembrandt's rare painted landscapes, no specific influence from Rembrandt can be seen. Ruisdael's technique, which derives much of its impact by marrying a broad, majestic massing of forms with a very detailed characterization of individual elements, could certainly be called Baroque; however, in realizing landscape as an equivalent of the tragic human condition, Ruisdael was profoundly original, and his empathy with the rhythm of transient and inexorable Nature is akin to that of Romantic poets such as Wordsworth.

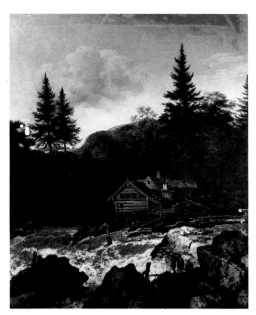

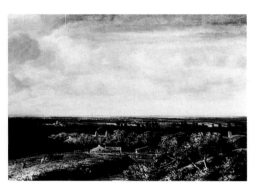

EVERDINGEN (left)
A waterfall, 1650
Everdingen was probably taught by Savery, who had travelled in the Tyrol. He himself travelled to Scandinavia with a patron in 1640, and in the 1650s he introduced into his pictures the waterfalls and log huts he had sketched there.

KONINCK (below)
View over flat country, 1650s or 1660s
Typical of Koninck is the bisecting horizon: no house or church joins land and sky. The slightly raised viewpoint stresses the endlessness of the plain: and Ruisdael, too, was to exploit such an effect of panorama.

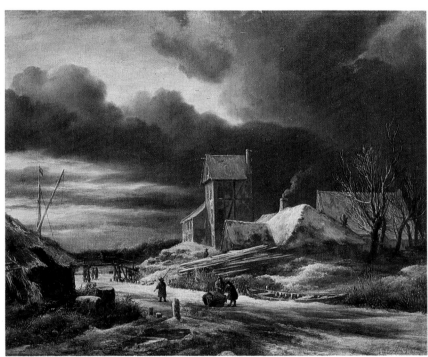

JACOB VAN RUISDAEL (above) *Winter landscape*, c. 1670
Desolate figures tramp the frozen river in the freezing dusk. The river slants against an ominous counter-diagonal into a void: even in this homely scene there is a sense of the insignificance of man.

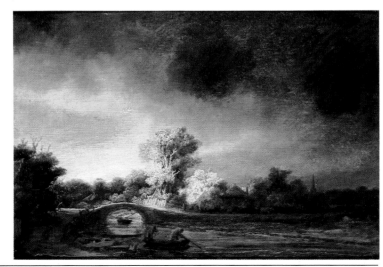

REMBRANDT (right)
The stone bridge, c.1637
The lighting is not naturalistic: it erupts into the dark of the painting, and blanches the tree it strikes. It is a theoretical landscape, like those of Seghers, not a sublimation of natural landscape like, for instance, Ruisdael's picture (above).

Dutch Genre and Portraiture 1

In the seventeenth century, genre – broadly, the painting of scenes from everyday life, even of the humblest kind – became separated out, like landscape or still life, as a subject in its own right. Secular, even low-life, subjects had been painted before, but in order to illustrate an allegory, a proverb or a moral. Caravaggio in Italy had painted still life or peasant characters as interesting in themselves or worthy of high art, but the emergence of Dutch genre was probably an independent development, for the favourite themes of the earliest Dutch genre painters can be traced back into previous Netherlandish religious and allegorical painting. In fact, there are probably moralizing undertones in many Dutch genre scenes that today seem to have no other subject than what they so realistically show.

Dutch genre, like Dutch landscape, made its most promising beginning in Haarlem, as an extension of the naturalism of Frans Hals' vivid portraiture. Its first subjects were what the Dutch called *Merry companies*, groups of drunken roisterers. Hals in his early career painted one or two such genre scenes, and Willem Buytewech (c. 1591-1624), who worked closely with him for a time, popul-arized the *Merry company* set in an interior. However, though he was a prolific and elegant etcher and draughtsman, Buytewech's rare paintings seem stiff and studious beside Frans Hals' portraiture; so do those even of Frans' brother Dirck Hals (1591-1666). The *Merry company* theme was soon extended to include guardroom scenes or tavern scenes featuring soldiers. The specialists in this form, such as Willem Duyster in Amsterdam or Pieter Codde, also introduced light effects from the Utrecht Caravaggisti, as did Judith Leyster (1609-60). She, however, more closely than anyone else, could occasionally catch the spirit and the crisp vivacity of Frans Hals' paint in her small genre works. In 1635 she married Jan Molenaer, who also specialized in genre, which by this time encompassed almost every kind of social or domestic activity.

The genius among the early genre painters was Adriaen Brouwer (1605/6-38). Though he worked most of his brief life in Antwerp, he was born Dutch and he was in Haarlem in the 1620s. His pictures – always small-scale – show a knowledge both of Bruegel and of Frans Hals, and he observed his chosen subjects, peasants squalid both in aspect and in setting, with scrupulous objectivity. His

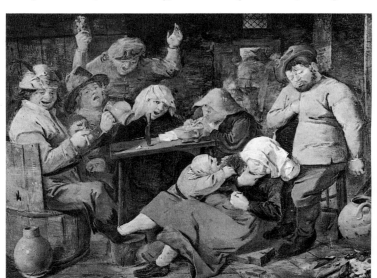

BROUWER (right)
Peasants in an inn, c. 1627-31
The squat figures and their vividly caught expressions (surely showing Frans Hals' influence) are typical of Brouwer. His coarse figures are both reprehensible and laughable – for instance, the mother who nods off while her child howls – but each figure is an individual, and, as such, sympathetic. The detail is particular and rich, indicated with a swift and broad brush, related consummately to the whole. Glowing greys and browns set the atmosphere: tonal modulations are extremely sensitive. It was Brouwer's achievement to transform subject matter quite the reverse of ideal or beautiful into a major work of art.

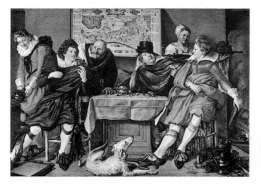

BUYTEWECH
Merry company, c. 1617-20
The bearded man left of centre is the very one that Frans Hals also painted in his *Shrovetide revellers* of about 1615 (not shown) – confirming links between Buytewech and Hals and Hals' crucial influence in the emergence of Dutch genre. The picture perhaps represents the Five Senses, but the exaggerated stances of the figures show a clear attempt at vivid realism.

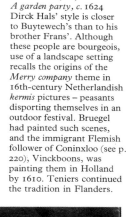

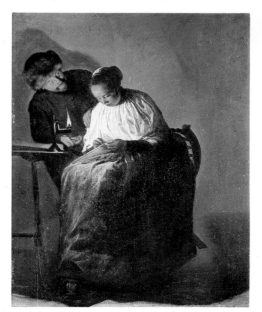

LEYSTER (left)
The offer, c. 1635?
The man offers her gold, but the seamstress seems determined to preserve her virtue. The man's leer, and the woman's concentration on her task, are caught in a frozen moment with an art anticipating Vermeer's.

ADRIAEN VAN OSTADE
(right) *Inside an inn,* 1653
The room has shadowy depths into which creep patches of light, in a style learnt from Rembrandt. The figures are dumpy and are painted briskly and in movement, like Brouwer's, but this is a kind of respect-able version of his low life.

DIRCK HALS (left)
A garden party, c. 1624
Dirck Hals' style is closer to Buytewech's than to his brother Frans'. Although these people are bourgeois, use of a landscape setting recalls the origins of the *Merry company* theme in 16th-century Netherlandish *kermis* pictures – peasants disporting themselves in an outdoor festival. Bruegel had painted such scenes, and the immigrant Flemish follower of Coninxloo (see p. 220), Vinckboons, was painting them in Holland by 1610. Teniers continued the tradition in Flanders.

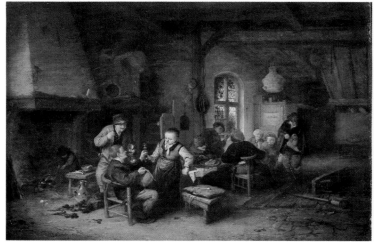

scenes could be comic, but neither caricatured nor condescending. He painted his people, in their weaknesses and their passions, as one of them, and the known facts of his Bohemian life suggest a strong sympathy with them. Brouwer has always been "a painter's painter": Rubens, for instance, had 17 of his paintings and Rembrandt owned six paintings and many of his very free drawings, which clearly influenced Rembrandt's own drawing style.

Those who followed in Brouwer's wake included some artists of talent approaching genius and a remarkable number of unusual competence. Characteristic was the prolific Adriaen van Ostade (1610-85). Early on he showed not only Brouwer's influence but also Rembrandt's, but later moved towards a more picturesque but less vital version of low life, probably one that was more acceptable to an ever-widening clientèle. His brother Isaack (1621-49; not shown), who started along similar lines, later developed his own vision of landscape and genre combined. Gerrit Dou (1613-75), a pupil of Rembrandt in his early Leyden days, continued all his life to paint small, highly finished and increasingly cosy domesticities, often a single figure set in a

window. His example was followed by the prolific painter Gabriel Metsu (1629-97) and by Frans van Mieris the Elder (1635-81).

Nicholaes Maes (1634-93), one of the most talented of Rembrandt's later pupils, worked with distinction very much in his master's Amsterdam manner, but turned about 1660 to painting society portraits and metamorphosed his style into an international Baroque almost indistinguishable from that of English or French counterparts such as Lely or Bourdon. Throughout the seventeenth century, the demand by the Dutch for portraits was constant, and was answered by a whole range of extremely able portraitists. Their work, to be sure, was less disturbing than Rembrandt's shadowy psychological probings, and tended to concentrate on rich superficial textures of flesh and costume. At their best the best among them – Thomas de Keyser, Bartholomeus van der Helst (1613-70) – were of high quality.

The crowning splendour of Dutch genre painting was the Delft school (see over), but the Leyden-born Jan Steen (1626-79) is more generally representative of its final phase. The son of a brewer, his sympathies were somewhat akin to Brouwer's. He was briefly a publican

and brewer himself in Delft between 1654 and 1657, where he was doubtless aware of Vermeer, and he was in Haarlem between 1661 and 1670, where Frans Hals' art had a pronounced effect on his own. Steen's popular reputation rests on his vigorous, bustling portrayals of carousing gatherings, in which he himself, relaxed and unbuttoned, is sometimes a participant. His output, however, was much more varied, though not always of high quality – packed with detail and colour yet freely and rhythmically painted, and always psychologically coherent. He painted not only genre but also historical, biblical and allegorical pictures (he was a Catholic), and in his genre paintings the moralizing or allegorical element is more evident than in most of his contemporaries' pictures. He depicted his figures not only in contemporary costume with domestic props, but also in theatrical guise, as if they were enacting a scene from the *Commedia dell'Arte*. Many critics have compared Steen to Molière, and his control of production is indeed worthy of a great dramatist-actor-manager. The elegant lightness and wit of his late pictures have almost an accent of Rococo, suggesting that Watteau is not far off.

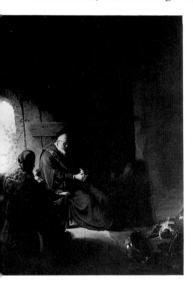

DOU AND REMBRANDT (left)
The blind Tobit and his wife Anna, c. 1630
The finish marks the work as Dou's, but the design, the chiaroscuro and the subject are more typical of Rembrandt. Rembrandt made many studies from the life but seldom painted genre; his biblical subjects, however, are often almost indistinguishable from it.

MIERIS THE ELDER (right)
Soap bubbles, 1663
The composition, a figure confronting the spectator from a window, had been popularized by Dou. Mieris has added even more detail, and hints of *vanitas* typical of still life (see p. 232).

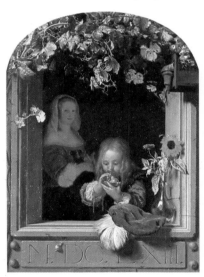

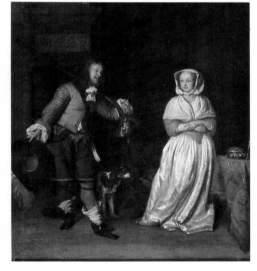

METSU (above)
The hunter's gift, c. 1661-67
Metsu was probably taught by Dou, but his varied art reflects other influences often more strongly. The grace of the figures recalls Steen; the subject, though it is more politely and subtly mentioned, is once more the trial of a woman's virtue.

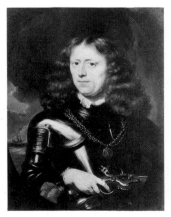

MAES (above)
Admiral Binkes, c. 1670-77
Later Dutch portraitists adopted Baroque devices, even if his attributes fail to energize the Admiral; perhaps the need for a good likeness inhibited fluency.

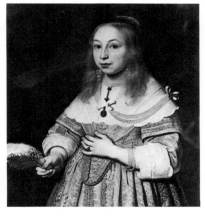

VAN DER HELST (above)
A young girl, 1645
The general run of Dutch portraiture – Rembrandt and Hals excepted – has a naive quality, though the likeness is probably exact and the stiffness often charming.

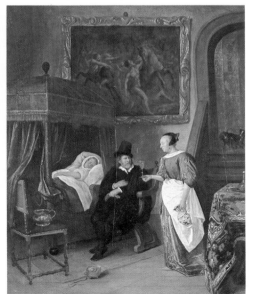

STEEN (left)
The doctor's visit, c. 1665
The bowl of charcoal on the floor contains an apron-string, burnt as a remedy for the girl's illness. The doctor will be of no better use, for she is sick of love; the picture above the bed indicates her passion. In his approach and in some of his devices Steen offered precedents for Hogarth.

Dutch Genre and Portraiture 2: Delft and Deventer

The brief harvest of genius between about 1654 and 1670 in the small town of Delft is an astonishing phenomenon in European painting; it can be compared in Dutch art only with the achievement of Rembrandt. Though it coincides with Rembrandt's last years, it is quite different in vision – in its classic poise, its restraint, its clarity. In Vermeer it produced the one artist in Holland who can equal Rembrandt's intimations of mystery and immortality – within a more restricted range.

There is in fact a link between Rembrandt and Vermeer, in the elusive personality of Carel Fabritius (1622-54). He was working with Rembrandt in the 1640s and was by far the most gifted of his pupils. By 1650 he was in Delft, but there he was tragically killed by an explosion in a gunpowder magazine in 1654. Very close to Rembrandt in his understanding of the possibilities of paint textures and tonal contrasts, in a sense he reversed Rembrandt's vision: he worked in darks against light, rather than in lights against a dark ground, his subjects becoming coolly luminous in a pervasive natural light. He also experimented with perspective effects – as in his topographically exact little *View of Delft*, 1652.

These two interests, in the reflections of cool light and in optics and illusionism, have an important place in the mature work of Jan Vermeer (1632-75), who owned at least three paintings by Fabritius. Further, Antony van Leeuwenhoek, an exploratory genius of the microscope and the science of optics, was Vermeer's fellow-citizen and exact contemporary, and ultimately his executor. Contemporary assessment of Vermeer is almost non-existent, and after his death he remained unrecognized for almost 200 years. His works are rare – doubtless he worked very slowly: only some 40 paintings by him are known, and no drawings that are certainly his at all. His very few early paintings are in the tradition and manner of the Utrecht Caravaggisti – religious or genre subjects relatively large in scale, for example *The procuress* of 1656. Even before 1660, however, his mature style was established – small-scale paintings, featuring one or two figures (most characteristically a single one) in a mildly lit, serene domestic interior. Some moral or allegorical significance, as well as a hint of narrative or latent drama, seems to persist: *A girl asleep at a table* is said to be drunk; *A woman weighing pearls*

possibly embodies a reflection on human vanity, her action paralleled in the picture of the Last Judgment hanging behind her.

Vermeer's greatness lies in his unique ability to invest the simplest pose or transient gesture of ordinary life with a monumental, spellbinding permanence. In his utterly calm, detached observation of domestic intimacy, he achieves a celebration of the simple marvel of human life unmatched before or since. Part of his achievement is the precise structure, the "architecture" of his compositions, and the subtle answering relationships between their component elements – the still life, the rich pattern and texture of materials, the modulation of light from an open window across the wall, of reflected light everywhere. The colour range is cool; a favourite colour chord is blue and yellow. The solidity of the forms is both intensified and offset by a highly original use of scattered highlights, virtually dots of light with a *pointillé* effect that makes the surface vibrant. The perspective is calculated so as to involve the spectator, compelling the eye back from the immediate foreground deep into the picture, but also suggesting that the picture extends forward into the spectator's own

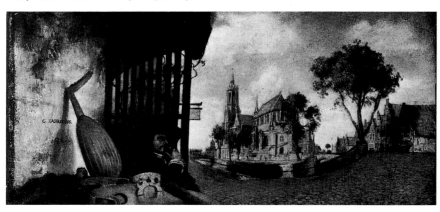

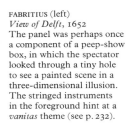

FABRITIUS (left)
View of Delft, 1652
The panel was perhaps once a component of a peep-show box, in which the spectator looked through a tiny hole to see a painted scene in a three-dimensional illusion. The stringed instruments in the foreground hint at a *vanitas* theme (see p. 232).

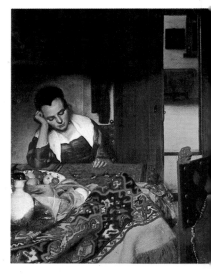

VERMEER (right)
A girl asleep at a table, c. 1656
This is thought to be an early work because there is an emphasis on still life, as in *The procuress*; there is an opening into another room, probably derived from de Hoogh, seldom repeated by Vermeer; there seems to be strong moralizing though the import is not certain.

FABRITIUS (below)
A goldfinch, 1654
In Rembrandt's work, light plays suggestively about the forms; here the light strikes the form and is obstructed: there is no interpenetration. Fabritius uses Rembrandt's techniques to paint a more literal, more material truth.

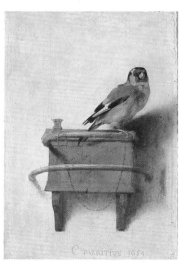

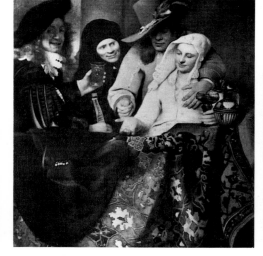

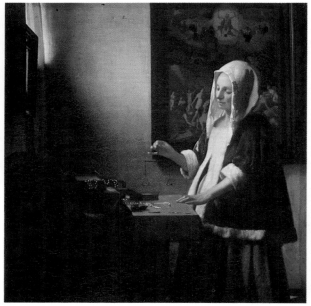

VERMEER (above)
The procuress, 1656
The figures are crowded; there is little of the haunting stillness of Vermeer's maturity. Only one other of his pictures is dated, and this is a rare certainty in his development – it was painted when he was 24.

VERMEER (right)
A woman weighing pearls, c. 1665
The pearls are specks of light – an obvious instance of Vermeer's "pointillism"; the tiny sprinkled dots are usually apparent only on close inspection. Here is Vermeer's art fully mature.

space. The staging of his pictures owes something perhaps to experimentation with mirrors (though mirrors are seldom shown in his pictures); it is certainly an indication of the artist's special fascination with the techniques of perspective, most evident in *"The Artist's Studio"* (see over). Though the characteristic Vermeer is an interior, he brought the same qualities to two remarkable urban views, one, his *View of Delft*, unparalleled in Dutch landscape, the other a street scene, in which he handled the subject much as de Hoogh did.

Pieter de Hoogh (1629-84) of Rotterdam was in Delft from about 1653 until the early 1660s, and thereafter in Amsterdam. His early work consisted of low-life subjects – peasants, soldiers, tavern scenes; his later works show a falling-off in quality. His masterpieces – demonstrating Delft's catalytic artistic climate – almost all date from his decade there. In Delft he was surely aware of Vermeer, although it may well be that in some respects he anticipated Vermeer; both alike responded to the values and patronage of a secure and prosperous urban bourgeoisie. De Hoogh's compositions are usually rigidly constructed, sometimes almost geometrically organized: his

figures are housed firmly within the horizontals and verticals, within the rectangular definitions of his interiors or courtyards. Yet he is also the master of the "escape route" – of vistas leading from one enclosed space to another, rich with invitations to further exploration, suggesting a whole town of domestic interiors, the whole fabric of an urban society. He uses more figures than Vermeer, and very often children, in enchanting evocations of family contentment. His pictures are warmer in tone than Vermeer's, and lack Vermeer's supreme, magical intensity.

Comparable in quality and mood, though he did not work in Delft, is Gerard Terborch (1617-81). Terborch painted not only domestic interiors but also portraits, and finally settled after wide travel (perhaps in Rome, certainly in Spain and in London) in Deventer, a community even smaller than Delft. His pictures are a bewitching amalgam of highly subtle sophistication and a very direct and fresh grasp of character. His small-scale, almost miniature, portraits are like Velazquez in little; their decorum and gravity – even monumentality – are remarkable, not least in relation to their scale.

TERBORCH (below)
*A boy picking fleas from a dog, c.*1655
Psychological delicacy and virtuosity in the painting of stuffs are the virtues of

Terborch's painting. Boy and dog are vividly observed, and the open book and hat beside add a context: he has returned from school and should be at his homework.

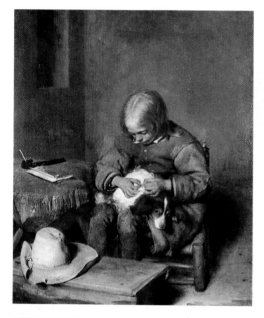

VERMEER (right)
*View of Delft, c.*1660
Its bold colours, its quiet composition without any of the forceful diagonals and accentually placed figures usual in landscapes of the "classic" phase (see p. 222), above all the naturalism of its air and light set this painting apart. *"Pointillé"* dots mark glints of light, and all the horizontals and verticals seem to have been softened in the gentle air.

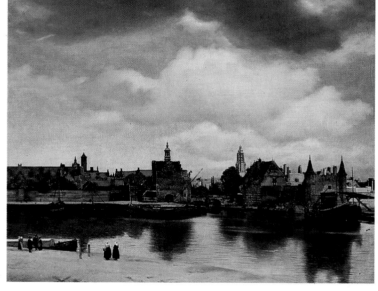

DE HOOGH (below)
The backgammon players, 1653
The subject and treatment are in the tradition of Duyster and Codde (see preceding page); there is no firm articulating framework of the kind typical of de Hoogh's Delft compositions.

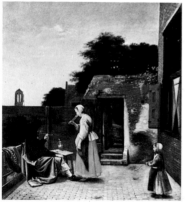

DE HOOGH (above)
*A man smoking, a woman drinking and a child in a courtyard, c.*1656
The static figures have

a quiet repose typical of de Hoogh's Delft period. The textures of things glitter with phosphorescent light a little like Vermeer's (left).

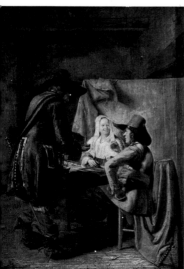

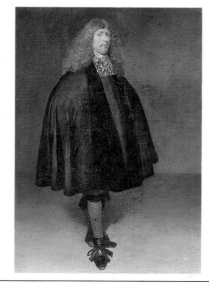

TERBORCH (left)
*Self-portrait, c.*1668
There is a sort of lively pomposity in the figure, pushing forward his bowed shoe and with arms akimbo beneath his cloak. The light on his lace front and long hair is beautifully handled. The picture is only about 60cm (28in) in height.

DE HOOGH (right)
*A musical party, c.*1677
De Hoogh's later work is quite different in feeling: he leaves behind quiet women and their children, to show rather grander settings – here the "escape route" is more elaborate, and perhaps the most successful element.

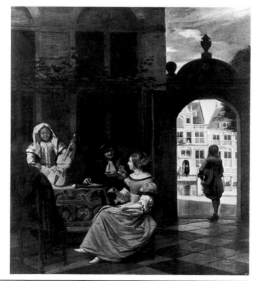

Vermeer: The Artist's Studio

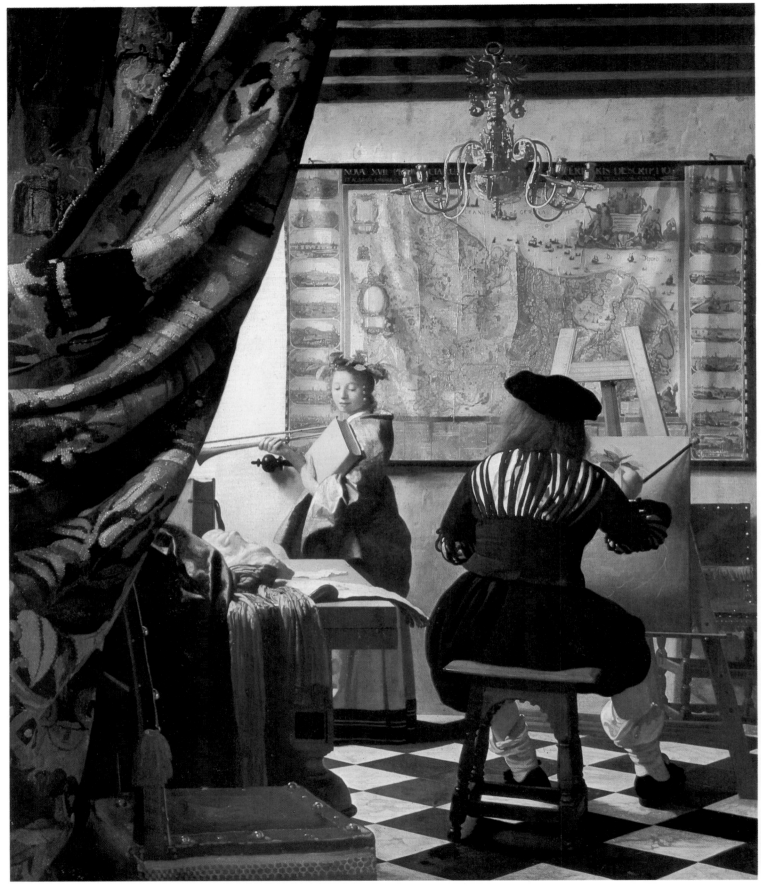

VERMEER
"The Artist's Studio"
(The art of painting),
c. 1665-70

The subject matter is detailed with all Vermeer's firm modelling and luminous, cool serenity: a painter, seen from behind, is in the act of painting on the easel before him the figure of a young girl who stands in the gentle light of a window in the corner of the room. It is a rich and typically Dutch interior – the black and white marble pattern of the floor; the sumptuously textured curtains; the fine brass chandelier; a map of Holland on the wall – inhabited by an inimitable element, Vermeer's pervasive and all-creating light.

On inspection, however, several questions about the picture begin to arise. This is no ordinary working painter's studio, cluttered and untidy; the painter is dressed in a costume that is certainly not studio garb. His model's shoulders are clad in a rather indeterminate drapery; her head is wreathed with what seem to be laurels, and though she has the features of a typical Vermeer girl (a daughter perhaps) she is accoutred with a fine trumpet and a large tome (that will soon surely be uncomfortably heavy). She must represent either a Muse – the Muse of History, Clio – or Fame, both of

whom earlier artists had shown with these accessories. Vermeer painted other allegories, and his widow is known to have referred to this painting under the title *The art of painting*. But this work celebrates the triumph of the painter's art far more movingly and convincingly than any Baroque contrivance of allegorical females could ever do, partly just because Clio, or Fame, is also a simple Dutch girl, dressed up rather touchingly and awkwardly; the artist in the picture, however, has not yet started with her person, he is beginning on his canvas with the laurels of fame.

But then, how did Vermeer himself set about the painting we see? There is no evidence in this or in any other painting that he worked otherwise than *alla prima*, directly on to the canvas, without preliminary studies or drawings – and this in spite of the absolute certainty with which the very elaborate structure and detail of the picture is established. He could, however, have framed his composition on a two-dimensional surface – ready to trace as it were – by the ingenious disposition of two mirrors, one behind the artist, the other in

front, so placed as to include the image of his own back as he painted. If so, this is a self-portrait, characteristically rejecting any self-revelation. There is still some ambiguity about the exact scope of the painting, a query, for example, as to whether the foreground curtain and chair are inside or outside the main subject of the picture. There are also ambiguities in the significance of the subject matter – the map of Holland, for instance, so ostentatious on the wall, looks like an assertion of Dutch national pride, but is beyond doubt of the Dutch provinces under the old Spanish rule.

The painting is signed (though for long it was attributed to de Hoogh), and is thought to be late within Vermeer's mature period, somewhere between 1665 and 1670. Some elements restate established motifs: painters at work (and seen from behind), the transitional device of the foreground curtain drawn back between the picture and the spectator – these occur in Rembrandt or in masters such as Dou or Mieris. What is unique to Vermeer is the monumental whole into which they are bound – entirely credible and yet unfathomable.

VERMEER (below)
The head of a girl, c. 1666
Though the girl may well be Vermeer's daughter, it is an impersonal portrait.

It seems to have been made chiefly to experiment with a favourite colour contrast, or to explore a fascination with the behaviour of light.

VERMEER (left)
An allegory of Faith,
c. 1669
This seems stilted. "*The Artist's Studio*" is instead really a genre picture of an artist painting an allegory: hence its greater success.

VERMEER (below)
Diana and her nymphs,
c. 1654
The subject, like that of the *Allegory* (left), is essentially Italian; classical myths and theatrical allegories were not main Protestant themes.

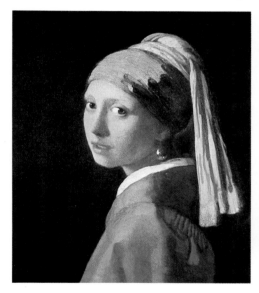

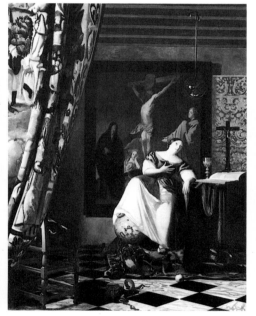

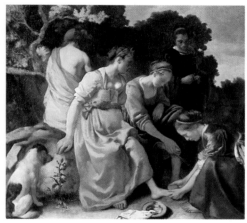

REMBRANDT (right)
The artist in his studio,
c. 1628-29
There is no high-flown allegory about this little genre work – it is hardly even a self-portrait. In Rembrandt's picture there is both a comic element and a debunking realism – the opposite of Vermeer's quiet, high seriousness.

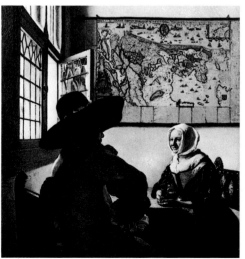

VERMEER (left)
A soldier and a laughing girl, c. 1657
Both the Italianate subject and the composition of "*The Artist's Studio*" owe much to the Utrecht school – even if the Utrechtian device of silhouetting a foreground figure against the light in the picture is more bluntly used in this early work.

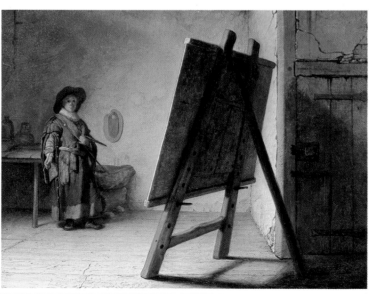

Dutch Still-Life Painting

The expression "still life", used to describe a category of painting, does not appear until about 1650, and then, significantly, in its Dutch form. It eventually became the habitual term for paintings of any kind of inanimate object – flowers, fruit, food of all kinds; tableware (from the grandest of gold or silver goblets to Venetian glass and Delft plates, or cutlery and the infinitely subtle white tones of napery); books, manuscripts, musical instruments. Yet still-life elements have recurred in Western art since classical times, and Netherlandish artists especially had long delighted in dwelling with vivid, doting accuracy on such objects, though not of course as the prime subject of their illuminations or pictures. In the sixteenth century, however, artists such as Aertsen (see p. 162) had painted detailed kitchen interiors in which the still life predominates, while the nominal pretext for the painting – Christ with Mary and Martha, for instance – is merely glimpsed in the rear.

In earlier pictures still-life objects were often, perhaps generally, introduced for their symbolic value. These values underlie much seventeenth-century still-life painting in Holland – the *vanitas* theme, for instance, announced in its most obvious form by a skull, reminding the viewer of the transience of all things; or references to the Five Senses (which occur, too, in genre painting) But while the vanity of all pleasures of this world is acknowledged by the Dutch, the admonition *memento mori* (remember death) always goes hand in hand with the celebration – remember life – implicit in the act of painting itself. The enduring enchantment of still-life painting rests in the paradox that the ephemeral subject – the cut flower, the emptied glass, the frailty of the butterfly – is translated by the illusionistic skill of the painter into immortality.

In seventeenth-century Holland, painters, and whole families of painters, tended to specialize in one aspect of the art – in flower-pieces or in "breakfast" and the more elaborate and complex "banquet" pieces; in studies of game or of fish; or in more overtly symbolic variations on the *vanitas* theme. All these subjects embodied a particularly Dutch pleasure, nourished in a hugely successful commercial society, in sensuous materialism – but these bourgeois took as much delight in a spiral of lemon peel as in the splendour of gold or silver plate. Certainly the price of the

CLAESZ.
Breakfast piece, 1637
The objects are bound in a spell of light that joins them in an intimate unity. It preserves about

them a lingering aura – as if they had just been handled by someone. Their textures are delicately evoked and contrasted – this is no dry inventory!

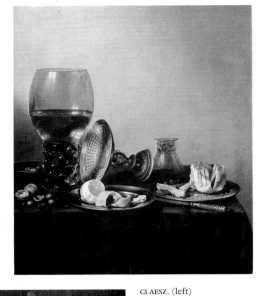

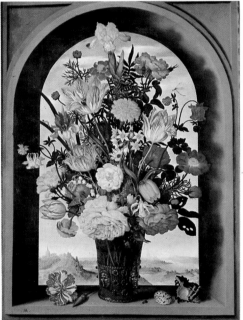

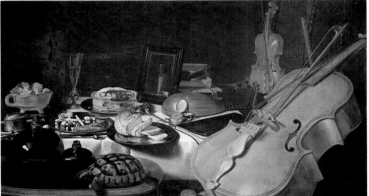

CLAESZ. (left)
Still life, 1623
Numbers of symbolic references can be discovered in the objects shown. All Five Senses are present – touch in every object; sight particularly in the mirror; hearing in the musical instruments; smell in the stoppered and unstoppered jars; taste in the half-eaten food. There are also many *vanitas* references to the passing of Time – the long-lived tortoise, symbol of old age; the lamp wick; the watch; the half-empty glass that once was full and soon will be empty.

AMBROSIUS BOSSCHAERT
THE ELDER (left)
A vase of flowers, c. 1620
Bosschaert habitually included flowers from all seasons in one picture, and often the very same bloom recurs from picture to picture. He must have worked from a portfolio of drawings rather than from the life.

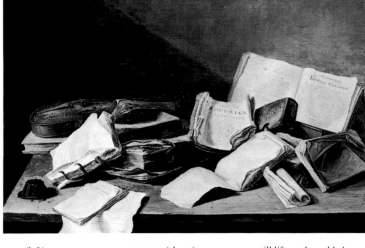

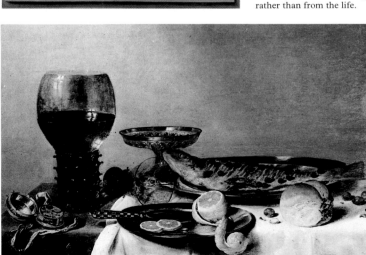

HEDA (left)
Breakfast piece, *c.* 1634
Claesz. and Heda painted similar delicately balanced compositions, and similar motifs. Heda's touch was slightly more meticulous, and his later works tended to be grander, like Kalf's.

DE HEEM (above)
Still life of books,
c. 1625-29
Still lifes of books were a local speciality of Leyden, a university town; de Heem was there as a young man. Unlike others, he did not specialize in one type of

still life, and, could change his style: the quite emphatic chiaroscuro of this picture was a passing interest. In Antwerp he tried a more Baroque style, comparable to that of Snyders (see p. 200) but rather cooler, as befitted a Dutchman.

objects painted was never forgotten: even flowers might be more than a simple pleasure, for this was the period of the great Dutch tulip boom, when the bulb itself might well cost much more than a painting of it. Still-life painters were as highly esteemed as other painters, and fed a rich export market.

Foremost amongst the early flower-specialists was Ambrosius Bosschaert the Elder (1573-1621), born in Antwerp but working mainly in Middelburg. His characteristic compositions consist of a vase of flowers set centrally in a niche through which a landscape can be seen. Each flower is described, "spelled out", with exact and impartial literalness in an even light. His tradition was carried on by many painters (including his own three sons and his brother-in-law, Balthasar van der Ast), though the subject matter increasingly included insects, shells, lizards or toads. In step with the general development of Dutch painting, their compositions became more naturalistic, modelled in terms of light and shade, with the illusion of depth and air. Modern eyes, glutted with ubiquitous colour photographs, cannot realize the delighted astonishment that such illusionist reproductions of the

elements of everyday life evoked in contemporaries – especially perhaps those faithful portrait likenesses of food on a table, seen from a high viewpoint to get in as much as possible.

The ablest popularizers of the breakfast piece were Pieter Claesz. (1597/8-1661) and Willem Heda (1599-1680/2), both based mainly in Haarlem. Like their contemporary, van Goyen, working in landscape, they were able to distil drama out of unspectacular objects by the calculated interrelationships between the elements of their composition, and the subtlest transitions of tone. Theirs was a tonal rather than a colouristic painting.

Slightly younger, Jan de Heem (1606-83/4) won an international reputation in a variety of kinds of still life; working mainly in Antwerp from 1636, he had an instinctive affinity with Flemish Baroque exuberance, a delight in movement and colour. Later again, the outstanding figure in the so-called "classic" phase of Dutch still life (corresponding to the "classic" phase of landscape painting) was the wonderfully talented Willem Kalf (1619-93). Though he worked briefly (1642-46) in Paris, his career was mainly in Amsterdam. His luxurious paint – influenced surely by Rem-

brandt's chiaroscuro, but also by Vermeer's scintillating treatment of light – is matched by a new richness of subject matter – plate, glass, exotic pearly-gleaming nautilus shells – answering the taste of a wealthy, patrician rather than bourgeois clientèle. Luxury, however, is always controlled by the most delicate feeling for compositional unity.

Kalf's contemporary Abraham van Beyeren (1620/21-90) specialized rather in more sumptuous banquet pieces, crowded with incident and variety, yet subtle in colour harmonies. Van Beyeren also painted fish-pieces, though paintings of dead game are rare in Dutch art till late in the century (there are two by Rembrandt). A "moving" variant on still life was developed later in the century by artists such as Melchior de Hondecoeter (1636-95), who depicted domestic or exotic birds and animals. Flower-painting, however, was perhaps always the most popular, and remained popular until well into the eighteenth century, sustaining its quality in the hands of successive generations of Dutch art; some of the later flower painters, such as the van Huysum family, fell little short of their predecessors in talent.

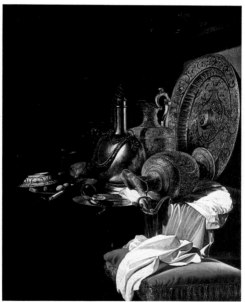

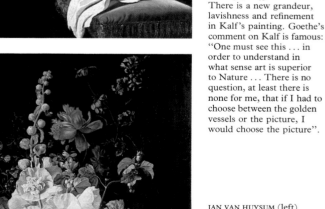

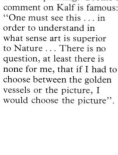

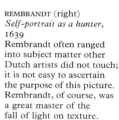

VAN BEYEREN (left)
Still life, undated
Van Beyeren's work seems a more modest, restrained version of the exuberant displays of the Flemish artists, or even de Heem.

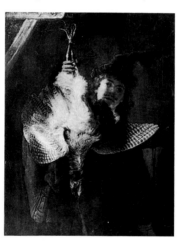

REMBRANDT (right)
Self-portrait as a hunter, 1639
Rembrandt often ranged into subject matter other Dutch artists did not touch; it is not easy to ascertain the purpose of this picture. Rembrandt, of course, was a great master of the fall of light on texture.

KALF (left)
Still life, 1643
There is a new grandeur, lavishness and refinement in Kalf's painting. Goethe's comment on Kalf is famous: "One must see this ... in order to understand in what sense art is superior to Nature ... There is no question, at least there is none for me, that if I had to choose between the golden vessels or the picture, I would choose the picture".

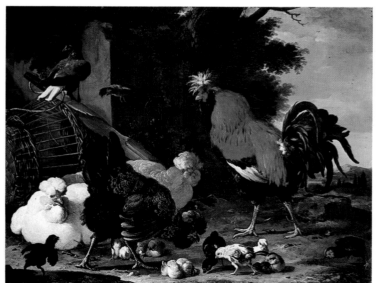

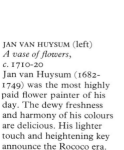

JAN VAN HUYSUM (left)
A vase of flowers, c. 1710-20
Jan van Huysum (1682-1749) was the most highly paid flower painter of his day. The dewy freshness and harmony of his colours are delicious. His lighter touch and heightening key announce the Rococo era.

HONDECOETER
Cocks, hens and chicks, with other birds, c. 1668
Hondecoeter's interest in

texture, his nicely blended colours and his naturalism are praised; his fowls had an international reputation.

There is often in them an allegory – of the Nations of Europe at War, or here, more simply, Family Life.

Late Baroque in Italy

Baroque painting in the Grand Manner, in particular decorative painting in the churches and, to a lesser extent, in the great aristocratic palaces, had been practised in Italy throughout the second half of the seventeenth century, and it continued into the eighteenth. In central Italy it remained within the tradition established by Pietro da Cortona (see p. 189), and perhaps its main development was towards an ever-increasing virtuosity in illusionism, in dissolving solid domes and vaults into celestial visions spiralling up into endless heavens. In Rome, a spectacular climax was reached in the

Allegory of the missionary work of the Jesuits with which Fra Andrea Pozzo (1642-1709) exploded the nave vault in S. Ignazio in the early 1690s. In sculpture, the influence of Bernini remained paramount, and his emotive style was continued in the work of his former assistant Antonio Raggi (1624-86) and others. Raggi's carving and stuccowork, for instance in the church of Il Gesù at Rome, is of a brilliance and colour almost comparable to that of his master.

Rome remained the fountain-head of sculpture until well into the eighteenth century,

even though in painting its importance as a centre of ambitious decorative projects waned. Nevertheless in central Italy, in Rome, Florence and Bologna, the principles of classicism and *disegno* were sustained: painters such as Carlo Maratta (1625-1713) continued to model their figures firmly and solidly and to evolve their compositions by means of painstaking preliminary drawings. The tradition was to culminate in the relatively sober vision of the German-born Mengs (see vol. 3 p. 56), whose Neoclassical figure painting is often strikingly reminiscent of the Carracci.

The important developments in decorative painting occurred elsewhere – to the south, in Naples, blossoming artistically under foreign domination, and to the north, in Venice, which was clearly in decline as a commercial or political power, but, like Rome, was already drawing tourists irresistibly from all over Europe. In both Naples and Venice painters exulted in the rhetoric of the Grand Manner with a new freedom: for these artists the movement of the brush, conjuring aerial rhythms of line, in strokes of brilliant colour suffused in light, became predominant – more important than literal accuracy of drawing.

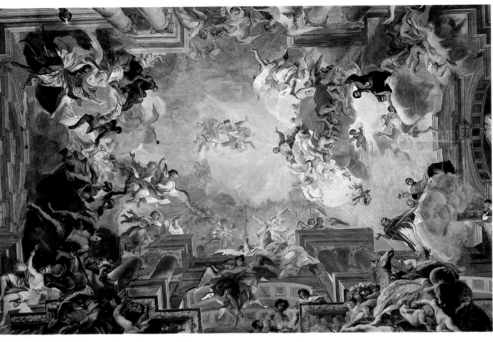

POZZO (left)
Allegory of the missionary work of the Jesuits, 1691-94
Padre Pozzo's ceiling for S. Ignazio, celebrating the developed strength of the Jesuit order, has crowded figures hurtling in a space deeper than any by Pietro da Cortona. Padre Pozzo's perspective, fully effective only from a single spot in the nave, was imitated in Germany and in Austria, where he settled in 1702.

GIORDANO (below)
Venus, Cupid and Mars, undated
One need only compare the Venus with a female nude by Annibale Carracci (see p. 187) to see how Giordano has infused the classicist tradition with the sensuality of Venetian art. Luca was consistent only in the zest with which he painted; he painted with great speed, being known as "Luca fa presto" (Luke quick-hand).

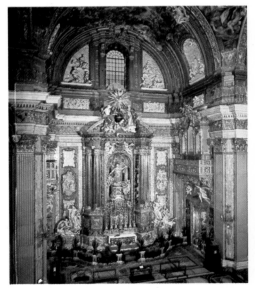

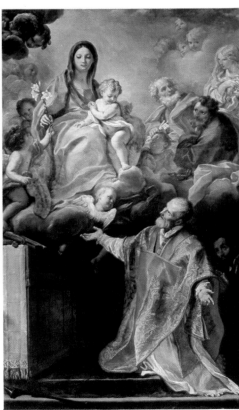

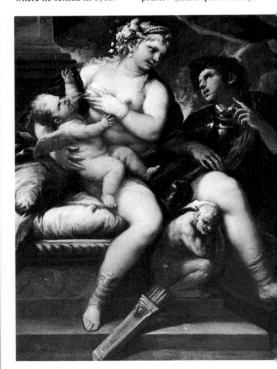

RAGGI
St Ignatius' Chapel, Il Gesù, 1683
Raggi's stucco sculptures, so rapturous in gesture, so turbulent in movement, set in such a rich setting, typify the increasingly decorative development of Bernini's union of all the arts revealed (see p. 190) in the Cornaro Chapel.

MARATTA (right)
The Virgin and Child with St Philip Neri, c. 1690
Maratta was the leading painter in Rome, and his prestige was enormous. He continued the classicizing trend of Andrea Sacchi, who taught him: his version of this subject is much more sober than that of the Neapolitan Solimena.

In Naples the prototype artist of the new fashion was Luca Giordano (1634-1705). Probably a pupil of Ribera, and therefore an heir to the Caravaggesque tradition, he became an endlessly inventive and prolific virtuoso in many styles, approaching each project as a problem to be solved by the application of whatever style might seem most fitting. Luca borrowed ideas impartially from the Venetians or from Pietro da Cortona, from Rembrandt or Dürer. He led a life typical of the leading late Baroque and Rococo artists, answering the calls of patronage wherever they might promise most richly; thus he worked in Naples, Madrid, Rome, Florence and Venice. His longest stay was in Madrid, where he was painter to the Spanish king for ten years from 1692, and where he decorated ceilings in the Escorial (not shown). He was succeeded in Naples by Francesco Solimena (1657-1747), who tended to revise Giordano's spirited manner back to a more sober reliance on academic drawing and composition, though his pictures were still often dashingly painted.

In Venice the major exponent of the late Baroque style was Sebastiano Ricci (1659-1734). Early study in Bologna, Parma and Rome established him in a tradition of relatively solid modelling, which he never entirely abandoned, but to it he brought a fluent bravura and a freedom of movement that he had learnt from older Venetian painters. He pitched his colour and tone ever higher in key, towards that magical luminosity and heady atmosphere for which Venetian eighteenth-century decorative painting soon became internationally renowned, above all in the work of Tiepolo (see over). In his verve, and his intelligent and wide-ranging eclecticism, he is the Venetian parallel to Luca Giordano, and like him was mobile, working in Milan, Vienna, Bergamo and Florence as well as in Venice. Quite late in life, for four years from 1712, he was in London with his nephew Marco Ricci (1676-1730), and then in Paris, where he met Watteau, and copied some of his paintings. He and Marco, often collaborating, answered the taste of Europeans on the "Grand Tour" of Italy for landscapes, and they were early practitioners of the *capriccio*, or "ruinscape".

The more classicistic strain in Venetian painting is better exemplified by Giovanni Battista Piazzetta (1683-1753): he worked, in a more staid and "academic" manner, not on grand decorations but mostly on altarpieces, and was firmly resident in Venice, where his large studio became an influential school. He, too, had been trained in Bologna, where the early work of Guercino made an impression on him, and he continued to rely on solid but dramatic modelling. His initially fairly sombre key (sometimes exploiting a Caravaggesque chiaroscuro) lightened in the 1730s. There was a large demand, especially from abroad, for his pastoral genre works (see p. 244).

In the eighteenth century foreign commissions, not only for genre and landscapes, not only for easel-pictures but also for ceiling paintings, became increasingly important for Italian artists. They provided the main market for Venetian painters in particular, and many of the most gifted were prepared to travel extensively to fulfil them. Like the Ricci, Giovanni Antonio Pellegrini (1675-1741; not shown) was peripatetic, working in Baroque palaces and country houses in England, Austria and Germany; so were Jacopo Amigoni (1682-1752) and others, all exporting a brilliant, hedonistic idiom of decoration, which often has clear affinities with French Rococo.

SEBASTIANO RICCI (right)
Pope Paul III reconciles Francis I with Charles V, 1686-88
Reference to Titian's *Paul III* (see p. 143) explains the oddly Mannerist elongation.

SOLIMENA (below)
The Virgin and Child with St Philip Neri, 1725-30
Solimena created majestic, dramatically lit altarpieces, influential and in demand both in Naples and abroad.

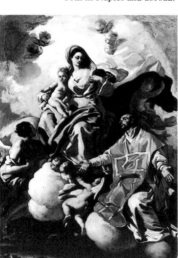

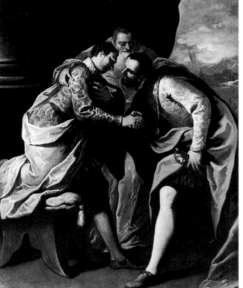

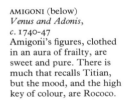

SEBASTIANO AND MARCO RICCI (right)
Allegorical tomb for the Duke of Devonshire, c. 1720
The Riccis' agglomerations of items from the classical past were a precedent for the *capricci* of Canaletto or Panini (see p. 254). This was one of a series, organized by an impresario, Owen McSwiny, of "tombs" for the leading English Whigs – in fact pastiches of well-known antiquities combined with gratifying allusions to the coats of arms and achievements of the living patrons.

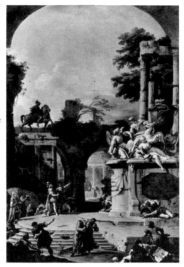

AMIGONI (below)
Venus and Adonis, c. 1740-47
Amigoni's figures, clothed in an aura of frailty, are sweet and pure. There is much that recalls Titian, but the mood, and the high key of colour, are Rococo.

PIAZZETTA (right)
The Adoration of the shepherds, c. 1725
In an era that rejoiced in bravura, Piazzetta's art was intense and introspective. His figures are quite firmly modelled – in a style learned not in Venice but in Bologna – yet they are enlivened by highly tactile dragged brushstrokes. The flickering light and shade are Caravaggesque, but make the figures more homely than monumental.

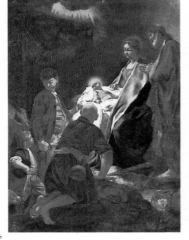

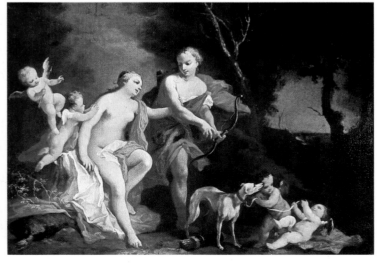

Tiepolo: The Residenz at Würzburg

One of the most spectacular achievements of eighteenth-century art is the decorative ensemble of about 1750 in the Prince-Bishop's Palace, or Residenz, at Würzburg. It is the work of the great German architect Balthasar Neumann and the last of the great Venetian painters, Giambattista Tiepolo (1696-1770), and its two main elements are the staircase, or *Treppenhaus*, and the salon, or *Kaisersaal*.

In the *Kaisersaal* marble, gold, stucco and glass come together with the colour, light and fluency of Tiepolo's paint to achieve a masterpiece of *Gesamtkunstwerk*, that union of the arts that lacks only music to become opera. On the ceiling are painted incidents from the life of Emperor Frederick Barbarossa, who had invested the Bishop of Würzburg in 1168 – almost in the Dark Ages. In Tiepolo's interpretation the action is transported into the sixteenth century, into the Venetian costume of Veronese, and has been rendered incandescent with light. The ceiling shows an exultant Apollo conducting across the heavens a triumphal chariot bearing Beatrice of Burgundy towards Frederick, her husband-to-be, who is enthroned on a steeply towering edifice on the other side, while Glory with a flaming torch hovers above. The *Treppenhaus*, with its complex iconography, *Olympus with the four quarters of the Earth*, is hardly less luminous.

Tiepolo's art in his maturity was the consummation of Baroque fresco, as complex and inventive as that of any of his predecessors, yet controlled and disposed with crystal clarity. The illusion in the *Kaisersaal* is complete – from the real, solid floor the eye travels up into the intricacies of art and so to the apparent dissolution both of the real and of art: the gilt stucco, now real, now a painted imitation indistinguishable from the real, melts into a heaven flooded with light and with an air that is almost breathable. Tiepolo's magic is most telling in the foreshortened horses that surge across the sky; their ancestors are to be found in Reni, Guercino (see p. 185) or Giordano, but only Tiepolo could inspire the spectator with a sense of almost interplanetary "lift-off". The glorious white creatures retain all their physical and massive presence, yet are superbly and triumphantly indifferent to gravity. In the frescos on the walls Tiepolo had less scope for such aerial heights of fantasy, and presented the scenes on stages revealed behind heavy curtains raised by angels; yet the quality of painting is equally high, and illusion interpenetrates reality equally deftly.

Tiepolo's earlier work had been influenced by the sculptural modelling and heavy chiaroscuro of his older contemporary Piazzetta, and was mostly in oil. Fresco, with the opportunity

for working over vast areas at great speed, released his genius, and for it he developed his characteristic high tonal key, within which he could make even his shadows glow with light. His frescos, whether religious or secular, are so joyfully radiant that to some nineteenth-century critics they seemed intolerably frivolous. There is no doubt, however, of Tiepolo's religious sincerity. Later in his life a strain of melancholy became stronger and his altar-pieces could strike a grave and elegiac mood, for instance in the ashen blues of the *modello* for an altarpiece of *St Thecla* for the Cathedral at Este. Yet the overwhelming impact of his art is its heart-lifting colour and light.

At the end of his career, in the service of Charles III in Madrid, his aerial perspectives became even more free, his figures sporting in their heavens became as light as bubbles in champagne, but this climax was attended by indications that new fashions were on the way. His almost equally brilliant son and collaborator, Domenico, painting in fresco what was in fact genre at the Villa Valmarana (see p. 244), was by 1757 "burying the Grand Manner right under his father's vigilant eye", as the historian Wittkower has put it, and the end of Tiepolo's life in Madrid was clouded by lapse from favour, when the King came to prefer the Neoclassical manner of Mengs.

TIEPOLO (below)
Abraham visited by the angels, c. 1732
Even after Tiepolo had developed his light-filled fresco style, he retained a more sombre and emphatic approach (conditioned in part by the medium) in his large-scale canvases in oils.

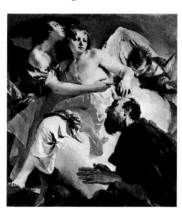

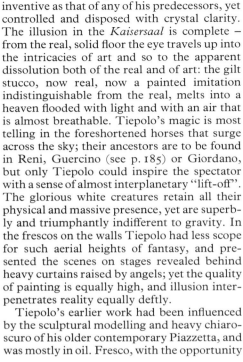

TIEPOLO (left)
St Thecla delivering the city of Este from the plague, 1759
Instead of the typically Baroque drama of the early altarpieces, Tiepolo's late *modelli*, or prior sketches, for religious canvases show airy, shimmering brushwork. (He left the full-scale work to be done by assistants.) They are, however, more solemn than his frescos – in approach recognizably Counter-Reformation art.

TIEPOLO (right)
The banquet of Cleopatra and Anthony, detail of the Palazzo Labia ballroom, 1745-50
The greatest influence on Tiepolo was Veronese: his complex illusionism at the Villa Maser (see p. 171) and the animated spectacle of his famous vast *Banquet* pictures lie behind the Palazzo Labia frescos.

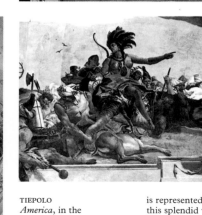

TIEPOLO (right)
Olympus with the four quarters of the Earth, detail of the ceiling of the *Treppenhaus*, Würzburg, 1752-53
Tiepolo exalts the four continents then known – Africa, Europe, America, Asia – in a cosmorama of races, costumes, flora and fauna, in which mythical and allegorical figures commingle with living persons. Apollo, in the middle, pays homage before the portrait of the Prince-Bishop. The group below, symbolizing Europe, includes the artist and his son Domenico.

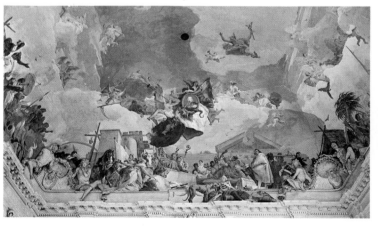

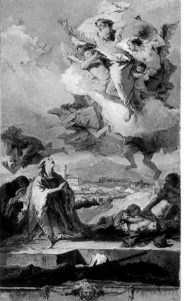

TIEPOLO
America, in the *Treppenhaus*, Würzburg
On each of the four walls is represented a continent: this splendid woman in a feathered head-dress is the personification of America.

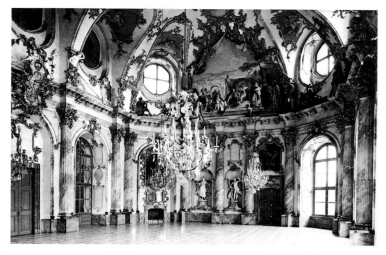

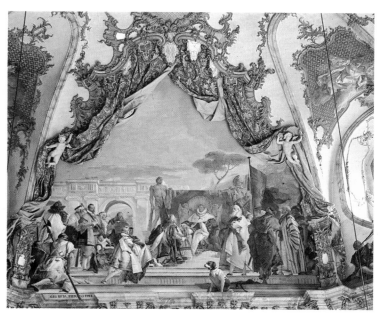

NEUMANN AND TIEPOLO
(above) The *Kaisersaal* in
the Residenz, Würzburg,
1751-52

TIEPOLO (below)
*Apollo leads Beatrice
to Barbarossa*, in the
Kaisersaal, Würzburg

TIEPOLO (right)
*The marriage of Beatrice
and Barbarossa*, in the
Kaisersaal, Würzburg

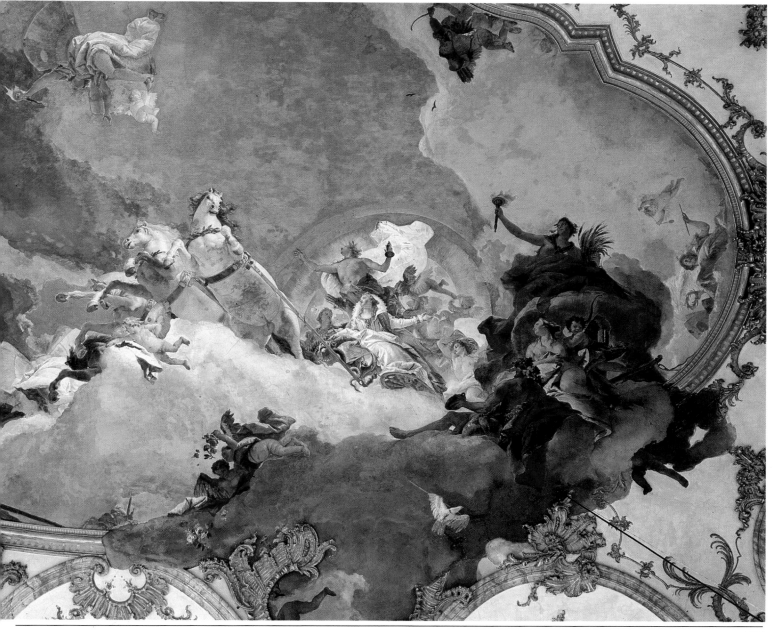

Watteau: The Embarkation for Cythera

Men and women in pairs, almost afloat in their silks against the haze of the sunset sky and the distant misty peaks, ebb down from the right of the painting, where stands a sculptured bust of the goddess Venus wreathed with roses and convolvulus, towards a boat awaiting them at the shore of an inlet of the sea. The picture is all autumnal gold, with a certain lilt of melancholy, a dying fall of farewells, and echoes of unheard music.

Of the two slightly different versions of *"The Embarkation for Cythera"*, one in Berlin and one in the Louvre, the earlier one in the Louvre was the enrolment picture which Jean-Antoine Watteau (1684-1721) deposited with the Académie in 1717 – a little belatedly, as he had become an Academician in 1712. He called it originally *Le pèlerinage à l'Ile de Cythère*, translatable as "the pilgrimage to, or on, or towards the island of Cythera". The title by which it has long been known, *"The Embarkation for Cythera"*, came later, and, though it was universally adopted, it is surely wrong, as has recently been shown. In legend, Cythera is the island where Venus rose from the sea, and here indeed she is, in statue form. But clearly the pilgrims are not setting off for the island but about to leave after a day's enchanting dalliance on it.

Fêtes galantes, showing lovers in a pastoral setting, sometimes banqueting, often with music, had attracted painters since the sixteenth century at least: an obvious prototype for Watteau's version is Rubens' *Garden of Love*,

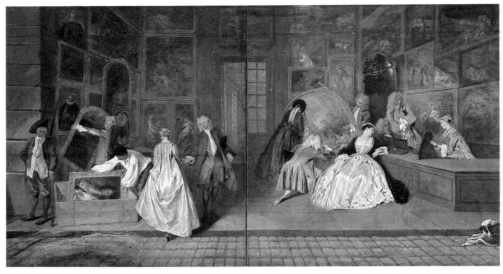

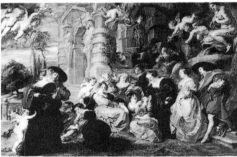

RUBENS (left)
The Garden of Love, c. 1632
Rubens' *fêtes galantes* (but not yet called that) were an inspiration to Watteau and other 18th-century painters – although they transposed his extrovert sensuality into an intimate, more graceful, Rococo key.

WATTEAU (above)
"L'Enseigne de Gersaint" (Gersaint's signboard), 1721
Watteau's "shop sign" has a greater realism, a more specific setting than his earlier pictures. Flemish artists hang recognizably on the walls; the man in the middle may be Watteau.

WATTEAU (below)
The Louvre *"Embarkation*

for Cythera", properly *The pilgrimage to Cythera*, 1717

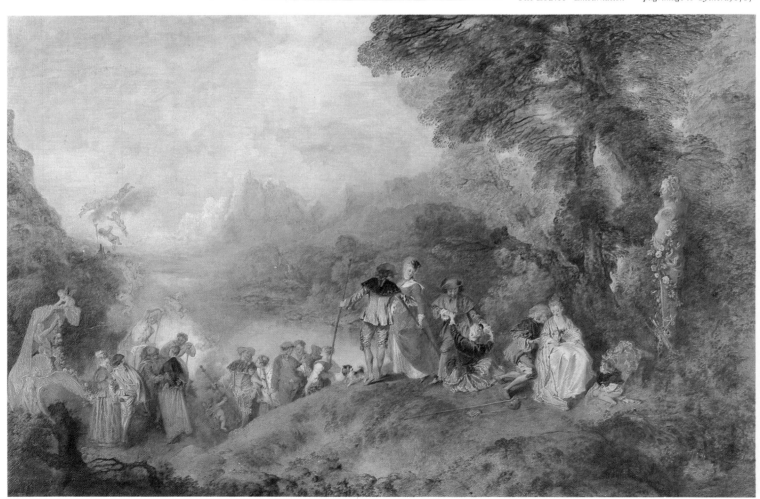

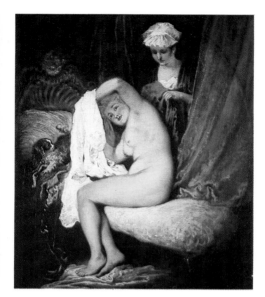

which Watteau certainly knew. His literary source was probably a musical entertainment, *The Three Cousins*, by Florent Dancourt, which appeared in 1700. It had pilgrims journeying to a temple of Love in Cythera, whence, a couplet pointed out, no girl returned without a lover or a husband. In Watteau's picture – which is very like a stage presentation, almost an opera – this consummation has clearly been brought about, as the couples turn lingering to the boat; yet pleasure is shadowed by the approach of evening. Time is not to be denied, and the transience of youth, the bittersweet of love itself, is only just below the surface.

The inspiration of the stage is obvious in most of Watteau's work, and in particular that of the Italian *Commedia dell'Arte*, with its costumed stock characters, of whom the best-known is Pierrot – he typifies its element of pathos and its occasional edge of satire. These qualities are indeed almost always present in Watteau's painting. But the enduring fascination of his artificial never-never world must be due in great part to the brilliance of his technique. From his very early days, he kept sketchbooks with swift notations of figures from the life, and these he used again and again in his paintings. He is one of the world's most bewitching draughtsmen, marrying strength and fragility, power and delicacy into his swallow's-wing line; this quality he transposed into his painting with no loss of grace. Over an underpaint of pearly white, sometimes hazing to blue or palest pink, he drifted on trees in washes of green and golden brown; then the figures, in a thick impasto modelled with incisive gesture; over this, transparent glazes, in a technique based on that of the sixteenth-century Venetians, so that the overall impression is of shimmering depths. His Flemish origins, however (he was born in Valenciennes, which until a few years before his birth was part of Flanders), are apparent in the rhythm and colour of his compositions, and his debt to Rubens was never forgotten. When Watteau arrived in Paris in 1702 the argument among French painters between "Rubenisme" and "Poussinisme" (see p. 198) was already swaying back towards Rubens.

The tinge of melancholy in Watteau's work is matched by his life. His health was undermined by early hardships, and he had less than ten years left when he became an Academician. In 1719-20 he was in London, partly in hopes that the famous Dr Mead might cure his consumption, partly perhaps from a desire to extend his sphere of action. He was already, however, fatally ill. On his return to France, as his death approached, he destroyed a large number of his more erotic paintings. One of his last paintings, however, *"L'Enseigne de Gersaint"* (Gersaint's signboard), for a picture dealer called Gersaint, who looked after him, was a new departure.

After his death, Watteau's style in *fêtes galantes* was carried on by Jean-Baptiste Pater and Nicolas Lancret, both of whom had competence but not Watteau's unique magic.

WATTEAU (below)
The Berlin *"Embarkation for Cythera"*, 1718
Here the moral lurking in the first version is made explicit: lovers turn to leave with a more obvious regret. The lyric haze of the first version has turned to a brighter clarity. The lady with the fan beneath the statue of Venus (now *"The Medici Venus"*) has a face of clearly Rubensian type.

WATTEAU (above)
"La Toilette", c. 1720
The picture is superbly ambiguous: the lady seems to have been surprised in the privacy of her chamber, but is she undressing or dressing? Her pose reveals as much as it conceals. Why the onlooking maid, if not to reinforce the erotic atmosphere? The moral laxity, the shell couch-head, her body's oval, are Rococo.

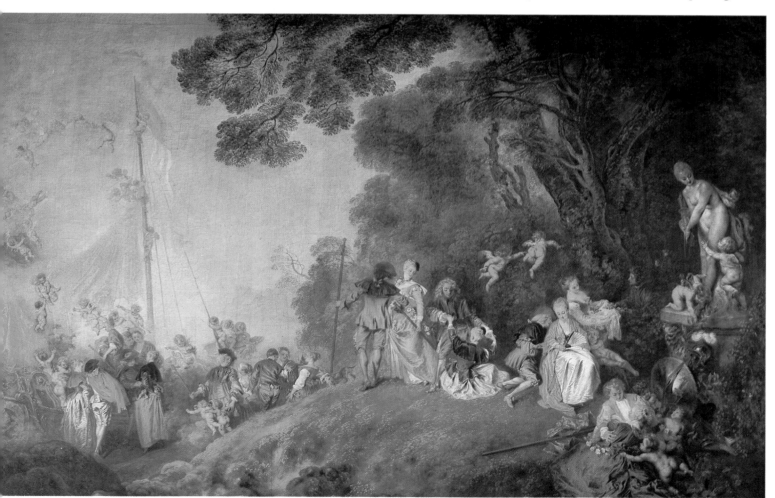

French and German Rococo

The word "Rococo" appears to derive from the French *rocaille*, perhaps in a kind of rhyming analogy with *barocco* (the Portuguese word for an irregular pearl, and arguably the source of the word "Baroque"). *Rocaille* means literally "rock work", but Rococo has come to describe primarily a style of decoration exploiting irregular or at least asymmetrical forms, and shell, rock or plant motifs linked by C- and S-scrolls. This style of interior decoration developed in France in reaction to the grandiose formality of Louis XIV's reign, and its roots were in the "grotesque" ornament of Italy and in the decorative tradition of the school of Fontainebleau, which had never entirely faded during the seventeenth century – it had been sustained by illustrators and especially perhaps by theatrical designers.

The dividing line between Baroque and Rococo is as difficult to establish as the exact moment when the surge of a wave breaks into its own spray. Rococo continues the movement of the Baroque, but tends to fragment it and to express itself on a smaller scale (even, at its most elegant, a miniature one); the surface becomes all-important; monumentality and pomp give way to relative informality, to gaiety and often to frivolity. In painting and sculpture, these stylistic qualities are to be found with a correspondingly less solemn subject matter – characteristically Rococo are mandarins in spindly pagodas, cavorting monkeys and shepherds and shepherdesses in pastoral idylls. It coincides with a new current in French manners and morals, and embodies the sensitive and highly sophisticated feeling for the visual arts of a society that valued elegance and artifice and light-hearted wit. Although Watteau (see preceding page) is always called a Rococo artist and indeed has some essential characteristics of the style, his underlying seriousness of mood transcends it. The archetypal painter of the French Rococo was François Boucher (1703-70).

Boucher began his career making engravings of Watteau's pictures, but during four years spent in Italy (1727-31) learnt much from Veronese and Tiepolo: though he was never to attempt the scale and sweep of the Grand Manner, his characteristic palette of light but rich pastel colours reflects Tiepolo's impact. In France, his most steadfast patron was the highly influential royal mistress Madame de Pompadour, whom he portrayed many times (see over). She induced him to extend his range to the designing of ambitious decorative schemes for the royal châteaux, and of spectacular stage productions; his resulting involvement with tapestry design brought him the directorship of the Gobelins factory, and in due course he became the King's painter. In his pictures, he transformed classical mythology into scenes of erotic gallantry, copiously populated with nubile nudes (some of whom were recognizable to contemporaries as fashionable beauties of the court). His apparently effortless erotic charm is, however, based on a formidably sure draughtsmanship. If in mood and colour he was both repetitive and unfailingly artificial, his execution was always brilliant and his inventiveness inexhaustible. He perfectly answered the needs of the sophisticated society of Louis XV's reign, even though after 1760 changing taste found him unserious and even immoral – the critic Diderot reluctantly admired his art as *"un vice si agréable"* (so delightfully wicked).

Jean-Honoré Fragonard (1732-1806) was briefly and not happily Chardin's pupil, and then more aptly Boucher's. Like Boucher, he saw Tiepolo's work in Italy, and was a protégé

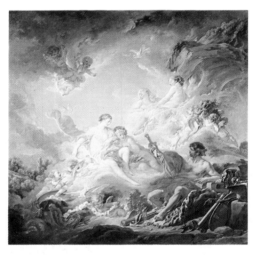

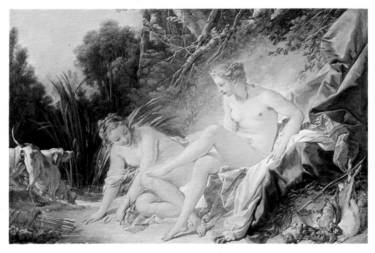

BOUCHER (left)
Vulcan presenting the arms of Aeneas to Venus, 1732
In the years up to about 1750 Boucher painted a large number of unheroic mythological pictures, all vigorous, erotic, poetic and decorative – they were in fact part of decorative schemes. In these qualities he is the intimate, informal equivalent of Tiepolo.

BOUCHER (right)
Diana bathing, 1742
The mythological settings eventually became no more than a pretext for painting gorgeous female nudes, set off, as here, by glowing draperies and a fine still life at bottom right.

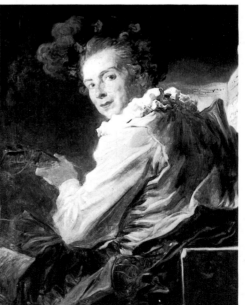

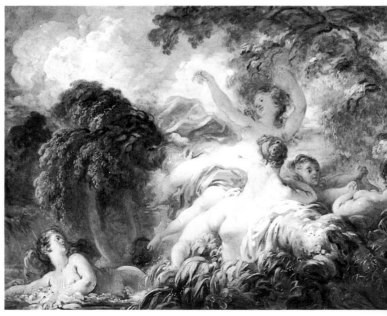

FRAGONARD (left)
Music, or M. de la Bretèche, 1769
The inscription states that the picture was painted in one hour. It is a sketch, but the characterization is fully realized, and the light and shade finely gradated; in its bravura handling it recalls Frans Hals, whom Fragonard greatly admired.

FRAGONARD (right)
Women bathing, 1777
Painted *alla prima* in a blend of translucent thin washes and dense impasto, this picture by Fragonard recalls the brushwork and curvilinear composition of Rubens – see the nymphs in *The disembarkation of Marie de Médicis* (p. 203). In the emphatic bare bottom there is conscious prurience.

of Madame de Pompadour. His themes, in their erotic gaiety, often have much in common with Boucher's, and appealed to the same clientèle, but his style developed differently: more like Watteau, he responded to the colour and free handling of Rubens and to the verve of Frans Hals. Though his pictures are often full of creams and pinks, they are never merely pretty effervescences: the dash and fluent freedom of his brushwork find their nearest counterparts in Gainsborough and Goya, and there is usually an edge of prurience or satire. Like Boucher, he sometimes delighted in nostalgic landscapes, with or without ruins, which can seem precociously romantic in mood, like the landscapes and "ruinscapes" of his gifted friend Hubert Robert (1733-1808).

The French Rococo style was exported by itinerant French artists, but also, through engravings, by a new generation of virtuoso printmakers. It influenced all Europe – it was only in England that it was not so pervasive. In Germany, however, particularly Catholic south Germany, Rococo took its own distinct form. It flowered relatively late but continued longer, from about the second quarter of the century to its end, and it was religious rather

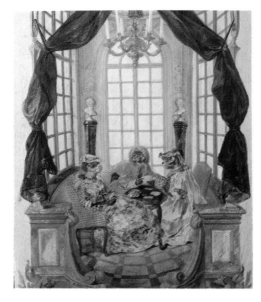

HUET (above)
The monkeys' salon, 1735
Christophe Huet (died 1759) was a master of the informal decorative scheme,

using to good effect the graceful and light-hearted arabesque, chinoiserie and *singerie* ("monkey-game") that typify Rococo décor.

than secular. Often, in its large scale and even massiveness, and particularly in its fascination with spatial complexities, it was very much within the framework of Baroque; many indigenous artists had been trained in Italy, or had visited it, while Italians from Padre Pozzo to Tiepolo had brought Italian Baroque north. There was also, not to be ignored, already a strong tradition of stucco decoration in south Germany, and an established delight in light, bright tonalities and colours.

These chief factors combined to produce an exuberant and heady hybrid, and especially brilliant concerts of the arts in the Catholic churches. Artists such as the Zimmermann brothers, Dominikus (1685-1766) and Johann Baptist (1680-1758), and the Asam brothers, Cosmas Damian (1686-1739) and Egid Quirin (1692-1750), produced interior spectaculars unsurpassed in their kind anywhere. They introduced visual opera (even at times visual musical comedy) into the repertoire of church décor. The exhilarating, airy and spacious effects obtained, often in small churches, are usually combined with a sweet simplicity, and in the artful sophistication of the Asams there was remarkable religious sincerity.

ROBERT (right)
Felling trees at Versailles, 1778?
Robert had visited Italy with Fragonard, and his landscapes, with their ruins, frond-like trees and tiny figures, have an Italianate charm. Also a landscape gardener, he designed some of the parks at Versailles.

THE ASAM BROTHERS
(below) The altar of the church of Maria Victoria, Ingolstadt, 1734
The close derivation from Roman Baroque is clear, but here the brothers have chosen delicate colours in a high key rather than rich marbling or dramatic light. Every inch is decorated.

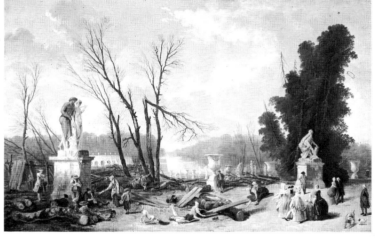

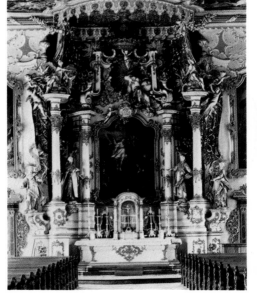

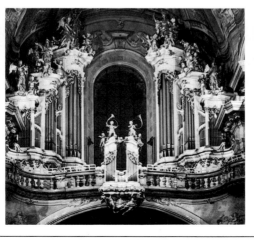

ST NICHOLAS MALA STRARIA, PRAGUE (below)
Detail of the upper nave, frescoed 1760-61
Swirling movement and an interplay of advancing and receding masses surround the delightfully posturing figures in the Jesuit church.

THE ASAM BROTHERS
(right) St John Nepomuk, 1733-46
The skilful relationship of sculpture to architecture creates a sense of spacious grandeur in this church, set on a tiny site next to Egid Quirin Asam's own house.

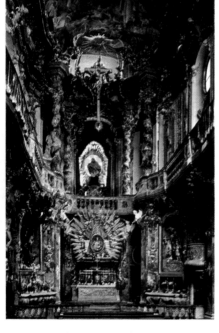

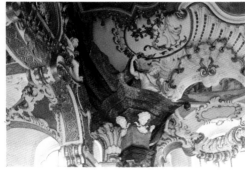

THE ZIMMERMANN BROTHERS
Detail of the ceiling of Die Wies, Bavaria, 1745-54

The church was stuccoed by Dominikus with luxuriant, colourful fronds and scrolls proliferating asymmetrically.

French Rococo 2: Portraiture and Sculpture

By the time that Louis XIV died, in 1715, after more than 70 years on the throne of France, the pomp and splendour of Versailles had become old-fashioned, though it was still the pattern for most European courts. During the Regency (1715-23) of the Duke of Orleans, Versailles virtually closed down and the boy-king Louis XV was housed in the Tuileries in Paris. An aristocratic taste succeeded the royal one: instead of the palace, the private house became the frame of culture. It was here that Rococo belonged, which, as we have seen, was primarily a style of interior decoration – even the frame of a work of art had an importance, often equal to that of the work itself. Mirrors were never long out of sight in this scheme of things; in them the self-conscious denizens of the salons could confirm their elegance, and naturally the portraitists flourished.

Two long-lived and superb professionals had become established in the previous reign, Rigaud, who had painted the aging Louis XIV (see p. 199) and Nicolas de Largillière (1656-1746). Rigaud continued to paint the court, but Largillière's clientèle was as much middle-class as aristocratic, though the flourishing *haute bourgeoisie* aspired to an elegance hardly less lavish; Largillière also painted sumptuous still lifes (see over). Although both artists answered the continuing demand for the formal "parade" portrait, their work shows the start of a clear movement away from the stupendous and magnificent towards the lively and informal. Their portraiture was always conditioned by the need of their clients to be seen at their best, but the gestures become less grandiose and robes, wigs and lace are more negligently agitated. The fashion for presenting sitters in allegorical terms – the females particularly, as the heroines or goddesses of some classical mythology, clothed in becoming (and sometimes rather scanty) fancy dress – continued to flourish. This element of role-playing, stemming especially from the Baroque portraiture of van Dyck, and prevailing also in Holland and England (Largillière had worked in Lely's studio), was well suited to the make-believe society of Louis XV's Paris; its level could vary from the realms of the gods to the Arcadian idyll of milkmaids and shepherdesses later aped by Marie Antoinette.

Following Largillière and Rigaud, the leading portraitist was Jean-Marc Nattier (1685-1766), endlessly in demand both in Parisian

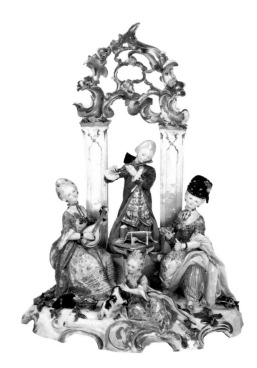

THE MEISSEN FACTORY (above) *The concerto,* c. 1760
Rococo was as much a mood as a style, affecting all the arts; indeed the fragile grace of porcelain attracted sculptors rather more than noble marble. Advances in techniques of firing and enamelling made possible such rich, deep and exquisite colours.

NATTIER (below)
Mlle Manon Balletti, 1757
The lady was the daughter of a successful actress of the Italian company in Paris. Nattier has enclosed her in an enchanting purity, suggesting palpitating flesh within the subdued colours of the rose and her gown.

LARGILLIERE (right)
The painter with his wife and daughter, c. 1700
Despite his daughter's airs, his wife's prim face and his own haughty mien, there is an easy informality about Largillière's family portrait. The artist-gentleman sits with gun, hunter and brace.

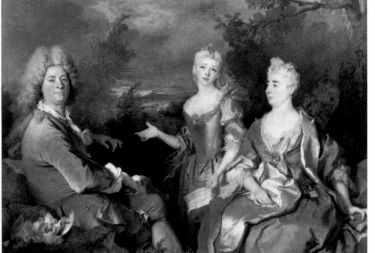

DROUAIS (below)
Comte and Chevalier de Choiseul, 1756
The Dauphin's two sons are dressed as Savoyards in national costume (of velvet, with gold buttons), beside a hurdy-gurdy. The spirit and mood prefigure Marie Antoinette's, enacting the tasks of a milkmaid in the dairy she had at Versailles.

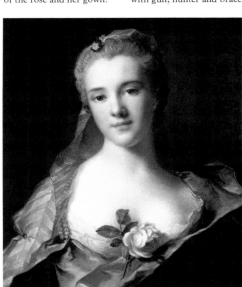

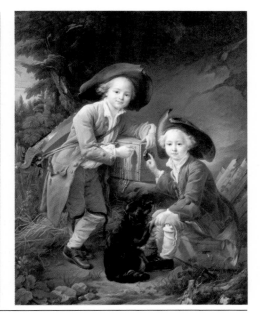

CARRIERA (right)
Self-portrait with an image of the artist's sister, 1709
In a quick, skilled hand, coloured chalks, or pastels, can be both decorative and spontaneous; it is a most direct medium, in which loose squiggles, melting planes and soft colours are characteristic. Rosalba has a pastel chalk in the holder between her fingers.

high society and at Louis XV's court. In keeping with the scale of the salon or boudoir, he painted mainly head-and-shoulders or half-length portraits, often in elaborately carved oval frames. In his pastel colouring, and a certain soft (though usually vivacious) sweetness of expression, he reflects the influence of the Venetian painter Rosalba Carriera (1675-1757). Though she spent most of her life in Venice, where she was much in vogue among tourists, a visit to Paris from 1719 to 1721 was extremely successful, and the mood of her both elegant and intimate portraiture was carried on by most of the successful French portraitists of the time. The prolific Louis Tocqué (1696-1772; not shown), Nattier's son-in-law, even exported the style eastwards in extended visits to Russia and Denmark. Both Tocqué and the younger François-Hubert Drouais (1727-75) were patronized by the Dauphin, and the quintessence of their "feminine" style is illustrated in a series of portraits of Madame de Pompadour, who was also painted many times by her protégé Boucher. This kind of portraiture was often most successful less than lifesize, and even on an almost miniature scale.

The artist, however, who reflected most

brilliantly the alert wit and sensibility of educated Parisian society, who could match its intellectual as well as its fashionable sparkle, was Maurice-Quentin de La Tour (1704-88). Following Carriera, he worked in pastel, and perhaps has hardly been surpassed in his ability to catch the movement of life in each particular sitter's features and gesture.

In sculpture, there was a parallel movement away from the grandiose and the monumental style of the established Baroque. Even though the production of classic statuary – that white progeny of nymphs, heroes and deities peopling the gardens of Versailles – did not entirely cease, the Rococo taste for the small-scale soon expressed itself. Most characteristic, perhaps, are the animated, rhythmic groups produced by the booming porcelain factories – Sèvres, Meissen and many others. Established sculptors began to produce terracotta models for mass-production. The trend is clearly illustrated in the work of Etienne-Maurice Falconet (1716-91), who began in monumental, classicizing terms, but gradually tempered especially his smaller works with a softer charm, often introducing markedly erotic overtones – almost the three-dimensional

equivalent of Boucher's painting. His style is seen at its most purely Rococo in the figures he made for the Sèvres factory, where he was director of sculpture from 1757 to 1766. He never entirely lost his interest in the monumental, however, and his most famous work, the bronze of *Peter the Great*, in St Petersburg, is heroic in scale and mood.

The culmination of erotic Rococo figure sculpture comes with Claude Michel, known as Clodion (1738-1814). There is a remarkable virtuosity in his flesh-pink terracottas, and a sensuality as rich as Boucher's, but fermented by a dynamism that can be compared to Fragonard's verve in paint. The portraiture of Quentin de La Tour had its counterpart in the busts of Jean-Baptiste Lemoyne the Younger (1704-78; not shown) or of Louis-François Roubiliac (c. 1705-62), a Huguenot from Lyons who, from about 1732, worked in England (his bust of Hogarth is illustrated on p. 248). Roubiliac, too, worked for a porcelain factory, in Chelsea, but his most spectacular works are his splendidly animated funerary monuments, which, on a simpler and smaller scale, sustain the rhetoric of the tradition stemming from Bernini.

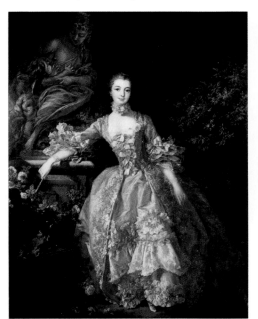

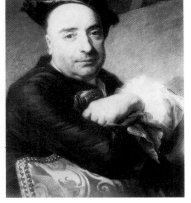

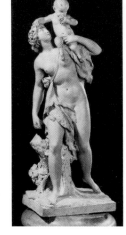

CLODION (right)
Bacchante, c. 1760
The classicism is clear in the pose and attributes of this small terracotta. But it is transformed by a finesse, a flowing grace, a smooth, elegant titillation.

QUENTIN DE LA TOUR
(left) *M. Claude Dupouch*, 1739
La Tour's pastel portrait of his drawing-master, leaning so casually on the back of an armchair, seems as instant as a snapshot, but also conveys a warm and sympathetic presence.

FALCONET (right)
Erigone, 1747
Falconet's nymph, a model for a porcelain figurine, has an animated softness and warmth, which Falconet (as he stated in numerous essays, published in 1781) found to be lacking in the sculpture of antiquity.

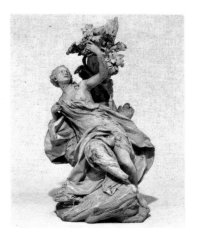

BOUCHER (above)
Mme de Pompadour, 1759
Boucher's brush enhanced the charms of the King's famous mistress in a series of ravishing portraits. He also decorated her rooms in the same sumptuously weightless manner, soon dubbed "*style Pompadour*"

FALCONET (right)
Peter the Great, 1766-68
In depicting the Tsar on a horse rearing dramatically on a rock, Falconet kept alive the Baroque tradition that Bernini had brought to Louis XIV's Paris, and to which the Empire would return. But he obtained no such commission in France. To set the horse rearing – diminishing its support – was a great technical feat.

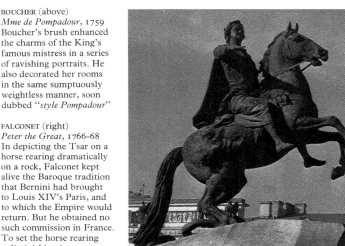

ROUBILIAC (right)
Monument to Lady Elizabeth Nightingale, 1761
Vainly her husband tries to save Lady Elizabeth from Death, leaping from below like a jack-in-the-box. The idea is taken from Bernini's tomb of Pope Clement VII in St Peter's (not shown).

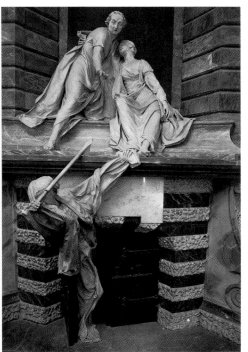

Genre and Still-life Painting

By the eighteenth century pictures of small to medium size, in handsome but not too large urban houses, had become a normal and integral part of interior decoration. Already in the late seventeenth century Netherlandish immigrants in England are recorded supplying landscapes and other subjects for lintels or mantels at a fixed price per foot. It was above all in Holland, with its prosperous, middle-class society, that painters had explored the subject matter suitable for this sort of picture – the prosaic aspects of everyday life, landscape, still life and genre scenes, often with some anecdotal interest.

Although the ever-growing market for paintings was answered mainly by exercises in the conventions established by the Dutch, in virtually all countries there was already present an indigenous tradition. In Italy, a taste for genre is already apparent in the late fifteenth-century paintings of Carpaccio. Caravaggio had raised genre to high art; later, the Bolognese painter Giuseppe Maria Crespi (1665-1747; not shown) had reduced even the most solemn biblical themes to the terms of peasant life, in humble, indeed sordid settings. Crespi's many pupils included the Venetians

Pietro Longhi (1702-85) and Giambattista Piazzetta (see p.235), and even in his altar-pieces, in the restraint of their colour and their rustic characterizations, Piazzetta seems nearer to genre than to Baroque exaltation. Throughout his career he also painted and made finished genre drawings, especially half-lengths and heads of peasant characters, which were widely popular, and about 1740 painted some highly evocative and mysterious pictures, hovering between allegory and genre.

Pietro Longhi, on the other hand, was the daily chronicler of incident and gossip in the pleasure-loving and carnival-going Venetian society of his time, and worked in a much more Dutch vein. His little paintings, haunted by black-swathed revellers in white-beaked masks, have a repertoire ranging from such trivia as a visit to the doctor to more exotic, headline-catching events – such as the visit to Venice of a rhinoceros. Then Giandomenico Tiepolo (1727-1804), the son and collaborator of the great Giambattista, raised genre to a grander scale in his frescos for the Villa Valmarana near Vicenza. Here, as in Longhi, there is no more than an occasional spice of satire, and their mood is almost mysterious,

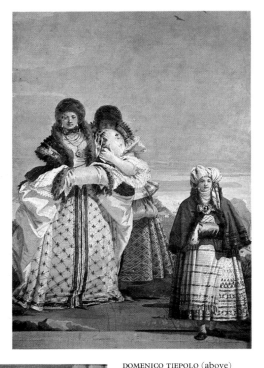

PIAZZETTA (right)
The fortune-teller, 1740
The figures are portrayed with something of the ripe sentimentalism that made Murillo's *Urchins* popular. The clear suggestiveness of the figures' gestures is in accord with the Rococo love of tastefully prurient pictures of peasant girls in states of *déshabillé*.

TROOST (below)
The city garden, c.1742
Troost is often compared to Hogarth, with whom he was exactly contemporary, but he lacks Hogarth's moral intention. This charming, highly finished painting, which combines a Rococo elegance with elements of traditional Dutch genre, is a tribute to a new concept of civilized, bourgeois living.

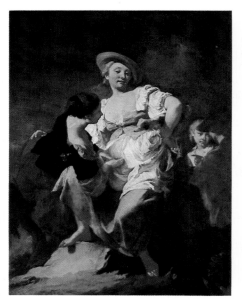

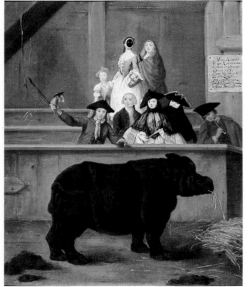

DOMENICO TIEPOLO (above)
The winter promenade, 1757
In the 18th century the boundary between genre and "history" painting was slowly eroded; the process was completed in the 19th. Domenico's subjects – this is one of a pair representing Summer and Winter – were thought suitable only for the guest house of the Villa Valmarana. Delight in trivial details of every-day life is thinly disguised in an allegory of the Seasons.

LONGHI (left)
The rhinoceros, 1751
Longhi's paintings have an airless quality, reflecting the claustrophobia of upper-class life in Venice – the "parade of appearances", as Lorenzo da Ponte, Mozart's librettist, called it. Manners and dress are described with unremitting decorousness.

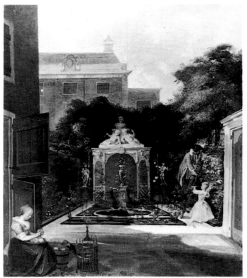

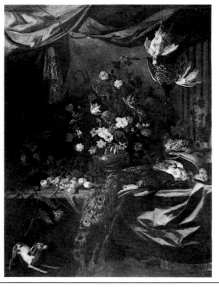

LARGILLIERE (left)
Still life, c.1690
Largillière was trained in the Flemish tradition under Lely in London, and the heaped-up sumptuousness, the rich textures, even the dog in movement beneath, all recall Flemish still life.

OUDRY (right)
The white duck, 1753
The accuracy of natural detail reflects a growing scientific interest in the world, and in the late 18th century private menageries became popular. Oudry is best known for his still life with virtuoso surface effects, though his book illustrations are notable, and he had a successful career as a designer at the famous Gobelins factory.

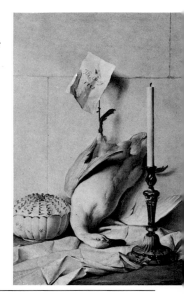

strangely poised between the comic and the melancholic; his astonishingly original tumblers, clowns and other figures seem to foreshadow not only Goya but also early Picasso.

A host of painters in Holland pursued the themes set in the seventeenth century. Many were capable, but none was of great originality, with the exception perhaps of Cornelis Troost (1697-1750), who recorded little portrait and genre groups with a charming, somewhat Italianate, elegance. In France, Dutch and Flemish genre and still-life paintings were collected with avidity, and some French artists, such as Largillière, the portraitist (see preceding page), painted brilliant still lifes of dead game in a very Flemish manner. France produced the supreme master of still life, the painter who seems both to sum up and to transcend the achievements of his predecessors in Holland, Chardin (see over). Jean-Baptiste Oudry (1686-1755), a pupil of Largillière, early on developed a distinct style, depending little on the Netherlandish traditions – light and open, with a most subtle command of tone: he specialized in game pieces for the royal hunting lodges, and in the most delicate modulation of white on white.

It was in France, too, that genre themes with a moral sentiment found for a time an appreciative audience. The leading master was Jean-Baptiste Greuze (1725-1805). From 1755 on, he produced a long series of subject pictures, the nature of which is indicated by their titles (such as *The grandfather reading the Bible to his family*, or *The paralytic tended by his children*). In these he attempted to reconcile the values of genre with those of "history" or epic painting, while in mood he answered the "sensibility" of the time – that ready compassion and eager emotional conscience characteristic of the 1760s and 1770s, of a society a generation away from revolution. Greuze's "sensibility", his moralizing and sentimental didacticism, was exactly in key with the theories of the leading writer on art, Denis Diderot (1713-84), who diagnosed in Greuze "the painter of virtue and the saviour from moral degradation". In a sense, Greuze reacted against the frivolities of the followers of Watteau, and his compositions, emphatic with meaningful gesture, paying homage to Poussin, foreshadow the Neoclassicism of David. Yet his single-figure studies of girls and children have a sometimes mawkish sweetness that is another aspect of

the erotic taste of the Rococo. His influence in Europe, propagated by engravings, was enormous, and inspired much of the sentimental genre of the nineteenth century.

Many of Greuze's genre figures are portraits, and some qualities of genre could also be applied to portraiture, notably small-scale group portraiture. The "conversation piece", in which the sitters are seen in their domestic setting, engaged in some leisurely pastime, was essentially a Dutch invention but became an English speciality, associated above all with William Hogarth (see p. 248). The conversation piece reflected pride in family and property, the secure status of a prosperous landed gentry and merchant class, and many artists exploited it in the eighteenth century. Arthur Devis (1711-87) is the "primitive" among them, preserving his rather doll-like sitters with awkward charm in a silvery silence; both Francis Hayman (1708-76) and the young Gainsborough (see p. 252) produced masterpieces in the genre. Hayman also painted bucolic allegories and scenes from the stage; Hogarth, however, was the restless, endlessly inventive master of genre, extending its capacity to story-telling and biting satire.

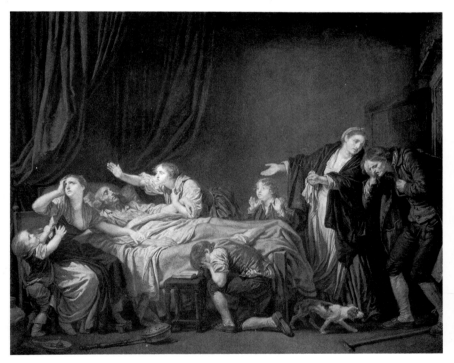

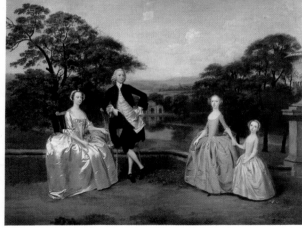

GREUZE (left)
The son punished, c. 1777
The over-emphatic effects may be due to Greuze's study of the theatre. The wicked son returns to find his father dying – as at the end of a play: one expects the actors to cease their posturing and take a bow.

DEVIS (below)
The James family, 1752
The figures are presented in quiet isolation before a landscape: this so-called conversation piece is an inventory of family and possessions, more Rococo than robust in the grand old tradition of Kneller.

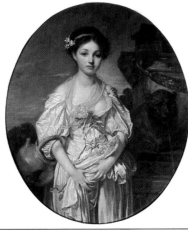

GREUZE (left)
The broken pitcher, c. 1773
The artist's beautiful but heartless wife, Gabrielle Balbuty, posed for this unambiguous allegory of lost innocence. Greuze does not hesitate to titillate while mourning for her virtue.

HAYMAN (right)
The wrestling scene from Shakespeare's As You Like It, c. 1744
Figures and setting reflect the staging conventions of contemporary theatre. This is an early example of the later vogue for paintings and prints of episodes in plays.

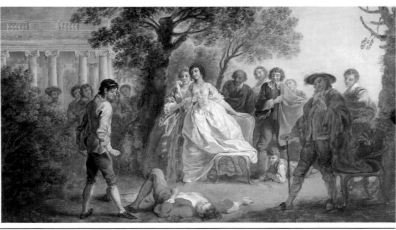

Chardin: The House of Cards

Jean-Baptiste-Siméon Chardin (1699-1779) developed only two main themes throughout his long career – still life, and domestic genre subjects. The still life is usually observed in the kitchen, rather than in the opulent dining-room implied by so many Dutch and Flemish still lifes; the genre scenes, too, are often sited "below stairs" – servants about their chores or – a favourite focus – children at play.

The boy building a house of cards is a subject to which Chardin returned several times. The concentration of the child, the delicacy of the operation on which he is engaged, are matched by the painter's concentration and subtlety. The image is essentially of transience, expressing the brevity and innocence of childhood: the cards will collapse and be put away in the half-open drawer; the child will grow up. This is observed with the utmost objectivity, though bourgeois values are implicit – a leisured society in which a house of cards is practicable, a secure family context. But there is no moralizing intent, as in Greuze; no sly overtones, as in Fragonard; and no trace of Boucher's Rococo fantasy.

Chardin's approach to his subjects was direct, relying not on preparatory drawings but on painting from nature straight on to the canvas: the density and richness of his paintings comes from an elaborate building up of the paint itself. For this there were precedents (there was the example, for instance, of Rembrandt's impasto), but it was noted by contemporaries as entirely new. The arbiter of contemporary taste, Diderot, commented: "There is a magic in this art that passes our understanding. Sometimes thick coats of colour are applied one above the other so that their effects seep upward from below. At other times one gets the impression that a vapour has been floated across the canvas, or a light sprayed over it. Draw near, everything becomes confused, flattens out, disappears, but step back and everything takes shape again, comes back to life" – effects achieved by a combination of broad and very fine brushwork, sensitive both to the textural qualities of the objects and to the pictorial qualities of the canvas. But the handling is supported by an ability to select a composition in which modern eyes can diagnose an abstract structure underlying the vivid reality of the images.

Chardin's beginnings were unorthodox: he did not pass through the Academy, and he had difficulty in establishing his artistic status. He was constantly being compared with Dutch and Flemish predecessors. The move from still life to scenes of domestic genre was prompted in part by this need to "elevate his art" and his prestige. For a time he further expanded his range to paintings that have elements of portraiture, but characteristically his subjects perform some undramatic, domestic action. Although these seem not to have met with such general favour, all aspects of his work were very successful, not so much among the middle classes as among his fellow-artists and with aristocratic connoisseurs. He repeated many subjects in replicas, and there was a widespread demand for engravings of his work, surpassing, it was noted at the time, the demand for the hitherto more fashionable allegorical and historical pieces.

CHARDIN (below)
Skate, cat and kitchen utensils, 1728
Exhibition of this early still life led to Chardin's election in 1728 to the Académie Royale. It shows, consummated for the first time, a sensuous pleasure in the substance and texture of paint which soon became characteristic of the French school. Chardin lies behind the still lifes of Courbet, Manet, Monet and Cézanne.

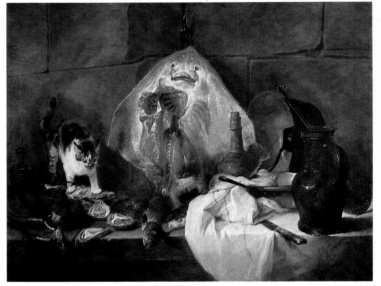

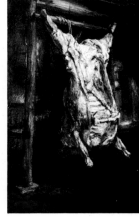

REMBRANDT (above)
The flayed ox, 1655
Rembrandt's picture was surely known to Chardin, and probably a precedent for the aggressive realism of Chardin's lurid *Skate*, disembowelled and bloody on its hook. Rembrandt's glow of light against dark was a more lasting lesson.

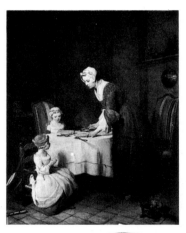

CHARDIN (left)
Saying grace, c. 1740
Chardin's modesty seems stark beside Boucher's sparkling gaiety (right). Perhaps he needed such unassuming, uninteresting domestic settings (so they perhaps appeared to those who preferred Boucher) to set off the voluptuousness of his paint. He depended, as Boucher did not, on the perspicacity of connoisseurs.

BOUCHER (right)
Breakfast, 1739
The very close similarity in composition between the two pictures emphasizes the difference in approach.

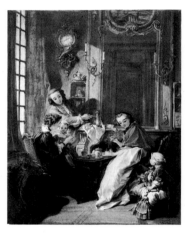

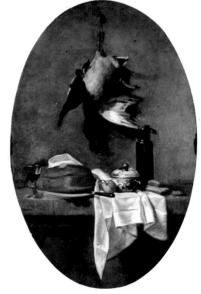

CHARDIN (above)
Still life with a wild duck, 1764
Chardin's reversion to still lifes in his latter years was due perhaps partly to his second marriage, to a rich wife, who brought him a new financial independence and thus artistic freedom.

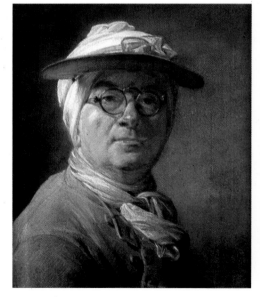

CHARDIN (above)
Self-portrait with an eyeshade, 1775
Neither illness nor failing eyesight stopped the aged Chardin painting, though he was forced to work in pastel. His very late *Self-portraits* are outstanding in their naked directness.

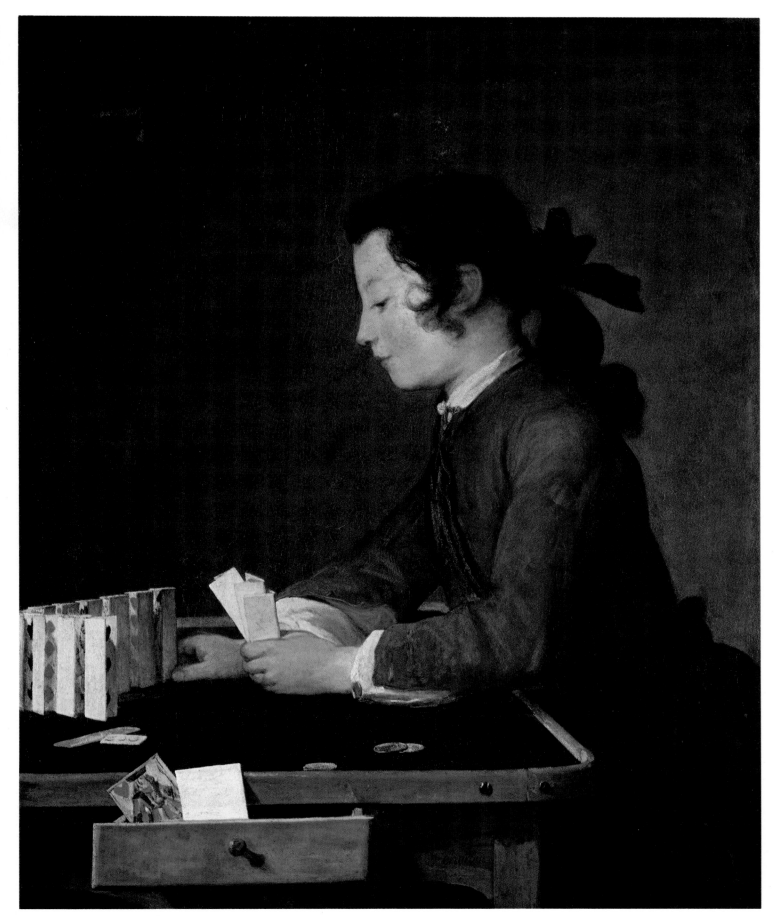

CHARDIN: *The house of cards* (in the National Gallery, Washington), *c.* 1741

William Hogarth

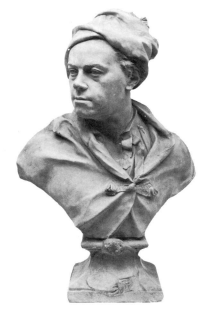

William Hogarth (1697-1764) was the first British-born painter to achieve an international influence and stature: artists such as Holbein, van Dyck, Lely, Kneller had all been immigrants. Highly individual and independent, truculent and frankly chauvinistic in his distrust of Continental art and artists, Hogarth asserted the validity of an English genius in art. Yet his spiritual allegiance was as much to literature, with the novel and the drama, as to painting, and his influence on the direction later painters would take was small. By his example, however, he helped his profession on its way to independence from a narrow aristocratic patronage, especially by his success in protecting the copyright of engravings, which increasingly became a source of income for artists. It was through engraving – the discipline in which he was trained – that Hogarth was primarily known, in Britain and abroad.

His character is reflected faithfully in his forthright *Self-portrait* of 1745. A touch of traditional pomp persists in the drape of the red curtain, but he presents himself otherwise informal, in his cap, with the tools of the trade, palette and brushes; with his English pug-dog Trump, and his spiritual associates, the works of the heroes of British culture, not Homer or Virgil but Shakespeare, Milton and Swift. The allusion to Swift, the biting satirist, is more obviously significant, since Hogarth's enduring fame derives from his satirical genre and his portraits. But the allusion to Shakespeare and Milton may be a reminder that he also saw himself as the first truly British exponent of epic and dramatic painting. His ventures into more traditional fields are little remembered, but posterity has admitted the claim of his friend, the novelist Henry Fielding, that Hogarth was the first great comic-history painter, just as *Tom Jones* established Fielding as a comic-history writer in prose. For Fielding, comedy was no less "serious" than tragedy, and Hogarth's busy scenes are not mere burlesques, but moral and social satires in key with the philanthropic, reforming mood of Henry Fielding's novels.

On the palette in the portrait is the "line of beauty", reference to Hogarth's treatise *The Analysis of Beauty*, and in its broken curve a patent recognition of Rococo. Although he ridiculed the English connoisseur's obsession with foreign art, and "the ship-loads of dead Christs, Madonnas and Holy Families" arriv-

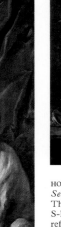

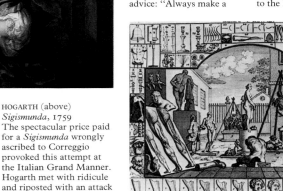

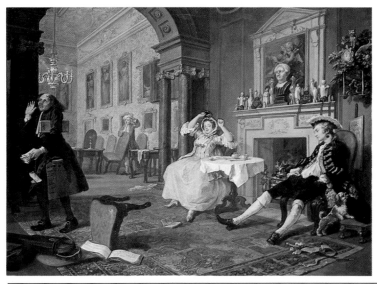

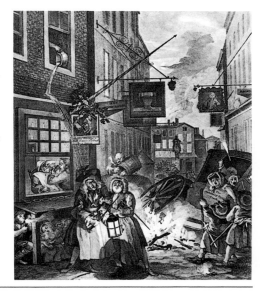

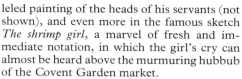

ing on the London market, he visited Paris in 1743, and the influence of Watteau and especially Chardin can be detected in the vigorous delicacy of his handling of paint.

Hogarth found his material not only in the swarming streets of contemporary London, but also on the stage: like a drama, *The Rake's Progress* unfolds the story of the destruction of its hero in eight separate paintings, each a crucial scene in the development of the plot. The moral of the whole, the Rake's destruction, is soon obvious, and the delight of the paintings is their satirical observation, endlessly inventive and intricate in detail, and with many targets, of contemporary taste in pictures and furnishings, as well as morals and manners. However, the quality of the paintings is uneven, since they were primarily intended as designs for engravings. Artistically, the finest set is *Marriage à la Mode*, where both the formal composition and the "stage-craft" – the dramatic impact – are at their best (this series was perhaps aimed at a more middle-class market, though likewise intended for engraving). His last series, *An Election*, is the largest in scale, the most broadly Baroque in composition and Hogarth's

clearest acknowledgment of his Dutch and Flemish ancestors, but it is unsurpassed by any genre painter in its teeming dynamism. This set satirizes corruption in public affairs; there are others in which the satirical comment is milder, such as *The Four Times of Day*, which has no continuous theme other than the element of time and of London topography. However, Hogarth's characters are always firmly rooted in the grossness of contemporary London life, and many of them were immediately identifiable as portraits of contemporary celebrities.

Not only a similar directness, but the same instinct for theatre, is found in Hogarth's portraiture. His conversation pieces are enlivened by the atmospherics of a domestic drama, overt or latent, far surpassing that of his rivals – indeed it is sometimes uncertain whether his little groups are portraits or pure genre. In his life-scale single portraits, working usually within the conventional head-and-shoulders format of the time, he produced honest, vivid, direct characterizations, suggesting the opening of a new, bourgeois chapter in the history of portrait painting. This directness is most remarkable in an unparal-

leled painting of the heads of his servants (not shown), and even more in the famous sketch *The shrimp girl*, a marvel of fresh and immediate notation, in which the girl's cry can almost be heard above the murmuring hubbub of the Covent Garden market.

Hogarth never followed up this exploration of "democratic" portraiture, but in at least one case he produced a quite deliberate, and brilliantly successful, attempt to marry the Grand tradition of formal portraiture with his own frankness of vision. The painting of *Captain Coram*, 1740, repeats very closely a design used by the French Baroque painter Rigaud (otherwise an object of Hogarth's scorn), and derived by Rigaud ultimately from van Dyck; amidst the Baroque swirl, the drapes, the column, the many accessories, the bluff sea-captain presides, benign and homely, sitting in a chair with his feet barely touching the floor.

Popular response to Hogarth was keen, but that of British connoisseurs was not. Posterity, however, has ranked him ever higher, while through the medium of his prints he was recognized and admired, especially as a social commentator and reformer, throughout Western Europe.

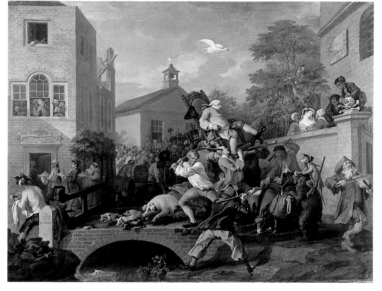

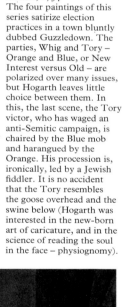

HOGARTH (left)
An Election: Chairing the member, 1754
The four paintings of this series satirize election practices in a town bluntly dubbed Guzzledown. The parties, Whig and Tory – Orange and Blue, or New Interest versus Old – are polarized over many issues, but Hogarth leaves little choice between them. In this, the last scene, the Tory victor, who has waged an anti-Semitic campaign, is chaired by the Blue mob and harangued by the Orange. His procession is, ironically, led by a Jewish fiddler. It is no accident that the Tory resembles the goose overhead and the swine below (Hogarth was interested in the new-born art of caricature, and in the science of reading the soul in the face – physiognomy).

HOGARTH
The Rake's Progress:
(above) *The orgy*; (below)
The madhouse, 1733-35
All Hogarth's gifts as a story-teller attend his spirited *Orgy*, in which the "serpentine line" of his aesthetic theory can be traced in the arrangement of figures. In *The madhouse*, stark lighting accents the tragic drama of the Rake, burned out in syphilitic body and brain, and dying in the company of lunatics – one thinks himself a king, another thinks he is God.

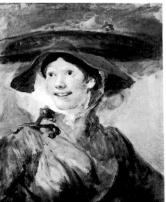

HOGARTH (left)
The shrimp girl, 1745
Hogarth's gifts as a story-teller may easily obscure the spontaneous skill of his painting, vivid in rare oil-sketches anticipating the verve of Manet; but this one is probably unfinished.

HOGARTH (right)
Captain Coram, 1740
A brilliant adaptation of Baroque state portraiture to a middle-class idiom, Hogarth's portrait, painted for the Foundling Hospital which Coram had founded, had a further significance: through it he induced other artists to donate pictures to the Hospital. They were shown publicly, initiating the institution of London exhibitions and ultimately of the Royal Academy.

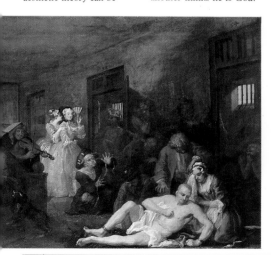

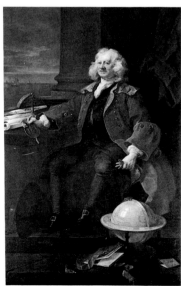

British Portraiture and Genre

The coming of age of British painting is marked by the foundation in London of the Royal Academy of Arts in 1768. Hogarth, the "father" of British painting, had been a solitary figure, and left no school of followers. It was one of the Academy's roles to establish British painting as a significant current within the mainstream of the European tradition.

The intellectual and theoretical creed of the Academy was set out by its founding President, Sir Joshua Reynolds (1723-92), in a series of remarkable *Discourses*, delivered one each year to the students. These still stand as a lucid statement of the case for eclecticism, for formulating a composite style, drawing from the best of antiquity as well as from the masters of the Renaissance and after. Reynolds had studied the Old Masters during an extended and crucial visit to Italy (1750-52), and his knowledge of them informed and influenced his work for the rest of his life. Among British artists of the time, only the landscapist Richard Wilson (see p. 255) and Reynolds' early rival Allan Ramsay (1713-84) had a similarly cosmopolitan artistic education.

In London from 1753, Reynolds rapidly established a successful portrait practice, becoming involved in the literary circle of Dr Johnson, Boswell, Edmund Burke, the playwright Goldsmith and the actor Garrick. His reliance on the Old Masters in his painting was comparable to a writer's use of the classics, more a matter of giving his work a richer resonance by quotation and cross-reference than of straight copying or plagiarism (though some contemporaries accused him of that). The tenets of his *Discourses* were firmly based on a characteristically eighteenth-century rationalism and morality, and his aims were the Sublime and the Ideal. Thus, for him, the supreme achievement of painting could be found only in epic or "history" painting, the grandest of subjects matched by the grandest of styles. This doctrine was to remain like an albatross about the shoulders of English painting for the next century. Reynolds' own attempts at history painting are not great successes, and his true achievement was to raise humble "face-painting" to the imaginative level of high theatre. He borrowed and integrated classical poses into his portraiture, and created a new kind of portrait, halfway between literal likeness and traditional mythological painting – as in *Lady Sarah Bunbury*

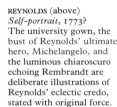

REYNOLDS (below)
The Hon. Augustus Keppel, 1753-54
Striding in classical pose and yet quick with genuine naturalism, the Admiral seems actively involved in the shifting weather of life.

REYNOLDS (right)
Sarah Siddons as the Tragic Muse, 1784
Reynolds' "Grand Style" was nicely suited to Mrs Siddons' fame in London as a tragic heroine, in its astute sense of theatre.

REYNOLDS (above)
Self-portrait, 1773?
The university gown, the bust of Reynolds' ultimate hero, Michelangelo, and the luminous chiaroscuro echoing Rembrandt are deliberate illustrations of Reynolds' eclectic credo, stated with original force.

REYNOLDS (left)
Lady Sarah Bunbury sacrificing to the Graces, 1765
Props from mythology and antiquity embellish a literal likeness of the sitter, who, with classical gesture, worships at the altar of beauty.

RAMSAY (below)
Margaret Lindsay, c. 1775
The artist's wife is painted with a graceful intimacy Reynolds emulated; but he had little sympathy for Ramsay's Rococo delicacy.

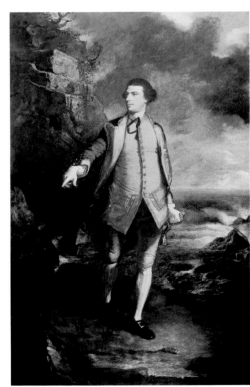

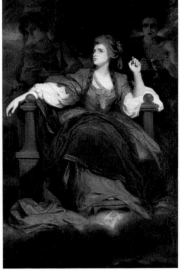

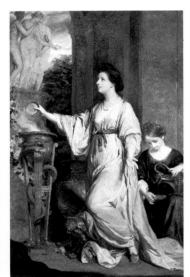

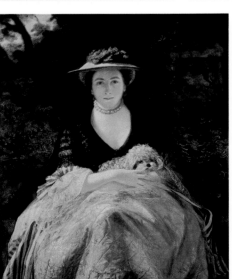

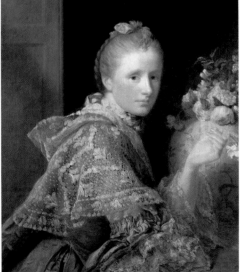

REYNOLDS (right)
Nelly O'Brien, 1760-62
Reynolds' simpler portraits are more to modern taste, especially those of well-known friends such as this famous demi-mondaine. She often sat for him: her haunting beauty is evoked

with an informality that reflects a close relationship. The delicate handling of the different textures, the delight in soft shadows and reflected lights upon the face, recall Rubens' portraits of Hélène Fourment (see p. 202), not by chance.

sacrificing to the Graces – culminating in his tremendous vision of the actress *Sarah Siddons* as a Michelangelo Sybil. Yet he could still extract the sublest nuances of character, and he was inexhaustibly flexible in his approach to each new sitter – in this he was without peer, and his rival Gainsborough (see over) admitted ruefully: "Damn him: how various he is!"

Reynolds' work became widely known through mezzotints, which could reproduce more of the richness of tone of oil-paintings than could line-engravings, and in which a few English engravers were the supreme virtuosi. His reputation has since suffered from various shortcomings – overproduction, with much work done by the studio; his use of perishable techniques (due to his restless search for new effects and for the lost secrets of the Venetian colourists); perhaps, too, a personal failing of charm. His ambition, his reasonableness, a certain cool at the heart of his character, may seem unattractive. Yet this was not apparent to contemporaries. Urbane and strong-willed, he raised the artist's calling to a new dignity by his personal example; his portraiture provided generations of English artists with a grammar and syntax of form; and the Academy he was

largely responsible for founding proved an enduring institution.

Within the Academy there grew up, in fact, a solid tradition of draughtsmanship, technique and professional conduct, and this in spite of an uneasy relationship between it and the more original of Reynolds' contemporaries. For Reynolds, the landscape painting which Wilson practised, which was the true but frustrated love of Gainsborough, was a lesser form of art. Lesser still was genre or animal painting. George Stubbs (1724-1806), primarily a horse-painter, could command prices sometimes higher than Reynolds', but has been recognized only in this century as an artist of comparable stature. Indifferent to cultural precept, he visited Italy briefly to confirm his view that Italian art had nothing to teach that could not be learned from Nature. His true "academy" was eighteen months spent drawing equine anatomy from the appalling carcases of decaying horses in a remote farmhouse in Lincolnshire, resulting in a scientific and artistic landmark – the etchings in his remarkable treatise *The Anatomy of the Horse*, 1766. The knowledge he gained was applied to his paintings of horses and animals, but was

controlled by a mastery of space, form and colour unmatched in his time.

Stubbs, too, had epic yearnings, as his many studies of horrific animal conflict witness – his images of lions assaulting horses influenced Delacroix. The provincial painter Joseph Wright of Derby (1734-97), who like Stubbs never became a full Academician, only an Associate, succeeded in raising genre to almost heroic proportions, though he, too, has waited till this century for reappraisal. Fascinated with candlelit or moonlit effects, he applied them sometimes to industrial or scientific subjects, but also to landscape, treated sometimes apocalyptically, foreshadowing Romanticism. He was also a forthright portraitist.

It is also as a portraitist that George Romney (1734-1802) is primarily remembered. Holding aloof from the Academy, he specialized in somewhat sweetly generalized portraits, with statuesque poses and broadly handled draperies. The Hogarthian tradition of the conversation piece was carried on by several competent painters, most notably by the German-born Johann Zoffany (1734/5-1810), reflecting eighteenth-century domesticity with a stolid, but still often sprightly charm.

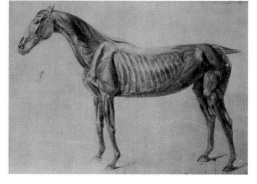

STUBBS (above)
Flayed horse, 1766
The tradition of sporting pictures recording the English gentry's love of

horses, hunting and dogs did not satisfy Stubbs, a natural scientist whose study of structure informs his drawings and canvases.

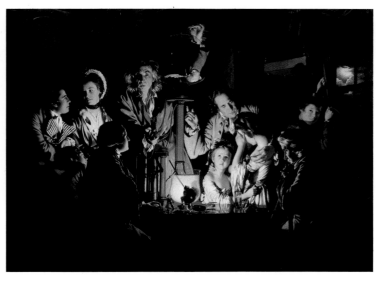

STUBBS (left)
The reapers, 1786
Landscape and human activity are observed with a direct simplicity which had scarcely been seen since Bruegel. The capacity for rendering form in space is classic; the rhythmic movement of the workers across the surface of the picture has a frieze-like quality; yet the composition is transformed by the naturalism of the figures. Like the landscape itself, they are emphatically English – far removed from the artifice of idealized Italianate pastorals. The light evokes the drawing-on of evening, an understated melancholy.

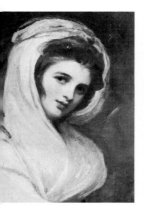

ROMNEY (above)
Emma Lady Hamilton, 1785
Romney's portraits are not usually searching; he projected a glamorous, simple handsomeness, not unlike that of early Hollywood publicity photographs. Emma, the famous mistress of Nelson, had lowly origins but a Hollywood-like career.

WRIGHT (left)
The experiment on a bird in an air pump, c. 1767-68
A new "historical" genre is created to express the contemporary collision of science and humanity as the child's pet bird is asphyxiated to demonstrate the creation of a vacuum. Wright's chiaroscuro lends an almost religious feeling.

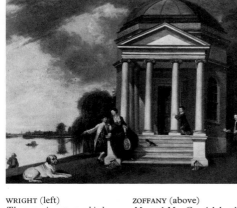

ZOFFANY (above)
Mr and Mrs Garrick by the Shakespearean temple at Hampton, 1762
Garrick employed Zoffany for self-publicity; Zoffany made his name painting Garrick in his stage roles. Garrick's elegant villa by the Thames, with its Adam temple and its Capability Brown park, is the setting.

Gainsborough: Mary, Countess Howe

Thomas Gainsborough (1727-88) painted Lady Howe's portrait about 1763-64. The sitter, the wife of a naval officer later to become one of Britain's heroes, was in her early thirties, the painter a little older, just settling into his assured maturity. The portrait was painted in the fashionable spa of Bath, where Gainsborough had moved from his native Suffolk in 1759. His early portraits in Suffolk had been of the provinces, a little naive and tending to the awkward, but both direct and delicately sensitive. He had already produced masterpieces with these qualities, such as the small-scale *Mr and Mrs Andrews* of about 1748, doubtless a marriage portrait, which unites the vivid young couple with an equally vivid portrait of the fertile sunlit Suffolk corn country. For the fashionable clientèle of Bath a more fully resolved sophisticated elegance was necessary, and for it Gainsborough deliberately evolved an appropriate style, inspired above all by the example of van Dyck.

In a very early portrait of his Bath period, the *Mrs Philip Thicknesse* of 1760, the pose is developed from a precedent by van Dyck into spiralling Rococo movement. Original and essentially informal compared with most society portraiture, it was disconcerting as such to some contemporaries. "A most extraordinary figure, handsome and bold", commented one, "but I should be very sorry to have anyone I loved set forth in such a manner." Four or five years later the image of Lady Howe, no less original and equally paying homage to van Dyck, is stabilized in a more orthodox decorum, but with that bewitching ease of informality within formality, in which none have surpassed Gainsborough. The difficult marriage of a literal likeness ("the principal beauty of a portrait", said Gainsborough once, perhaps in peevish response to his rival Reynolds' insistence on generalizing) with the urgency of his almost fluid handling of colour in paint is here magisterially consummated. Lady Howe is at once of flesh and blood, and a shimmering cascade of pinks and greys. The hat, so lovingly dwelt upon, adds a touch of chinoiserie. The landscape has dissolved away from the factual account of the Andrews painting, and is perhaps the least satisfactory part of the composition: the silver birch, a complementary vertical to the sitter's figure, is an afterthought.

A little later, in his most famous portrait, "*The Blue Boy*", Gainsborough made his most explicit homage to van Dyck. It was painted not as a commission but for the artist's own pleasure, though he showed it at the Academy in 1770. The subject was a friend, Jonathan Buttall, the dress a van Dyckian studio prop – the fancy dress fashionable with sitters at the time and used by many painters other than Gainsborough, including Reynolds. The result, a sophisticated romantic vision, shows all the fluency with which Gainsborough's style was opening out. Here landscape and figure are fully integrated, echoing each other in their rhythm. Gainsborough had a passion for music, and in contrast to Reynolds' more theoretical and literary bent, his genius demands a musical analogy. "One part of a picture ought to be like the first part of a tune ... you can guess what follows, and that makes the second part of the tune." Reynolds, in his tribute to Gainsborough after his death, indicated much the same, praising "his manner of forming all the parts of his picture together; the whole thing going on at the same time, in the same manner as Nature creates her works".

In the final phase of Gainsborough's career, in London, where he moved in 1774, his style became ever more fluent, free and open. His loyalty to the likeness remained – as in *Mrs Siddons*, seen as an imperious lady of fashion in remarkable contrast to Reynolds' apotheosis of the same sitter (see preceding page). Gainsborough at his most inspired, his most original, as in the flickering, shimmering vision of "*The Morning Walk*", seems to merge his sitters into the landscape as in a happy dream.

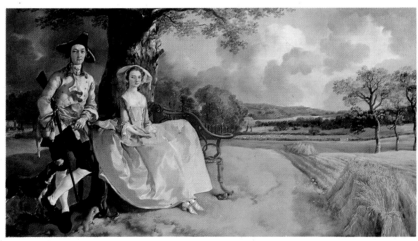

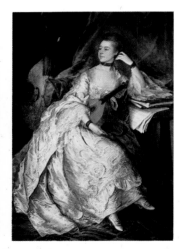

GAINSBOROUGH (left)
Mrs Philip Thicknesse, 1760
Gainsborough's style was nourished by van Dyck and some French Rococo. This portrait could be set beside Boucher's images of *Mme de Pompadour* (see p. 243), but its nervous intensity differentiates it.

GAINSBOROUGH (below)
"*The Morning Walk*"
(Mr and Mrs Hallett), 1785
Gainsborough's animated brushwork drew comment from Reynolds – "those odd scratches and marks ...this chaos which by a kind of magic at a certain distance assumes form".

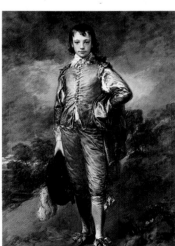

GAINSBOROUGH (above)
Mr and Mrs Andrews, c.1748
At heart a landscapist who earned his living "in the Face way", Gainsborough started his career painting precise conversation pieces closely comparable with the work of Devis (see p. 245).

GAINSBOROUGH (left)
"*The Blue Boy*", c.1770
Gainsborough worked with very long brushes, in oils thinned to the consistency of watercolour, to achieve his shimmering effects.

GAINSBOROUGH (right)
Mrs Sarah Siddons, 1785
"Damn the nose, there's no end of it", Gainsborough is reported to have remarked. He uses it to enhance the presence of the sitter, shapes it into the nature of her imposing beauty.

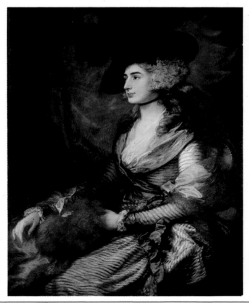

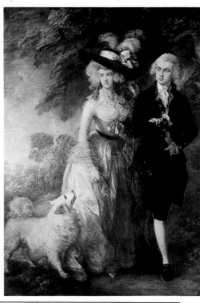

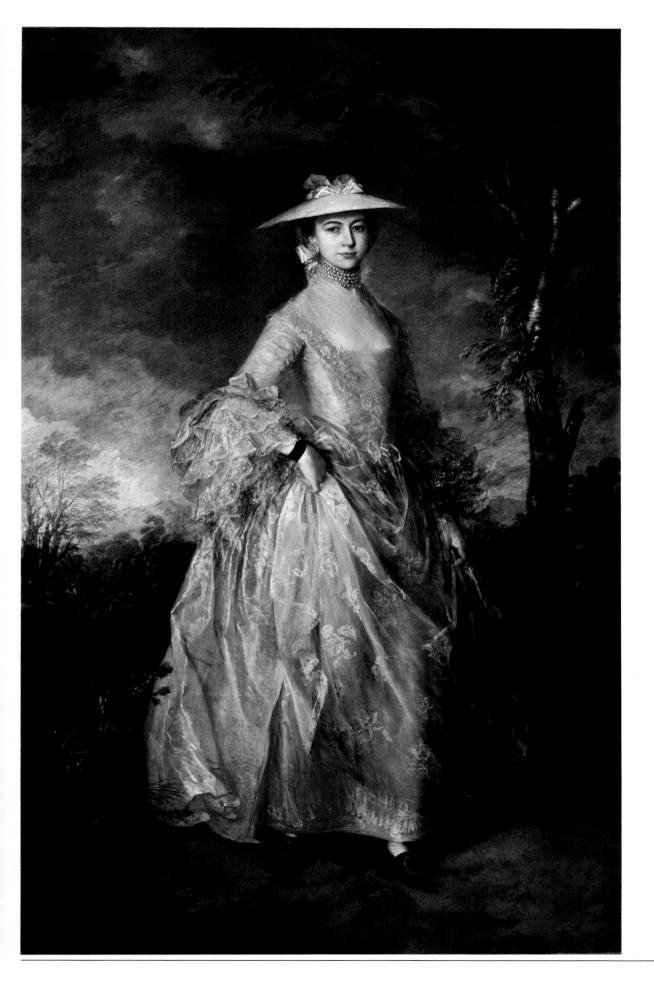

GAINSBOROUGH
Mary, Countess Howe,
c. 1763-64

Landscape: View-Painting and the Grand Tour

Landscape painting in its own right, established in the seventeenth century, persisted and ramified during the eighteenth, although the supreme example of the great Dutch masters was not to be taken much further until the early nineteenth century, by Constable. In topography, the major contribution came from Venice. The subject matter was urban rather than rural, but the stones of Venice, rising like a dream from the waters of the lagoon, are no ordinary urban prose. Canaletto (Giovanni Antonio Canal, 1697-1768) was the finest transcriber of its poetry on to canvas.

Canaletto began by painting views in a broad and dramatic style, very far from picture postcards. The masterpiece of this phase is *The stonemason's yard* of about 1730. The view is of S. Maria della Carità, now the Accademia, Venice's famous gallery. The focus, however, is more on the activity in the foreground; there is a feeling almost of genre. Canaletto's later, more familiar pictures show the Venetian scene more grandly; they are set pieces displaying her architectural splendours, drawn with the greatest accuracy but also, at their best, capturing the atmosphere of the city – her light, air, water and sky – in glorious harmony.

Venice had been for some time a magnet for tourism, and tourism of a grand and moneyed kind: the well-to-do of all northern Europe might spend two or three years of their youth on the Grand Tour, of which the prime goal was Italy, and in Italy Rome and then Venice. This steady stream provided the greater number of Canaletto's patrons, and when his clients could not come to him, because of war, he had to go to them – hence, probably, his sojourns in England, 1746-56, revealing London as radiant as Venice, in Venetian weather. In England, his work produced several competent imitators, while the peripatetic Bernardo Bellotto (1720-80; not shown), his very able nephew and pupil, exported his style to Germany, Austria and Poland.

Canaletto's equivalent in Rome was Giovanni Paolo Panini (*c.*1692-1765), recording contemporary Rome and its ceremonial but also, for the fashionable, classically-minded tourist, its archaeology. He painted ruins in the same mood of inquisitive awe that set Gibbon to write *The Decline and Fall of the Roman Empire*. He also popularized the *capriccio*, or "ruinscape", grouping several famous monuments of antiquity together in one compo-

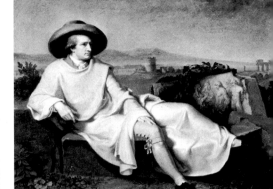

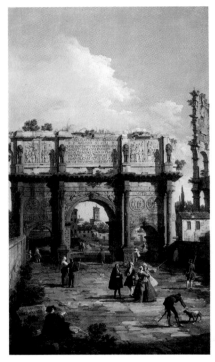

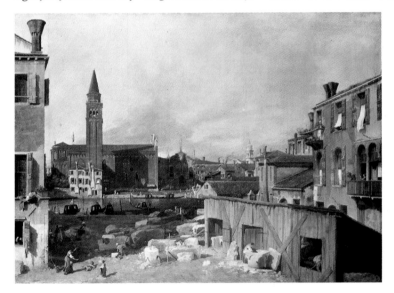

CANALETTO (left)
The stonemason's yard,
*c.*1730
Warm, luminous tones
envelop the concentrated
detail; Canaletto's views
could be much drier later.
The picturesque ramshackle
and domestic disorder of the
foreground are a glimpse of
a working Venice "behind
the scenes", and could even
be compared with Cornelis
Troost's genre (see p.244).

CANALETTO (right)
*The Arch of Constantine,
Rome*, 1742
Canaletto re-created the
scene from studies made
on an earlier visit to Rome:
five such views were bought
by the English consul in
Venice, Joseph Smith, his
chief patron. Smith was
the connection by which
Canaletto came to England.

PIRANESI (right)
*View of the Villa of
Maecenas at Tivoli,
c.*1760-65
Piranesi's highly influential
Vedute di Roma (Views of
Rome) began to appear in
about 1748. Many of the
plates faithfully recorded
archaeological minutiae;
others evoke a Romantic

vision of departed Rome:
primeval ruins rear heroic
against the assaults of Time
and Nature; diminutive
troglodytes, refugees from
Arcadia, caper among them.
Piranesi defended Roman
art against the preference
given by Winckelmann to
the Greeks, stressing the
awe and grandeur of Rome.

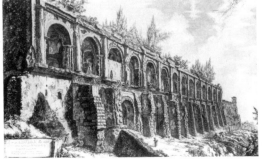

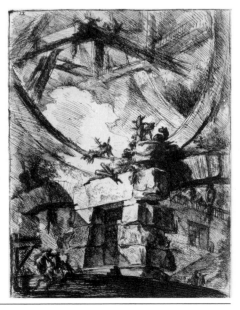

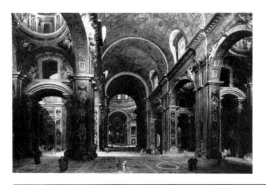

PANINI (left)
*The interior of St Peter's,
Rome*, 1731
The tiny figures and the
dramatic viewpoint, amplifying the grandeur of the
architecture, are typical
of Panini's views of ancient
and modern Rome, which
transform the eternal city
into a colossal stage-set.

PIRANESI (right)
Etching from the *Carceri
d'Invenzione* (Imaginary
prisons), *c.*1745
Exploring a theme set by
earlier stage designers,
notably the Bibiena family,
Piranesi gave a Romantic
scope to his imagination,
using dizzying perspectives
to create haunting scenes.

sition, offering the tourist three or more for the price of one. The tourists were eager buyers and Panini's work was exported all over Europe. Canaletto also made *capricci*, sometimes of juxtaposed ruins, sometimes purely fanciful picturesque concoctions. Probably more influential than either, however, was Giovanni Battista Piranesi (1720-78), whose etchings were best-sellers well into the next century. His dramatic use of light and shade is strikingly successful in his famous *Views of Rome*, but even more so in his fantastic and vertiginous *Carceri d'Invenzione* (Imaginary prisons), begun about 1745.

These found a ready response with the Romantics, but Piranesi was also a learned (though controversial) archaeologist and a seminal influence on the growth of Neo-classicism. His *Views* were the source from which cultivated Europeans, especially if they had not been to Rome, formed their image of the eternal city. The preoccupations of the visitors are crystallized in the portrait of the greatest of them all, Goethe, by Johann Heinrich Wilhelm Tischbein (1751-1829). The poet is shown, half-reclining in contemplation, in the lowlands outside Rome, the Campagna:

here is antiquity, the fragment of a classical frieze trailing a grape-heavy vine of today.

Not only Grand Tourists but artists came to Rome; in fact artists swarmed to it, to stay for years at a time, sometimes for ever. Their studios formed part of the sightseers' round, and in them the Claudeian tradition, the expatriate vision of an ideal Italy, was also sustained. Claude-Joseph Vernet (1714-89) was for years in Rome, and, when he went back to France, applied a fairly pure version of Claude's style to a royal commission to paint the French ports. The Venetian painter Francesco Zuccarelli (1702-88; not shown) exported a more sentimental, Rococo variant to London, where he was more popular than his friend, the Welsh Richard Wilson (1713-82). After some years in Rome in the 1750s, Wilson applied classical principles, an austere and grave dignity, to British landscape, in classics of a kind not known before, accurate in the particular, but raising the particular to the ideal, the general. British patrons, however, preferred their landscapes to come from abroad, and their real contribution lay in their treatment of the landscape itself: a succession of highly gifted landscape gardeners trans-

posed damp English earth into visions of Arcadian pastoral – an ordering of nature based on classical principle, but inspiring a distinctly Romantic nostalgia.

British patronage failed likewise adequately to support the landscapes of Thomas Gainsborough. Gainsborough, who had early captured a Suffolk harvest countryside that one can almost smell (see preceding page), moved thence to a more Rococo sophistication, acknowledging Dutch example. In this he abandoned descriptive portraiture (referring a prospective patron to the topographical artist, Paul Sandby (1725-1809; not shown), a seminal watercolourist). Gainsborough's mature landscapes are almost the equivalent of musical improvisations; as a starting-point for the composition he might arrange sticks, stones and scraps of foliage on a table.

Gainsborough's rhythm and felicity of colour had in some degree a Venetian counterpart in the work of Francesco Guardi (1712-93). Not so successful as Canaletto's, Guardi's visions of Venice as a figment of dream materializing amidst the irradiant mist and sky of the lagoon would find a more sympathetic response in eyes used to Impressionism.

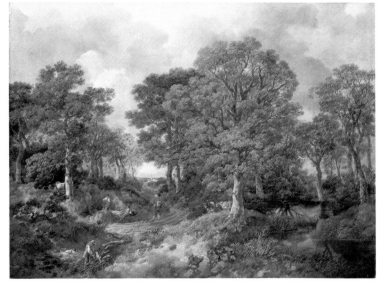

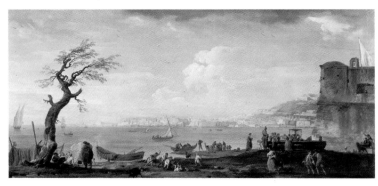

VERNET (above)
View of the Bay of Naples, 1742
Low, flat, panoramic sea-shores had been painted by Salvator Rosa and others. Vernet's are freer in handling, lighter in tone, rather more atmospheric.

WILSON (right)
Snowdon, c.1770
Wilson has interpreted the Welsh mountain and its crater-like lake in a mood of classical calm. He was active just before Britons discovered the Picturesque in their native landscape.

GAINSBOROUGH (above)
"Cornard Wood", c.1748
The wood is probably not a real one; Gainsborough stressed that landscape

painting was a creative act. It can be compared both to Dutch and to French landscapes, but notable is the liveliness of the light.

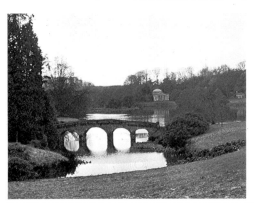

STOURHEAD, WILTSHIRE
View of the park
The temple is straight out of a Claude painting (see p. 197). The park was created in the mid-18th century by a banker with a good collection of Claudes.

GUARDI (right)
View of a canal, c.1750
Guardi's sketchily painted, often rather low-life scenes of Venice are as delicate as Chinese landscapes. His choice of views, sometimes seemingly fragments, also anticipates Impressionism.

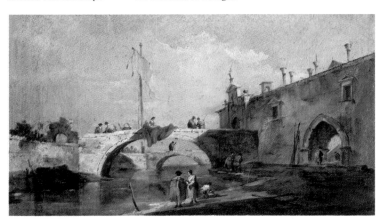

List of Illustrations and Acknowledgments

Works of art illustrated are listed in the order in which they appear in the book. In general, the order runs from top to bottom and left to right on each page, though works by the same artist or of the same origin are grouped together.

The name of the artist (or, if the artist is not known, the place of origin) and the title or description of each work are followed by its medium, its dimensions (metric) and its present location and ownership. Photographic credits are given in brackets, unless the photograph has been supplied by the owner. Scala, the major supplier of photographs, is abbreviated as S.

Though every effort has been made to check the accuracy of these specifications, it has not always been possible to verify all of them.

2–3 Frontispiece
TITIAN: *Charles V at Mühlberg*, 1548, oil on canvas, 332 × 279 cm, Madrid, Prado (S). AFTER APELLES: *Aphrodite wringing her hair*, original *c.* 350 BC, marble, height 30.5 cm, Philadelphia, University of Pennsylvania, University Museum.

8–9 Ancient Worlds
PAESTUM, ITALY: The Temple of Neptune, *c.* 470-460 BC (Michael Holford). PALENQUE, MEXICO: The Pyramid of the Inscriptions, *c.* AD 700 (Michael Holford).

10–11
(Map by Colin Salmon and Dinah Lone)

12–13 Palaeolithic Art
LAKE TRASIMENE: "*Venus*" figure, Aurignacian period?, stone, height about 13 cm, Florence, Private Collection (S). BRASSEMPOUY: Female head, *c.* 22000-20000 BC, ivory, height 3.5 cm, St-Germain-en-Laye, Musée des Antiquités Nationales (S). LESPUGUE: "*The Venus of Lespugue*", *c.* 20000-18000 BC, ivory, height 14 cm, Paris, Musée de l'Homme (S). LA MADELEINE: Bison, *c.* 12000 BC, reindeer antler, length 10 cm, St-Germain-en-Laye, Musée des Antiquités Nationales (Photoresources). LAUSSEL: "*The Venus of Laussel*", *c.* 20000-18000 BC, stone slab, height 45 cm, Musée d'Aquitaine (S). WILLENDORF: "*The Venus of Willendorf*", *c.* 30000-25000 BC, limestone, height 11 cm, Vienna, Kunsthistorisches Museum (Photoresources). THE DORDOGNE: *Reclining woman*, *c.* 12000 BC, stone, length 71 cm, *in situ* (S). LASCAUX: "The Hall of Bulls" (Colorphoto Hans Hinz); detail, *Man and bison*, rock-painting, length of bison 109 cm, *in situ* (Colorphoto Hans Hinz). ALTAMIRA: *Two bison*, *c.* 13000 BC, rock-painting, length of each bison about 1.85 m, *in situ* (S). ADDAURA: *Human figures*, *c.* 10000 BC, rock engraving, height of engraved area about 1 m, *in situ* (S). SKARPSALLING: Decorated bowl, 3rd millennium BC, terracotta, height 17 cm, Copenhagen, National Museum.

14–15 African Art 1
TANZANIA: Rock-painting from a neolithic site (Werner Forman Archive). TASSILI: Rock-painting: *Masked figure*, at Sefan, height about 2.5 m, *in situ* (Robert Harding Picture Library); Rock-painting of the "Pastoralist" type, at Jabaren, height of painted area about 20 m, *in situ* (Robert Harding Picture Library); Rock-painting of the "Wheeled chariot" type, length of image about 50 cm, Algiers, Musée de Préhistoire et d'Ethnographie (Werner Forman Archive). BRANDBERG: "*The White Lady*", San, rock-painting, figure about 40 cm high, *in situ* (Gerald Cubitt). IVORY COAST: Embroidered cotton representing a fertility dance, Senufo, The Hague, van Bussel Collection (Werner Forman Archive). NIGERIA: *Human head*, Ife, bronze, height 36 cm, London, British Museum; *Human head*, Nok, terracotta, height 23 cm, Lagos, National Museum (Werner Forman Archive); *Queen Mother head*, Benin, bronze, height 91 cm, London, British Museum (Werner Forman Archive); *Human head*, Ife, terracotta, height about 10 cm, Berlin, Museum für Volkerkunde (Werner Forman Archive); *A Benin king and his retinue*, Benin, bronze relief, height 46 cm, Kansas, Nelson Gallery of Art (S); Salt-cellar, Afro-Portuguese, ivory, height 30 cm, London, British Museum (Werner Forman Archive). GHANA: A weight, Ashanti, brass, height about 5 cm, British Museum (Werner Forman Archive).

16–17 African Art 2
MALI: Dogon dancers (Robert Harding Picture Library); *Walu* mask: *An antelope*, Dogon, wood, fibres, height 54 cm, Paris, Vérité Collection (Werner Forman Archive); *Chi wara* head-dress: *An antelope*, Bambara, wood, height about 90 cm, Private Collection (Werner Forman Archive). IVORY COAST: Weaving pulley, Baule, wood, height about 20 cm, New York, Mr and Mrs Harold Rome Collection (Werner Forman Archive). ZAIRE: *Kifwebe* mask, Basongye, painted wood, height 60 cm, Zurich, Rietberg Museum (Werner Forman Archive); A mask: *Woot*, for a young man's society, Bakuba, wood, beads, shells and fibre, height 60 cm, Tervueren, Musée Royal de l'Afrique Centrale (Werner Forman Archive). NIGERIA: Shango cult figure, Yoruba, wood, height 71 cm, New York, Museum of Primitive Art (S); Egungun cult mask, Yoruba, painted wood, height about 1 m, London, British Museum (Michael Holford); Bead embroidered crown, Yoruba, glass beads, height (not including fringe) 30 cm, London, British Museum (Michael Holford). CONGO: A chief's stool, Buli (Baluba), wood, height 53 cm, Tervueren, Musée Royal de l'Afrique Centrale (S). MALI: Granary door, Dogon, wood, height about 1.5 m, New York, Museum of Primitive Art (Robert Harding Picture Library).

18–19 Pre-Columbian Art
TLATILCO: *Female figure*, Pre-Classic period, Olmec, terracotta, height 11 cm, Mexico City, Museum of Anthropology (Vautier-Decool). TIKAL: Door lintel, *c.* AD 747, Mayan, wood, about 1.5 × 2 m, Basel, Museum für Volkerkunde. MEXICO: *Head*, *c.* 1200-600 BC, Olmec, basalt, height about 3 m, Vera Cruz, University (Werner Forman Archive). BONAMPAK: *Two warriors*, *c.* AD 750, Mayan, mural, height of figures 114 cm, *in situ* (Norman Hammond). JAINA: *Priest* or *Official*?, *c.* AD 600-900, Mayan, clay, height 18 cm, Mexico City, Museum of Anthropology (Werner Forman Archive). PERU: Ceremonial knife, *c.* AD 1100-1470, Chimu, gold and turquoise, height 43 cm, Lima, Museum (Joseph P. Ziolo); *Ex voto: An alpaca*, *c.* AD 1500, Inca, silver, height 10 cm, Cuzco, University of San Antonio (South American Pictures); *Head*, portrait vase with stirrup spout, *c.* AD 500, Moche, clay, London, British Museum (Robert Harding Picture Library). MEXICO: *Tlazolteotl*, *c.* AD 1300-1500, Aztec, stone, height 20.5 cm, Washington, Woods Bliss Collection (S). TULA: "Atlas figures", *c.* 900-1200, Toltec, stone, height about 4.5 m, *in situ* (Werner Forman Archive).

20–21 A Tlingit House-post
NORTH PACIFIC COAST: Carved house-post, Tlingit, painted wood, height 230 cm, Philadelphia, University of Pennsylvania, University Museum. THE SOUTH-EAST: pipe bowl, from Ohio, stone, length 10 cm, London, British Museum. EASTERN WOODLANDS: "False-face" mask, Iroquois, wood and hair, height 28 cm, New York, Museum of the American Indian, Heye Foundation (Carmelo Guadagno). THE PLAINS: *Blackfoot dignitaries* (Bird Rattler, Curly Bear and Wolf Plume), photograph (Peter Newark's Western Americana); Shield, Crow, painted buffalo hide, diameter 61 cm, New York, Museum of the American Indian, Heye Foundation (Carmelo Guadagno). THE SOUTH-WEST: *Kachina* doll, Pueblo, wood and fibre, height 33 cm, New York, Brooklyn Museum; *Weaving a blanket*, Navajo, photograph (Peter Newark's Western Americana). ARCTIC REGIONS: Arrowshaft straighteners, Eskimo, ivory, length varying from 13 to 18 cm, London, British Museum.

22–23 Oceanic Art
NEW IRELAND: *Uli* figure, wood, mother of pearl, snail-shells and roots, height 124 cm, Basel, Museum für Volkerkunde (S); *Malanggan*, painted wood, bark and cloth, height 85 cm, Basel, Museum für Volkerkunde (S); "Soul-boat", painted wood, length about 6 m, Stuttgart, Linden Museum. SEPIK: Ancestor figure (ceremonial seat), wood, hair and shells, height 76 cm, Zurich, Rietberg Museum (S); *Crocodile head*, wood, length about 1 m, Paris, Musée de l'Homme (S). NEW ZEALAND: House-post, wood, height 120 cm, New York, Museum of Primitive Art (S). HAWAII: *Kukailimoku*, feathers, shells, teeth and wicker, height 82 cm, Honolulu, Bishop Museum (S). EASTER ISLAND: Ancestor figure, stone, height about 8 m, *in situ* (Ardea). *Tattooed warrior*, Engraving, plate 100 in G. H. von Langsdorff, *Voyages and Travels in Various Parts of the World*, 1803-07, London, British Library. NUKURO: *Tino*, wood, height 30 cm, Leyden, Rijksmuseum voor Volkerkunde. AUSTRALIA: *A kangaroo*, bark-painting (Werner Forman Archive).

24–25 Egyptian Art 1
MEMPHIS: The Palette of Pharaoh Narmer, *c.* 3100 BC, stone, height 63.5 cm, Cairo, Egyptian Museum (Werner Forman Archive). SAQQARA?: *Servant straining beer*, *c.* 2400 BC, painted wood, height 25 cm, Florence, Museo Archeologico (S). GIZA: Giant Sphinx, *c.* 2530 BC, sandstone, height 73 m, *in situ* (Ronald Sheridan). SAQQARA: *Hesy-ra before an offering table*, *c.* 2650 BC, from the tomb of Hesy-ra, wood, relief, height 115 cm, Cairo, Egyptian Museum (S); *Cutting a hyena's throat*, *c.* 2400-2150 BC, painted limestone relief, *in situ* (William Macquitty); The tomb of Mereruka, *c.* 2400-2150 BC, relief and free-standing figure painted limestone, height of figure about 1.6 m, *in situ* (S); The tomb of Ptah-hotep, *Funerary procession*, *c.* 2400 BC, painted limestone relief, *in situ* (William Macquitty). GIZA: *Pharaoh Chephren*, *c.* 2585-2560 BC, diorite, height 160 cm, Cairo, Egyptian Museum (Werner Forman Archive). MEIDUM: *Prince Rahotep and his wife Nofret*, *c.* 2550 BC, painted limestone with inlaid eyes, height 120 cm, Cairo, Egyptian Museum (Werner Forman Archive); "*The Geese of Meidum*", *c.* 2550 BC, from the tomb of Nefermaat, painted gesso, height of field 27 cm, Cairo, Egyptian Museum (Werner Forman Archive). SAQQARA: *Seated scribe*, *c.* 2450 BC, painted limestone, height 54 cm, Paris, Louvre (S).

26–27 Egyptian Art 2
AMARNA: *Akhenaten with his baby daughter*, *c.* 1379-1361 BC, limestone relief, height about 1 m, West Berlin, Staatliche Museen (Photoresources); *Nefertiti*, *c.* 1379-1366 BC, painted limestone, height 50 cm, Florence, Museo Archeologico (S). THEBES: *A banquet*, *c.* 1413-1367 BC, from the tomb of Nebamun, painted relief, height 61 cm, London, British Museum; One of four cases for Tutenkhamun's viscera, *c.* 1361-1352 BC, from the tomb of Tutenkhamun, gold, cornelian and glass, height 21 cm, Cairo, Egyptian Museum (S); *Tutenkhamun hunting ostriches*, *c.* 1361-1352 BC, flabellum, incised gold, width 94 cm, Cairo, Egyptian Museum (S); A panel of Tutenkhamun's throne, before 1361 BC, wood plated with gold and silver, inlays of glass and paste, height 104 cm, Cairo, Egyptian Museum (Werner Forman Archive). KARNAK: *Akhenaten*, *c.* 1379-1361 BC, fragment of a column, sandstone, height of statue when complete about 4 m, Cairo, Egyptian Museum (S). DEIR EL MEDINA: *Cha' and Mere pay homage to Osiris*, *c.* 1405-1367 BC, from a *Book of the Dead* in the tomb of Cha' and Mere, painted papyrus, total length 14 m, Turin, Museo Archeologico (S). ABU SIMBEL: The Temple of Ramesses II, *c.* 1304-1237 BC, height of figures about 20 m, *in situ* but raised above original location (Ronald Sheridan). SAQQARA?: *Cat*, after 30 BC, bronze, nose and earrings gold, breast inlaid with silver, height 33 cm, London, British Museum (Ronald Sheridan). EDFU: *The Falcon of Horus*, 3rd century BC, from the Temple of Horus, stone, height about 3 m, *in situ* (Ronald Sheridan).

28–29 Western Asian Art
ERIDU: Male figure, *c.* 4500 BC, terracotta, height 14 cm, Baghdad, Iraqi Museum (Holle Bildarchiv, Baden-Baden). MESOPOTAMIA: Cylinder seal, stone, height 5 cm, Baghdad, Iraqi Museum (S). UR: Panel from the sound-box of a harp, *c.* 2600 BC, gold and shell inlaid on wood, height 39 cm, Philadelphia, University of Pennsylvania, University Museum (Holle Bildarchiv). NINEVEH: *Sargon?*, *c.* 2340 BC, bronze, height 30 cm, Baghdad, Iraqi Museum (S). WARKA: "*The Lady of Warka*", *c.* 3500 BC, marble, height 20 cm, Baghdad, Iraqi Museum (Holle Bildarchiv). LAGASH: *The ruler Gudea*, *c.* 2100 BC, diorite, height 106 cm, Paris, Louvre (Holle Bildarchiv). MESOPOTAMIA: *The goddess Lilith*, *c.* 2000-1800 BC, terracotta, height 50 cm, Colonel Norman Colville Collection (Holle Bildarchiv). LURISTAN: Horse bit, 9th century, bronze, length 10 cm, Baltimore, Walters Art Gallery (Holle Bildarchiv). PERSEPOLIS: The processional stair in the Palace of

Darius, *c.* 500 BC, stone (Holle Bildarchiv). MESOPOTAMIA: Enamelled vase, *c.* 700 BC, clay, height 43 cm, New York, Metropolitan Museum of Art, J. Pulitzer Bequest (Holle Bildarchiv); Ewer, 6th/7th century AD, silver on gold, height 34 cm, Paris, Bibliothèque Nationale (Holle Bildarchiv).

30–31 The Lion Hunt Reliefs from Nineveh
KHORSABAD: *Lamassu, c.* 710 BC, limestone, height about 4 m, Paris, Louvre (S). NIMRUD: *Bird-headed god, c.* 865-860 BC, alabaster relief, height 110 cm, Louvre (S). NINEVEH: *A herd of gazelles, c.* 645-640 BC, stone relief, height 53 cm, London, British Museum (Photoresources); *A lion springing at King Assurbanipal, c.* 645-640 BC, stone relief, height 157 cm, British Museum. NIMRUD: *Cooks in a fortified camp, c.* 858-824 BC, stone relief, height about 1 m, London, British Museum (Ronald Sheridan).

32–33 Cycladic, Minoan and Mycenaean Art
THE CYCLADES: *Female figure, c.* 2300 BC, from Naxos, marble, height 58 cm, Athens, National Museum (S); "Fiddle" figurine, *c.* 2800-2500 BC, marble, Eleusis, Museum (S). MINOAN CRETE: *Two goats, c.* 1700 BC, impression of chalcedony seal, diameter 2 cm, London, British Museum (Ronald Sheridan); Beaked jug, "Kamares" style, from Phaistos, terracotta, height 26 cm, Heraklion, Archaeological Museum (Photoresources). KNOSSOS: *An acrobat leaping over a bull, c.* 1600 BC, bronze, length 15.5 cm, London, British Museum (Michael Holford); *"Snake Goddess", c.* 1600 BC, faience, height 34 cm, Heraklion, Archaeological Museum (Photoresources); Bull's head *rhyton, c.* 1500 BC, stone, wood, crystal and shell, height 21 cm, Heraklion, Archaeological Museum (Sonia Halliday); *"La Parisienne", c.* 1600 BC, fresco, height 25 cm, Heraklion, Archaeological Museum (S). THERA: An interior: *Rocks and lilies, c.* 1500 BC, fresco, Archaeological Museum (Ronald Sheridan). MYCENAE: Gold face mask, *c.* 1500 BC, gold, height 29 cm, Mycenae, National Museum (S); Decorated bronze dagger; *Ramping lions, c.* 1500 BC, gold and bronze, length 23 cm, Mycenae, National Museum (S).

34–35 Archaic Greek Art
ATHENS: Protogeometric amphora, 10th century BC, clay, height 52 cm, Athens, Kerameikos Museum (The Mansell Collection); Geometric amphora, *c.* 750 BC, clay, height 155 cm, Athens, Archaeological Museum (Giraudon). CORINTH: Stoppered *oinochoe* (wine cruet), 7th century BC, clay, height 16 cm, Syracuse, Museo Archeologico Nazionale (S). EXEKIAS: *Aias and Achilles play draughts, c.* 550-540 BC, black-figure amphora, clay, height 61 cm, Rome, Vatican (S). EUPHRONIOS: *Herakles strangling Antaios, c.* 510-500 BC, red-figure *krater*, clay, height 48 cm, Paris, Louvre (Giraudon). UNKNOWN GREEK SCULPTOR: *"The Lady of Auxerre", c.* 630 BC, limestone, height 62 cm, Paris, Louvre (Giraudon). ATHENS, ACROPOLIS: *"The Peplos Kore", c.* 540-530 BC, marble, height 122 cm, Athens, Acropolis Museum (Photoresources); *"The Kritios Boy", c.* 490-480 BC, marble, height 82 cm, Athens, Acropolis Museum (S). SOUNIUM, ATTICA: *Kouros, c.* 600-580 BC, from the Temple of Poseidon, marble, approximate height 3 m, Athens, National Museum (Ronald Sheridan). ANAVYSOS, ATTICA: *Kouros, c.* 540-515 BC, marble, height 193 cm, Athens, National Museum (S). CORCYRA, TEMPLE OF ARTEMIS: West pediment, *A gorgon and two lions, c.* 600-580 BC, limestone, height 275 cm, Corfu, Archaeological Museum (Photoresources). CERVETERI, ETRURIA: *Reclining couple*, 550-520 BC, painted terracotta, length 201 cm, Rome, Villa Giulia (Giraudon). VEII, ETRURIA: *"The Apollo of Veii", c.* 500 BC, marble, height 178 cm, Rome, Villa Giulia (S).

36–37 The Artemisium Zeus/Poseidon
AFTER KRITIOS AND NESIOTES: *Harmodios and Aristogeiton*, original 477-476 BC, marble, height of figures 203 and 195 cm, Naples, Museo Nazionale (S). DELPHI: *A charioteer*, fragment of a group, *c.* 475-470 BC, bronze, height 180 cm, Delphi, Archaeological Museum (Sonia Halliday and (detail) S). CAPE ARTEMISIUM: *Zeus?* or *Poseidon?, c.* 460 BC, bronze, 210 cm, Athens, Archaeological Museum (S and (detail) Ronald Sheridan). AFTER KRESILAS: *Perikles*, original *c.* 429 BC, marble copy of bronze original, height 48 cm, West Berlin, Staatliche Museen (Archiv für Kunst und Geschichte). AFTER AN ATHENIAN SCULPTOR: *Anakreon*, original *c.* 450 BC, marble, height 198 cm, Copenhagen, Ny Carlsberg Glyptotek.

38–39 Classical Greek Art
OLYMPIA, THE TEMPLE OF ZEUS: Metope: *Herakles' twelfth Labour*, 465-457 BC, marble, height 156 cm, Olympia, Archaeological Museum (S); The west pediment, 465-457 BC, marble, height of Apollo 305 cm, Olympia, Archaeological Museum (S). AFTER MYRON: *"Diskobolos"* (The discus thrower), original *c.* 450 BC, marble, height 147 cm, Rome, Museo delle Terme (S). ATHENS, THE ACROPOLIS: *"Mourning Athene", c.* 470-450 BC, marble relief, height 54 cm, Athens, Acropolis Museum (S). OLYMPIA: *Zeus carries off Ganymede, c.* 470 BC, painted terracotta, height 110 cm, Olympia, Archaeological Museum (S). UNKNOWN ARTIST: "The Ludovisi Throne": *The birth of Aphrodite, c.* 470-460 BC, this face 140 × 102 cm, Rome, Museo delle Terme (S). ATHENS, THE PARTHENON: Fragment of the east pediment: *Aphrodite and two other goddesses*, 438-432 BC, marble, overall length 315 cm, London, British Museum (S); the frieze, *c.* 440 BC, marble, height 106 cm, London, British Museum (S). THE PENTHESILEA PAINTER: *Greeks and Amazons, Achilles killing Penthesilea? c.* 455 BC, *kylix*, glazed clay, diameter 43 cm, Munich, Staatliche Antikensammlungen und Glyptothek. ATHENS, THE ERECHTHEION: Caryatid, before 409 BC, marble, height of caryatid 216 cm, *in situ* (S). PAIONIOS: *Nike, c.* 420 BC, marble, height 216 cm, Olympia, Archaeological Museum (S).

40–41 Fourth-century Greek Art
HALICARNASSUS, THE MAUSOLEON: Frieze: *Greeks and Amazons, c.* 353 BC, marble, height 90 cm, London, British Museum (Michael Holford); *"Mausolos", c.* 353 BC, marble, height 301 cm, London, British Museum (S). (AFTER?) PRAXITELES: *Hermes and the infant Dionysos, c.* 350-330 BC, marble, height 216 cm, Olympia, Archaeological Museum (S). UNKNOWN ARTIST: *"The Anticythera Youth", c.* 350-330 BC, bronze with glass, limestone and copper, height 196 cm, Athens, National Museum (S). AFTER PRAXITELES: *"The Cnidian Aphrodite"*, original *c.* 350-330 BC, marble, height 204 cm, Vatican, Museum (S). AFTER LYSIPPOS?: *Alexander the Great* ("The Azara Herm"), original *c.* 325 BC, the head 25 cm high, Paris, Louvre (Giraudon); *"Apoxyomenos"* (Youth scraping down), original *c.* 325-300 BC, marble, height 206 cm, Vatican (Archiv für Kunst und Geschichte); *"The Farnese Hercules"*, original *c.* 350-300 BC, marble copy of bronze, height 306 cm, Naples, Museo Nazionale (S). SYRACUSE: Tendrachma piece, *c.* 479 BC, silver, diameter 3.2 cm, London, British Museum. AFTER LEOCHARES?: *"The Apollo Belvedere"*, original 4th century BC, marble, height 215 cm, Vatican (S). UNKNOWN ARTIST: *Comic actor, c.* 350 BC, terracotta, height about 15 cm (Ronald Sheridan).

42–43 Hellenistic Art
AFTER POLYEUKTOS: *Demosthenes*, original *c.* 280 BC, marble, height 202 cm, Copenhagen, Ny Carlsberg Glyptotek. PERGAMUM: The Altar of Zeus, outer frieze, east side: *The battle of the gods and giants, c.* 180 BC, marble, height 230 cm, East Berlin, Pergamon Museum (Archiv für Kunst und Geschichte); inner frieze, *Telephos and companions, c.* 165-150 BC, East Berlin, Pergamon Museum (Bildarchiv Preussischer Kulturbesitz). AFTER A PERGAMENE SCULPTOR: *A dying Gaul*, original *c.* 200 BC, marble, height 73 cm, Rome, Capitoline Museum (S). SAMOTHRACE: *Nike, c.* 190 BC, marble, height 240 cm, Paris, Louvre (S). AFTER AN UNKNOWN SCULPTOR: *"The Aphrodite of Cyrene"*, original *c.* 100 BC?, marble, height 149 cm, Rome, Museo delle Terme (S). MYRINA: *Two women gossiping, c.* 100 BC, painted terracotta, height 20 cm, London, British Museum (Michael Holford). AFTER AN UNKNOWN SCULPTOR: *"The Medici Venus"*, original *c.* 150-100 BC?, marble, height 153 cm, Florence, Uffizi (S). POMPEII: Candelabrum support: *Silenos, c.* 100 BC-AD 69, bronze, height 61 cm, Naples, Museo Nazionale (S). AGASANDROS OR ALEXANDROS: *"The Venus de Milo"*, late 2nd or 1st century BC, marble, height 180 cm, Paris, Louvre (Michael Holford). AFTER AN UNKNOWN SCULPTOR: *Antiochos III of Syria*, original *c.* 200-150 BC, marble, height 35 cm, Paris, Louvre (Documentation Photographique de la Réunion des Musées Nationaux).

44–45 The Lost Riches of Classical Painting
PAESTUM: *A banquet, c.* 480 BC, wall-painting, Paestum, Museum (S); *A diver, c.* 480 BC, wall-painting, height of field 98 cm, Paestum, Museum (S). THE ACHILLES PAINTER: *A Muse, c.* 440 BC, white-ground *lekythos*, clay, height 37 cm, Munich, Staatliche Antikensammlungen und Glyptothek. AFTER PHILOXENES?: The Alexander mosaic, *Alexander meets Darius in battle*, original *c.* 300 BC, mosaic, height 3.7 m, Naples, Museo Nazionale (S). AFTER APELLES: *Aphrodite wringing her hair*, original *c.* 350 BC, marble, height 30.5 cm, Philadelphia, University of Pennsylvania, University Museum; *Zeus enthroned, c.* 350 BC, from Pompeii, House of the Vettii, wall-painting, height 51 cm, *in situ* (Mauro Pucciarelli). AFTER NIKIAS?: *Perseus and Andromeda*, original *c.* 350 BC, from Pompeii, House of the Dioskurides, wall-painting, height of field 106 cm, Naples, Museo Nazionale (The Mansell Collection). ROME, ESQUILINE: *Odysseus enters Hades*, original *c.* 150 BC, wall-painting, height about 1.5 m, Vatican, Museum (S). DIOSKOURIDES: *Street musicians, c.* 100 BC, from Pompeii, Villa of Cicero, mosaic, height 62 cm, Naples, Museo Nazionale (S). ROME: The garden painting in the house of Livia at Prima Porta, *c.* AD 25, wall-painting, height of wall about 3 m, Rome, Museo delle Terme (S). POMPEII: *A cat with a bird, ducks and fish*, original *c.* 250 BC, mosaic, height 53 cm, Naples, Museo Nazionale (S).

46–47 Roman Art 1
HAGESANDROS, POLYDOROS AND ATHENODOROS: *Laocoön*, 1st century AD?, marble, height 244 cm, Vatican, Museum (S). APOLLONIOS: *"The Belvedere Torso", c.* 100 BC, marble, height about 1.4 m, Vatican, Museum (S). ROME: *"The Capitoline Brutus"*, 3rd century BC, bronze, height 69 cm, Rome, Capitoline Museum (S); *Ampudius, his wife and daughter*, 1st century BC, relief from a tomb near Porta Capena, Rome, marble, length 164 cm, London, British Museum; *Pompey* (Pompeius Magnus), *c.* 50 BC, marble, height 25 cm, Copenhagen, Ny Carlsberg Glyptotek; *Augustus*, after 27 BC, marble with traces of purple paint, height about 2 m, Rome, Museo delle Terme (S); Gold coin, with head of Nero on obverse, *c.* AD 60-68, diameter 20 mm, New Haven, Harvard University, Fogg Art Museum, Van Nest Bequest; The Gemma Augustea, 1st century AD, onyx cameo, 18 × 23 cm, Vienna, Kunsthistorisches Museum (Archiv für Kunst und Geschichte); The Altar of August Peace (*Ara Pacis Augustae*), 13-09 BC, marble, width of front 10.5 m, Rome, Lungotevere in Augusta (S); The Arch of Titus, interior relief panel: *Triumph with the spoils of Jerusalem, c.* AD 81, marble, height of relief 239 cm, Rome, Forum (S). POMPEII: *Paquius Proculus and his wife*, before AD 79, wall-painting, height of field 58 cm, Naples, Museo Nazionale (S); A room in the House of the Vettii, before AD 79, length 6.5 m, width 3.5 m, *in situ* (S).

48–49 Trajan's Column
BENEVENTUM: Trajan's Arch, AD 114-17, marble, height 14.5 m, width 13.1 m, depth 5.1 m, *in situ* (S). ROME: *Trajan, c.* 98-117, porphyry, life-size (Ronald Sheridan); Trajan's Column, 106-13, marble, height 38 m, length of relief 198 m, height of relief band about 120 cm, *in situ* (Photoresources; (*Decebelus' suicide*) Ronald Sheridan; (base and other details) S).

50–51 Roman Art 2
DELPHI: *Antinoüs, c.* 130, marble, height about 1.7 m, Delphi, Archaeological Museum (S). ROME: *Hadrian, c.* 117-38, marble, Rome, Museo delle Terme (S); *Commodus as Hercules, c.* 180-92, marble, height 106 cm, Rome, Capitoline Museum (Archiv für Kunst und Geschichte); The Column of Marcus Aurelius, *c.* 181, marble, height 42 m, diameter 3.8 m, *in situ* (Alinari); The Ludovisi sarcophagus; *Romans fight Germans*, mid-3rd century, marble 1.5 × 2.7 × 1.3 m, Rome, Museo delle Terme (S); The Velletri sarcophagus, early 2nd century, marble, 1.4 × 2.7 × 1.4 m, Velletri, Museo Archeologico (Mauro Pucciarelli); *Marcus Aurelius, c.* 161-80, bronze with traces of gilt, height 3.5 m, Rome, Campidoglio (Michael Holford); *Septimius Severus as Serapis, c.* 200, bronze, about life-size, Brussels, Musées Royaux des Beaux-Arts; *Alexander Severus, c.* 222-35, marble, about life-size, Vatican, Museum (S); *Philip the Arab, c.* 244-49, marble, about life-size, Vatican, Museum (S). EGYPT: *Septimius Severus and his family, c.* 199-201, tempera on wood, diameter 30.5 cm, West Berlin, Staatsbibliothek (Bildarchiv Preussischer Kulturbesitz). LEPTIS MAGNA: The Arch of Septimius Severus: *Triumphal procession, c.* 202, marble, overall dimensions of frieze 1.7 × 7.4 m, Tripoli, Museum (R. Wood).

52–53 Early Christian Art
ROME: *The Emperor Constantine, c.* 313, marble, height about 2.5 m, Rome, Capitoline Museum (S); The Arch of Constantine, *c.* 312-15, marble, height about 21 m, height of frieze with *largitio* 104 cm, *in situ* (S; (frieze) The Mansell Collection). ROME, CATACOMB OF PRISCILLA: *The breaking of bread*, late 2nd century, wall-painting, height 36 cm, *in situ* (S); *The Good Shepherd, c.* 250-300, wall-

painting, *in situ* (S). CONSTANTINOPLE: *The Tetrarchs, c.* 303, porphyry, height 130 cm, Venice, Piazza (S). ROME, CATACOMB IN THE VIA LATINA: *Hercules and the Hydra*, 4th century, wall-painting, height 84 cm, *in situ* (S). ROME, S. COSTANZA: An apse: *Christ gives the law to SS. Peter and Paul*, 5th century, mosaic (S); Detail of the vault of the ambulatory: *Putti harvesting grapes, c.* 350, mosaic (S). ROME, S. SABINA: Panel of a door: *Moses and the burning bush, c.* 432, wood, panel 85 × 40 cm, *in situ* (S). UNKNOWN ARTIST: *The three Marys at the tomb*; *the Ascension*, late 4th or early 5th century, ivory, 18 × 11 cm, Munich, Bayerisches National Museum.

54–55 Medieval and Early Renaissance Art
AMIENS, FRANCE: Interior view, facing east, of the Cathedral, begun 1220 (A. F. Kersting). URBINO, ITALY: The courtyard of the Ducal Palace, by Luciano Laurana, 1465-69 (S).

56–57
(Map by Colin Salmon and Dinah Lone)

58–59 Byzantine Art 1
ROME, SS. COSMA E DAMIANO: *Christ with saints, c.* 530, mosaic (S). RAVENNA, S. VITALE: *The Emperor Justinian*, before 547, mosaic (S); *The Empress Theodora*, before 547, mosaic (S); View of the apse (S); Detail of a capital (S). RAVENNA: *Theodora*? *c.* 530, marble, height 27 cm, Milan, Castello Sforzesco (S). MT SINAI, ST CATHERINE: *The Transfiguration, c.* 548-65, mosaic (Ronald Sheridan). SYRIA: The Rabula Gospel: *The Ascension*, 586, folio 13v, ink on vellum, Florence, Biblioteca Laurenziana (S). CONSTANTINOPLE: The Barberini diptych: *The Emperor as defender of the faith*, 6th century, 18 × 13 cm, Paris, Louvre (Documentation Photographique de la Réunion des Musées Nationaux). SALONIKA, ST DEMETRIOS: *St Demetrios and the Virgin*, late 6th or early 7th century, mosaic (A. Held/Joseph P. Ziolo). RAVENNA: Archbishop Maximian's Throne, *c.* 550, wood with ivory panels, height 1.5 m, width 60 cm, Ravenna, Museo Arcivescovile (S).

60–61 Byzantine Art 2
CONSTANTINOPLE, HAGIA SOPHIA: *The Virgin and Child enthroned*, 867, mosaic (Photoresources). DAPHNI, CHURCH OF THE DORMITION OF THE VIRGIN: *The Crucifixion, c.* 1100, mosaic (Ken Takase/Joseph P. Ziolo); *Christ Pantocrator, c.* 1100, mosaic (Sonia Halliday). TORCELLO CATHEDRAL: *The Virgin and Child*, 12th century, mosaic (S). CEFALU CATHEDRAL: View of the apse, *c.* 1148 (S). CONSTANTINOPLE: The Paris Psalter: *David harping, c.* 950, folio 378v, colour on vellum, 38 × 28 cm, Paris, Bibliothèque Nationale (Immédiate 2); The Joshua Roll: *The stoning of Achan, c.* 950, ink on papyrus, 30 × 1050 cm, Vatican, Library; The Veroli casket: *The rape of Europa*, 10th or 11th century, ivory, 11.5 × 40.5 × 15.5 cm, London, Victoria and Albert Museum. CONSTANTINOPLE, HAGIA SOPHIA: *The Deesis, c.* 1261?, mosaic (Sonia Halliday). SOPOCANI: *The dormition of the Virgin, c.* 1265, fresco, Church of the Trinity (S). KIEV, HAGIA SOPHIA: View of the apse, 1042-46 (Cercle d'Art/Joseph P. Ziolo). THEOPHANES THE GREEK: *The Holy Trinity*, 1378, fresco, Novgorod, Church of Our Saviour and of the Transfiguration (Cercle d'Art/Joseph P. Ziolo).

62–63 The Virgin of Vladimir
FAYOUM: *Artemidorus*, portrait on a mummy-case, 2nd century AD, encaustic on panel, height of image 31 cm, London, British Museum. MT SINAI: *The Madonna among saints*, 6th century, encaustic on panel, 68.5 × 50 cm, Monastery of St Catherine (Ronald Sheridan); *St Peter*, early 7th century, encaustic on panel, 93 × 53 cm, Monastery of St Catherine (Percheron/Joseph P. Ziolo). NOVGOROD SCHOOL: *The Presentation in the Temple*, 16th century, panel, 89 × 58 cm, Moscow, Tretyakov Gallery (S). ANDREI RUBLEV: *The Holy Trinity, c.* 1411, panel, 140 × 112 cm, Moscow, Tretyakov Gallery (G. Mandel/Joseph P. Ziolo). CONSTANTINOPLE: *St Michael, c.* 950-1000, silver inlaid with ivory, gold, jewels and enamel, 44 × 36 cm, Venice, Tesoro di S. Marco (S); *"The Virgin of Vladimir"*, *c.* 1131, panel, 78 × 55 cm, Moscow, Tretyakov Gallery (Cercle d'Art/Joseph P. Ziolo).

64–65 Christ in Chora
The Anastasis, fresco, height of Christ 163 cm (Sonia Halliday); *The miracle at Cana*, mosaic, width of vault 3.9 m (Sonia Halliday); View of the apse (Sonia Halliday); *Theodore Metochites presenting the church to Christ*, mosaic, height of Christ 140 cm (S); *The Last Judgment*, fresco, width of Christ's mandorla 98 cm (Sonia Halliday); *Scenes from the life of the Virgin*, mosaic, width of vault about 2.5 m (Sonia Halliday); all *in situ* in Istanbul, Museum of Kariye Camii.

66–67 Celtic art
PFALZFELD: Carved stone, 4th century BC, height 148 cm, Bonn, Rheinisches Landesmuseum (S). HOCHDORF: *Lion*, ornament from a bronze vessel, *c.* 500 BC (Deutsche Presse Agentur). SUTTON HOO: Purse lid, *c.* AD 650, gold and enamel with garnets, width 19.5 cm, London, British Museum. MOONE: High Cross, 9th century AD, granite, height 5.3 m (Photoresources). BEWCASTLE: High Cross, late 7th century AD, sandstone, height 5.1 m (Photoresources). IRELAND: The Book of Durrow: *St Matthew, c.* AD 680, folio 21v, colour on vellum, height 16.5 cm, Dublin, Trinity College. JARROW: The Codex Amiatinus: *Ezra restoring a damaged bible, c.* AD 690, folio 5r, colour on vellum, 50 × 34 cm, Florence, Biblioteca Laurenziana (S). LINDISFARNE: The Lindisfarne Gospels: *St Mark, c.* 690, folio 93v; Carpet page, *c.* 690, folio 94v, both colour on vellum, 34 × 24 cm, London, British Library. IONA: The Book of Kells: *St John, c.* 800, folio 291v; The Incarnation Initial, *c.* 800, folio 34r, both colour on vellum, 32 × 25 cm, Dublin, Trinity College. IRELAND: The Lichfield Gospels: Carpet page, early 8th century, folio 3, colour on vellum, 29 × 22 cm, Lichfield, Cathedral.

68–69 Carolingian and Ottonian Art
AUXERRE, ST GERMAIN: *St Stephen preaching*, begun 851, fresco (Faillet/Joseph P. Ziolo). RHEIMS: The Utrecht Psalter: Psalm 108, *c.* 816-823, folio 54r, ink on vellum, height 33 cm, Utrecht, University Library; The Ebbo Gospels: *St Mark, c.* 816-35, folio 60v, ink and colouring on vellum, 26 × 20 cm, Epernay, Bibliothèque Municipale. AACHEN: The Godescalc Evangelistary: *Christ in benediction*, 781-83, folio 3r, colour, gold and silver on vellum, 30.5 × 21 cm, Paris, Bibliothèque Nationale; The Coronation Gospels: *St John, c.* 795-810, folio 178v, colour on vellum, 32 × 25 cm, Vienna, Kunsthistorisches Museum (Photo Meyer); The Lorsch Gospels: *Christ between angels*, early 9th century, back cover, ivory, 37 × 27 cm, Vatican, Library (Ronald Sheridan). MILAN, S. AMBROGIO: The Golden Altar of St Ambrose, central panel: *Christ in majesty with the Evangelists and the apostles, c.* 824-59, gold with silver, jewels and enamel, height of this panel 84 cm, *in situ* (S). HILDESHEIM CATHEDRAL: Bernward's Column, *c.* 1010, bronze, height 3.7 m, *in situ* (S); The bronze doors, detail: *The Nativity* and *The Adoration of the Magi*, 1015, width of panel 59 cm (S). ECHTERNACH: The Speyer Gospels: *St Mark*, 1045-46, folio 61v, colour on vellum, 31.5 × 25.5 cm, Madrid, Escorial (Ampliaciones y Reproduciones Mas). COLOGNE CATHEDRAL: Gero's Crucifix, 969-76, height 213 cm, *in situ* (Bildarchiv Foto Marburg).

70–71 Romanesque Sculpture
MOISSAC ABBEY: *St Peter, c.* 1100, stone relief in the cloister (S); *The Apocalypse, c.* 1115-20, stone relief in the portal tympanum (Photo Bulloz); *Jeremiah*?, stone jumeau of the portal (Ronald Sheridan). TOULOUSE, ST SERNIN: *Christ in majesty*, 1094-96, marble relief in the ambulatory (S). CONQUES, STE FOY: *The Last Judgment*, stone relief in the portal tympanum (S). CLUNY, ST PIERRE: *The third tone of plainsong*, 1088-95, stone capital, Cluny, Musée du Farinier (Photo Bulloz). RENIER DE HUY: The brass font of Nôtre Dame des Fonts: *The baptism of Christ, c.* 1110, brass, height of font 63.5 cm, Liège, St Barthélemy (Bildarchiv Foto Marburg). GLOUCESTER ABBEY: The Gloucester candlestick, *c.* 1110, gilt bronze, height 58.5 cm, London, Victoria and Albert Museum. MERSEBURG CATHEDRAL: *Rudolf of Swabia*, after 1080, bronze, height 197 cm, *in situ* (Bildarchiv Foto Marburg). VERONA, S. ZENO: The bronze doors, detail: *The Crucifixion*, *c.* 1140, bronze plaque nailed on wood (S). BARI, S. NICOLA: The Archbishop's Throne, *c.* 1098, marble inlaid with colour pastes, *in situ* (S).

72–73 Gislebertus: The Sculpture at Autun
ST PIERRE: *The fourth tone of music*, 1088-95, stone capital, Cluny, Musée du Farinier (Photo Bulloz). AUTUN, ST LAZARE: *The flight into Egypt, c.* 1125-35, stone capital, Autun, Cathedral Museum (Sonia Halliday); *The dream of the Magi, c.* 1125-35, stone capital, Autun, Cathedral Museum (S); *The fourth tone of music*, *c.* 1125, stone capital, *in situ* (S); *Eve*, fragment of the north transept lintel, before 1132, stone, height 72 cm, Autun, Musée Rolin (S); The west tympanum and lintel: *The Last Judgment, c.* 1135, stone, width 6.4 m, *in situ* (M. Babey/Joseph P. Ziolo); The west portal, *c.* 1135 (M. Babey/Joseph P. Ziolo). VEZELAY, STE MADELEINE: The tympanum of the central west narthex portal: *The mission to the apostles, c.* 1130, stone (S).

74–75 Romanesque Painting
MASTER HUGO: The Bury Bible: *Moses expounding the law, c.* 1130-40, folio 94r, colour on vellum, height 51 cm, Cambridge, Corpus Christi College. BERZE-LA-VILLE: The apse: *Christ in majesty with apostles*, before 1109, mural, Berzé-la-Ville Priory (A. Held/Joseph P. Ziolo). WINCHESTER: The Winchester Psalter: *The mouth of Hell, c.* 1150, folio 39v, colour on vellum, 29 × 21 cm, London, British Library. CITEAUX: *St George*, initial from a *St Gregory's Moralia in Job*, before 1111, folio 156, colour on vellum, 52 × 37 cm, Dijon, Bibliothèque Municipale. ST-SAVIN-SUR-GARTEMPE: *Scene from the life of St Savin, c.* 1100, fresco, St Savin (Pelissier/Joseph P. Ziolo). FLANDERS: The Stavelot Bible: *Christ in majesty*, folio 136r, ink on vellum, 44 × 27 cm, London, British Library. MEUSE DISTRICT: The Floreffe Bible: *The Crucifixion; the sacrifice of Isaac, c.* 1155, folio 187, colour on vellum, height 28 cm, London, British Library. STEPHANUS GARCIA: The St-Saver Apocalypse: *The torture of souls*, mid-11th century, folio 84v, colour on vellum, 36.5 × 28 cm, Paris, Bibliothèque Nationale. CITEAUX: *The Tree of Jesse*, from a *St Jerome's Explanatio in Isaiam*, folio 4v, ink and colour on vellum, 38 × 12 cm, Dijon, Bibliothèque Municipale. URGEL: Altar frontal: *Christ in majesty with apostles*, early 12th century, painted wood, 130 × 150 cm, Barcelona, Museo de Arte Cataluña (S). CANTERBURY?: The Bayeux Tapestry: *King Edward of England*, *c.* 1080, embroidered cotton, height 50 cm, length 69 m, Bayeux, Town Hall (S).

76–77 Gothic Art in Northern Europe
CHARTRES CATHEDRAL: Detail of west portal figures: *A queen and king, c.* 1150, stone (Sonia Halliday); Detail of south portal figures: *St Gregory, c.* 1215-20, stone (Sonia Halliday). NICHOLAS OF VERDUN: The Klosterneuberg Altar: two of the 45 enamel plaques with biblical scenes, completed 1181, each panel 20 × 16 cm, Vienna, Kunsthistorisches Museum (Toni Schneiders/Joseph P. Ziolo). PARIS, SAINTE CHAPELLE: Interior looking east, 1243-48 (Sonia Halliday). BAMBERG CATHEDRAL: *"The Bamberg Rider", c.* 1236?, stone, *in situ* (S). RHEIMS CATHEDRAL: *The Annunciation* and *The Visitation, c.* 1230-40, stone (K. Takase/Joseph P. Ziolo); The west façade, begun *c.* 1225 (Candelier-Brumaire/Joseph P. Ziolo). NAUMBERG CATHEDRAL: *Eckhart* and *Uta, c.* 1250, stone, *in situ* (S). MASTER HONORE: *The death of the Virgin*, from the Nuremberg Book of Hours, *c.* 1290?, folio 22r, colour of vellum, Nuremberg, Stadtbibliothek. MATTHEW PARIS: *The Virgin and Child*, frontispiece to *A History of the English, c.* 1250, folio 6, ink and colour on vellum, 36 × 24 cm, London, British Library. ST-DENIS: Tomb of Philippe IV, begun 1327, marble, St Denis (Archives Photographiques/Joseph P. Ziolo).

78–79 The Genesis of Italian Painting
ROME, S. MARIA ANTIQUA: *The Crucifixion*, 8th century, mural (S). COPPO DI MARCOVALDO: *The Madonna and Child*, 1261, tempera on panel, 220 × 125 cm, Siena, S. Maria dei Servi (S). GIOTTO?: *St Francis makes the first crib, c.* 1290-1300, fresco, 2.3 × 2.7 m, Assisi, S. Francesco, Upper Church (S). CAVALLINI: *Four apostles*, detail of *The Last Judgment*, *c.* 1293, mural, height of figures about 1 m, Rome, S. Cecilia in Trastevere (S; detail of head S). CIMABUE: Crucifix, *c.* 1285, tempera on wood, 450 × 390 cm, Florence, S. Croce (S); *"The S. Trinita Madonna", c.* 1280, tempera on panel, 380 × 220 cm, Florence, Uffizi (S). DUCCIO: The *Maestà*, rear face: *Scenes from the life of Christ*; front face: *The Virgin in majesty*, 1308-11, tempera and gilt on panel, 210 × 430 cm (panel of *Christ's Arrest* and *The Agony in the Garden* 102 × 76 cm), Siena, Museo dell' Opera del Duomo (both sides and detail S); *"The Rucellai Madonna"*, 1285, tempera and gilt on panel, 470 × 290 cm, Florence, Uffizi (S). GIOTTO: *"The Ognissanti Madonna", c.* 1305-10?, tempera on panel, 320 × 200 cm, Florence, Uffizi (S).

80–81 Italian Gothic Sculpture
PISA, CAMPO SANTO: *Phaedra*, detail of a sarcophagus, 3rd century, marble, *in situ* (S). NICOLA PISANO: *The Adoration of the Magi*, detail of the Pisa Baptistery pulpit, 1260, marble, field 85 × 113 cm, *in situ* (S); *The Visitation*, detail of the Siena Cathedral pulpit, 1265-68, marble, field 85 × 97 cm, *in situ* (S); *December*, detail from the Great Fountain, Perugia, 1278, marble, field 49 × 30 cm (S). GIOVANNI PISANO: *The Massacre of the Innocents*, detail of the Pistoia pulpit, 1301, marble,

field 84 × 102 cm, Pistoia, S. Andrea Fuorcivitas (S); *Temperance* and *Chastity*, detail from the base of the Pisa Cathedral pulpit, 1302-10, marble, height of figures 1.2 m, *in situ* (S); Fragments of the tomb of Margaret of Luxembourg, 1313, marble, height of Empress 65.5 cm, Genoa, Palazzo Bianco (S). ARNOLFO DI CAMBIO: Detail of a crib: *The Three Magi*, *c.* 1290, marble, height of figures about 1 m, Rome, S. Maria Maggiore (S); Tomb of Cardinal de Braye, after 1282, marble, Orvieto, S. Domenico (S). TINO DI CAMAINO: *The Madonna and Child*, 1321, marble, height 78 cm, Florence, Bargello (S). ANDREA PISANO: *The death of St John the Baptist*, panel of the Florence Baptistery doors, 1330-37, bronze, panel 50 × 43 cm (S). MAITANI: The centrepiece of the façade of Orvieto Cathedral: *The Madonna enthroned*, 1330, the figure marble, height about 1 m, the baldachino and the angels bronze (S).

82–83 Giotto di Bondone
GIOVANNI PISANO: *The Madonna and Child and two angels*, *c.* 1302-10, marble, height of the Madonna 129 cm, Padua, Arena Chapel (S). GIOTTO: *The Last Judgment* in the Arena Chapel, Padua, detail: *Scrovegni presents the chapel*, before 1306, fresco, size of wall 10 × 8.4 m (S); Crucifix, *c.* 1290-1300, tempera on wood, 590 × 410 cm, Florence, S. Maria Novella (S); *St Francis, praying in S. Damiano, receives divine instruction*, *c.* 1290-1300, fresco, 2.7 × 2.3 m, Assisi, S. Francesco, Upper Church (S); The Arena Chapel, Padua: interior, looking east, dedicated 1306 (S); *Moses*, fresco, height of field 70 cm (S); *The expulsion of Joachim*, *The feast at Cana*, *The mocking of Christ*, fresco, each 200 × 185 cm (all S); The death of *St Francis*, detail from the Bardi Chapel, S. Croce, Florence, *c.* 1320, fresco, 2.8 × 4.5 m (S); *The dance of Salome*, detail from the Peruzzi Chapel, S. Croce, Florence, *c.* 1325, fresco, 2.8 × 4.5 m (S).

84–85 Italian Gothic painting
SIMONE MARTINI: *Maestà* (The Madonna in majesty), 1315-21, fresco, 7.6 × 9.7 m, Siena, Palazzo Pubblico (S); *St Louis*, 1317, tempera and gilt on panel, 200 × 140 m, Naples, Museo di Capodimonte (S); *The Annunciation*, 1333, tempera and gilt on panel, 260 × 300 cm, Florence, Uffizi (S); *Guidoriccio da Fogliano*, 1328, fresco, 3.4 × 9.7 m, Siena, Palazzo Pubblico (S). AMBROGIO LORENZETTI: *The Presentation in the Temple*, 1342, 260 × 170 cm, tempera on panel, Florence, Uffizi (S). PIETRO LORENZETTI: *The Virgin and saints*, 1320, tempera and gilt on panel, 300 × 330 cm, Arezzo, Pieve di S. Maria (S); *The birth of the Virgin*, 1342, tempera on panel, 190 × 180 cm, Siena, Museo dell' Opera del Duomo (S). TADDEO GADDI: *The Presentation of the Virgin*, *c.* 1332-38, fresco, Florence, S. Croce, Baroncelli Chapel (S). MASO DI BANCO: *St Sylvester and the dragon*, late 1330s, fresco, width 5.35 m, Florence, S. Croce, Bardi Chapel (S). ORCAGNA: *The Redeemer*, detail of the Strozzi altarpiece, 1354-57, tempera and gilt on panel, 160 × 290 cm, Florence, S. Maria Novella (S).

86–87 Lorenzetti: The Good Commune
AMBROGIO LORENZETTI: *The effects of Good Government on town and countryside; Allegory of Good Government; Allegory of Bad Government; Grammar*, 1338, all fresco, Siena, Palazzo Pubblico (all S); *Landscape*, *c.* 1335, tempera on panel, 23 × 33 cm, Siena, Pinacoteca (S). SIENA: *Winged Victory*, 2nd century?, stone relief, Siena, Pinacoteca (S). NICOLA PISANO: *The Liberal Arts*, detail of the Siena Cathedral pulpit, 1265-68, marble, height of figures 61 cm, *in situ* (S).

88–89 The International Gothic Style
GENTILE DA FABRIANO: *The Adoration of the Magi*, 1423, tempera and gilt on panel, 300 × 280 cm, Florence, Uffizi (S). PISANELLO: *St George and the Princess*, *c.* 1435, fresco, Verona, S. Anastasia (S); *Horses*, undated, pen on paper, 20 × 16.5 cm, Paris, Louvre (The Mansell Collection); *Filippo Maria Visconti*, 1440, bronze medal, diameter 10 cm, Florence, Bargello (S). UNKNOWN ARTIST: The Wilton diptych, *c.* 1377-1413, London, National Gallery (Michael Holford). SASSETTA: *The Adoration of the Magi*, *c.* 1430?, tempera on panel, 32 × 35 cm, Siena, Chigi-Saraceni Collection (S). STEFANO DA VERONA: *The Virgin in a rose garden*, *c.* 1405-10, tempera on panel, 127 × 93 cm, Verona, Museo di Castelvecchio (S). THE MASTER OF THE UPPER RHINE: *The Garden of Paradise*, *c.* 1420, tempera on panel, 26 × 33 cm, Frankfurt, Städelsches Kunstinstitut. MASTER THEODORIC: *Charles IV receiving fealty*, detail of frescos in Karlstein Castle, Czechoslovakia, *c.* 1348-70 (Faillet/Joseph P. Ziolo). THE LIMBOURG BROTHERS: Les *Très Riches Heures du Duc de Berri: February*, 1413-16, folio 2v, colour on vellum, 21.6 × 13.9 cm, Chantilly, Musée Condé (Giraudon). PUCELLE: The Belleville Breviary: *Strength and Weakness*, *c.* 1325, folio 37, colour on vellum, 24 × 17 cm, Paris, Bibliothèque Nationale (Photo Bulloz).

90–91 Netherlandish Art 1
BROEDERLAM: *Scenes from the life of Mary*, altarpiece for the Chartreuse de Champmol, 1396-99, oil and tempera on panel, each wing 167 × 124 cm, Dijon, Musée des Beaux-Arts (S). SLUTER: The tomb of Duke Philip the Bold, 1385-1405, painted stone, Dijon, Musée des Beaux-Arts (Pelissier/Joseph P. Ziolo); The Well of Moses, 1395-1403, stone, height of figures 182 cm, Dijon, Chartreuse de Champmol (R. Roland/Joseph P. Ziolo). CAMPIN?: The Mérode altarpiece: *The Annunciation*, *c.* 1425, oil on panel, centre panel 63.5 × 63.5 cm, New York, Metropolitan Museum of Art, Cloisters collection. THE BOUCICAUT MASTER: *The Visitation*, from the Hours of the Maréchal de Boucicaut, *c.* 1405, folio 65v, tempera on vellum, 28 × 18 cm, Paris, Musée Jacquemart-André (Photo Bulloz). JAN AND HUBERT VAN EYCK: The Ghent altarpiece, oil and tempera on panel, overall height 340 cm, Ghent, St Bavo (*The Virgin* (height of panel 170 cm) S; *The adoration of the Lamb* (height of panel 140 cm) S; *The Virgin Annunciate* (height of panel 160 cm) S). JAN VAN EYCK: *The Madonna with Canon van der Paele*, 1436, oil on panel, 122 × 157 cm, Bruges, Groeningemuseum (S); *The Madonna with Chancellor Rolin*, *c.* 1435, oil on panel, 66 × 62 cm, Paris, Louvre (S).

92–93 Jan van Eyck: The Arnolfini Marriage
JAN VAN EYCK: "*The Arnolfini Marriage*", 1434, oil on panel, 82 × 60 cm, London, National Gallery; *Giovanni Arnolfini*, *c.* 1437, oil on panel, 29 × 20 cm, West Berlin, Staatliche Museen (Archiv für Kunst und Geschichte); *A man in a turban*, 1433, oil on panel, 25.5 × 19 cm, London, National Gallery; *Cardinal Albergati*, *c.* 1431, silverpoint, 21 × 18 cm, Dresden, Staatliche Kunstsammlungen (Gerhard Reinhold, Leipzig-Molkau/Joseph P. Ziolo); *Cardinal Albergati*, *c.* 1432, oil on panel, 34 × 26 cm, Vienna, Kunsthistorisches Museum (Photo Meyer).

94–95 Netherlandish Art 2
AFTER CAMPIN: *The Deposition*, *c.* 1430-35?, oil on panel, 59 × 60 cm, Liverpool, Walker Art Gallery. VAN DER WEYDEN: *St Luke painting the Virgin*, *c.* 1434-35? oil on panel, 135 × 122 cm, Boston, Museum of Fine Arts, Gift of Mr and Mrs Henry Lee Higginson; *The Last Judgment*, *c.* 1450?, oil on panel, width 560 cm, Beaune, Musée de l'Hôtel-Dieu (Photo Bulloz); *The Deposition*, *c.* 1430-35?, oil on panel, 220 × 260 cm, Madrid, Prado (S); *The Madonna and saints*, *c.* 1450, oil on panel, width 32 cm, Frankfurt, Stadelsches Kunstinstitut; *A young woman*, *c.* 1440?, oil on panel, 35.5 × 26.5 cm, Washington, National Gallery of Art, Andrew W. Mellon collection. CHRISTUS: *St Eligius and two lovers*, 1449, oil on panel, 98 × 85 cm, New York, R. Lehman Collection; *Edward Grimston*, 1446, oil on panel, 33 × 24 cm, London, the Gorhambury Collection, St Albans, on loan to the National Gallery (by permission of the Earl of Verulam). BOUTS: *The Last Supper*, 1464-68, oil on panel, central panel, 180 × 151 cm, Louvain, St Pierre (S); *A young man*, 1462, oil on panel, 31 × 20 cm, London, National Gallery.

96–97 Netherlandish Art 3
VAN DER GOES: The Portinari altarpiece: *The Adoration of the shepherds*, *c.* 1474-76, oil on panel, height 310 cm, Florence, Uffizi (S); The Monforte altarpiece: *The Adoration of the Magi*, early 1470s, oil on panel, 147 × 241 cm, West Berlin, Staatliche Museen (Bildarchiv Preussischer Kulturbesitz); *The death of the Virgin*, *c.* 1480, oil on panel, 145 × 120 cm, Bruges, Groeningemuseum (S). MEMLINC: The Donne triptych: *The Virgin and Child with saints and donors*, *c.* 1480, oil on panel, height 71 cm, London, National Gallery. JUSTUS OF GHENT: *The Institution of the Eucharist*, 1473-75, oil on panel, 330 × 330 cm, Urbino, Galleria Nazionale delle Marche (S). LOCHNER: *The Adoration of the shepherds*, 1445, oil on panel, 120 × 80 cm, Munich, Alte Pinakothek (S). THE MASTER OF THE CUER D'AMOUR ESPRIS: *How Hope rescued Heart from the water*, 1457, *Le Livre du Cuer d'Amour Espris*, folio 21v, tempera and oil on vellum, 29 × 20 cm, Vienna, Österreichische Nationalbibliothek. WITZ: *The miraculous draught of fish*, *c.* 1444, oil on panel, 132 × 157 cm, Geneva, Musée d'Art et d'Histoire (S). AVIGNON SCHOOL: "*The Avignon Pietà*", *c.* 1460, oil on panel, 160 × 220 cm, Paris, Louvre (S). FOUQUET: "*The Virgin of Melun*", *c.* 1450, oil on panel, 93 × 104 cm, Antwerp, Musée Royal des Beaux-Arts (S).

98–99 Bosch: The Garden of Earthly Delights
BOSCH: *The Garden of Earthly Delights*, *c.* 1505-10, oil on panel, wing panels 220 × 97 cm, centre panel 220 × 195 cm, Madrid, Prado (all details S); *The Crowning with thorns*, undated, oil on panel, 73 × 59 cm, London, National Gallery. GEERTGEN TOT SINT JANS: *Christ as the Man of Sorrows*, *c.* 1490, oil on panel, 24.5 × 24 cm, Utrecht, Rijksmuseum het Catharijne Convent. MASTER OF THE VIRGO INTER VIRGINES: *The Annunciation*, *c.* 1495, oil on panel, 57 × 47 cm, Rotterdam, Museum Boymans-van Beuningen.

100–101 Italian Renaissance Sculpture 1
GIOVANNI PISANO: "*The Ballerina*", from the parapet of Pisa Baptistery, 1297-98, stone, height 132 cm, Pisa, Museo Nazionale (S). ANDREA PISANO: Bronze doors of Florence Baptistery, 1330-37, height about 4 m (S). GHIBERTI: *The sacrifice of Isaac*, 1401, bronze plaque, 45 × 38 cm, Florence, Bargello (S); *The Annunciation*, *c.* 1405-10; *The Flagellation*, *c.* 1415-20, both panels of the north Baptistery doors, bronze, 52 × 45 cm (both S); *Self-portrait*, detail of the "Paradise" doors, *c.* 1450 (S); *Joseph in Egypt*, panel of the "Paradise" doors, *c.* 1425-47, bronze, 79 × 79 cm (S). BRUNELLESCHI: *The sacrifice of Isaac*, 1401, bronze, 45 × 38 cm, Florence, Bargello (S). *Leon Battista Alberti*, bronze medal by Matteo de'Pasti, width 7 cm, Paris, Louvre (S). *Filippo Brunelleschi*, detail of a panel attributed to Uccello, tempera, height 42 cm, Paris, Louvre (Documentation Photographique de la Réunion des Musées Nationaux). NANNI DI BANCO: *Four martyr saints*, *c.* 1414-18, marble, height of figures 182 cm, Florence, Orsanmichele (S). JACOPO DELLA QUERCIA: The Great Door of S. Petronio, Bologna, *c.* 1425-35 (S); a relief from it, *The sacrifice of Isaac*, marble, 87 × 70 cm (S). LUCA DELLA ROBBIA: *Musicians*, panel from the *Cantoria* (Singers' Gallery), *c.* 1430-38, marble, 103 × 93 cm, Florence, Museo dell'Opera del Duomo (S); *The Madonna and Child*, *c.* 1455-65, enamelled terracotta, diameter 180 cm, Florence, Orsanmichele (S).

102–103 Donatello
DONATELLO: *St George*, *c.* 1415-17, marble, height of figure 209 cm, Florence, Bargello (S); *The feast of Herod*, detail of the Siena Cathedral font, 1423-27, gilt bronze relief, 60 × 61 cm, *in situ* (S); *The Annunciation*, *c.* 1430?, sandstone with residual gilt and polychrome, 4.2 × 2.5 m, Florence, S. Croce (S); *Jeremiah?*, 1423, marble, height 191 cm, Florence, Museo dell'Opera del Duomo (S); The High Altar, S. Antonio, Padua, 1443-54, artwork after J. White by MB Studio; its central statue, *The Madonna and Child*, bronze, height 159 cm, *in situ* (S); *Mary Magdalen*, *c.* 1456?, wood, height 188 cm, Florence, Baptistery (S); *David*, undated, bronze, height 159 cm, Florence, Bargello (S); *Gattamelata*, 1443-48, bronze on marble and limestone base, height of statue 340 cm, Padua, Piazza del Santo (S); *Lamentation on the dead Christ*, detail of one of the pulpits in S. Lorenzo, Florence, *c.* 1465, bronze, height of panel 137 cm, *in situ* (S).

104–105 Masaccio: The Holy Trinity
MASACCIO: *The Holy Trinity*, 1428, fresco, 6.7 × 3.2 m, Florence, S. Maria Novella (S); detail of the Virgin (S); artwork after P. Sanpaolesi by MB Studio; *The Crucifixion*, fragment of the Pisa altarpiece, 1426, tempera on panel, 76 × 63.5 cm, Naples, Museo di Capodimonte (S). DONATELLO: *St Louis*, *c.* 1422-25, gilt bronze, height 266 cm, reinstated in its niche outside Orsanmichele, Florence, now in S. Croce, Florence (S). BRUNELLESCHI?: *Crucifix*, *c.* 1412, wood, height about 1 m, Florence, S. Maria Novella. LORENZO DI NICCOLO GERINI: *The Holy Trinity*, late 14th century, tempera on panel, Greenville, South Carolina, Bob Jones University. MASOLINO: *The Crucifixion*, *c.* 1428, tempera on panel, 53 × 32 cm, Vatican Gallery (S).

106–107 Italian Renaissance Painting 1
MASACCIO: *The tribute money*, 1425-28, fresco, 2.5 × 6 m, Florence, S. Maria del Carmine, Brancacci Chapel (S); detail of heads (S); *The expulsion of Adam and Eve*, 1425-28, fresco, 2 × 0.9 m, S. Maria del Carmine, Brancacci Chapel (S). MASOLINO: *Adam and Eve under the Tree of Knowledge*, 1425-28, fresco, 2 × 0.9 m, S. Maria del Carmine, Brancacci Chapel (S). UCCELLO: *The Battle of San Romano*, *c.* 1455, tempera on panel, 180 × 320 cm, London, National Gallery; *The Flood*, *c.* 1445, fresco, 2.2 × 5.1 m, Florence, S. Maria Novella (S); *The night hunt*, *c.* 1460, tempera on panel, 65 × 165 cm, Oxford, Ashmolean Museum. FILIPPO LIPPI: *The*

Madonna and Child with two angels, *c.* 1460, tempera on panel, 92 × 64 cm, Florence, Uffizi (S); *The Annunciation*, *c.* 1440, tempera on panel, 175 × 183 cm, Florence, S. Lorenzo (S); One of the Prato frescos: *The feast of Herod*, 1452-64, Prato, Cathedral (S). DOMENICO VENEZIANO: *St John the Baptist in the desert*, predella panel from the St Lucy altarpiece, *c.* 1445-48, tempera, 28 × 32 cm, Washington, National Gallery of Art, Samuel H. Kress collection; The St Lucy altarpiece, *c.* 1445-48, tempera on panel, 209 × 216 cm, Florence, Uffizi (S). DONATELLO: *St Louis*, *c.* 1422-25, gilt bronze, height 266 cm, Florence, S. Croce (S).

108–109 Fra Angelico: The Annunciation
FRA ANGELICO: *The Annunciation*, at the top of the dormitory stairs in S. Marco, Florence, *c.* 1450?, fresco, 2.2 × 3.2 m (S); *The Deposition*, *c.* 1440?, tempera on panel, 105 × 164 cm, Florence, S. Marco; *The Annunciation*, for S. Domenico, Cortona, *c.* 1428-32, tempera on panel, 175 × 180 cm, Cortona, Museo Diocesano (S); *The Annunciation*, in Cell 3 of the dormitory of S. Marco, *c.* 1441, fresco, 1.9 × 1.6 m (S); *St Stephen preaching and addressing the Jewish council*, *c.* 1447-49, fresco, 3.2 × 4.1 m, Vatican, Chapel of Nicholas V (S).

110–111 Italian Painting 2
GOZZOLI: *The journey of the Magi*, 1459-61, fresco, Florence, Palazzo Medici-Riccardi (S); *Man treading grapes*, detail of the Campo Santo frescos, 1468-97, Pisa, Campo Santo (S). CASTAGNO: *God the Father*, detail of S. Zaccaria apse, 1442, fresco, Venice, S. Terasio presso S. Zaccaria (S); *The Last Supper*, *c.* 1445-50, fresco, Florence, Museo di S. Apollonia (S). PIERO DELLA FRANCESCA: *The Compassionate Madonna*, begun 1445, tempera on panel, 134 × 91 cm, Borgo San Sepolcro, Palazzo Communale (S); *The baptism of Christ*, *c.* 1440-50, tempera on wood, 167 × 116 cm, London, National Gallery (Angelo Hornak); Details from the Arezzo frescos, 1452-64, *The old age and death of Adam; The victory over Khosroes; The dream of Constantine; The Annunciation*, S. Francesco (all S); *The Resurrection*, *c.* 1463, fresco, 2.25 × 2 m, Borgo San Sepolcro, Palazzo Communale (S).

112–113 Piero della Francesca: The Flagellation
BERRUGETE?: *Federigo da Montefeltro*, 1477, tempera on panel, 135 × 79 cm, Urbino, Galleria Nazionale delle Marche (S). PIERO DELLA FRANCESCA: *Federigo da Montefeltro*, *c.* 1465, tempera on panel, height 47 cm, Florence, Uffizi (S); *The flagellation of Christ*, undated, tempera on panel, 59 × 81.5 cm, Urbino, Galleria Nazionale delle Marche (S); artwork by Peter Courtley. UNKNOWN ARTIST: *Ludovico Gonzaga*, *c.* 1450, bronze, life-size, West Berlin, Staatliche Museen (S). URBINO, DUCAL PALACE: The *Cappella del Perdono*, 1468-72 (S). ALBERTI: The Holy Sepulchre in the Rucellai Chapel, Florence, 1467, marble (S).

114–115 Italian Sculpture 2
BERNARDINO ROSSELLINO: *Leonardo Bruni*, *c.* 1445-50, marble, height of tomb about 6 m, Florence, S. Croce (S). ANTONIO ROSSELLINO: *Giovanni Chellini*, 1456, marble, height 51 cm, London, Victoria and Albert Museum; *The Cardinal of Portugal*, 1460-66, marble with some paint, height of tomb 5 m, Florence, S. Miniato al Monte (S). MINO DA FIESOLE: *Piero de' Medici*, 1453, marble, height 55 cm, Florence, Bargello (S). DESIDERIO DA SETTIGNANO: Tabernacle in S. Lorenzo, *c.* 1460, marble, Florence, S. Lorenzo (S). POLLAIUOLO: *St Sebastian*, 1475, tempera on panel, 290 × 200 cm, London, National Gallery; *Ten nudes fighting*, *c.* 1460, engraving, Florence, Uffizi, Gabinetto Nazionale dei Disegni e Stampe (S); *Hercules and Antaeus*, *c.* 1475-80, bronze, height 45 cm, Florence, Bargello (S). VERROCCHIO: *Bartolommeo Colleoni*, 1481-90, bronze, height about 4 m, Venice, Campo SS. Giovanni e Paolo (The Mansell Collection); *The doubting of Thomas*, 1465, bronze, height of Christ 230 cm, Florence, Orsanmichele (S); *Putto with a fish*, *c.* 1470, bronze, height 69 cm, Florence, Palazzo Vecchio (S). MATTEO DE' PASTI?: *Botany*, *c.* 1460-68, marble, Rimini, Tempio Malatestiano, Chapel of the Liberal Arts (S).

116–117 Italian Painting 3
PERUGINO: *The giving of the Keys to St Peter*, 1481-82, fresco, 3.5 × 5.5 m, Vatican, Sistine Chapel (S). GHIRLANDAIO: *The birth of St John*, 1485-90, fresco, Florence, S. Maria Novella (S); *The calling of the first apostles*, 1481-82, fresco, 3.5 × 5.5 m, Vatican, Sistine Chapel (S). BOTTICELLI: *"The Madonna of the Magnificat"*, *c.* 1480-90, tempera on panel, diameter 116 cm, Florence, Uffizi (S); *The punishment of Corah*, 1481-82, fresco, 3.5 × 5.5 m, Vatican, Sistine Chapel (S); *Lamentation over Christ*, *c.* 1490-1500, tempera on panel, 140 × 207 cm, Munich, Alte Pinakothek (S); *A young man*, *c.* 1482?, tempera on panel, 37 × 28 cm, Washington, National Gallery of Art, Andrew W. Mellon collection. FILIPPINO LIPPI: *The vision of St Bernard*, *c.* 1480, tempera on panel, 206 × 192 cm, Florence, Badia (S). GHIRLANDAIO: *Old man and his grandson*, *c.* 1475?, tempera on panel, 60 × 45 cm, Paris, Louvre (S).

118–119 Botticelli: Primavera
BOTTICELLI: *Primavera*, 1478, tempera on panel, 203 × 314 cm, Florence, Uffizi (S; detail S); *The birth of Venus*, *c.* 1482-84, tempera on canvas, 172 × 287 cm, Florence, Uffizi (S); *Abundance*, undated, pen, chalk and body-colour on paper, 31 × 24 cm, London, British Museum; *Mars and Venus*, late 1480s, tempera on panel, 69 × 173 cm, London, National Gallery. PIERO DI COSIMO: *The discovery of honey*, *c.* 1500, on panel, 79 × 128 cm, Worcester, Massachusetts, Worcester Art Museum (S).

120–121 Renaissance Painting in North and Central Italy
DONATELLO: Relief from the Santo altar: *The miracle of the mule*, *c.* 1447, bronze, 52 × 123 cm, Padua, *in situ* (S). MANTEGNA: Fresco from the Eremitani: *The martyrdom of St Christopher*, 1448-51, fresco, width 332 cm, Padua, Church of the Eremitani, Ovetari Chapel (S). MANTEGNA?: *Self-portrait*, *c.* 1490, bronze, life-size, Mantua, S. Andrea (S); The *Camera degli Sposi*, *c.* 1474, fresco, Mantua, Palazzo Ducale (ceiling and general view S); *The Triumph of Caesar*, *c.* 1486-94, tempera on canvas, 274 × 274 cm, Hampton Court (by gracious permission of Her Majesty the Queen); *St Sebastian*, undated, tempera on panel, 275 × 142 cm, Paris, Louvre (Documentation Photographique de la Réunion des Musées Nationaux). COSIMO TURA: *The Virgin Annunciate*, 1469, tempera on canvas, 400 × 150 cm, Ferrara, Museo dell' Opera del Duomo (S). CRIVELLI: *Pietà*, 1493, tempera on panel, 128 × 241 cm, Milan, Brera (S).

122–123 Renaissance Painting in Venice
JACOPO BELLINI: *Christ before Pilate*, undated, silverpoint and pen on vellum, 42 × 29 cm, Paris, Louvre (Documentation Photographique de la Réunion des Musées Nationaux). CARPACCIO: *St Ursula taking leave of her parents*, 1495, tempera and oil on canvas, 280 × 611 cm, Venice, Accademia (S). GENTILE BELLINI: *Sultan Mehmet II*, *c.* 1480, canvas, 70 × 52 cm, London, National Gallery; *The miracle at Ponte di Lorenzo*, 1500, canvas, 316 × 611 cm, Venice, Accademia (S). ANTONELLO DA MESSINA: *St Jerome in his study*, *c.* 1460, oil on panel, 46 × 36 cm, London, National Gallery; *A young man*, 1478, oil on panel, 20 × 14 cm, West Berlin, Staatliche Museen (Archiv für Kunst und Geschichte). GIOVANNI BELLINI: *Doge Loredan*, *c.* 1502, oil on panel, 61 × 45 cm, London, National Gallery; The Brera *Pietà*, *c.* 1470, tempera on panel, 86 × 107 cm, Milan, Brera (S); *St Francis in ecstasy*, *c.* 1470-80, oil and tempera on panel, 124 × 142 cm, New York, The Frick Collection (copyright); *"The Sacred Allegory"*, *c.* 1490-1500, oil and tempera on panel, 72 × 117 cm, Florence, Uffizi (S).

124–125 The Sixteenth Century
VENICE, ITALY: Interior view of S. Giorgio Maggiore, by Palladio, begun 1565 (A. F. Kersting). PRAGUE, BOHEMIA: Vladislav Hall, Prague Castle, by Benedict Ried, begun 1487 (Architectural Association).

126–127
(Map by Colin Salmon and Dinah Lone)

128–129 The High Renaissance 1
MELOZZO DA FORLI: *Sixtus IV ordering his nephew Palatina to reorganize the Vatican library*, 1475-77, fresco, 3.6 × 3.1 m, Vatican, Pinacoteca (S). ANDREA SANSOVINO: *The baptism of Christ*, 1502-05, marble, height of Christ 340 cm, Florence, Baptistery (S). PINTORICCHIO: *Susannah and the Elders*, lunette from the Borgia apartments in the Vatican, *c.* 1492-94, fresco and gilt gesso, *in situ* (S). LEONARDO: *"Vitruvian Man"*, *c.* 1490, ink on paper, 34 × 24.5 cm, Venice, Accademia (S); *The Last Supper*, *c.* 1495, oil, tempera and fresco, 4.2 × 9.1 m, Milan, S. Maria delle Grazie (S); *The Virgin and Child with a cat*, *c.* 1478-81, ink and wash over stylus drawing on paper, 13 × 9.5 cm, Florence, Uffizi, Gabinetto Nazionale dei Disegni e Stampe (S). AFTER LEONARDO: *The Battle of Anghiari*, 1503-06, copy by Rubens, chalk and ink on paper, 43.5 × 36.5 cm, Paris, Louvre (Documentation Photographique de la Réunion des Museés Nationaux). RAPHAEL: *"The Madonna della Sedia"* (The Virgin enthroned), *c.* 1515-17, oil on panel, diameter 71 cm, Florence, Palazzo Pitti (S); *Baldassare Castiglione*, *c.* 1516, oil on canvas, 82 × 67 cm, Paris, Louvre (S). MICHELANGELO: *"The Pitti Madonna"*, 1504-05, marble, 86 × 82 cm, Florence, Bargello (S). FRA BARTOLOMMEO: *The Entombment*, 1515, oil on panel, 157 × 203 cm, Florence, Palazzo Pitti (S).

130–131 Leonardo da Vinci
VERROCCHIO AND LEONARDO: *The baptism of Christ*, *c.* 1472, oil on panel, 177 × 151 cm, Florence, Uffizi (S). LEONARDO: *Self-portrait*, *c.* 1512, chalk on paper, 33 × 21 cm, Turin, Biblioteca Reale (S); *The Adoration of the Magi*, 1481, underpaint on panel, 243 × 246 cm, Florence, Uffizi (S); *Landscape*, 1473, ink on paper, 19 × 28.5 cm, Florence, Uffizi, Gabinetto Nazionale dei Disegni e Stampe (S); *Ginevra de' Benci*, *c.* 1474?, oil on panel, 42 × 37 cm, Washington, National Gallery of Art; *The Virgin of the rocks*, *c.* 1483-85, oil on panel transferred to canvas, 197 × 119.5 cm, Paris, Louvre (S); *The Virgin and Child with St Anne*, *c.* 1495, chalk on paper, 139 × 101 cm, London, National Gallery; *Flying machine*, *c.* 1486-90, from Manuscript B, folio 80r, ink on paper, 23 × 16 cm, Paris, Institut de France (S); *Mona Lisa*, *c.* 1503-06, oil on panel, 77 × 53 cm, Paris, Louvre (S); Anatomical drawing: *Sexual intercourse*, *c.* 1492-94, from Anatomical Manuscript C, folio 3v, pen and ink, 27 × 20 cm, Windsor, Royal Collection (by gracious permission of Her Majesty the Queen).

132–133 Michelangelo Buonarroti
Michelangelo Buonarroti, portrait attributed to Jacopino del Conte, oil on panel, 98.5 × 68 cm, Florence, Casa Buonarroti (S). MICHELANGELO: The Vatican *Pietà*, 1499, marble, height 174 cm, Vatican, St Peter's (S); Study for *Leda*, *c.* 1530?, chalk on paper, 35 × 27 cm, Florence, Uffizi, Gabinetto Nazionale dei Disegni e Stampe (S); *Tityus*, 1532, chalk on paper, 19 × 31.5 cm, Windsor, Royal Collection (by gracious permission of Her Majesty the Queen); *David*, 1501-04, marble, height 434 cm, Florence, Accademia (S); *Moses*, 1513-16, marble, height 235 cm, Rome, S. Pietro in Vincoli (S); *"Dying slave"*, 1513-16, marble, height 215 cm, Paris, Louvre (S); The tomb of Giuliano de' Medici in the Medici Chapel, S. Lorenzo, 1534, marble, Florence (S); *The crucifixion of St Peter*, 1546-50, fresco, 6.2 × 6.6 m, Vatican, Cappella Paolina (S); *The Last Judgment*, 1534-41, fresco, 13.7 × 12.2 m, Vatican, Sistine Chapel (S); *"The Rondanini Pietà"*, *c.* 1555-64, marble, height 195 cm, Milan, Castello Sforzesco (S).

134–135 Michelangelo: The Sistine Chapel Ceiling
MICHELANGELO: The Sistine Chapel ceiling, 1508-12, fresco, 13 × 36 m, Vatican (S); Interior of the Sistine Chapel (S); Details of the ceiling (S).

136–137 Raphael
RAPHAEL: *The marriage of the Virgin*, 1504, oil on panel, 118 × 170 cm, Milan, Brera (S); *"La Belle Jardinière"* (The Madonna and Child with St John), *c.* 1506, oil on panel, 122 × 80 cm, Paris, Louvre (S); *Agnolo Doni*, 1505, oil on panel, 63 × 45 cm, Florence, Palazzo Pitti (S); *"The Sistine Madonna"*, 1512, oil on canvas, 265 × 196 cm, Dresden, Gemäldegalerie (S); *"The School of Athens"* in the *Stanza della Segnatura*, 1509-11, fresco, width at base about 7.7 m, Vatican (S); *Self-portrait*, detail (S); *The triumph of Galatea*, *c.* 1513, fresco, 2.95 × 2.25 m, Rome, Villa Farnesina (S); *The expulsion of Heliodorus*, 1511-13, fresco, width at base about 7.5 m, Vatican, *Stanza d'Eliodoro* (S); *Two apostles*, study for *The Transfiguration*, chalk on paper, 50 × 36 cm, Oxford, Ashmolean Museum.

138–139 Bellini: The S. Zaccaria Altarpiece
GIOVANNI BELLINI: The S. Zaccaria altarpiece: *The Virgin and Child with saints*, 1505, oil on panel transferred to canvas, 500 × 235 cm, Venice, S. Zaccaria (S); *The Madonna and Child*, *c.* 1465-70, tempera on panel, 72 × 46 cm, New York, Metropolitan Museum of Art, Bequest of Theodore H. Davis; *"The Madonna of the Meadow"*, *c.* 1501, oil on panel, 67 × 86 cm, London, National Gallery; The S. Giobbe altarpiece, *c.* 1490, oil on panel, 471 × 258 cm, Venice, Accademia (S). GIORGIONE: *"The Castelfranco Madonna"*, *c.* 1504, oil on panel, 200 × 152 cm, Castelfranco Veneto, S. Liberale (S).

140–141 Giorgione: The Tempest
GIORGIONE: *"The Three Philosophers"*, after 1505?, oil on canvas, 123 × 144.5 cm, Vienna, Kunsthistorisches

Museum (Photo Meyer); *"Laura"*, 1506, oil on canvas, 41 × 33.5 cm, Vienna, Kunsthistorisches Museum (Photo Meyer); *Venus, c.* 1509-10?, oil on canvas, 108 × 175 cm, Dresden, Gemäldegalerie (S); *The tempest,* 1st decade of the 16th century, oil on canvas, 83 × 73 cm, Venice, Accademia (S).

142–143 Titian
TITIAN: *An allegory of Prudence, c.* 1570, oil on canvas, 76 × 69 cm, London, National Gallery; *"Noli Me Tangere"* (Christ with Mary Magdalen), *c.* 1512, oil on canvas, 109 × 91 cm, London, National Gallery; *"Le Concert Champêtre"* (Pastoral music-making), *c.* 1510, oil on canvas, 110 × 138 cm, Paris, Louvre (S); *The Assumption of the Virgin,* 1516-18, oil on panel, 690 × 360 cm, Venice, S. Maria dei Frari (S); Apse of S. Maria dei Frari (S); *"The Pesaro Madonna"*, 1519-26, oil on canvas, 485 × 270 cm, S. Maria dei Frari (S); *The girl in a fur wrap, c.* 1535, oil on canvas, 95 × 63 cm, Vienna, Kunsthistorisches Museum (S); *"The Young Englishman", c.* 1540, oil on canvas, 111 × 93 cm, Florence, Palazzo Pitti (S); *Charles V at Mühlberg,* 1548, oil on canvas, 332 × 279 cm, Madrid, Prado (S); *Pope Paul III and his grandsons,* 1546, oil on canvas, 200 × 173 cm, Naples, Museo di Capodimonte (S); *Pietà,* 1576, oil on canvas, 353 × 248 cm, Venice, Accademia (S).

144–145 Titian: The Rape of Europa
TITIAN: *The rape of Europa,* 1562, oil on canvas, 178 × 204 cm, Boston, Isabella Stewart Gardner Museum; *Sacred and Profane Love, c.* 1514, oil on canvas, 118 × 279 cm, Rome, Galleria Borghese (S); *The Andrian Bacchanal,* 1518-23, oil on canvas, 175 × 193 cm, Madrid, Prado (S); *"The Venus of Urbino", c.* 1538, oil on canvas, 119.5 × 165 cm, Florence, Uffizi (S); *Diana and Actaeon,* 1558, oil on canvas, 188 × 206 cm, Edinburgh, National Gallery of Scotland (S); *The death of Actaeon,* after 1562, oil on canvas, 179 × 198 cm, London, National Gallery.

146–147 The High Renaissance 2
SEBASTIAN DEL PIOMBO: The Viterbo *Pietà, c.* 1515, oil on panel, 270 × 190 cm, Viterbo, Museo Civico (S); *Pope Clement VII,* 1526, oil on canvas, 140 × 98 cm, Naples, Museo di Capodimonte (S). PALMA VECCHIO: *The three sisters, c.* 1520-25, oil on panel, 88 × 123 cm, Dresden, Gemäldegalerie (S); *Venus and Cupid, c.* 1520, oil on panel, 118 × 209 cm, Cambridge, Fitzwilliam Museum. LOTTO: *The Madonna and Child with St John and St Peter Martyr,* 1503, oil on panel, 55 × 85 cm, Naples, Museo di Capodimonte (S); *Andrea Odoni,* 1527, oil on canvas, 101 × 104 cm, Hampton Court, Royal Collection (by gracious permission of Her Majesty the Queen). TULLIO LOMBARDO: *Bacchus and Ariadne, c.* 1520-30, marble, 56 × 72 cm, Vienna, Kunsthistorisches Museum (Photo Meyer). RICCIO: *Pan,* 1st quarter of the 16th century, bronze, height 150 cm, Oxford, Ashmolean Museum; The Easter Candlestick, 1507-15, bronze, height 3.9 m, Padua, S. Antonio (S). JACOPO SANSOVINO: *Mercury, c.* 1540-45, bronze, height 149 cm, Venice, Loggetta (S).

148–149 The High Renaissance 3
CORREGGIO: *"La Notte"* (The Adoration of the shepherds), *c.* 1527-30, oil on panel, 256 × 188 cm, Dresden, Gemäldegalerie (Gerhard Reinhold, Leipzig-Molkau/Joseph P. Ziolo); *The vision of St John on Patmos* in the dome of S. Giovanni Evangelista, 1521, fresco, Parma (S); *The Assumption* in the dome of Parma Cathedral, 1526-30, fresco (S); *Danaë, c.* 1531, oil on canvas, 193 × 161 cm, Rome, Galleria Borghese (S). MORETTO: *St Justina, c.* 1530, oil on panel, 98 × 137 cm, Vienna, Kunsthistorisches Museum (Photo Meyer); *A gentleman,* 1526, oil on canvas, 198 × 88 cm, London, National Gallery. MORONI: *"Titian's Schoolmaster"*, undated, oil on canvas, Washington, National Gallery of Art, Widener collection. SAVOLDO: *Mary Magdalen, c.* 1530?, oil on canvas, 86 × 79 cm, London, National Gallery. DOSSO DOSSI: *Melissa, c.* 1523, oil on canvas, 176 × 174 cm, Rome, Galleria Borghese (S). PORDENONE: *The Crucifixion,* in Cremona Cathedral, 1520-21, fresco (S).

150–151 Dürer and Grünewald
DURER: *The piece of turf,* 1503, watercolour and gouache on paper, 41 × 31.5 cm, Vienna, Albertina (S); *The Adoration of the Magi,* 1504, oil on panel, 99 × 113.5 cm, Florence, Uffizi (S); *A young Venetian woman,* 1505, oil on panel, 33 × 26 cm, Vienna, Kunsthistorisches Museum (Photo Meyer); *The Adoration of the Trinity,* 1511, oil on panel, 144 × 131 cm, Vienna, Kunsthistorisches Museum (S); *Erasmus of Rotterdam,* 1526, drypoint etching, 25 × 19 cm, Vienna, Albertina (S); *Self-portrait,* 1498, oil on panel, 52 × 41 cm, Madrid, Prado (S); *"The Four Apostles"*, 1526, oil on panel, 214.5 × 76 cm, Munich, Alte Pinakothek (S). GRUNEWALD: The Isenheim altarpiece, 1515, oil on panel (*The Crucifixion,* 269 × 307 cm; *The Resurrection* and *The Annunciation,* both 269 × 143 cm; *The temptation of St Anthony,* 265 × 139 cm), Colmar, Musée d'Unterlinden (all details S).

152–153 Dürer: The Four Horsemen of the Apocalypse
DURER: The Apocalypse: *The angels staying the four winds; The Whore of Babylon; The four horsemen,* all 1498, woodcuts, all 39 × 28 cm (*The angels* and *The Whore,* London, British Museum; *The Horsemen,* Florence, Uffizi, Gabinetto Nazionale dei Disegni e Stampe (S); *Melancolia 1,* 1514, drypoint etching, 24 × 19 cm, Vienna, Albertina (S); *Adam and Eve,* 1504, drypoint etching, 25 × 19 cm, London, British Museum.

154–155 Painting in Germany
SCHONGAUER: *"Noli Me Tangere"*, after 1471, oil on panel, 115 × 84 cm, Colmar, Musée d'Unterlinden (Colorphoto Hans Hinz); *The temptation of St Anthony, c.* 1470, drypoint engraving, 31 × 23 cm (The Fotomas Index). PACHER: *The Four Doctors of the Church,* central panel, *c.* 1483, oil, 212 × 200 cm, Munich, Alte Pinakothek (S). CRANACH: *Martin Luther,* 1521, oil on panel, 37.5 × 23.5 cm, Florence, Uffizi (S); *Adam and Eve,* 1526, oil on panel, 117 × 80.5 cm, London, Courtauld Institute Galleries. THE MASTER OF THE ST BARTHOLOMEW ALTARPIECE: *St Bartholomew with SS. Agnes and Cecily,* central panel, *c.* 1505-10, oil, 129 × 161 cm, Munich, Alte Pinakothek (S). ALTDORFER: *St George and the dragon,* 1510, oil on panel, 28 × 22.5 cm, Munich, Alte Pinakothek (S); *The battle of Alexander and Darius on the Issus,* 1529, oil on panel, 158 × 120 cm, Munich, Alte Pinakothek (S). BURGKMAIR: *Hans Baumgartner,* 1512, chiaroscuro woodcut, 29 × 23 cm, London, British Museum (The Fotomas Index). BALDUNG GRIEN: *Death and the Maiden,* 1517, oil on panel, 28 × 16 cm, Basel, Offentliche Kunstsammlungen (Colorphoto Hans Hinz).

156–157 Holbein: The Ambassadors
HOLBEIN: *"The Ambassadors"*, 1533, tempera on panel, 206 × 209 cm, London, National Gallery; *The dead Christ,* 1521, tempera on panel, 30.5 × 200 cm, Basel, Offentliche Kunstsammlungen (Colorphoto Hans Hinz); *The Virgin and Child with the Meyer family, c.* 1528, tempera on panel, 146.5 × 102 cm, Darmstadt, Schloss Darmstadt (S); *Sir Thomas More,* 1527, tempera on panel, 74 × 59 cm, New York, The Frick Collection (copyright); *Jane Seymour, c.* 1535, chalk and primer on paper, 50 × 29 cm, Windsor, The Royal Library (by gracious permission of Her Majesty the Queen); *King Henry VIII,* 1542, tempera on panel, 92 × 67 cm, Castle Howard, Howard Collection.

158–159 Sculpture in Germany
GERHAERTS: *"Self-portrait", c.* 1467, sandstone, height 43 cm, Strasbourg, Musée de l'Oeuvre de Notre Dame (S). RIEMENSCHNEIDER: The altar at St Jakob, Rothenburg, 1501-05, varnished wood, height of figures about 1 m (Tony Schneiders/Joseph P. Ziolo). PACHER: The high altar of St Wolfgang, *c.* 1471-81, gilded and painted wood, central field 3.9 × 3.3 m (Snark International/Joseph P. Ziolo). STOSS: The high altar at St Mary's, Cracow, 1477-89, painted wood, height of tallest figure 2.8 m (Almasy Archives/Joseph P. Ziolo); *The Virgin and Child, c.* 1520, painted stone, height about 2 m, Nuremberg, Germanisches Nationalmuseum (S). KRAFT: The Tabernacle at St Lorenz, 1493-96, sandstone, Nuremberg, *in situ* (S). THE VISCHER FAMILY: The Shrine of St Sebaldus, 1507-19, bronze, height of free-standing figures 90 cm, Nuremberg, St Sebaldus (Bildarchiv Preussischer Kulturbesitz). MEIT: *Judith with the head of Holofernes,* 1510-15, alabaster, height 30 cm, Munich, Bayerisches Nationalmuseum (S). LOSCHER: Fragments from the Fugger chapel in Augsburg: *Putti,* 1515 height about 30 cm, Vienna, Kunsthistorisches Museum (S). FLOTNER: The Apollo Fountain, 1532, bronze, height of Apollo 76 cm, Nuremberg, Hof Pellerhaus (S).

160–161 Netherlandish and French Painting
MABUSE: The Malvagna triptych: *The Virgin and Child, and saints,* 1510-15, oil on panel, height 45 cm, Palermo, Galleria Nazionale (S). MASSYS: *The banker and his wife,* 1514, oil on panel, 74 × 68 cm, Paris, Louvre; *Egidius (Peter Giles),* 1517, oil on canvas, 224.5 × 219 cm, Private Collection. ORLEY: *Georges de Zelle,* 1519, oil on panel, 39 × 32 cm, Brussels, Musées Royaux des Beaux-Arts (S). PATENIER: *The Flight into Egypt,* undated, oil on panel, Antwerp, Musée Royal des Beaux-Arts (S). MASSYS AND PATENIER: *The Crucifixion; saints and donors, c.* 1520-30, oil on panel, central panel 156 × 92 cm, Antwerp, Musée Mayer van den Bergh (S). VAN SCOREL: Mary Magdalen, *c.* 1540, oil on panel, 67 × 76.5 cm, Amsterdam, Rijksmuseum. HEEMSKERK: *Self-portrait beside the Colosseum,* 1533, oil on panel, 44 × 54 cm, Cambridge, Fitzwilliam Museum. CLOUET: *A lady in her bath, c.* 1550?, oil on panel, 92 × 81 cm, Washington, National Gallery of Art, Samuel H. Kress collection. VAN LEYDEN: *The engagement, c.*1520-30, 30 × 32 cm, Antwerp, Musée Royal des Beaux-Arts (S). FONTAINEBLEAU SCHOOL: *Three minions, c.* 1580-89, oil on slate, 57 × 57 cm, Milwaukee, Art Center, Gift of the Women's Exchange.

162–163 Bruegel: August
AERTSEN: *Christ in the house of Martha and Mary,* 1559, oil on panel, 126 × 200 cm, Rotterdam, Museum Boymans-van Beuningen. BRUEGEL: *January (The hunters in the snow),* 1565, oil on panel, 117 × 162 cm, Vienna, Kunsthistorisches Museum (S); *August (The corn harvest),* 1565, oil on panel, 118 × 161 cm, New York, Metropolitan Museum of Art, Rogers Fund; *The peasant wedding, c.* 1567, oil on panel, 114 × 163 cm, Vienna, Kunsthistorisches Museum (S); *The procession to Calvary,* 1564, oil on panel, 124 × 177 cm, Vienna, Kunsthistorisches Museum (S); *The Adoration of the Magi,* 1564, oil on panel, 111 × 83 cm, London, National Gallery.

164–165 Mannerist Painting in Italy 1
RAPHAEL: *The Transfiguration,* 1520, oil on panel, 400 × 279 cm, Vatican, Pinacoteca (S). MICHELANGELO: *Victory, c.* 1530, marble, height 145.5 cm, Florence, Palazzo Vecchio (S). ANDREA DEL SARTO: *"The Madonna of the Harpies"*, 1517, oil on panel, 208 × 178 cm, Florence, Uffizi (S). GIULIO ROMANO: The *Sala dei Giganti,* 1534, fresco, Mantua, Palazzo del Té (S). PONTORMO: *Joseph in Egypt, c.* 1515, oil on panel, 96.5 × 109.5 cm, London, National Gallery; *The Deposition, c.* 1526-28, oil on panel, 313 × 109 cm, Florence, S. Felicità (S); *The halberdier, c.*1529-30, oil on panel, 92 × 72 cm, New York, Private Collection, on loan to the Frick Collection. ROSSO: *The Deposition,* 1521, oil on panel, 375 × 196 cm, Volterra, Galleria Communale (S). BECCAFUMI: *The birth of the Virgin, c.* 1543, oil on panel, 233 × 145 cm, Siena, Pinacoteca (S). PARMIGIANINO: *"The Madonna of the Long Neck", c.* 1535, oil on panel, 216 × 132 cm, Florence, Uffizi (S); *"The Priest", c.* 1523, oil on panel, 89 × 64 cm, London, National Gallery (Angelo Hornak).

166–167 Mannerism 2
BRONZINO: Chapel of Eleanora of Toledo, Palazzo Vecchio: *The crossing of the Red Sea,* 1542-44, fresco, Florence (S); *Venus, Cupid, Folly and Time, c.* 1545, oil on panel, 146 × 116 cm, London, National Gallery; *Eleanora of Toledo, c.* 1546?, oil on panel, 83 × 60 cm, Florence, Uffizi (S). SALVIATI: Frescos in the Palazzo Sacchetti: *Bathsheba going to David, c.* 1552-54, Rome (S). VASARI: *Alessandro de' Medici, c.* 1533, oil on panel, Florence, Museo Mediceo (S); Cosimo I's *studiolo,* Palazzo Vecchio, 1570-73, Florence (S). ROSSO AND PRIMATICCIO: The Gallery of Francis I, Château de Fontainebleau (Giraudon). PRIMATICCIO: The Room of the Duchesse d'Etampes, Château de Fontainebleau (René Roland). GOUJON: Panel from the Fountain of the Innocents: *Nymphs and tritons,* 1547-79, marble, height about 1 m, Paris, Louvre (Documentation Photographique de la Réunion des Musées Nationaux). CELLINI: *"The Nymph of Fontainebleau"*, 1540-43, bronze, 203 × 408 cm, Paris, Louvre (Documentation Photographique de la Réunion des Musées Nationaux). PILON: The tomb of Henri II and Catherine de Médicis, 1563-70, marble with bronze effigies, St-Denis, St Denis (René Roland).

168–169 Mannerist Sculpture in Italy
FLORENCE: The Piazza della Signoria (S). AMMANATI: The Fountain of Neptune, 1571-75, marble with bronze figures, Florence, Piazza della Signoria (S). CELLINI: *Perseus,* finished 1554, bronze, height of statue with base 3.2 m, Florence, Loggia dei Lanzi (S); The salt-cellar of Francis I, *c.* 1540, gold and enamel, height 33.5 cm, Vienna, Kunsthistorisches Museum (Photo Meyer). GIAMBOLOGNA: *Mercury, c.* 1564, bronze, height 180 cm, Florence, Bargello (S); *Apollo,* 1570-73, bronze, height 88 cm, Florence, Palazzo Vecchio (S); *Hercules and the centaur,* 1594-1600, marble, height 270 cm, Florence, Loggia dei Lanzi (S); *Duke*

Cosimo I, 1587-95, bronze, height 450cm, Florence, Piazza della Signoria (S); *The rape of the Sabine*, 1579-83, marble, height of statue with base 410cm, Florence, Loggia dei Lanzi (both views S).

170–171 Painting in Venice
TINTORETTO: *St Mark frees a Christian slave*, 1548, oil on canvas, 410 × 545cm, Venice, Accademia (S); *Bacchus and Ariadne*, 1578, oil on canvas, 146 × 167cm, Venice, Doge's Palace (S); *The finding of the body of St Mark*, 1562-66, oil on canvas, 399 × 399cm, Milan, Brera (S); *The Last Supper*, 1592-94, oil on canvas, 366 × 568cm, Venice, S. Giorgio Maggiore (S); *Susannah and the Elders*, *c.* 1557, oil on canvas, 147 × 193cm, Vienna, Kunsthistorisches Museum (S). BASSANO: *The Adoration of the shepherds*, 1568, oil on canvas, 238 × 149cm, Bassano, Museo Civico (S). VERONESE: *The feast in the house of Levi*, 1573, oil on canvas, 554 × 1280cm, Venice, Accademia (S); *Mars and Venus united by Love*, *c.* 1580, oil on canvas, 205 × 160cm, New York, Metropolitan Museum of Art, Kennedy Fund; A fresco from the Villa Maser: *Giustiniana Barbaro and her nurse*, *c.* 1561, width 1.6m, Maser, Villa Barbaro (S).

172–173 Tintoretto: The San Rocco Crucifixion
TINTORETTO: *The Crucifixion*, 1565, oil on canvas, 536 × 1224cm, Venice, Scuola di San Rocco (The Mansell Collection; detail S); *Self-portrait*, 1573, oil on canvas, 72 × 57cm, Scuola di San Rocco (S); *The Flight into Egypt*, 1583-87, oil on canvas, 422 × 580cm, Scuola di San Rocco (S); *The road to Calvary*, 1566, oil on canvas, 515 × 390cm, Scuola di San Rocco (S); *The temptation of Christ*, 1579-81, oil on canvas, 539 × 330cm, Scuola di San Rocco (S).

174–175 Art in Spain
MORO: *Mary I of England*, 1554, oil on panel, 109 × 84cm, Madrid, Prado (Bildarchiv Preussischer Kulturbesitz). LEONI: The tomb of Charles V, 1593-98, bronze, Madrid, Escorial. EL GRECO: *Christ driving the money-changers from the temple*, *c.* 1572, oil on canvas, 117.5 × 150cm, Minneapolis, The Minneapolis Institute of Arts; *Guilio Clovio*, *c.* 1570, oil on canvas, 65 × 95cm, Naples, Museo di Capodimonte (S); "*El Espolio*" (The disrobing of Christ), 1577-79, oil on canvas, 285 × 173cm, Toledo, Cathedral (S); *The burial of Count Orgaz*, 1586, oil on canvas, 487.5 × 360cm, Madrid, Prado (Bildarchiv Preussischer Kulturbesitz); *Cardinal Fernando Nino de Guevara*, *c.* 1600, oil on canvas, 171.5 × 108cm, New York, Metropolitan Museum of Art, H.O. Havemeyer collection; *View of Toledo*, *c.* 1595-1600, oil on canvas, 121.5 × 108.5cm, New York, Metropolitan Museum of Art, H.O. Havemeyer collection; *The Immaculate Conception*, *c.* 1607-13, oil on canvas, 236 × 118cm, Toledo, Museo de Santa Cruz (Salmar).

176–177 The Baroque Era
VERSAILLES: *The Galerie des Glaces*, begun 1678, by Lebrun (A. F. Kersting). TWICKENHAM: Strawberry Hill, begun 1747, by Horace Walpole (A. F. Kersting).

178–179
(Map by Colin Salmon and Dinah Lone)

180–181 Michelangelo da Caravaggio
CARAVAGGIO: *Boy bitten by a lizard*, *c.* 1596-1600, oil on canvas, 66 × 50cm, Florence, Longhi Collection (S); *The fortune teller*, *c.* 1594-95, oil on canvas, 99 × 131cm, Paris, Louvre (S); *St John the Baptist*, 1597-98, oil on canvas, 132 × 97cm, Rome, Capitoline Museum (S); *The Supper at Emmaus*, *c.* 1596-1600, oil on canvas, 141 × 196cm, London, National Gallery; *The Supper at Emmaus*, *c.* 1605-06, oil on canvas, 141 × 175cm, Milan, Brera (S); *St Matthew and the angel* (1st version), *c.* 1599, oil on canvas, 223 × 183cm, formerly Berlin, Staatliche Museen, destroyed (S); *The Calling of St Matthew*, *c.* 1597-99, oil on canvas, 338 × 348cm, Rome, S. Luigi dei Francesi (S); *The death of the Virgin*, 1605-06, oil on canvas, 369 × 245cm, Paris, Louvre (S); *The Resurrection of Lazarus*, 1609, oil on canvas, 380 × 275cm, Messina, Museo Nazionale (S).

182–183 Caravaggio: The Conversion of St Paul
CARAVAGGIO: *The crucifixion of St Peter*, 1600-01, oil on canvas, 230 × 175cm, Rome, S. Maria del Popolo (S); *The conversion of St Paul*, 1600-01, oil on canvas, 230 × 175cm, S. Maria del Popolo (S). DURER: "*The Large Horse*", 1505, etching, 17 × 21cm, London, British Museum. MICHELANGELO: *The conversion of St Paul*, 1546-50, fresco, 6.1 × 6.5m, Vatican, Cappella Paolina (S). MANTEGNA: *The dead Christ*, *c.* 1505, tempera on canvas, 66 × 81cm, Milan, Brera (S). ANNIBALE CARRACCI: *The Assumption of the Virgin*, 1600-01, oil on panel, 245 × 155cm, Rome, S. Maria del Popolo (S).

184–185 The Carracci and their Pupils
ANNIBALE CARRACCI: *The butcher's shop*, *c.* 1582, oil on canvas, 185 × 266cm, Oxford, Christchurch Picture Gallery (Angelo Hornak); *Landscape with the Flight into Egypt*, *c.* 1604, oil on canvas, 122 × 230cm, Rome, Palazzo Doria Pamphili (S); *Pietà*, *c.* 1599-1600, oil on canvas, 156 × 149cm, Naples, Museo di Capodimonte (S); *A prisoner*, early 1590s, red chalk, 42 × 35cm, Florence, Uffizi (S). AGOSTINO CARRACCI?: *Annibale Carracci*, late 1580s, oil on panel, 16 × 13cm, Florence, Uffizi (S). AGOSTINO CARRACCI: *The last communion of St Jerome*, 1593-94, oil on canvas, 375 × 224cm, Bologna, Pinacoteca (S). LUDOVICO CARRACCI: *The Madonna and Child with saints*, *c.* 1590, oil on canvas, 219 × 144cm, Bologna, Pinacoteca (S). LANFRANCO: *The Virgin in glory*, detail of dome of S. Andrea della Valle, 1625-27, fresco, Rome (S). GUIDO RENI: *Atalanta and Hippomenes*, *c.* 1620, oil on canvas, 194 × 264cm, Naples, Museo di Capodimonte (S). GUERCINO: *Profile head of a man*, undated, red chalk on paper, 18 × 16cm, London, British Museum (John Freeman); *Aurora*, 1621-23, fresco, Rome, Villa Ludovisi (S). DOMENICHINO: *The martyrdom of St Cecilia*, 1611-14, fresco, Rome, S. Luigi dei Francesi (S).

186–187 Annibale Carracci: The Farnese Gallery
AGOSTINO CARRACCI: Cartoon for *Glaucus and Scylla* on the inner wall of the Farnese Gallery, *c.* 1597-99, on paper, 203 × 410cm, London, National Gallery. ANNIBALE CARRACCI: The Farnese Gallery: *The loves of the gods*, 1597-1600, fresco, length of ceiling 20m, width 6.4m (details, *Venus and Anchises*, S; *The triumph of Bacchus and Ariadne*, S), Rome, Palazzo Farnese (S). *View of the inner wall of the Farnese Gallery*, engraving by Giovanni Volpato, London, Victoria and Albert Museum (A. C. Coopers). RAPHAEL: The ceiling of the Villa Farnesina *loggia*, detail: *The marriage of Cupid and Psyche*, 1518, fresco, Rome (S).

188–189 The High Baroque in Rome
BERNINI: *Neptune and Triton*, 1620, marble, height 182cm, London, Victoria and Albert Museum; *Apollo and Daphne*, 1622-24, marble, height 243cm, Rome, Borghese Gallery (S); *David*, 1623, marble, height 170cm, Rome, Borghese Gallery (S); *Cathedra Petri* (St Peter's Chair), 1656-66, stucco and bronze, Vatican, St Peter's (S); *Louis XIV*, 1665, marble, height 80cm, Versailles, Salon de Diane (Documentation Photographique de la Réunion des Musées Nationaux); *Costanza Buonarelli*, *c.* 1635, marble, height 72cm, Florence, Bargello (S); *The four rivers*, 1646-51, marble, Rome, Piazza Navona (S). *The Piazza and Basilica of St Peter's, Rome*, engraving by Francesco Piranesi, 38 × 54cm, London, British Museum. PIETRO DA CORTONA: *Allegory of divine Providence and Barberini power*, 1633-39, fresco, Rome, Palazzo Barberini (S).

190–191 Bernini: The Cornaro Chapel
BERNINI: The Cornaro Chapel, S. Maria della Vittoria, 1647-52, marble, bronze, stucco, gilt wood and fresco, Rome (whole and details S).

192–193 French Art 1
LOUIS LE NAIN: *The peasants' meal*, 1642, oil on canvas, 211 × 122cm, Paris, Louvre (S). ANTOINE LE NAIN: *A woman and five children*, 1642, oil on copper, 22 × 29.5cm, London, National Gallery. MATHIEU LE NAIN: *The guardroom*, 1643, oil on canvas, 115 × 134cm, Paris, Louvre (Photo Bulloz). THE LE NAIN BROTHERS: *The Adoration of the shepherds*, *c.* 1640, 120 × 90cm, sold Christie's, London, 1979 (Photo Bulloz). GEORGES DE LA TOUR: *St Jerome*, 1621-23, oil on canvas, 157 × 100cm, Grenoble, Musée des Beaux-Arts (Cooper-Bridgeman Library); *A woman crushing a flea*, *c.* 1645, oil on canvas, 120 × 90cm, Nancy, Musée Historique Lorrain (Cooper-Bridgeman Library); *The new-born child*, *c.* 1650, oil on canvas, 76 × 91cm, Rennes, Musée des Beaux-Arts. VOUET: *St Charles Borromeo*, late 1630s, oil on canvas, 360 × 260cm, Paris, Louvre (S). CHAMPAIGNE: *Ex voto*, 1662, oil on canvas, 165 × 229cm, Paris, Louvre (Documentation Photographique de la Réunion des Musées Nationaux); *Cardinal Richelieu*, *c.* 1635-40, oil on canvas, 221 × 154cm, Paris, Louvre (S).

194–195 Poussin: The Holy Family on the Steps
POUSSIN: *The Holy Family on the steps*, 1648, oil on canvas, 69 × 97.5cm, Washington, National Gallery of Art, Samuel H. Kress collection (S); *Self-portrait*, 1649-50, oil on canvas, 98 × 74cm, Paris, Louvre (S); *The poet's inspiration*, *c.* 1628-29, oil on canvas, 184 × 214cm, Paris, Louvre (S); Preparatory drawing for *The Holy Family*, 1648, pen and bistre and chalk on paper, 18 × 24cm, Paris, Louvre (Documentation Photographique de la Réunion des Musées Nationaux). RAPHAEL: "*The Madonna of the Fish*", *c.* 1513, 215 × 158cm, Madrid, Prado (S). ROME, ESQUILINE: "*The Aldobrandini Marriage*", 1st century BC, fresco, 91 × 242cm, Vatican, Museum (S).

196–197 Landscape Painting in Italy
ELSHEIMER: *Rest on the Flight to Egypt*, 1609, oil on copper, 31 × 41cm, Munich, Alte Pinakothek (S). PAUL BRIL: *Landscape with hunting scene and the Baths of Titus*, *c.* 1620, London, Private Collection (S). POUSSIN: *The burial of Phocion*, 1648, oil on canvas, 114 × 175cm, Ludlow, Earl of Plymouth Collection (S); *Summer, or Ruth and Boaz*, 1660-64, oil on canvas, 118 × 160cm, Paris, Louvre (S). CLAUDE: *Tree*, *c.* 1650, chalk and wash on paper, 25 × 18cm, London, British Museum; *Ulysses returning Chryseis to her father*, 1644, oil on canvas, 119 × 150cm, Paris, Louvre (S); *Egeria mourning over Numa*, 1669, oil on canvas, 155 × 199cm, Naples, Museo di Capodimonte (S); *Self-portrait*, after 1644, frontispiece to the Liber Veritatis, drawing, 15 × 12cm, London, British Museum. SALVATOR ROSA: *Landscape with a bridge*, *c.* 1640, oil on canvas, 106 × 127cm, Florence, Palazzo Pitti (S). GASPARD DUGHET: *View near Albano*, *c.* 1630-40, oil on canvas, 48 × 66cm, London, National Gallery.

198–199 French Art 2
LE SUEUR: *The Muses*, *c.* 1647-49, from the *Cabinet d'Amour* in the Hotel Lambert, oil on canvas, 128 × 128cm, Paris, Louvre (Documentation Photographique de la Réunion des Musées Nationaux). LEBRUN: *Louis XIV visiting the Gobelins factory*, 1663-75, oil on canvas, height 256cm, Paris, Louvre (Documentation Photographique de la Réunion des Musées Nationaux); *Louis XIV adoring the risen Christ*, 1674, oil on canvas, 473 × 261cm, Lyons, Musée des Beaux-Arts (Giraudon). COYSEVOX: *Louis XIV*, 1687-89, marble, height about 2.5m, Paris, Musée Carnavalet (Photo Bulloz). SARRAZIN: Caryatids on the Pavillon d'Horloge of the Louvre, 1641, marble (Giraudon). MICHEL ANGUIER: *Amphitrite*, 1680, marble, height about 2m, Paris, Louvre (Photo Bulloz). GIRAUDON: *Apollo tended by nymphs*, 1660, marble, height of figures about 1.7m, Versailles (Ken Takase/Joseph P. Ziolo). BOURDON: Mythological drawing, undated (Photo Bulloz). LEBRUN AND COYSEVOX: The *Salon de la Guerre* (Hall of War) at Versailles, 1681-83, marble and mixed media, Versailles (S). PUGET: *Milo of Crotona*, 1683, marble, height 269cm, Paris, Louvre (S). RIGAUD: *Louis XIV*, 1701, oil on canvas, 274 × 177cm, Paris, Louvre (S).

200–201 Art in Flanders
RUBENS AND "VELVET" BRUEGHEL: *The Virgin and Child in a garland*, *c.* 1620, oil on panel, 79 × 65cm, Madrid, Prado (S). PAUL DE VOS: *The stag hunt*, *c.* 1630-40, oil on canvas, 212 × 347cm, Madrid, Prado (S). VAN DYCK: *Marquesa Caterina*, *c.* 1625, oil on canvas, 230 × 170cm, Paris, Louvre (S). SNYDERS: *The fruit-seller*, before 1636, oil on canvas, 153 × 214cm, Madrid, Prado (S). CORNELIS DE VOS: *The artist and his family*, 1621, oil on canvas, 188 × 162cm, Brussels, Musées Royaux des Beaux-Arts (S). JORDAENS: *The riding academy*, *c.* 1635, oil on canvas, 90 × 153cm, Ottawa, National Gallery of Canada; *The King drinks*, *c.* 1645, oil on canvas, 156 × 210cm, Brussels, Musées Royaux des Beaux-Arts (S). TENIERS: *The country fair*, *c.* 1650, oil on canvas, 77 × 99cm, Madrid, Prado (S); *The picture gallery of the Archduke Leopold*, *c.* 1650, oil on canvas, 106 × 129cm, Madrid, Prado (S).

202–203 Peter Paul Rubens
RUBENS: *Self-portrait*, *c.* 1639, oil on canvas, 109 × 85cm, Vienna, Kunsthistorisches Museum (S); *The Duke of Lerma*, 1603, oil on canvas, 289 × 205cm, Madrid, Prado (S); *The horrors of war*, 1638, oil on canvas, 206 × 342cm, Florence, Palazzo Pitti (S); *Self-portrait with Isabella Brandt*, 1609, oil on panel, 178 × 136cm, Munich, Alte Pinakothek (S); *Hélène Fourment in a fur wrap*, *c.* 1638, oil on panel, 175 × 96cm, Vienna, Kunsthistorisches Museum (S); *The rape of the daughters of Leucippus*, *c.* 1618, oil on canvas, 222 × 209cm, Vienna, Kunsthistorisches Museum (S); The ceiling of the Banqueting House: *The apotheosis of James I*, 1629-34, London, Whitehall (Cooper-Bridgeman Library);

The Château de Steen, c. 1636, oil on panel, 131 × 229 cm, London, National Gallery; The Luxembourg Palace cycle: *Marie de Médicis lands at Marseilles,* 1622-25, oil on canvas, 394 × 295 cm, Paris, Louvre (S).

204–205 Rubens: The Descent from the Cross
RUBENS: *The Descent from the Cross,* 1611-14, oil on panel, 240 × 310 cm, Antwerp, Cathedral (S); *The raising of the Cross,* 1610-11, oil on panel, 240 × 310 cm, Antwerp, Cathedral (A. De Belder/Joseph P. Ziolo); Drawing of the *Laocoön, c.* 1606, black chalk on paper, 43 × 25 cm, Milan, Biblioteca Ambrosiana; Copy after Caravaggio's *The Entombment, c.* 1600, reworked *c.* 1613, oil on panel, 88 × 65 cm, Ottawa, National Gallery of Canada. DANIELE DA VOLTERRA: *The Descent from the Cross,* 1541, fresco, Rome, S. Trinita ai Monti (S).

206–207 Art in England
EWORTH: *Queen Mary I,* 1554, oil on panel, 21 × 17 cm, London, National Portrait Gallery. HILLIARD: *Young man in a garden, c.* 1588, watercolour on vellum, 13.5 × 7 cm, London, Victoria and Albert Museum. VAN DYCK: *William Fielding, Earl of Denbigh, c.* 1633, oil on canvas, 248 × 149 cm, London, National Gallery; *Lady Elizabeth Thimbleby and Dorothy, Viscountess Andover, c.* 1637, oil on canvas, 130 × 140 cm, London, National Gallery; *Charles I hunting, c.* 1638, oil on canvas, 272 × 213 cm, Paris, Louvre (Documentation Photographique de la Réunion des Musées Nationaux); *Charles I on horseback, c.* 1638, oil on canvas, 367 × 292 cm, London, National Gallery; *Charles I from three angles, c.* 1636, oil on canvas, 84.5 × 100 cm, Windsor, Royal Collection (by gracious permission of Her Majesty the Queen). COOPER: *Oliver Cromwell,* 1656, colour on card, height 7 cm, London, National Portrait Gallery. LELY: *Anna, Countess of Shrewsbury, c.* 1670, oil on canvas, 100 × 61 cm, London, National Portrait Gallery. DOBSON: *A cavalier, c.* 1643, oil on canvas, 95 × 76 cm, London, National Maritime Museum. KNELLER: *Jacob Tonson, c.* 1717, oil on canvas, 91 × 71 cm, London, National Portrait Gallery. BARLOW: *Buzzards about to attack some owlets,* undated, oil on canvas, 106 × 137 cm, London, Tate Gallery.

208–209 Art in Spain
RIBALTA: *St Bernard embracing Christ, c.* 1620-28, oil on canvas, 158 × 113 cm, Madrid, Prado (S). RIBERA: *The bearded woman,* 1631, oil on canvas, 196 × 127 cm, Toledo, Hospital Tavera, Fondacion Lerma (S); *The martyrdom of St Bartholomew, c.* 1630, oil on canvas, 234 × 234 cm, Madrid, Prado (S); *The mystic marriage of St Catherine,* 1648, oil on canvas, 201 × 152 cm, New York, Metropolitan Museum of Art, Samuel D. Lee Fund. MENA: *Mary Magdalen,* 1644, painted wood, height about 1.5 m, Valladolid, Museo Nacional de Escultura (S). ZURBARAN: *St Anthony of Padua with the infant Christ,* 1650s, oil on canvas, 148 × 108 cm, Madrid, Prado (S); *Hercules seared by the poisoned robe,* 1634, oil on canvas, 136 × 167 cm, Madrid, Prado (S); *Still life, c.* 1664?, oil on canvas, 46 × 84 cm, Madrid, Prado (S). MURILLO: *Boys playing dice,* undated, oil on canvas, 146 × 108 cm, Munich, Alte Pinakothek (S); *The Immaculate Conception, c.* 1655-60, oil on canvas, 206 × 144 cm, Madrid, Prado (S). VALDES LEAL: *The triumph of Death,* 1672, oil on canvas, 220 × 216 cm, Seville, Hospital de la Caridad (S).

210–211 Velazquez: Las Meninas
VELAZQUEZ: *Christ in the house of Mary and Martha,* 1618, oil on canvas, 60 × 103 cm, London, National Gallery; *The tapestry weavers, c.* 1654, oil on canvas, 220 × 289 cm, Madrid, Prado (S); *The Infanta Margarita, c.* 1656, oil on canvas, 70 × 59 cm, Paris, Louvre (S); *Philip IV,* 1634-35, oil on canvas, 191 × 126 cm, Madrid, Prado (S); *"Las Meninas"* (The maids of honour), 1656, oil on canvas, 318 × 276 cm, Madrid, Prado (S).

212–213 Art in the Dutch Republic
HOOGSTRATEN: *The slippers, c.* 1660-75, oil on canvas, 103 × 71 cm, Paris, Louvre (Documentation Photographique de la Réunion des Musées Nationaux). SAENREDAM: *St John's Church, Haarlem,* 1645, oil on canvas, 49 × 42 cm, Utrecht, Centraal Museum. VAN DE CAPPELLE: *The large ferry,* 1660s, oil on canvas, 122 × 154.5 cm, London, National Gallery. REMBRANDT: *The syndics of the Cloth Guild,* 1662, oil on canvas, 191 × 279 cm, Amsterdam, Rijksmuseum; *Two women teaching a child to walk, c.* 1637, chalk on paper, 10 × 13 cm, London, British Museum (The Fotomas Index); *Four orientals beneath a tree, c.* 1654, pen and bistre, wash on paper, 19 × 12 cm, London, British Museum (The Fotomas Index); HONTHORST: *The banquet,* 1620, oil on canvas, 138 × 204 cm, Florence, Palazzo Pitti (S); *William of Orange,* after 1637, oil on canvas, 130 × 108 cm, The Hague, Mauritshuis (S). LASTMAN: *Juno discovering Jupiter with Io,* 1618, oil on panel, 54 × 78 cm, London, National Gallery. REMBRANDT: *A girl sleeping, c.* 1656, pen and bistre on paper, 22 × 20 cm, London, British Museum (The Fotomas Index).

214–215 Hals: A Banquet of the St George Civic Guard
VERONESE: *The feast at Cana,* 1559-60, oil on canvas, 660 × 990 cm, Paris, Louvre (S). CORNELIS VAN HAARLEM: *The banquet of Haarlem guardsmen,* 1583, 156.5 × 222 cm, Haarlem, Frans Hals Museum. FRANS HALS: *The banquet of the St George Civic Guard,* 1616, oil on canvas, 175 × 324 cm, Haarlem, Frans Hals Museum; *The regents of the St Elizabeth Hospital, c.* 1641, oil on canvas, 153 × 252 cm, Haarlem, Frans Hals Museum; *"The Laughing Cavalier",* 1624, oil on canvas, 86 × 89 cm, London, Wallace Collection; *The banquet of the St George Civic Guard, c.* 1627, oil on canvas, 179 × 257.5 cm, Haarlem, Frans Hals Museum; *Willem Croes, c.* 1660, oil on canvas, 47 × 34 cm, Munich, Alte Pinakothek (S).

216–217 Rembrandt van Rijn
REMBRANDT: *Self-portrait in studio attire, c.* 1650-60, oil on canvas, 25 × 31.5 cm, Amsterdam, Rembrandt Huis; *Balaam,* 1626, oil on panel, 65 × 47 cm, Paris, Musée Cognacq-Jay (Photo Bulloz); *The blinding of Samson,* 1636, oil on canvas, 236 × 302 cm, Frankfurt, Städelsches Kunstinstitut (S); *The anatomy lesson of Dr Tulp,* 1632, oil on canvas, 169.5 × 216.5 cm, The Hague, Mauritshuis (S); *The Descent from the Cross,* 1633, oil on panel, 89 × 65 cm, Munich, Alte Pinakothek; *The return of the Prodigal Son,* 1636, etching, 15.5 × 13.5 cm, Amsterdam, Rijksmuseum; *Nude on a mound,* 1631, etching, 18 × 16 cm, Paris, Bibliothèque Nationale (Immédiate 2); The Hundred-Guilder Print: *Christ healing the sick, c.* 1648-50, drypoint and burin etching, 28 × 40 cm, London, British Museum (The Fotomas Index); *"The Night Watch" (The Company of Frans Banning Cocq and Willem van Ruytenburch),* 1642, oil on canvas, 359 × 438 cm, Amsterdam, Rijksmuseum; *"The Jewish Bride", c.* 1665, oil on canvas, 121.5 × 166.5 cm, Amsterdam, Rijksmuseum.

218–219 Rembrandt: The Self-Portrait at Kenwood
REMBRANDT: *Self-portrait* in Munich, detail, *c.* 1629, oil on panel, 18 × 14 cm, Alte Pinakothek (S); *Self-portrait with Saskia, c.* 1635, oil on canvas, 161 × 131 cm, Dresden, Gemäldegalerie; *Self-portrait* in Berlin, 1634, 55 × 46 cm, West Berlin, Staatliche Museen; *Self-portrait after Titian's "Ariosto",* 1640, oil on canvas, 102 × 80 cm, London, National Gallery; *Self-portrait drawing by a window,* 1648, drypoint and burin etching, 16 × 13 cm, Paris, Bibliothèque Nationale (Immédiate 2); *Self-portrait* in Kenwood, London, *c.* 1665, oil on canvas, 114 × 95 cm (The Greater London Council as Trustees of the Iveagh Bequest, Kenwood); *Self-portrait* in Vienna, 1652, oil on canvas, 113 × 81 cm, Kunsthistorisches Museum (Photo Meyer); *Self-portrait* in Cologne, *c.* 1669, oil on canvas, 82 × 63 cm, Wallraf-Richartz Museum; *Self-portrait* in London, 1669, oil on canvas, 86 × 70.5 cm, National Gallery.

220–221 Dutch Landscape 1
CONINXLOO: *The forest, c.* 1660, oil on panel, 56 × 85 cm, Copenhagen, Statens Museum fur Kunst. SAVERY: *Orpheus charming the animals, c.* 1625, oil on panel, 62 × 131 cm, Verona, Museo di Castelvecchio (S). SEGHERS: *Landscape, c.* 1630, oil on panel, 55 × 100 cm, Florence, Uffizi (S). AVERCAMP: *Winter landscape, c.* 1610, oil on panel, 36 × 71 cm, The Hague, Mauritshuis (S). ESAIAS VAN DE VELDE: *The ferry-boat,* 1622, oil on panel, 75.5 × 113 cm, Amsterdam, Rijksmuseum. BOTH AND POELENBURGH: *Landscape with the Judgment of Paris,* undated, oil on canvas, 97 × 129 cm, London, National Gallery. BERCHEM: *The crab-fishers,* undated, oil on panel, 31.5 × 40 cm, York, City Art Gallery. REMBRANDT: *Landscape with a village, c.* 1650, ink and wash on paper, 16 × 23 cm, London, British Museum (The Fotomas Index); *"Six's Bridge",* 1645, etching, 13 × 22 cm, London, British Museum (The Fotomas Index).

222–223 Dutch Landscape 2
VAN GOYEN: *View of the village of Overschie, c.* 1645, oil on panel, 66 × 96.5 cm, London, National Gallery. SALOMON VAN RUYSDAEL: *View of a river,* 1630s or early 1640s, 33 × 51 cm, The Hague, Mauritshuis (S). JACOB VAN RUISDAEL: *View of Haarlem,* 1660s, oil on canvas, 55 × 61 cm, The Hague, Mauritshuis (S). SAENREDAM: *St Bavo's, Haarlem,* 1660, oil on canvas, 70 × 55 cm, Worcester, Massachusetts, Art Museum. CUYP: *View of a road near a river,* mid-1650s, oil on canvas, 112 × 165 cm, London, Dulwich College Gallery (by permission of the Governors). POTTER: *Cows resting,* 1649, oil on canvas, 53 × 66 cm, Turin, Galleria Sabauda (S). HOBBEMA: *The avenue at Middelharmis,* 1689, oil on canvas, 103.5 × 141 cm, London, National Gallery. VAN DE CAPPELLE: *View of the mouth of the river Scheldt, c.* 1650?, 69 × 91 cm, New York, Metropolitan Museum of Art, Michael Friedsam collection. WILLEM VAN DE VELDE THE YOUNGER: *The cannon shot, c.* 1660, oil on canvas, 78.5 × 67 cm, Amsterdam, Rijksmuseum.

224–225 Ruisdael: The Jewish Cemetery
JACOB VAN RUISDAEL: The Dresden *Jewish cemetery,* 1660s, oil on canvas, 84 × 95 cm, Dresden, Gemäldegalerie (G. Reinhold, Leipzig-Molkau/Joseph P. Ziolo); The Detroit *Jewish cemetery,* 1660s, oil on canvas, 142 × 189 cm, Detroit, Institute of Arts, Gift of Julius H. Haass in memory of his brother; *Tombs in the Jewish cemetery at Ouderkerk, c.* 1660, chalk and wash on paper, 19 × 27.5 cm, Haarlem, Teylers Museum; *Winter landscape, c.* 1670, oil on canvas, 41 × 49 cm, Amsterdam, Rijksmuseum. REMBRANDT: *The stone bridge, c.* 1637, oil on panel, 29 × 42.5 cm, Amsterdam, Rijksmuseum. EVERDINGEN: *A waterfall,* 1650, oil on canvas, 112 × 58 cm, Munich, Alte Pinakothek (S). KONINCK: *View over flat country,* 1650s or 1660s, 118 × 166 cm, Oxford, Ashmolean Museum.

226–227 Dutch Genre and Portraiture 1
BUYTEWECH: *Merry company, c.* 1617-20, oil on panel, 49 × 68 cm, Rotterdam, Museum Boymans-van Beuningen. LEYSTER: *The offer, c.* 1635?, oil on panel, 31 × 24 cm, The Hague, Mauritshuis (S). DIRCK HALS: *A garden party, c.* 1624, oil on panel, 78 × 137 cm, Amsterdam, Rijksmuseum. BROUWER: *Peasants in an inn, c.* 1627-31, oil on panel, 19.5 × 26.5 cm, The Hague, Mauritshuis (S). ADRIAEN VAN OSTADE: *Inside an inn,* 1653, oil on panel, 40 × 56 cm, London, National Gallery. DOU AND REMBRANDT: *The blind Tobit and his wife Anna, c.* 1630, oil on panel, 64 × 48 cm, London, National Gallery. MAES: *Admiral Binkes, c.* 1670-77, oil on canvas, 44 × 33 cm, New York, Metropolitan Museum of Art, Gift of J. Pierpont Morgan. VAN DER HELST: *A young girl,* 1645, oil on canvas, 75 × 65 cm, London, National Gallery. MIERIS THE ELDER: *Soap bubbles,* 1663, oil on oak, 25.5 × 19 cm, The Hague, Mauritshuis (S). STEEN: *The doctor's visit, c.* 1665, oil on panel, 48 × 41 cm, The Hague, Mauritshuis (S). METSU: *The hunter's gift, c.* 1661-67, oil on panel, 56 × 50 cm, Florence, Uffizi (S).

228–229 Dutch Genre and Portraiture 2
FABRITIUS: *View of Delft,* 1652, oil on panel, 15.5 × 32 cm, London, National Gallery; *A goldfinch,* 1654, oil on canvas, 33.5 × 23 cm, The Hague, Mauritshuis (S). VERMEER: *The procuress,* 1656, oil on canvas, 143 × 130 cm, Dresden, Gemäldegalerie; *A woman weighing pearls, c.* 1665, oil on canvas, 41.5 × 35 cm, Washington, National Gallery of Art, Widener collection; *A girl asleep at a table, c.* 1656, oil on canvas, 42.5 × 38 cm, New York, Metropolitan Museum of Art, Benjamin Altman Bequest; *View of Delft, c.* 1660, oil on canvas, 98.5 × 117.5 cm, The Hague, Mauritshuis (S). DE HOOGH: *The backgammon players,* 1653, oil on canvas, 46 × 33 cm, Dublin, National Gallery of Ireland; *A man smoking, a woman drinking and a child in a courtyard, c.* 1656, oil on canvas, 78 × 65 cm, The Hague, Mauritshuis (S); *A musical party, c.* 1677, oil on canvas, 83.5 × 68.5 cm, London, National Gallery. TERBORCH: *Self-portrait, c.* 1668, oil on canvas, 61 × 42.5 cm, The Hague, Mauritshuis (S); *A boy picking fleas from a dog, c.* 1655, oil on panel, 34 × 27 cm, Munich, Alte Pinakothek (S).

230–231 Vermeer: The Artist's Studio
VERMEER: *"The Artist's Studio"* (The art of painting), *c.* 1665-70, oil on canvas, 120 × 100 cm, Vienna, Kunsthistorisches Museum (Photo Meyer); *The head of a girl, c.* 1666, oil on canvas, 47 × 40 cm, The Hague, Mauritshuis (S); *A soldier and a laughing girl, c.* 1657, oil on canvas, 50.5 × 46 cm, New York, The Frick Collection (copyright); *An allegory of the New Testament, c.* 1669, oil on canvas, 113 × 88 cm, New York, Metropolitan Museum of Art, Michael Friedsam collection;

Diana and her nymphs, c. 1654, oil on canvas, 98.5 × 105 cm, The Hague, Mauritshuis (S). REMBRANDT: *The artist in his studio, c.* 1628-29, oil on panel, 25 × 32 cm, Boston, Museum of Fine Arts, Zoe Oliver Sherman collection.

232–233 Dutch Still-life Painting
AMBROSIUS BOSSCHAERT THE ELDER: *A vase of flowers, c.* 1620, oil on canvas, 64 × 46 cm, The Hague, Mauritshuis (S). HEDA: *Breakfast piece, c.* 1634, oil on panel, 46 × 69 cm, The Hague, Mauritshuis (S). CLAESZ.: *Still life,* 1623, oil on canvas, Paris, Louvre (S); *"Breakfast",* 1637, oil on panel, 83 × 66 cm, Madrid, Prado (S). DE HEEM: *Still life of books, c.* 1625-29, oil on panel, 36 × 48.5 cm, The Hague, Mauritshuis (S). KALF: *Still life, c.* 1643, oil on canvas, 115 × 86 cm, Cologne, Wallraf-Richartz Museum (S). JAN VAN HUYSUM: *A vase of flowers, c.* 1710-20, oil on canvas, 62.1 × 52.3 cm, London, National Gallery. VAN BEYEREN: *Still life,* undated, oil on panel, 98 × 76 cm, The Hague, Mauritshuis (S). HONDECOETER: *Cocks, hens and chicks, with other birds, c.* 1668, oil on canvas, 85.5 × 110 cm, London, National Gallery. REMBRANDT: *Self-portrait as a hunter,* 1639, oil on panel, 121 × 89 cm, Dresden, Gemäldegalerie (Archiv für Kunst und Geschichte).

234–235 Late Italian Baroque
POZZO: *Allegory of the missionary work of the Jesuits,* 1691-94, fresco, Rome, S. Ignazio (S). RAGGI: *St Ignatius' Chapel,* Il Gesù, 1683, stucco and other materials, Rome (S). MARATTA: *The Virgin and Child with St Philip Neri, c.* 1690, oil on canvas, 197 × 343 cm, Florence, Palazzo Pitti (S). GIORDANO: *Venus, Cupid and Mars,* undated, oil on canvas, 152 × 129 cm, Naples, Museo di Capodimonte. SOLIMENA: *The Virgin and Child with St Philip Neri,* fresco, Naples, Museo di Capodimonte (S). PIAZZETTA: *The Adoration of the shepherds, c.* 1725, oil on canvas, 73 × 53 cm, Padua, Museo Civico (S). SEBASTIANO RICCI: *Pope Paul III reconciles Francis I with Charles V,* 1686-88, oil on canvas, 108 × 94 cm, Piacenza, Museo Civico (S). SEBASTIANO AND MARCO RICCI: *Allegorical tomb for the Duke of Devonshire, c.* 1720, oil on canvas, 217 × 138 cm, Birmingham, University of Birmingham, The Barber Institute of Fine Arts. AMIGONI: *Venus and Adonis, c.* 1740-47, oil on canvas, 52 × 73 cm, Venice, Accademia (S).

236–237 Tiepolo: The Residenz at Würzburg
TIEPOLO: *Abraham visited by the angels, c.* 1732, oil on canvas, 140 × 120 cm, Venice, Scuola di San Rocco (S); *St Thecla delivering the city of Este from the plague,* 1759, oil on canvas, 80 × 44 cm, New York, Metropolitan Museum of Art, Rogers Fund; *The banquet of Cleopatra and Anthony,* detail of the Palazzo Labia ballroom, 1745-50, fresco, Venice (S); *Olympus with the four quarters of the Earth,* detail of the ceiling of the *Treppenhaus,* Würzburg, 1752-53, fresco (S); *America,* in the *Treppenhaus* (S); *Apollo leads Beatrice to Barbarossa,* in the *Kaisersaal,* Würzburg, fresco (S); *The marriage of Beatrice and Barbarossa,* in the *Kaisersaal* (S). NEUMANN AND TIEPOLO: The

Kaisersaal in the Residenz, Würzburg (S).

238–239 Watteau: The Embarkation for Cythera
RUBENS: *The Garden of Love, c.* 1632, oil on canvas, 198 × 283 cm, Madrid, Prado (S). WATTEAU: *"L'Enseigne de Gersaint"* (Gersaint's signboard), 1721, oil on canvas, 182 × 307 cm, West Berlin, Staatliche Museen (S); The Louvre *"Embarkation for Cythera",* properly *The pilgrimage to Cythera,* 1717, oil on canvas, 129 × 194 cm, Paris, Louvre (Documentation Photographique de la Réunion des Musées Nationaux); *"La Toilette", c.* 1720, oil on canvas, height 44 cm, London, Wallace Collection; The Berlin *"Embarkation for Cythera",* 1718, oil on canvas, 130 × 192 cm, West Berlin, Staatliche Museen (S).

240–241 French and German Rococo
BOUCHER: *Vulcan presenting the arms of Aeneas to Venus,* 1732, oil on canvas, 320 × 320 cm, Paris, Louvre (S); *Diana bathing,* 1742, oil on canvas, 55 × 72 cm, Paris, Louvre (S). FRAGONARD: *Music, or M. de la Bretèche,* 1769, oil on canvas, 80 × 65 cm, Paris, Louvre (S); *Women bathing,* 1777, oil on canvas, 63 × 79 cm, Paris, Louvre (S). ROBERT: *Felling Trees at Versailles,* 1778?, Lisbon, Fundacão Calouste Gulbenkian. THE ASAM BROTHERS: The altar of the church of Maria Victoria, Ingolstadt, 1734, stucco and other materials (Claus and Liselotte Hansmann); St John Nepomuk, 1733-46, interior, stucco and other materials, Munich (Claus and Liselotte Hansmann). ST NICHOLAS MALA STRARIA, PRAGUE: Detail of the upper nave, frescoed 1760-61 (S). THE ZIMMERMANN BROTHERS: Detail of the ceiling of Die Wies, Bavaria, 1745-54, stucco and other materials (S).

242–243 French Rococo 2
NATTIER: *Mlle Manon Balletti,* 1757, oil on canvas, 54 × 46 cm, London, National Gallery. LARGILLIERE: *The painter with his wife and daughter, c.* 1700, oil on canvas, 147 × 208 cm, Paris, Louvre (S). CARRIERA: *Self-portrait with an image of the artist's sister,* 1709, pastel on card, 71 × 57 cm, Florence, Uffizi (S). THE MEISSEN FACTORY: *The concerto, c.* 1760, painted porcelain, height about 17 cm (S). DROUAIS: *Comte and Chevalier de Choiseul,* 1746, oil on canvas, 139 × 107 cm, New York, The Frick Collection (copyright). BOUCHER: *Mme de Pompadour,* 1759, oil on canvas, 91 × 69 cm, London, Wallace Collection. FALCONET: *Peter the Great,* 1766-68, bronze, height of statue about 3.5 m, Leningrad, Square of the Decembrists; *Erigone,* 1747, terracotta, height about 27 cm, Sèvres, Musée National de Céramiques (Documentation Photographique de la Réunion des Musées Nationaux). QUENTIN DE LA TOUR: *M. Claude Dupouch,* 1739, pastel, 60 × 50 cm, St-Quentin, Musée A. Lecuyer (Photo Bulloz). CLODION: *Bacchante, c.* 1760, terracotta, height about 20 cm, Orléans, Musée des Beaux-Arts (Giraudon). ROUBILIAC: Monument to Lady Elizabeth Nightingale, 1761, marble, Westminster Abbey, London (Angelo Hornak).

244–245 Genre and Still-life Painting
TROOST: *The city garden, c.* 1742, oil on canvas, 66 × 56 cm, Amsterdam,

Rijksmuseum. PIAZZETTA: *The fortune-teller,* 1740, oil on canvas, 160 × 114 cm, Venice, Accademia (S). LARGILLIERE: *Still life, c.* 1690, oil on canvas, Chatsworth, Trustees of the Chatsworth Settlement. LONGHI: *The rhinoceros,* 1751, oil on canvas, 60 × 47 cm, Venice, Ca' Rezzonico (S). DOMENICO TIEPOLO: *The winter promenade,* 1757, fresco, Villa Valmarana (S). OUDRY: *The white duck,* 1753, oil on canvas, 93 × 62 cm, Houghton Hall, Collection of the Dowager Lady Cholmondeley (Eileen Tweedy). GREUZE: *The son punished, c.* 1777, oil on canvas, 127.5 × 157.5 cm, Paris, Louvre (S); *The broken pitcher, c.* 1773, oil on canvas, 108 × 84 cm, Paris, Louvre.

246–247 Chardin: The House of Cards
CHARDIN: *Skate, cat and kitchen utensils,* 1728, oil on canvas, 114 × 145 cm, Paris, Louvre (S); *Saying grace, c.* 1740, oil on canvas, 49.5 × 38.5 cm, Paris, Louvre (Documentation Photographique de la Réunion des Musées Nationaux); *Still life with a wild duck,* 1764, oil on canvas, 133 × 97 cm, Springfield, Massachusetts, Museum of Fine Arts, James Philip Gray collection; *Self-portrait with an eyeshade,* 1775, pastel, 46 × 38 cm, Paris, Louvre (Documentation Photographique de la Réunion des Musées Nationaux); *The house of cards, c.* 1741, oil on canvas, 81 × 65 cm, Washington, National Gallery of Art, Andrew W. Mellon collection. BOUCHER: *Breakfast,* 1739, oil on canvas, 80 × 61 cm, Paris, Louvre (Documentation Photographique de la Réunion des Musées Nationaux). REMBRANDT: *The flayed ox,* 1655, oil on canvas, 94 × 69 cm, Paris, Louvre (S).

248–249 William Hogarth
ROUBILIAC: *William Hogarth, c.* 1741, terracotta bust, height 70 cm, London, National Portrait Gallery. HOGARTH: *Self-portrait,* 1745, oil on canvas, 86.5 × 69 cm, London, Tate Gallery; *Marriage à la Mode: Soon after the marriage,* 1743-45, oil on canvas, 70 × 90.5 cm, London, National Gallery; *Sigismunda,* 1759, oil on canvas, 100 × 124 cm, London, Tate Gallery (John Webb); Engraving from *The Analysis of Beauty,* 1753, 36 × 47 cm, London, British Museum (John Freeman); *The Four Times of Day: Night,* 1738, oil on canvas, 76.5 × 61 cm, London, British Museum (John Freeman); *The Rake's Progress: The orgy; The madhouse,* 1733-35, both oil on canvas, 61 × 74 cm, London, Sir John Soane's Museum (courtesy of the Trustees); *The shrimp girl,* 1745, oil on canvas, 63.5 × 51 cm, London, National Gallery; *An Election: Chairing the member,* 1754, oil on canvas, 101 × 131 cm, London, Sir John Soane's Museum (courtesy of the Trustees); *Captain Coram,* 1740, oil on canvas, 37.5 × 23 cm, London, The Coram Foundation (Cooper-Bridgeman Library).

250–251 British Portraiture and Genre
REYNOLDS: *The Hon. Augustus Keppel,*

1753-54, oil on canvas, 231 × 297 cm, London, National Maritime Museum; *Sarah Siddons as the Tragic Muse,* 1784, oil on canvas, 236 × 144 cm, San Marino, California, Henry E. Huntington Library and Art Gallery; *Nelly O'Brien,* 1760-62, oil on canvas, 315 × 250 cm, London, Wallace Collection; *Lady Sarah Bunbury sacrificing to the Graces,* 1765, oil on canvas, 235 × 150 cm, Chicago, Art Institute; *Self-portrait,* 1773?, oil on canvas, 125 × 100 cm, London, Royal Academy of Arts. RAMSAY: *Margaret Lindsay, c.* 1775, oil on canvas, 74 × 61 cm, Edinburgh, National Gallery of Scotland. STUBBS: *Flayed horse,* 1766, engraving, 48 × 61 cm, London, Royal Academy of Arts; *The reapers,* 1786, 88 × 113 cm, London, Tate Gallery (Angelo Hornak). ROMNEY: *Emma, Lady Hamilton,* 1785, oil on canvas, 54 × 61 cm, London, National Portrait Gallery. WRIGHT: *The experiment on a bird in an air pump, c.* 1767-68, oil on canvas, 182 × 243 cm, London, Tate Gallery (Angelo Hornak). ZOFFANY: *Mr and Mrs Garrick by the Shakespearean temple at Hampton,* 1762, oil on canvas, 100 × 125 cm, London, National Portrait Gallery.

252–253 Gainsborough: Mary, Countess Howe
GAINSBOROUGH: *Mr and Mrs Andrews, c.* 1748, oil on canvas, 70 × 119 cm, London, National Gallery; *"The Blue Boy", c.* 1770, oil on canvas, 175 × 120 cm, San Marino, California, Henry E. Huntington Library and Art Gallery; *Mrs Sarah Siddons,* 1785, oil on canvas, 126 × 100 cm, London, National Gallery; *Mrs Philip Thicknesse,* 1760, oil on canvas, 44 × 132.5 cm, Cincinnati, Art Museum, Mary M. Emery Bequest; *"The Morning Walk",* 1785, oil on canvas, 236 × 179 cm, London, National Gallery; *Mary, Countess Howe,* 1763-64, oil on canvas, 240 × 150 cm, London, Kenwood House (Greater London Council as Trustees of the Iveagh Bequest).

254–255 Landscape Painting
CANALETTO: *The stonemason's yard, c.* 1730, oil on canvas, 123.5 × 163 cm, London, National Gallery; *The Arch of Constantine, Rome,* 1742, oil on canvas, 184 × 105 cm, London, Royal Collection (by gracious permission of Her Majesty the Queen). PANINI: *The interior of St Peter's, Rome,* 1731, oil on canvas, 150 × 223 cm, London, National Gallery. PIRANESI: *View of the Villa of Maecenas at Tivoli, c.* 1760-65, etching, 44 × 66 cm, London, British Museum (The Fotomas Index); Etching from the *Carceri d'Invenzione* (Imaginary Prisons), 1744-48, 55 × 41 cm, London, British Museum (The Fotomas Index). TISCHBEIN: *Goethe in the Campagna,* 1787, oil on canvas, 162 × 205 cm, Frankfurt, Städelisches Kunstinstitut. VERNET: *View of the Bay of Naples,* 1742, oil on canvas, Alnwick, Collection of the Duke of Northumberland (Cooper-Bridgeman Library). STOURHEAD, WILTSHIRE: View of the park (Simon Pugh). WILSON: *Snowdon, c.* 1766?, oil on canvas, 101 × 124 cm, Nottingham, Castle Museum (Cooper-Bridgeman Library). GAINSBOROUGH: *"Cornard Wood",* 1748, oil on canvas, 122 × 155 cm, London, National Gallery. GUARDI: *View of a canal, c.* 1750, oil on canvas, Florence, Uffizi (S).

Index

Page numbers in **bold** refer to
the main entries; *italic* numbers
refer to the illustrations